(33919   )   .$15.00

MW00989559

Review

Jans 2/99

Reg G. Boulton
23 Stafford Road
Sidcup Kent DA14 6PX
Tel: 0181 300 3485 Fax: 0181 302 7644
Mobile: 0589 172319
e-mail: reg@tcwuk.idiscover.co.uk

The Aesthetics of Music

The Aesthetics of Music

ROGER SCRUTON

CLARENDON PRESS · OXFORD
1997

Oxford University Press, Great Clarendon Street, Oxford OX2 6DP

Oxford New York Athens Auckland
Bangkok Bogota Bombay Buenos Aires
Calcutta Cape Town Dar es Salaam Delhi
Florence Hong Kong Istanbul Karachi
Kuala Lumpur Madras Madrid Melbourne
Mexico City Nairobi Paris Singapore
Taipei Tokyo Toronto Warsaw
and associated companies in
Berlin Ibadam

Oxford is a trade mark of Oxford University Press

Published in the United States
by Oxford University Press, New York

British Library Cataloguing in Publication Data
Data available

Library of Congress Cataloging-in-Publication Data
Scruton, Roger.
    The aesthetics of music / Roger Scruton.
        p.   cm.
    Includes bibliographical references and index.
    1. Music—Philosophy and aesthetics.   I. Title.
ML3845.S3975   1997   781.1'7—dc21   96-49339
ISBN 0-19-816638-9

10 9 8 7 6 5 4 3 2 1

Typeset by Seton Music Graphics

Printed in Great Britain
on acid-free paper by
Biddles Ltd
Guildford & Kings Lynn

Designed by John Trevitt

No time to rejoice for those who walk among noise and deny the voice

(Ash-Wednesday, V)

Preface

The philosophy of music is the oldest branch of aesthetics, and also the most influential, being responsible for the cosmology that came down from the Pythagoreans, via Plato, Ptolemy, St Augustine, Plotinus, and Boethius, to the poets and philosophers of the Middle Ages. The Copernican revolution that destroyed the old cosmology, destroyed also the philosophy which inspired it. Although Schopenhauer wrote brilliantly of the 'metaphysics of music', modern philosophers have ventured into this terrain, as a rule, with little confidence that it will cast light on anything outside itself, and even Schopenhauer's theories depend more on his global system than on a detailed study of the musician's art. As for Kant and Hegel—the two giants of modern aesthetics—no person with an ear can read the observations of the first on music without being acutely aware that he was more or less deaf to it, while the second, who confessed to being little versed in the art, seems to be improvising during much of the chapter devoted to music in his lectures on aesthetics. Finally Croce, their greatest successor, ignored the subject altogether. It is an odd experience, indeed, to read Croce's essay on the relationship between the Countess and Cherubino in Beaumarchais's *Marriage of Figaro*, and to discover that the author makes no mention of Mozart, whose music made this relationship so moving and so clear.

This neglect of musical aesthetics has characterized modern philosophy throughout its history. Although Descartes wrote a short treatise on music, he discovered nothing in the subject to alert his philosophical powers, and merely regurgitated standard Renaissance theories of harmony. Leibniz made a few obscure and interesting remarks about this, as about every subject; but in Spinoza, Locke, Berkeley, and Hume music is hardly mentioned. The rebirth of musical aesthetics in the eighteenth century was the work of such minor figures as Johan Mattheson and Charles Batteux, and it was not until the *Essai sur l'origine des langues* and the *Dictionnaire de musique* that a great, if erratic, philosopher turned his attention to the field.

Rousseau was not only a philosopher: he was a novelist and essayist, who found the words, images, and characters that would give form to his prodigious sensibility. He was also a composer, whose little opera *Le Devin du village*, put together as an illustration of his theories, was performed over 400 times between 1752 and 1829, and earned the praise of so great a master as Gluck. Yet Rousseau's writings on music, for all their verve and insight, provide no philosophy of the subject, and are now of largely historical interest.

Rousseau was not the only philosopher-composer in modern times. Nietzsche and Adorno enjoy the same distinction, while the greatest philosopher of our century—Wittgenstein—was, if not a composer, nevertheless profoundly musical. But the writings of those last three, even when they announce, like Adorno, a new 'philosophy of music', have little to say about the problems which I believe to be central to the discipline: the relation between sound and tone, the analysis of musical meaning, and the nature of the purely musical experience. The recent history of these questions belongs more to the work of talented amateurs like Hanslick and Gurney, or to the studies of the *Gestalt* psychologists and those critics (such as Victor Zuckerkandl) who were immediately influenced by them.

In the last decades, however, there has been an upsurge of interest in musical aesthetics, among both musicologists and philosophers. This interest has been especially marked among those who practise what is known, for want of a better word, as 'analytical' philosophy, by which is meant the painstaking process of arguing about fundamental questions, without the benefit of any prearranged or systematic answer to them. Prominent among current writers in the field are Jerrold Levinson, Peter Kivy, Malcolm Budd, Stephen Davies, Michael Tanner, Nicholas Wolterstorff, Kendall Walton, and Diana Raffman, whose names I mention here by way of acknowledging their influence on my thinking, and apologizing for the many places in which I ignore their arguments, in order to press on with my own.

Mention should also be made of two philosophers who, despite strong links to the analytical tradition, have approached the subject in Schopenhauer's spirit, by applying a global system whose plausibility does not depend upon the truth about music. The first—Suzanne Langer—drew on the early work of analytical philosophers, in order to reforge a somewhat Crocean aesthetic, of a kind that has little surviving appeal. The second—Nelson Goodman—stunned the philosophical world by rewriting the agenda of aesthetics in terms of the nominalism expounded in his logical works. The impact of these two writers on the philosophy of music has been such, that it may seem remarkable that I devote so little space to discussing them. However, I am convinced that recent criticisms have so effectively undermined their arguments, that it is no longer necessary (as once perhaps it was) to make a long and tedious detour in order to rebut them.

In this book, therefore, I have begun from first principles, and allowed the subject, rather than those who have discussed it, to dictate the direction of the argument. It came as a surprise that so dry a question as 'what is a sound?', should lead at last to a philosophy of modern culture. Had I. thought more about the Pythagorean cosmology, and the true meaning of *harmonia*, I should perhaps have known beforehand, that the ordering of sound as music is an ordering of the soul.

The text began life as a course of lectures, delivered in Boston University in the Fall Semester of 1992, and again in 1993 and 1994. I wish to record my gratitude to the students who attended those lectures, and whose lively encouragement helped me to overcome the inertia that might otherwise have consigned these thoughts to a desk drawer. I am particularly grateful to John Howland, Simon Keefe, and Margaret MacAllister, who collaborated so generously in my musical education, and to Holly Mockovack, music librarian at Boston University, for her unfailing kindness and encouragement.

Previous versions of the text have been read, either in whole or in part, by Fiona Ellis, Sebastian Gardner, John Howland, James Johnson, Simon Keefe, Jerrold Levinson, Graeme Mitchison, Charles Rosen, James Schmidt, and David Wiggins. I am grateful to them for saving me from so many errors.

R. S.

Malmesbury,
Spring 1996

Contents

List of Music Examples

Note to the Reader

In what follows I adopt the following conventions.

The arabic numerals 1, 2, 3, surmounted by carets denote the scale degrees—i.e. $\hat{1}$ denotes the tonic of the key, $\hat{2}$ the next note higher on the scale, $\hat{3}$ the next note, and so on.

The large Roman numerals, I, II, III, IV, etc. denote the major triads built on the notes of the scale—i.e. the three-note chords constructed by adding major third and fifth to each of the notes of the scale. Thus in the key of C, the symbol III denotes the triad of E major, V the triad of G major.

The small Roman numerals, i, ii, iii, iv etc. denote the minor versions of those triads, so that vi in C major is the triad of A minor. Hence the six perfect triads in the major are I, ii, iii, IV, V, vi.

1 *Sound*

Sounds and Colours

Like colours, sounds are presented to a single privileged sense-modality. You can hear them, but you cannot see them, touch them, taste them, or smell them. They are objects of hearing in something like the way that colours are objects of sight, and they are missing from the world of deaf people just as colours are missing from the world of the blind.

A deaf person could recognize sounds by sensing the vibrations that produce them: this would be a kind of tactile lip-reading. But *sounds* (the sounds of things) would nevertheless be absent from his experience; he could no more gain an acquaintance with sounds by this method than a blind person could become acquainted with colours by reading a Braille spectroscope. A blind person can know many facts about colours, and know which colour any given object is (for example, by asking those with normal eyes to tell him), while not knowing colour. For the knowledge of colour is a species of 'knowledge by acquaintance', a knowledge of 'what it is like', which is inseparable from the experience that delivers it. In the same way a deaf person could know much about sounds, and about the particular sounds emitted by particular objects, while not knowing *sound*.

Primary qualities can be perceived in other ways than by sight, and a blind person is also familiar with them. The shape of a coin can be the object of touch, as much as the object of sight. And it is qualities which are objects of sight, smell, or sound alone that philosophers have traditionally described as 'secondary'. Being red may not be exactly a matter of looking red to the normal observer; nevertheless, how things look to the normal observer in normal conditions is our principal test of colour: for what other access do we have to the colours of things? And now it begins to seem as though colours and other such secondary qualities lie closer to the surface of the world than the primary qualities on which they depend. It is as though they form the 'phenomenal skin' of things, which is peeled away by science.

Colours lead a double life: as properties of light, and as features of the things which stand in it. A room may be suffused with a red light; and this means that everything in the room will be redder than otherwise. There is a deep and difficult question as to which application of the idea of colour—to the light, or to the things which stand in it—is primary.[1] In either case, however, colours are properties; and our knowledge of colours stems from our encounter with the things that have them—with *coloured* things. We are familiar with the colour blue from the look of blue things, and every bit of blue in our world is a blue *something*. In this sense, colours are dependent on the things which possess them, even if one of those things—light—is a thing of a very peculiar kind.

Sounds, however, are not secondary qualities, for the reason that they are not qualities at all. Objects do not have sounds in the way that they have colours: they emit sounds. You could identify a sound while failing to identify its source, and there seems to be nothing absurd in the idea of a sound occurring somewhere without an identifiable cause. If we say that the sound must nevertheless *have* a cause, this would reflect a metaphysical view about causation (namely, that every event—or every event of a certain kind—has a cause), rather than the belief that sounds are qualities. Besides, even if every sound must have a cause, it does not follow that it must also be *emitted* by its cause, or that it must be understood as the sound *of* that cause.

The Acousmatic Experience

The separability of sound and cause has important consequences. Pythagoras is reputed to have lectured to his disciples from behind a screen, while they sat in silence attending to his words alone, and without a thought for the man who uttered them. The Pythagoreans were therefore known, Iamblichus tells us, as *akousmatikoi*—those willing to hear. The term has been redeployed by Pierre Schaeffer, to describe the character of sound itself, when considered in the context of the musical experience.[2] In listening, Schaeffer argues, we spontaneously detach the sound from the circumstances of its production,

---

[1] See L. Wittgenstein, *Remarks on Colour*, ed. G. E. M. Anscombe, tr. L. J. McAlister and M. Schattle (Oxford, 1977), and J. Westphal's illuminating discussion in *Colour: A Philosophical Introduction* (2nd edn., London, 1991). There are those who doubt that colours are properties, believing that we need finer metaphysical distinctions in order to map this territory. (See, e.g., J. Levinson, 'Properties and Related Entities', *Philosophy and Phenomenological Research*, 39 (1978), 1–22.) I retain the terms 'property' and 'quality', and use them loosely to denote that which corresponds, at the ontological level, to an adjective. This loose usage may be questioned; but it enables me to make the distinctions that I need, and I shall therefore ignore some of the metaphysical niceties.

[2] *Traité des objets musicaux* (Paris, 1966).

and attend to it as it is in itself: this, the 'acousmatic' experience of sound, is fortified by recording and broadcasting, which complete the severance of sound from its cause that has already begun in the concert hall.

The precise tenor of Schaeffer's argument does not concern us. But his primary intuition is surely of the first importance. The acousmatic experience of sound is precisely what is exploited by the art of music. (It is to the music, and not the instruments, that Ferdinand refers, when he says 'This music crept by me upon the waters'.) Imagine a room (call it the 'music room'), in which sounds are heard; any normal person entering the room is presented with sounds which are audible only there, but which can be traced to no specific source. For instance, you may hear a disembodied voice, or the pure note of a clarinet. Notice that I have described those sounds in terms of their characteristic causes: but I do not *have* to describe them in that way. The history of music illustrates the attempt to find ways of describing, notating, and therefore identifying sounds, without specifying a cause of them. A specific sound—middle C at such and such a volume, and with such and such a timbre (these qualities identified acoustically, as part of the way the note sounds)—can be heard in the room. Yet there are, let us suppose, no physical vibrations in the room: no instrument is sounding, and nothing else happens there, besides this persistent tone.

The case seems to be conceivable, whether or not a real possibility from the point of view of physics; so too is it conceivable that the sounds of an orchestra should exist in this room, and that the person entering it should be granted a musical experience, even though nothing is present or active there, besides the sounds themselves. The one who hears these sounds experiences all that he needs, if he is to understand them as music. He does not have to identify their cause in order to hear them as they should be heard. They provide the complete object of his aural attention.

Physics, Phenomena, and Secondary Objects

Are these sounds *physical* objects? Well, they exist and are perceived in a certain region of physical space: they are part of the 'world of extension' as the Cartesians would say. But the concept of the physical is not as clear as the old Cartesian idea of extension would make it. Is a rainbow, for example, a physical object? It is visible, certainly, in a region of space, and from a certain point of view in space. But does it really exist 'in' that space, as I do? It seems odd to say so, partly because you cannot *encounter* the rainbow at the place in which you locate it through sight: approach that place and the rainbow disappears. Or, if it does not, it was not a real, but only an illusory rainbow, so to speak. Moreover, the rainbow does not exactly *occupy* the place in which we see it, since it excludes nothing from that place. All we can say, and perhaps all that we need to say, is that a rainbow is *visible* to someone of normal sight from a certain point of view: a rainbow is a way that the world appears. It occupies no place, but is only visible in certain places. But it really does exist in the region where it can be seen.

On the other hand, rainbows are not secondary qualities: for, like sounds, they are not qualities at all. An Aristotelian would hesitate to classify them as substances: but in a less demanding sense of the term, they are certainly objects, the bearers of properties, things about which there are objective truths, and concerning which we might be mistaken. We too may hesitate to call them physical objects; but they are not mental objects either. A rainbow is not reducible to my experience of it; it is a 'well-founded phenomenon' in Leibniz's sense—an appearance which is also real. To use the scholastic jargon, rainbows are material, and not intentional, objects: an intentional object being defined by the mental state that 'intends' or focuses upon it.

Are sounds material objects in that sense? Suppose that I enter the music room, and hear the first bars of Beethoven's Second Symphony, Op. 36 sounding there. I leave the room and return, to discover that the sound has advanced to exactly the point that I would expect, had the symphony been sounding in my absence. Suppose that you too have the same experience, and that in general the 'constancy and coherence' (as Hume described it) of our impressions causes us to speak of the sound as existing *there*, in the room, and not in the heads of those who stand in it. Might we not be justified in speaking in this way?

The case is reminiscent of the argument of chapter 2 of *Individuals*, in which Strawson imagines a pure sound world, a world which contains *nothing* but sounds, and in which, nevertheless, under certain conditions (Strawson suggests) the hearer may find a use for the distinction between being and seeming, between the real world of sounds, and the merely apparent one. I do not say that Strawson's argument is right; but it is surely plausible to assume that, in *our* world, with its independently established spatial framework, sounds may be as real for us as smells or rainbows are. If you ask whether they are also *really* real, then the answer will parallel the one that might be supplied for smells or rainbows. From the point of view of physics, the reality consists in this: that changes occur in the primary properties of things, which cause systematic effects in the perceptual experiences of normal people. (Light waves are refracted in raindrops and make their divided progress to the eye; vapours are emitted by objects and linger in the nose; vibrations are produced in the air, and communicate themselves to our sense of hearing.) But there can be objective and decidable judgements about something, even if it is not, from the point of view of physics, part of the ultimate reality. Secondary qualities are an instance of this; so too are 'secondary objects', as I shall call them, like rainbows, smells, and sounds. Moreover, aesthetic interest (which is our real subject in this discussion) is an interest in appearances: its object is not the underlying structure of things, but the revealed presence of the world—the world as it is encountered in our experience (the *Lebenswelt*, to use Husserl's term for it). (I ask the reader to take this claim on trust, since only later can I offer a proof of it.) An aesthetic interest in sound need attribute to sounds no more than the qualified reality that they have in my example: the reality of a well-founded phenomenon, of a 'material' (as opposed to 'intentional') object that is not strictly part of the underlying physical order.

A difficulty arises at this point which parallels certain difficulties that arise in the discussion of secondary qualities. If someone asks what *is* it, to be red, the temptation is to follow Locke, and describe the quality as a power or disposition. To be red is to be disposed to produce in the normal observer the experience of seeing red. (The definition is of course circular: but we need not decide, for present purposes, whether the circle is vicious.) But, it might be said, you cannot stop there; dispositions must be 'grounded': there must be some structural feature of the object, by *virtue* of which it is disposed to present this appearance. And if that is so, should we not say that redness consists in possessing this structural feature, that this is what it is to *be* red?

It would take us too far afield to explore all the avenues that are opened by this suggestion. But it is worth bearing the following countervailing arguments in mind: first, the assumption that dispositions must be 'grounded' in structural features has never been persuasively defended. Indeed, it is very hard to reconcile with quantum mechanics, which shows precisely that our desire to replace dispositional by occurrent properties cannot, in the end, be satisfied. (Such, at any rate, is the conclusion that a philosopher is likely to draw from Bell's theorem, which shows the untenability of Einstein's argument for the view that 'God does not play dice').[3]

Secondly, why should we assume, in the case of redness, that there is only *one* structural feature responsible for this appearance? Could there not be two or three, maybe indefinitely many? Only on the assumption that red things form a 'natural kind', in the sense made familiar by John Stuart Mill, and more recently by Putnam and Kripke, could we rule out such possibilities.[4] But if 'red' means 'looks as *this* looks' (pointing to an instance), it is plainly not a natural-kind term. It could become so only by ceasing to be the name of a secondary quality.

[3] See J. S. Bell, 'Bertleman's Socks and the Nature of Reality', *J. Phys.* (Paris), 42 (1981), 41–61.

[4] J. S. Mill, *A System of Logic* (London, 1943), Bk I, ch. 7 sect. 4; H. Putman, 'Is Semantics Possible?', in his *Collected Papers*, ii. *Meaning and Metaphysics* (Cambridge, 1975); S. Kripke, *Naming and Necessity* (Oxford, 1980).

Thirdly, the advance of physics has certainly made us familiar with a relevant natural kind: namely red light. It is now known that red things do, in fact, have something in common, namely that they emit or refract light in a certain range of wavelengths. But this is precisely not a structural feature of the objects themselves. And the redness of red light is again something that it possesses only by virtue of its appearance. Red light, defined as light of a certain range of wavelengths, might cease to appear red, and yet still be essentially what it is. Hence this natural kind does not provide us with a 'real essence' of redness, even if red light *has* a real essence, and even if that real essence is uniquely responsible for our seeing red.

The example is important, since it relates directly to the true physics of sound. As we know, sounds are also produced by waves: vibrations which are communicated to the ear. If I see a rainbow, I know that light waves are reaching my eyes from the direction in which they are turned: and *that* is the physical reality which explains what I see. Likewise, if I hear a tone, I know that sound waves are reaching my ears from the direction in which I locate the tone; and *that* is the physical reality which explains what I hear. If the example of the music room is to be physically possible, then it must be that such sound vibrations are occurring in the room: it cannot contain sounds without also containing sound waves. ('Cannot', here, denotes physical rather than metaphysical impossibility.)

But we should no more *identify* the sound with the sound wave than we identify the redness of an object with the light that comes from it. There is no better case for eliminating the phenomenal reality of sound in favour of the primary qualities of sound waves than there is for eliminating the phenomenal reality of colours and rainbows. By using the term 'phenomenal reality' I wish again to emphasize the distinction between an appearance and a *mere* appearance. Even in the realm of appearance we can distinguish what is objectively so, from what is merely apparently so to a particular observer. Red things are *really* red, even though redness is a matter of appearance. Some things are merely apparently red, because of a trick of the light or a defect in the observer. Hence there is a distinction between being red and merely looking red, even though redness is a matter of how things look.

Sounds as Secondary Objects

Likewise with sounds; the presence of a sound is established by *how things sound* to the normal observer, and by nothing else. But we can still distinguish between sounds which are really there to be heard, and sounds which are merely imaginary. And the case is additionally interesting on account of the fact that sounds are not properties of anything. We do not predicate them of other things, but regard them as the bearers of auditory properties (pitch, timbre, and so on). Gareth Evans doubts this, arguing (in the course of discussing Strawson's sound world) as follows:

> *We* can think of sounds as perceptible phenomena, phenomena that are independent of us, and that can exist unperceived, because we have the resources for thinking of the abiding stuff in whose changes the truth of the proposition that there is a sound can be regarded as consisting.[5]

And he goes on to locate the 'stuff' to which he refers as the source, whatever it might be, of the sound vibrations. But the argument is not persuasive. The phenomenal sound is indeed always the result of sound waves. But this does not show that the distinction between the sound that is there, and the sound that merely appears to be there, cannot be drawn *at the phenomenal level*, in just the way that we distinguish the real from the apparent colour of a thing. To be precise: to say that middle C really *is* sounding in the music room is to imply that any normal observer who entered there in normal conditions would hear middle C. This counterfactual condition is the ultimate fact of the matter—the fact in which the distinction between real and apparent sound is grounded—just as in the case of colours. However, sounds are not qualities of things, but independently existing objects. The conclusion must be that there is no 'abiding stuff' of which they are predicated. Their objective reality is phenomenal, but also intrinsic.

But what kind of objects are they? Notice, first, that we do not have clear identity-conditions for sounds. We can count them and individuate them in many ways, depending on our interests. Suppose, for example, that a middle C with the timbre of a clarinet is sounding in the music room. Suddenly the timbre changes to that of an oboe. Do we say that one sound was replaced by another, or merely that it changed its character? Neither description is forced on us, and everything will depend upon our interests. (If the change occurs in a context where orchestration matters, we are likely to say that there were two sounds; otherwise, it may be more natural to speak of one.)

Some might say that such arbitrariness is merely proof that the concept of numerical identity does not here apply, and that sounds are therefore objects only in a derivative sense: metaphysically speaking they are not objects at all, but properties of the regions in which they are heard. And again, from the metaphysical point of view, this robust Aristotelianism has much to be said for it. However, it fails to do justice to the phenomenal character of sounds, whose role in our perception and response cannot be adequately understood without the concept of numerical identity. Consider words, for example. These are identified in two ways—as types and as

---

[5] 'Things without the Mind', in *Collected Papers* (Oxford, 1993), 278.

tokens, to use C. S. Peirce's famous (though obscure) distinction.[6] The word 'man' is both present in this sentence, as a token, and exemplified as a type. And if the sentence is spoken aloud, we have an instance of the token utterance of 'man': the individual sound, recognition of which as the 'same again' is necessary if we are to understand the spoken type. Is not this token utterance an *individual*? It has properties which it shares with other sound individuals: it is loud, long-drawn-out, and finishes abruptly. But it is distinct from its properties, just as the token Ford Cortina car is distinct from the properties which inhere in it, at least some of which define the type of which it is an instance.

It is partly because we have such an interest in word-types, whose properties and relations constitute our language, that we treat the token utterance as an individual, whose properties are to be divided into those which belong to the type, and those which are merely 'accidents' of the token. And this interest in sound types is exemplified also in music: although in this case the types are defined in another way.

However, the case is clearly not like that of the Ford Cortina, whose tokens are individual physical objects, unproblematic bearers of a numerical identity that they would retain whether or not there were a type which partly conditioned it. I do not say that the numerical identity of my car can be fixed without reference to my interests: for plainly, the Ford Cortina is an artificial and not a natural kind, and criteria of token-identity do not in such a case lie 'in the nature of things'. Nevertheless, the concept of numerical identity seems far less problematic than in the case of sounds, partly because my car is an object in space, with definite boundaries, standing in clear physical relations to other such objects. A sound, on the other hand, lasts for a certain time and then vanishes without remainder. Its spatial properties are indeterminate or vague, and even its temporal boundaries may be unclear until fixed by convention. Thus Husserl, in his attempt to define the *individual* tone, as opposed to the character possessed by it, was inclined to identify a tone through the specific 'now point' at which it is heard. Only when circumscribed by the 'now' does the tone become an individual, whose identity is fixed to it for ever, and accompanies it on its endless journey into the past.[7] But this suggestion would remove the problem of the identity of sound events only if the boundaries of the now were fixed by nature—and this is clearly not so. 'Now' may designate this instant, this

---

[6] See e.g. the explanation given by Peirce to Lady Welby, in Charles S. Peirce, *Selected Writings*, ed. P. P. Wiener (New York, 1958), 406. Peirce's distinction has been interestingly applied in the musical context by R. S. Hatton, *Musical Meaning in Beethoven: Markedness, Correlation and Interpretation* (Indianapolis, 1994), 44–56.

[7] E. Husserl, *The Phenomenology of Internal Time Consciousness*, ed. M. Heidegger, tr. J. S. Churchill (The Hague, 1964), 69–70.

minute, this day, week, or era, depending upon the speaker's interests. And even if we think, with William James, that there is a phenomenal minimum in the experience of time—a 'specious present' which cannot be further divided—we can think of such a thing, only because we *do* divide it intellectually, regarding every now as infinitely divisible: and likewise for the events and processes that ride upon the present as it buoys them backwards to oblivion.[8]

Events and Processes

Whatever they are, sounds are either events or processes. But what exactly are events and processes, and what, if anything, is the distinction between them? Both events and processes *occur*; but in normal parlance only processes *endure*. Events happen *at* a time, processes last through a time. An event marks a change in the world; a process may last 'unchangingly'. Thus the beginning or ending of a process is an event.

Although we can, in this way, make a distinction between events and processes, the distinction is by no means hard and fast. It may be difficult to decide whether something is an event or a process: consider explosions, storms, emotions. Maybe events and processes belong to a single metaphysical category—the category of happenings or things which occur. Actions, for example, seem to include both events and processes; and one and the same action—eating an apple—may be described in either way. In thinking about these matters it is probably wrong to be too closely guided by 'ordinary language'. It may be better to adopt some general term to cover 'things which occur', and to leave the distinctions for the places where they are needed. Since the term currently favoured by philosophers is 'event', I shall adopt it—while asking the reader to remember that while all sounds, according to this usage, are events, some are also processes.

Events do not figure in Kant's Table of Categories, although Aristotle acknowledges them under the heading of 'action and passion' (*to poiein kai paschein*).[9] The sparseness of Aristotle's remarks is to some extent compensated for in his extended treatment of 'coming to be and passing away' (*De Generatione et Corruptione*); but it is power and causation that concern him, and he offers us nothing, so far as I can tell, about the metaphysical status of events. Kant is equally interested in causation, which features in two of his twelve categories; but nothing that he says casts any light whatsoever on the nature of events or their place in our ordinary scheme of things.

---

[8] *Principles of Psychology*, 2 vols. (New York, 1890), i. 608 ff. James takes the expression 'specious present' from E. R. Clay (ibid. 609).

[9] *Categories*, 11[b].

Nevertheless, events are fundamental items in our ontology, and no view of the world that excluded them would be complete. They are also intrinsically problematic. There is, for example, a problem about the individuation and identity of events which remains unsolved in the existing literature. Consider a car crash. How many events is this? The answer seems to be indeterminate. For the policeman it is one event; for the surgeon it is as many events as victims; for the spectator it is an inexhaustible multitude of horrors. But this indeterminacy in no way shows that there are no such things as individual events: it merely reminds us of our ontological priorities. Our world is a world of substances—things, organisms, and people; events and processes are what *happen* to those substances. There are philosophers who reverse this priority: the 'process' philosophers, such as Whitehead and Hartshorne, who regard substances as participants in processes, and process itself as the fundamental reality. But their philosophy notoriously comes to grief over the idea of the individual, and finds no anchor for language in the endless flow of happening.

More recent philosophers have tried to come to grips with the problem of events. Jaegwon Kim has proposed that we construe events as exemplifications of properties at times—thus making the identity of events parasitic upon the identity of properties.[10] (But do we really have a clear idea of *that* kind of identity?) Donald Davidson, whose 'ontology of events' is dictated by the desire to understand the logic of action and causality,[11] gives priority to the question of event-identity. But his suggestion—that an event is individuated by the totality of its causal relations—provides us with no criterion that *we* could apply in sorting one event from another. Moreover, there seem to be no grounds for accepting it, apart from the desire—by no means universal—to save the rest of Davidson's system. (Consider two uncaused events with no effects: for Davidson these must be one event— even if they occur in completely different regions and at completely different times: surely a *reductio ad absurdum*.)[12]

Granted the ontological priority of substances (the persons and material objects of Strawson's *Individuals*), we can in fact live happily with a fluid concept of the identity of events and processes. There is no problem presented by the fact that the car crash is as many events as our interests determine, since we do not have to *identify* the events in order to refer to the episode and communicate about it. We identify the individuals, and say what happened to *them*.

[10] 'Events as Property Exemplifications', in M. Brand and D. Walton (eds.), *Action Theory* (Dordrecht, 1980), 159–77. Kim's view has been effectively criticized by J. Bennett in *Events and their Names* (Oxford, 1988), 75–87.

[11] 'The Individuation of Events', in *Essays on Actions and Events* (Oxford, 1980).

[12] The argument here is spelled out at length by M. Brand, 'Identity Conditions for Events', *American Philosophical Quarterly*, 1 (1977), 329–77.

Moreover, there are good reasons for retaining a fluid concept of event-identity. Our world-view rests on three applications of the concept of identity: to abstract particulars, like numbers, to concrete individuals, like tables, animals, and people, and to natural kinds like the lion, the oak tree, or chlorine. Abstract particulars lie outside time, and, being immune to change, possess all their properties essentially. Concrete individuals are situated in the stream of time, subject to its unending erosion, and can be understood, therefore, only through a concept of identity-across-time. As Strawson has cogently argued, it is their reidentifiability which endows these elementary 'substances' with their being, and makes them the anchor to our thoughts.[13] But criteria for identity across time acquire their authority from the identity of kinds, and it is only because we sort the world into kinds that we can reidentify its individual occupants. It seems then that the concept of identity owes its importance to our unending, hopeless, but necessary struggle against the flow of time.

Events, however, do not stand against the current; on the contrary, the current is composed of them. To endow events with rigid conditions of identity would be precisely to lift them from the stream of time, like numbers, or else to anchor them in the midst of it, like rocks and stones and trees. In either case, it would be to denature them: to destroy their character as events. To deploy a strict criterion of event-identity, we might say, is to sacrifice becoming to being, and so to lose our sense of time's dominion.

The Pure Event

That brief excursus is highly speculative, and this is not the place to continue it. But it leads us to an interesting point. In the case of a car crash, the event is identified through its 'participants'. It consists in changes undergone by them. And this is something that we observe. In general, when we see an event or a process, we see the objects which participate in it. I cannot witness a car crash without witnessing a car crashing. And this applies to visible events generally: in seeing an event, I see objects which change; in seeing a process I see objects which act in a certain way.

In the case of sounds, however, we are presented with *pure* events. Although the sound that I hear is produced by something, I am presented in hearing with the sound alone. The thing that produces the sound, even if it is 'something heard', is not the intentional object of hearing, but only the cause of what I hear. Of course, in ordinary day-to-day matters, we leap rapidly in thought from the sound to its cause, and speak quite accurately of hearing the car, just as we speak of seeing it. But the phenomenal

---

[13] *Individuals* (London, 1959), ch. 1.

distinctness of sounds makes it possible to imagine a situation in which a sound is separated entirely from its cause, and heard acousmatically, as a pure process. This is indeed what happens in the music room. In hearing, therefore, we are presented with something that vision cannot offer us: the pure event, in which no individual substances participate, and which therefore *becomes* the individual object of our thought and attention. Although the assignment of numerical identity to such a thing remains arbitrary, or at least interest-relative, it comes to have a peculiar importance. We begin to treat sounds as the basic components of a 'sound world': a world which contains nothing else but sound. And we therefore begin to take an interest in the repeatable events which fill that world, availing ourselves of criteria of sameness and difference which enable us to reproduce the sound that strikes us, with all its salient features still intact.

Sound events take time. But being pure events, their temporal order is the *basic* order that they exhibit. It is through temporal divisions that we discompose them into parts, and the primary relations between events are temporal: before, after, and simultaneous define the positions of sounds in the acousmatic world. It is true that we locate sounds in space: as over there, nearby, far away, and so on. But as we come to focus on the sounds themselves, this feature is gradually refined away, and plays only an attenuated part in music. The off-stage trumpets in Mahler's first and second Symphonies are meant to evoke a sense of distance: but it is a distance of the imagination; these trumpets call to us from far away, and also from within, like the voices of the dead; their 'distance' is metaphorical, and they are as present in the musical structure as the other sounds with which they coincide. Similarly, the dialogue between cor anglais and oboe, in the third movement of Berlioz's *Symphonie fantastique*, in which the oboe is placed off-stage so as to create the effect of shepherds answering each other across a valley, is not a dialogue in physical space, even if it *uses* our perception of physical space, in order to remind us of the sense of distance. Musically speaking, there is no distance at all between the oboe and the cor anglais, both of which float in the same musical empyrean.

The point here may not be intuitively obvious. For one thing, the *physical* space between sounds plays an important part in the musical experience—as in the last example, or in the arrangement of orchestras, choirs, and chamber groups. Stereo reproduction make an important contribution to the musical experience, precisely because it reproduces the spatial array of sound. But the case should be compared with that of a picture, in which the spatial relations between brush-strokes on the canvas are indispensable to the experience, even though the space that we see in the picture has nothing to do with that in which the brush-strokes lie. We must notice the distance between this patch of red and that of yellow, so as to see the relation between the figures that they represent. The patches are inches apart in the space that we occupy. The figures are separated by half a mile, in an imagined space of their own. Likewise, the spatial array of the orchestra *induces* us into the musical space; but it is not part of it, and gives way to it, just as soon as we are gripped by the musical perception.

The Sound Space

The world of pure sound exhibits other interesting features. Sounds do not cut each other off from the ear, as visible objects cut each other off from the eye. A sound may 'drown out' its competitors, but this is because it saturates our hearing, so that we can no longer discriminate what is there. (The case should be compared with pain: a severe pain distracts me from lesser pains; but it does not 'hide them from view'.) A visible object, by contrast, may stand between me and another such object, thus veiling it. The physics of sight and sound explains this difference. An opaque object does not allow light to pass; but no sound wave can impede the passage of other sound waves, and therefore no sound can be opaque. (When we describe sounds in that way, we use a metaphor. For example, the chords which mark the opening rhythm in the second movement of the *Rite of Spring* are opaque. But there is no way of explaining what this means, without using another metaphor. Light does not pass through these chords; they block out the background; all other musical events are heard as 'in front of' them: and so on.)

This absence of opacity in the sound world means that, if no sound is too loud, I may be able to hear all the contents of that world (all that are audible *here*, that is) simultaneously. The world of sound may lie open before me, with none of its contents outside my awareness. The paradigm case of this is music, in which the sound world can be surveyed in its entirety, with its regions clearly defined: in music we obtain a God's-ear view of things. Thus a great contrapuntalist like Bach, or a great orchestrator like Ravel, presents us with an open soundscape, in which every musical element is directly audible.

However, we are not *part* of the world of sound, as we are part of the visual world. I see things *before* me, spatially related to me. But I do not stand *in* the world of sound as I stand in the world of sight. Nor is this surprising, given that the world of sound contains events and processes only, and no persons or other substances. (This point seems to me to show the flaw in the thought-experiment of Strawson's *Individuals*, chapter 2: the observer can neither exist *in* that world of sounds, nor out of it.) The sound world is inherently other, and other in an interesting way: it is not just that we do not belong in it; it is that we *could* not belong in it: it is metaphysically apart from us. And yet we have a complete view of it, and discover in it, through music, the very life that is ours. *There* lies the mystery, or part of it.

Nevertheless, there is a temptation to say that the sound world has a spatial, or quasi-spatial order: a temptation yielded to by Strawson in his interesting attempt to construct the absent argument of Kant's Transcendental Aesthetic—the argument for the striking claim that space is the 'form of outer sense': i.e. for the claim that we cannot perceive something as existing objectively without situating it in a spatial frame. It is as though pitch formed a one-dimensional space, through which sounds can move much as physical objects move through physical space. But as soon as we take seriously the fact that sounds are not substances but events, whose identity-conditions are inherently contested, we see that we cannot speak of them in that way. There need be no clear sense attached to the idea of the same sound, now at this place, now at that; or to the idea of a place containing now this sound, now that. Of course, we can invent a use for these notions: but it will not confer on the pitch spectrum the property that it does not, and cannot have, of being a dimension, analogous to the dimensions of physical space. The essential feature of a spatial dimension is that it contains places, which can be *occupied* by things, and between which things can move. Sounds may be arranged on the pitch spectrum, but no sound can move from one place on that spectrum to another without changing in a fundamental respect. It would be as reasonable to say that it had changed into another sound (a semitone higher, for instance), as that it had moved through auditory space. Moreover, there is no clear orientation of sounds in auditory space: no way of assigning faces, ends, boundaries, and so on to them, so as to introduce those topological features which help us to make sense of the idea of 'occupying' a place. Far from confirming Kant's thesis, the acousmatic experience offers a world of objects which are ordered in space only *apparently*, and not in fact.

Of course, we speak of 'up' and 'down' in relation to the pitch spectrum, and higher and lower too. And these are very important descriptions, integral to the experience of music. But literally speaking these descriptions are false. High and low on the pitch spectrum are like high and low on the temperature scale, or the scale of the real numbers: they indicate the existence of a continuum, but not that of a dimension. There is no sense in which the temperature of a body 'occupies' a place on the Celsius scale: as though it could have occupied another place and still have been the temperature that it is! (We should note, too, that not every language is like English, in using 'high' and 'low' or their equivalents for the two ends of the pitch spectrum. French has *aigu* and *grave*, for example, while the Greeks used 'high' where we speak of 'low' and vice versa, since they were guided by the places of the strings on the lyre. On the other hand, all people recognize movement in music from low to high (in our sense) as an *upward* movement, and the opposite as *downward*, and it is this feature of the musical experience that stands in need of an explanation.)

Spatial metaphors permeate our experience of music, and the organization which produces music out of sound prompts us, almost inexorably, to think of sound in spatial terms. Why this is so, and the consequences of its being so, will occupy us in Chapter 2.

The Pitch Matrix

One final observation should be made concerning the world of sounds. Sounds are arranged on the pitch spectrum, which is a continuum: between any two pitches there lies a third. This is not merely a physical truth—a truth about pitch, construed as Helmholtz would construe it, as the frequency of a vibration.[14] It is also a phenomenal truth: while we may not be able to discriminate one pitch from its near neighbour, between any two pitches that we *can* discriminate, there will be a third, possibly indiscriminable. (Compare shades of red: there can be a phenomenal continuum, even when our capacities to discriminate are, as they must be, finite. In this way we acquire the *idea* of a phenomenal distinction, even though it is a distinction with no phenomenal reality for us.)[15] Nevertheless, it is an interesting fact that we do not treat the phenomenal continuum as a *mere* continuum. Like the colour spectrum, it has salient points and thresholds. Orange shades into red: but orange and red are *different colours*. Orange is not a shade of red, nor red a shade of orange. Likewise, one pitch shades into the pitch a semitone above: but, having got there, we recognize the new pitch as another pitch. In between the two we are likely to think of an 'out-of-tune version' of either. There is a kind of grid lying over the pitch continuum, divided—for us—into the semitones of the chromatic scale, which leads us to hear all pitches within the octave as versions of those twelve fundamental pitches: versions more or less 'out of tune'. This grid is not a static thing: it has changed since the introduction of equal temperament, and even now it shifts noticeably, for a string-player, from key to key. It is in part the centuries of music-making that have created this grid, and other civilizations have used other divisions of the scale—whether into

---

[14] H. Helmholtz, *On the Sensations of Tone*, tr. A. J. Ellis (London, 1885; repr. New York, 1954).

[15] Diana Raffman doubts this, and argues that the pitch spectrum is not dense, in Goodman's sense, but disjoint, since our powers of aural discrimination are finite. See *Language, Music and Mind* (Cambridge, Mass., 1993), 121. But she goes on to recognize that the pitch continuum is experienced *as if* it were dense. In fact, this 'as if' is what *constitutes* density, in the phenomenal realm.

twenty-four equal tones, as in classical Arabian music, or into the highly uneven divisions of the Greek modes,[16] or into the inflected and sliding tones of the Indian scales; but it is there in each of us, and has its basis in the experience of harmony. Cultural variations do not alter the fact that all musical people, from whatever tradition, will divide the octave into discrete pitches or pitch areas, and hear intervening pitches as 'out of tune'.

Sound and Tone

Those reflections on the nature of sound and the experience of sound already suggest some of the reasons for the special place accorded in our lives to music. Music is an art of sound, and much that seems strange in music can be traced to the strangeness of the sound world itself. Nevertheless, music is itself a special *kind* of sound, and not any art of sound is music. For instance, there is an art, and an aesthetic intention, in designing a fountain, and the sound of the fountain is all-important in the aesthetic effect. But the art of fountains is not music. For one thing, the sound of the fountain must be heard in physical space, and should be part of the charm of a place. Nor is it the work of a musician to write poetry, even though poetry too is an art of sound. So what distinguishes the sound of music?

The simple answer is 'organization'. But it is no answer at all if we cannot say what kind of organization we have in mind. Poetry too is organized sound: sound organized thrice over, first by the rules of syntax and semantics, secondly by the aesthetic intention of the poet, and thirdly by the reader or listener, as he recuperates the images and thoughts and holds them in suspension. And although we have paradigms of musical organization, in the canon of masterpieces, it is not obvious that these are all organized in the same way, or that they exhaust the possibilities. Some may argue that the electronic noises produced on a computer by such 'radical' composers as Dennis Lorrain are music; others may make similar claims for such purely percussive sequences as Varèse's *Ionisation*, or collections of evocative sounds in the style of George Crumb, as in his *Music for a Summer Evening*. Modernism has been so prolific of deviant cases that we hesitate to call them deviant, for fear of laying down a law which we cannot justify: even John Cage's notorious four minutes and thirty-three seconds of silence has featured in the annals of musicology. So how do we begin to define our theme?

Such questions have bedevilled aesthetics in our times—and unnecessarily so. For they are empty questions, which present no real challenge to the philosopher who has a full conception of his subject. Whatever it is, music

---

[16] See the discussion in M. L. West, *Ancient Greek Music* (Oxford, 1992), ch. 6.

is not a natural kind. What is to count as music depends upon our decision; and it is a decision made with a purpose in mind. That purpose is to describe, and if possible to extend, the kind of interest that we have in a Beethoven symphony. Other things satisfy that interest; and there is no way of saying in advance which things these will be—not until we have a clear idea of what exactly interests us in the Beethoven. The question whether this or that modernist or postmodernist experiment is a work of music is empty, until we have furnished ourselves with an account of our central instances of the art. Only then do we know what the question means. And even then we may feel no great need to answer it.

The best way of summarizing those central instances is to say that they each achieve, though not necessarily in the same way, a transformation of sounds into tones. A tone is a sound which exists within a musical 'field of force'. This field of force is something that *we* hear, when hearing tones. It may not be possible for all creatures to hear it; indeed, if subsequent arguments are right, it is only rational beings, blessed with imagination, who can hear sounds as tones. It may even be that the transformation from sound to tone is effected *within* the act of hearing, and has no independent reality. But it is a transformation that can be described, just as soon as we forget the attempt to find 'something in common' to all the works that critics have described as music.

This transformation from sound to tone may, nevertheless, be usefully likened to the transformation of a sound into a word. The word 'bang' consists, in its token utterances, of a sound. This sound could occur in nature, and yet not have the character of a word. What makes it the word that it is, is the grammar of a language, which mobilizes the sound and transforms it into a word with a specified role: it designates a sound or an action in English, an emotional state in German. When hearing this sound as a word I hear the 'field of force' supplied by grammar. The sound comes to me alive with implications, with possibilities of speech. I do not merely hear the sound of the voice: I hear *language*, which is an experience of meaning. When I 'hear what you say', I may be unaware of the sounds that you are making, unaware that you are speaking French, with an *accent du Midi*. Language causes us to hear the voice as in a certain sense outside nature: it is not a sound, but a message broadcast into the soundscape. (Cf. Aristotle's argument that the voice is distinct from all other objects of hearing, since we hear it in another way.)[17] Something similar happens when I hear middle C while walking, and take it for a note in music. Maybe it was only a bird, a child playing with a squeaky toy, a rusty hinge turning. It would then be the same sound; but to hear it as *those* sounds

---

[17] See *De Anima*, 420[b].

would be to situate it outside the order which is music. To hear a sound as music is not merely to hear it, but also to *order* it.

The order of music is a *perceived* order. When we hear tones, we hear their musical implications in something like the way that we hear the grammatical implications of words in a language. Of course, we probably do not know the theory of musical organization, cannot say in words what is going on when the notes of a Haydn quartet sound so right and logical. But nor do we know the theory of English grammar, or the principles of syntactical construction, even though we can identify a sentence as an intelligible piece of English. Maybe you could say that we have *tacit* knowledge of grammar, as Chomsky does. But in that sense we have tacit knowledge too of music. This knowledge is expressed not in theories but in acts of recognition.

It is possible, as I shall argue, to make too much of the analogy with language. But it is a useful analogy, and launches us on our path. It also reminds us of an all-important fact about sounds, which is that they have a *primary* occurrence in the lives of rational beings, as instruments of communication. It is in the form of sound that language is normally first learned; and it is through sound that we communicate most immediately and effectively when face to face. It is impossible to put this fact behind us. Every sound intentionally made is instinctively taken to be an attempt at communication. And this is as true of music as it is of speech. In the presence of sound intentionally produced, and intentionally organized, we feel ourselves within another person's ambit. And that feeling conditions our response to what we hear.

We are now in a position to explore some of the distinguishing marks of tones, and of the organization that creates them.

2   *Tone*

Music makes use of a particular kind of sound: an acousmatic event, which is heard 'apart from' the everyday physical world, and recognized as the instance of a type. This isolation of the pure sound event leads to a peculiar experience, which I have called the experience of tone. No longer does it seem as though the middle C that sounds is caused by someone blowing on the clarinet. Instead we hear it as a response to the B that preceded it, and as though calling in turn for the E that follows. When Brahms hands the second theme of the last movement of the Second Piano Concerto in B flat major Op. 83 from orchestra to piano and back again, we hear a single melody jump electrically across these poles. Each note follows in sequence as though indifferent to the world of physical causes and responding only to its predecessor and to the force that it inherits from the musical line (Ex. 2.1).

Ex. 2.1. Brahms, Second Piano Concerto in B flat major, Op. 83, last movement

The example illustrates three important distinctions: that between the acoustical experience of sounds, and the musical experience of tones; that between the real causality of sounds, and the virtual causality that generates tone from tone in the musical order; and that between the sequence of sounds and the movement of the tones that we hear in them. These distinctions are parts of the comprehensive distinction between sound and tone which is the subject–matter of this chapter. When we hear music, we do not hear sound only; we hear something *in* the sound, something which moves with a force of its own. This intentional object of the musical perception is what I refer to by the word 'tone', and in exploring the relation between sound and tone I shall be describing the contours of the musical experience.

It is tempting, as I have already pointed out, to say that music is distinguished by its organization: that sound becomes tone when organized in a musical way. In which case, to hear tones is to hear the implicit organization: as we hear the grammatical order that transforms 'bang' from a sound to a word, and which causes us to hear it differently when conversing in English or in German. And the suggestion is by no means absurd. However, as I shall later argue in more detail, there is no musical 'grammar' which generates the order that we hear, when we hear a sound as a tone.

Aaron Copland writes that 'music has four essential elements: rhythm, melody, harmony and tone colour'.[1] This division of the subject leaves out one of the elements—pitch—and imports another (tone-colour) which is rooted in the *character* of sounds rather than their organization. In what follows, therefore, I shall leave tone-colour to one side, and concentrate upon the other elements, since they display the organization which turns sound to tone, and so permits us to hear music, where other creatures hear only sequences of sounds. Pitch, rhythm, melody, and harmony are not the only forms of musical organization; but they provide the core musical experience in our culture, and perhaps in any culture that is recognizably engaged in music-making.

Pitch

The pitch of a sound is comparable to the colour of a light, in this respect: that it is a secondary quality, produced by, and from the point of view of physics reducible to, a vibration. Moreover, just as each change in the frequency of light waves produces a shift in colour, so does a change in the frequency of a sound wave produce a change in pitch. This change may not be noticeable—there are thresholds of discrimination here, as with every sensory experience. Nevertheless, our experience of pitch, like our experience of colour, presents us with a continuum: between any two colours or pitches, there lies a third, even if its character is not, to us, perceivably different from its neighbours.

There, however, the analogy ends. For the pitch continuum possesses certain features which are not possessed by the colour spectrum and vice versa. First, we hear the pitch continuum as though it were a dimension: pitched sounds are higher or lower, and this impression varies strictly in accordance with their frequency. Not every language deploys the idiom of

[1] *What to Listen for in Music* (New York, 1939), 33.

'high' and 'low' in describing relations of pitch. But whatever terms are used, they are understood in terms of a movement up and down, towards and away from, in two-dimensional space. A French person, for whom bass notes are *grave* and treble notes *aigu*, nevertheless hears the movement from the first to the second as a rising, and the movement back again as a fall. Imagine what it would be like, to hear the opening theme of Bruckner's Seventh Symphony (Ex. 2.2) as falling, or as moving from left to right or right to left in a horizontal plane, or as not moving at all. Surely, you could not understand the musical sense of this melody, if you did not hear the force which bears it aloft, and then allows it to subside to a brief quietus.

Ex. 2.2. Bruckner, Seventh Symphony in E major, first movement

Secondly, pitches are grouped by a pure 'between-ness' relation, and by nothing else. The distance between pitches provides our only way to compare them *as pitches*. There is no equivalent of colour-kinds—no areas of the pitch continuum which belong together as do blues or greens—even though there are shades of pitch *relations* (for example, the differences between the semitone interval in equal temperament, and the semitone interval between tonic and leading-note in a justly intoned scale).

Things did not *have* to be this way. It could have been that we heard all vibrations between 400 and 560 beats per second as sound-blue, shading into sound-green. And this might have provided our central experience of 'same pitch', so that blue pitches seemed to belong together, regardless of their frequency, while near neighbours seemed to belong apart, merely because one was blue and the other green. It so happens, however, that the secondary quality maps the underlying cause: pitches are organized in hearing in a manner that exactly parallels the physical order which produces them.

Finally, the pitch spectrum offers a peculiar experience of 'the same again'—namely the octave. Although audible pitches extend from 60 beats per second to 3,000 or more, they are all contained within the octave—the segment which reaches from 60 to 120, from 120 to 240, and so on. On reaching the octave, we return to our place of departure. This phenomenon is less marked when sounds slide up and down, like the glissando of a siren, than when they advance by discrete steps, as along the diatonic or chromatic scales. But, once the organization of the scale is imported, the experience is irresistible. Since the introduction of equal temperament into classical

Western music, therefore, only twelve pitch classes have been recognized: all the rest are derived from them by the rule of 'octave equivalence'.

This connects with the fact noticed in Chapter 1, that the pitch continuum is not experienced merely as a continuum: it is organized into discrete regions which shade into one another while remaining distinct. In between one pitch and the pitch a semitone above, we hear only 'out-of-tune' versions of either. The potential for musical order is already contained in this. This is not to say that a new musical idiom might not arise, in which the semitone matrix were replaced by a division into quarter-tones, say, as Alois Hába attempted. But this new idiom would depend as much as did the old one, on our disposition to hear intermediate tones as 'out of tune'.

Pitch, therefore, involves two distinct forms of organization. First, there is the continuum of frequencies, which orders sounds according to the process that produces them. Secondly, heard in, and imposed upon this continuum, is another: a quasi-spatial arrangement of tones, arranged in a pattern of discrete intervals, which repeats itself at the octave until vanishing at last over the horizon of perception. This second order is part of what we hear, when we hear sound as music.

Rhythm

Here is a suggestion: rhythm exists when sounds occur in regular succession, with accents that divide the sequence into definite measures. Against the background which such organization provides, we hear the sounds as arranged in order, and come to expect the repeated emphasis. In such circumstances a rhythm is heard: which is simply to say that our perceptions are informed by a particular expectation.

The suggestion is inadequate, for a variety of reasons. First we often hear these regular and self-repeating sequences of sound, without hearing them as rhythm. For example, the clicking wheels of a railway carriage emit sounds that are 'organized' in just this way. Yet it is only by a special effort of attention that we begin to hear rhythms in them. We must imagine the musical context which transforms the sounds into tones. (Gershwin first heard *Rhapsody in Blue* in the wheels of a train on which he was travelling.) Or consider the mechanical hammers in a factory: these too make regular blows, with repeated accents. But to hear them as rhythms we must hear something else: the something that Wagner provides, when he sets the anvils of Niebelheim in a musical context (Ex. 2.3). In this justly famous passage, Wagner *first* establishes the rhythm in the orchestra, as something irresistible, a demonic force that sweeps us into Niebelheim and animates what happens there. Then, when the anvils sound alone, the rhythm beats on in them, a ghostly residue of what began as life. This is not to say that pure

Ex. 2.3. Wagner, *Das Rheingold*, the descent into Niebelheim

percussive sounds could not be used to establish a rhythmic pulse. (Witness the mesmerizing rhythms of Varèse's *Ionisation*, or the inexpressibly delicate opening to the slow movement of Bartók's *Sonata for Two Pianos and Percussion*.) It is rather to show that, even when we hear only percussion, the perception of rhythm involves a movement to another perceptual level.

Nor is regularity required. One of the most rhythmical pieces of music ever written—the 'Sacrificial Dance' from the *Rite of Spring*—dispenses with small-scale repetitions altogether, changing time and accent with every bar (Ex. 2.4). The dense harmony and armoured orchestration press the music relentlessly across the barlines, like a horseman riding hard over fences.

We can hear rhythm in one tone, even in the first tone of a piece. As soon as a tone sounds, the perceptive listener will understand it as on or off the beat, as leading towards or away from a down-beat. You have to hear the first note of *Parsifal* as off the beat: the musical person instantly does this, and holds the beat in suspension, as it were, until the eighth note comes finally down on it (Ex. 2.5).

Rhythmic Organization

How, in the face of such examples, should we describe the organization that we hear in hearing rhythm? It is to Hegel's credit that he made the answer

Ex. 2.4. Stravinsky, *The Rite of Spring*, 'Sacrificial Dance'

Ex. 2.5. Wagner, *Parsifal*, prelude

to this question crucial to the philosophy of music.[2] I shall list what seem to me to be the most important variables in rhythmic organization, before examining how this extraordinary phenomenon should be understood.

1. Beat. This term, often used vaguely to denote either the whole of rhythmic organization, or at least organization of a regular and insistent kind, describes, in my use, the underlying pulse of music: the movement *with* which we move, when we enter into the 'spirit' of the piece. It is significant that I have been compelled to use metaphors in my attempt to describe this thing, which is nevertheless so familiar to us. The beat in music is comparable to the heartbeat—the regular, but flexible, throbbing upon which our life depends, and which we notice only when some great exertion has upset the natural function of the body.

The term 'beat' is therefore naturally used when describing:

2. Measure, or metre. Leibniz described music as 'a kind of unconscious calculation'.[3] This too is a metaphor. Rhythm plays with regularity, but is not reducible to it: the pulse is both counted and discounted. Psychological

---

[2] *Aesthetics: Lectures on Fine Art*, tr. T. M. Knox, 2 vols. (Oxford, 1975), ii. 913–19.

[3] *Principles of Nature and Grace*, in *Philosophical Essays*, tr. and ed. R. Ariew and D. Garber (Indianapolis, 1989), 212. See also 'On Widsom', vii. 86–7, in *Philosophical Papers and Letters*, tr. and ed. L. E. Loemker (2nd edn., Dordrecht, 1969), 425–6.

studies have shown, what is a priori obvious, that even the most exact performer will imbue a piece with a minute rubato, and this rubato is the mark
of a living organism—the unnoticed vacillation of the pulse.[4] When this
rubato is absent—as when someone plays in time to a drum machine or a
metronome—it is precisely rhythm that is the primary victim.

Nevertheless, Leibniz's observation points to a pivotal feature of our
experience of rhythm. In Western classical music the beat is *measured out*,
and rubato makes sense only on the assumption that this is so. Barlines
indicate a process that repeats itself through the music; and the bars themselves are subdivided into individual 'beats', which can be further divided.
In hearing a rhythm we order sounds in time by the recursive subdivision
of a primary sequence. This fact has suggested to Christopher Longuet-
Higgins a far-reaching theory with which to explain rhythmic ambiguity (as
when one and the same phrase can be heard in 3/4 or 6/8 time), the
distinction (evident from Ex. 2.5) between off-beats and on-beats, and the
phenomenon of beat itself.[5] Before considering this theory, it is necessary to
enumerate some the the phenomena that it might be called upon to explain.

3. The first of these is divisibility itself, which depends upon the temporal
value assigned to individual tones. Note-values indicate the duration of a
tone by specifying the interval between the beginning of one musical event
and the beginning of the next (which might be a silence). A few instances
are given in Ex. 2.6, which will serve simply to remind the reader of the

Ex. 2.6. Simple rhythms (*a*) Waltz; (*b*) Polka; (*c*) Siciliano; (*d*) March

[4] E. F. Clarke, 'Structure and Expression in Rhythmic Performance', in
P. Howell, I. Cross, and R. West (eds.), *Musical Structure and Cognition* (London
1985), 209–36; J. A. Sloboda, *The Musical Mind: The Cognitive Psychology of Music*
(Oxford, 1985), ch. 3.

[5] The relevant papers have been collected in J. C. Longuet-Higgins, *Mental
Processes: Studies in Cognitive Science* (Cambridge, Mass., 1987).

obvious fact, that time signature (the number of beats, of what value, per measure) determines rhythm only when the subdivisions within the bar are clear. The various ways of parcelling our four-beat bar in Ex. 2.6*d* provide familiar instances.

The temporal continuum is infinitely divisible, although there is a threshold below which we cannot perceive the divisions. Hence rhythms too are divisible, as far as that threshold permits, and each rhythm is heard as containing an indefinite potential for further subdivision. Jazz frequently takes an off-beat, divides it into quarter-notes, and places the accent on the fourth of those quarter-notes—an effect which impacts so violently against the measure, that we cling more firmly to the underlying rhythm, and throw ourselves into the movement. Sometimes we sense this dividing of time as a palpable effect of the musical utterance, an atomizing of the moment—as in Alberich's syncopated gesture of resentment (Ex. 2.7).

The first beat of the bar or measure is often called the 'down-beat'. Hence the distinction between:

4. Down-beat and up-beat. The rhythmic movement, which comes *down* on the first beat of the bar, is also raised in anticipation. This 'raising' of the beat is sometimes known as the up-beat; but while what counts as a 'down-beat' is relatively clear, and settled by the metre itself, the same is not true of the up-beat. An up-beat is most clearly heard as a *melodic* event—a 'leading into' the melody, which we know so well from English and German folksong: see Ex. 2.8, in which the first note lies on an up-beat, and contrast Czech and Russian folk-melodies, which characteristically begin on a down-beat, as in Ex. 2.9.[6] For this reason up-beats may comprehend more than one beat—as

Ex. 2.7. Wagner, *Götterdämmerung*, Act 2, prelude

[6] The influence of speech rhythm is all-important in the rhythmic structure of folksong. Slavonic languages make little use of articles, and often have truncated prepositions: in Czech, moreover, the accent is always on the first syllable of the word. These facts make the up-beat virtually redundant in Czech folksong. Bartók attributed the same down-beat character of Hungarian folksong to the fact that Hungarian places the accent, like Czech, on the first syllable (*Hungarian Folk Music*, tr. M. D. Calvocoressi (London, 1931), 13). Equally important, however, is the fact that cases in Hungarian are determined agglutinatively, by a suffix to the noun, and not by prepositions.

in their frequent (some would say cliché-ridden) use by Mahler (Ex 2.10)—or less than one, as in Ex. 2.11.

Certain theorists—notably Riemann[7]—have associated the distinction between up-beat and down-beat with that in ancient Greek orchestrics, between *thesis* and *arsis*, the first being the moment in dance when the foot comes down, the second the moment when the foot is raised. Riemann distinguishes the rhythmic motif, which is a succession of *arsis* and *thesis*, from the beat or measure which underlies it. From the same ancient lexicon comes the term *anacrusis*, to denote the moment of anticipation, which 'leads

Ex. 2.8. German folksong 'Sandmännchen', arr. Brahms

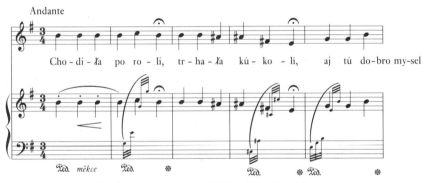

Ex. 2.9. Moravian folksong, 'Kvítí Milodĕjné, arr. Janáček

Ex. 2.10. Mahler, Fourth Symphony in G major, first movement

Ex. 2.11. Mussorgsky, *Pictures at an Exhibition*, 'Samuel Goldberg and Schmuyle'

[7] *System der musikalischen Rythmik und Metrik* (Leipzig, 1903).

into' the dance. In Riemann's usage these terms form the technicalities of a complete theory of rhythm—a theory now widely rejected, despite its commendable attempt to find the origin of rhythmic organization in the movements required by dancing.

The influence of Riemann endures, however, in the frequent application of the term 'up-beat' to *all* forms of rhythmical *anacrusis*. For instance, a Viennese waltz will normally begin with a passage in which indolent waltz rhythms exchange courtesies with fleeting polkas, in which slow marches cross the musical horizon, while local gallops twitter briefly and pass on. This might be described as an 'extended up-beat', which prepares the down-beat of the first danceable bar. (But what should we say of the first three notes of the 'Blue Danube' when it finally emerges? Are they not the *true* up-beat into the waltz?) A similar instance is provided by Beethoven's Eroica Symphony, Op. 55, which begins with two loud E flat chords, before launching into the melody. These too have been described as an up-beat, by Edward Cone, who popularized this use of the term.[8] An extended up-beat may also be, or include, a down-beat. There is no harm in this usage, provided we know exactly what we mean by it. In effect we imply that rhythmic organization occurs on several levels; hence a down-beat on one level—that of the measure—may be an up-beat at another level—the level of melodic organization or musical form.

It is nevertheless true that our experience of rhythm distinguishes, at the level of the bar, three quite different forms of beat: the down-beat, against which everything is measured, the up-beat which 'leads into' it, usually as part of a melodic sequence, and the beat which is neither 'down' nor 'up' but neutral.

5. Grouping. The phenomena that I have just discussed—measure, division, and the three kinds of beat—should be distinguished from the active 'grouping' of musical events into complex wholes. One and the same metre, involving the same divisions of the various beats, may be grouped in different ways. You can hear the elements in Ex. 2.12 with the quavers either trailing from or leading to the crotchets—a possibility vividly exploited by Sibelius, in the finale to his Violin Concerto. Some musicologists have been so impressed by the phenomenon of grouping, that they have tried to make it the cornerstone of rhythmic organization. 'To experience rhythm,' write Cooper and Meyer, 'is to group separate sounds into structured patterns. Such grouping is the result of the interaction among the various aspects of the materials of music: pitch, intensity, timbre, texture and harmony—as well as duration.'[9] For reasons that should already be evident,

---

[8] *Musical Form and Musical Performance* (New York, 1968), 23.
[9] *The Rhythmic Structure of Music* (Chicago, 1960), 1.

Ex. 2.12. Rhythmic groupings

this suggestion is far too narrow. Rhythmic grouping is a *Gestalt* phenomenon, like the perception of visual patterns. But it relies on an underlying temporal measure which it does not generate. For reasons that I shall later examine, grouping has the freedom of the imagination: the grouping of sounds is not dictated by their real relations, but is completed by us, in an act that is subject to the will. This is already evident from Ex. 2.12. However unambiguous the metrical organization of a piece of music, there will be subsidiary groupings, stresses, and boundaries which we impose on it, and which we can alter and emphasize at will. (Consider the constantly shifting rhythmic groupings of Ravel's *Boléro*, established against an unambiguous metrical background. Intelligent listening, and intelligent playing, here require active participation in the creation of the rhythmic structure.)

6. Accent. An accent may fall *on* or *off* the 'beat' (by which is meant the *down*-beat). Accent is the primary form of rhythmic emphasis, the bringing forward into consciousness of a particular *moment* in the rhythmic order. Although it can arise through a momentary increase in volume, this is neither necessary nor sufficient to create the accent. The difference between an accented and an unaccented note is a difference of *attack*, and is most clearly understood in those cases, like the bowing of a violin, in which the instrument itself is attacked in different ways.

The distinction between beat (in the sense of measure) and accent is clearly illustrated by syncopation. A syncopated rhythm is a *single* rhythm, in which the accent falls regularly off the beat—often on a note which lies between two beats, as in Ex. 2.13. Syncopated rhythms should be distinguished from melodic syncopations, in which the melodic line falls off the beat, creating a stress where there is no rhythmic accent. A moving example

Ex. 2.13. Paul Desmond and Dave Brubeck, 'Take Five'

of this occurs in Janáček's opera *Káťa Kabanová* when the heroine, alone in the darkness, and hesitating whether to yield to Boris, is disturbed by voices, and gives a guilty start. The melodic line stands against the rhythm in a way that portrays Káťa's life, arrested within her, and then comes down on the beat with the words 'srdce přestalo bít'—'my heart ceased to beat'—a statement which the rhythmic organization subtly denies (Ex. 2.14).

Ex. 2.14. Janáček, *Káťa Kabanová*, Act 2

7. Such examples suggest that we should distinguish accent from stress, by which I mean the audible *leaning* on a note which is neither a down-beat nor a rhythmic accent. It is very difficult to set a melody off the beat without creating a pattern of stresses which lie against the measure. The term 'syncopation' is therefore naturally used of examples like the last one from Janáček. Nevertheless, an account of rhythmic organization ought to be sensitive to the distinction between stress and accent, and ought to allow that a stress may fall even on the weakest of pulses—even on a silence. And here, by way of illustrating the distinction between beat, measure, accent, stress, and grouping, it is worth studying an example in which all five forms of organization are held apart, to create a prolonged and unresolved sense of anticipation. The example, Ex. 2.15, is from Ravel's *Rapsodie espagnole*, and beneath it I have made a tentative suggestion as to how this ought to be heard (and therefore played) in order to bring out its rhythmic complexity, with the rhythmic grouping following the repeated figure, so cutting across the barline, with the accent falling on the first or second beat of the bar, and with a stress moving constantly from one to another of the three beats.

8. Tempo. The division of the bar depends for its rhythmic effect on tempo—which is not, in itself, a form of organization, but a source of the energy by which rhythmic organization is driven. If rhythm were *simply* a matter of measure or grouping, then we could not explain the effect of tempo, any change of which strikes directly at our experience of rhythm, whether or not it changes the grouping, stress, or accent. The obvious explanation of this is that our experience of rhythm is an instance of, or runs parallel to, our experience of bodily life. In hearing rhythms, we are hearing a kind of animation.

Ex. 2.15. Ravel, *Rapsodie espagnole*

9. Simple and compound rhythm. Classical music theory distinguishes simple rhythms, in which beats are subdivided into half- and quarter-notes, from compound rhythms, in which beats are subdivided into odd-numbered parts—usually three, as in 6/8 time. The distinction here merely elaborates the considerations which I have listed under 3 above; and is only the first move in the task of classifying rhythms. Far more interesting from the philosophical point of view is:

10. Cross-rhythm, in which two rhythms are heard simultaneously. Acoustically speaking, a cross-rhythm presents the same profile as a compound rhythm. For example, the compound rhythm in Ex. 2.16*a* is acoustically identical with the cross-rhythm in Ex. 2.16*b*. In the context of the classical style, however, we could not regard the choice between these two ways of hearing as open. Ex 2.16*b* represents two simultaneous rhythmic groupings which sound across each other, with conflicting musical movements. The example provides us with a clear illustration of the distinction between sound and tone. Assuming that the notes are played staccato, the

Ex. 2.16. (*a*) compound rhythm; (*b*) cross-rhythm.

sound sequences are indistinguishable. But the second involves two musical processes, while the first involves only one. The distinction can be observed even in music without melody or pitch, in which organization is a matter of rhythm alone. Indeed, cross-rhythm is one of the most important devices in African drum music.

Hierarchy

Cooper and Meyer support their theory of rhythm by invoking the distinction between stressed and unstressed events. (They use the term 'accent' to denote what I have called 'stress'.) In one of their quasi-definitions they describe rhythm as 'the grouping of one or more unaccented beats in relation to an accented one', and they identify five basic groupings, which they describe in terms taken from classical prosody. These are:

iamb:	⌣ —
anapest:	⌣ ⌣ —
trochee:	— ⌣
dactyl:	— ⌣ ⌣
amphibrach:	⌣ — ⌣

Stress does not depend upon note-values, and may conflict with them, as in Ex. 2.17, the second subject of Schubert's String Quartet in G major D887, first movement, which Cooper and Meyer describe as a fully inverted amphibrach—an amphibrach in which the stress falls always on the shortest note in the group. (Their graph of the stress pattern appears beneath the example.)

It should already be obvious that rhythmic organization cannot be accounted for in terms of stress pattern alone: metre, note-value, accent, and the play of up-beat and down-beat are just as important in shaping the rhythmic character of this most subtle melody. Even in poetry, from the ancient theory of which Cooper and Meyer take their terms, rhythm involves a metrical background. In Helen Gardner's words, the music of the English heroic line 'arises from the counterpointing of variable speech stresses with regular metrical stresses'.[10] Nevertheless, Cooper and Meyer have an important motive for their emphasis on stress patterns. For this gives substance to their view that rhythmic organization is hierarchical—groupings at the basic level are reproduced at higher levels, where 'height' is a matter of time-span. The distinction between stressed and unstressed events radiates through the entire musical surface, as though the rhythmic organization of the piece were latent within each smallest cell. The example in Ex. 2.18 (Bach's Six Little Preludes, No. 5) illustrates the point. Here level (1) is, in

[10] *The Art of T. S. Eliot* (London 1949), 17 n.

Ex. 2.17. Schubert, String Quartet in G major, D887, first movement, second subject

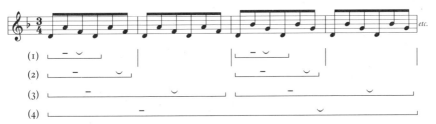

Ex. 2.18. J. S. Bach, Six Little Preludes, No. 5 in D minor, BWV935

Cooper and Meyer's terminology, the 'sub-primary' level, lying beneath the primary rhythmic organization.

A distinction should, however, be made between two kinds of hierarchy, which I shall call the cumulative and the generative respectively. In a cumulative hierarchy, lower-order elements are comprehended in themselves, and the higher-order elements understood in terms of them. In a generative hierarchy the lower-level order is perceived only because, and in so far as, it is *derived from* the higher. Cooper and Meyer's theory of rhythm postulates a cumulative hierarchy, in which grouping at the primary level is understood measure by measure, while higher levels are in turn derived from the primary organization by extrapolating over larger time-spans. Someone could fully grasp the primary organization, and yet have no knowledge—not even tacit knowledge—of the higher-level organization. Meyer and his followers are up to a point right in thinking that musical surfaces are organized hierarchically in this way: the same is true of patterns and ornaments in the decorative arts, as well as the classical Orders in architecture, and the high Gothic of the cathedrals. And as we shall see, this fact is of great significance. But it proves far less than Cooper and Meyer seem to think. Only a generative hierarchy would offer an explanation of our ability to grasp, from hearing a short passage, the rhythmic organization of the piece as a whole.

In any case, it is surely evident that metre is more fundamental to rhythm than stress. And metre, Longuet-Higgins has argued, exhibits a generative hierarchy.[11] Metrical organization arises through the repeated subdivision of

[11] See esp. H. C. Longuet-Higgins and C.S. Lee, 'The Rhythmic Interpretation of Monophonic Music', in Longuet-Higgins, *Mental Processes*, 150–68, and eid., 'The Perception of Musical Rhythms', *Perception*, 11 (1982), 115–28.

a temporal measure, as when a bar is divided into two crotchets, each of which is divided into two quavers, which in turn are divided into semi-quavers; and so on. The result is a 'tree' structure as shown in Diagram 2.1.

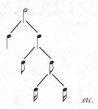

Diagram 2.1

The application of a recursive procedure enables the listener to derive all lower levels from the highest. To hear rhythm, on this view, is to grasp how events at the audible level are dispersed on the lowest branches of a generative tree. Thus I hear the first note of *Parsifal* (Ex. 2.5.) as the second of two semiquaver units, derived by division of a crotchet, derived by division of a bar into four crotchet measures. The generative process which I recuperate in listening also determines that the first note is an off-beat, and that the off-beat stress should endure through the first two bars. Of course, I do not carry out this calculation *consciously*. Nevertheless, by unconsciously latching on to the generative hierarchy, I am able to assign a measure, a beat, and a temporal value to the notes that I hear, and so begin to 'move with' the music as it steps across the charted territory of time.

Longuet-Higgins's theory marks the first appearance in this book of an influential idea. Language is organized by a generative syntax, so we now believe. To prove that music is organized in a similar way is therefore to give substance to the age-old analogy between music and language. In Chapter 7 I shall consider more fully what the suggestion means, and whether it can be substantiated. For the present it is sufficient to note that the theory, however plausible in its own terms, is incomplete. It gives no account of stress, accent, or grouping, and therefore offers no final theory of the *activity* that we hear, when we hear rhythm in music. A computer could discern and reproduce rhythms by means of Longuet-Higgins's syntax: indeed, that is how rhythm machines work, and it is one reason why they sound so profoundly unmusical. Metre is not rhythm, but the background against which rhythm is achieved. To account for rhythm we must add to the generative hierarchy discerned by Longuet-Higgins (and which is already implied in our musical notation), the cumulative hierarchies of Cooper and Meyer, together with groupings which exhibit no hierarchical organization at all. What I mean can best be illustrated by an example. Having presented the unforgettable melody of the woodbird's song, Wagner is able to reintro-duce it as a purely *rhythmic* structure, when Siegfried approaches the foot of Brünnhilde's rock (Ex. 2.19). The listener is grouping the repeated notes against both barline and accent, to form a bounded cell, the character of which has been emancipated from the original melodic movement. Such a rhythmic cell is not reiterated at higher levels, and although it is heard against the metrical background, it is understood as the ghost of a melody, rather than a metrical structure.

Ex. 2.19. Wagner, *Siegfried*, Act 3

Rhythm and Life

Longuet-Higgins's theory of rhythm is a piece of psychology (or 'cognitive science'): it offers to show how we perceive rhythmic organization in a sequence of sounds. The theory of Cooper and Meyer does not try to *explain* our experience of rhythm. Rather, it attempts to amplify that experience, by showing how the organization of a rhythmic cell may be heard in ever larger time-spans. It is, one might say, a critical rather than a psychological theory. A philosophy of music offers neither psychological explanations nor critical recommendations. It attempts to say *what music is*, prior to any explanation or amplification of our musical experience. Both the theories that I have considered are deficient, when it comes to the philosophical question. Cooper and Meyer substitute stress for metre, in order to reach the iterative hierarchy which for them provides so satisfying an account of musical order—at least of the order exhibited by the fifth of Bach's Little Preludes. But they achieve this result only by ignoring the generative hierarchy that is implied by metrical organization. Longuet-Higgins overlooks both grouping and stress, in order to provide a consistent theory of the remainder: a theory which treats music as perceptually organized sound. As I have implied, however, the experience of rhythm is something more than an experience of metrical structure. To hear rhythm is to hear a kind of animation. Rhythm involves the same virtual causality that we find in melody. Beats do not follow one another; they bring each other into being, respond to one another, and breathe with a common life. The organization that I have just described is not a possible organization of sounds, construed as material objects. But it *is* an organization of mental objects, and one that we know intimately from our own inner experience: the experience of life conscious of itself as life.

Regularity, hierarchical organization, relative loudness, and tempo, considered in themselves (i.e. acoustically, as properties of sounds), are as much properties of machines as of living beings. But they become rhythm and stress when our own life speaks to us through the sound. What we hear then becomes something more than sound for us, something more urgent, more immediate, and more intimately connected to processes that we know in ourselves. It is then that beat, accent, and grouping emerge. This is particularly obvious when we consider *silent* rhythm: rhythm that is not heard but sensed in some other way, as when we dance without music, or when we see another dancing, but do not hear the sound. Here we are observing a particular display of life, and the regularity that we see in the movements is minutely qualified by the style and phrasing that lead us to move in sympathy.

This is one reason why rhythm cannot, in the end, be studied as a thing apart from melody and counterpoint. The subtle rhythmic organization achieved by such composers as Haydn, Schubert, and Brahms depends upon our understanding of melody, theme, and motif, which cause us to break down the metre of the music into many smaller pulses, crossing and reinforcing one another. Thus arises the indescribable sense of a breathing organism which those whose sole acquaintance with rhythm derives from the more mechanical kind of pop music could never begin to imagine. Consider just one instance: the middle section of the slow movement of Schubert's String Quintet in C major, D956; and try to enumerate all the many pulses and accents that are synthesized in its extraordinary texture (Ex. 2.20). Each pulse here is associated with a melodic fragment, and is made noticeable by the impeccable rightness of its melodic line.

Foreground and background

The Schubert example illustrates the distinction between background and foreground in our experience of rhythm. Metre and accent create an underlying movement; but they do not determine the rhythmical groupings in the musical surface. Consider the opening of Mozart's Fortieth Symphony (Ex. 2.21). Here the rhythmic background is provided by the viola figure, with the accent (emphasized in the bass) falling regularly on the first beat of the bar. Against this background the violins play the opening phrase, whose rhythmic contour is then repeated in the three phrases which follow, before making way for the answering configuration which moves the melody onwards to its half-conclusion on the dominant. Much of the symmetry of this theme is due to the rhythmical foreground, which unifies the opening phrases, and enables Mozart to lengthen the melody without the faintest sense of strain. The very same foreground grouping occurs in Cherubino's aria 'Non so più' (Ex. 2.22), although set against a rapid and flowing back-

Ex. 2.20. Schubert, String Quintet in C major, D956, second movement

ground with two accents to the bar: and again Mozart is able to build a fourfold opening statement by this rhythmic device. Comparison of the two examples shows how immediate is our experience of these distinct levels of rhythmic order—and, as we see from the Schubert Quintet, there can be more than two of them.

Foreground organization might coexist with a hazy and indefinite background, as in the opening bars of *Parsifal*. Skriabin's early piano music often relies upon a rhythmical background that is so faint as to transfer the movement entirely to the foreground, where it sways in the gentle breeze of the composer's Chopin-intoxicated harmony. The first of the Preludes, Op. 15, for example, makes constant use of the little motif in Ex. 2.23, which straddles the barline, against a limp bass in 3/4 time. Here the rhythmic cell generates and controls the movement, and the metrical background is dissolved in a summer haze (Ex. 2.24).

Rhythms are quickly wearisome, unless refreshed by a countervailing foreground which groups the tones against the metre. The ever-so-slight rubato of a solo instrument playing in front of the beat is familiar to jazz-lovers. To play jazz properly it is not enough to move with the beat: you must also enter the 'groove' of it, which means riding alongside it with those playful gestures that ruffle the rhythmic surface and fill it with light. The distinction between beat and groove is a special case of the general distinction between foreground and background rhythm.

The distinction is fundamental to all music—even the music of the African drums, from which harmony and melody are absent. The rhythmic

Ex. 2.21. Mozart, Fortieth Symphony in G minor, K. 550

Non so   più co-sa son co-sa fac-cio, or di   fo-co, o-ra so-no di

ghiac-cio Og-ni don- na can-giar di co - lo - re,   Og-ni don- na mi fa pal-pi-(tar)

Ex. 2.22. Mozart, *Le nozze di Figaro*, 'Non so più'

Grouping:

Ex. 2.23. Rhythmic motif

Ex. 2.24. Skriabin, Five Preludes, Op. 15 No. 1

foreground in classical music is one of the principal generators of symmetry and asymmetry, of unity and diversity, and of parallels and disjunctions. Identity of rhythmical shape can make one set of pitches into the answering phrase required by almost any other: witness the twelve-tone melodies of Berg, in the Violin Concerto and *Lulu*. And when the rhythmic foreground is dissolved—as in the serialized rhythms of Luigi Nono—the result is a kind of punctilious shapelessness in which, in the absence of tonality, we search in vain for musical relations. Strangely, whole schools of musical analysis have emerged—among them that of Heinrich Schenker, which I discuss in Chapters 10 and 13—which make next to no mention of rhythm. Without rhythm, however, there is no musical surface to analyse.

Melody

We can now make a first attempt to place music in its metaphysical context. When we hear music, three things occur: there is a vibration in the air; by virtue of this vibration we perceive a sound, which is a 'secondary object', heard as a pure event; and in this sound we hear an organization that is not reducible to any properties of the sound, nor to any properties of the vibration that causes it. Hearing sound involves the exercise of the ear: it displays an *acoustic* capacity, and all that we hear when we hear sounds are the secondary properties of sound events. Animals also hear these properties, and respond to sounds and to the information contained in sounds. But to hear music we need capacities that only rational beings have. We must be able to hear an order that contains no information about the physical world, which stands apart from the ordinary workings of cause and effect, and which is irreducible to any physical organization. At the same time, it contains a virtual causality of its own, which animates the elements that are joined by it. Even so apparently simple a phenomenon as rhythm gives proof of this. A study of melody will show yet more clearly the distinction between acoustic and musical experience.

What happens when I hear a melody in a sequence of sounds? By 'melody' I do not mean tunes, but the musical kind of which tunes are an instance. I have in mind the experience of a musical unity across time, in which something begins, and then moves on through changes in pitch—perhaps to an audible conclusion. A melody has temporal boundaries, and a musical movement between them. It is a special kind of musical *Gestalt*, perceived as a unity, and functioning as a 'reidentifiable particular' in the world of sound. It is itself composed of such unities: phrases and motifs, which may import a highly complex organization to the melodic whole.

A chord is also a *Gestalt:* and yet to hear the unity of the nursery theme in Ex. 2.25, is not the same as to hear the unity of the chord that follows— even though each unity contains the same individual tones. The melodic *Gestalt* is a unity across *time*—a unity perceived in a continuous flux of sounds, and not one in which several elements are simultaneously held together in an organized totality. The melodic *Gestalt* also differs from the rhythmic 'grouping'. The rhythmic group is heard as unified, but not as an unbroken unity; unlike melody, it is not heard as a musical individual.

Ex. 2.25. 'Twinkle, twinkle', 'Ah, vous dirai-je maman', etc.

This unity and individuality in a temporal process have puzzled philosophers. Husserl asks the question: 'How does the unity of a process of change that continues for an extended period of time, a unity that comes to pass or develops in succession—the unity of a melody, for example—come to be represented?'[12] And he refutes the suggestion made by Brentano, that the components of such a process are retained in consciousness, so being united with their successors—a suggestion that would imply that our experience of a melody is indistinguishable from that of a chord.

One may doubt the cogency of Husserl's general question: there may be no such thing as an account of *how* we 'represent' temporal processes in consciousness—no account that does not assume already that we are doing just this. (Maybe that is the real moral of Kant's thesis that time is the form of inner sense: there is no such thing as thinking time away, in order to show how we construct it from something that is not temporally ordered. Certainly Husserl is unable to provide even the faintest hint of an answer to

---

[12] *The Phenomenology of Internal Time Consciousness*, 141.

the question how this is done. For whatever is done must be done in time: time must already exist for us, if there is to be the process that brings it into consciousness.)

Nevertheless, Husserl's *particular* question—what accounts for the experience of unity in the temporal *Gestalt?*—is significant. Consider our experience of sentences: here we certainly believe that an account can be given of our ability to hold them together as unities: a generative syntax would explain why it is that an uncompleted sentence, such as 'The cat sat on the', is experienced as 'unsaturated'—as possessing a valency, which in this case only a noun-phrase will satisfy. In Chapters 7 and 10 I shall return to the suggestion that the musical *Gestalt* can be accounted for in a parallel manner, through a generative syntax. But a more urgent task confronts us here, which is to characterize the melodic *Gestalt* as *phenomenon*. Consider the well-known melody that opens Rachmaninov's Second Piano Concerto in C minor, Op. 18 (Ex. 2.26). This is preceded by a sequence of subdominant chords, and two bars of accompaniment from the piano. But when the orchestra enters, it is not simply that we hear the sound of the strings: we hear something *begin* on that first note of C—something more than the note C itself. The experience is totally compelling, and wholly natural: and as the theme sways back and forth on C an impulse is developed which carries it forward from bar to bar until, at bar 16, it returns to its starting-point. But is this where the melody ends? Certainly you can *hear* an ending here, should you so choose. But notice Rachmaninov's bowing: he wishes you to hear the C in bar 16 not as an ending but as a new beginning: the C leads us into a new region of the melody, a new upwards movement which both answers and continues the movement of the opening bars. Even when the

Ex. 2.26. Rachmaninov, Second Piano Concerto in C minor, Op. 18, first movement, first subject

strings fade away and the piano takes over, it is not certain that the melody
has ended—rather, its life ebbs away; what is left of it evaporates as the piano
soars away into the upper register. Here, then, is a melody with a very clear
beginning, and with marked internal boundaries, but without a clear ending.
In such a case you, the listener, are required to place the ending where you
will: and part of the purpose of critical discussion will be to guide your choice.

Musical boundaries may be clear or vague; they are also highly permeable.
A melody can seep across into the surrounding material. What sounds for one
moment as an accompanying figure may suddenly become an up-beat: or it
may gradually permeate the melodic line until it is part of it. A lively instance
is provided by the slow movement of Beethoven's Fourth Symphony, in B
flat major, Op. 60, which begins with a repeated fourth, lasting for a whole
bar, until the melody takes over (Ex. 2.27). When did that melody begin? At
bar 2? Or a quarter-beat before (the last B flat being an up-beat into the
melody)? Or a beat, two beats, three beats before? The listener has a choice
here: and it is an important one, since that accompanying phrase is gradually
incorporated into the melody, and how the melody is heard depends crucially
on the history accorded to the rising fourth. (A similar case: those four opening drum-beats in the Violin Concerto: are they part of the melody or not?
You can hear them either way: but gradually you understand that they are the
leading motif, the seed from which the whole wonderful movement grows.)

Ex. 2.27. Beethoven, Fourth Symphony in B flat major, Op. 60, second movement

Musical boundaries may also overlap. One phrase may begin before
another has ended, and a single note may be heard both as the end of one
phrase and the beginning of another, much as a line in a drawing may serve
as the boundary to two distinct figures. (Consider the multiple overlapping in
the coda to Schubert's Eighth Symphony in B minor, D759, first movement,
Ex. 2.28. We hear the concluding note of a loud phrase, and, *simultaneously*,
the beginning of a soft one, emerging as it were from behind.)

Phrases may be dovetailed, so as to criss-cross through the texture of a
piece, stitching it together, as in the Mozart example, Ex. 2.29. Here we
see, in miniature, the process whereby music grows, develops, and diverges,
while remaining bound in a continuous texture. Our ability to perceive these

internal boundaries, and to hear them occurring in separate but concurrent phrases, is something that we take so much for granted, that we seldom pause to study it. As soon as we do so, however, we see how remarkable

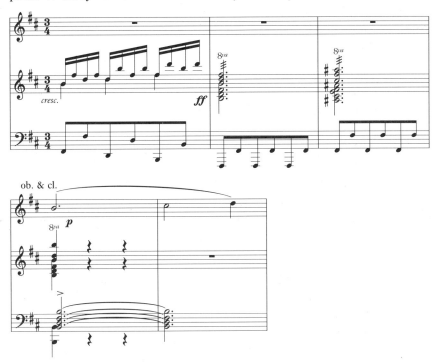

Ex. 2.28. Schubert, Eighth Symphony in B minor, D759, first movement, coda

Ex. 2.29. Mozart, String Quartet in D minor, K. 421, first movement

this ability is, and how strange it is that we should have acquired it: to what end, and by what process of selection?

Such observations again illustrate the relation between musical hearing and the perception of aspects (as exemplified by the well-known duck-rabbit and Necker cube). Musical hearing, like certain other forms of aspect perception, lies within the province of the will. Not that you can always or even generally make yourself hear a piece in some novel way, but that it makes sense to ask someone to do so. This is a request that might be obeyed. In Chapter 3 I will try to show why this fact is of such supreme importance for the philosophy of music.

Ex. 2.30. Janáček, *The Cunning Little Vixen*, prelude, bars 1–4

Sometimes short phrases and melodic fragments are all that a composer offers us: but still the experience of the boundary prevails. The overture to *The Cunning Little Vixen* begins with a scatter of animated phrases (Ex. 2.30). One of them seems to detach itself, being repeated at different pitches, and pressing itself on our attention (Ex. 2.31). And in that tiny phrase you hear not only a beginning and an end, but a movement between them, and even an upbeat, the F flat being a kind of preparation for the movement upwards from E flat to the fifth above. You could not call this a melody; yet it occupies our musical attention in the same way that melodies do; and before long, indeed, it amalgamates with the phrase of the first two bars to form a beautiful theme (Ex. 2.32). Such a musical gesture, pregnant with melodic suggestions and eager for companionship, yet complete in itself, would now be described as a motif. The widespread use of this term (intro-

Ex. 2.31. Janáček, *The Cunning Little Vixen*, prelude, bar 4

Ex. 2.32. Janáček, *The Cunning Little Vixen*, prelude, bars 10–11

duced in its modern sense by A. B. Marx)[13] stems from Wagner's theory of the Leitmotif, and Schoenberg's claim that motif, rather than theme, is the true atomic particle of modern music. I use the term more neutrally, and without giving it any more precise sense than it spontaneously acquires from examples like the Janáček.[14]

The phenomenon of the melodic boundary must be distinguished from another with which it is sometimes confused—that of melodic 'closure'. This term was introduced by the *Gestalt* psychologists, to describe the spontaneous tendency to complete the object of perception, by seeing temporally or spatially fragmented objects as uniform and continuous. It was popularized by L. B. Meyer (who was more influenced by the mathematical than the psychological uses of the term) and by certain followers of Heinrich Schenker, in order to describe the goal-directed character of music. Even the simplest folk-melody seems to be working towards a conclusion, which rounds off the musical gesture and gives an impression of completeness. The nursery theme of Ex. 2.25 (completed in Ex. 2.33) returns to the tonic in bar 4. But the listener instinctively feels that there is more to come, and is granted the experience of closure only four bars later,

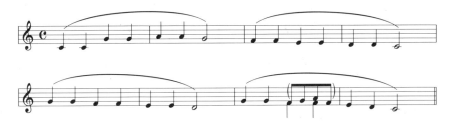

Ex. 2.33. Completion of Ex. 2.25

---

[13] *Die Lehre von der musikalischen Komposition*, 2 vols. (Leipzig, 1837–42), i. 27.

[14] Note that there are also rhythmic and harmonic motifs, and that my appropriation of the term in the present context implies only that there are melodic entities which are smaller than melodies.

after an episode which departs towards the dominant before returning. The experience of closure occurs, as in this example, on the smallest scale; it also occurs, as in the classical sonata-form movement, on a scale so vast that we cannot assume that it is always the *same* experience, or always to be explained in the same way, even though both Meyer and Schenker argue for this striking conclusion. Whether the experience of closure is one or many, however, it is fundamental to melodic organization in our tradition. Our classical music has devoted itself to extending the experience of closure as far as possible, building closed structures out of closed parts via closed sections.

It should be noted that the 'sense of an ending' belongs equally to harmonic and to rhythmic organization. The example I gave is of a closed melody: but it is a melody built according to an harmonic scheme which is also closed. It is one of the remarkable features of Western classical music, that it has developed a language in which rhythmic, harmonic, and melodic closure are achieved together, after a venture outwards in which each partner in the enterprise takes its own, often hair-raising, risks.

Closure creates a boundary—but only one kind of boundary, that which is heard as an end (in either or both senses of the word). Beginnings are not closures, nor are the boundaries of motifs and 'unsaturated' phrases, such as that given in Ex. 2.25. A theory of the musical *Gestalt* must therefore address not only closure, but a host of less prominent but no less important experiences. Indeed, without these other boundary experiences, there would be neither melody nor movement, and therefore nothing to close.

Motifs, phrases, and melodies may stand out more or less vividly from the surrounding music: not because of their loudness or timbre, but simply because they capture our attention. The musical *Gestalt* stands out in something like the way that a configuration stands out in a drawing or puzzle picture. This effect is vital to counterpoint, which depends upon the composer's ability to switch our attention from part to part, while maintaining an even texture. Yet even the most powerful musical *Gestalt* can be sent into the background and replaced by another. Consider Webern's orchestration of Bach's six-part 'Ricercar' from the *Musical Offering*: here the orchestration compels you to hear Bach's melodic line as *background*, the foreground being occupied by the short motifs which, for Webern, form the true substance of this extraordinary work: Ex 2.34. Sometimes a melody emerges from two or more voices which interweave—as in the two-part canon at the sixth from the 'Goldberg' Variations, BWV 988 (Ex. 2.35). Here neither of the two upper voices has a real tune, even though, sounding together, they produce a lively and emphatic melody. Here the melodic *Gestalt* emerges only for the person who gives equal weight to the voices which create it, and who therefore hears three simultaneous movements in the melodic foreground: the two upper voices, and their melodic synthesis. This effect

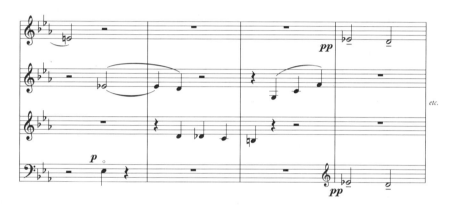

Ex. 2.34. Webern, orchestration of the six-part Ricercar from Bach's *Musical Offering*

is even more striking when a melody is provided with a counter-melody which can be heard through it, as in Ex. 2.36, the Quintet from *Meistersinger*. Sometimes a melody must be heard *as though* produced polyphonically, even though there is only one voice (acoustically speaking) involved in its production. The Bach Suites for solo cello are full of beautiful instances, such as that in Ex. 2.37*a*, which is heard as a one-dimensional projection of Ex. 2.37*b*.

In hearing a melody, we hear a beginning and an end, but also a *movement* between them. And this movement is still going on, even when

Ex. 2.35. J. S. Bach, 'Goldberg' Variations, BWV988, canon at the sixth

Ex. 2.36. Wagner, *Die Meistersinger*, Act 3, quintet

Ex. 2.37. J. S. Bach, Suite for cello in G major, BWV1007, second minuet

there is no sound, as in the theme from the last movement of Beethoven's *Eroica Symphony*, Op. 55, used also in the 'Eroica' Variations for piano, Op. 35, and taken from his ballet *Die Geschöpfe der Prometheus* (1801). In the orchestral version, this theme consists largely of silences (into which Beethoven inserts, when the theme is repeated, a cheeky echo) (Ex. 2.38). Yet we hear in these silences an intense musical movement, which is driving

Ex. 2.38. Beethoven, *Eroica Symphony*, Op. 55, last movement

onwards through them with all the greater force in that it is flying silently. The difference between musical and acoustical events can hardly be better captured than by this example, of a musical event which continues when sound has ceased. Consider too the use of silence in the Fifth Symphony in C minor, Op. 67. The first movement of this work ends with a silent bar, marked by Beethoven with a pause, while the last movement builds up such a momentum that only constantly repeated C major chords can finally bring it to a stop—and in the silences between those chords you hear the movement pressing onwards until stunned at last into submission.

Before completing the discussion of melody, however, we must examine more closely the phenomenon that has been gradually working its way into the foreground of the argument: the phenomenon of musical movement.

Movement

The phenomenon has seemed puzzling to many who have written about it. Gurney argues that musical motion is *ideal* (a motion whose only reality is in the mental sphere).[15] Zuckerkandl argues, by contrast, that musical motion is *pure* motion, a motion in which nothing moves; it is therefore *the most real motion*, motion manifest as it is in itself.[16] Bergson too writes of melody as a 'change in which nothing changes', a change which becomes the 'thing itself'.[17] Schopenhauer latches on to the same phenomenon in his bold theory of music as a manifestation in the world of appearance of the pure thing-in-itself, which is will. Music is a striving in which nothing observable strives.[18] In assessing these theories, however—and at this stage I wish neither to dismiss nor to dwell on them—we should be careful not to confound the mysteries. We should be clear that what we hear in melody is not just change but *movement*: a distinction to which Bergson, like many of the 'process philosophers' whom he inspired, was never as alert as he should have been. Movement involves three things: a spatial frame, an occupant of that frame, and a change of position within it. Change can occur, however, where there is no spatial frame, no dimension save that of time alone. Melody would be less mysterious if it were merely a sequence of acoustic changes; but it is change of a particular kind—the change that we know as movement.

Nor should we confound the movement that we hear in melody with the rhythmic organization studied in the first sections of this chapter. We speak

[15] *The Power of Sound* (London, 1880), 165.

[16] *Sound and Symbol*, tr. W. R. Trask (London, 1956), 139.

[17] 'The Perception of Change', in *The Creative Mind*, tr. M. Andison (Westport, Conn., 1946).

[18] 'On the Metaphysics of Music', in *The World as Will and Representation*, tr. E. F. J. Payne, 2 vols. (New York, 1969), ii. 447–57.

of rhythmic movement, as opposed to 'sequel' or 'pattern', and this is an important fact—an expression of our experience of rhythm, as a form of life. But rhythmic organization can occur without pitched sound, and therefore without the possibility of melody. The distribution of pitches in melody is also a conquest of tonal space, a movement from and towards.

Moreover, we should not attribute to *music* the kind of experience that is made available already by *sound*. It is sound that presents us with the 'pure event', and therefore with a 'change in which nothing changes', a change which is the *thing itself.* (See the argument of Chapter 1.) You do not need to hear tones, in order to experience the pure process: and the experience of this process is only part, and not the most mysterious part, of the experience of music.

The real question, therefore, is why should we speak of movement in describing melody? What moves, and where? Movement requires both a spatial dimension, and objects that occupy positions within it. It is true that we describe the pitch spectrum in spatial terms, and attribute to this auditory 'space' a phenomenal character that is derived from our experience as embodied and 'extended' beings. Things go *up* and *down* in auditory 'space': they move more or less rapidly from place to place; they span larger or narrower distances; and so on. The problem, however, is that we have no way of identifying the individual occupants of this space so as to capture the idea of musical movement. What resides, for example, at the place marked by middle C? Here are three possibilities:

1. The sound of C, produced, let us say, by a clarinet.
2. The tone that we hear in that sound, and in which we also hear musical movement.
3. Some other musical entity—a melody, for example—of which that tone is a part.

Consider suggestion (1). It is certainly possible for the clarinet to move from C to D: and there is no a priori reason why we should not describe this as the movement of a sound from C to D. Such a concept of 'sound identity' is coherent, and in certain circumstances useful to us. But it has two defects from our present point of view. First, it does not justify the idea of *movement*, as opposed to mere change in pitch. Secondly, it does not identify the change that we hear when we hear *musical* movement. When the clarinet plays C, and is replaced by a violin playing D, we hear the very same upwards movement. But here no sound (identified as we have identified the sound of the clarinet) changes its 'position' at all.

Let us now turn to possibility (2). It is surely evident that, whatever a tone is, it is inseparable from the pitch at which we hear it—it could not be the tone that it is, while sounding at another pitch. When we hear the tone sounding on middle C, we are hearing middle C, and hearing it *in a certain way* (as music). To hear a tone at another pitch is to hear another tone: hence no *tone* is ever heard as moving from C to D. There is no way of reidentifying a tone at another place from the one that it first occupied. Although we do have the sense of the 'same' tone at different places, there is no use for the idea of *numerical* identity here. The C one octave higher than middle C is heard as the 'same', but not because it has moved to that position from middle C; it is the same because, in an important sense, it *sounds* the same. Again, when a melody is transposed from C to G, the tone heard at G sounds 'the same' as that previously heard at C: but not because it moved there from C; rather, because this tone stands in the same musical relations to its neighbours as C originally stood.

Of course, transposition, and the doubling effect of the octave are highly significant musical phenomena. But they do not give us the sense of musical movement; rather they presuppose it. A transposition is precisely a transposition of the *movement* from one register to another. The movement was occurring at the original register, and has now been transferred to a fifth above. And that is why the third possibility will also fail to provide us with an account of musical movement. While melodies and thematic devices are understood in a way as musical individuals, it is not their movement through musical space that gives us our idea of musical motion. For the motion that we are seeking to define is *internal* to them, and remains the same when they are transposed.

I have laboured the point, partly because it is important to dismiss a major metaphysical temptation (to which Strawson all but yields in chapter 2 of *Individuals* and which is incipient in many theories of musical expression)— the temptation to think of the sound world as organized in the way that space is, and to situate tones and melodies in that world as the apes of our activity, moving in ways analogous to the way in which *we* move. Not only does the tone-world contain no mobile individuals; its 'spatial' character is a mere appearance. All that constitutes space as a frame *in* which objects are situated as occupants is absent from the pitch continuum: orientation, motion, congruence, and incongruence, and the topological structure that gives sense to the idea of place. I shall say more about this shortly; but it should be already apparent that the idea of musical movement is something of a paradox: for how can we speak of movement, when nothing moves? Musical space, and musical movement, are not even *analogous* to the space and movement of the physical world.[19]

[19] Ernst Kurth, who makes in his own way many of the points that I endorse, nevertheless concludes that musical space is analogous to physical space—even though a feature of the purely psychic realm. (See *Musikpsychologie* (Bern, 1947), 116–36.)

Someone might say that the word 'movement' is being used metaphorically: that we do not really mean movement, but a certain kind of sequence
or change. We could therefore describe what we hear without using spatial
metaphors.

To argue in that way, however, is to argue from no basis. First, do we
know what a metaphor is? To say that a given usage is metaphorical is to
say nothing definite, without some theory of metaphor that will allow us to
assess the damage. Moreover, as I shall argue in Chapter 3, we must distinguish among metaphors between luxuries and necessities. And we are here
dealing with a necessity. For suppose someone said that, for him, there *is* no
up and down in music, no movement, no soaring, rising, falling, no running
or walking from place to place. Could we really think that he experienced
music as we do, that it was, indeed, *music* for him, rather than some other art
predicated upon the interest in sounds? Surely, the temptation is to say that
we *must* hear the movement in music, if we are to hear it as music. (Cf.
again the example from Bruckner, Ex. 2.2.) If we have a metaphor here, it is,
to adapt the happy phrase of Johnson and Lakoff, a 'metaphor we hear by'.[20]

The Dynamics of Tone

It often seems apt to describe musical movement in terms of the dynamic
properties of the tone itself. Tones seem to incline towards each other, fall
away from each other, as though they were incomplete entities which are mag-
netized by their neighbours and eager to cling to them. To a certain extent
they resemble words in a language, which are restless and ambiguous until
surrounded by a completing sentence. But words do not exhibit the peculiar
tension that leads us, on hearing one tone, to want its resolution in another.
To some writers—notably Zuckerkandl—this is the core phenomenon of
musical movement.

Sounds do not contain this tension until heard as tones, and tones contain
it only in context. It is no intrinsic property of sounds pitched on B that they
lean towards C. Nor are they always heard as doing so. In the context of C
major, where B is the leading-note, this experience of leaning towards C is
certainly vivid: although by no means constant, since any tone, even in the
strictest tonal context, can tend in any direction. But in the key of B major,
the tone B has no tendency to lean towards C at all: on the contrary, it
actively excludes C, and as it were defends itself against the very thought of it.

Zuckerkandl rightly argues that there is no way of reducing these
musical experiences to their acoustical basis.[21] When I hear intervals, for

---

[20] *Metaphors We Live By* (Chicago, 1980).

[21] *Man the Musician* (vol. ii of *Sound and Symbol*), tr. Norbert Guterman
(Princeton, 1976), ch. 12.

instance, I always hear more than the interval itself. I hear the dynamic properties of the tones that compose it. This means that, in the key of C major, the interval C–G is heard differently from the interval E–B, even though both are perfect fifths (ignoring, since they are here irrelevant, the complications introduced by temperaments other than the twelve-tone equal temperament which now prevails). The first fifth has a solid, motionless character, a character of home; while the second has an ethereal waif-like sound, the sound of foreign regions.

Zuckerkandl attempts an explanation of our experience of movement, as a response to the logic of tonality. In hearing dynamic properties, he suggests, we are recognizing the intrinsic order of tonal music, the relations of tension and release that are contained within the diatonic scale itself. The key establishes those expectations, leading us to want C after B, as we feel the melodic tension of the leading-note, and perhaps also the harmonic tension which sounds through it, as V calls for its resolution in I. The tonal language enables a composer to delay those expectations, to play on them, to stretch out the tension so that a whole paragraph of tones can be threaded on it.

Agreeable though such speculations may be, they do not really account for the experience of movement. All that I have said in discussing the tonal melodies of classical music could be said of atonal music too. The agonizing but beautiful opening of Schoenberg's *Erwartung* contains just as many boundaries in musical space, just as many beginnings and ends, soarings and leapings, as any comparable tonal piece (Ex. 2.39). But here, from the very first measure, our tonal expectations are cancelled by the harmony. I don't doubt that in much modern music the experience of movement, which is naturally generated by tonal melody, is absent or subdued. But it is not the rejection of tonality that causes this phenomenon, so much as the disag-

Ex. 2.39. Schoenberg, *Erwartung*, Op. 17

gregation of the melodic line, as in Harrison Birtwistle's *Verses for Ensembles*, for example, in which neighbouring notes lie too far apart to be held in relation. Scatter Beethoven's 'Ode to Joy' over four octaves and you would achieve a comparable effect. Some of the greatest musical achievements of our century have arisen from the discovery of new forms of musical *movement*, in which boundaries are shifting or non-existent, so that we can no longer hear individual melodies, but only a kind of unceasing melodiousness. In the sixth movement of the *Turangalîla symphonie*, for instance, the strings and *ondes Martenot* sound an unbroken line, in dense F sharp major harmony, against an atonal background. The melodic line begins at the beginning of the movement, and carries through to the end, without any perceivable boundary. But the beautiful effect that Messiaen achieves depends once again upon the spatial properties of music: the music seems to rest in tonal space, moving without effort among familiar things, like the undulating waters of a sun-spangled lake (Ex. 2.40).

There are precedents, of course, for this 'unbordered' music—in plainsong, in certain kinds of oriental music, and even in Bach (notice, for example, the Prelude in E flat major from the First Book of the Forty-Eight). But it is new sounds, new colours, and new harmonies that created Messiaen's absolute repose.

Movement and boundary are, then, intrinsic to the musical experience, and not peculiar to tonal music—even though tonality may enliven them. In any case, the idea of a dynamic property is not really much clearer than the concept of movement that it is supposed to explain. If B leans towards C in the key of C major, then it certainly does so in a way unlike that in which 'the' leans towards 'mat' in the utterance 'a cat sat on the'. It is not just *any* sort of magnetism that we have in mind when referring to the dynamic properties of the tone. It is the special kind which we hear in hearing musical movement. We do not capture *that* peculiar idea, either through the concept of a dynamic property, or through the theory of tonality that supposedly explains it (while in fact explaining nothing of the kind). (Nothing moves through the sentence 'A cat sat on the mat', in the way in which the clarinet stalks through the orchestra in *Peter and the Wolf*.)

In fact we should be careful precisely to *distinguish* the experience of tension in music, from the experience of movement. We can hear a melody move from B to C, without hearing a tension in B that is resolved in C. It is surely exaggerated to write, as Zuckerkandl does, of tensions within the diatonic scale itself, which lead to the desire for resolution. Everything here depends upon the harmony, which is the prime generator of musical tension. And it is only when harmony is conceived uniquely in tonal terms, that the movement of the melodic line could be understood as Zuckerkandl understands it.

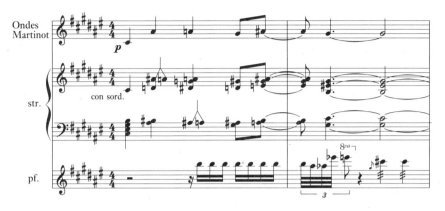

Ex. 2.40. Messiaen, *Turangalîla symphonie*, sixth movement: 'Jardin du sommeil d'amour'

Melodic Organization

Musical movement is the background reality against which melodies are formed. But it is exemplified in all musical organization, even where there is no tune. Whenever we hear music, we hear movement; but sometimes, as in Gregorian chant, this movement flows uninterrupted through tonal space, with no internal boundaries.

When internal boundaries are weak or non-existent, the experience of melody vanishes: a chant may be melodious, but it has no *melody*. Medieval secular music, however, has iterated tunes, which show a move towards the melodic organization of classical music. From Monteverdi onwards, our music has been composed from bounded phrases and motifs, ordered sometimes as melodies, sometimes as contrapuntal sequences with permeable boundaries, as in the final duet of *L'incoronazione di Poppea* (Ex. 2.41).

Ex. 2.41. Monteverdi, *L'incoronazione di Poppea*, final duet

Melodies move in many ways. They may advance to and from adjacent notes on the scale—i.e., by 'neighbour-note' movement, as in the melody from Sibelius's *Karelia* suite, Op. 11, in Ex. 2.42. They may move by arpeggiation—i.e. by passing from one note to another along a chord (usually a fundamental triad of the key). Arpeggiation is a fundamental device in the classical style, with countless symphonic and sonata-movement themes deriving from the consecutive arpeggiation of the tonic and dominant triads—as in the opening of *Eine Kleine Nachtmusik*, K. 525 or of Beethoven's first piano sonata, Op. 2 No. 1 (Ex. 2.43). In such themes melodic and

Ex. 2.42. Sibelius, *Karelia* suite, Op. 11

Ex. 2.43. Beethoven, Piano Sonata in F minor, Op. 2 No. 1, first movement

harmonic organization tend in the same direction. Harmonic values are important also in melodies which move by 'consonant skips'—i.e. by advancing from one tone to another which rhymes with it harmonically, as in the opening motif of *Der Rosenkavalier*, Ex. 2.44.

Ex. 2.44. Richard Strauss, *Der Rosenkavalier*

Those three forms of melodic movement play an important role in the theory of Heinrich Schenker, whose names for them I have therefore borrowed. And they are associated by Schenker with a distinction which will occupy us in several later discussions, that between 'structural' tones, and their 'prolongations'. The distinction here is not a matter of emphasis, accent, or boundary, but is entirely *sui generis*. In Schenker the distinction is predicated upon a theory of tonal organization, according to which harmonic progressions lie always in the background of any melodic device. And this theory, at least when applied locally and on a small scale, has an intuitive appeal. Consider, for example, the celebrated melody of 'Dalla sua pace' (Ex. 2.45). The listener hears the A in bar 9 as a destination, a place towards which the melody moves, and at which it rests before continuing with a new impetus; but the A in bar 6 has no such character. On the surface, at least, each of these tones occurs over a dominant harmony: so what explains the difference between them? Schenker's own theory—which I examine in later chapters—implies that the underlying harmony of the A in bar 6 is not V⁷ but I, and that the V⁷ chord is merely a 'prolongation' of the tonic harmony. But this explains the distinction between structure and prolongation only by assuming it—as a distinction made at the harmonic rather than the melodic level.

In fact the experience to which Schenkerians refer is present in all music, regardless of its harmonic structure. Consider the folk melody ('Lovely Joan') in Ex. 2.46—a melody in the Dorian mode. Most listeners will assign structural importance to the first D in bar 5, to the second G in bar 7, and to the C in bar 8. This upper C is the last of four occurrences; but it is only at this fourth attempt, so to speak, that the melody really arrives there,

Ex. 2.45. Mozart, *Don Giovanni*, 'Dalla sua pace'

to fall away at last with a gesture of homecoming. A Schenkerian might wish to harmonize this final C on the dominant—i.e. as part of the chord of A minor. But it is not the implied harmony that would prompt such a decision, so much as the structure of the melody itself. In any case, modal music of this kind bridles at a dominant-to-tonic conclusion, and is vulgarized

Ex. 2.46. 'Lovely Joan'

and denatured by the attempt to supply it. A folksinger would either eschew harmony altogether, or accompany that final C with its own triad—the chord of the leading-note. (It is the rival demands of romantic polyphony that lead Vaughan Williams, in the *Fantasia on Greensleeves*, to harmonize this C with an F major triad, construed as the subdominant of the leading-note.)

Schenker made the bold suggestion that the distinction between structural tones and prolongations contains the secret of all musical order in our classical tradition. That highly controversial claim need not be accepted, however, in order to recognize that the movement of melodies and phrases is often, perhaps always, fixed to tones which stand out as 'points of arrival and departure' or 'stations on the way'. As the example of 'Lovely Joan' seems to show, the phenomenon here is not a matter of implied harmonic structure, but resides in the melodic line itself.

The distinction between structure and prolongation is related to, though distinct from, that between thematic and ornamental devices. An apoggiatura is heard, as a rule, as an *embellishment* to a melody, and the 'grammar' of ornament in seventeenth- and eighteenth-century music is so rich, precisely because the ear was, and to some extent still is, trained to hear a melody through the decorative incrustation. An ornament is such only in context. Details which begin life as ornaments may become important melodic elements in their own right—like the turn, which, by the time of the overture to *Rienzi*, has become an independent melodic motif, and which can be heard in the last movement of Mahler's Ninth Symphony as a *structural* device: the very essence of the music, from which all else derives.

The encapsulation of musical movement in melodic events, with boundaries that may be closed or permeable, and with structural episodes heard as 'stations on the way', is the most important source of thematic organization in classical music. This organization spreads outwards through the entire musical surface. Starting from motifs, which are the smallest unities generally recognized, we encounter, in order of increasing length, first phrases, which act like the clauses in a sentence, presenting incomplete but bounded units of melodic thought, and then periods, which consist of two consecutive phrases, the second offering a conclusion to the movement begun in the first. This bipartite structure of the period already has harmonic implications: for it brings to the fore the implicit cadence of the melodic line, at the end of the first phrase (which might well imply a dominant harmony), and then at the end of the second (where the tonic would be normal) (see Ex. 2.47, Beethoven, Piano Sonata in C major, Op. 2 No. 3). Already all kinds of subtleties can be introduced into the musical line, by enlarging the period, or repeating one of the motifs in the second phrase (see Ex. 2.48, Schubert, 'Frühlingsglaube'). Melodies may be built from two answering periods (Beethoven's 'Ode to Joy', for example), and so create an effect of symmetry. Or a composer may rely on our sense of symmetry precisely in order to disrupt it, so that the melody seems to have broken free from its boundaries, to run out into musical space. Consider Ex. 2.49, for example—'Ungeduld' from *Die Schöne Müllerin*. After four phrases based on a single dotted motif, the composer adds a fifth—and at the same time lengthens it, causing the melody to lie open and incomplete, awaiting the four soaring gestures which convey the innocent fullness of the miller's emotion.

Ex. 2.47. Beethoven, Piano Sonata in C major, Op. 2 No. 3, last movement

Ex. 2.48. Schubert, 'Frühlingsglaube', D686: (*a*) what a lesser composer might have written; (*b*) what Schubert wrote

Ex. 2.49. Schubert *Die Schöne Müllerin*, D795, 'Ungeduld': (*a*) figure and bass;
(*b*) melody

Melodic organization, like rhythmic organization, exists in both foreground
and background spaces. We distinguish the voices of an accompaniment
from those of the melody, even when the accompanying voices are singing
melodically, and make tunes of their own. This distinction between foreground and background can be heard in the most meticulous polyphony—
even in Victoria, Schutz, and Palestrina, where the voices are entirely equal
in their cogency and expressive role. The distinction of foreground and
background is a distinction of aspect, and can often be changed at will: as
when we listen for the inner voice, and allow it to dominate the melody.

We should also distinguish melodic motifs from figures. A figure resembles
a moulding in architecture: it is 'open at both ends', so as to be endlessly
repeatable. In hearing a phrase as a figure, rather than a motif, we are at the
same time placing it in the background, even if it is as strong and melodious
as the figures used by Stravinsky in *The Rite of Spring* (Ex. 2.50). A phrase
which we hear first as a melodic motif may suddenly be thrown into the
background to transform itself into a figure, when repeated beneath another
and more expansive melodic line. An example occurs at the beginning of the

Ex. 2.50 Stravinsky, *The Rite of Spring*, figures

Ex. 2.51. Debussy, String Quartet, second movement

second movement of Debussy's String Quartet (Ex. 2.51). A composer who offers nothing *but* figures, as in the endless daisy-chains of Philip Glass, invites us to hear only background: in such cases the music slips away from us, and becomes a haze on the heard horizon. It is interesting to compare the interminable figurations of *Ekhnaton*, for example, with the little motif from *The Cunning Little Vixen* (Ex. 2.31), discussed earlier. Janáček's three notes are neither 'open at both ends' nor endlessly repeatable: they long for development, and attract to themselves from the surrounding tonal space the phrases that complete the melody.

'Ungeduld' provides a good illustration of those various kinds of melodic ordering. Here the accompanying figure consists of triplets on one chord, whose motion is brilliantly etched into the musical surface by the bass-line (Ex. 2.49a). The bass-line itself is built from a motif which finally conquers the melody and brings it to earth. The extent and subtlety of organization here is so great that words can hardly begin to capture it: but the listener spontaneously hears the multitude of boundaries, some weak, some strong, some open, some closed, some ending, some beginning, by which the musical surface is crossed.

Melodic organization enables a composer to treat a melody or a motif as a 'subject': it becomes a musical individual with a history. Phrases can be varied, inverted, set in counterpoint; motifs can be extracted from their context and augmented or diminished; the melody itself can be broken up or prolonged—and always the listener will recognize these unities as musical individuals, journeying through the tonal space which is their element. Melodic organization can be elaborated and extended, to generate all the familiar forms of music: the binary and ternary structures which provide so many settled melodies; and the larger forms, such as theme and variations, sonata, rondo, sonata-rondo, and the mixed forms of the suite, overture, or symphony. Although these musical forms are of immense intrinsic interest, it would take us too far from our present concerns to study them. Moreover, for the philosopher, they raise no questions, and suggest no answers, that are not raised and suggested by motifs, phrases, and tunes.

Harmony

The experience of harmony should be distinguished from two other experiences to which it is closely related: the experience of pitched sounds occurring together ('simultaneities'); and the experience of concord and discord.

The ancient theory of music that we owe to the Pythagoreans, which is endorsed by Plato in the *Timaeus* and by Plotinus, St Augustine, and Boethius in their treatises on music, and which survives in Al-Farabi, in Aquinas, and even in such Renaissance theorists as Zarlino, is centred on the experience of harmony. Having noticed that the elementary concords—

octave, fifth, and fourth—are produced by strings whose lengths are propor-
tioned according to perfect fractions, those writers concluded that our experience of music is an experience of number. Number, and the relations of
number, provide the hidden order of the universe; and numbers are known
through the intellect, and known with a certainty that pertains to no other
thing. When understanding mathematics we have access to the order of
creation, and this order is eternal, like the numbers themselves. In music we
know through experience, and in time, what is also revealed to the intellect as
outside time and change. Just as time is, for Plato and Plotinus, the moving
image of eternity, so is the experience of music the revelation in time of the
eternal order. The beauty of music is the beauty of the world itself, revealed
to the sense of hearing—a 'point of intersection of the timeless with time'.

Leaving that suggestion where it was, let us at least note that the
acoustical science of Helmholtz led to a modern variant of the Pythagorean
theory. Helmholtz argued that harmonic relations are indeed relations of
number, and he offered a physical theory that would prove Pythagoras'
speculation concerning the perfect concords. These occur when the
frequencies of concurrent vibrations are related as 1:2, 2:3, and so on, since
in such cases the lower overtones of the components coincide, while the
'upper partials' do not 'beat' against one another. Beating is the result of
interference patterns created between the sound waves, and it is the beating
of the upper partials that explains the experience of discord.

All that is familiar. But it does not account for the experience of
harmony. For Helmholtz is describing the *acoustical* phenomenon of discord
and concord, not the *musical* phenomenon of dissonance and consonance.
What we hear in hearing a harmony is not simply two or more sounds
occurring together. We hear also a relation between them, and sometimes a
new entity that is formed by their conjunction. Thus musical consonance is
frequently heard when triads sound in the bass—not because the resulting
chords contain less distorting overtone patterns than any discord (for this is
not so), but because we hear the musical organization, which assigns to
these chords a particular harmonic function. Nor are acoustical concords
always heard as consonant harmonies: for they may not be heard as harmonies at all. Someone may be playing the clarinet next door, while I listen
to a violin sonata on my record-player. I hear the clarinet through the wall,
as a sound which is simultaneous with the sound of the sonata: but I may
not hear the two as harmonizing—even if they are, by some chance, in the
same key and sounding concordantly.

There are interesting examples in music itself, of sounds which are
simultaneous while not being harmonically related. In 'Putnam's Camp'
from *Three Places in New England*, Ives introduces the sound of two bands
playing simultaneously; the effect is one neither of encumbered harmony,

nor of unmusical cacophony. It is an effect of happy contest between tones which resolutely stay apart, each enjoying its local harmony, so to speak, and quite satisfied with that. Of course, there *is* a clash of key, and many a combination of sounds which, by Helmholtz's standard, would be considered highly discordant. But that is not what we notice. Indeed, this separation of tones can occur even when the sound pattern consists of recognized concords. Consider the brilliant use of the three orchestras on the stage, in the conclusion to Act I of *Don Giovanni*. The tension that is created throughout the scene is largely due to the fact that we hear three musical processes, not as parts of a single harmonic whole, but as contesting against each other, refusing to join in harmony, even though the sounds that emerge are acoustical concords.

In harmony it is as though two or more melodic events had come together and coalesced. We should distinguish two forms of this coalescence: chords, in which separate tones are arranged 'vertically', to form a new musical entity; and polyphony, in which the component parts are melodies, rather than tones, and the resulting entity is not a sequence of chords, but a musical movement *through* chords. For the purpose of the present chapter I shall concentrate on chords.

Hindemith writes that

> A chord is by no means an agglomeration of intervals. It is a new unit which, although dependent on the formative power of the single interval, is felt as being self-existent and as giving to the constituent intervals meanings and functions which they otherwise would not have.[22]

So understood, consonant chords are only one kind of harmony. To hear harmony is to hear a unity of tones; but this unity may be more or less consonant, more or less tense or explosive. When we hear consonance, we hear the tones as resting together, belonging, as though something in each were satisfied by the others. Consonance is something that we hear in the sounds: and it is therefore maximally sensitive to context, like every musical, as opposed to merely acoustical, phenomenon. In the context of classical tonal music, the second inversion of a triad will sound slightly dissonant, even though it is acoustically as much a concord as the same triad in root position. For the second inversion is a 6–4 chord, which 'demands resolution', by downward motion over a pedal, usually with a suspension along the way. Fourths, which were paradigms of consonance in medieval music, for this reason began to sound dissonant as the classical style emerged, so that the parallel fourths in the melodic line of Mozart's Piano Sonata in A minor, K. 310, last movement, have a decidedly unsettled character (Ex. 2.52). In jazz, this slightly dissonant character is overcome by the use of chromatic

---

[22] *A Composer's World* (Cambridge, Mass., 1952), 72.

Ex. 2.52. Mozart, Piano Sonata in A minor, K. 310, last movement

harmony, so that the fourth regains its character as a primary concord: witness the once famous melody by Billy Mayerl, in Ex. 2.53.

More obviously, a chord that sounds dissonant in Haydn may sound consonant in Stravinsky. No doubt the opening of Mozart's 'Dissonance' Quartet, K. 465, does not sound so dissonant to us as it it did to Mozart's contemporaries. The passage from the *Rite of Spring* in Ex. 2.54 is heard by almost everyone as sweetly consonant. Yet the harmonies are stacked full of semitones and warring intervals. The example illustrates an important principle: the tension introduced by dissonance can be negated, by orchestration, rhythm or—as here—by the creation of rival harmonic expectations. In such a case the experience of dissonance has a tendency to vanish. Thus in jazz, where accessory notes are usually added to the chords, it is not

Ex. 2.53. Billy Mayerl, 'Marigold', Op. 78

Ex. 2.54. Stravinsky, *The Rite of Spring*, Part II

normal to experience dissonance. An all-pervading relaxation of harmony is more often the effect, so that sonorities considered highly dissonant in other contexts are felt to require no resolution. Ex. 2.55 shows how Art Tatum harmonizes the first bar of 'Aunt Hagar's Blues'; from the first cluttered chord you feel the force of D flat major. The little gesture to the bass simply reinforces an existing sense of lazy consonance and delicious relaxation. Nevertheless, that fairly standard jazz augmentation of a major chord would be an intolerable dissonance even in Wagner.

When describing harmonies, we acknowledge their context-dependence. The chord in Ex. 2.56, which would sound dissonant in Mozart, but which is perfectly consonant in the Chopin Nocturne, Op. 27 No. 1, would be described in its actual context, as a diminished seventh on an A flat pedal. Had it occurred in a Schoenberg quartet, you could not have so described it. For the description I have given characterizes the chord in terms of its harmonic *function*, its contribution to the musical movement, and not just in terms of the intervals that compose it.[23] That is why the famous 'Tristan' chord has so many rival descriptions: for it occurs in a thousand different contexts, and in each case seems to function differently, according to the

Ex. 2.55. Art Tatum, 'Aunt Hagar's Blues'

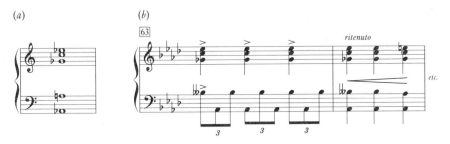

Ex. 2.56. Chord (*a*) out of context; (*b*) in context: Chopin, Nocturne in C sharp minor, Op. 27 No. 1

[23] The functional account of harmony, advocated by Hugo Riemann in his *Elementar-Schulbuch der Harmonielehre* (Leipzig, 1906) and *Musiklexikon* (Leipzig, 1909), originally attempted to reduce the functions of chords to three basic varieties: tonic, dominant, and subdominant. The extension of this functional idea to take account of modern and romantic harmony is now common, though it is not at all clear how it should be stated. See the discussion in Ch. 10, below.

field of force surrounding it. In the prelude to *Tristan und Isolde* it leads into the dominant of A minor, and is related to the dominant of the dominant: its tonal implications are subsumed by the A minor tonality. But it is the very same collection of tones, neither transposed nor inverted, which, at the end of the opera, resolves into a glorious B major. Do we say that this is the *same* chord in this new relation, or another? And is it the same chord when used in the context of *Götterdämmerung*, to form the agonizing synthesis of Alberich's 'Wehe!' and the Rhinedaughters' 'Rheingold!'? (see Ex. 2.57).

Ex. 2.57. Wagner, *Götterdämmerung*, Act 2

Perhaps we should give up the attempt to describe the chord in tonal terms, and treat it, as Milton Babbitt treats it, as that unique four-tone chord in which the intervals of 2, 3, 4, 5, and 6 semitones are all exemplified.[24] But Babbitt's description seems more acoustical than musical—a description of the sounds, which is deliberately neutral concerning the tones that we hear in them. Having reviewed the standard descriptions of the 'Tristan' chord, as half-diminished seventh, as minor triad with augmented sixth, and so on, Schoenberg tells us to abandon the attempt at a definition. Such chords, he tells us are 'spies, who seek out weaknesses in order to introduce confusion; runaways in flight from their own personality; in every respect bringers of disquiet, but above all—highly amusing fellows'.[25] And here we see the effect of the virtual causality that governs the world of music. Just as an event is the event that it is partly on account of the causal relations in which it is embedded, so is the musical object the object that it is by virtue of the apparent causality that shows it rising from one thing, and leading to another. (Cf. again Donald Davidson's criterion of event-identity.[26])

Polyphony

A chord may be heard as a limiting case of polyphonic organization: the case in which the voices are stationary. That is how the novel chords in Wagner should be heard, and it is why they admit of several descriptions. The 'Tristan' chord is not one chord but many, and its identity depends

[24] *Words about Music* (Madison, Wisc., 1987), 155.
[25] *Harmonielehre* (3rd edn., Vienna, 1922), 311.
[26] 'The Individuation of Events', in *Essays on Actions and Events*, 163–80.

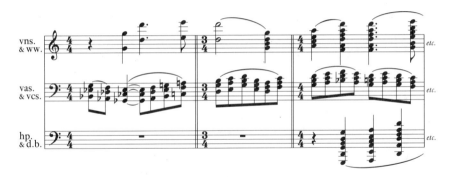

Ex. 2.58. Vaughan Williams, *Pastoral Symphony* (No. 3)

upon the movement implicit in its four component voices: whence do they come, and where are they going?

At the same time, the hearing of a chord as a musical unity is not reducible to the experience of counterpoint. While I may hear the major triad, for example, as the effect of three simultaneous voices, I may also hear it as a single 'chordal' voice, from which the parts have no tendency to flow out in directions of their own. This is shown by the existence of chordal melodies, which may stand in polyphonic relation to other chordal melodies, as in the example from the Vaughan Williams *Pastoral Symphony* in Ex. 2.58. Here there are three voices—violins and woodwind together, lower strings, and harp with bass and bassoon—each voice sounding massive chords, which must be heard nevertheless as the atoms of a melody.

In counterpoint our experience of harmony involves the coalescence of *movements*. Seldom do the chords themselves capture our attention, as we hear the simultaneous melodies in a canon or fugue. Yet here too we distinguish harmony from simultaneity. Consider Ligeti's Horn Trio, in which the three instruments, playing in different keys, seldom harmonize, even though the composer for the most part avoids acoustical discords (Ex. 2.59).

In normal contrapuntal writing, although we do not hear a sequence of chords, we nevertheless hear a sequence of harmonic *regions*, through which the voices move. The very same harmonic order that may be produced through a sequence of chords, can result from polyphony. Maybe polyphony, rather than the chord, is the essential harmonic phenomenon in our tradition. (Such, at least, will be the burden of later arguments.) Nevertheless, harmonic organization is common to the two kinds of writing.

Ex. 2.59. György Ligeti, Trio for violin, horn and piano, second movement

Harmonic Organization

The context-dependence of harmony entails that harmonic tension is not intrinsic to a chord, any more than melodic tension is intrinsic to a tone. The 'dynamic' properties of harmonies, like those of tones, vary according to the field of force in which they are placed. A chord that demands resolution in Beethoven (the opening chord of the last movement of the Ninth Symphony, for instance), could actually *be* the resolution of a sequence in a composer like Walton. (Consider the magnificent first movement of Walton's First Symphony, in which tension is built up through dissonant harmonies, and then released into harmonies which are themselves chock-full of augmented fourths and semitones.)

At the same time, there are harmonic relations which remain constant across musical styles. There are chord sequences which sound natural and logical in Renaissance polyphony, in Bach fugues, in Mozart sonatas, Smetana overtures, Strauss waltzes, and jazz. Undeniably, there is all the difference in the world between harmonic organization achieved through voice-leading in full polyphony, and that which derives from block chords strummed on a guitar. Nevertheless, even in polyphony, harmonic organization can be described and understood independently of the melodic lines, in terms of progressions which make sense regardless of voice-leading.

So understood, harmonic organization displays features which complement the melodic organization described earlier. Chord sequences increase and decrease in tension, causing individual chords to lean towards and away from one another. We distinguish 'structural' harmonies from their prolongations, and are prepared to discount all kinds of intrusive voices, in order to identify the true underlying harmony of a section or element. These are matters of such importance that I shall return to them in later chapters. For the present purposes, it is sufficient to recognize harmony as an independent form of musical organization, which may exist in friendly or adversarial relation to the melodic and rhythmic structure. When the relation between harmony and melody is friendly, we experience the harmonic progression as though it were a 'working-out' in the vertical dimension, of forces that are also exerting themselves 'horizontally' in the melody. Antagonism can arise either expressly—as in Stravinsky's buoyant harmonization of Russian street-songs in the last act of *Petrouchka*—or unwittingly, through the catastrophic failure of taste that destroyed the language of English folksong, by pressing tonal progressions on to modal melodies.

Only in later chapters will I be able to explore harmonic organization in the detail that it requires. For present purposes we should note the dependence of this organization on spatial metaphors, and metaphors of movement. Chords are spaced, open, filled, or hollow. They spread over the stave, strain asunder, tend away from or towards their neighbours. They provide the primary experience of a spatial (as opposed to a temporal) *Gestalt* in music: of a unity which crosses distances, and which can be grasped all at once. And like melodies, they are objects of musical, rather than merely acoustical, perception. Only a musical creature could hear them, and even if animals may respond favourably to concordant sounds, it does not follow that they are hearing and enjoying harmony. It seems that deaf people can discriminate concords from discords, in the acoustical sense: but they cannot hear consonance or dissonance, for the simple reason that they cannot hear.

The Musical Individual

Our discussion has provided us with examples of musical individuals: entities that exist in musical space, and which may be reidentified as the 'same again'. Tones provide the simplest example; but almost invariably they are understood as the parts of other entities, the atoms from which the true objects of musical understanding are composed. These true objects include motifs, melodies, and chords. And these objects have a history: they are affected by the musical process, and acquire a character from it. This is one of the most interesting features of the musical *Gestalt*. Consider the melody from Schubert's Piano Sonata in B flat major of 1828, D960, in Ex. 2.60. This is a powerful statement in C sharp minor, of a theme whose contours are carefully outlined by the harmony. No sooner does it end, however, than it begins again, almost note for note the same, but now harmonized in E major (Ex 2.61). The heartbreaking effect of this is hard to describe in words. But it would not exist, if we did not perceive the melody as an individual, a thing which can reappear in another context, and undergo change. And this is change of a radical kind: not just the change from song to march that is undergone by Beethoven's 'Ode to Joy', but a change of musical substance. For now the melody begins on $\hat{3}$ instead of $\hat{5}$, it sinks to $\hat{2}$ instead of $\hat{4}$. Harmonically, and tonally, it has been completely recomposed, like the ship of Theseus. Yet it is the same.

   The example is an extreme case of something on which all music depends: repetition, not of sound only, but of phenomenal individuals. The return of a theme, or a chord, or a phrase, in some new harmonic or melodic context, the entry of a theme in another voice or at another pitch, the transposition of phrases and harmonies in musical space—these are the phenomena which create the musical experience. They compel us to think of music as spread out in acousmatic space, where a new kind of individual is born and lives out its life: an individual whose character is constantly changing in response to the musical surroundings.

Ex. 2.60. Schubert, Piano Sonata in B flat major, D960, second movement

Ex. 2.61. Schubert, Piano Sonata in B flat major, D960, second movement

These musical individuals are not, of course, concrete particulars, like tables and chairs. One and the same musical individual can be in two places at the same time, as in an overlapping canon. They are heard as individuals; but any attempt to identify them must lean upon acoustical criteria—according to which they are not individuals at all, but repeatable patterns or types.

Time, Space, and Causality

It is at this point, however, that we need to become a little clearer about the two concepts which I have taken for granted in this chapter: the concepts of time and space. Kant denied that space and time are concepts, believing that they do not have, as concepts must have, a plurality of instances. For Kant they were 'forms of intuition', imposing a preconceptual order on our experience. To translate Kant's claim into modern idiom, it is this: every object of experience is situated in time. I cannot have a sensation, nor can I perceive an object, without experiencing those things as belonging to the order of before and after. Some things, however, are experienced as objective (or 'transcendent', to use Husserl's idiom): the house that I see is not a mental object; it is represented in my perception as something *other* than me. That is how I *see* it, as an objective item which might not be as it seems, and which does not depend on me for its existence. I see it in that way, even if it is in fact an hallucination. To experience something as objective, I must situate it not only in time but also in space: it is 'out there', and stands to me in a spatial relation. The objective world is therefore an extended world— and this is the deep reason for the view that physics is the science of 'things in space'.

The intrinsic plausibility of that thesis has never been matched by an argument in support of it. It is hard to doubt that all experience occurs, and must occur, in time—although to give a reason for this has proved to lie beyond the powers of philosophers, perhaps, as I suggested earlier, because the temporal nature of experience is so deep a fact, that it can never be explained without assuming it. (Consider the hopeless attempts of Fichte, Hegel, and Schopenhauer, to envisage time as a requirement of self-consciousness, which has its origins 'in me': *in whom?*) Be that as it may, there is much more room for doubt concerning the second part of Kant's thesis—the doctrine of space as the 'form of outer sense'. The only argument that comes close to sustaining the doctrine is that offered by Strawson in chapter 2 of *Individuals*, and partly endorsed by Jonathan Bennett.[27] Strawson argues that in an auditory universe (a universe containing only sounds) the concept of objectively existing sound objects gains a purchase provided that these objects can be *located* in a place. But the argument collapses, just as soon as we reject the possibility that the sound spectrum should literally admit of the distinction between a place and its occupant.

The distinction between place and occupant is, however, fundamental to the concept of space. It also marks an important difference between space and time. Times are not occupied or filled by the things that occur in them, as spaces are. An event takes time: but it does not compete with other events for the time required; indefinitely many events can take place simultaneously.

Those observations help to explain the spatial metaphor that lies embedded in our experience of music. They also endorse the view that music presents us with the nature not of space but of time—time lifted from the tangle of causes and presented in all its mystifying simplicity, as the impossible but necessary condition under which our existence is granted. For the acousmatic realm is separated from the physical world by an impassable metaphysical barrier. The horn that opens Brahms's Second Piano Concerto in B flat major, Op. 83, sounds in the concert hall—and the sound that it makes is an event in the physical world, occurring just before, and twenty feet away from, the sound of the piano that answers it. But the tones that we hear when the horn is sounding are not twenty feet from the B flat arpeggio on the piano: they stand to the tones that follow them in a quite different relation, even if it is one that has, for us, a spatial character. The horn-call summons the piano to enter the place that it has just vacated; and the final F on the horn brings the bottom B flat of the piano into existence, drawing it from the silence with a gesture of command. Those relations between tones are both spatial and causal; but they have nothing to do with physical space, or physical causality. At the same time the acousmatic realm is heard as objective. I do not encounter the Brahms Concerto as an inner process of mine, like a sensation or an image; it is *out there*, independent, and could be other than it seems to *me*. It is testimony to the truth of Kant's insight that, in so conceiving tones, we find ourselves compelled to situate them within a spatial framework—albeit a framework spun from metaphor. The apparent spatiality of the acousmatic realm is of a piece with its transcendence (with the fact that we encounter it as something *other*, something observed, rather than as an inner process). There is no *real* space of sounds; but there is a phenomenal space of tones. It is modelled on the phenomenal space of everyday perception—the space in terms of which we orientate ourselves. It has 'up' and 'down', height and depth; its single dimension is understood not only geometrically but also in terms of effort and motion, attraction and repulsion, heaviness and lightness. It is permeated by a phenomenal gravity, to the law of which all tones are subject, and against which they must strive if they are to move at all.

Yet, try as we might, we cannot advance from this phenomenal space to an objective spatial order. The topological character of space, as a system of places and surfaces, is not reproduced in the acousmatic realm. In that realm we confront only a succession of events, ordered in time but not in space, and retaining the directionality and placelessness which are the marks of the temporal dimension. This explains, I believe, the frequently encountered view that, in the musical experience, we are confronted with time: not just events in time, but time itself, as it were, spread out for our contemplation as space is spread out before us in the visual field. For in the acousmatic realm temporal order is dissolved and reconstituted as a phenomenal *space*. We transfer to it the familiarity and the sense of freedom which characterize our experience of the spatial order. For a while it seems as though we can *wander in time*, with the same sovereignty that we exercise in our wanderings through space. Music is not bound to time's arrow, but lingers by the way, takes backward steps, skips ahead, and sets the pace that *it* requires. Of course, all this is a sophisticated illusion—which is why Suzanne Langer describes the order of music as involving not real but 'virtual' time.[28] But it is, to adapt Leibniz's idiom, a 'well-founded illusion'—and one which constantly and irrepressibly resurges in our experience of music.

The spatializing of the temporal order is also a release from it: we are granted a sensuous intimation of something that we can otherwise grasp only in thought, and which therefore fails to persuade us of its real possibility: namely, an order outside time and change. Plato in the *Timaeus*, and following him Plotinus, described time as the moving image (*eikōn*) of eternity. We can think of *virtual* time in such a way. For it is time emancipated from itself; time in which we move freely from one illusory location

[28] *Feeling and Form* (New York, 1953), ch. 7, esp. p. 108.

to another, and in which all process is reversible. There are forms of music—the Indian raga is an instance—which cultivate this experience and which impart a consolation that is tinged, in consequence, with a religious tranquillity.

Let it be said, however, that these speculations cast no light on the meaning or value of music. For the spatialized time of the acousmatic realm is exemplifed by all its occupants: by the good and the bad, the beautiful and the ugly, the meaningful and the meaningless. The acousmatic dimension is the background against which musical meaning is achieved. But its vast metaphysical promise remains unfulfilled, and while it beckons to the Platonic imagination, it will never persuade the sceptical philosopher.

The phenomenal space and phenomenal time of music are matched by the phenomenal causality that orders the musical work. We have already studied this strange causality, in two masterly instances from the Brahms Second Piano Concerto. But it should be added that the causality that binds tone to tone in music is not the dead causality of a machine, but the causality of life, whose principal manifestation, for us, is in the world of human action. The notes in music follow one another like bodily movements—with a causality that makes immediate sense to us, even though the *how* of it lies deep in the nature of things and hidden from view.

Our perception of human life is distinguished from our perception of mechanism in another respect also. When we understand another's gesture it is not, as a rule, because we have discovered its physical cause. It is because we have found a *reason* for it, an answer to the question 'why?' which, even if we cannot put it into words, shows us the order, meaning, and goal of the other's behaviour. Human conduct manifests both life and reason: the order of reason is imposed upon, and seen in, the order of life, in the way that the scene depicted in a picture is imposed upon and seen in the shapes and colours that compose it. And this duality in our understanding of each other is reflected too in our experience of music. The background in music is heard as a kind of life: the music is a living, breathing, moving organism. But against this living background there dawns the light of rational agency. A tone is heard as the *response* to its predecessor, as tending towards its successor, as continuing an action which makes sense as a whole.

The causality that we hear in the musical foreground is therefore the 'causality of reason' which, for Kant, was the ground of human freedom. It is the more easy to hear this 'causality of reason' in music, in that the world of physical causes—the 'causality of nature'—has been set aside, discounted, hidden behind the acousmatic veil. In music we are given an unparalleled glimpse of the reality of freedom; and because, as Kant reminds us, reason deals only in necessities, we hear the free order of music as a necessary order: it is when each note *requires* its successor, that we hear freedom in music.

Freedom is the consciousness of necessity; but it is a necessity imposed upon life. Kant observed that our understanding stops at the threshold of this paradox, and cannot resolve it. Yet the solution seems to be ineffably contained in those triumphs of musical organization, such as the fugues of Bach and the late quartets of Beethoven, in which the 'must be' of reason orders and redeems the 'is' of life.

A Note on Timbre

I have not yet touched upon a phenomenon which many would count among the basic variables of musical utterance, and which has become increasingly important as a consequence of Schoenberg's attempt to jettison the constraints of traditional tonality: the phenomenon of timbre. Once again, the physical cause of the phenomenon is well understood: the timbre of a tone is a product of the overtones. If we are to describe timbre itself, however—by which I mean, the thing that we hear when we hear timbre— we find ourselves baffled. Either we identify the timbre through its physical cause (the sound of a clarinet), or we have recourse to metaphor. (Consider, for example, the extraordinary sound of the E major chord that announces the triumph of Brünnhilde's plea to Wotan, Ex. 2.62. How can we capture this in words, except as something like a sudden golden blaze?) In describing the timbre of a tone we are not situating it in the musical space; nor are we identifying anything that is essential to it as a musical individual. This is why orchestrations, reductions, and so on are, as a rule, heard as *versions* of a piece, rather than as new musical entities. When orchestration creates a new musical entity, it is because it has been used to disrupt, or alter, the organization of the tones—as in Webern's orchestration of Bach's six-part 'Ricercar', mentioned earlier.

That is not to deny the importance of timbre, as a contribution to musical meaning; but it is to imply that timbre, and tone-colour generally, presents no parallel system of musical organization, on a par with rhythm, melody, and harmony. Those last three weave the musical surface together, and create the tonal space in which its movement is heard. Nothing will be lost

Ex. 2.62. Wagner, *Die Walküre*, Act 3

if, at this stage in our investigation, we set timbre to one side, as a secondary characteristic of the musical object.

Filling the Tonal Space

Many qualities of tones are, by contrast, directly connected to their spatio-temporal appearance. For example, a tone has *volume*: it seems to fill another dimension of musical space, a dimension of 'thickness', quite independent of that established by the pitch continuum. Volume is not the same as loudness;[29] some of the most voluminous pieces of music are—like the first movement of Bruckner's Ninth Symphony—relatively quiet, while the thin textures of Ravel's *Boléro* are spread over one huge crescendo.

Tones also have weight, and are subject to a kind of gravity. Heavy music is not merely music that moves slowly—think of the sheer mass of a Brahms symphony, compared with the lightness of Haydn.

Chords are heard as 'open', 'hollow', 'filled', 'stretched'—and again the spatial metaphors identify qualities of the things we hear, which are essential to their musical identity.

In what follows it will be necessary to bear such qualities in mind: for they show us how deeply our experience of music is penetrated by the spatial metaphor, and how difficult it would be to remove the metaphor, so as to organize pitches in some other way.

Summary

I shall conclude with a revised (but still far from complete) description of the musical experience and its cause.

1. When sounds are heard as music, three processes occur:

(*a*) The physical vibrations in the air (the sound waves) which are the sole physical reality. Pythagoras made a guess at the nature of these vibrations; Helmholtz completed the work with a true physical theory.

(*b*) The sound produced by those vibrations, which is isolated in music as a pure event. This is a 'secondary object', just as colour is a secondary quality. That is to say, it exists *for* the sense of hearing, and not otherwise.

(*c*) What I hear in the sound, when I hear it as music. This is the intentional object of musical perception, and is characterized through variables

[29] See G. Revesz, *Introduction to the Psychology of Music*, tr. G. I. C. De Courcy (Norman, Okla., 1945), 102; J. C. R. Licklider, 'Basic Correlatives of the Auditory Stimulus', in S. S. Stevens (ed.), *Handbook of Experimental Psychology* (New York, 1951), pp. 1002 f. The matter has been discussed in more phenomenological terms by J. Wilson Coker, *Music and Meaning* (New York, 1972), 39.

(pitch, rhythm, melody, and harmony), which organize the tonal surface, and outline an acousmatic space.

2. This acousmatic space is associated with a virtual causality: tones act upon one another, regardless of the physical causes of the sounds in which we hear them. A melody can therefore be passed from instrument to instrument without interruption, each note being heard as the effect of the one preceding it.

3. This virtual causality is sometimes perceived as physical relations are perceived: namely, as law-like and inevitable. More often, however, the order that we hear in tones is an order of *action*: one tone does not merely give rise to its successor; it creates the conditions which make the successor a right or appropriate response to it. The order that we hear in music is one that is familiar to us from our own lives: the order of intention, in which one thing serves as the reason for another.

4. Finally, we should not think of sounds and tones as distinct individuals—as though tones really existed apart from sounds. Perhaps the best way of understanding the relation between the two is in the way that Spinoza understood the relation between mind and body. For Spinoza reality can be conceptualized in two ways: as mental or as physical. But that which we conceptualize in these two ways is *one*. Moreover, the two ways of conceptualizing the world (the two attributes) are incommensurable. I cannot pass from one to the other, or use the one to explain or predict the other: each is self-contained, autonomous, and self-sufficient. In a similar way, acoustical and musical events are identical. But you cannot slip back and forth between one way of understanding sound and the other. We hear the sound world as a whole when we hear it musically: but what we hear has ceased, in our understanding, to affect us as sound. Thus when a sound enters the musical world it is heard in another way—like the cowbells in Mahler's Sixth Symphony, which lose their character as sound and are swamped in music. It is music that you hear in those bells, not sound. This is equally true of such extramusical resources as the wind-machine in Vaughan Williams's *Sinfonia Antartica*.

All those observations return us to the same persistent metaphor: that of musical space, and the movement that occurs in it. But what exactly *is* a metaphor? And what is the significance of the claim that this particular metaphor is indispensable to the experience of music?

3   *Imagination and Metaphor*

In Chapter 2 I argued that our experience of music involves an elaborate system of metaphors—metaphors of space, movement, and animation. But this leaves us with three very difficult questions to answer: what is a metaphor? What does it mean to say that an experience 'involves' a metaphor (and is the word 'involves' the right one)? Could we eliminate the metaphor, and describe the object of the musical experience without depending on it? These questions are so important that we must confront them now. Much of what I say in this chapter draws on previous arguments—notably those put forward in *Art and Imagination*—amended in the light of recent discussions.

Metaphor

Metaphors are figures of speech, often classed as one kind among many, to be contrasted with metonymy, synecdoche, prosopopoeia, and so on. However, from the philosophical point of view, it is the similarities between the figures of speech that are of central concern—and in particular, the *figurative use of language* which they exemplify, and which is manifest most clearly in metaphor. In developing a philosophical theory of metaphor, I shall be attempting to account for figurative language generally. And much as the study of the various tropes and their distinguishing marks may be of interest to rhetoric and literary theory, the single instance of metaphor will introduce issues which almost all of them raise for the philosopher. By metaphor I shall mean what Aristotle meant: the deliberate application of a term or phrase to something that is known not to exemplify it. (If you don't like this wide usage, just substitute some other term for 'metaphor'.)

At once we have a problem. If you deliberately apply some predicate to an object, are you not thereby assuming that it *does* apply? What is the content of the expression 'known not to apply'? If you are a nominalist, and believe that there is no further explanation for the fact that we classify things as we do, that the application of predicates is the ultimate fact, then it is indeed hard to distinguish metaphorical from other usages. The only distinction we could have in mind is between old uses and new ones. A metaphorical use is one of which we have yet to acquire the habit. Such is the theory of metaphor espoused by the arch-nominalist Nelson Goodman, in *Languages of Art*, and it is one that conveniently brings discussion to a close.

Too conveniently, however. If anything were to show the incoherence of nominalism, it is metaphor. It is precisely our consciousness of metaphor that enables us to distinguish the case when something really *is* blue, say, from the case when our judgement that something is blue depends for its point upon its falsehood. So clearly are we conscious of this that the word 'literally' has all but replaced 'truly' and 'really' in everyday speech.

Again someone might have qualms about a theory of metaphor that concentrates only on the metaphorical application of *predicates*. For is it not the whole sentence that bears the burden of falsehood, and not merely the predicate that is 'misapplied'? To cut a long story short, I believe that metaphorical predication is, if not the only, at least the central, example of the phenomenon that I wish to analyse. There can be metaphorical names— as when I call my horse 'Apollo' for his beauty—but their being *names* is precisely what is not metaphorical about them. Apollo is so called because of his beauty: but he really (literally) *is* Apollo: not the god, of course, but that particular horse. This animal is what the name 'Apollo' refers to; and it is plausible to suppose, with Kripke and Putnam,[1] that, in the case of proper names, reference determines sense, so that there is no such thing as a metaphorical name—or rather, that the metaphor in a name is no part of its function *as a name*. If there is a metaphor here, it resides in a crypto-predication: I convey the thought that this horse has the attributes of the god of music, even though of course no such thing is true. And when a metaphor is achieved through the use of nouns rather than adjectives, it is still via an act of predication, as in Macbeth's immensely expressive muddle of equestrian imagery:

---

[1] Kripke, *Naming and Necessity*; Putnam, 'Is Semantics Possible?', in *Mind, Language and Reality: Philosophical Papers*, ii (Cambridge, 1975). The view is associated with Russell, and attributed to him explicitly by G. E. M. Anscome, *An Introduction to Wittgenstein's Tractatus* (London 1959; 3rd edn., London, 1967), ch. 2. For a more cautious approach, in sympathy with Kripke and Putnam, see J. McDowell, 'On the Sense and Reference of a Proper Name', in Mark Platts (ed.), *Reference, Truth and Reality* (London, 1980). The theory that metaphor consists always in a shift in a deviant *predication* is implicit in I. A. Richards's seminal account in *The Philosophy of Rhetoric* (London, 1936), and has been elaborated in a series of works by Paul Ricœur—see esp. *La Métaphore vive* (Paris, 1976).

> I have no spur to prick the side of my intent
> Save vaulting ambition, which
> O'erleaps itself and falls on the other side.

In isolating the predicate as the crucial part of the metaphor, I follow Max Black's distinction between the *focus* of the metaphor (the crucial predicate) and the sentential frame.[2] But there is a deeper reason for this, and one which was perceived by Aristotle. Metaphors are, as their Greek name implies, transferred from another context—from the central context which gives their sense. We learn the predicate 'blue' by learning to apply it to what is literally blue: and then we transfer the predicate to things (such as music) which are not or cannot be blue. This act of transference has a purpose for us, a role in a language game, to use Wittgenstein's idiom. A theory of metaphor should tell us what this purpose is.

There is a distinction between metaphor and simile which helps to clarify the argument. In a simile, A is likened to B, the implication being that the likeness could be spelled out, that there is some respect in which the two objects agree. To say that 'the Assyrian came down like a wolf on the plain' is to say something that is literally true (assuming the story is not a fiction). Everything resembles everything else in *some* respect: and the greater or more significant the resemblance, the greater the 'degree of truth' in the simile. Many of the elaborate figures in Homer, Virgil, and Milton take the form of similes: indeed, in epic poetry metaphor is used sparingly, since it curtails those great arches of comparison which give the narrative its breadth and universality.

All the same, the point of a simile is not exhausted by its truthfulness—not even by its 'truth to life'. Like a metaphor, the simile has to 'work', and its *working* consists in an alchemical transformation of the reader's response. Critics have disputed whether Addison's comparison of the Duke of Marlborough to an avenging angel, in this famous passage from 'The Campaign', is really apt:

> 'Twas then great Marlbro's mighty soul was prov'd
> That, in the shock of charging hosts unmov'd,
> Amidst confusion, horror, and despair,
> Examin'd all the dreadful scenes of war;
> In peaceful thought the field of death survey'd,
> To fainting squadrons sent the timely aid,
> Inspir'd repuls'd battalions to engage,
> And taught the doubtful battle where to rage.

[2] Black, 'Metaphor', in *Models and Metaphors: Studies in Language and Philosophy* (Ithaca, NY, 1962) and 'More about Metaphor', in A. Ortony (ed.), *Metaphor and Thought* (2nd edn., Cambridge, 1993).

> So when an angel by divine command
> With rising tempests shakes a guilty land,
> Such as of late o'er pale Britannia past,
> Calm and serene he drives the furious blast;
> And, pleas'd th'Almighty's orders to perform,
> Rides in the whirlwind, and directs the storm.

According to Dr Johnson,[3] while the sentiments of this passage are just and noble, the simile is a failure: not because it is untrue, but because it is too obviously *true*. The action attributed to Marlborough, and that attributed to the angel, he argued, are one and the same, while 'a poetical simile consists in the discovery of likeness between two actions, in their general nature and disposition dissimilar'. You do not have to agree with Johnson's judgement of Addison's lines, in order to see the rightness of his meaning. The success of figurative language consists precisely in bringing dissimilar things together, in creating a relation where previously there was none. And this relation is created in the reader's experience; the success of a simile, therefore, is no different from that of a metaphor. The presence or absence of a comparative, such as 'like' or 'as', is of little significance besides the fusion that is achieved in the perfect metaphor, and equally in the successful simile. In neither case is the point of the figure displayed by *spelling out* the analogy, showing that just this or that feature is shared between Marlborough and the angel, the Assyrian and the wolf. Consider the following sequence of similes:

> If I can stave off thought, which—as a whelp
>   Clings to its teat—sticks to me through the abyss
> Of this odd labyrinth; or as the kelp
>   Holds by the rock; or as a lover's kiss
> Drains its first draught of lips:—but, as I said,
> I *won't* philosophize, and *will* be read.

> (Byron, *Don Juan*, 10. 28)

The three similes draw on the same analogy: between the tenacity of thought and the tenacity of other things. But as the mind ranges over the comparisons, encountering animal, vegetable, and human attachment, maternal warmth, sea-cold, and erotic passion, and all the time comparing these with a tenacity that is not physical at all, the result is precisely one of supreme ironic *de*tachment. It is not the analogy that creates this effect, but the dislocating nature of the images, fused one by one with the thing that half-rejects them.

The surface grammar of a simile may belie a metaphorical intention, as when Eliot writes:

[3] 'Addison', in *Lives of the English Poets* (Everyman edition, London, 1925),   i. 353.

> Midnight shakes the memory
> As a madman shakes a dead geranium.

('Rhapsody on a Windy Night', in *Prufrock, and Other Observations*)

Midnight does not literally shake, nor is the memory literally shaken; the comparison implied by 'as' assumes a prior metaphorical transfer. And even so, it cannot be carried through. Midnight is not like a madman, nor memory like a dead geranium. Nor do the lines imply the contrary; rather, they bring the image of a madman shaking a dead geranium into proximity with the poet at midnight, helplessly and uselessly 'remembering things'. The result is not a comparison but a highly imaginative fusion, of the kind we know from metaphor.

Even when the comparison is genuine, a simile may owe its power to metaphors and images which crowd in under its protection, as when Shakespeare writes:

> nor can
> Her heart inform her tongue: the swan's downfeather
> That stands upon the swell at full of tide
> And neither way inclines.

(*Antony and Cleopatra*, III. ii. 47–50)

The comparison of the tongue to a feather imports another and more impressive image—that of the tide, and thereby the vastness of human passion, the unknown depths from which feeling springs, and the impotence of reason (the swan's downfeather) in the attempt to master it.

To appreciate the proximity of simile and metaphor is to see the insufficiency of theories which assign to metaphors a secondary meaning, saying that while they are false when taken literally, they may be true when taken metaphorically—that in their metaphorical use they attribute to a subject properties which it actually *has*, and which we are able to see that it has, thanks to the comparison. It is not simile that is the paradigm of transferred predication, but metaphor; and it is in terms of metaphor that simile should be explained. The point of a simile is identical with the point of a metaphor: not to describe an object, but to *change its aspect*, so that we respond to it in another way.

This is possible precisely because terms used metaphorically, like those which occur in a simile, are used with their ordinary sense. This point may be appreciated from an example of Wittgenstein's:[4] suppose someone asks himself the following question: 'Which is fat and which lean, Tuesday or Wednesday?' He will at once seize upon an answer that seems right to him: Wednesday is fat, say. Asked what he means by 'fat' he will reply, 'What

---

[4] *Philosophical Investigations*, tr. G. E. M. Anscombe (Oxford, 1953) pt 2, §11.

I have always meant'. The point is that he wishes to use precisely *this* term, with its ordinary meaning, *here*. The central examples *show the meaning* of the term, and this is the meaning that it has, even when applied in a metaphor.

This observation has great significance in the philosophy of art, as I tried to show in *Art and Imagination*. It rules out many theories of metaphor, but also many theories of expression and aesthetic description. Someone might argue, for example, that the word 'sad' in the sentence 'The music is sad' has a secondary meaning, going on to spell out what this meaning is—what features of a work of music must be present if it is truly to be sad. But that misses the whole point of the judgement, which is that I should wish to use *this* word, with its ordinary meaning, *here*, where it does *not* (literally) apply. Nor could someone learn the meaning of the word 'sad' by attending exclusively to sad pieces of music: it is to the central examples that he must turn, even in order to know what is meant when the predicate is used of music.

A distinction is sometimes made between dead and living metaphors. The idea is that a metaphor, when too much used, *does* change the meaning of the term, so that it comes to extend quite literally to the new examples. The sign of this is that you could learn the meaning of the term from examples which were once only metaphorically described by it. Many people learn the meaning of the word 'bastard' in this way, without knowing what it originally referred to. In such a case the metaphor has not merely died: its death has split the sense of the word in two. It now has two independent meanings, which could be grasped without reference to each other. A dead metaphor is part of the archaeology of living usage.

Most effective metaphors could never die in that way, since the connection that they make is unique to the context of their utterance, and incapable of being severed from it. When Mallarmé describes a trinket as 'aboli bibelot d'inanité sonore', he creates a fusion of senses that is irrepeatable. Inanity cannot be sonorous: yet here it resounds in a cavernous hollow of negation.

The Point of Metaphor

As I have suggested, we should not try to translate such a metaphor into its 'literal' equivalent. In understanding a literal sentence, I acquire a grasp of its truth-conditions. In understanding a metaphor I come to see its point— or, when it fails, its pointlessness. The intention of the speaker is to bring me to share the experience that prompts his description: the experience of seeing and responding to one thing in terms suggested by another.

This is the aim, too, of a simile. Consider Milton's description of Satan, as he stands before his defeated army, summoning them to counsel:

> As when the Sun new ris'n
> Looks through the horizontal misty Air
> Shorn of his Beams, or from behind the Moon
> In dim Eclips disastrous twilight sheds
> On half the Nations, and with fear of change
> Perplexes Monarchs. Dark'n'd so, yet shon
> Above them all th'Arch Angel: but his face
> Deep scars of Thunder had intrencht, and care
> Sat on his faded cheek, but under Browes
> Of dauntless courage, and considerate Pride
> Waiting revenge . . .

(*Paradise Lost*, 1. 594–604)

The point of such a comparison lies not so much in the analogy, which is merely a vehicle, but in the transformation of the reader's experience. Satan comes before us in another aspect; in his face we see the eclipsed and thwarted sunlight, and the menace of his vengeance is received as that primeval menace, in which the light of nature glows black and half-extinguished, threatening the end of all. In metaphors, such vast transformations are condensed into a single word or phrase, as when Rilke writes: 'so reißt die Spur der Fledermaus durch Porzellan des Abends', and the lightning hair-crack along a piece of porcelain fuses with the unseen flutter of a bat in the twilight.

To describe this fusion of experience, and its effect on us, is not easy. But here, briefly, is the theory that I defended in earlier work and which I shall adopt now as a working hypothesis. We are able to attend not only to the inner reality of objects, but also to their appearance. In aesthetic experience our senses are saturated by the appearances of things, which take on a fascination that is especially significant, in that its origin lies in *us*. We are appreciating objects as they are *for us*, and so bringing them into a kind of personal relation. The jar as it is for me is not the jar as it is in itself, but rather a bridge between me and the outer world, so that 'a Chinese jar still / Moves perpetually in its stillness'. Sometimes, however, I can concentrate on the appearance of one thing, while attending equally to the appearance of another, and my response to the second is transferred to the first. I come to vibrate in sympathy with both simultaneously. I thereby make a connection between them—a connection that is real in my emotions, but only imagined in the objects themselves.

The resulting experience is one with a 'double intentionality'. It is directed towards two appearances simultaneously, and forbids their separation. A simple case of this—which Richard Wollheim[5] has called 'representational seeing', but which, for reasons that will become apparent, I prefer to call

[5] *Painting as an Art* (London, 1987).

'aspect perception'—is the case in which one thing is seen in another. This is a clear instance of double intentionality. When I see a face in a picture, then, in the normal aesthetic context, I am not seeing a picture *and* a face; nor am I seeing a resemblance between the picture and a face. The face and the picture are fused in my perception: which is not to say that I confuse the one with the other, or mistake the reality of either. I am presented with two simultaneous objects of perception: the *real* picture, and the *imaginary* face. And my response to each is fused with my response to the other. For example I respond to the flowing lines and flesh-tints with emotions and expectations that derive from my experience of faces, and to the face with emotions and expectations that arise from my interest in colour, harmony, and expressive line. The fusion is effected at the highest level of rational interest, while being transcribed into the perception itself.

A parallel experience arises in the understanding of metaphor. I am not merely thinking of the bat's flight *in terms of* a hairline crack in porcelain; nor am I making analogies, or confusing objects that are simultaneously imagined. On the contrary, as in the case of the picture, the effect depends upon my recognizing the impassable difference—the metaphysical gulf—between the two objects of my response. In no way can the crack and the bat's flight be confused in reality, since the two experiences belong to different contexts and even different sense-modalities. (You sense the bat through a kind of subliminal cringe of the body.)

Just as every line, shade, and nuance of the painted surface enters into and conditions my experience of the face, so does the very syntax and sound of the metaphor inhabit my experience of the thing described. Mallarmé's internal rhymes, inverted syntax, and sudden emptying of sound into the abysmal vowels of *sonore* transform the appearance of that 'abolished trinket', so that its triviality becomes also a poignant 'pastness', a thing mindlessly cherished, now gone for ever.

Of course, there are important differences between aspects and metaphors, and I do not claim to have given in those few paragraphs a complete theory of either. But I hope that aspect perception provides sufficient proof of double intentionality to suggest a plausible way of looking at metaphor. David Cooper, in his study of metaphor, dismisses the comparison, arguing that when we predicate a term of an object metaphorically, it is absurd to say that we are seeing the object *as* that term suggests, or that we have the particular experience of the 'dawning of an aspect'.[6] And that is certainly true. Nevertheless, aspect perception provides a paradigm of double intentionality;

[6] *Metaphor* (London, 1986), 227–38. For the contrasting view, which makes aspect perception *central* to the understanding of metaphor, see Marcus B. Hester, *The Meaning of Poetic Metaphor* (The Hague, 1967).

and it is *this* feature which is important in our understanding of metaphor. Before returning to music, something should be said about the mental capacity which is exercised whenever intentionality doubles itself in this way.

Imagination

Everyday cognitive activity involves perception, belief, and information-gathering. It is an activity that is common to many animal species, and certainly not distinctive of man. However, rational beings—of which man and his gods are the only known examples—have capacities which are not to be found elsewhere. Imagination is one of them.

Rationality involves the ability to represent to ourselves absent or hypothetical situations, to project our thought in a speculative arch away from the immediate present, into regions which are past or future, possible or impossible, probable or improbable, and from which it returns with insight into the nature of things. Animals draw conclusions from their experience: else why should the horse jump the fence and not go crashing through it? But this 'drawing of conclusions' is confined to the immediate data, and the rules of thumb that transform the data into premises for action. Rational beings think in terms of past, future, and possible worlds—even impossible worlds, as is shown by fiction. And we do this because we can think in symbols. Language represents the not-now and the not-here, and spreads them before us on equal terms with the here and now.

In our normal commerce with the world, we move like the animals among things that we perceive, gathering information and pursuing our desires with the robust sense of actuality that guides the cat to the mouse, the fox to the pheasant, and the horse to his stable. In these circumstances perception is informed by belief, and thought seeks the truth about the world before us. Some philosophers argue, indeed, that perception must be understood *in terms of* the gathering of information. At any rate, the intentionality of ordinary perception is like that of belief—it involves a mental affirmation of a proposition about the perceivable world.

Propositions may be affirmed; but they may also be entertained without affirming them. The capacity to do this—and to do it constructively—is part of what I mean by imagination. It is necessarily true that every rational being has this capacity to some degree; for it is exemplified by inference itself. As Frege argued, the fact that a sentence is *asserted* cannot be part of its meaning; else how would the inference from p and p implies q to q be valid, when p is asserted in the first step, and unasserted in the second?[7]

---

[7] Frege, 'The Thought', in P. F. Strawson (ed.), *Philosophical Logic* (Oxford 1967); P. T. Geach, 'On Assertion', in *Logic Matters* (Oxford, 1972).

Every inference involves this capacity to entertain a proposition in its unasserted form: and it is the very same proposition that is asserted or affirmed when we believe it to be true.

'Unasserted thought' plays an important role also in imagery. When I form an image of some absent or fictitious thing, my image stands to my thought much as the memory image stands to my beliefs about the past. It is the 'sensuous shining', to use a Hegelian phrase, of an unasserted thought, just as the memory image is the sensuous shining of a belief about the past. As to what images *are*, this is a question that we need not explore.[8] For present purposes it is not imagery, but imaginative perception that we must analyse.

Suppose I see a man standing before me in a threatening posture. My instinct is to be on my guard. I *expect* something, and fear it; and I respond accordingly. My behaviour is adequately accounted for by the fact that what I see I also believe to be there. Indeed seeing, in such a case, is believing. The visual experience has the intentionality of a belief: it is an unqualified affirmation that *this* is how things are.

Suppose now that I see a man standing with the same threatening posture, but in a picture. My instinct is to look, to study, to enjoy this meditation on the phenomenon of anger. I expect nothing, fear nothing, and am given over entirely to the way things look. Here my behaviour is accounted for by the fact that what I see I also believe *not* to be there. I am 'seeing without belief'. The visual experience has the intentionality of an unasserted thought: it speaks to me of possibilities, not actualities, and contains no affirmation that this is how things are.

From the cognitive point of view, the two experiences are as different as can be. The one is linked to fear and flight, the other to peaceful meditation; the one fixes me in the here and now, in a condition of maximum alertness; the other allows me to drift free of the present reality, and to lose myself in thought. At the same time, there is surely a great resemblance between them. There is a sense in which the world looks the same in ordinary perception, and in its 'unasserted' version. The image in the picture is the image precisely of a man, who stands and threatens, and who is indistin-guishable from the real man who had seemed to threaten me. What I see in the picture corresponds exactly to all that is revealed to me as I stand on my guard: the same colours, outline, and so on. (Such could be the case, at any rate.) Yet the intentional content is so different that the experiences can be compared in no other way.

But now we see why the experience of aspect perception is available to the rational being, and why it is important to him. When I see the picture, and the man portrayed in it, the intentionality of perception can double

---

[8] I address this question in *Art and Imagination* (London, 1974), pt II.

itself, precisely because there is no conflict between the images. I am not being torn between rival beliefs, as I would be by a *trompe l'œil* mural, wondering whether this is a painting *or* a man. I can approach it as both a painting *and* a man, precisely because the man does not belong to the world in which the painting is situated. I believe this thing before me is a painting, and merely *think of* the man within it. This is the peculiar experience that imagination makes available—the coming-together in a single perception of asserted and unasserted thought.

The very same capacity is exercised in the making and understanding of metaphor. This is why the *falsehood* of a metaphor is so important a part of it. It is the impossibility of believing that the evening really *is* porcelain that enables me to think of it *as* porcelain: to hold this thought in suspension before my mind, until the imagined perceptions of a bat flitting through the evening air, and a crack running through porcelain coalesce in a single image. In the examples that I have given, both of metaphor and of simile, we encounter the singular freedom that is gained by thought, when emancipated from the duty of believing things. Thoughts entertained simultaneously can coalesce in single images—images of which we can venture no better description than is provided by the metaphor itself. For the metaphor is the verbal expression of an experience made available precisely by *that form of words.*

The freedom of imaginative thought-processes is manifested in another way namely, in the voluntary character of the experiences that depend on them. You cannot command someone to believe that the moon is made of cheese, but you can command him to imagine it. Similarly, you cannot command someone to see a dagger before his eyes, but you can command him to form an image of it. Likewise, standing before a painting, I can ask you to see it, not as a portrait of a child, but as the portrait of a dwarf with child-like features, not as the portrait of a woman, but as the portrait of a man in woman's clothing. The familiar examples of ambiguous figures, which we can see now one way, now another, are not the exceptions: they are simply the clearest instances of a universal freedom that we have, when that which we see is seen without believing. The change of aspect is a change from one experience to another: but it is not precipitated by any change in visual information; it involves the transition from one unasserted thought to another, each embodied in a visual image whose sensory contours remain unchanged.

This does not mean that I have *total* freedom: for of course, my perception is constrained by the material object. Nor does it mean that every way of seeing a picture is equally *right*. On the contrary, here as elsewhere, freedom implies the possibility of criticism. Reasons can be given for a 'way of seeing', and criticism has the production of those reasons as its goal.

The Indispensable Metaphor

When I use a metaphor in order to describe the real world, it is often shorthand for a complex truth. Eliminating the metaphor will then reveal that truth, laid bear to the eye of pure believing. I can spell out *homo homini lupus*, for instance, by describing the known facts of man's aggression towards his fellows, and in one sense this is what the metaphor means. Of course, I have not captured the 'point' of the metaphor, in the particular context of its utterance. For there may still be the peculiar coalescence which comes from our knowledge that whatever else man may be, he is not, literally, a wolf. But it has to be a very special context that would bring *this* tired metaphor to life again. For all intents and purposes, it is now dispensable.

The same can be said about any metaphor that is used to convey a truth about the material world. There are no metaphorical facts, since all metaphors are false—or true only 'in passing', as in John Donne's famous 'No man is an island', which touches truth on its way to the magnificent falsehood that we are all parts of a continent. In so far as we are interested in describing the reality, we could dispense with metaphors, even those 'metaphors we live by' that have been agreeably (though contentiously) surveyed by Mark Johnson and George Lakoff.[9] There are those who doubt that this is so— who argue with Derrida that language is fundamentally metaphorical, and that every literal use is founded on a metaphor that undermines it.[10] But life is too short to mount the full refutation of such a view, which if true, must also be false, since at least one thing would then be literally true. A metaphor comes about when a term is transferred from the use which gives its meaning, to a context where it does not, or even cannot, apply. There can be metaphors, therefore, only where there are also literal uses; to deny this is to deny the possibility of meaning anything at all. (A denial that Derrida's writings illustrate but in no way justify.)

Nevertheless, there are contexts in which metaphors seem indispensable: not merely because they are part of some unique literary experience, as in the examples that I have considered, but because we are using them to describe something other than the material world; in particular because we are attempting to describe how the world *seems*, from the point of view of the active imagination.

Kant maintained that every experience that is referred to the material world must also be 'brought under concepts'. Intentionality requires the application of concepts, which determine *how* the world appears in the perspective of my attention. But Kant did not directly distinguish two kinds of concept-application: in a judgement, as he called it, and in imagination.

---

[9] *Metaphors We Live By.*
[10] 'La Mythologie blanche', in *Marges de la philosophie* (Paris, 1972).

In my example, when I see the man standing before me, my perception is informed by concepts—and in particular by the concept: *man*. But here the concept is applied in a judgement: seeing is believing, and I am disposed to take the world *for* what I see. When I see the man in the picture, the concept *man* likewise informs my perception. But it is not applied in a judgement: appearance is all, and while I entertain thoughts about this man before me, I do not affirm them to be true. Here we might say that a concept is applied in a perception, but transferred from its central use. Moreover, it is impossible to eliminate the transferred usage, and still describe the way the world seems. This transferred usage defines the intentional object of my perception, as nothing else can define it.

The peculiar intimacy of concept and experience in perception has often been commented upon. A perceptual experience is not an *interpretation* of some raw 'intuition': it is animated and informed by thought. Hence many philosophers speak of perception as a kind of 'representation', and seek to explain intentionality (here as elsewhere) in terms of the mental representation of the world. To enter this debate would take us too far from our purpose: although I shall have something to say about it in Chapter 7. The important point is to recognize that, however intimate the connection between experience and concept may be, it does not fully define the intentionality of an experience. In order to complete the account of intentionality, we need to know whether the concept is asserted in the experience, or merely entertained. And if it is merely entertained, how is it entertained? The indispensable metaphor occurs when the way the world seems depends upon an imaginative involvement with it, rather than on our ordinary cognitive goals. And this is the case when we listen to music.

The Life in Music

I argued in Chapter 2 that there lies, in our most basic apprehension of music, a complex system of metaphor, which is the true description of no material fact, not even a fact about sounds, judged as secondary objects. The metaphor cannot be eliminated from the description of music, because it defines the intentional object of the musical experience. Take the metaphor away, and you cease to describe the experience of music. Perhaps the metaphors could be revised in certain respects. It may be that we could regard the descriptions 'high' and 'low' as dispensable, replaceable by other metaphors, such as the French *aigu* and *grave*. But this local variation involves no rejection of the spatial metaphor, nor of the sense that movement to higher frequencies is a movement *upwards*—a movement which *lifts* the melodic line *above* its former location. Indeed, what would it be like to dispense altogether with the experience of space? We should then cease to hear orientation in music; tones would no longer move towards or away from each other; no phrase would mirror another, no leaps be bolder or larger than others, and so on. In short, the experience of music would involve neither melody nor counterpoint as we know them. Musical movement would have been reduced to a static pulse: in which case, why should we continue to talk of music? If the metaphors are dispensable, it is only for the trivial reason that our world might not have contained the experience of music. But that too could be doubted: for perhaps it is in the nature of reason, to hear sounds in just this way?

If the description of music is so dependent on metaphor, then we might go on to conclude that music is not, strictly speaking, a part of the material world of sound. A scientific description of the world of sound would not mention, as an independent fact of the matter, the phenomenon of music. There is no explanatory function to be filled by the concept of music that will not equally be filled by the concept of organized sound: no scientific method could discriminate between the two, the extension of each concept in the material world being the same. If there is an additional *fact* of the matter, it is that we (beings of a certain kind) hear music. Music belongs uniquely to the intentional sphere, and not to the material realm.

Someone might object, however, that the argument shows no more than that musical properties and relations are secondary, rather than primary, properties of sounds. To deny on such grounds that they are part of the material world in some significant sense (some sense that does not merely reiterate the scientific realist's commitment to the explanatory priority of primary qualities) is to repeat a mistake at least as old as Berkeley. It is to think that because the sense of a term ('red', for example) is to be specified in terms of a certain experience involved in its application, its reference must therefore be to the experience—the 'idea'—and not to any material reality.

It is true that the terms used to describe music *refer* to material sounds. But they refer to them under a description that no material sound can satisfy. Sounds do not move as music moves (so as to 'reach into the silence'). Nor are they organized in a spatial way, nor do they rise and fall. Yet this is how we hear them when we hear them as music.

The case is quite different from that of secondary qualities for another reason. The ability to perceive a secondary quality is a sensory capacity, and depends only upon the power of sensory discrimination. Many animals discriminate sensory qualities better than we do (bees, for example, perceive a wider range of colours, birds a wider range of sound qualities). This ability does not depend upon superior intellect, nor upon any other faculty that might be improved or impaired through education. It is this that leads us to think of secondary qualities as *inherent* in the objects that possess them. For no reasoning or discussion of the matter can lead us to perceive or dissuade us from perceiving them: they are inexorably there, for any creature blessed, or cursed, with the appropriate apparatus.

Musical qualities, however, are not secondary qualities. They are like aspects—what might be called tertiary qualities, in recognition of the fact that, while part of the appearance of something, they are not objects merely of sensory perception. Such tertiary qualities are neither deduced from experience nor invoked in the explanation of experience. They are perceived only by rational beings, and only through a certain exercise of imagination, involving the transfer of concepts from another sphere.

In what sense such qualities are really *in* the object in which they are heard is a difficult question, to which I shall return. But their objectivity is at least *put in question* by the fact that only imaginative beings can perceive them. Like every object of imaginative perception, they are subject to the will, and the object of conscious and subconscious choices. That is why criticism is possible, here as in the case of painting. You can give arguments for hearing the drum-beats that open Beethoven's Violin Concerto, Op. 61, as a sustained up-beat, or as part of the melody; and the choice lies with the listener. Look carefully at the parallel with pictures, and you will see that musical perception involves all those features that I have attributed to the imagination, and could not exist in the mind of a creature incapable of imaginative thought.

Non-Conceptual Content

Kant argued that experience involves a synthesis of intuition (the sensory component) and concept; it is by virtue of this synthesis that perceptions are also 'representations'. However, he also argued that intuition exhibits a preconceptual order, which is the order of space and time. Space and time, for Kant, were not concepts but 'forms of intuition', and experience is ordered spatially and temporally prior to any representation of its object.

In a similar vein, recent philosophers (notably Christopher Peacocke)[11] have distinguished the 'conceptual' from the 'non-conceptual' content of experience, arguing that an object may be presented to a person's perception, even though he cannot identify it through concepts. This act of presentation is also a 'content', and implies a non-conceptual ordering—as when a figure emerges from a background, for someone who can say nothing whatsoever about the figure's nature.

The suggestion encourages us to distinguish the perceptual *Gestalt* from the interpretation placed upon it, and revives the Kantian notion of a 'unity of the manifold' which is 'given' preconceptually. Needless to say, the

[11] *Sense and Content* (Oxford, 1983).

suggestion has not escaped vigorous criticism,[12] and I find no great reason to accept it. Nevertheless, a philosopher who *did* accept it, might find himself sceptical of the position advanced in this chapter, according to which we hear music under an indispensable metaphorical description.[13] Why is the unity of a motif or melody not given 'preconceptually', like that of the visual *Gestalt*? Why assume that the metaphor with which we describe such unities, is also the intellectual act that creates them? Could we not hear melodies and harmonies as musical individuals, and fail to hear them in terms of space and movement?

The real question here is not whether there might be a preconceptual organization exhibited by the musical *Gestalt*, but whether it would be sufficient to hear this organisation in order to hear the music as *music*. And this I doubt. Consider the first phrase of 'Baa, Baa, Black Sheep', beginning on C. The phrase is composed as follows: two crotchets on C, two on G, and then four quavers on A, B, C, and A, leading again to G where the melody rests. It is quite possible that a listener should hear this as a unity, without hearing the movement that *we* hear in it. For him, as for us, the melody begins on C and pauses on G, with the intervening notes leading from the first note to the last. But he could organize the notes in this way, even though they had, for him, no direction: even though he discerned no upward movement from C to G; even though he did not hear that the quavers were moving the melody on in the *same direction*; even though the return to G thereafter involved no loss of the 'upward' impulse. Such a case would parallel that in which a person recognized a figure as standing against a ground, but had no knowledge of the figure's nature. Surely, however, we should say that our listener, even if he has perceived a musical unity, has not perceived it *as music*. He has heard the outline, but not the substance, and the crucial act of recognition, which is a recognition of movement, has yet to occur.

The point here is fundamental. You can imagine a person who heard and grouped adjacent sounds in ways that are quite different from those described in Chapter 2. You could, if you like, use the word 'music' to describe what he hears, simply in order to emphasize the similarity with our own experience. But *I* use the word precisely to emphasize the difference: the difference between hearing temporally organized sounds, and hearing *tones*.

[12] e.g. J. McDowell, *Mind and World* (Cambridge, Mass., 1994).
[13] See e.g. M. Budd, 'Understanding Music', *Proceedings of the Aristotelian Society*, suppl. vol. (1985), 239–45.

The Imagined World of Tones

The picture at which we have arrived is this. In hearing sounds, we may attend to them in the way that we attend to pictures, on the look-out, or listen-out, for imaginative perceptions. There then arises the peculiar double intentionality that is exemplified in the experience of metaphor: one and the same experience takes sound as its object, and also something that is not and cannot be sound—the life and movement that is music. We hear this life and movement *in* the sound, and situate it in an imagined space, organized, as is the phenomenal space of our own experience, in terms of 'up' and 'down', 'rising' and 'falling', 'high' and 'low'.

Phenomenologists will draw their own conclusions from that theory. For they tell us that our everyday concept of space is not geometrical but phenomenal: it is derived from the experience of movement and the sense of the world's resistance to our will. At a deep level the sense of 'up' and 'down' are understood in terms of the toils and strains of our activity. (Hence those absurd attempts to explain the experience of *musical* movement by reference to the strain on the larynx as it ascends the scale.[14]) The metaphor of musical movement, since it has no other ground than the way things appear to us, and cannot give way to a theory of musical space, is the pure phenomenal residue of our ordinary experience of space. And what is this phenomenal residue, other than a sense of the world's complex resistance to our will, and our own being-in-the-world as active organisms? Such, at least, would be the likely conclusion of a Sartre or a Merleau-Ponty. And they would be in broad agreement with Schopenhauer, although beginning from quite different premisses, that music is the presentation in appearance of the will.

It is too early, however, to draw such radical conclusions; and besides, the premisses of phenomenology are as dubious as those of Schopenhauer's idealism, accepted, like Schopenhauer's, for the ease with which they deliver results and not from any persuasive argument. So I shall rest, for the moment, with a minimal conclusion from the discussion of this chapter. Music is the intentional object of an experience that only rational beings can have, and only through the exercise of imagination. To describe it we must have recourse to metaphor, not because music resides in an analogy with other things, but because the metaphor describes exactly *what* we hear, when we hear sounds as music.

[14] C. Stumpf, *Tonpsychologie*, 2 vols. (Leipzig, 1883), vol. i. The suggestion is taken seriously by C. C. Pratt, *The Meaning of Music: A Study in Psychological Aesthetics* (New York, 1931), and even so penetrating a thinker as Paul Hindemith, in *A Composer's World*, 52 f, tries to understand musical movement in terms of the physical energies of the performer who produces it.

4 Ontology

In describing the *phenomenal* nature of music, I have avoided raising the ontological question: what exactly *is* a work of music? When is work A the same as work B, and what hangs on the answer? And with this question of identity come others, no less interesting and no less difficult: what is the relation between a work and a (true) performance of it? What is the relation between a work and an *arrangement* of it? What do we mean by 'versions' of the same work? When judging a work of music, how do we separate the qualities of the music from those of the performance? If an improvisation is written down and played again, is that a performance of the very same work? And so on. Such questions may not be equally important, and they may also be less important than they have seemed to recent philosophers. Nevertheless we must answer some of them before we can give a clear account of the meaning of music.

Before beginning, however, there is a point of method that needs to be borne in mind. Several writers (notably Carl Dahlhaus, Edward Said, Lydia Goehr, and others influenced by Adorno)[1] have argued that the habit of identifying individual *works* of music is a recent one, coinciding with the rise of a listening public, and with the institution of concert-going as a cultural practice. Music was not always the solemn occasion that it has become in the culture of bourgeois Europe and America. Far more often in the history of mankind it has been part of a larger event: worship, dancing, ceremony, even battle. In such circumstances people do not stand back and focus on the piece itself, nor do they savour the sounds as modern listeners do. Some argue further, that aesthetic interest is not a human universal, as Kantian philosophers claim, but part of the ideology of bourgeois culture.[2]

[1] Dahlhaus, *Esthetics of Music*, tr. W. Austin (Cambridge, 1982), and *The Idea of Absolute Music*, tr. R. Lustig (Chicago, 1989); Said, *Musical Elaborations* (London, 1991); Goehr, *The Imaginary Museum of Musical Works* (Oxford, 1992).

[2] See esp. P. Bourdieu, *Distinction: A Social Critique of the Judgement of Taste*, tr. R. Nice (London, 1984); and T. Eagleton, *The Ideology of the Aesthetic* (Oxford, 1990).

Only in the context of that culture does the practice of identifying individual works of art and their authors make sense.

To both these claims I shall return in Chapters 14 and 15. But a preliminary response is called for, if we are to venture with confidence into the realm of musical ontology. It is an important and interesting observation, that the practice of *listening* to music, and in particular of listening to it in the reverent hush of a concert hall, is neither a human universal, nor the whole of musical experience. It is also an interesting observation (should it be true) that the habit of identifying specific musical works arose precisely in the context of a 'listening' culture. The fact remains, however, that we *do* identify individual works, and identify them as the particular objects of aesthetic interest. Even when the habit of identifying works of music was not yet established, people had an aesthetic interest in performances: the writings of Plato, St Augustine, and Boethius abundantly testify to this. And while people then listened in a different way, nevertheless they listened, and heard at least some of the musical phenomena that I described in Chapter 2. The questions that now concern us will not dissolve merely because such people did not notice them. For they are questions that may be raised whenever people listen to music, and whenever they experience the thing listened to as 'the same again'.

There is a general question, too, about the bearing of historical theories on philosophy. Many writers—particularly those from a Marxian background—remark on the 'historicity' of intellectual problems, implying that they become problems only in certain historical contexts, and cease to be intelligible outside the cultural conditions from which they arose. (Consider the question: What is virtue? as discussed by Plato and Aristotle; or the question: How is private property justified? as posed by Locke.) The implication is that the problems arise always within the ideology of a period, from concepts which are neither necessary to us as human beings, nor useful when lifted from their cultural roots.

I doubt that any such thing is ever true of a philosophical question. It is not merely that history has shown that philosophical questions, once discovered, do not dissolve with a change of the cultural climate. It is that they are not of a nature to dissolve, any more than are the questions of mathematics. People in our culture take an intense interest in works of music. They listen to them for their intrinsic qualities, and are eager to compare one work with another. The philosophical question is this: *what* are they listening to and assessing with such fervour? That question will not dissolve, just because people at some future time should cease to listen, or cease to notice the existence of individual works, any more than the question 'What are numbers?' will disappear, when people lose all skill in mathematics. Our ability to notice philosophical questions may change with historical conditions; the questions themselves do not.

Some Puzzles about Identity

Although we distinguish works of music from their performances, we are by no means clear as to how the works themselves should be counted. Is an arrangement of a work *another* work, or just the same work adjusted? You might say that it depends on the adjustment. For example, Mahler made an arrangement for string orchestra of Schubert's 'Death and the Maiden' Quartet, D810. He did very little to the quartet, apart from preventing the double basses from swamping the lower register, and for pages the two scores look almost identical. Is this arrangement a new work, or merely a 'version' of the old one? Or consider a piano reduction of a symphonic score: does this bring a new musical work into being, or is it merely a 'version' of the old one?

I put the word 'version' in inverted commas, precisely because the question will not be solved by the distinction between a work and its versions: for we have no clear conception of what a 'version' is. Certainly there are arrangements which are something more than 'versions': Liszt's arrangements of operatic scenes for the piano, for example, or Percy Grainger's incredible two-piano meditation on Bach's 'Sheep May Safely Graze', entitled *Blithe Bells.* Likewise we distinguish among orchestrations, between those which are merely orchestral *versions* (such as the versions made by Mahler or Vaughan Williams of their early songs for voice and piano), and those which are something more than that—which involve a creative act that changes the character of the piece and raises again the question of identity: for example, Schoenberg's orchestration of Brahms's Piano Quartet in G minor, Op. 25, which is sometimes referred to as Brahms's Fifth Symphony, so much does it take on a symphonic character in this transformation. (Though Brahms would surely not have used a xylophone!) More modest orchestrators than Schoenberg may yet add creative touches which change the character of a piece entirely. One of the many contributors to *Les Sylphides* (not Glazunov) orchestrated the Waltz in C sharp minor, Op. 64 No. 2, with the inner voice of Ex. 4.1. This voice is added to, and also in a sense discovered in, the musical line, and represents a real creative achievement. Perhaps we should speak of a variation, rather than a version, in such a case. (I heard this on a record the label of which contained no indication of the arranger's identity.)

Another puzzling example should once again be considered: Webern's orchestration of the six-part 'Ricercar' from Bach's *Musical Offering*, in which the melodic line is broken into motifs, and stuttered out in timbres so opposed that the piece seems as though pulverized and reconstituted out of tones that Bach would never have imagined (Ex. 2.34). The result is reminiscent of the famous story by Borges, 'Pierre Menard, Author of *Don*

Ex. 4.1. Chopin, arr. anon., *Les Sylphides*, Waltz in C sharp minor, Op. 64 No. 2, in original key, second episode

NB. Orchestrators of this waltz tend to follow Glazunov's example, and transpose it up a semitone to D minor, often preceding it with a cello solo derived from the C♯-minor study Op. 25 No. 7. The inner voice is not present in Glazunov's version: it may be due to Roy Douglas.

Quixote'. This tells of the writer Pierre Menard, who set out to compose a work which would be word-for-word identical with Cervantes's classic, but written out of the experience and the sensibility of a modern writer. Similarly, it is as though Webern had set himself the task of composing anew the 'Ricercar', from the sensibility of the serial composer, but arriving *at the very same notes* that Bach wrote. Not surprisingly, the result is not a version of Bach's great fugue, but another work—and a minor masterpiece.

Add to such puzzle cases the vast differences that we notice between performances, the effects of transposition (necessary at times in vocal music), the indeterminacy of musical scores, and the fact that much music is improvised and enjoyed *as* an improvisation (as in jazz), and you will begin to see that there are real puzzles about the identity of musical works, and that we ought to try to solve them. At least we should try to give some procedure for relating the work to its performances, and distinguishing versions of a work from departures that are so radical as to be versions of something else. In this chapter I shall explore the background metaphysical questions, returning to the concepts of performance and arrangement in Chapter 14.

Numerical Identity

We can proceed only if we can avail ourselves of a concept of numerical identity. When two objects have all their properties in common, they are qualitatively identical; but if they are two, then they are not numerically identical. (Leibniz famously denied the possibility that they *could* be two, thus reducing numerical to a special case of qualitative identity, with interesting but highly counter-intuitive results.) Could there be a useful concept of numerical identity applied to musical works? Why should we require it, and what disadvantages would follow should we abandon it?

Numerical identity is not always a clearly defined notion, so let us consider the various metaphysical categories, in order to ascertain what is required in order to define it.

1. Things. I use this vague term to cover, not only the 're-identifiable particulars' discussed by Strawson in *Individuals*, but any of the following:

(*a*) Ordinary physical objects.
(*b*) Organisms, including animals.
(*c*) Persons, including human beings.
(*d*) Theoretical entities, such as atoms and quarks.

Modern philosophy has shown that these are not all in the same boat, as far as identity goes. Sometimes the question whether *a* is identical with *b* seems to be answered by a convention or decision; at other times the answer seems to lie in the nature of things. Consider Hobbes's example of the ship of Theseus,[3] the planks of which are replaced one by one until not a plank remains unchanged. Suppose now the old planks are re-assembled in their original form. Which is the ship of Theseus—the one that emerged as the result of successive repairs, or the one that is put together from the debris? It does not matter which you say—though you cannot say both.

In the case of personal identity we are presented with the opposite paradigm: here it really *does* matter what we say—legally, morally, and personally. Although one philosopher—Derek Parfit[4]—has argued vigorously that the concept of personal identity is just as unfounded as that of the identity of ships, and indeed that it would be better not to employ the concept at all because of the moral confusion that it engenders, his arguments have not found general favour. The person, after all, is the thing that I identify as myself: it is that which I pick out incorrigibly as the subject of my first-person avowals, which stares from these eyes and hears with these ears: the very thing that fears for the future and learns from the past.

---

[3] Hobbes, *De corpore*, bk. 2 ch. 1—p. 136 in *Thomas Hobbes opera philosophica*, ed. Sir Thomas Molesworth, ii.
[4] *Reason and Persons* (Oxford, 1984).

Surely it is not arbitrary for *me* that I should be identical with a particular past or future person?

In between those two cases are the non-rational animals: members of natural kinds, whose identity is established by their continuity as living beings. And it is in the life of the animals that we gain access to *one* secure conception of identity through time—an identity that is neither bestowed by us nor a matter of convention. When we turn to the physical world, we find the 'individuals' that abound in it all too ready to crumble before our enquiries, to dissolve into heaps of atoms, which in turn fragment into the bewildering entities of subatomic physics—entities that seem hardly to be things at all. It is at the level of systems (animals and people especially) that we seem most convinced that numerical identity lies in the nature of things, and is irreducible to an identity of qualities. The real puzzle about personal identity comes about because persons exemplify two different forms of organization: they are animals, members of a natural kind, organized by the principle of life; and they are also persons, members of a peculiar moral kind, organized according to a principle of intention and responsibility. And we seem to have no a priori guarantee that the two forms of organization will always coincide.

2. Properties. Thing-identity is not reducible, I have suggested, to quality- or property-identity. But what about properties themselves? Is it ever true to say that property *F* is numerically identical with property *G*? The problem, of course, is that we do not have any reason, in normal discourse, to *count* the properties of things. An object has as many properties as there are true ways of describing it; nothing is added by saying that one of these descriptions attributes precisely the *same* property as some other. Besides, what would be our criterion of identity? It is a truth of biology that the description 'has a heart' is true of all and only those things that have a kidney. But this coextensiveness of two predicates seems to fall far short of proving that they attribute the same property. Maybe we should get nearer to a criterion of identity if we think in terms of necessity: property *F* is identical with property *G* if *F* and *G* are coextensive in all possible worlds. But that too might be questioned, since it implies that 'having equal angles' and 'having equal sides' denote one and the same property of Euclidean triangles—a result that we suppose to be counter-intuitive, since we can understand and attribute the one property, without having acquired any competence in the other. (Yet are we justified therefore in asserting that the properties are really *two*?) It is likewise a truth of physics that all and only blue things emit or reflect light within a certain range of wavelengths. Does this mean that blueness is the same property as that of emitting light of that wavelength, or merely that the two properties are always conjoined? In Chapter 1 I gave reasons for thinking that this fact would not establish the

identity of blueness and the property of emitting light of the relevant wavelength. But what *would* establish such an identity? And what hangs upon the answer to such a question?

I have dwelt on the case of properties for two reasons: first because identity cannot here mean identity across time—time and change make no inroads on the being of properties—but only an eternal unity. Secondly, because properties show us that the question of numerical identity may be undecidable. We have no clear criterion of the identity of properties; but we can cheerfully attribute properties to objects, and describe the objects themselves as identical in their properties. A paradox? I do not know.

3. Kinds. There has been a growing recognition among philosophers, ever since John Stuart Mill and C. S. Peirce introduced the topic, that there is a distinction among properties between those which identify a kind and those which do not. A kind is defined in such a way as to determine the nature of the things which fall under it. Blue things do not form a kind: elephants and tables do. Some kinds are natural; like the kind *elephant*, their nature is not bestowed upon them by us, but is inherent in the things themselves. Other kinds are artificial, like the kind *table*, defined in terms of a function. Not all kinds are kinds of object: there are also kinds of stuff, like water, carbon, or ice-cream, and again the distinction can be made between the natural and the artificial among them.

While the identity of properties in general remains obscure, the same is not always true of kinds. For the nature of a kind is the nature of its instances, and kind *a* is identical with kind *b* if and only if, in all possible worlds, something is an *a* only if it is a *b*, and vice versa. Numerical identity is here parasitic on the numerical identity of objects.

4. Types. A particular kind of kind has proved interesting to students of aesthetics: namely the *type*. The distinction between type and token was made by C. S. Peirce,[5] though it is to this day unclear how we ought to define it. The relation he had in mind was that between the letter 'a' of the alphabet, and all the individual inscriptions of it. But the example is unhelpful, since no one quite knows what it is that we recognize, when we see that a letter is an 'a'. Consider all the many ways of writing an 'a': is it a *shape* that we notice? Which shape? Or a movement of the hand? Or a fixed contrast with other letters? Think of the Arabic alphabet, where to recognize a letter may be to recognize *where the script is going*, a notion that is itself far from transparent. One person's *a* may look like another person's *d*: only in the system of a person's handwriting is its identity as a letter determined. Our ability to recognize that one person's *a* is the same letter as another's is therefore predicated upon our ability to recognize identity of

[5] *Selected Writings*, 406.

actions: itself a highly problematic application of the concept of identity, as we shall see.

A better instance might be the relation that obtains between a particular model of a car, and the many instances of it. The Ford Cortina is a type; its instances are tokens of the type. The Ford Cortina is also a kind. So what makes a kind into a type? Here is my suggestion: a kind is a type when its definition lists all the salient features of an individual token: all the features in which we should naturally take an interest, if interested in that kind of thing. (For example, all the features that contribute to the performance of its function.) On this view the elephant is not a type: nor is any other natural kind, since natural kinds are not defined by their functions, nor by their salient features.

5. Patterns, structures, and abstract particulars. When describing a type, we tend to use a singular term, as though identifying a particular rather than a universal: *the* Ford Cortina. Yet the type has instances, which are its tokens, and there is no limit to the number of these instances. Types seem to straddle the ontological divide between particular and general: we can describe them either as abstract particulars (like numbers or sets), or as universals which are instantiated in their individual tokens.

Each type is associated with a genuine abstract particular, which is the pattern, or set of instructions, from which it derives. When Henry Ford invented the Model T, he produced a pattern: a formula for producing the tokens of a type. This pattern is not identical with any concrete object. But nor is it a universal—a predicate of other things. It is an abstract object, which itself bears the predicates of the individuals that exemplify it. The Model T Ford has four wheels, a 25 hp engine, and a maximum speed of 60 miles an hour, just like the car that is standing in your drive (which is a token Model T).

Patterns are sometimes called designs—in order to emphasize the creative act that produced them. The fact that we understand them as the *product* of a human *action* explains some of the problems about their identity, as I argue below. But there are abstract particulars which are not designed in this way, yet exemplified by objects in the natural world. For example, the structure of the human skeleton is exemplified by all normal humans. It can be displayed in a model, and described independently of its instances. It is something shared by indefinitely many individuals, and yet described as a particular, a bearer of properties, which can be varied and changed. It would not be normal to describe its instances as tokens of a type, since that would imply that we identify the structure through its function, and that we have a prior sense of its salient characteristics. Nevertheless, its instances stand to the structure very much as the tokens of a type stand to the design that produced them.

In ordinary thought and action, we do not bother to distinguish the token, the type, and the pattern: since we always have the same salient features in mind. But we are more concerned to distinguish the structure from its instances. This is because the pattern is *realized in* its instances (in the tokens of the relevant type), while the structure is *abstracted from* its instances. We always know what we are talking about, when we describe a design or pattern: about a structure we may be half in the dark. Still, designs and structures are alike abstract particulars, and their identity-conditions are determined in the same way as the identity-conditions of kinds in general. Design or structure A is identical with design or structure B when every realization or instance of A is identical with some realization or instance of B, and vice versa. Hence a design can be identical with a structure. (You could produce a design which is identical with the structure of the human skeleton.)

6. Events. I have already argued (see Chapter 1) that the concept of numerical identity can be applied only problematically to events. The case is in fact reminiscent of case (2) above. Events are happenings: they take time. This means that we may be uncertain as to how we should reidentify them through time. Much depends on the circumstances. Presumably my neighbour's noisy party is an event: and I awake in the night to find that the very *same* event is still in being. The next night's party is presumably another event. In such cases events are *processes*: and a process is characterized by a governing causal influence. My neighbour's party lasts so long as it sustains itself through the gregarious acts of its participants. At a certain point the interaction ceases, and the party is over.

Event-identity cannot always be reduced to process-identity, however, even when a process is continuously occurring. The wind constantly waves the branches of the tree outside. But how many events are involved here, when does each one start and finish, and when do we reidentify an event across time? The answer is surely arbitrary: the movement of that frond of leaves was one event: or two if you consider the movement first to the left, and then to the right. In such circumstances we have as little use for the concept of event-identity as for that of property-identity (case (2) above). This is not to say that a philosopher committed to an ontology of events—the process philosophers such as William James and Hartshorne, or Donald Davidson in his quixotic attempt to imprison reality in the predicate calculus—could not devise a criterion of numerical identity that would deliver consistent and systematic results. But, as I suggested in Chapter 1, the most plausible attempt so far made—Davidson's theory of events, as identified through the totality of their causal relations—is a far cry from any test that *we* could apply, and suggests an almost Schopenhauerian contempt for the world of appearance, and for the things that figure in it.

The insecurity of identity is even more evident when we turn to pure events, as I have called them—events which do not happen *to* any thing, but which are identified in themselves, and not through other things. Sounds and smells are the paradigm cases: secondary objects that are produced by things, but do not inhere in them. We certainly speak of numerical identity here. The question 'Did you hear that sound?' implies that I heard a sound, and that I am wondering whether you too heard a sound, and, if so, whether the sound heard by you is the same as that heard by me. But here our concept of numerical identity is that of identity at a time. When it comes to identity over time the case is far less clear. We could adopt various criteria of course: for example, we might say that a sound lasts as long as the physical process that produces it. But this will not fit the normal case of musical sounds, which endure through radical changes in the mode of their production, as when a sustained tremolando on the violins is maintained by handing it from one desk to the next in the orchestra. From the point of view of music, as we have seen, the mode of production of a sound sinks away into the background, and our experience of duration and change resides in the tones themselves. And here there seems to be nothing independent that constrains our decision to say that a given sound is numerically the same, but changed, rather than a new individual.

In the pure sound world it is qualitative identity that determines numerical identity; identity is then merely the last stage of similarity. Our experience of 'same again' is really an experience of similarity, and not the 'recognition of an individual' in any strict sense. Yet we have a version of the latter experience too, as when we recognize a theme or a chord, changed in this or that respect, but still the same. What exactly is going on here?

Two facts should be borne in mind. The first is that sounds belong to recognized types. Sounds have salient features which fill our attention; and when identified in terms of those features, they are identified as types. Each token of the type will then be recognized as the same again. Music exploits these salient features: pitch and timbre in particular, and the notation devised for music is devised precisely so that sound tokens can be prescribed and reproduced in accordance with a type.

The second fact is that the individuals which we hear in music do not exist in the material world of sounds: they are not sounds, nor even sound types, but tones. The theme is an intentional object, and to recognize a theme as 'the same again' is to make a judgement of 'intentional identity'. There is no way of specifying 'sameness of sound' which will capture what we mean by the identity of a musical individual. To this point I shall return.

In the musical context, the most salient features of a sound are pitch and duration of pitch. The primary experience of 'same again' is an experience of these two. For a musical experience however, we require temporal organization of successive sounds: and that means not merely measure and tempo, but the experience, far more vivid than that of pitch itself, of the relative pitches of neighbouring sounds. These provide other dimensions of 'same again': the dimensions that we perceive as rhythm and movement. When we have prescribed pitches, durations, tempo, and measure, we have specified a type of sound event that will be a recognizable vehicle of the musical experience. This is what a piano score presents: pitches and durations are specified by the notes, measure by the barlines. Of course those are not the only relevant variables from the musical point of view. But they are the features that form our primary way of identifying the sound types which interest us as music. They are identified in terms of a design: instructions that are realized in a performance, when a particular instance of a sound pattern is produced. If there are problems about the identity of musical works, I suggest, it is not because the idea of such a design is vague or incoherent. It is in part because the individuals that are produced in *realizing* it—the individual sound events—have only fuzzy conditions of identity. They suffer from the metaphysical insecurity that surrounds the concept of a pure event. But it is also because musical designs are the products of human actions.

7. Actions. Actions are events, and share the identity-problems of events. But they have further problems of their own, which stem from their intentionality. Wittgenstein's well-known rhetorical question—'What is left over if I subtract the fact that my arm goes up from the fact that I raise my arm?' (*Philosophical Investigations*, §621)—reminds us of the distinction between movement and action. The same action can be performed by different movements, and one and the same movement can be made when performing two quite different actions. And an action depends for its identity on the intention behind it: a movement which causes death may be a murder; in the absence of *mens rea* however, that is certainly the wrong description.

The problems of action-description and identity are familiar to students of philosophy and law, and their complexity must excuse me from discussing them. Nevertheless, we should recognize that works of music, whatever they are, originate in human actions, and are understood as *intended* objects. The design which determines the performances of a work of music is an intended design, and the intention is underdetermined by the score which records it. Whether we count an arrangement as a version of the original or as a new work, will depend in part on the intention of the arranger. And the difference between a performance and a travesty lies in our sense of the distance between the composer's intention and the performer's product.

Moreover, we perceive human action differently from the way in which we perceive other events. The *Verstehen* with which we grasp the intention and reasoning behind an action is part of our unconscious dialogue with the agent. Actions are shaped in our perception by the question 'why?', asking for a reason rather than a cause. And the same is true of the musical design. A sense of the composer's intention inhabits our musical perception, and influences the translation of sound into tone.

The Identity of the Musical Work

What in the world is a work of music? In one sense the work of music has no identity: no *material* identity, that is. For the work is what we hear or are intended to hear *in* a sequence of sounds, when we hear them as music. And this—the intentional object of musical perception—can be identified only through metaphors, which is to say, only through descriptions that are false. There is nothing in the material world of sound that *is* the work of music. But this should not prompt those metaphysical fantasies that lead philosophers to situate the work of music in another world, or another dimension, or another level of being.[6] Rather, it reminds us that questions of numerical identity are sometimes of no importance.

Let us take a parallel case: painting. What is a painting, and when is painting *a* identical with painting *b*? We are on slightly firmer ground here, since the temptation is to say that paintings are ordinary physical objects, located in space, which can be identified and reidentified by our normal criterion, of spatio-temporal continuity. But such a criterion does not capture the *salient* feature of a painting, which is the aspect that we see in it, when we see with understanding. Suppose water cascades over Giorgione's *Sleeping Venus* and washes the image away: would this physical object still be Giorgione's *Sleeping Venus*? Surely, we should say that Giorgione's painting had been destroyed by this calamity, and that whatever remains is something else, not the painting. (It is like the case of an animal that dies: what remains, the dead body, is not old Fido the dog.)

Suppose, on the other hand, a device had been discovered that could read the image from a painting and exactly reproduce it, colours, textures, and all. And suppose, before the calamity, Giorgione's painting had been read by this device, and transferred to another canvas. Should we not be disposed to say that the painting had been *saved* from destruction? At least, we should think that nothing important had been lost, and if identity had been lost, then identity is not important.

This kind of thought might lead us to suppose that, when treating paintings as representations, we are really considering them as *types*, whose salient features reside in the coloured surface and all that pertains to it

---

[6] See e.g. R. Ingarden, *The Work of Music and the Problem of its Identity* (1928), tr. A. Czerniawski, ed. J. G. Harrell (Berkeley & Los Angeles, 1986).

when we see its pictorial quality.[7] All that interests us in a painting can be specified by describing the salient features that enable us exactly to reproduce what we see in it, when we see it as a painting. If we cannot quite rest with that suggestion, it is because it is indifferent to one of the most important aesthetic features of paintings: namely, that they are understood as the *unique* tokens of the type. What is appreciated in a painting is a design realised in a single instance.

But that suggests an equally straightforward answer to the question of identity. What we see *in* a painting, when we see it pictorially, is an intentional object of sight, defined by a description that is literally false. The content of the painting is no part of the material world, and as suspicious as a subject of identity-statements as any other member of the intentional realm. The painting itself is a uniquely exemplified design, defined by its salient features: those features that would enable us to reproduce precisely *this* pictorial experience. We could imagine a set of coordinates drawn across the surface of the picture, specifying all the colours and visual textures that occur on every point of it. This would be a complete specification of the design: and it would not mention what is seen in the picture by the one who sees with understanding. It would be a painterly equivalent of the musical score, and would identify the painting completely, as the painting that it is. This suggestion is quite compatible with the view that, if we were to reproduce this pattern again and again, and so convert the painting from a unique realization into a type, we should radically change its aesthetic character. (The *Mona Lisa* as dishcloth.) But there is no way in which identity conditions can be made to follow aesthetic character, in this case or in any other. For aesthetic character is part of the intentional, rather than the material, reality of the object. We cannot require, therefore, that a change in aesthetic character, is always and necessarily a change in the identity of the material object that possesses it.

Here then is an answer to our original question: to identify the work of music in the material world is to identify the sound pattern intended by the composer, which is realized in performance by producing sound events. This sound pattern defines the salient features of the musical work, and can be written down in the form of a score.

The puzzles that we encountered in the first section arise for a simple reason: namely, that some features are more salient than others. There is a prominent foreground in the musical sound type, which is given by relative pitch, duration, measure, and tempo, and any reproduction of those features will bring a forceful impression of 'the same again'. The reason for this is

---

[7] See the discussion in R. Wollheim, *Art and its Objects*, sects. 35–7, and the important qualifications added in the appendix to the 2nd edn.

clear: when these features are determined, so too are rhythm, melody, and harmony—in so far as these intentional objects can be determined by material means. The salient features of a musical work, in other words, are those which contribute to its tonal organization: the organization that we hear, when we hear sounds as tones. This is why we distinguish *versions* of a work, without denying their identity with the original. The piano reduction, orchestral arrangement, transposition, all coincide with the organizational foreground: and hence we describe them as versions of a single work, and assume that we do no violence to the composer's intention. It is precisely when a work is arranged so as to disrupt or reorder its rhythmic, melodic, or harmonic organization that we feel inclined to deny its identity with the original—as with Webern's orchestration of the six-part 'Ricercar'.

We could adopt a stricter criterion, and add colour and timbre to the specification of the relevant sound pattern. Nothing whatsoever hangs on the decision, since the concept of numerical identity is here entirely a matter of convenience. We should not worry that the versions of a work are qualitatively so different: for it is quality that interests us in any case, and the assignment of identities serves no purpose except that of distributing the credits. If we say that Chopin's C sharp minor Waltz is another work as it appears in the *Sylphides*, it is because we wish to draw attention either to the recomposition that has changed its aesthetic character, or to the changed artistic intention.

The question of the relation between work and performance is rather more difficult. A performance is an attempt to determine the intentional object of a musical experience, by realizing the salient features of a sound pattern. If performances vary it is partly because there are features of any performance that are not specified in the pattern, even though the musical experience depends upon them, and partly because the sound pattern under-determines the intention which originally produced it. The performer therefore has an important part to play in the production of the aesthetic experience, completing the transition from the intended design to its realization, and in doing so completing the musical experience. What are the constraints that bind him, and how do we understand his contribution? To those questions I shall return in Chapter 14.

Notation and Identity

It follows from what I have said, that a work of music can be fully identified through a system of notation: any notation which unambiguously identifies the salient features of the sound pattern will identify the work. Now not every notation *does* do this. For example, the figured bass which leaves out the inner parts leaves a freedom to the performer which must be filled by tradition, convention, and education if the pattern is to be realized as a musical event. Alternatively, we may wish to adopt a looser condition of identity here, and say that it suffices to follow the chord patterns of the figured bass-line to achieve a 'version' of the work. (Compare the many versions of a Bach cantata.) Opting for the stronger identity-condition is a way of saying that the performer is not as free as he might like to think, that tradition and convention are here all-important, and that there are ways of ruining the work that have not been ruled out by the score.

In aleatoric music the performer's freedom may be part of the point, although it is a freedom constrained by incomplete instructions which leave a residue to chance. In improvisation, the freedom of the performer is greater still—and here notation follows performance, rather than preceding it. In jazz the writing down of a piece may consist merely in the specification of a melody and an harmonic sequence. To follow the sequence, while improvising around the melody, is to give a 'version' of the piece. Versions will be so different that very few listeners would wish to say that they are instances of a single composition. Indeed, composition and performance are inseparable. The work consists in what the performer *does*. The performance rules the work, and even if it is recorded or written down, so as to become familiar as a pattern, it is appreciated nevertheless as a single sound event. When performance and work are fused in this way, recording does not transfer our interest from the performance to the abstract structure. We are interested, not in an action-type, but in an individual action.

The history of classical music would be inconceivable without the invention of the notational system which has enabled the composer to specify the work before its performance. It is not surprising, therefore, that Nelson Goodman has looked to this notational system as providing the answer to questions of musical ontology.[8] He proposes a strict criterion of identity, according to which the score uniquely identifies a work of music, so that any performance that exactly follows the score, and obeys all the instructions contained in it, is a performance of the individual work. No other performance 'complies' with the work, which can be defined either intensionally, through the score, or extensionally, as the 'compliance class' which that score determines.

Of course much that the performer does is not commanded by the score: but the performance complies with the score—i.e. it is a performance *of* the work—just so long as all the instructions in the score are followed. A performance with a mistake in it is therefore not a performance of the work, any more than one that takes Horowitz-like liberties.

---

[8] *Languages of Art: An Approach to a Theory of Symbols* (Oxford, 1969), chs. 4 and 5, esp. pp. 177–91.

Should we accept this stringent criterion? Commentators have waxed hot under the collar about it, especially about the counter-intuitive implication that an incorrect performance is really a correct performance of another work (although one that has yet to be written down). But Goodman can say that if he wishes: he neither misrepresents the facts in doing so, nor constrains our musical perception. It is up to us to determine which features of the sound token are features of the pattern. And after all, the score is designed precisely to settle that question; so why not allow to it the last word? If the result is counter-intuitive, it is only because we have failed to realize that numerical identity is at our behest, and that it is qualititative similarity that really concerns us. We wish to know how far two tokens can vary without violating our sense of the 'same again'. And that is not determined by a criterion of numerical identity ranging over 'material' objects, not even if those objects are abstract particulars or items of notation. The 'identity' that concerns us is an intentional identity—an identity in appearance, which translates into no material fact.

On the other hand, one might reasonably object to Goodman's priorities, and to the bias towards writing that his strict criterion betrays. Whole traditions of music-making have grown and perpetuated themselves without the benefit of scores; and even if it is true that here, as elsewhere, the habit of writing has greatly expanded the possibilities of learning from one's predecessors, writing is nevertheless no more than a device for recording what exists independently—the sound pattern—so facilitating the production of future instances. The musical work exists in the habit of its repro-duction. While this habit is facilitated by notation, it would seem strange to allow notation to dictate the nature of the thing itself. Better perhaps to allow our concept of numerical identity to be shaped by the live tradition, by our sense of what matters in a true performance, and of the distinction between trivial and serious departures. It might be very important to us that we consider Schubert's 'Death and the Maiden' Quartet and Mahler's arrangement to be versions of the same work, and attribute that work to the creative genius of Schubert. And it might be equally important to us that we distinguish Brahms's arrangement for piano left-hand of the Bach Chaconne in D minor from Bach's original, from Busoni's two-hand version, and from Schumann's little-known version for violin and piano. These three works are animated by three quite different artistic intentions. They are not versions of one work, but four works with a single source—albeit a source so great that it has filled four channels with its unbrookable creative energy. Those are the kinds of consideration that are likely to determine our choice of identity-conditions.

Platonism

What I have said would be acceptable, with a few modifications, to many of those who have recently considered the question of musical ontology—notably to Nicholas Wolterstorff,[9] with his conception of works of music as 'performance kinds'. (Although John Bender, arguing along lines similar to those that I have followed, gives reasons for rejecting the idea that performances are *instances* of a work, rather than realizations of it.)[10]

Jerrold Levinson, however, does not share this point of view. For him a great danger lurks for all who would specify the identity of a musical work in abstract terms—as a 'sound structure' or sound type.[11] (His own use of 'sound structure' is of no significance in the present context, and I shall ignore his unwarranted desire to include the 'performance means' among the conditions of a work's identity.) The danger is this: if the work is an abstract object or a universal, then it is, like all such entities, eternal. It no more comes into being when the composer writes it down than did blueness come into being with the first blue thing. The best we can say is that the composer discovered it: but it might have been discovered by another composer at some other time, like a mathematical proof.

This result seems paradoxical to Levinson, for the reason that it seems to mislocate one of the most important of a work's aesthetic qualities: namely its originality. This is something that we appreciate in the Overture to *A Midsummer Night's Dream,* for example, because we believe that Mendelssohn *created* the work, and created it at a certain time. It was hard to do that, a great achievement, something requiring genius, taste, and inspiration. It was not so hard for Weinberger to write the Polka in *Švanda Dudák,* given the existence of Dvořák's *Slavonic Dances* (particular the A flat major dance from the First Book). Originality is something that we observe and appreciate in the music: an indispensable feature of music as an art.

In response to this worry, Levinson tries to build into the conditions for a work's identity a reference to the composer's activity: a work is a sound structure (and performance means) *as specified by* so-and-so at such a time. And he is surely right to imply that the musical design is understood and appreciated as the outcome of an *action*. On the other hand, reference to this action does nothing to answer Levinson's difficulty. An abstract object does not become time-bound merely because we relate it to a particular

[9] Wolterstorff, 'The Work of Making a Work of Music', in P. Alperson (ed.), *What is Music?: An Introduction to the Philosophy of Music* (University Park, Pa., 1994).

[10] 'Music and Metaphysics: Types and Patterns, Performances and Works', *Proceedings of the Ohio Philosophical Association* (Apr. 1991).

[11] 'What a Musical Work Is', in *Music, Art and Metaphysics* (Ithaca, NY, (1990), 63–88.

person's encounter with it. It is still the case that this work, construed in just this way, exists timelessly, and did not come into being with the gesture that is incorporated into its definition.

There is indeed something strange in Levinson's worry, as in the extended defence of musical Platonism embarked on by Peter Kivy, who happily endorses the 'conclusion' that works of music are discovered rather than made.[12] For one thing we should recognize that the problem is not specific to music: works of literature too are designs, realized in their spoken and written instances. But they too are appreciated for their originality. As I have shown above, we might also be constrained to confer a similar kind of identity on a painting. So did Giorgione's *Sleeping Venus* precede his painting her?

Let us take another case. Every time I do something or say something, I have performed a particular action; I have also indicated a pattern. Somebody else could do or say the same thing, by producing another instance of the pattern. Does this mean that nothing that I say or do is my *doing*, but at best only my discovery? Surely, common sense tells us that there is such a thing as doing something *for the first time*, and that this is what we mean by originality, even if the thing done can be described (as is logically unavoidable) as the instance of a pattern? Moreover, things done are done in response to other things done. The first performance of an action is likely to be regarded as a peculiarly important instance: being a first instance of a pattern, or a model for a type, is the kind of feature that *must* spring to our attention, if we are to understand the world of human conduct.

Moreover, the argument—both Levinson's defence of his view and Kivy's attack on it—shows precisely what is wrong with a certain kind of Platonism. The sense in which types, kinds, structures, and patterns are eternal does not prevent them from having a history, any more than the kind: *tiger* is prevented by its status as a kind from having a history, from coming into existence and passing away. The history of a kind is the history of its instances. It would be small consolation to the ecologist to learn that the tiger exists eternally, so that nothing need be done to ensure its survival. The eternal nature of the type consists merely in the fact that, considered as a *type*, temporal determinations do not apply to it; it does not imply that it *preceded* its first token, for it is only through its tokens that it can precede or succeed anything.

Often when writers notice that this or that feature of a work of art is an immovable part of its aesthetic character, they feel tempted to say that the feature must therefore belong to the identity-conditions of the work. (Thus Strawson in an early article, who defines the criterion of identity for a work

---

[12] 'Platonism in Music: A Kind of Defense', in *The Fine Art of Repetition: Essays in the Philosophy of Music* (Cambridge, 1993), 35-58.

of art as 'the totality of the features relevant to an aesthetic appraisal'.)[13] But if you take this line you will end by saying that every observable feature of a work belongs among its identity-conditions, since nothing observable can be discounted from the aesthetic effect. Once again you have run qualitative identity and numerical identity together.

There is another reason for resisting the temptation. The aesthetic character of a musical work does not reside in the sounds, but in the tones that we hear in them. It is reasonable to identify works of music as sound patterns, only because we thereby identify the vehicle of the musical experience. But that experience is sensitive to many things besides the salient features of the sound, and to attempt to build all those things into a criterion for the identity of the *sound* is to embark on a task that has no conclusion. Because we know that Mendelssohn composed his overture when he did, we hear it differently. The intentional object of musical perception is affected by this knowledge, just as it would be affected by the knowledge that we had all along been wrong, since the overture was written by Mendelssohn's sister Fanny. But the way I have chosen to express myself in that last sentence is surely the right one: I am supposing that this overture, this very same piece, might have been written by Fanny.

The Marxists think of the aesthetic experience as having 'historicity'—it is a transient manifestation of human life, dependent upon those particular economic conditions that create the ideological interest in 'mere appearances'. Whether they are right is a matter to which I return in Chapter 15. But the aesthetic experience is certainly *sensitive* to history: a sense of our historical position, however rudimentary, is contained within it, and leads us to endow works of music with indelible historical characters. No periodization is easier or more natural than that which comes to us with our experience of music. Our sense that a given piece just *must* have been composed exactly then and there, and by that composer, is one of the most vivid historical experiences that we have. Why is that? The answer must be sought in the nature of musical perception. The acousmatic realm is structured by virtual actions and virtual intentions. We hear these with the same immediacy as we perceive the actions and motives of our fellows. A work of music directly acquaints us with a form of human life, and with the style and mannerisms of a period—just as do the expressions, and the forms of dress that we witness in an Elizabethan portrait. Hence we can hear the originality of a work, with the same immediacy as we hear its composer's style.

---

[13] 'Aesthetic Appraisal and Works of Art', in *Freedom and Resentment and Other Essays* (London, 1974), 178–88.

Intentional Identity

Levinson's theory of musical works identifies them as sound 'structures'. He situates them unambiguously in the material world of sounds, as complex secondary objects, though somewhat eccentrically described. And there is in truth no useful concept of the identity of a musical work that does not operate in that way, as a specification of a structure or pattern that is realized in physical *sounds*.

Yet his qualms stem from the fact that the intentional character of the musical work is not fixed by the identity conditions of the sound-structure. To identify musical works in that way is to identify the things in which we hear music. It is comparable to the method I proposed for identifying a picture, through a graph which assigns coordinates to all the colours and textures of the painted surface, but which says nothing about the figure of Venus that we see in them. And, someone might suppose, the real question is about *her*: where and what is *she*?

Is there anything to be said in answer to this question? And is it a real question of ontology? We certainly use the concept of identity when describing the intentional objects of our mental states. It is perfectly coherent to say, for example, that I saw my mother in my dream last night—i.e. that the woman of whom I dreamed was my mother. There are even cases of pure 'intentional identity', as Geach has pointed out in a distinguished paper.[14] (For example, 'John thinks that the witch who blighted Harry's mare is the same as the one who, Dan believes, blighted his cow.' The identity sign is here strung between terms in intentional contexts—contexts which, for Quine and many of his followers, must be understood as referentially opaque. And it is a queer kind of identity sign that lies between terms that do not refer!)

In the case of music, the experience of 'same again', which prompts us to speak of numerical identity, is associated with those strange quasi-individuals in the world of tones to which I referred in the preceding chapters: to melodies, phrases, gestures, and movements. In musical quotation, for example, these quasi-individuals appear to us, lifted from their context and shown in another light—as the opening phrase of *Tristan und Isolde* is mocked in Debussy's 'Golliwog's Cake-Walk', or the Seventh Symphony of Shostakovich in Bartók's *Concerto for Orchestra*. Is this not a case of pure intentional identity? For certainly the sound patterns are here not the same, by any of the criteria that I have so far deferred to. The only sense we can make of these cases is this: that what we hear in the one work is numerically identical with what we hear in the other, but qualitatively different.

---

[14] 'Intentional Identity', in *Logic Matters*, 146–52.

The same theme in another context. And yet there is no way to spell out that identity in terms of the material properties of the sounds.

There is a parallel in the world of painting, when the person whom I see in one picture is seen as identical with the person whom I see in another, but transformed. But there is a difference: in the case of the paintings I am deploying a concept of identity—identity of persons—that derives from the material world, and which I learn by applying it to genuine individuals. It is not so clear that the individuals in the world of tones can be encountered elsewhere. Our sense of their individuality is primitive and irreducible.

But for that very reason, we should not expect a theory of musical ontology to give us an account of the intentional object of hearing. If it strays into the world where the musical individual is encountered, it is a world of metaphor—of things that do not and cannot exist. If it stays in the world of sound, then it can do no more than specify the sound patterns that make the musical experience available. There is no third possibility, which means that there is nothing further to be said.

5 *Representation*

I have given a preliminary sketch of the experience of music, and the nature of music as an intentional object of perception. I now wish to explore the question of the meaning of music: a question that is frequently posed, but seldom in the terms that enable us to answer it. To put the question very simply: is there anything, other than itself, that music means? Even that simple version contains a puzzle, however; when and why does something 'mean itself'?

I shall begin with an exploration of the simplest kind of artistic meaning: representation. Theorists, philosophers, and composers have continually disagreed as to whether music has representational properties, and the question is not without interest, since it compels us to make serious comparisons between music and the other arts.

Mimēsis

When ancient philosophers considered the meaning of the various art forms, it was usually in the context of discussing *mimēsis*, or imitation: an activity which is far wider than its artistic instances. Both Plato and Aristotle believed that music too is a form of *mimēsis*. The music that they had in mind was sung, danced to, or marched to. The thing imitated in the music was, they thought, automatically imitated by the person who 'moved with' it. If the music was imitating the wrong things, therefore, those who moved with it would also be imitating the wrong things. Since imitation is the way in which we form our characters, it follows that music has a vast moral significance. This was the basis for Plato's suggestion that certain modes should be banned from the ideal republic, in which no music would be permitted that did not contribute to the growth of virtue among the youth. Plato drew this stark conclusion because he believed that music imitates *character*. It copies those dispositions which we know as virtues and vices: it can be noble or profane, chaste or dissipated, manly or effeminate. And the same is true of those who dance to it.

Plato's theory is not without interest, and I shall offer a kind of defence of it in later chapters. Clearly, however, it is incomplete as it stands. For it assumes an understanding of the crucial term—*mimēsis*—a term which, in this context at least, Plato makes no effort to define, and which may very well not be the right one. The word was used not only to cover all the many kinds of imitation in life—from the imitation by which I learn from another, to the imitation with which I ridicule him—but also to describe all forms of artistic meaning. In Plato's usage it is insensitive to the principal distinctions—between representing, expressing, and merely copying: three quite distinct ways in which a work of art can be related to a 'subject-matter' or 'content'.

The distinction between representation and expression was introduced by Croce, although he was making explicit something that had been implicit in aesthetic theories since Kant: namely, that there are at least two kinds of artistic meaning. The one is displayed by narratives, stories, and descriptions, while the other may exist even in the absence of storytelling. We are frequently tempted to describe this second kind of meaning—for which Croce coined the term 'expression'—as ineffable, or not fully effable. Making this distinction clear is one of the major tasks of aesthetics; but since the terms 'representation' and 'expression' are technicalities, introduced by Croce in the context of a wildly implausible theory of art, it is impossible to assume any common understanding of them. Each philosopher who has discussed the terms has used them in his own way, and for his own theoretical purposes, and in the absence of established results, I shall have to make a fresh start.

The matter of terminology is additionally complicated by the history of our subject. Few developments in the history of Western music have been more important than the discovery of opera—at first no more than an idea in the minds of Florentine humanists, but soon becoming, in the works of Monteverdi, one of the highest of art forms. The new manner of composing for voices, so as to shape the musical line according to the motives and passions of the characters, was called *stile rappresentativo* by Monteverdi, since it was a style dedicated to the representation of dramatic action and character. But the feature of music which called forth this terminological innovation was not what I shall call representation. If music has a role to play in the theatre, it is not because it represents things, but because it expresses them.

Likewise, when Schopenhauer, using a Kantian term (*Vorstellung*), describes music as a representation of the Will, or when Hanslick, using the same term, denies that music can represent our inner emotions, they are really writing about expression; it is an accident of history that they should use the term whose meaning for the modern philosopher will be my subject in this chapter.

Representation and Imitation

Imitation occurs in many contexts, and I shall consider imitation only as it exists in art. A work of art may involve imitation in two ways: it may imitate artistic forms and details; or it may imitate the forms and details of other things. The voices of a fugue imitate one another: but that is scarcely a candidate for representation. A melody can imitate the sound of a bird: and that *is* a candidate for representation.

This second kind of artistic imitation occurs very widely: in architecture, in decoration, in textile-weaving, and furniture-making. If I say that it is not representation, this is because there is another and more interesting phenomenon, which better deserves the name. Consider the leaf-mouldings in Gothic architecture. There is no doubt that these are of great aesthetic significance: by the use of these mouldings the Gothic architect was able to transform stone into something as full of light and movement as a tree in summer. But the resulting building conveys no thought about *leaves*. It is not asking us to think of the mouldings as leaves, or to understand the column as a forest narrative. *Nothing* is being said about the leaves: they are there 'for the effect'.

The same is true of the stylized flowers in a dress or a piece of wall-paper. There is all the difference in the world between the pattern of a wallpaper, and a picture of the thing used in the pattern: *even if they look exactly the same*. The wallpaper is not asking us to think of the flowers contained in it. Put a frame around one of the flowers, however, and a signature beneath it, and at once it jumps out at you, not as a pattern, but as a *flower*, asking to be understood as such. You can say that the pattern and the painting are both representations: for what's in a word? But you will then need another word to describe the distinction between them: the distinction between copying the form of a flower, and presenting a *flower* for our contemplation.

This is why Muslim law, which forbids representation as a form of idolatry, can nevertheless tolerate the weaving of carpets in which natural patterns are exploited: carpets like those of the Caucasus, which incorporate stylized trees and animals.[1] As the case suggests, man's attitude towards representation has been complex and troubled: the fear, awe, and sense of blasphemy associated with the 'graven image' has persisted as one of the

---

[1] Koran, 16. 71—though the text tells us only not to 'make likenesses concerning God'.

deepest undercurrents in human feeling, since the law of Moses first forbad us to make gods of our creations.[2] But man's attitude to *patterns* has retained its primeval innocence. Our interest in patterns is quite different from our interest in representation: even when the patterns are derived from natural forms, and imitate them closely, like the leaf-mouldings in architecture. True, we should not perceive these patterns as harmonious were we not familiar with the things themselves. It is important to the effect of the Gothic column that *leaves* are imitated on its capital; seeing the column in this way, we transfer to our perception a pre-existing experience of light and movement and a pre-existing sense of being at home in the natural world. Nevertheless, we do not see the leaves as *leaves*, as we should see leaves in a painting. Rather, we see the stone as leaf-like: an imitation which delights us precisely as an imitation, and not through some thought about the thing itself. (Conversely, we do not see the *Mona Lisa* as face-like: we see it as a face. We are not delighting in an imitation, but in the portrait of a lady, about whom we have a thousand thoughts.)

Representation and Abstraction

Representation becomes clearer through the phenomenon with which it is normally contrasted: abstraction. Consider a Poussin landscape. This presents a scene, and contains an implicit narrative about it. Someone who sees the painting may have only incomplete information about this narrative: but his eyes present him with the essentials. Looking at the picture he is conducted by his eyes into a 'fictional world', and given a wealth of information about this world. If he did not encounter the world of the picture, that would show that he did not understand what he was seeing. Someone who delighted in the shapes and colours displayed on the canvas, but did not see the land-scape, would be blind to the representation, and blind to the painting's character as a work of art.

Abstract painting does not present a scene or tell a story. There is nothing that you have to understand about a fictional world in order to see the painting correctly. Indeed, the attempt to *imagine* a fictional world in an abstract by Mondrian shows a misunderstanding as great as that which is shown by the person who sees no landscape in the Poussin. This does not imply that an abstract painting is meaningless, or without 'content'. The term 'expression' has gained such wide currency partly because critics have sought for a word with which to convey the residue of meaning that may be present in a work of art, even when all representation has been abstracted away. In an abstract expressionist painting there is something to be understood—namely the expression. And that is the content of the painting.

[2] See A. Besançon, *L'Image interdite* (Paris, 1993).

One reason for denying that music is a representational art is that it provides our paradigms of pure abstraction: of forms and organizations that seem interesting in themselves, regardless of any 'fictional world' which this or that listener may try to attach to them. When Walter Pater wrote that all art aspires to the condition of music, he had this pure abstract quality foremost in mind: music inspires and consoles us partly because it is unencumbered by the debris that drifts through the world of life.

Representation in General

If you were to think only of painting, then you might be tempted to describe representation as a kind of resemblance: *a* represents *b* by resembling it. It is clear, however, that, while resemblance of a kind may be a *route* to representation, it is not the relation itself. For resemblance is a symmetrical and reflexive relation, whereas representation is both non-symmetrical and non-reflexive. Besides, the resemblance in question is a queer sort of resemblance. The picture that Leonardo painted of the Mona Lisa resembles a picture of a dog far more than it resembles a woman. The salient resemblance is not between the picture and a woman, but between what we *see in* the picture and a woman. (That is our criterion of realism in painting.) This relation of 'seeing in' is what a theory of pictorial representation needs to analyse, and what it therefore cannot assume.

The resemblance theory loses its appeal in any case, just as soon as we turn our attention to literature. Poetry, drama, and prose are all representational, and affect us through the presentation of fictional worlds, peopled with events and characters that must be understood by anyone who reads with understanding. The world of a poem or novel may be very elaborate— like that of the *Divine Comedy* or *Anna Karenina*. Or it may be very confined, as in the brief evocative lyrics of a Blake or a Verlaine. But there is no work of literature that does not refer beyond itself, to a world that is other than the text itself. Even in those paradoxical novels of Beckett, in which the characters are brought into being and dissolved by their own reckless syntax, 'the narrator narrated' as Beckett describes it, the distinction is real and necessary, between the words that we understand, and the world described by them. Only if you thought that fictional worlds must also be possible worlds would you regard these novels as non-representational. But impossible worlds have been the prerogative of fiction since *Gilgamesh*.

Literature is representational by virtue of an essential feature of language— namely, that it refers to things other than itself. And here there arises a temptation similar to that yielded to by the resemblance theory of pictorial representation—the temptation to suppose that representation is identical with the route to it. Reference is the *route* to representation in literature, just as resemblance (between things seen in pictures, and things seen elsewhere) is the *route* to representation in painting. Nelson Goodman, who analyses representation in terms of 'denotation' (the relation between name and object in a language) understands paintings too as semantic devices, and describes their pictorial properties as you might describe the narrative properties of language.[3] Paintings are described as bearing syntactic and semantic features, just like sentences. Appealing though such a theory may be to a nominalist of Goodman's persuasion, it overlooks precisely what is most important about paintings: namely, that we *see* their content. If there is a semantic mastery involved in this, it is that which is involved in *seeing*, not that which is generated by convention, through a system of symbols. (I here remain neutral on the question whether there is a 'semantics of perception', and leave this idea to those Fodor-inspired cognitive scientists whom I shall discuss in Chapter 7.)

What is common to narrative literature and figurative painting is to be found in our way of understanding them. In both cases we understand the works through recuperating *thoughts* about something other than themselves. By thought I mean what Frege meant: the sense of a sentence; the entity that is identified through its truth-conditions, and which is grasped by knowing how the world must be if the sentence is to be true.[4] As I have already suggested, aspect perception involves the entertaining of unasserted thought: so too does the understanding of poetry, drama, and the novel. A fictional world is a world identified by such thoughts, and the point of representation in art is that it presents a fictional world for my attention, by compelling me to think in imaginative ways. It can do this in the manner of literature, by drawing on my semantic understanding. Or it can do it in the manner of painting and sculpture, by causing me to see a fictional world before my eyes. Since aspect perception is informed by unasserted thought, the cognitive result is the same. But the route to cognition is not.

Much more can and should be said on the topic of representation. But enough has been said to enable us to evaluate the status of music.

Musical Imitation

In what follows it is necessary to distinguish the following questions: can music represent things? Does music sometimes represent things? Is representation ever an important property of a musical work—important, that is, to its nature as music? And finally, is music a representational art?

---

[3] *Languages of Art*, ch. 1.
[4] 'The Thought: A Logical Enquiry', in Strawson (ed.), *Philosophical Logic*, 17–38.

It is clear that the novel is a representational art form, and that the art of prose is a representational art. That is how we understand it, and how we must understand it, if we are to grasp its nature as an art. Painting too is a representational art; for while there are non-representational paintings, they form a byway from the main avenue of painting, and are in any case scarcely intelligible without reference to the great tradition of depiction which made them possible and upon which they provide a diluted commentary.

The weakest claim on behalf of musical representation would be that music *can* represent things. Of course, it is easy to imagine music being given a representational use. For example, I could play a game in which I communicate with my partner through a musical code: we assign signature tunes to characters, events, properties, and states of affairs, and use them to communicate about an imaginary world. This would show musical representation to be possible, however, only if the nature of the tunes *as music* were essential to the game. And that is precisely what would be disputed by the sceptic. Someone who heard only sounds and never tones could play this game; and no musical understanding is involved in recuperating the representational content from the 'musical' signs. If the possibility of such a game shows that music can be representational, then it would show the same of abstract painting too. In which case we should have proved nothing interesting about music.

The best way to show that music can be representational (as *music*) is to show that it sometimes *is* representational. My brief discussion of painting and literature suggests that we must first identify a musical *route* to representation: a feature of music that will enable it to present thoughts about something other than itself. Evidently sounds can resemble other sounds, and there is a perceivable similarity between sounds which causes the hearer of one sound to be sometimes reminded of the other. Could the 'sounds like' relation suffice to provide the vehicle of representational meaning?

One philosopher has suggested that it could. Peter Kivy argues at length that music *is* (at least sometimes) representational, on the basis of musical examples which manifestly *sound like* other things.[5] He quotes at length from Honnegger's *Pacific 231*, a piece of music in which the sound and movement of a steam train is imitated. This, for Kivy, is a paradigm of musical representation.

Notice how different the case is from that of painting. How strange it would be to say that Mantegna's Crucifixion *looks like* the crucifixion of Christ. It looks like nothing of the kind; indeed, it looks like nothing so much as a wooden board smeared with oil-paint. The resemblance that

[5] *Sound and Semblance: Reflections on Musical Representation* (Ithaca, NY, 1991). Kivy is taken to task at great length by S. Davies, in *Musical Meaning and Expression*, 79–122.

serves as a route to representation obtains between the crucifixion of Christ
and the scene that we *see in* the painting. Similarity of appearance is neither
necessary nor sufficient for pictorial representation: so why should it be
sufficient in the case of music?

Kivy's argument makes no reference to the distinction between sound
and tone; and it is clear from what I have said in the first two chapters
that, if we do not acknowledge that distinction, we shall in all probability
not succeed in talking about *music*, as opposed to the sounds in which
music is heard. Even if it is true that the Honegger *sounds like* a steam
train, it does not follow that the musical listener will hear a steam train *in*
the music. Nor do we really know what is meant by this. Do I hear a steam
train in the music when I hear the *sound* of a train in the notes, or the
movement of a train, or what? (Do I hear a steam train in the sound of a
steam train? Or do I just hear the sound of a steam train? The question
suggests that we should again remind ourselves that sounds are not *qualities*
of the objects that emit them, but secondary objects, in the sense defined in
Chapter 1.)

That there is much imitation in music cannot be doubted: think of the
imitation of birdsong, in Beethoven's Sixth Symphony in F major, Op. 68,
in Wagner's *Siegfried*, and in Handel's 'Sweet Bird'. Or think of the musical
insects in Bartók's Third Piano Concerto, the clock in Couperin's 'Tic-toc
Choc', the bells in the last movement of Mussorgsky's *Pictures at an
Exhibition*. Examples can be adduced *ad infinitum*; but unless we can show
that imitation here is something more than *mere* imitation, of the kind that
we find in wallpaper, architecture, and textile-weaving, we shall not have
found an argument for the existence of musical representation. Notice too
that imitation, in these standard cases, is always imitation of *sound*, and
depends upon the 'sounds like' relation for its effect. Even if we could
prove that imitation of this kind can be tantamount to representation, it
would be a defect of music that it could represent only the sounds of things—
only those things which it also reproduces. In literature and painting an
object of thought is presented through forms which do not resemble it, and
whose sensuous properties irradiate it with a meaning that it otherwise
could not have. In the vertical flat surface of a Bonnard I see a horizontal
table, laden with fruit, and spreading away from me towards a light-filled
window. The canvas is a door on to another world; yet the painter compels
me to see the flatness, the surface, and the unbending verticality which
imprison that world and interrogate it. In such a representation the medium
transfigures the content, by its deliberate refusal to resemble it.

The point is of glancing significance. Nevertheless, it is important to
understand the peculiar relation that obtains, between music and the sounds
of everyday life, when the latter are 'imitated' in a musical form. One of

two things seems to happen. Either the sounds intrude completely, so as to become present in the music—not so much represented as reproduced, like the birds in Respighi's *Fountains of Rome*. Or else the music gathers them up and overrides their character as sound, so that we begin to hear music in them. They cross the barrier between sound and tone, and become part of the musical structure, like the cowbells which tinkle on the slopes in the slow movement of Mahler's Sixth Symphony: bells which may *suggest* the life of nature in the valleys below, but which are in fact a distant but definite part of the percussion section. To say that these cowbells represent the thing that they suggest is again to confuse two quite distinct relations. Any argument for saying this would apply equally to every instrument of the orchestra. The horn always suggests the horn—and with that suggestion come many more: the hunt, the post, and other slowly fading things. But the horn does not represent the horn or its ordinary uses, even when deliberately used to suggest them, as in Mozart's 'Posthorn' Serenade in D major, K. 320, or in the many passages of music inspired by hunting.

There are exceptions to that observation: but they are in the nature of the case rare, often dependent upon some theatrical context for their success. The light orchestra placed on the stage by Mozart in *Don Giovanni* imitates the sound of popular music only by reproducing it. Representation is achieved through the purely theatrical, non-musical convention that what is on the stage is part of the *action*. The 'representational' status of Mozart's music could be understood by someone with no *musical* understanding whatsoever: it is therefore not a *musical* property of the sounds. In Act 2 Scene 4 of *Wozzeck*, by contrast, we find the remarkable effect of an imitation of Viennese dance music written in the prevailing atonal idiom of the work (Ex. 5.1). The music has a part to play in the total representation over and above the fact that it is performed on the stage. For the music must be understood as atonal, even while we *hear in* it the robust tonality of Johann Strauss. The atonality of the medium renders it opaque to the tonal 'subject-matter', so that the sounds imitated are not merely reproduced in the music. Nor are they gathered up and absorbed by the musical structure, so as to lapse from imitation to a mere suggestiveness.

This striking and unusual example casts a certain light on what happens in the more central cases of musical imitation—as in the imitation of birdsong. It is undeniable that birdsong *can* be imitated in music. But imitation is always part of a musical pattern, which develops according to its own inner logic. Just compare the examples in Ex. 5.2: Handel's 'Sweet Bird', the cadenza of birdsong in Beethoven's Sixth Symphony, Wagner's woodbird, Vaughan Williams's *Lark Ascending* and, for good measure, the 'Merle bleu' from Messiaen's *Catalogue des oiseaux*. It is possible for a listener to recognize the imitation in all of these (although some may have

Ex. 5.1. Berg, *Wozzeck*, Act 2, Scene 4

severe difficulty with the last). But the imitation is in each case the starting-point for a musical structure, and quickly relinquishes any attempt to guide or influence the melodic line. Handel's bird is soon cadencing according to the laws of figured harmony; Beethoven's birds stand briefly apart from the structure before melting into the symphonic flow. Wagner's bird is Wagnerian, singing one of those melodies built out of thirds which are so important in the musical structure of the *Ring*, while Vaughan Williams's lark is a product of English folksong, melismatic and pentatonic. Messiaen's blackbird is likewise pure Messiaen, singing massive six-voice chords which surpass the reach of any natural organ. In each case the imitation serves a purpose comparable to the imitation of leaves in Gothic architecture: it takes a detail from nature, in order to exploit its associations. But it emancipates that detail from any narrative: the musical line is not *about* the birdsong, any more than the Gothic moulding is *about* the leaves.

Reference and Predication

Representation involves, I have argued, the presentation of thoughts about a fictional world. Thoughts have structure: they refer to objects, and predicate properties of them. This structure exists not only in language, but also in every intentional state: in perceptions, beliefs, and imaginings. Sometimes, however, the element of predication may be vague or inexplicit: as when I point to something in order to draw your attention to it, or think of something without dwelling on its properties. Musical imitation seems to have

Ex. 5.2. (a) Handel, 'Sweet Bird', from *L'allegro, il penseroso e il moderato*; (b) Beethoven, Sixth Symphony, Op. 68, second movement, cadenza; (c) Wagner, *Siegfried*, Act 2; (d) Vaughan Williams, *The Lark Ascending*; (e) Messiaen, 'Merle bleu', as quoted in 'Le Traquet rieur', from *Catalogue des oiseaux*, 12

more in common with this kind of mental ostension than it has with the fictional narratives of literature and the visual arts. There is a gesture towards something, in the course of a musical argument: but the music quickly goes on its way, without developing the thought. Call this representation if you like: but acknowledge too that the incompleteness of the thought sets the phenomenon apart from the description or depiction of fictional worlds.

Peter Kivy doubts the point, arguing, for example, that a musical representation of a cuckoo might convey the following thought: 'here is a cuckoo: it sounds a descending major third'.[6] But if the only ground for saying such a thing is that the *music* sounds a descending major third, we can hardly take this as proof of musical predication. Is Messiaen saying 'Here is a blackbird, and it sounds like *this*: Ex. 5.2e'? Surely, he is saying nothing of the kind. He is asking us to recall the song of the blackbird, while attributing to it nothing specific apart from its atmosphere. In such a case it would be surely more reasonable to speak of the music as wearing a certain *expression*. It neither sounds like a blackbird, nor represents it: rather, it is itself a response to the blackbird's call, a musical expression of the bird-lover's emotion, as he is carried away by its song. (The best way of understanding the piece is as a *descant* on the song of a bird, when that song is heard as music.)

Often, when examples of musical representation are proposed, they turn on examination into examples of musical expression. This is especially so when the 'subject' is not a sound. For example, Strauss's *Don Quixote* opens with a portrait of the Don, alone in his study, reading tales of chivalry. The music presents the knightly character and sentimental emotion of a good person corrupted by fables. But does it *represent* this character? How? What, exactly, is Strauss *saying* about the Don, and how might he have varied the story? These questions, pertinent to Cervantes, are not at all pertinent to Strauss. For the music is not saying anything specific: it wears a certain expression, and that expression, the composer tells us, is the expression of Don Quixote's soul.

The example is interesting for another reason: for it shows the immense importance of titles in establishing the subject-matter of a musical portrait— just as it is left to the title to tell us what an abstract painting is 'about'. Imagine that Strauss's great theme and variations for orchestra had never been called *Don Quixote*. Should we have suspected that it was nevertheless *about* the Don, or someone like him, and that it narrated the events of Cervantes's novel? What exactly would be missed by the person who either failed to make the connection, or connected the music to another theme—thinking of

---

[6] *Sound and Semblance*, 158.

it, perhaps, as the day's adventures of a dog? One is tempted to reply: nothing much. Or at least: nothing *musical*. And this is the crucial point.

Representation and Understanding

While someone may look at an untitled picture and know immediately what it represents, it is most unlikely therefore that he should do the same with a symphonic poem. The relation between a work of music and its 'subject' is determined only by the presence of an ancillary text: the title, the lyrics, the action on stage. A quarrel between husband and wife might be 'represented' by music that could equally be used to 'depict' a forest fire. This is very clearly seen in the ballet, where the action is left so far indeterminate by the music that several incompatible choreographies may exist side by side as accepted members of the repertoire, as in the *Rite of Spring*. Hence, while the aspect of a painting and the meaning of a sentence are publicly recognized facts, which make possible the intention of representing things, there is no such basis for representation in music.

On the other hand, when we learn of a piece of music that it is supposed to depict something, then its aspect may change for us: we begin to hear things *in* it, which we did not hear before. This may happen even when the subject is not itself a sound, and not even something that *has* a sound. Consider the sparkle on the silver rose that Strauss conveys by scattering unrelated triads on flute and harp through the upper spaces of his score (Ex. 5.3). Or consider the depictions of the sea in Debussy's *La Mer* and Britten's *Sea Interludes*. Debussy placed a title at the end of each of his preludes, with the clear expectation that the words would 'click' in the listener's mind. 'That's exactly right' is the response invited. And this sentiment would surely be impossible if we could not hear the music as the title suggests.

But what if someone did *not* hear the music in the way suggested? Suppose he heard in Debussy's *La Mer* not the sea but the waving of a

Ex. 5.3. Richard Strauss, *Der Rosenkavalier*, Act 2

forest in the wind; or suppose he heard nothing at all, apart from the musical movement. Should we say that he misunderstood the music? That he was deaf to its meaning as *music*? I doubt it. Return for a moment to the case of painting. The suggestion that one might understand a figurative painting, and yet not perceive the figures, is inherently absurd. Of course, there may be many unanswered questions and ambiguities that trouble the spectator. Consider Giorgione's famous picture known as the *Tempest*. Who are these figures? Why are they standing like that? What explains the strange atmosphere of the scene? But if you did not see the figures as people, placed in a storm-troubled landscape, you would not have the first understanding of the picture. To claim that you could have a partial understanding of such a painting without attending to its nature as a representation, you should have to ignore everything significant about it. There *is* such a thing as appreciating a painting as an abstract composition: enjoying the balance of the lines, the resolution of forces and the harmony of colours. But these important aesthetic properties cannot be detached from whatever representation is present in the painting. You could not perceive the balance that Giorgione achieves between the figures in this painting if you did not perceive them as people. Try imagining the left-hand figure as a statue, or a cardboard cut-out, and the tension and force of the composition will at once disintegrate. Take away the representation and the formal perfection would dissolve. (Consider also the difference between painting a moustache on to a Mondrian abstract, and painting it on to the *Mona Lisa*, as Duchamp did in his 'conceptualist' work entitled *LHOOQ* (1919).)

To understand a representational work of art, therefore, I must grasp the represented content. In such a case the aesthetic interest lies *in* the representation, and cannot be detached from it. This is not true of music. We can have a considerable, even perfect, understanding of a piece like *La Mer* while being ignorant of, or dismissive towards, its representational claims. Of course, to hear with understanding you must perceive the musical movement: those vast heavings of bottomless sound which can indeed be likened to the swell of the sea. But you do not have to hear this movement as the movement of the sea or even to notice the likeness. You may hear it as you hear the movement in Chausson's *Poème* for violin and orchestra, or the movement in a Bach prelude: as a purely musical phenomenon, to which you attach no subject in your thoughts. If there is anything that you *have* to hear in it, in order to hear with understanding, then it is the *expression*. It is only by confusing representation and expression that Kivy, for example, is able to argue that music should sometimes be understood as depicting things.

But what precisely is the distinction between representation and expression? It is my contention that we need to distinguish two kinds of aesthetic interest. Both are forms of interest in a work of art, for its own sake, as a significant appearance. But one kind of interest involves thoughts about a fictional world, where these thoughts are not merely associations, but conveyed and developed by the work itself. In thinking of Aeneas and his adventures I am also attending to the *Aeneid*, and receiving the impact of those mighty hexameters. This double intentionality in the reader's response enables us to think of representation here as an *aesthetic* phenomenon, and part of the meaning of the *Aeneid* as a work of art. The subject of a representational work is the subject of our thoughts when we respond to the work with understanding.

Clearly not all aesthetic interest is like that. And this is reflected in the fact that *understanding* may exist, even when there are no thoughts about a fictional world: as in music. Extramusical thoughts certainly occur in the appreciation of music; but they are either generated independently, through lyric and drama, or belong to the expressive effect. A passage of music may seem to carry a reference to grief, to a flight of birds, to something we know not what. These extramusical thoughts have an 'ostensive' character, as though the music were making a gesture towards something that it cannot define. We have difficulty in putting such thoughts into words; nor do we believe that it is necessary to do so. There is a peculiar 'reference without predication' that touches the heart, but numbs the tongue. This kind of aesthetic meaning was familiar to people, long before Croce coined a term for describing it. And if there is meaning in music, then surely it is meaning of this kind.

I have claimed that we do not understand music in the way that is necessary if music is to be representational. But it will be asked: what is meant by 'understanding' here? And it may be thought that my claims are purely legislative, that I am simply defining away the possibility of representation, without examining the case for it. The objection helps us to grasp what is at stake. I am not concerned to show that works of music, considered as sound patterns, can or cannot represent things. For the question that I am considering concerns how we think of music, when we hear it and appreciate it *as music*. The question is: do we ever understand music in the way that we understand representational works of art? It is clear that we could invent new ways of understanding music, according to which musical works become articulate utterances in a code, as in the game that I considered earlier. Music would then become an inherently information-bearing medium, and its capacity to represent the world could no longer be disputed. But the intuitive idea of musical understanding, which has informed my discussion throughout this work, makes no contact with that use of music. Only by developing a rival account of musical understanding, could the hypothesis that music represents things be vindicated. But I can see no path to such an account. Suppose that someone were to develop a musical semantics, in the full sense of a theory that assigns truth-conditions to musical utterances. Then there would still be no argument for saying that music is a representational medium. For we should still have to show that this semantic theory provides an account of the way in which music is understood.

This is not to say that associations and suggestions do not play an important part in the musical experience. Of course they do; and they may be integral to the musical experience. Consider, for example, the last of *Pictures at an Exhibition*, 'The Great Gate of Kiev' (in Mussorgsky's original version for piano—Ex. 5.4). Here there is a deliberate imitation of two familiar sounds: cathedral bells and a distant hymn. Their combination leads to a splendid effect of musical unity, but it is a unity that could not exist were it not for our prior disposition to associate the two kinds of sound. But to see how far even this case is from ordinary representation we need only ask ourselves what a person must lack who fails to recognize the extramusical reference. Even *he* may experience the musical unity; and for him too the association of bells with hymn-tunes may be leading him to hear the inevitability with which the musical elements are combined and synthesized. In no sense is his musical understanding diminished by his failure to entertain the thought that is here suggested by the 'representation'.

Quotation and allusion can likewise create a kind of subliminal 'narrative'. In Ex. 5.5, from an evocation for piano of a woman friend, the listener hears a reference to Debussy's prelude entitled 'La Fille aux cheveux de lin'—with harmonic and melodic invocations of childhood and spring. It is easy to deduce that the woman is young, happy, and blonde. But the web of allusion passes obliquely, through titles and quotations; and the listener who missed it might understand the music as well as the one who did not. The narrative here, like that in Berg's Violin Concerto, is a matter of suggestion, rather than representation.

The claim was made by Liszt, that music could be tied to a programme, in such a way that it would be necessary to understand the programme in order to understand the music.[7] Such 'programme music' must be heard as the unfolding of a poetic narrative. And that, he claimed, is the inner logic of his tone poems. But was he right? How many of those who listen with understanding to Liszt's *Tasso*, and appreciate all that there is of musical life and feeling in it, know the story of Tasso's life, or think of Tasso as they attend to the music? The history of music abounds in such examples, from Jannequin's chanson 'La Bataille', through Biber's 'Mystery' Sonatas and Kuhnau's *Biblische Historien*, down to the evocations of places and

---

[7] *Gesammelte Schriften*, ed. L. Ramann (Leipzig, 1880–3), iv. 69 (essay on Berlioz).

Ex. 5.4. Mussorgsky, *Pictures at an Exhibition*, 'The Great Gate of Kiev'

people in Copland, Vaughan Williams, and Ives. But it is one thing for a piece to be *inspired* by a subject, another for it to imitate the subject, another for it to evoke or suggest a subject, another for it to express an experience of the subject, and yet another for it to *represent* the subject. It is only by revising our concept of musical understanding that we could describe any of the well-known programmatical compositions as representations; Liszt's claims on behalf of the musical programme therefore remain wholly unsubstantiated.

Ex. 5.5. R. Scruton, *Portraits and Weddings*, No. 4

The Leitmotif

My argument suffices to show, I think, that music, as we know and understand it, is not a representational art form. Even if there are occasions when
music acquires a representational character, these are exceptional, and almost
always dependent upon some extramusical context. The representation of
the Viennese Waltz in *Wozzeck* depends upon the convention that what is
placed on the stage is not presented but *re*presented. This cannot be used
to prove that music is representational: for if you place an abstract painting
on the stage, it too would become a representation—of an abstract painting.

Even so, it would be a mistake to think that the operatic context
automatically turns music into a representation. The music in the orchestra
pit is in a crucial sense no part of the action: it was likened by Wagner, with
some truth, to the chorus in the Greek theatre. The music is responding to
what occurs on the stage, feeding from it, and feeding into it. When the
characters sing, they attach their feelings to the musical line, borrow the
great force of sympathy with which the orchestra surrounds their action,

and project their emotions into our hearts. But this is not representation. Rather, it is a special case of expression, in which the orchestra sometimes joins in the feelings expressed, sometimes withdraws from them—resonating, as Wagner perceived, like the chorus in a play.

Nevertheless, it was Wagner who did most to change our musical understanding, so as to approach the representational paradigm. Although his use of the leitmotif had been anticipated, he transformed the device into something very like an orchestral language, permitting the musical articulation of thoughts that could be conveyed in no other way: like the thoughts conveyed by the Greek chorus, which show the defective understanding of the protagonist, by supplying what the protagonist himself cannot conceive. Consider the closing scene of *Walküre*. Wotan, having summoned the god of fire to protect the sleeping Brünnhilde, points his spear and sings:

> *Wer meines Speeres*
> *Spitze fürchtet,*
> *durchschreite das Feuer nie!*

The melodic line, at once repeated by the orchestra, gives the theme which had been sung by Brünnhilde herself, when she revealed that Sieglinde is pregnant by Siegmund, with a child who will be the greatest of heroes (Ex. 5.6). This is the leitmotif that henceforth will be associated (in one of his aspects) with Siegfried, the unborn hero who is the only mortal acceptable to Brünnhilde as a husband.

In understanding this passage we recuperate from the music a complex and indeed astonishing thought, namely this: Brünnhilde has chosen mortality through her defiance, precisely in order to love the child of Siegmund with a human love; while Wotan has conferred mortality on her precisely so that the hero of whom he stands in need should enjoy her help and protection; at the same time, Brünnhilde does not consciously intend what is now inevitable, just as Wotan does not consciously understand that the hero to whom he half refers is already in existence. Both characters are swept along by a force whose nature they comprehend completely, while refusing to comprehend it.

Ex. 5.6. Wagner, *Die Walküre*, Act 3

Had the thoughts which I have just sketched been expressed by either of the characters, the drama would have collapsed entirely. The wonderful climax of this opera depends entirely on the subconscious nature of the forces that are coming to fruition, now in this character, now in that—how else is it possible for the tragedy of Siegmund and Sieglinde to find its resolution here, between two quite different characters? It is the music which completes the reference that Wotan begins, and which fills his words with the sense of destiny.

Debussy famously criticized Wagner's use of the leitmotif as a 'visiting card': the example shows just how wrong that criticism is. The leitmotif is not attached by a convention to its subject, as is a code. Or rather, if it is attached by convention, it must inevitably cease to be musically significant. The true leitmotif *earns* its meaning, from the dramatic contexts in which it appears. The theme that I quoted no more means 'Siegfried', than does the descending scale of Wotan's spear-theme mean 'spear' or 'treaty'. The theme is creating an expressive link between dramatic contexts, which compels the listener to bring one situation to bear on another, so that their atmospheres fuse. By the time that we have reached Siegfried's funeral music, the theme has acquired a resonance not merely of heroism, but of the whole sad process, whereby the warm-hearted innocence of Siegfried presses undaunted towards its own destruction. A leitmotif is not a symbol in a code, but a musical magnet, around which meaning slowly accumulates. And if it permits us to complete the dramatic thought, this is largely because it serves as an expressive link. The leitmotif works like a metaphor, coalescing with the dramatic idea and dragging it into the music, where it is subjected to a musical development—a development, however, that it does not resist. If the motif were musically inept, a mere counter, it would not succeed in conveying the thought. For it would not compel us to attribute the thought to the characters on the stage. It is only because Wagner's music is so intensely expressive, and so cogently organized as music, that it can perform its ancillary role, as chorus in the drama.

Whether we wish to call this musical representation is a moot point. Outside the context provided by the stage, the Wagnerian leitmotifs would surely not acquire their representational potential even if they retained their expressive power. If they work, it is because they work as *music*, as instruments of expression, set within the great force field of a drama. In such a force field almost anything can convey a dramatic thought: even costumes, facial expressions, abstract shapes upon the stage. Nevertheless, we do not understand Wagner's music as we understand the representation: we respond to it as expression, and we could miss the meaning of all that happens on the stage and yet have a complete understanding of the music. (Bruckner, who understood Wagner's music better than anyone, is reported to have looked up from the orchestra pit during this scene to ask 'why are they burning that woman?'.)

Musical Understanding

I have argued that music is not representational, since thoughts about a subject are never essential to the understanding of music. But, it might be said, I have done nothing to show that we *must* understand music as we presently understand it, nothing to show that there could not be a new way of understanding music which yet had the character of an aesthetic (rather than, say, a practical or scientific) interest, and which accorded to music the status of a narrative.

Throughout this chapter I have been concerned to point out specific differences between music and the other arts, specific properties of music that seem to distinguish it from the other arts precisely in those respects that are required by representation. The objection would be answered if it could be shown that these features are not accidental features derived from our present mode of interest in music, but on the contrary essential features, arising from the very nature of music as an art of sound.

Now it would be wrong to say that sounds simply cannot be understood as representations: for what is poetry if not sound? But the representational nature of poetry is a consequence of the medium of language; poetry achieves representation by describing things, according to the pre-established semantic rules. If the sounds of music were likewise to be put to a linguistic use—if there were literally a musical language—then of course music would be capable of representation. But then it would cease to be music. It would be poetry written in a language of absolute pitch (a kind of superlative tonic language). You could understand that language without having the experiences that I described in Chapter 2, and without crossing the barrier between sound and tone. If we think that there is a mystery in music, it is precisely because we know that it is meaningful, and know that its meaning cannot be understood in such a way.

To show that music is representational, we should have to show how we could hear the music in sounds, in which we also hear a 'subject'. There should have to be a single act of attention, in which both the music and its subject-matter are heard, and in which a description of the subject is unfolded through the music, just as the aspect is displayed by a painting. For this to be possible there should have to be the same kind of relation between sound and subject-matter as exists between a painting and the thing that we see in it, or between a text and the world that it describes. But could this ever be so? There is a crucial difference here between acoustic and visual appearances. You cannot see a visual appearance without attributing it to something: it is the appearance *of* a woman, a horse, or a landscape. Indeed, a visual appearance may present us with an identifying description of an object: so that what we see in a painting leads us infallibly to a narrative of some fictional world. Things heard, however, are not attributed to an object, as one of its properties. They *are* objects—albeit the peculiar secondary objects that I described in Chapter 1. A sound does not contain within itself the description of the thing that emits it, or of any other thing beside itself. If we hear movement in sounds this is not because the sounds convey to us the thought of a fictional world, in which things are moving. The experience of movement is here *primitive*, and depends upon no representational thought. Nor is such a thought made available by the sounds, which appear in music detached from all physical causes, unattributed and related only to one another.

Such speculations are inconclusive, of course. Moreover, they can scarcely carry conviction until we have explored the two concepts that I have been taking for granted: expression and understanding. It is to these topics that we now must turn.

6 *Expression*

I have argued that music is not a representational art, since it has no narrative content. It will at once be said that the meaning of a work of art is never reducible to its narrative content in any case. Figurative paintings and novels are representations: but their significance does not reside merely in the story, which might have been told in other and less artistic ways—indeed, in ways that are artistically meaningless. (Think of the difference between one of Hesiod's narratives of the gods, and the equally informative entry in a dictionary of mythology.) Even a work of *belles-lettres*, which feeds us with information, means something more than information.

Hence there arises the belief—expressed in many ways—that works of art have an 'aesthetic' meaning over and above their representational content. Following Croce, it is normal to use the term 'expression' as a name for this aesthetic meaning. Maybe there is more to aesthetic meaning than expression. But a theory of expression would explain the impact of art, and its place in the lives of moral beings like us.

The present chapter is largely negative: the purpose is first to introduce the concept of musical expression, and secondly to clear the ground for the theory of content developed in Chapters 10 and 11.

The Term 'Expression'

The term 'expression' has been used to denote several features of works of art, only one of which concerns me. The term figures prominently in eighteenth-century aesthetics; but its centrality is due to the distinction, made categorically for the first time by Croce,[1] between expression and representation. The distinction has been taken up by almost every subsequent

---

[1] *Aesthetic as Science of Expression and General Linguistic*, tr. D. Ainslie (New York, 1922).

writer in the field. But it is a distinction made at the theoretical level and aesthetic theories are as various as their authors. We should not assume, therefore, that it is *one* distinction, or that we can understand what a writer means by it in advance of his arguments.

In particular, we should not assume that 'expression' always denotes a relation between a work of art and a state of mind. It is natural to use the term in this way; but because the term is so frequently made to bear the full burden of aesthetic meaning, philosophers have extended its range. Nelson Goodman, for example, whose radical nominalism provides him with a short cut to a complete theory of aesthetic meaning, argues that works of art can express any property (or 'predicate').[2] A work might express sadness, joy, or adoration. But it can also express blueness, solidity—maybe even grueness. For Goodman, a work of art expresses P by 'metaphorically exemplifying' the predicate 'P'. This intriguing suggestion has given rise to considerable controversy. But an example will help us to see the point of it. Consider the lovely moonlight sequence from Smetana's 'Vltava' (Ex. 6.1). This is not a representation of the Vltava in the moonlight, for reasons that I have already given. But it wears a certain expression, and predicates like 'shining', 'silken', 'shimmering' suggest themselves as an apt description of it. It is fairly obvious that these predicates are applied metaphorically; it is Goodman's contention that the music also *exemplifies* them, in the way that a tailor's sample exemplifies a pattern. It does not seem strained to suggest that Smetana's music expresses the shining and silken qualities that we hear in it, just as the opening chords of Beethoven's Fourth Piano Concerto in G major, Op. 58, express a tranquil gratitude. Smetana's music is not *literally* shining or silken. But its expressive power is revealed in its ability to compel these metaphors from us, and to persuade us that they fit exactly. Of course, it is a mystery that they fit. But the mystery is immovable. Every metaphor both demands an explanation and also refuses it, since an explanation would change it from a metaphor to a literal truth, and thereby destroy its meaning. The mystery therefore lies equally in my description of the Beethoven.

The burden of Goodman's theory does not lie in the claim that aesthetic meaning is identified through metaphors: *this*, I shall argue, is true. Rather, it lies in the theory of exemplification, according to which we learn from works of art in something like the way we learn from colour charts. In opposition to the Kantian tradition, which explicitly distinguishes aesthetic from cognitive interests, Goodman assimilates them. And this assimilation forms the background to his generalized semantic theory of art, of which his concept of expression forms a part.

---

[2] *Languages of Art*, ch. 2.

Ex. 6.1. Smetana, *Má Vlast*, 'Vltava'

Goodman's approach has considerable appeal—not least because it promises a method for identifying the content of works of art. One critic[3] has relied upon it in order to attribute the most adventurous metaphysical meanings to various works of Beethoven, largely because he finds himself using complex Heideggerian metaphors when describing them. The promise, however, is illusory. Nothing that Goodman says enables us to determine when a work of art *exemplifies* the predicates that we metaphorically apply to it. And, as a licence to elevate every metaphorical description of a work into a revelation of its meaning, the theory does a disservice to criticism.

I shall return to Goodman, whom I mention here only because of the broad domain that he ascribes to the relation of expression. Other philosophers restrict the domain to states of mind, either treating works of art as expressions of emotion, or, like Croce, inventing a special mental category as the subject-matter of art. Croce believed that works of art express 'intuitions'—a term that he took from Kant, and to which he gave sense, like Kant, through a distinction between intuition and concept. An intuition, for Croce, is a preconceptual mental particular, an apprehension of reality in its uniqueness. About intuitions as they are in themselves nothing can be said: to describe is to generalize, and so to replace intuition by concept. But intuitions can be communicated by *expressing* them in artistic form. The uniqueness of the work of art is then explained by the uniqueness of the intuition that is expressed by it: these two forms of uniqueness are one and the same phenomenon, seen now from within, now from without.

Having launched himself on this path, Croce has no difficulty in proceeding to his desired conclusions: first, that the meaning of a work of art can be captured in no other way, since it resides in *this* particular work, and is understood through *this* particular experience (the intuition). Secondly, that form and content are inseparable, since each intuition corresponds to one and only one expression. Thirdly, that no two works of art mean the same thing. And finally that the interest in a work of art is an interest in the work itself, for its own sake, and not as a means to an end. Although I am interested in a work on account of the intuition that it expresses, this intuition is not something separable from the work, and not something to which the work is a means. Hence art is an end in itself, and each work of art is appreciated as the unique individual that it is. Every work has a meaning; but no work can be severed from its meaning, and no concepts can capture what it means. Aesthetic meaning is real but ineffable. To attempt to make it effable, is to reduce expression to representation, and therefore to lose sight of the essence of art.

[3] D. B. Greene, *Temporal Processes in Beethoven's Music* (New York, 1982).

Three important ideas remain with us, as the legacy of Croce's *Aesthetic*:

1. The distinction between representation and expression.
2. The term 'express'—with its implication that artistic meaning is to be compared with the communication of our states of mind.
3. The suggestion, which tends in an opposite direction, that the meaning of a work of art is, after all, ineffable, and in any case available only through its *particular* expression in the work of art.

(2) suggests that aesthetic meaning is a relation; (3) suggests that it is not. A similar tension seems to arise in other theories of expression, and one merit of Croce's account is that it brings the tension so vividly to the surface, forcing us to confront the question whether expression really is a relation, and if so, what are its terms?

Elementary Errors

There are three theories of expression which are so evidently erroneous that it would be pointless to refute them, were it not for the fact that all three have been advocated in recent literature. I shall therefore quickly dispose of them, for clarity's sake.

1. The biographical theory. According to this view, a work of art expresses a state of mind because the artist 'puts his state of mind *into*' the work. In understanding the product, we recuperate the mental state that went into making it.

In everyday life we use the verb 'to express' in two quite different ways: to refer to the revelation of a mental state in behaviour, and to describe a particular kind of *action*, in which a person does not merely reveal his mental state, but also draws attention to it. The first case is sometimes called 'evincing';[4] it is something that we share with the animals, and has nothing to do with artistic expression. The second case is more interesting, since it looks very like a case of *meaning* something. You might even propose to analyse it in the manner of Grice:[5] in terms of the intention to communicate something through the recognition of intention.

No theory of expression will be adequate that does not make the connection between artistic expression and the expression of feeling in everyday life. For how else do we understand this word, if we break the connection with its central use? Nevertheless, we should not attribute the expressive content of a work to the artist who created it. Mozart was deeply unhappy when he wrote the 'Jupiter' Symphony, K. 551; but what higher expression

---

[4] e.g. by W. Alston, *The Philosophy of Language* (Englewood Cliffs, NJ, 1964).
[5] 'Meaning', *Philosophical Review*, 66 (1957), 377–88. See the expansion of Grice's view by J. R. Searle, in *Speech Acts* (Cambridge, 1969).

of joy than the last movement of that work? Mozart disappears behind his work, as every artist must disappear when the work is judged aesthetically. What we find in the 'Jupiter' symphony we find in *it*, without enquiring into the biography of its composer.

It does not follow that we are indifferent to the composer's intentions. On the contrary: works of art are saturated with human intention, and are understood as intricately purposeful. But the intention is revealed *in* the work, and is sealed off from the artist's biography. If we are to create a bridge to the artist's real emotions, it will be possible only when we have first understood the work in its own terms, as *containing* its expression.[6]

2. The evocation theory. Turning away from the artist, one may attend instead to the audience, and identify the emotion expressed by a work with an emotion induced in the listener. Hence someone may argue that to say that the Mozart *Masonic Funeral Music*, K. 477, expresses grief is to say that I feel, or ought to feel, or would ideally feel, grief in response to it. (The very real distinctions between those ways of formulating the theory do not matter for present purposes.)

Again the theory has a point. For if we did not respond in some way to works of art, why should we trouble to describe them in these terms: as expressive, moving, troubling, and so on? Surely, the 'recognition of expression' in art is not the dispassionate diagnosis of another person's feeling, but involves a sympathetic response to it. But that shows precisely what is wrong with the evocation theory. To respond sympathetically to grief is not to feel *grief*: sympathy has a logic of its own, and does not imitate its object. Moreover, how can I respond sympathetically to the grief in the *Masonic Funeral Music* if I do not attribute grief to the *music*? That question shows the evocation theory to be incoherent.

It is important to distinguish the meaning of a work of art from its associations. We do not always do this, since we are not always concerned to distinguish the meaning of a work from its *meaning for me*. Nevertheless, to say that a work of music is associated for me with certain feelings, experiences, memories, etc., is to say nothing about its musical character. Expression, by contrast, belongs to the aesthetic character of a work of art if anything does. And this is borne out by an interesting distinction: you can appreciate the

---

[6] This paragraph raises the unwelcome spectre of the 'intentional fallacy'—the supposed fallacy of studying a work of art through the intentions of the artist, rather than through its own intrinsic nature (W.K. Wimsatt and M. C. Beardsley, 'The Intentional Fallacy', in W. K. Wimsatt, *The Verbal Icon: Studies in the Meaning of Poetry* (Lexington, 1954)). There is probably no such fallacy, since there is no real distinction between studying an artist's intentions and studying his work—see S. Cavell, 'A Matter of Meaning it', in *Must We Mean What We Say?* (New York, 1969). Nevertheless, the 'intentional fallacy' was such an inspiration to the 'New Critics' in America, that the controversy rages still.

expression of a work only by attending to *it*, and hearing the emotion in *it*. Turn your attention away and the experience vanishes. But you can appreciate the associations of a work of art long after you have shut your mind to it. They are 'triggered' by the aesthetic experience, but linger beyond it.

Sometimes an association seems to fuse with the aesthetic experience. When you hear the opening of Vaughan Williams's Fifth Symphony you are likely to think of the English landscape: and this thought is one in which the uncritical listener might wallow unscrupulously, since it is the occasion of so many comfortable emotions. For such a listener, the music is an excuse for his own emotion, a means to reverie. A more critical listener may also be reminded of the English landscape: but he will think of it only in so far as the thought involves attention to the music. The evocation fuses with the musical experience, and association then becomes expression. This passage from evocation to expression lends force to Goodman's idea, that *any* property, and not just states of mind, can be expressed by a work of art. For certainly, there are no obvious limits to what a work of art may evoke, and if evocation can pass into meaning, meaning too should not be limited.

The contrast between evocation and expression can be observed in critical discourse. The critic for whom the evocation of the English landscape is part of the expressive content of Vaughan Williams's movement will 'write the meaning into' the work. He will show how the precise character of the evocation is determined by the music, and can be understood only through attention to the music. Those pastoral horn chords, for instance, calling from far away, with the seventh sounded in the bass, suggesting the flattened leading-note of English folk-music; the pentatonic melody on the violins, with its folkish phrases, and spacious intervals, recalling the slow-moving clouds in an English sky. (See Ex. 9.3.) The attempt to make the description 'stick' to the music also accords to the purely musical processes an indispensable role in defining the content of the piece. Evocation becomes expression only by becoming a property of the musical surface. Here we see the point of Croce's intuition, that expression and form are in the end inseparable—whether or not ineffable. And we see too how important the critical sense becomes, in identifying the content of a work of art. Does Vaughan Williams really succeed in expressing the heartfelt but undemonstrative love of the Englishman for his native landscape? Or is the music just a little too banal, too much dependent on worn-out pastoral gestures from which the realities of country life in the modern world have been expurgated? Arguing in this way, you could come to the conclusion that the music is evocative, but also inexpressive, since the evocation is no part of its musical sense.

3. The resemblance theory. This tells us that expression in music is founded in analogy or resemblance between a piece of music and a state of

mind. In saying that the music *expresses* the state of mind I am simply drawing attention to the resemblance. The theory[7] parallels the attempt to derive a theory of musical representation from the 'sounds like' relation. Indeed, it is the same theory in another guise, and not only is it insensitive to the distinction between representation and expression, but also, like analogy theories generally, it confuses expression with the *route* to it. When I say that the last movement of the 'Jupiter' expresses a radiant joy, I am using 'express' in the same way as I use it when I describe Tennyson's 'Morte d'Arthur' as expressing a profound death-wish. But poetry does not *resemble* what it expresses.

Nor, of course, does music. Consider, for example, the slow movement of Beethoven's String Quartet in F Major, Op. 135—the 'Heilige Dankgesang'. Beethoven gives us a very precise description of a state of mind by way of preface to the movement: the sacred song of thanksgiving of the convalescent to the Godhead. We may disagree with this description (after all, the composer is only one critic among many). Nevertheless, suppose it to be right. Is the piece of music in any way *like* this state of mind? If you say that the sounds and the state of mind resemble each other, then you must also admit that they resemble each other less than the sounds resemble other things—and other states of mind. So why is *this* resemblance so important? In any case, what does 'resemblance' mean? If you say that the music 'sounds like' a state of mind, then that too is nonsense: how do states of mind sound? (Cf. the pithy observation of Carroll Pratt, that music

---

[7] which Kivy seems to be defending, at least fitfully, in *The Corded Shell: Reflections of Musical Expression* (Princeton, 1980) although the rewriting of the book as *Sound Sentiment: An Essay on the Musical Emotions* (Philadelphia, 1989) considerably shifts the emphasis from hearing a resemblance, to 'hearing in'. It is astonishing to discover the frequency with which theories of musical meaning, deploying the most sophisticated apparatus, reduce in the end to a lame idea of analogy between music and emotion. Consider Coker (*Music and Meaning*, 152): 'Music is a metaphor for life values . . .' where a metaphor is 'an icon that links two distinct objects by analogy involving qualitative and structural similarities'. The invocation of metaphor is here as redundant as the use of Charles Morris's theory of the icon. Both are rhetorical gestures designed to render interesting the theory—as banal as it is false—that music resembles our states of mind. The same obfuscation occurs in M. Budd, *Values of Art* (London, 1995), in which he describes the 'expressive perception of music' as 'a form of cross-categorial likeness perception'—one that consists in the experience of a likeness between, on the one hand, the objects of a sense modality and, on the other hand, "internal" psychological states' (p. 147). Once again, the massive investment in technicalities falls instantly away, and leaves one with the bare assertion that music (the 'object' of hearing) resembles our states of mind. Yet no argument is given to tell us how any such thing could be true. The same is true of Suzanne Langer's theory in *Philosophy in a New Key* (Cambridge, Mass., 1942), with its redundant invocation of the 'logical form' of feelings, in order to dignify with the theories of Wittgenstein's *Tractatus*, the same old idea of resemblance.

sounds as emotions feel.)[8] If you say that what you hear in the sounds resembles the state of mind, then that may be true: but only because you hear the state of mind in the music. And what does *that* mean? Surely, that is precisely what we have to explain.

Some Crocean Thoughts

Before returning to the resemblance theory, we should briefly examine the origins of the concept of expression, in the writings of Croce and his disciple Collingwood.[9] Although both philosophers set the concept of expression within a discredited metaphysical framework, they begin from certain intuitions about the work of art and its significance that we should do well to respect, even if we cannot endorse them entirely.

It seemed clear to Croce that the kind of meaning for which he reserved the term 'expression' is grasped in and through the aesthetic experience: it could be made available in no other way, and certainly not by some biographical study of the artist, or by decoding the work according to the imagined rules of its construction. Moreover, he believed expression to be an aesthetic value—indeed *the* aesthetic value, the single criterion of aesthetic success.

Croce and Collingwood designed their theories of art so as to vindicate this intuition. But we do not need to accept their theories in order to see the point of it. For there would be no reason to accord such prominence to expression, if we did not think of it as central to aesthetic interest. And there may be a truth too in the suggestion that it is only *through* aesthetic experience that expression can be grasped: *this* kind of expression at least. (Consider again the discussion of Vaughan Williams's Fifth Symphony above—the shift from evocation to expression occurs precisely when the evocation fuses with the musical experience.)

Croce's intuition therefore suggests a useful test that any theory of expression ought to pass: the 'value test', as I shall call it. When we say that a piece of music has 'expression', we mean that it invites us into its orbit. Expression is intrinsically an object of aesthetic interest. It does not follow that expressive works of art are by nature beautiful or good. The unctuous narcissism of the César Franck Piano Quintet is certainly an expressive feature: but not a virtue in the work that possesses it. Nevertheless, it is part of the *power* of this work, that it so successfully conveys this somewhat disreputable state of mind.

Croce and Collingwood believed representation to be of no *aesthetic* significance; in their view successful representation could accompany aesthetic

---

[8] *Meaning of Music*, 203.
[9] Collingwood, *The Principles of Art* (Oxford, 1938).

disaster, and the pursuit of representational accuracy or completeness was a derogation from the aims of art. They were no doubt wrong in that, although right in the weaker claim that representation can be the object of non-aesthetic interests, and valued in non-aesthetic ways. Their concept of 'expression' was designed, by contrast, to pass the value test: expression was to be an intrinsic object of aesthetic interest, and one that could be understood in no other way. For Croce and Collingwood the aesthetic experience is nothing more nor less than the 'recognition of expression'.

We see here another weakness in the theories that I briefly dismissed in the preceding section. For example, those who argue that musical expression is a matter of 'analogy' or 'resemblance' to human states of mind, must face the objection that you could, in that case, notice the expression while being aesthetically unaffected, and that a successful expression may be an uninteresting piece of music. But if that were so, what remains of the idea that the expressive properties of a piece are part of its meaning as music?

Someone might propose an amended version of the 'resemblance' theory, arguing as follows. When we refer to analogies between music and our states of mind, we do not imply that these analogies can be noticed and appreciated independently of the musical experience. Music does not languish in the way that people languish; it does not droop, revive, palpitate, and strain in the fashion of a human gesture, but in its own fashion. It is only through the musical experience that these features can be grasped. You have to hear the emotion *in* the music, and that means attending to the music, in an act of aesthetic interest.

As we have seen, however, the reply is also a capitulation. For it amounts to saying that the features we notice in expressive music are precisely *not* those that we observe in the human psyche. If they were the same features, then we should not need this quite special experience (the appreciation of music) in order to notice them. We must hear these features *in* the music, by an act of musical understanding. And it is precisely this capacity, to hear emotion in music, that needs explaining. To say that we 'hear resemblance' is either false (if it implies that the expression could be grasped without the aesthetic experience), or empty (if the resemblance has to be described in terms of the experience it was supposed to explain).

Expression and Ideology

By way of further clearing the ground, we should notice a use of terms like 'expression' in the sociology of art, which is sometimes confused with their use in aesthetic judgement. When a sociologist describes Heavy Metal, for example, as expressing the alienation and frustration of modern youth, this might sound like an aesthetic judgement—and perhaps one with a positive import. If the grounds for making it, however, make no distinction between the expressive and the inexpressive, ignore all issues of musical competence, and are based on the role of Heavy Metal in general, in the lives of its followers in general—as in Robert Walser's study[10]—then we cannot take the description as an aesthetic judgement at all. It has become a sociological hypothesis, concerning the state of mind evinced by a style of music, regardless of whether any of its instances succeed in giving real expression, in the aesthetic sense, to that state of mind or to any other.

The influence of Adorno and Critical Theory has led to much sociological criticism of this kind. The goal is usually to expose the 'ideological' content of a musical style—its function in endorsing and stabilizing the power-relations that require just *this* kind of music. Even tonality itself has been described in these terms, as an ideological instrument, of no more permanent significance than the 'bourgeois' class whose musical image it is.[11] Susan McClary, for example, describes tonality as 'a set of structural and syntactical procedures that emerged in Western music during the course of the seventeenth and that underlies the concert music of the eighteenth and nineteenth centuries . . . The social values it articulates are those held most dear by the middle class: beliefs in progress, in expansion, in the ability to attain ultimate goals through rational striving, in the ingenuity of the individual strategist operating both within and in defiance of the norm.'[12] The term 'articulates' belongs with 'expresses', as part of the language of aesthetic judgement. But McClary is not making an aesthetic judgement. What she says, if true, applies equally to Beethoven and Leopold Mozart, to Wolfgang Amadeus Mozart and Arthur Sullivan. It has no bearing on the expressive content of any particular work of music, and neither affirms nor denies the judgement that the *Eroica Symphony* really does articulate the striving of bourgeois man, in a way that the feeble symphonies of Leopold Mozart, or the piano concertos of Hummel, do not.

Exactly what should be made of this kind of sociological criticism and the theory of ideology that goes with it, are questions that I shall consider in later chapters. For our present purposes it is important to remark only on their irrelevance.

[10] *Running with the Devil: Power, Gender and Madness in Heavy Metal Music* (Hanover, 1993).

[11] See R. Norton, *Tonality in Western Culture: A Critical and Historical Perspective* (Unversity Park, Pa., 1984).

[12] 'On Blasphemously Talking Politics during Bach Year', in R. Leppert and S. McClary (eds.), *Music and Society: The Politics of Composition, Performance and Reception* (Cambridge, 1987), 21–2.

Form and Content

Croce had another intuition about expression, and one to which I have already referred. He supposed that the expression of a work of art is integral to the form in which we discover it: indeed, that it is not detachable. If a painting represents a landscape with cows, then I could describe its representational content in words, as I have already done in part. But any attempt to translate the expressive meaning of a work of art, Croce thought, would detach it from the artistic form in which it lives, and therefore detach it from itself. Expression must be grasped in the *particular* experience of the *particular* work, if it is to be grasped at all. In which case, the only way to identify *what* is expressed by the last movement of the 'Jupiter' Symphony, is to play the last movement of the 'Jupiter' Symphony.

This intuition corresponds both to Hegel's view that in art 'form' and 'content' are inseparable, and to the attack on the 'heresy of paraphrase', mounted by Cleanth Brooks and the New Critics in America.[13] As I have already suggested, however, it is in tension with the belief that expression is a real relation. To allow no other way of referring to the content of a work of art than by pointing to the work that 'expresses' it, is to demote expression to a pseudo-relation, and to lose the idea of an aesthetic content. Much of Hegel's aesthetics is vitiated by this; and much of Croce's too. Hegel's description of art as the 'sensuous shining of the Idea' strikes a chord. But when it transpires that the same Idea shines through all works of art, and that its individual versions are inseparable from the sensuous forms which express them, we feel cheated. On the other hand, the desire to speak in this way is so firmly established in critical practice, that we must at least find an explanation for it, and try to accommodate it within our theory.

There is another thought that emerges from the study of idealist aesthetics. It is a fundamental contention of Hegel's philosophy of mind, that the inner life comes into being through successive 'realizations'. States of mind that are otherwise inchoate and embryonic, come to full reality by achieving objective expression in the public realm. The process of expression is largely a matter of appropriating the outward forms of public discourse, and making them one's own. The state of mind precedes this process only in the way that the Aristotelian potential precedes its actualization. The emotion comes into being through its objectification (*Entäußerung*) in social life, and the emotional dialogue with the Other.[14] On this view, the expression of emotion is also the creation of emotion: or at any rate, its transformation into something known, conscious, and part of the discourse of social life.

[13] Brooks, *The Well Wrought Urn* (London, 1949).
[14] See esp. *The Phenomenology of Spirit*, tr. A. Miller and J. N. Findlay (Oxford, 1977), 111–18.

If this were true, then we should be inclined to say that an emotion is indeed inseparable from its expression—*even in everyday life*—since we could not identify the emotion prior to its successful realization. We should not therefore be surprised that emotion and expression are also inseparable in art: for this is merely the special case where our most difficult and elusive feelings are captured and transfixed in symbols, so falling from the airy sphere of potentiality into the really real. (Collingwood used this thought as the premiss for his distinction between art and craft, and for his original explanation of the nature of art as an 'end in itself'.)[15]

Such an Hegelian view of expression would not only explain the value of art; it would also give grounds for a fully cognitive theory of aesthetic interest. For it would imply that we are interested in works of art because they are the realizations of our mental potential. Through them we come to understand what we could understand in no other way: namely, the actuality of those states of mind which we otherwise sense only in their latent forms. This is a very attractive suggestion. Art becomes the mirror in which we confront ourselves, not as we are, but as we should be if our nature were fully realized.

Unfortunately, however, the theory depends upon something that has never been provided: namely, a criterion of identity, that would permit us to say that an artistic expression of feeling is the realization of that very thing—an emotion—which in another and more inchoate form motivates our daily existence. Without that criterion, the description of a work as an expression remains empty—since there is no answer to the question 'expression of *what?*'.

The Language of Emotion

The strength of Croce's theory lies in its ability to explain certain enduring intuitions, such as the ones I have briefly reviewed. That is why the term which Croce (and following him Collingwood) made central to aesthetics has been so widely adopted. Before committing ourselves to the concept of expression, however, it is well to look at the *other* ways in which the relation between art and the mind is described.

The term 'expression' suggests a connection between music and the emotions; but this connection can also be made in other ways, none of which seems forced on us:

1. Directly, when we apply mental predicates to art. For instance we may describe a piece of music as sad, brooding, angry, joyful. We all understand these descriptions, even if we can give no theory of their meaning.

[15] *Principles of Art*, ch. 6.

2. By the use of 'affective' terms, such as 'depressing', 'moving', 'uplifting', which refer to the mental effect of art.

3. By the use of quasi-relational terms, such as 'evocative', 'expressive', 'atmospheric', 'resonant', 'suggestive'. The choice of term here may very well seem arbitrary: though it *ought* not to be arbitrary, given the evident distinctions, in normal usage, between expressing and evoking, meaning and suggestion, content and atmosphere.

It is a remarkable fact about the recent literature on musical expression, that writers almost invariably assume that they *must* use this term, if they are to capture what they mean. And this assumption is made even by those who recognize that the term is borrowed from another context, and used obliquely to capture a phenomenon which no one has yet identified. However, maybe the term is not necessary at all—a relict of Crocean aesthetics, which could be discarded with the rest of Croce's theory.

Kivy, who does not clearly distinguish the first and the third kind of description, proposes a version of the similarity theory in order to explain what they mean.[16] We call music sad, he suggests, because it moves slowly, stumbles, droops, and so on—just as sad people do. But these are not real analogies, since music does not *literally* droop or stumble, any more than it is *literally* sad. The 'analogy' is simply the substitution of one metaphor for another. As I argued in Chapter 3, metaphors do not have to be grounded in similarities; nor do they merely compare things. Their sense can be described only by reference to the literal meaning of the terms deployed in them; and their point is captured by the *experience* that leads us to adopt them: the experience of 'fit' between two mental contents. What, in the present case, would such an experience be?

The difficulty here should not be lightly dismissed. For one thing, it rules out the possibility of giving clear-cut definitions of the terms used to characterize works of art. The language of aesthetic description is (to use a metaphor) shot through with metaphor. Almost every term deployed in describing the aesthetic character of something (its character as an object of aesthetic interest) is transferred from some other context. This is true too of the term 'expression'. To give a definition of the term in *this* use is to break the connection with its central use, and so to undermine the metaphor.

This observation leads to another: namely, that a certain kind of 'realist' or 'cognitivist' theory of aesthetic description becomes untenable. Someone might argue that the sadness that we hear in music is a *property* of the music, in just the way that the blueness of a shirt is a property of the shirt. We hear the sadness by hearing *that it is there*. This combination of realism and cognitivism has been endorsed in later writings by Kivy, and more

---

[16] *The Corded Shell*; but see n. 7, above.

ambivalently by Sibley, in a well-known series of articles.[17] But it is open to a serious objection. If we say that the Countess's aria 'Dove sono' from *Le nozze di Figaro* actually possesses the sadness that we hear in it, we face the question whether this sadness is the same property as that possessed by a sad person or another property. It surely cannot be the *same* property: the sadness of persons is a property that only conscious organisms can possess. But it cannot be *another* property either, since it is precisely *this* word—'sad'—with its normal meaning, that we apply to the music, and that is the whole point of the description. To say that the word ascribes, in this use, another property, is to say that it has another sense—in other words that it is not used metaphorically but ambiguously. If that were so, we could equally have used some other word to make the point, and someone could be an expert at noticing the property we describe as musical sadness, even though he vehemently denies that music can be sad. (He might even say that it makes no sense to describe music as sad.) But that is surely absurd: if he refuses to describe the music as sad, then he has not noticed the sadness. It follows that the word 'sad' attributes to the music neither the property that is possessed by sad people, nor any other property. It therefore attributes no property at all.

That argument is by no means the last word. But it provides part of the motive for the anti-realist and non-cognitivist account of aesthetic judgement which I shall defend in later chapters. Another motive is provided by the affective terms (case (2) above). These are not metaphors; but nor are they plain descriptions, either of the listener's emotion or of the thing that causes it. When I describe a work as moving, I do not mean merely that *I* am moved by it: I am also recommending my response. Otherwise there would be no disagreement between us, when you maintain that the work is not moving at all, but merely sentimental. Whatever these affective terms mean, they are used in a kind of open-ended dialogue, whose purpose lies in our attempt, as rational beings, to achieve some coordination in our responses. Why we should make that attempt, and whether success can ever attend it, are questions of the greatest importance in aesthetics. I shall therefore return to them in the final chapters.

Some affective terms are applied to aesthetic objects only in the context of aesthetic approval: 'exciting', 'stirring', 'moving'. Other terms, similarly, are negative or ambivalent: 'depressing', 'sickening', 'disturbing'. A work can *express* depression, of course, like the finale of Tchaikovsky's Sixth Symphony in B minor, Op. 74, without being depressing: even if this very

[17] Kivy, *Music Alone: Philosophical Reflections on the Purely Musical Experience* (Ithaca, NY, 1990); Sibley, 'Aesthetic Concepts', *Philosophical Review*, 68 (1959), 421–50, and 'Aesthetic and Non-Aesthetic', *Philosophical Review*, 74 (1965), 135–59.

movement has led critics to wonder whether depression is an emotion that art *should* try to express. Depressing music is not normally depressed, and muzak in a restaurant is depressing largely because of its asinine cheeriness.

Expression and Structure

Granted that we spontaneously extend our mental predicates to music, what need have we of the term 'express'? Is there any difference between the judgement that a work is sad, and the judgement that it expresses sadness? *Both* of these descriptions are metaphorical: hence we can use them to make the same point, or different points, depending on context. Nevertheless, the use of the term 'express' seems to imply human agency of some kind, and also the attempt to *articulate* something. (There are sad landscapes, sad colours, and so on: but only of human artefacts does it make sense to distinguish their being sad, from their expressing sadness.)

Hence it is quite reasonable to distinguish an empty work of music (the choruses from John Adams's *Death of Klinghoffer*, for example), from one that *expresses* emptiness, like the prelude to Act 3 of *Tristan und Isolde*, or a jolly work, like Grainger's *Shepherd's Hey*, from one expressive of jollity, like the overture to *The Bartered Bride*. An expressive work does not merely possess a certain atmosphere: it has a content, upon which it meditates, and which it sets before us in articulate form. Hence the plausibility of Goodman's suggestion, that an expression of sadness is not merely (metaphorically) sad, but stands in a semantic relation to sadness: the relation that he calls 'exemplification'.

This is another reason for rejecting the three primitive theories dismissed at the beginning of this chapter. The expression in Beethoven's 'Heilige Dankgesang' does not arise simply through evocation, or through the fleeting resemblance (whatever that might be) with a state of mind. The expression penetrates the musical structure, and is worked out through it. In hearing expression in music, we are hearing a distinctively musical process: a kind of musical *interrogation* of human feeling, and not the feeling itself. Tovey begins his account of the first movement of the *Eroica* in the following way:

> After two introductory chords, the violoncellos state the principal theme. It is simply the notes of a common chord, swinging backwards and forwards in a quietly energetic rhythm. Then, as the violins enter with a palpitating high note, the harmony becomes clouded, soon however to resolve in sunshine [Ex. 6.2].[18]

[18] *Essays in Musical Analysis*, 7 vols. (London, 1935), i, 30.

Ex. 6.2. Beethoven *Eroica Symphony*, Op. 55, first movement, first subject

And he adds:

> whatever you may enjoy or miss in the *Eroica*, remember this cloud: it leads eventually to one of the most astonishing and dramatic strokes in all music.

Tovey is here referring to the reappearance of the main theme at the end of the development, where the C sharp (all of modern music is contained in that C sharp, said Wagner to Cosima[19]) is used to throw the music out of the orbit of E flat into F major and thence into D flat, before the home key of E flat triumphantly reasserts itself. The implication is clear: the emotion belonging to the 'cloud' is part of a musical process, which captures our attention and our sympathy, leading us by musical means to see an entirely unexpected meaning in the hesitation from which it began. The meaning of the 'cloud' is provided by the great arch of musical argument that subsumes it.

Tovey gives only a rudimentary description of the 'content' of Beethoven's movement. What is important, he implies, is the musical process, the alchemy whereby something is first given in the music, and then worked out, through a magnificent structure of paragraphs, until its character is shown in all its inherent richness and all its comprehensive humanity. To describe the process in emotional terms is far less important than to identify the crucial transitions. At the same time, the success of the first movement is in part a *dramatic* success. It consists in the utterly unforced and sincere manner in which the little cloud of doubt is worked into the joyful dynamism that precedes it, and gradually taken through its musical paces, until finally hesitation is swept away and the seed of doubt proves to be a seed of triumph.

This suggests another test that a theory of expression must pass: the *structure* test, as I shall call it. A theory of expression must show how the organization of a work of music serves to articulate the emotional content.

---

[19] *Diaries*, ed. M. Gregor-Dellin and D. Mack, tr. G. Skelton, 2 vols. (London 1978–80), i. 378.

It must show how an emotional *demand* can be resolved by a musical argument. Croce's theory, which makes the content of a work dependent upon every detail of its form, does pass this test: but only by throwing the idea of content into doubt. In so far as we have any intuitions here, they prompt us to believe that expressive music is expressing something other than itself, but through a purely musical process, a process that must be understood as *music*, and not merely as some kind of code. (Nelson Goodman's theory fails as it stands to pass this test, since clearly a piece of music could be sad, and could also exemplify sadness, even though the *musical* structure has nothing to do with the exemplification.)

Expression, Expressing, and Expressiveness

The reader will have noticed the ease with which I have substituted the phrase 'is expressive of' for 'expresses' in the previous section. This reflects a general observation concerning artistic expression. In everyday life people often express themselves in inexpressive ways: indeed, the decline of popular culture leads precisely to an impoverishment in the means of expression, with the result that ordinary emotions are crusted over with a stagnant film of cliché. In such circumstances people cease to be transparent to each other and to themselves; emotion persists in an inchoate and disordered underworld, seldom shining forth in speech or step or gesture. Maybe one of the purposes of high art is to preserve the memory of something better: of that absolute giving of the self in speech or song that we find in Shakespeare and Mozart.

In any case, we certainly do not allow to art the licence that is seized by modern life: the licence to express inexpressively. If a work of art is inexpressive, then we decline to say that it expresses anything. Expression and expressiveness here coincide—an interesting fact that tells us something about our interest in expression. For expressiveness is a kind of success: a success in communication. The expressive word or gesture is the one that awakens our sympathy, the one that invites us into a mental orbit that is not our own. If we think that all artistic expression is also expressive, that is surely a fact about how we *respond* to expression in art. It is plausible to suppose, therefore, that a theory of expression must incorporate a theory of our response to it.

I remarked earlier that there are two ways in which the verb 'express' is used in ordinary life: to describe a kind of behaviour (the evincing of mental states), and to describe a kind of action (the communication of mental states). There is also a use of the noun 'expression' which is not cognate with these and which is of some importance. We may speak of the expression on a face, without meaning to imply that there is any particular state of mind that is evinced by it: it may be a purely 'physiognomic' quality of the face. In this case the term 'expression' is used, so to speak, 'intransitively', without implying that the expression is an expression *of* some state of mind.

There is also a transitive use of the noun, according to which the expression on a face is *expressing* something: an emotion, say. To be an expression, in this sense, is to stand in a certain relation to a state of mind: it is to be part of the process of evincing or communicating something. An expression in the intransitive sense might also be an expression *of* something: a state of character, for example, or an emotion. And the two may diverge in interesting ways—as when a person, expressing his grief, adopts a jocular expression. As that example shows, we may describe the character of an expression in the intransitive sense *in terms of* a state of mind, without implying that it is an expression (in the transitive sense) *of* that state of mind.

Matters are further complicated by the fact that we attribute expressions to entities which could never really express *anything* in the transitive sense. For his groom a horse wears a certain facial expression: his lips smile and his eyes dance. But horses express nothing through their faces, and if they sometimes *evince* their primitive emotions, it is largely through their ears and their tail. Our habit of seeing expression where there is none (in the transitive sense) is irresistible, and we extend it to the whole of nature: to fish and plants, to clouds and trees and landscapes. And it is not implausible to argue that it is expression in *this* (intransitive) sense that we hear in music.

Certainly, when we consider the use of the term *espressivo* in a musical score, we are inclined to believe that we are dealing with the intransitive concept. The pupil, asked to play with more expression, may ask 'More expression of *what*?' But he has no right to an answer; nor would he necessarily be helped by one. We understand the difference between playing with expression and playing in a wooden or inexpressive way, and the difference between the right and wrong expression, without even thinking about a *content* which is to be expressed.

This does not mean that the expression cannot be described—as we would the expression on a face. But an expression can be described as cheerful, lugubrious, and so on, without implying anything about a state of mind that is being expressed through it. On the other hand, such descriptions may, at times, seem entirely inappropriate to us. We may wish to say that a piece of music expresses a 'quite peculiar' emotion: an emotion that we cannot put into other words, but for which we need no other words, since *this*—the song—is its exact expression. (Wittgenstein calls this use of 'peculiar' or 'particular' also an intransitive use.)[20] It is tempting to say that when a

---

[20] *The Blue and Brown Books* (Oxford, 1958), 158 f. See the illuminating discussion of this passage in R. Wollheim, *Art and its Objects*, §41.

philosopher writes in such a way, the use of a transitive concept of expression is really a pretence, and that what he has in mind ought to be captured in the intransitive idiom. For what is the difference between saying that 'x is an expression of y', and 'x has a particular expression', when y can only be defined in terms of x?

It seems to me, in fact, that we use both concepts in describing works of art, and with good reason. We might attribute to a passage of music a certain atmosphere without implying that it is really *articulating* anything: and then we use the intransitive concept of expression. (For instance, the atmosphere that attaches to a Debussy prelude: which can certainly be *described* (as the titles indicate), but which is not an expression *of* the state of mind that may be implied in the description.) But we may also attribute expression in the transitive sense to a work of music, even when we find ourselves at a loss to identify the content. We have the sense that an emotion, a character, a conception is being articulated through the musical argument: as in the example, from Tovey, of Beethoven's *Eroica Symphony*. And, even if we find no words to describe it, this does not destroy our sense that there is a meaning to this music, which relates it to things *other than itself*.

The oscillation between transitive and intransitive uses of 'express' and its cognates seems natural, almost inevitable. The fact that we are intuitively pulled in these two conflicting directions is also something that a theory of expression must explain. It is a defect of Goodman's theory that it not only does not explain this fact, but also renders the intransitive use of 'expression' quite mysterious. If Goodman's theory were correct, we should be tempted to describe a work of art as expressive only in those circumstances where the predicate is available to identify exactly what it is expressing (the predicate that is 'metaphorically exemplified'). Far more usual, however, is the encounter with an expressive work of art whose meaning remains allusive and elusive, resisting any attempt to convey it in words.

And so we arrive by another route at Croce's intuition: that the content of a work of art is real but ineffable. Croce's theory offers an explanation, therefore, of our constant retreat from the transitive to the intransitive use of the term 'express'. Equally interesting in this regard is the theory propounded by Schopenhauer in *The World as Will and Representation*. According to Schopenhauer, music is a direct presentation of the will. The will, as thing-in-itself, is not knowable through concepts, and nothing therefore can be said about *it*: we can speak only of its 'representations' in the world of appearance, in which the will is portrayed indirectly, and through a resisting medium. Music, however, is a non-conceptual art, and is able to present to us, in objective form, a direct picture of the will itself. Yet what it presents to us cannot be described, nor presented in any other medium. The content of music is again real but ineffable.

I shall return to Schopenhauer's theory in Chapter 11. Like Croce, Schopenhauer leans on Kant's transcendental idealism to resolve the paradox of musical meaning—the paradox that music means or refers to something other than itself, but that there is no access to this 'other' thing through concepts, and therefore no answer to the question *what* music means. Here is a sublime metaphysical explanation of the fact that the term 'expression', applied to music, tends towards both a transitive and an intransitive grammar. It is not an explanation that I shall endorse. But it is one that should be taken far more seriously, I believe, than is customary.

Tertiary Qualities and Tertiary Objects

Schopenhauer and Croce seek to explain the ineffability of musical meaning by referring to that which cannot be conceptualized, either because it lies beyond the empirical world (Schopenhauer), or because it is bound up with a form of non-conceptual awareness (Croce). These Kantian ideas provide short cuts towards theories that explain our intuitions, only by demanding precarious metaphysical commitments. In what follows I shall try to explain those very intuitions, but in a more plausible way.

A few pages back I sketched an argument against any realist interpretation of emotional and affective qualities in works of art. Even if we do not accept that argument, we must recognize, I believe, that these qualities are of a very special kind. The sadness of a piece of music is certainly not a primary quality of anything. Nor is it a secondary quality. If it *were* a secondary quality, then any creature with the requisite sensory powers could discern it. But surely, although animals may perceive the redness of a flower, the loudness of a sound, the bitterness of a leaf, they do not hear the sadness of a melody. To hear such a quality you need not only sensory capacities, but also intellect, imagination, perhaps even self-consciousness. This is what I mean by describing the sadness of a song as a 'tertiary' quality.

Tertiary qualities are peculiar in several respects. For one thing, we can be argued into and out of perceiving them. I can describe a piece of music in such a way that another person, following my argument, comes to hear it as serene rather than tragic, as obsessively destructive rather than life-affirming (for instance, Don Giovanni's 'Finch'han dal vino'). This fact is of immense importance in aesthetics.

As with aspects, which are paradigms of tertiary qualities, the experience of perceiving them may be subject to the will. I can (within limits) choose what to hear, when hearing emotion in music. Consider 'Good Night', from the first book of Janáček's *On an Overgrown Path*. Attend to the triadic harmony and the innocent C major melody, and you will probably hear a serene tenderness, as the title suggests. Attend to the constant downward shift from C major to B minor, the inner voice sounding a sixth below the melody at the climax, the pulsating heartbeat of the semiquaver figure, and you will hear an apprehension that wipes all serenity away (Ex. 6.3). To hear such a piece as it should be heard, you must be able to shift at will between these contrasting aspects; and it is part of Janáček's genius that he makes the choice so natural, and each interpretation so compelling.

In Chapter 1, I argued that sounds are secondary objects—analogous to secondary qualities, in the sense that they are really there, but that their nature is given by our way of hearing them. The primary object is the vibration in the air, which (unlike the sound itself) could be perceived without hearing it. The sound does not feature in the theories of physics: which is not to say that it is unreal, but only that there are more objects in the world than are featured in the book of physics (the book which *explains* the world). I went on to suggest that tones are not to be confused with sounds. Tones are what we hear in sounds, when we hear sounds as music. They have properties that no sound could have: for example, they occupy positions in an acousmatic space; they attract and repel one another; they point towards and away from one another, and carry the mysterious movement that flows through music.

We might say that a work of music is a tertiary *object*, as are the tones that compose it. Only a being with certain intellectual and imaginative capacities can hear music, and these are precisely the capacities required for the perception of tertiary qualities. The mystery of musical meaning lies partly in this: that it is a tertiary quality of a tertiary object. No wonder that people are tempted to deny that musical meaning exists.

Ex. 6.3. Janáček, *On an Overgrown Path*, 'Good Night'

It is not only in the aesthetic context that we encounter tertiary qualities. The expression (intransitive) in a face is such a quality. No animal has the power to perceive facial expressions—even if it can perceive the features in which those expressions reside, and even if it is able to glean from them reliable information about the identity and state of mind of their owner. When an animal recognizes a person, it is not by recognizing his *expression*, but by interpreting primary and secondary qualities (shape, movement, smell, etc.) in the normal way.

The example points to another peculiarity of tertiary qualities, namely their supervenience. The expression in a face is supervenient upon its primary and secondary qualities: it is not something 'over and above' those qualities, which could be added to or taken away from them without any other change. A rule for the reproduction of all the primary and secondary qualities of a face, would automatically reproduce the expression, even though it makes no mention of the expression. Conversely, if two faces differ in their expression, they must differ in some other respect as well. Supervenience is a widespread phenomenon, and has been used to support antirealist theories of moral qualities, as well as physicalist theories of the mind.[21] It certainly seems to me that the three features of tertiary qualities that I have just outlined tend to support the antirealist argument given earlier.

The supervenience of expression (in its intransitive reading) implies that 'likeness of expression' is not reducible to likeness among primary and secondary qualities. When I say of a face that it has the same expression as my father's face, I do not mean that the two faces *express the same thing*. A face with just this expression could belong to a person whose states of mind never coincided with my father's. This 'likeness of expression' can exist, even though there is the greatest physical disparity between the faces, while two faces that are almost indiscernible may nevertheless wear entirely different expressions: one small blemish, one extra wrinkle, one lock of hair can totally transform an expression, like the tiniest moustache painted on the Mona Lisa. Likeness of expression is not secured by any rule.

This phenomenon carries over into music. For instance, we recognize a similarity between the climactic passage of Beethoven's *Eroica*, first movement, and a passage in the first movement of Stravinsky's *Symphony in Three Movements*, despite radical disparity in the sounds (Ex. 6.4). Conversely, the smallest difference in sound may lead to a complete transformation or even

[21] See I. McFetridge, 'Supervenience, Realism and Necessity', in *Logical Necessity and Other Essays*, ed. J. Haldane and R. Scruton (London, 1990), 75–90. For the application of the concept in the philosophy of mind, see J. Kim, 'Causality, Identity and Supervenience in the Mind–Body Problem', *Midwest Studies in Philosophy*, 4 (1979), 31–49; and 'Psychophysical Supervenience', *Philosophical Studies*, 41 (1982), 51–70.

Ex. 6.4 (a) Beethoven, *Eroica Symphony*, Op. 55, first movement; (b) Stravinsky, *Symphony in Three Movements*, first movement

loss of expression. Consider the theme of Beethoven's 'Ode to Joy' (Ex. 6.5). Often one may hear the twelfth and thirteenth bars hummed or whistled as on the lower staff: a very small change, but one that destroys the expression entirely. The 'uplifted heart' of the tied note is replaced by a vulgar jollity.

Such examples illustrate two important points: first, the extreme sensitivity of expression (in the intransitive sense) to the surrounding context, and secondly, the impossibility of providing rules of expression, in the sense of instructions which, if followed, will infallibly produce the *same expression*.

Ex. 6.5. Beethoven, Ninth Symphony in D minor, Op. 125, 'Ode to Joy'

The only conceivable rule is that which reiterates the supervenience relation: which says, reproduce all the features of Beethoven's theme, and you will reproduce its expression. But that is not a rule for producing other works with the same expression. Expression is tied to the particular work, and the sharing of expression is a creative outcome that cannot be foreseen.

Consider the 'Todesklage' from Wagner's *Ring* (Ex. 6.6). This theme contains a tense, tragic, and yet questioning expression. It is a normal exercise of the critical intelligence to look for the features which are responsible for so powerful an effect: the accumulated suspensions, and the final Neapolitan cadence finishing on a seventh chord, with its 'unsaturated' and yearning character. Remove the suspensions, and the tension goes (Ex. 6.7). Alter the final cadence and we have (with a slight change of rhythm) the serene introduction to Mendelssohn's 'Scottish Symphony' in A minor, Op. 56 (Ex. 6.8). But could one really have predicted that expressive transformation outside the context provided by Wagner's (and Mendelssohn's) melody? And could one have known, in advance of the particular case, that, in removing Wagner's suspensions, one would arrive at an effect of serenity

Ex. 6.6. Wagner, *Die Walküre*, Act 2, 'Todesklage', transposed

Ex. 6.7. The same, without suspensions.

Ex. 6.8. Mendelssohn, Third ('Scottish') Symphony in A minor, Op. 56, opening

rather than insipidity, or that in adding suspensions to Mendelssohn's theme one would arrive at an effect of tragic tension rather than cluttered portentousness? These are surely idle speculations: all we can know is that, *in context*, the suspensions contribute to the tragic expression. But the context includes everything else that might be heard as part of the musical *Gestalt*.

Hanslick's Objection

Hanslick made a famous objection to the theory that music can 'represent' emotions.[22] (This pre-Crocean use of the term 'represent' should not mislead us; he meant 'express'.) What, he asked, are the objects of the feelings expressed by music? Most forms of art said to express emotions are also representational: they describe, depict, or refer to a fictional world. It is at first sight difficult to see how emotions can be expressed in the absence of representation. For every emotion requires an object, and any attempt to distinguish emotions from one another, whether in general or in the particular instance, is doomed to failure if we cannot identify either the intentional object or the characteristic 'description under which' the object is conceived. It would seem to follow that an artistic medium which, like music, can neither represent objects nor convey specific thoughts about them, is logically debarred from expressing emotion. If people have so frequently doubted the expressive potential of music, it is largely on account of its *narrative* incompetence. When the objection is made, that the feelings conveyed by music can never be put into words, and therefore that no serious agreement can ever be reached as to their nature, the point in mind is usually Hanslick's: that without the object, the feeling cannot be identified. To say, as Mendelssohn did,[23] that musical emotion is indescribable because it is too precise for words, is not to answer Hanslick's objection. Precision of emotion is always and necessarily consequent upon precision of thought—such is the lesson of literary criticism. Precise emotion requires a precise situation: without it, there is no focus to what we feel. And the complementary

---

[22] *On the Beautiful in Music*, tr and ed. G. Payzant (Indianapolis, 1986), 9.
[23] Letter of 28 Oct. 1842.

view—espoused by Mahler when he asserted that the need to express himself in music, rather than in words, came only when indefinable emotions made themselves felt[24]—risks once again a return to a purely intransitive notion of expression. For how can we distinguish an indefinable expression, from the expression of an indefinable thing?

There is a response to this objection that I should like to dismiss immediately—the response typified by Suzanne Langer in her writings on this subject.[25] It might be argued that really emotions have two parts—the direction outwards towards the object, which indeed could be captured only if the object could also be portrayed, and the inner movement of feeling, which has a form and structure that can be comprehended without reference to its intentionality. It is this form or structure that is mirrored, symbolized, or 'presented' by expressive music, which gives the dynamic movement of our feelings, while leaving their intentionality unexplored.

I reject that view for several reasons. First, it seems to reflect a Cartesian conception of the inner life. Three massive and powerful arguments have been levelled against any such conception. First, there is the Wittgensteinian argument against the very idea of an 'inner' realm—an argument rooted in the proof of the impossibility of a 'private language'. Secondly there is the Hegelian argument that our 'inner' life is realized in, and constituted by, its *Entäußerung* in social life. Finally, there are the arguments of Brentano, Husserl, and their followers for the conclusion that intentionality is not an *addition* to a mental state, but a part of its structure. It seems to me that a philosopher who had worked through those three impressive contributions would find it impossible to describe mental states as Langer does.

Secondly, Langer's theory makes extraordinary claims about the nature of emotions—claims reminiscent of the speculations of nineteenth-century psychologists. The emotions are portrayed as sensations might be portrayed: as consisting of crescendos and diminuendos, surges and releases, tensions and plateaux; and these peculiar 'formal' features are then isolated as the *things that matter* in our emotional life. As though loving someone mattered because of those inner rushes of blood to the heart (if that is how it feels) and not because the person himself matters a million times more!

Thirdly, Langer seems set on a futile path, towards some version of the resemblance theory (which is indeed where she unknowingly ends up).[26]

---

[24] Alma Mahler, *Memories and Letters* (2nd edn., London, 1968).

[25] Esp. in *Philosophy in a New Key*, and the theory of the 'presentational symbol' there developed. But see also *Feeling and Form* (New York, 1953).

[26] She argues, borrowing in an eccentric way from Wittgenstein's *Tractatus*, that a work of music and a feeling may have the same 'logical form', and that this is what we notice in noticing expression (*Philosophy in a New Key*). Since no content can be given here to the expression 'logical form', the suggestion amounts to no more than this: that musical processes resemble emotional processes. See n. 7, above.

For she is trying to extract from emotions the features that might be *imitated* in music, by virtue of a correspondence between structures.

In Chapter 11 I shall show why Hanslick's objection is not as devastating as it might appear. But it is important to counter it in part, before summarizing the argument of this chapter. First, we should remind ourselves of the many contexts in which the object of musical emotion is defined—by the text of a song, by the action of an opera, by a title, or by a perceivable custom. Surely the objection falls to the ground, if we can show that music is sometimes used—as in a song—to express emotion towards some object that the song also describes? Nor do we need words to complete the reference. A certain use of the voice—as in the polyphony of Palestrina or Victoria—automatically transports us into the religious context. We hear the God-wards intentionality in religious music, just as we see it in the upturned face of the sculpted saint. And the example is all the more telling in that God cannot be represented, except in forms that misrepresent him. He is always, from the point of view of representation, 'off-stage'.

Secondly, we should remind ourselves that emotions are not identified only through their objects, but also through their subjects, and the behaviour whereby a subject expresses them. Suppose you are walking in a quiet place; turning a corner, you come across a woman who sits on a bench, head in hands, quietly weeping. Your heart goes out in sympathy towards her emotion: you know nothing of its object; but you have a strong and immediate sense of its intentionality—as you might see an arrow pointing, without knowing where. The release of sympathy here is not irrational or confused: it is a clear response to a clear situation.

Suppose now that you are studying a fresco of Masaccio. One of the figures is looking out of the picture to the right, his hands raised in astonishment, and his face radiated with emotion. Here you know that the object is 'off-stage', and unknowable. But you can respond to the emotion portrayed, and once again you have a clear sense, through the subject and the way that he is presented, of its intentionality.

Something similar may occur in poetry, as in these lines by Paul Celan:

> *Fahlstimmig, aus*
> *der Tiefe geschunden:*
> *kein Wort, kein Ding,*
> *und beider einziger Name*
>
> *fallgerecht in dir,*
> *fluggerecht in dir,*
>
> *wunder Gewinn*
> *einer Welt.*

(Fallow-voiced, lashed out of the depth: no word, no thing, and the unique name of both, ready for falling in you, ready for flying in you, wound-winning of a world.)

Celan gives us an intense emotion, but with only imprecise indications of the object. Yet we know that the object *is* precise—unbearably so: it is as though reality itself had crowded into the poet's feeling, and blotted out its name.

If there is expression of emotion in instrumental music it should perhaps be likened to those cases: we hear the emotion in the music, even though we can identify neither subject nor object, but only a wordless intentionality—a bridge between these absent things. How we do this, and why it should so deeply interest us, are questions to which I return.

Expression and Understanding

In the last chapter I argued that music is not representational, because that is not how we *understand* it. The considerations that I presented against representation, would weigh against expression too, if we could not show that expression must be *understood* by the one who understands music. An example will, I hope, illustrate the importance of this point.

Suppose John and Henry live at either end of a railway tunnel, and, sharing an interest in trains, send messages to each other about their common hobby. When a train enters the tunnel at John's end, he fires a semaphore rocket, so that Henry can prepare himself for the train that will soon emerge. This is an act of communication, like the game envisaged in Chapter 5, which also has the structure made familiar by Grice:[27] John intends Henry to understand that a train has entered the tunnel, by recognizing that this is John's intention.

The game develops to the point where Henry can deduce from the height, trajectory, colour, etc., of the rocket, a wealth of information about the expected train. Henry watches with awe and wonder as the rocket explodes in mid-air, showering the countryside with its multicoloured sparks. His pleasure in watching this performance is, we should be inclined to say, an aesthetic pleasure: its object is the *appearance* of the exploding rocket, contemplated for its own sake. (Whether this is an entirely accurate delineation of aesthetic pleasure is a question that I must here postpone.) But Henry also feels a pleasure of anticipation: soon, he has deduced, a passenger express will hurtle from the tunnel in the vigorous way that always surprises and delights him. The two pleasures are in principle separable, and Henry might have enjoyed one without the other. Furthermore, Henry interprets the rocket: he assigns to the explosion a meaning. This meaning is constituted independently of the aesthetic pleasure, being equally apparent to John, who takes no aesthetic interest in the rockets that he fires. Furthermore, the aesthetic experience is available both to Henry and to his

[27] 'Meaning'.

neighbour Jane, who, not being part of the game, has no awareness of the meaning.

A theory that assigned meaning to music as Henry assigns meaning to John's rocket—without reference to the aesthetic experience—would not be a theory of musical meaning, and therefore not a theory of expression. The expression of a piece of music is part of its meaning as *music*—which means, as an object of a particular kind of aesthetic experience. To grasp the meaning of a piece of music is already to respond to its quality as music. Hence a theory that succeeded in providing rules of syntax and semantics for music would not yet be a theory of musical meaning. It would have to be shown that these rules were active in producing the aesthetic experience, and that the aesthetic experience was involved in applying them.

The thoughts that I have just adumbrated will become clearer in Chapter 7. But already we have the idea of a further test that a theory of expression must pass. Any theory that severs the connection between the understanding of expression and the aesthetic experience should be rejected. This means that a theory of expression which attaches expression to rules that may be understood by the person who has no appreciation of music, is not a theory of musical expression.

The meaning of a sentence is what you understand when you understand it. There are ways of *attaching* meaning to any object (pebbles on the seashore, scratches in a tree-trunk, constellations of the stars). But these do not tell us what the object means. (Imagine someone who reads a text of Arabic from left to right, and succeeds in deriving a semantic theory that coherently interprets it in accordance with such a reading. He would not be understanding the text, for his theory is not a theory of the language in which it is written.) To put the point directly, and in terms made familiar by Dummett in his commentaries on Frege,[28] a theory of musical meaning is a theory of what we understand when we hear with understanding.

Since expression is held to be part of the meaning of music, expression too must be something that is understood by the one who understands a piece of music. Any theory of musical expression which allowed musical understanding and the grasp of expression to diverge, so as to become related only accidentally, would not be a theory of expression.

Summary

Many questions have been raised in this chapter, and few answered. However, we are in a position to define the concept of expression, not positively, but negatively, in terms of the tests that a theory of expression must pass. A theory of expression must explain or justify all of the following claims:

[28] See esp. *Frege: Philosophy of Language* (London, 1973).

1. Expression is (in the normal case) an aesthetic value. (The value test.)
2. Expression and expressiveness coincide.
3. The term 'expression' vacillates, in the aesthetic context, between transitive and intransitive uses.
4. Expression is a tertiary quality, and therefore supervenient.
5. There are no rules for expression.
6. Expression is *developed* through a musical argument. For a work of music to be expressive, it must provide a musical articulation of its content. (The structure test.)
7. Music cannot acquire expression merely by convention, or by being put to a semantic use.
8. Expression is part of what is understood, when a piece is understood as music. If a piece of music is expressive, then this must be understood by the one who hears with understanding. (The understanding test.)

Those intuitions provide strong constraints on a theory of expression, as I shall show. But before returning to this topic in Chapter 11, we need to make an extended detour. In the four chapters that follow I hope to give a theory of musical understanding which will show just what we understand, when we understand music as expressive.

7 *Language*

Music has been called a 'language of the emotions'. Musicologists often describe tonality as a language, with its own grammar and syntax. Theories used to explain the structure of natural languages have been adapted to music; some writers—notably Deryck Cooke in *The Language of Music*—have ventured to explain the meaning of music by interpreting its 'vocabulary'. This vast intellectual investment in the analogy between music and language deserves an examination: if it is a good investment, then we should follow it; if it is a bad one, then we should know the reason why.

Analogies are based in resemblance and they are illuminating only if the resemblance is deep, so that the knowledge of the one thing casts light upon the other. Language has many features; and may resemble music in one respect without resembling it in another. We should therefore begin by considering some of the many ways in which music and language *might* be compared, and then work out which of the comparisons bears intellectual fruit. Obviously, if music had a grammar in exactly the sense that a natural language has a grammar, this would have enormous significance for the theory of musical understanding. But there are other features of language, equally interesting from the philosophical viewpoint, which might also motivate the comparison.

For example, language is unique to rational beings: maybe it is the thing which *makes* them rational. It is language which provides us with an articulate picture of the world, and which permits us to think abstractly, so emancipating our thought from present experience and present desire. Hence the attempt to say what is distinctive of the rational being will pay great attention to language. At the same time, there are many things besides language which are unique to rational beings. For example, only rational beings are persons; only rational beings are self-conscious; only rational beings are moral agents; only rational beings laugh, fall in love, cast judgement. And only rational beings make and listen to music. Here lies a connection between music and language which is surely of the greatest philosophical significance.

One kind of rational being is known to us: namely the human kind. (Philosophically speaking, gods and angels do not belong to another kind: for either we are made in their image or they in ours.) Language is therefore a human institution, and is marked by human life. Other animals communicate: but, so far as we know, they do not *represent* the world to each other, or describe their situation within it. A dolphin language would be very different from ours: it would have no true equivalents for 'up' and 'down', 'standing' and 'lying', 'falling' and 'rising'. Human perception, human action, and human desire have shaped the concepts that we use to express them, and moulded our world accordingly. Music, too, is a human institution, and bears the imprint of our creaturely desires. And the shape that these desires impose on language is mirrored in the forms of music: our music is the music of upright, earth-bound, active, love-hungry beings. Words move, music moves, 'so as to reach into the silence'—so as to claim for our humanity the speechless space surrounding us.

Hence, in comparing music and language, we might be drawing attention to the way in which our nature is expressed and realized in each of them. Interesting though the comparison might be, however, it casts little light on the problems that have motivated the argument of earlier chapters. Language is essentially an information-carrying medium, intelligible in principle to every rational being, and governed by rules which organize a finite vocabulary into a potential infinity of sentences. It is not obvious that any of those things is true of music. Although music can be used in communication—as when we sing or dance together—it is not (or at any rate, not obviously) used to convey information. Moreover, there are rational beings who are tone-deaf; certainly many who are deaf to the meaning of music. And even if music has an apparently rule-guided structure, it is by no means obvious that the rules are comparable to the rules of grammar, nor that they operate over a finite musical 'vocabulary'.

Still, it might be said, even if the comparison is hasty, so too would be its rejection. The rule-guided nature of music is too impressive a fact to be dismissed as a mere surface phenomenon—a mere matter of style. Moreover, the experience of musical meaning which I described in Chapter 6 seems to be intimately connected with this rule-guided character: it is afforded only to the listener who is *following* the music, and seems bound up with an awareness of the musical 'argument'. It is doubtful that music conveys information as language does; but it shares with language another and equally important feature—the fact of inhabiting the human face and voice. We hear music as we hear the voice: it is the very soul of another, a 'coming forth' of the hidden individual. These descriptions may be metaphors, but they seem to be forced upon us, and invite us to treat the relation between music and language as something more than a passing accident.

Semiology

There have been many false starts in the theory of musical syntax, and it is worth considering one of them, since it brings vividly to our attention what a theory would have to prove if it were to cast light on the understanding of music. So far I have considered the linguistic analogy as an attempt to explain music through the comparison with language. In his *Cours de linguistique générale* Saussure made another suggestion, and one that proved for a while to be highly influential.[1] Language, he argued, is a system of signs: but it is only one possible system. Rather than see other systems as special cases of language, or derived from language by analogy, we should treat all systems of signs as genera of a single species, with none enjoying the special privileges of a paradigm case. Thus was born the 'general science of signs', or 'semiology', which, according to Saussure, has a 'right' to exist.

What, then, are the general characteristics of signs? Two in particular have been singled out by the proponents of semiology. First, the relation between a sign and its meaning—between signifier and signified; secondly the existence of syntactic structure. Under the influence of Saussure—and in particular of the deviant reading of Saussure introduced by Roland Barthes[2]—critics and literary theorists began to think of works of art and literature as signs, built according to structuralist principles. It was supposed that the artistic meaning of a work is to be found 'encoded' in its 'structure', to be recuperated (perhaps at an unconscious level) by the reader who grasps the structure and identifies its elements. The key assumption was that meaning and structure are connected. Hence, if you could find syntactic or quasi-syntactic structure, you would find meaning encoded within it. Nicholas Ruwet, for example, proposed to treat music as a 'semiotic system' because it 'shares a certain number of common features—such as the existence of syntax—with language and other systems of signs'.[3] The idea of a musical 'syntax' therefore came to assume enormous prominence in the theory of music—syntactic structure would be sufficient proof that music is a semiotic system: a system of signs, which could be interpreted by the one who knew the code. J.-J. Nattiez repeats the idea,[4] accepting syntactic structure as sufficient proof of semiotic content. (The term 'semiotics', taken from Charles Morris and C. S. Peirce, has largely replaced the term 'semiology', in recognition that this general 'science' of signs may not deserve the name.)[5]

[1] (Paris, 1966), sect. 3, ch. 3, p. 33.
[2] See esp. his *Éléments de sémiologie* (Paris, 1959).
[3] *Langage, musique, poésie*, Paris, 1972, 44.
[4] *Fondements d'une sémiologie de la musique* (Paris 1975).
[5] Peirce, *Selected Writings*, 407; C. W. Morris, *Foundations of the Theory of Signs* (New York, 1938).

The problem, however, is that Saussurian linguistics gives no persuasive theory of syntax, and no theory as to *how* syntactic structures encapsulate meaning. Ruwet and Nattiez regard music as a 'system', with 'paradigmatic' and 'syntagmatic' structure, for the sole reason that in music, as in language, every item limits what may precede or follow it. At any point in a sentence words from a given syntactic category may be substituted for one another, without loss of syntactic cogency. In 'John loves Mary' you can substitute 'kicks' for 'loves', but not 'thinks that', 'swims', 'but', or 'elephant'. If you have proceeded to a certain point in a sentence, you have placed limits on what may come next: there is a right and a wrong way to proceed, and this right and wrong are determined by rules of grammar. And it is clear that music has a syntax in that sense: at least in certain of its manifestations. Take a simple chord sequence, such as that of the 12-bar blues. This has syntagmatic structure: each point in the sequence is a syntagma, in which only certain musical elements, drawn from a paradigm class, may be substituted. If that is what we mean by syntactic structure, then much traditional music has a syntax. Of course, music is spread out in several dimensions—rhythmic, melodic, and harmonic. But each dimension has such a structure, and the syntax of the whole is like the solution of three simultaneous equations, each musical event limiting the values of the three variables in the next one.

But can we really believe that the presence of this kind of structure shows music to be a system of 'signs', or casts light on its meaning? Consider one of Nattiez's examples—the opening bars of the prelude to *Pelléas et Mélisande* (Ex. 7.1). The task for the *sémiologue*, according to Nattiez, is to arrive at a correct description of the chords which occur in bars 5 to 6—the description which will justify their place in the syntactic structure, by showing how they follow from the preceding harmonies, and how they compel the harmonies that come after them. Now the key signature, and the opening four bars, point unmistakably to the key of D minor—or at least, the D minor mode with flattened leading-note. So how does the first chord of bar 5 fit into that description? How are we to *parse* it, so as to show its place in the D minor 'syntax'? René Leibowitz has described it as the dominant seventh chord of G with a flattened fifth; Van Appledorn prefers to view it as a second inversion of a French sixth; while Nattiez himself has no settled opinion.[6]

---

[6] Leibowitz, 'Pelléas et Mélisande ou les fantômes de la réalité', *Temps modernes*, 305 (1971), 891–922; Van Appledorn, 'Stylistic Study of Claude Debussy's Opera, *Pelléas et Mélisande*', Ph. D. diss., Univ. of Rochester, NY; J.-J. Nattiez, *Fondements*, 90–3. See also the comparative study of eight accounts of the passage in question by J.-J. Nattiez and L. Hirbour-Paquette, 'Analyse musicale et sémiologie: A propos du Prélude de Pelléas', *Musique en jeu*, 10 (1973), 42–69.

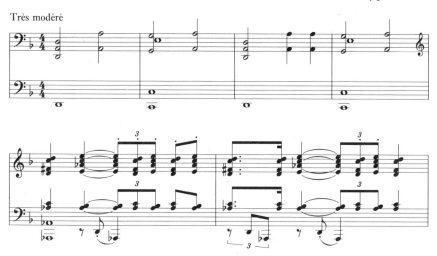

Ex. 7.1. Debussy, *Pelléas et Mélisande*, prelude

The contest here is not between rival descriptions, but between rival ways of hearing. For musical syntax is something that we hear: it resides in the experience of music, in our intuitive recognition that this note or chord or rhythm is right, and that one wrong. The description of a chord will capture its syntactic value if it explains why we hear it as right or wrong, and how we hear it in relation to the surrounding harmonies. (Leibowitz, for example, suggests a chord out of Fats Waller: Debussy rarely *flattened* a fifth, as a jazz musician might; what is important in this passage and in the chord that opens it is not the flattened fifth, but the tritone, with which it is acoustically, *but not musically*, identical.)

The example shows that, at the very least, there is more to musical 'syntax' than syntagmatic structure. For what exactly is *heard* in these bars of music, by the person who hears with understanding? Surely the most striking fact about bars 5 and 6 is that they are not in D minor at all—nor in any other key. For they are composed from the notes of the whole-tone scale, the rocking tritone in the bass being used, as in the prelude to *Siegfried*, Act 2, to deny the sense of key, by ruling out the possibility of a dominant. The whole-tone harmony supports the whole-tone melody (perhaps the greatest melody ever to have been composed from just two notes); it gives to the melody that wandering, poignant air which Debussy exploits throughout the opera. Somebody who fails to understand can be given other examples of the whole-tone scale, used to a similar effect—as in the prelude called 'Voiles' in Debussy's First Book.

The effect of the chord in bar 5, therefore, will be misrepresented by any description which aligns it with the D minor tonality of the previous bar. Indeed, there seems to be no way of identifying, in terms of 'grammatical' rules which prevail in the first four bars, a class of syntactically permissible harmonies that must follow thereafter. The first chord in bar 5 breaks away from the D minor tonality, without sounding wrong. Nor is Debussy's prelude like a piece of macaronic verse, in which we switch from language to language as we pass from line to line. There is a smooth musical transition from bar 4 to bar 5, as well as a contrast. This transition sounds right to us, but its rightness was surely not predictable before Debussy achieved it.

This is not to deny the existence of syntactic structure in Debussy's prelude, but rather to cast doubt on the Saussurian description of it—and, incidentally, on the whole project of semiology, as a general 'science of signs'. Syntagmatic structure exists in menus, fences, table-settings, and railway trains, all of which are composed of 'places' filled from a finite list of substitutional equivalents. But if these objects are also signs, it is not for *this* reason. A moment's reflection tells us that, in such examples, structure and meaning fall apart, so that the one is no guide to the other. In language, by contrast, syntax and semantics go hand in hand—the syntactic composition of a sentence is explained by the semantic goal. Furthermore, syntax is generative. Syntactic rules are not merely rules of substitution. They include rules of transformation—rules for the generation of surface structure from underlying 'deep' structures. And this is precisely what we should expect, when the goal of syntax is to articulate a *meaning*. The 'general science of signs' depends upon connecting structure and meaning wherever meaning exists. But the connection has been made only in those *special* cases, typified by language, in which structure is the result of generative syntax.

Syntax and Semantics

Those last observations return us to ideas that we have already glimpsed in Chapter 2, in the discussion of rhythm. Linguistics has moved on since Saussure's day, and the reader of Barthes or Ruwet will naturally wonder whether any serious thinker could have written as they wrote, had he been acquainted with Tarski's semantics, Chomsky's syntax, and the model theory of Kripke and Montague.[7] Just what are we to make of the suggestion that music has a syntax, when we mean by 'syntax' what Chomsky means, or of the suggestion that music has semantic import, when semantics is

[7] Tarski, 'The Concept of Truth in Formalized Languages', in *Logic, Semantics, and Metamathematics*, tr. J.H. Woodger (new edn., Oxford, 1956); Chomsky, *Syntactic Structures* (The Hague, 1969), and *Aspects of the Theory of Syntax* (Cambridge, Mass., 1964); Kripke, 'Semantic Considerations on Modal Logic', *Acta Philosophica Fennica*, 16 (1963), 83–94; Montague, *Formal Philosophy*, ed. and introd. R. H. Thomason (New Haven, 1979).

understood in Tarski's way? One thing at least is clear: if we have no answer to those questions, then the analogy between music and language will cast no light on understanding music.

It is well known that the distinction between syntax and semantics is not hard and fast—a generative theory of English syntax will almost certainly rely, at some level, on a theory of semantic structure. Only in the case of artificial languages, such as the predicate calculus, is the distinction between syntax and semantics—between the well-formed formula and its interpretation—theoretically defined, and even there the syntax owes its structure to the intended interpretation. Nevertheless, at the surface level, we can distinguish syntactic from semantic intuitions, and it is at this level that the comparison between language and music should first be made. Syntactic intuitions tell us whether a sentence is a possible sentence of English, which of its component sounds is a word rather than a phoneme, and how the words are linked. Semantic intuitions tell us whether a sentence has meaning, and what the meaning is. A theory of syntax offers to explain our syntactic intuitions, by showing how we can derive sentences of English, by finite transformation rules, from a finite vocabulary and a repertoire of deep structures. We recognize the syntactically correct sentences by grasping their derivation; deviant sentences are those which we cannot derive from our repertoire of rules and structures. When we hear a sentence as 'wrong' it may be because it has no evident meaning—as in 'the borogoves were mimsy, and the mome wraths outgrabe', a sentence which is, from the point of view of syntax, quite impeccable. It may also be because, even if we can assign a meaning to it, it violates the rules of syntax. 'The magician up looked at the sky' and 'The magician looked at the sky up' sound wrong to native English speakers; but they know what the sentences mean.

Drawing the contrast between 'to look up at' and 'to look up' is one way of explaining the importance of transformational grammar. For the native speaker will accept 'John looked Mary up', and also 'John looked up Mary'. 'Looked' and 'up' are heard as belonging together, however far they may stray from each other in the sentence, so long as 'up' comes after 'look' and is separated from it by a noun phrase: consider the inelegant but syntactically accepted sentence 'John looked the girl he had met at William's party up'. Such intuitions can be explained on the assumption that the two sentences 'John looked up Mary' and 'John looked Mary up' are derived from a common underlying structure. Transformation rules explain our ways of grouping words in a sentence; they also explain how we *hear* the sentence—a fact that is of considerable interest when it comes to extending the modern conception of syntax to the case of music.

Consider the following sentence:

That he was angry was evident from the way he frowned.

English speakers will hear the distance between 'angry' and the second occurrence of 'was' as greater than that between 'angry' and the first occurrence, regardless of the actual time interval between the words. This is because they will hear the first clause as grouped together. This recalls the experience of the musical *Gestalt* as I described it in earlier chapters. For instance, the listener to

Ex. 7.2. Mozart, *Don Giovanni*, 'Batti, batti'

'Batti, batti' will hear a greater distance between the second and third notes of bar 3 than between the first and the second, although they have the same rhythmic value (Ex. 7.2). The experience has an explanation in the linguistic case. For consider the tree analysis of the quoted sentence in Diagram 7.1.

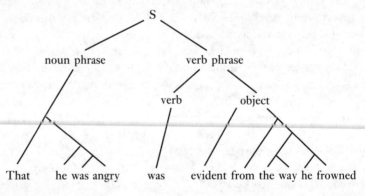

Diagram 7.1

The felt distance between 'angry' and the 'was' that follows can be understood from this tree, which shows the 'was' to belong to a quite different part of the sentence, derived by transformation rules from another section of the underlying structure. This simple example shows three things: first, how the deep structure of a sentence may be barely reflected in its surface grammar; secondly, how a subliminal awareness of the deep structure, and of the transformation rules that are applied to it, can explain our syntactical intuitions, without reference to the meaning of the words; thirdly, how the audible 'grouping' of words might be explained.

Generative Grammar and Musical Syntax

Rules which generate syntagmatic structure of the kind observed in menus or railways trains, do not explain our grammatical intuitions, for they are 'context-independent'. For example, a rule that allows both 'himself' and 'herself' to follow 'washes' would be suggested by a structuralist analysis of English syntax. The result would be that 'The boy washes himself' and 'The girl washes herself' are both well formed; so too, however, is 'The boy washes herself'. Clearly our rules of grammar must take into account more than the surface position of a word if they are to generate a natural language. The point is brought out, too, by reflecting on the intransitivity of syntax. A word may be acceptably joined to its successor, and the successor to *its* successor, and yet the result be ill-formed. For example, 'fish eat' is acceptable; so is 'eat three', and so is 'three ideas': but 'fish eat three ideas' is not an acceptable sentence of English.

The examples suggest that *semantic* considerations are at work in generating our intuitions about syntax. Nevertheless, they have their parallels in music. Much of Hindemith's *Gebrauchmusik* sounds like 'fish eat three ideas'— each bar leading smoothly into its successor, yet the whole thing a kind of nonsense (Ex. 7.3).

So perhaps there *are* rules of grammar in music, which could be evoked to explain at least some of our intuitions of right and wrong, and lend support to the view of music as a rule-governed art, whose meaning is

Ex. 7.3. Hindemith, Concerto for trumpet, bassoon, and strings, second movement

worked out through its structure. Before examining generative grammar in more depth, therefore, it is worth reflecting on the nature of musical 'syntax', and on the intuitions that a theory of syntax might be called upon to explain.

As in language, our intuitions concerning what is 'right' and 'wrong' in music exist in three dimensions, which we might without too much distortion describe as syntax, semantics, and style. A piece of music can be syntactically quite in order, even though bland and meaningless. Consider the simple syntax of 'Baa, baa, black sheep', and compare it with the equally simple syntax of the highly meaningful 'Wiegenlied' of Schubert—both poised on the major scale, without accidentals, between tonic and dominant, using only tonic, dominant and (in the first case) subdominant harmonies, and moving stepwise between them (Ex. 7.4). It seems quite reasonable to suggest that the meaningful quality of the Schubert is something more than mere syntactical correctness, even though the music depends on this syntactical correctness for its blissful repose. Conversely, a wrong note may strike us as exactly right from the point of view of meaning, forcing our syntactical and semantical intuitions apart. Consider the D sharp that occurs at the beginning of the second measure in the passage from Chopin, Ex. 7.5, where 'syntax' demands C sharp. You hear that it is wrong, and also that it is right—like the distorted syntax in Milton.

Likewise, composers can write in the same syntax, but with a different style, as did Handel and Bach, or Mozart and Beethoven. True, the distinction between syntax and style has broken down in much twentieth-

Ex. 7.4 (*a*) 'Baa, Baa, Black Sheep'; (*b*) Schubert, 'Wiegenlied', D498

Ex. 7.5. Chopin, Nocturne in E major, Op. 62 No. 2

century music, as each composer strives to impress his individuality on the raw material of sound. But this breakdown of the distinction between style and syntax can be observed in much twentieth-century literature too (consider *Finnegan's Wake*), and it may seem more reasonable to think of the phenomenon as showing something about twentieth-century art and the modernist project, rather than as distinguishing the language of music from language of other kinds.

We have already encountered the suggestion that the metrical aspect of rhythmic organization is governed by a kind of generative syntax. But for the analogy with language to be sustained, we must provide something like a rule-governed syntax for the other dimensions of musical organization also. Our first requirement must therefore be to generalize the notion of 'syntactic correctness' to melody and harmony. Suppose I hear regular beats of the same duration, accented in the following way:

$$ - \smile \smile - \smile \smile - \smile \smile - \smile \smile - \smile \smile \smile - \smile \smile - \smile \smile $$

And suppose that I parse these beats in waltz time. At bar 5 I am jolted into an awareness of 'something wrong'. The incorrectness of this bar has to do with the fact that it cannot be derived using rules that I have recuperated from the measures that precede it. Even if there is a musical rightness in it, there is a syntactical wrongness.

We could add to the waltz rhythm a tune, and again it is natural to make a distinction between syntactically correct and syntactically incorrect ways of doing so. The tune in Ex. 7.6 is a syntactically acceptable sequence in C major. The tune in Ex. 7.7 is not: it sounds wrong at almost every juncture, even though it stays in the key of C major, and even though it complies with the 3/4 rhythm of the waltz. In the vacuous tune of Ex. 7.6

Ex. 7.6. Syntactically acceptable waltz theme

Ex. 7.7. Syntactically unacceptable waltz theme

each note follows from the preceding with the ease with which words follow in a well-formed sentence. The three rising notes followed by a fall, repeated thrice, with the fall each time slightly greater; the stasis on the dominant before the closing phrase which inverts and diminishes the initial motive: these stock devices engage our expectations in just the way that they are engaged by the rhythm. We can treat each bar as a syntagma, in which substitutions may be made—some of which make sense, others of which do not. For example, we can substitute a falling fourth for the descending phrases in the second, fourth, and sixth bars, as in Ex. 7.8.

The case is unlike language in several ways. For example, the phrase in bar 2 is answered by those in bars 4 and 6: if we substitute a falling fourth in 2 for the original descending scale, we feel a pressure to do the same in 4 and 6. The 'slots' in the melody are, in other words, constantly redefined, depending upon how the first of them is filled. Nothing like this is true of a natural language. Likewise, there is no musical equivalent of 'parts of speech'. In the sentence 'John kicks Mary angrily', the fourth slot is occupied by an adverb, for which other adverbs (but not nouns or verbs) can be substituted without loss of syntax. There is no equivalent in music: no 'adverbial' or 'adjectival' phrase. True, certain places in a melody might be heard as 'up-beats', or 'conclusions'; but the phrases that fill these slots could occur elsewhere with another syntactical force.

Such differences between language and music should not deter us in our search for a musical syntax. That the rules of musical grammar should be quite unlike those which define the grammar of a natural language is precisely what we should expect. What matters is that the rules should exist, and that they should have the same generative character as the rules of syntax. Obviously, a single body of rules will not suffice to generate every kind of music. But simple melodies like Ex. 7.6 can certainly be generated in such a way. Sundberg and Lindblom, for example, have proposed a grammar, which seems to generate themes that are instantly recognized as possible nursery tunes in the style of Alice Tegnér.[8] Some such grammar could be proposed for the acceptable permutations on Ex. 7.6.

Similar considerations apply to harmony. A bass-line for Ex. 7.6 can be derived directly, on the assumption that the tune is heard in C major. The

---

[8] Sundberg and Lindblom, 'Towards a Generative Theory of Melody', *Svensk Tidskrift för Musikforskning*, 52 (1970), 71–88.

Ex. 7.8. Substitutional variant of Ex. 7.6

first and last notes will be the tonic, C; a rise to the dominant at bar 6 will be heard as correct; and according to the rules of part-writing, the bass should move to the dominant by stepwise progression, while an octave drop on the dominant will prepare the way for the concluding tonic. Ex. 7.9 gives the resulting bass-line, and, filling in the harmonies, we arrive at the opening phrase of a vapid but grammatical waltz (Ex. 7.10). Add a consequent phrase to this antecedent, a middle section, a reprise, and a coda, and the thing will stand alone, as a finished piece of music.

The game of substitutions can be extended. The alternative tune (Ex. 7.8) can be substituted for Ex. 7.6 without changing the bass; or another melody entirely (Ex. 7.11) can take the place of the vocal line. Likewise, we can hold the melody constant and alter the harmony, as in Ex. 7.12, in which a chromatic sequence replaces bars 1 to 5, introducing references to other keys. It is even possible, as in Ex. 7.13, to harmonize the original tune so that it sounds in another key—in this case D minor. These substitutions are second nature to the tonal composer, and also to his audience. They are heard as correct or permissible, regardless of whether the result is truly meaningful. It would be a simple exercise to write a little waltz for piano, based on the melodies and harmonies that I have given, in which faultless

Ex. 7.9. Bass-line to Ex. 7.6

Ex. 7.10. Opening phrase of 'grammatical' waltz

Ex. 7.11. Alternative melody for Ex. 7.10

Ex. 7.12. Alternative bass for Ex. 7.10

Ex. 7.13. Ex. 7.6, sounding in another key

syntax is combined with an undemanding vacuousness. It seems to me that many jazz improvisations are of that kind. The distinction between syntax and meaning can be readily grasped, by comparing my waltz with the sequences of piano waltzes composed for the drawing-room by Schubert, illustrated in all their exquisite simplicity in Exx. 7.14 and 7.15. The compositional grammar here is the one that I have used—although without chromatic harmonies. But Schubert's utterance is highly charged, while mine is bland and meaningless.

Ex. 7.14. Schubert, a waltz in A flat, from Op. 9a

Of course, I have not provided a generative grammar for the waltz, nor could I do so. Nevertheless, the familiar facts to which I have referred in constructing the example remind us that the intuitions of right and wrong upon which the musician builds in composing are remarkably like the

Ex. 7.15. Schubert, another waltz in A flat, from Op. 9a (*a*) theme; (*b*) second
episode; (*c*) third episode

intuitions of right and wrong which the linguist tries to explain through a
transformational grammar. To that observation we should add the following:

1. Music—or at any rate tonal music of the kind to which we all
respond—embraces an infinity of utterances. Once someone has begun to
understand tonal music, he finds himself able to understand any number of
pieces that he might never have heard before. This recalls the ability of
language-users to understand and construct indefinitely many new sentences.

2. Although the number of potential musical utterances is infinite, the
'vocabulary' is finite. This fact is more extraordinary than it seems. For the
acoustical realm is not in itself disjoint: between every two pitches, for

example, there is a third. Like the visual realm, the sound world is a many-layered continuum. Painting reproduces this feature, in images that are as continuous as the objects depicted in them. Music, however, does not. The pitch spectrum is divided into discrete tones, and the interesting thing is that we *hear* it in that way. As I argued in Chapter 1, we do not regard the twelve semitones as arbitrarily chosen points on a continuum, but as *categories* of pitch: a tone between C and C sharp is not heard as another tone, but as an out-of-tune version of one of its neighbours. (Only by a great effort are we able to hear the quarter-tone quartets of Hába, for example, as syntactically organized, and this special case merely reminds us of the normal grammar.)

3. Listening to music is clearly a cognitive process, in which we attend to what we hear, and in which every element is connected in our hearing with the whole structure.

4. Our sense of musical syntax is not of a step-by-step substitution of syntactically equivalent components, but of a context-dependent *affinity* between tones. Certain elements belong together, even when separated by intervening material—like the dominant and the tonic chords in a lengthy cadence. Organization in music is *sui generis*, based on variation, imitation, parallels, and the heard distinction between structural and prolonging episodes that was briefly described in Chapter 2.

5. As in other cognitive activities, there is a recognizable 'chunking' of information: we group tones, beats, and harmonies together, and hear them as unitary. This phenomenon, which I explored in Chapter 2, is fundamental to the understanding of music, and resembles the grouping of words into sentences in ordinary speech.

6. We seem to hold a piece of music together in our memory and attention as we listen: as though we were attempting to find the structure from which the whole is derived. This experience, hard to put into words, is fundamental to music: without it, we should be deaf to the formal perfection of Bach or Mozart, in whose music every note seems to be exactly where it should be, held in equilibrium by the surrounding grammar.

7. Many of our musical intuitions suggest a 'generative' explanation. For example, the major triad on C can be heard either as I of C major, as V of F major, as III of A minor, and so on. How it is heard reflects an hypothesis as to how it is *derived*. Or consider again the Debussy example (Ex. 7.1) discussed above. To hear the problematic chord as involving the flattened fifth of D is to attach it to the wrong generative process. We must hear it as involving a tritone, derived from the whole-tone scale: and this experience, while in itself purely musical, is reasonably seen as based in a generative hypothesis. Not that the sensitive listener is consciously *aware* of the derivation, or of the musicologist's preferred way of describing it. The hypothesis forms part of the tacit framework of musical cognition.

Some of those features were noticed by the *Gestalt* psychologists, and it is significant that the development of transformational grammar has given rise to a renewed interest in the theory of the 'good *Gestalt*'. Many cognitive scientists argue that the processing of linguistic information is not, or ought not to be, different in kind from the processing of visual or acoustical information. Maybe a similar process occurs when we hear music: the musical surface is processed according to a transformational grammar, whose rules serve to generate the surface by a finite recursion from some underlying 'deep structure'. If this were so, then many of the seven features that I have referred to would be explained—and explained in the most natural and satisfying way, by showing that they are special cases of a more general phenomenon.

The Generative Theory of Tonal Music

What would a generative theory of music look like? First, it would begin from a characterization of the musical 'intuitions' that need to be explained, which would be the primary evidence for the theory. There are at least five kinds of musical intuition that seem relevant:

1. Intuitions concerning the grouping of musical elements: the horizontal grouping into phrases, melodies, and the like, and the vertical grouping into chords. (See Chapter 2.)

2. Metrical intuitions, against which the experience of grouping plays. Consider the passage from Schumann's fourth Symphony in D minor, Op. 120, in Ex. 7.16. Because the 3/4 beat is only weakly affirmed by the string chords, which begin from a syncopation, we may be tempted to hear the melodic line as sounding in 6/8 time. When this happens we are suddenly jolted into recognition at the end of the phrase, when our mistake becomes apparent. Metrical intuitions, like grouping intuitions, represent choices among rival structures. The effect of Schumann's trio section depends in part upon its rhythmic ambiguity: this is the one moment of limpness in the driving momentum of the symphony. But the ambiguity is heard only if you go on counting three in a bar.

3. Intuitions concerning the melodic line: how it divides into episodes which elaborate, answer, or continue one another. Consider the phrase-structure and period-structure discussed in Chapter 2. Again we can mishear: dividing at the wrong point, not noticing the overlaps, or treating as an accompanying figure what is really a motif—like the three notes that open Brahms's Second Symphony in D major, Op. 73.

4. Intuitions concerning the tension and relaxation of a musical sequence: we hear a tone as pointing towards, or requiring another, a chord as being incomplete or 'unsaturated', a passage as moving towards a conclusion, or requiring resolution. Many of these intuitions suggest that we are always

Ex. 7.16. Schumann, Fourth Symphony in D minor, Op. 120, third movement, trio section

'hearing structurally', building up an account, so to speak, of musical tension, that requires compensation in a final cadence.

5. Intuitions concerning the part–whole relationship: which parts of a piece of music answer to which, which must be taken together as independent episodes, and so on. Under the Stalinist regime it was normal to reverse the last two movements of Tchaikovsky's Sixth Symphony in B minor, Op. 74, so as to bring the work to a triumphal, rather than a despairing, conclusion. But almost all musical listeners found this intolerable. It proved impossible to hear the third movement as an *answer* to the fourth: on the contrary, the third movement displays the false humour of distraction, which plunges the music into the depth of despair, and so summons that final bleak negation.

If we are to make sense of those intuitions, as the linguist makes sense of grammatical intuitions, then we should require a theory that generates just those patterns that sound right to us, and excludes just those patterns that sound wrong. Such a theory would *explain* our musical intuitions: it would therefore be a prime candidate for a theory of musical understanding. It would show not only how we understand music but also what there *is* to be understood. At the same time it would be the first step in a cognitive psychology of music, since the structures that it discerns would serve as a model of the mental operations that we deploy in hearing music, and which enable us to organize a piece of music into an auditory *Gestalt*.

The search for such a generative theory has occupied many recent writers—notably John Sloboda, Fred Lerdahl, and Ray Jackendoff. And the first shot at producing the theory was made in 1983, by Lerdahl and Jackendoff, in their highly influential book, *A Generative Theory of Tonal Music* (a book which more or less coincided with John Sloboda's more empirical *The Musical Mind* (1985)). I shall have cause to return to Lerdahl and Jackendoff's arguments. But it is well to survey them now, in order to assess what a generative theory might have to offer to the philosophy of music.

Lerdahl and Jackendoff are themselves extremely cautious concerning the linguistic analogy. Nevertheless, they believe that the analogy is significant, and that their generative 'syntax' is comparable in many ways to a transformational grammar of a natural language. It is perhaps worth pointing out that no transformational grammar for a natural language has ever been produced; and that there are reasons for thinking that it could be produced only with the aid of theoretical devices that make a radical *distinction* between language and music.[9] Nevertheless, the attempt to provide a grammar of tonal music is of intrinsic interest, whether or not the comparison with language is ultimately sustainable.

Lerdahl and Jackendoff distinguish two kinds of grammatical rule: those which specify when a given complex is *well formed*, and those (the preference rules), which specify the preferred or favoured musical structures: the structures which the listener prefers to hear, and which he strives to hear in the musical surface. (For example, most listeners, hearing triplets in 4/4 time, prefer to hear *two* metrical patterns: 3 *against* 2, rather than a single dotted rhythm.) Lerdahl and Jackendoff emphasize the great importance of these preference rules, the bulk of the rules that they specify for their musical syntax being of this kind: the concept of 'well-formedness', which is the equivalent of syntax in most formal languages, is marginalized by the theory.

Why is this? One reason is that Lerdahl and Jackendoff are seeking for a theory of the 'good *Gestalt*' in music: they even describe their theory as a *Gestalt* theory, concerned to explain the way in which we comprehend musical *wholes*.[10] They argue that the organization of the visual field in perception provides an analogy with musical understanding that is at least as good as the analogy with language. *Gestalt* psychologists, such as Köhler

---

[9] e.g. the near shot offered by Montague ('English as a Formal Language', and 'The Proper Treatment of Quantification in Ordinary English', in *Formal Philosophy*, 188–221 and 247–70 respectively), depends heavily upon a theory of semantic structure, which draws on the semantics of modal logic.

[10] *A Generative Theory of Tonal Music* (Cambridge, Mass., 1983), 304.

and Koffka,[11] argued with some plausibility that the visual field is organized into figure and ground, so as to produce the most 'stable' figuration, and that our preference for stable figures is active in determining how we see the world, even when the world itself is visually unstable. Some cognitive scientists see the organization of visual information in perception as precisely parallel to the organization of information in language: for there is a 'language of thought' which provides the underlying structure of intentionality.[12] Nevertheless, this speculative theory would be worthless, if we could not show exactly how the organization of the visual field is derived, and how it compares with the derivation of syntactic wholes in language. The contrast between depiction and description, touched on in Chapter 5, shows some of the important dissimilarities that must be taken into account: notably, the density of the visual field, and its presentational character. In my view, these dissimilarities make it extremely implausible to suggest that the semantic articulation that we observe in language, can also be observed in visual perception.

But let us return to music. Music is not dense, as pictures are, but disjoint, like language. The good *Gestalt* in music is an order among discrete components rather than a form discovered in a continuous field. This is the critical fact, and the ultimate ground for thinking that music has a syntax. Lerdahl and Jackendoff propose four parallel and mutually rein-forcing structures in tonal music: grouping, metre, the organization of pitches according to their structural importance, and the order of tension and release (the 'breathing in and out of music', as they pertinently describe it). Groupings, rhythms, 'time-span' organization, and tension and release are represented by strict hierarchies, which derive perceivable musical phenomena from underlying structures, in much the way that the word order in a sentence is derived from the deep structure by rules of transformation.

The first step in a transformational grammar of natural language is to represent, by means of 'trees', the derivation of the word order from the underlying syntax, as in the example that I gave earlier: 'That he was angry was evident from the way he frowned.' The tree analysis of this sentence showed which parts of it are subvervient, and which dominant. Lerdahl and Jackendoff construct similar trees to explain which musical elements are heard as subordinate to which.

The analysis proposed by Lerdahl and Jackendoff has the following layers:

1. The grouping structure, which divides the piece into motifs, phrases and sections, derived hierarchically as in a tree diagram;

[11] K. Koffka, *Principles of Gestalt Psychology* (New York, 1935); W. Köhler, *Gestalt Psychology: An Introduction to New Concepts in Modern Psychology* (New York, 1947).

[12] J. A. Fodor, *The Language of Thought* (New York, 1975).

2. The metrical structure, which implants a regular alternation of strong and weak beats at various levels into the grouping structure.

3. The 'time-span reduction', which assigns to the pitches a hierarchy of structural importance;

4. A 'prolongation reduction', which derives the tension and relaxation of the harmonic and melodic elements hierarchically, from an underlying harmonic and melodic structure (the Schenkerian *Ursatz*).[13]

Each structure is described independently, although Lerdahl and Jackendoff regard it as an important result of their theory that the intuitive segmentation of the musical surface derived from the time-span reduction has a tendency to coincide with that derived from the prolongation reduction. Each structure is characterized largely by 'preference' rules: rules which tell us, for example, to prefer as the most important event (the 'head') in a time-span, the event which leads to the more stable metrical order. Having laid down a highly complex set of rules, and tested them against their intuitive hearing of certain well-known tonal examples, the authors go on to suggest that there are musical universals, just as there are linguistic universals, and that the ability to organize musical structures is to a large extent innate—a striking claim, given the absence of any clear reason why musical understanding should have found evolutionary favour. (What benefit has it been to our species, that we should have the power to organize sound on tonal principles? If there is a benefit here, it is to the human soul—that redundant by-product of the evolutionary tragedy.)

However nearly such a theory may coincide with our 'syntactical' intuitions, we should hesitate to call it a theory of musical syntax. First, the rules do not determine any musical surface uniquely, nor could they. This is because preference rules, unlike rules of well-formedness, can conflict. You could imagine rules for resolving conflicts, but those rules too would have to be preference rules, equally liable to be ensnared in conflict. Indeed, one may wonder whether preference rules are really rules at all, or what function they could perform in the explanation of musical structure.

According to Lerdahl and Jackendoff 'it is the task of preference rules to select, out of the possible . . . structures, just those that the listener hears'.[14] There is no implication that anybody—either listener or composer—actually follows such a rule, in the way that you might follow the rule 'Add 4' in writing down an arithmetical series. Consider the following rules, which allegedly govern the perception of rhythm: 'strongly prefer a structure in

[13] Although the contrast between structure and prolongation, as adopted by Lerdahl and Jackendoff, stems from Schenker's controversial theory (which I discuss in Chs. 10 and 13), there is no need for any more explanation, at this juncture, than was given in Chapter 2.

[14] *Generative Theory*, 84.

which cadences are metrically stable'; 'prefer metrical structures in which at each level every other beat is strong'.[15] It is impossible to think of these as rules which one might *obey*: the listener acts in accordance with these rules, but not from them, to borrow Kant's distinction. But what, in that case, is meant by 'strongly prefer'?

Lerdahl and Jackendoff admit that preference rules have no parallel in a natural language—at least, so far as the theory of syntax is concerned. This is partly because the rules of a language do not merely generalize over the behaviour of competent speakers: they are also *obeyed* by competent speakers. They are the 'rules of the game', and the game is information. True, obedience is tacit and automatic, and the rules are not objects of conscious knowledge. Nevertheless, any description of these rules presents them as a set of instructions, which are *followed* by the competent speaker.

The problem of preference rules touches on the nature of Lerdahl and Jackendoff's enterprise, and the aims of a generative theory of syntax as they conceive it. Such a syntactical theory, they assume, forms part of 'cognitive science': it tells us how a piece of music is organized in the brain of the listener, reduced to the operations which generate it, and so comprehended. By showing that each piece can be derived from certain basic musical structures, by the iterated application of a finite number of rules, we offer a model of the cognitive mechanism that is at work, when we spontaneously hear some novel musical gesture as right or wrong. The key assumption is that 'the listener attempts to organise all the pitch-events of a piece into a single coherent structure, such that they are heard in a hierarchy of relative importance' (the 'reduction hypothesis').[16] The reduction of any piece therefore acquires the tree structure familiar from generative theories of syntax, shown in Diagram 7.2.

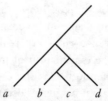

a   *b*   *c*   *d*

Diagram 7.2

Here *d* is a prolongation of *a*, *b* of *d*, and *c* of *b*: the prolongation being subordinate to (leading towards or away from) the principal musical event.

The authors admit that in one sense this tree notation is misleading, 'because linguistic syntactic trees relate grammatical categories, which are absent in music';[17] in music it is the individual events that are (they suppose) hierarchically related. Nevertheless, the hypothesis remains, that

[15] *Generative Theory*, 90.   [16] Ibid. 106.   [17] Ibid. 112.

the surface structure of any acceptable tonal piece can be derived in this rule-governed way. We thereby explain how it is that a listener with finite capacities may be able to recognize and comprehend indefinitely many novel musical episodes. The four 'reductions' can overlap, interact, and enter into conflict. Nevertheless, Lerdahl and Jackendoff claim, a listener comprehends any piece of tonal music by an act of unconscious analysis, so reducing it to a familiar deep structure in finitely many steps. The question for us, is whether a theory of tonal music, conceived in these 'cognitive science' terms, will really show how we understand tonal music.

Suppose that there existed an art form, of long-established usage, which consisted in arranging dots on a screen, so as to make aesthetically interesting patterns. Some of the resulting 'dot-works' are rejected as nonsensical; others appear wrong in detail—a dot out of place, perhaps, or an entire area botched; others still are accepted as correct but vacuous. Significant dot-works are rare; and when they occur they are highly regarded, even if they violate the 'rules of grammar'. In enjoying and judging a dot-work it is the *Gestalt* which is most important—the surface form which is seen in the disposition of dots. However, each *Gestalt* is *composed*: the viewer sees the form as derived in a certain way from the organization of the dots, and his pleasure is enhanced by this. The aspiring artist learns certain rules of thumb, comparable to the rules of musical 'syntax' which guided the little waltz of Ex. 7.10. But these rules relate to the surface order only; they are summaries of successful practice, but can be broken with impunity should the artistic intention require. They certainly give no 'generative syntax' from which all and only acceptable dot-works can be derived.

Such a generative syntax could certainly exist, however. This possibility is a trivial consequence of the fact that the number of dots which compose any given dot-work is always finite. Consider all the acceptable dot-works that have been produced to date. Whatever shapes they present, and however the dots are distributed, there will be a set of rules whose iterated application to some basic structure or structures produces just this class of dot-works— just as there is an algebraic equation which generates any given geometrical curve. Even if we make the requirement that the rules should derive the dot-works from a suitably small set of deep structures, it is still trivially true that, given sufficiently many rules, the derivation will always be possible. And if we allow ourselves the use of 'preference rules' in addition to rules of well-formedness, we can very quickly translate our intuitions concerning the surface forms of the dot-works, into rules for their derivation. But what exactly does this prove?

The dot-works themselves are understood like pointillist paintings: in terms of an organization that is *seen in* the surface. The composition of the surface too is something that is seen in it. You learn to understand dot-works not by grasping rules for producing them, but by comparing the surface forms of successful examples, and by acquiring a feel for shape and composition. Even if this 'feel' can be correlated with a generative grammar, knowledge of the grammar would not tell us *what* we understand when we understand a dot-work, nor would it show why dot-works are important. It would be a curious but ultimately trivial fact that there is such a grammar, a fact which casts no light whatsoever on the meaning of dot-works. There is a complete lack of fit between the order perceived in dot-works, by the one who understands them, and the grammar which is supposed to generate those works, but which is in fact derived from them.

A similar lack of fit occurs between the musical surface as described by Lerdahl and Jackendoff's syntax, and the musical surface as we hear it when we hear with understanding. Each of the four reductions proposed by Lerdahl and Jackendoff offers to explain our experience of sequence: why this sounds right after that, why this leads naturally to that, and so on. And of course, this is an important element in the musical *Gestalt*. However, just as important from the syntactic point of view, and of far greater significance in our experience of musical meaning, is counterpoint. Tonal music in the Western tradition is formed by the confluence of voices, each developing according to its own logic, and yet in harmony with the rest. Consider the simple canon in Ex. 7.17. Theories of harmonic tension, of tonal sequence, or of phrase prolongation may explain why the implied A minor triad at the beginning of bar 3 sounds right. But we explain this fact more readily without their aid. In listening to a canon we register the leading voice and its history; we register the canonical voice beneath it; and as a result we know that the lower voice will land on the A at the beginning of bar 3. (Of course, we may not know this fact under precisely that

Ex. 7.17. A simple canon

description: knowledge here is a matter of musical expectation.) We listen for such contrapuntal patterns, and are pleased by them, as when light chases light across the surface of water.

This difficulty points to another. Consider the 'prolongation reduction', as Lerdahl and Jackendoff describe it, which gives a hierarchical derivation of the 'breathing' of music from a simple cadence, in the manner of Schenker. Here we notice a most important fact: that the relations described require that the listener has already processed the music into intelligible elements. The first of Schubert's 'Suleika' songs begins as in Ex. 7.18. For three bars there is no harmony apart from an ambiguous G major seventh. But the listener is already hearing B minor, so that the eleventh chord on F sharp comes as no surprise. Lerdahl and Jackendoff would parse these three bars as prolonging and subordinate to, and therefore hierarchically derived from, the cadence on to the dominant, which is itself subordinate to the tonic chord that follows, as in Ex. 7.19. That is indeed what musical intuition requires. But *why*? Surely, because the listener has already assigned a key to the unharmonized first bar, where the emphasis on the tonic and dominant of B is heard through the musical movement. We can treat the passage as subordinate to the cadence only because we are already perceiving the temporal *Gestalt*. Those three bars would sound in B minor even if the cadence that followed affirmed the key of D, as in Ex. 7.20. When we hear B minor in those phrases, it is because we hear a movement that is suspended on the frame of B and F sharp. Hearing that movement involves recognizing the parallel between the three phrases of the first measure, and sensing the force that is passed through them so as to arrive on G and B simultaneously. These basic experiences—recognizing parallels, movement,

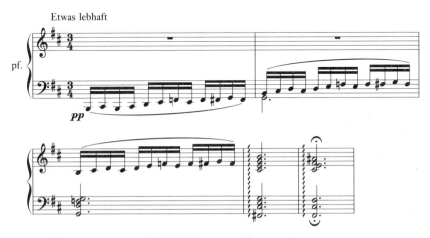

Ex. 7.18. Schubert, 'Suleika I', D720, opening

Ex. 7.19. Prolongation tree for Ex. 7.18

Ex. 7.20. Schubert 'Suleika I', cadencing in D

and force—are not explained by the hierarchical theory of the piece's structure, but assumed by it. Yet it is *they* which govern our sense of the important events in the piece.

Lerdahl and Jackendoff admit that they can provide no theory of musical parallelism, and rightly compare the recognition of parallels to the recognition of a face by its expression.[18] But this creates the greatest difficulty for their theory. First, the recognition of expression (in a face, for example) is a paradigm of *Gestalt* perception. A prior conception of the musical *Gestalt* is therefore required before the generative theory of prolongation can get off the ground. Secondly 'sameness of expression' is, as we have seen, irreducible to any rule, and not amenable, therefore, to syntactical or quasi-syntactical treatment. There is something primitive in our ability to recognize the second phrase in the Schubert as 'the same again', or to hear

[18] *Generative Theory*, 287.

the parallel—so important to the effect of this song—between the two phrases in Ex. 7.21.

Ex. 7.21. Schubert, 'Suleika I'; (*a*) mid-stream (Etwas lebhaft); (*b*) concluding phrase (Etwas langsamer)

There is another way of bringing the point home. Lerdahl and Jackendoff rightly draw our attention to musical grouping, and assimilate this phenomenon to other instances of *Gestalt* perception. But they do not mention the key component of the grouping phenomenon. Our intuitions about grouping are subordinate to an experience of movement—of phrases beginning, moving on, and coming to an end—and to an experience of the phenomenal space in which this movement spreads before us. Metrical experiences too are subordinate to this experience of movement, which has a primitive character, like the experience of parallels.

To notice the movement in music, you must perceive the notes not merely as organized into groups, but as moving; and that means perceiving the music under an irreducible metaphor (see Chapter 2). A generative theory of grouping is necessarily blind to this fact: it can, perhaps, explain the grouping; but it cannot explain the metaphor—nor the fact that *this* is how the music is heard. The crucial component in our understanding of music will therefore not be touched by the theory. But since it is the component from which our more important musical intuitions derive, it is unlikely that the theory will explain our intuitions.

Syntax and Semantics

The reader of Lerdahl and Jackendoff will be struck by the number, variety, and *ad hoc* character of their transformation rules; he will also notice that, apart from a perfunctory adoption of Schenker's suggestion (which I discuss in Chapter 12) that tonal pieces derive, or should derive, from a tiny class of background structures or *Ursätze*, there is no real attempt to explain the 'deep structure' of tonal music. Just what might such a structure be, and why should the musical surface derive from it?

Here we enter a controversial area, where philosophers, logicians, and linguists often vehemently disagree, and where I can do no more than take a speculative stand. It seems to me that we can obtain a coherent conception of deep structure in a natural language, only if we think of such a structure as semantically grounded—that is, tied to a semantic interpretation. Although linguists make a distinction between syntax and semantics, it is not clear that the distinction can really be made at the deeper level. Our syntactic intuitions, which tell us that 'John thinks that Mary' is ill-formed, are dependent on our semantic intuitions. We know, for example, that 'John' and 'Mary' are names of people, and that 'thinks that' denotes the relation between a person and a proposition. This is what makes the sentence so incongruous. (Cf. 'fish eat three ideas', discussed above.) Although we can, in formal languages, state rules for well-formedness without venturing into a semantic interpretation, this is a result of the artificiality of the system. And even in a formal language, the syntax is always modelled on an implicit interpretation, a recognition that these signs will at some stage acquire a meaning. It would be of no interest to us that $(x)(Fx \supset . Fx \lor Gx)$ is a well-formed formula of the predicate calculus, if it were not thereby marked out as a candidate for interpretation, a sentence which, under some possible assignment of semantic values, might be true or false. In natural languages, we discover both syntax and semantics after the event, so to speak, and discover them together. There is no way in which we could begin to build a theory of English syntax which did not depend upon intuitions about the meaning of English words. We simply would not know what we are doing, in tracing surface structure back to deep structure, if we did not see the generative process as an instrument for *meaning* things—a device for expressing indefinitely many thoughts by means of a finite number of symbols.

Indeed, plausible theories of language rely upon semantic assumptions from the beginning, explaining the structure of English sentences in terms of a theory of truth, or a model theory, for English.[19] This suggests that music could be described in syntactic terms only if we could also propose a musical semantics. The weakness of the semiological approach lay in its inability to combine syntax and semantics into a unitary theory. Music has a quasi-syntactic structure; it also has a kind of meaning. But unless the first articulates the second, and is interpreted in terms of it, there is no reason to believe that the structure is genuinely syntactical, or that *structure* is the vehicle of meaning. The same goes for the generative grammar proposed by Lerdahl and Jackendoff.

It is one of Frege's great insights, that the semantic structure of a sentence must show how its meaning is generated from the meaning of its parts.[20] The meaning of any term, he argued, consists in its systematic

[19] Montague, cited in n. 9, above.

[20] See esp. 'On Sense and Reference', in M. Black and P. T. Geach (eds.), *Translations from the Philosophical Writings of Gottlob Frege* (2nd edn., Oxford, 1960), 56–78.

contribution to the meaning of the sentences that contain it. This is why we can understand indefinitely many sentences that we have never previously encountered. Although the truth-theory of Tarski, and the model theory of Kripke and Montague, make use of contrasting theoretical devices,[21] they both respect this original insight, as must every theory of language that has the remotest chance of explaining how we understand it. The first question to ask about music, therefore, is whether there could be a musical semantics which had this generative character: a semantics which showed how the meaning of musical complexes could be derived from the meaning of their parts?

A Curious Theory of the Ineffable

Not all philosophers have been as critical of Lerdahl and Jackendoff as I have been. Indeed there is one philosopher—Diana Raffman[22]—who not only accepts the theory (at least in outline) as providing a genuine account of musical understanding, but also uses it to propose an ingenious explanation of the 'ineffability' of musical meaning—of the fact that the meaning of music always and inevitably eludes our attempts to express it in words.

The explanation, in its bare essentials, is this: the quasi-syntactical structure of music, as unravelled by Lerdahl and Jackendoff, 'misleads us into semantic temptation'. We are led unconsciously but inevitably to postulate the existence of a semantic interpretation of the musical syntax. Our experience of understanding creates in us the sense that the music is 'about' something, while at the same time there is no possibility that this should be so. Our semantic instincts are aroused by the music and also baffled by it, so that we are led to hear meaning precisely where meaning cannot be heard. In fact, however, the meaning of music consists merely in the 'feelings that result . . . from the experienced listener's unconscious recovery of structures constitutive of the work',[23] even though these structures can be assigned no semantic value. So *does* music have a meaning? Raffman is nonchalant:

> do the musical feelings constitute a quasi-semantics? I leave it to the reader to decide. If you require of any semantics, quasi or otherwise, that it specify truth conditions for well-formed strings, or that its values be established by convention, or that it be explicitly represented in the grammar of the language, then you will be inclined to answer in the negative. If on the other hand you are impressed by the fact that the musical feelings result in systematic ways from grammar-driven operations defined over representations of acoustic stimuli, are clearly distinguishable from those operations and the representations operated upon, are creative in Chomsky's sense, sustain robust notions of correctness and error . . . underwrite the

---

[21] See n. 7, above.   [22] *Language, Music and Mind.*   [23] Ibid. 53.

beginnings of a plausible theory of musical communication, and play the explanatory and guiding roles characteristic of meaning in the natural language, then you may well answer in the affirmative. If 'independent' musical meaning exists at all, these feelings lie at the heart of it.[24]

Should she be so nonchalant? Surely not, if it is true, as I have suggested, that transformational grammar requires a semantic interpretation, and if deep structure must be specified in semantic terms. A theory which assigns deep structure to music, while at the same time cancelling the possibility of a semantic interpretation, fails to identify a purpose in listening. Why should we be interested in recuperating from every piece of tonal music an underlying structure to which no interpretation could be assigned? To say that there are 'feelings' involved in this process of recuperation, and that *these* are the meaning of music is to make an empty claim. You might just as well say that there are 'feelings' involved in attending to the musical surface, and *these* are the meaning of music—for how would you specify those feelings, except as the feelings we have when listening to music?

But suppose Lerdahl and Jackendoff are right in proposing a transformational grammar for tonal music, and Raffman right in suggesting that our musical feelings derive from the mental representation of this grammar. Would her explanation of musical ineffability, as arising from the bafflement of semantic expectations, be persuasive? I think not, and this for two reasons. First, the sense of an ineffable meaning is a rare phenomenon, in comparison to the abundance of tonal music. Unlike Schenker, who set out to provide a theory of tonal masterpieces, Lerdahl and Jackendoff propose a grammar to which even the most empty exercise in tonality will conform. The listener to Bach's Double Violin Concerto, to Beethoven's late quartets, or to Bruckner's Ninth Symphony, will certainly be granted an experience of a meaning 'too deep for words'. If Raffman is right, however, the same experience should attend the hearing of 'Yankee Doodle' and 'Three Blind Mice'.

Secondly, the experience of 'ineffability' may occur, even when our search for a semantic interpretation is rewarded. Take any powerful poem, and ask yourself what it means. What for example is meant by 'Tyger, tyger, burning bright'? Of course, you can translate it into other words, give truth-conditions for its component sentences, assign a semantic value to every word. But in doing so you miss the ineffable meaning that attaches to just *these* words, in just this arrangement. This ineffability is a mark of the aesthetic experience, in all its higher forms. Since expressive poetry usually has semantic structure, and in no way baffles our semantic desires, it follows that ineffability must have some other explanation than the one offered by Raffman.

[24] *Language, Music and Mind*, 55–6.

The comparison with poetry and poetic meaning returns us to the question of whether preference rules can really provide a theory of syntax. Lerdahl and Jackendoff, as we have seen, remark that there is no parallel to such rules in the generative syntax of a natural language. But this is in fact misleading. For although the syntax of natural language is a matter of well-formedness, there is an order in language which parallels that which Lerdahl and Jackendoff are trying to explain in music—the order of *style*. And if there were rules of style in any meaningful sense, they would largely consist of preference rules. A generative syntax would explain why both of the following are acceptable in English:

1. Mary phoned the man she had been talking to up.
2. Mary phoned up the man to whom she had been talking.

But it would not necessarily explain why (2) sounds better. Still less would it explain why

3. 'What of soul was left, I wonder, when the kissing had to stop?'

is preferred to

4. 'I wonder what remained of soul, when the kissing had to come to an end?'

The preference for (2) over (1) can perhaps be accounted for by rules; but surely not that for (3) over (4). Although Lerdahl and Jackendoff at one point compare their grammar to the rules of prosody (a revealing comparison),[25] it is not true that prosody can really capture the finer points of style. According to those rules

5. 'What of soul remained, I wonder, when the kissing had to stop?'

would be equivalent to (3). But Browning's line is still to be preferred—it sounds exactly *right* on the lips of the imagined speaker, while (5) sounds just slightly wrong.

With such examples we are clearly in the same region as we are with the rules of composition—rules which tell us to avoid parallel fifths, to move stepwise in the bass, to resolve a Neapolitan sixth on to the dominant seventh, and so on. These are rules of thumb, which guide without determining our actions; and they point towards those finer details in which the meaning of a work (its meaning as a work of art) resides. In approaching this kind of meaning, however, we are precisely leaving ordinary syntax and semantics behind—whether in poetry or in music. And such rules as remain to guide us have nothing to do with the rules of grammar.

---

[25] *Generative Theory*, 315 ff.

Rules in Music

There are many lessons to be drawn from the attempt to give a musical syntax. In particular, it has reminded us of the status of musical rules, and warned us against taking too simple a view of how these rules shape our musical practice. In what follows we should bear the following points in mind:

1. The order that we hear in music may be likened to syntax, but it is not truly syntactical. Although it resembles the order that we know as style, it is less individual than that implies—the tradition of tonal music contains something that is shared, trustworthy, established, and it is this strange thing that reminds us so vividly of a natural language.

2. There are rules in music, but they are not usually prescriptive. Most of them are derived *post facto*, like the laws of classical harmony. They are generalizations from a musical tradition, rather than rules of grammar.

3. There are no 'parts of speech' in music: no syntactic elements which play a single specifiable role in forming the musical *Gestalt*. The contribution made by any one element will be affected by the presence of the others. In music, as in language, it is only in the whole context of the utterance that any element has meaning. (Frege's 'context principle'.)[26] But in music, unlike language, the contribution is not and cannot be constant.

4. In language, speaker and hearer have the same competence, and the rules used by the speaker to form his utterance are also deployed by the hearer in comprehending it. While the composer must have the hearer's competence, he must also have much more than this if his music is to be meaningful. Even if there were a 'generative grammar' of tonal music, it would not tell us how tonal music is composed.

5. Rule-governed music is, in general, uninteresting. Even in the most grammatical utterance of a Haydn or Mozart, it is the unexpected nuance that counts—the detail which seems inevitable only in retrospect.

Musical Semantics

Where does this leave the question of musical meaning? The least that can be said, is that the linguistic analogy is more metaphor than simile. We certainly cannot use it to found a theory of musical understanding.

Nevertheless, as we have seen, the analogy is not entirely empty, and the concept of musical 'syntax' is not entirely without a use. The real question is whether we can find any equivalent to the passage from syntax to semantics. If the linguistic analogy is to be of any help to us, it should

---

[26] As it is called by Dummet, in *Frege: Philosophy of Language*, and C. Wright, *Frege's Conception of Numbers as Objects* (Aberdeen, 1983).

enable us to move from the vague premiss that music is meaningful, to a more concrete sense of *how* and *what* music means.

Now in language meaning is developed structurally: the meaning of any complex sign is a function of the meaning of its parts. A semantic theory shows exactly how to derive the meaning of complex signs from the meaning of their components—as we derive the truth-conditions of a sentence in a formal language from the references of its individual terms. We could use the linguistic analogy to cast light on the meaning of music, therefore, only if we could also think of music in the same structural terms—in other words, only if we could envisage the meaning of any piece of music as in some way *composed* from the meanings of its elements. We should need some musical equivalent of a *vocabulary*—phrases, harmonies, progressions, and so on with a fixed and repeatable significance, whose contribution to the meaning of any musical whole is, if not exactly rule-governed, at least regular and predictable. We should then be as close to the idea of a musical semantics as we have come to that of a musical syntax.

If Deryck Cooke's *The Language of Music* is worth reading, it is not only because of the brilliant critical insights—entirely characteristic of this writer—which it contains. It is also because it explores the meaning of music in the only way that takes the analogy with language seriously—by attempting to find the musical equivalent of a vocabulary. As we should expect from the preceding argument, the attempt is a failure. But it is an interesting failure, which will help us towards a better attempt.

Cooke proceeds by analysing certain recurrent elements in classical tonal music, and showing, through well-chosen examples, that the elements have been used to similar effect by different composers. For example, the ascending major scale, from tonic to dominant, expresses an outgoing, assertive emotion—an emotion of joy, as in the passages from Handel's *Israel in Egypt*, Beethoven's *Missa Solemnis*, and Stravinsky's *Oedipus Rex* (the one moment of joy in an otherwise gloomy oratorio) quoted in Ex. 7.22. Those are just three of more than twenty examples. It is instructive to read Cooke's explanation of their expressive power:

> We have postulated that to rise in pitch is to express an out-going emotion; we know that, purely technically speaking, the tonic is the point of repose, from which one sets out, and to which one returns; that the dominant is the note of intermediacy, towards which one sets out, and from which one returns; and we have established that the major third is the note which 'looks on the bright side of things', the note of pleasure, of joy. All of which would suggest that to rise from the tonic to the dominant through the major third . . . is to express an outgoing, active, assertive emotion of joy. Composers have in fact persistently used the phrase for this very purpose.[27]

[27] *The Language of Music* (Oxford, 1959), 115.

Ex. 7.22. Quotations of composers by Deryck Cooke: (*a*) Handel; (*b*) Beethoven; (*c*) Stravinsky

Cooke's interest is aroused primarily by word-settings, since these seem to him to settle unambiguously the question of what the music *ought* to mean. And if the setting is successful, it really does mean what it ought. Cooke's examples are therefore of striking and powerful works, in which a verbal message is conveyed with maximum musical force. This might lead the reader to be sceptical of the claim that Cooke has isolated a genuine vocabulary: a set of phrases and gestures which have a standard meaning for those who are competent to deploy them, regardless of any accompanying text.

It may be appropriate here to recount the experience of an amateur composer, faced with the desire to express a serious emotion, and possessing only those resources which the love of music had bestowed. A friend had been struck down with a rare illness which left her with little chance of recovery. She had been placed in isolation in St Thomas's hospital, in a brightly illuminated room above the busy Thames. Visiting her there, and listening to her conversation as I looked out over the sunlit river, I recalled Lorca's 'Despedida': 'Si muero, dejad el balcón abierto' ('if I die, leave the balcony open'). When, a few days later, I learned of her death, I felt an urge to set the poem to music. The opening melody is given in Ex. 7.23. I wrote it down, and the rest of the song followed quickly and logically. Later I recalled Dido's aria from Berlioz's *Les Troyens*: 'Je vais mourir', with its descending minor triad. I returned to Deryck Cooke, and sure enough discovered that the descending minor triad is featured in his vocabulary as 'meaning' a 'passive sorrow', and seems to be associated in many of his examples with the recognition and acceptance of impending death. The major second that follows in 'Despedida' does indeed 'look on the bright side of things'—on the beauty that survives and justifies. And the parallel tenths which are introduced at this juncture—these, too, surely form a standard item of the tonal language. They do not occur in Cooke's lexicon,

Ex. 7.23. R. Scruton, *Three Lorca Songs*, 'Despedida'

but surely it would not be hard, for someone with Cooke's tenacity and knowledge, to find a host of instances of this figure, associated as here with the feeling of tender regret. Indeed, one such instance comes immediately to mind—'Ruckblick' from *Winterreise*, Ex. 7.24.

But what does this prove? I happen to be attached to 'Despedida', although I make no claims for it as a work of art. Certainly, if it has any meaning, it is not because it uses Cooke's 'vocabulary': on the contrary, this may be precisely what is wrong with it. (I was not cheered but disturbed to discover the wealth of precedents: they seemed to cast doubt on the idea that

Ex. 7.24. Schubert, *Winterreise* D911, 'Ruckblick'

I had really *meant* something by this memorial. Maybe the piece is no more than a patchwork of musical clichés.) At the same time, it is indeed curious that precisely *these* phrases and devices came spontaneously to mind, as I looked for the notes that would convey the mood of Lorca's poem.

It is easy enough to refute the claim that the existence of this tonal 'vocabulary' proves music to have semantic structure. First, the meaning assigned to a given musical element is assigned not by convention, but by perception. Cooke believes that there is something inherent in musical perception which leads us to hear the falling minor triad, or the rising phrase from tonic to dominant as we do. He is not suggesting that some rival semantic rule could be devised, that would endow these phrases with another meaning. This is, of course, wholly unlike natural language, in which the connection between a word and its meaning is conventional.

Secondly, as I noted earlier, the constancy of meaning that Cooke discerns is tested against examples, all of which have accompanying texts. A sceptic might reasonably suggest that this is cheating: that the meaning of the musical elements should be apparent to us, without the words that suggest it. Furthermore, Cooke presents always the *confirming* instances for each hypothesis, and does not look for a counter-example.

Finally, the meaning of each element is located in its expression. Cooke marks out a unified semantic domain for music—the human emotions—and every element of the musical vocabulary acquires its reference from that domain. This has serious consequences for the resulting theory. First, the vocabulary exhibits no functional differentiation: there are no 'parts of speech', and therefore no clear procedures for deriving a semantic interpretation of a whole phrase or movement from the interpretation of its parts. Although, in a blind *tour de force*, Cooke attempts such an interpretation of the first movement of Mozart's fortieth Symphony,[28] the only procedure that he can follow is that of succession: the music means *first* this, and *then* that. Its meaning does not derive from the meanings of its parts: there is simply an accumulation of meaning, without articulate structure. The music is analysed as *following* the evolution of a feeling; not as describing it. Secondly, expressive meaning is maximally context-dependent, and irreducible to rules. This implies that constancy of meaning cannot really be assumed, and that the process of accumulation changes unpredictably the significance of each 'syntactical' part. Who would say that

---

[28] *Language of Music*, 232–52. Interestingly, Coker (*Meaning of Music*), who develops a theory similar to Cooke's, although heavily influenced by Morris's theory of the 'iconic sign', recognizes the need for musical parts of speech other than predicates—including the logical particles such as 'if', 'not', 'and', and 'or'. But these too he explains in terms of feelings—the feeling of disjunction, etc.—so reiterating a mistake which was decisively ridiculed by Frege and Russell.

the move from the minor sixth to the dominant in the minor key means the *same* in Alberich's lament, and in Mozart's Fortieth Symphony, K. 550 (Ex. 7.25)? This process of unpredictable feedback destroys the hypothesis of semantic structure, by destroying the possibility of a rule-guided derivation of the meaning of a piece from the meaning of its parts.

But those objections are, in a way, too obvious. Once we have recognized that the idea of musical syntax is at best a kind of metaphor, we are bound to conclude that the hypothesis of semantic structure in music, presented as a literal truth, is unsustainable. The fact remains that phrases, chords, progressions, and harmonic devices seem to acquire a 'constancy' of meaning in the tonal tradition which we can hardly dismiss as an accident.

The case should be compared with poetry, which *does* have syntactic and semantic structure. The words of a poem gain their meaning by convention, and are bound by rules which enable them to make systematic contributions to the meaning of sentences in which they occur. But the semantic structure is merely the foundation on which the true significance of a poem is built. The expressive properties of the poem come to it by another route: not by convention, but by our culturally influenced disposition to hear, in the words of a poem, the emotion of an imaginary speaker. The weight of a word in poetry can be compared to the weight of a phrase in music: it is the meaning that the word contains, over and above its semantic (rule-governed) content. And here too we find regularities, a certain constancy of choice among sounds, syllables and syntax, according to social and emotional connotations. Of course, the way a word sounds to the educated ear is influenced by its sense; the 'matching' of sound to sense is therefore not the straightforward thing that we observe in music. To the English speaker the word 'lapping' captures in its sound the very thing that it refers to; but so does 'clapotis' to the speaker of French. The universality of the musical 'vocabulary' cannot, therefore, be reproduced in poetry. Nevertheless, there is a process of adjustment between what is heard and what is meant which is common to the two arts; and it is this process which leads to the gradual emergence of the musical vocabulary discussed by Cooke, just as it generates a repertoire

We - he! ach, We - he! O Schmerz! O Schmerz!

Ex. 7.25. (*a*) Wagner, *Rheingold*, scene 1; (*b*) Mozart, Fortieth Symphony, K. 550, opening

of poetic idioms and effects, which are drawn on and added to by poets, although always warily, since what has been many times done may precisely *lose* its meaning by dint of repetition. (No poet since Valéry could repeat the words 'la mer'; no poet since Poe could use the word 'nevermore' unless in inverted commas, and no poet now could write 'thou' or ''twas' or 'poesy'.)

Cooke's primary sources are word-settings and music-dramas: contexts which define a meaning to which the music must fit. When composing 'Despedida' I was motivated by a text, and trying to find the phrases that would be most appropriate to it. This 'matching' of words to music is like the matching of clothes to an occasion—to a state ceremony, a private cele-bration, a wedding or a funeral. Although motivated by feeling, my aim was not to transcribe emotion into music, but to find musical forms that would *match* that emotion, by matching the text that matches it. The crucial relation here is not expression but appropriateness. It is through the constant search for the appropriate gesture that aesthetic conventions emerge. The musical vocabulary discerned by Cooke is the outcome of a long tradition of 'making and matching'; and his 'rules of meaning' are really habits of taste.

Goodman

Before leaving the comparison with language we must briefly return to the general science of signs. All that has been proved so far is that music has neither syntactic nor semantic *structure*: but are there not symbol systems without semantic structure? Are there not symbols which present their subject-matter directly, and without the kind of semantic 'composition' that is displayed by a sentence or a well-formed formula?

This brings us to an intriguing byway in aesthetics, associated with the name of Nelson Goodman, though present too in the writings of Suzanne Langer, and deriving ultimately from the theory of the 'iconic sign' given by Peirce and colonized by Charles Morris.[29] The intention is to formulate a concept of symbolism that will allow us to speak of music (and other art forms) as *signs*, while denying that they *describe* what they signify, as language does. As I pointed out in Chapter 6, Croce's contrast between representa-tion and expression went with a parallel distinction (derived and doctored from Kant) between concept and intuition. Representation, according to Croce, is conceptual—it describes a content in generalizing terms, by deploying con-cepts. Representation, therefore, can be translated from work to work and medium to medium. Expression, by contrast, is untranslatable; for its content is an *intuition*, something which is inherently particular, and which must be

---

[29] Peirce, *Selected Writings*; and Morris, *Foundations*. Langer, *Philosophy in a New Key* and *Feeling and Form*; Nelson Goodman, *Languages of Art*.

conveyed in its particularity if it is to be conveyed at all. Hence we arrive at the 'untranslatable sign', whose meaning, nevertheless, is not identical with itself.

In similar manner, Suzanne Langer has argued that art is a system of 'presentational' rather than discursive symbols.[30] The artistic symbol *presents* an object (usually an emotion) for our attention, but does not describe it. This is supposed to offer some explanation of why the thing presented is inseparable from the mode of presentation: it would be separable only if *described*, so permitting the translation into a conceptual equivalent. Such explanations of 'ineffability' are generalizable across the many art forms, and therefore are not vulnerable to the objection I raised earlier, against Diana Raffman.

The latest venturer down this path, Nelson Goodman, goes armed with a nominalist theory of meaning. Symbolism, for Goodman, means labelling: and the ultimate ground of the labelling relation is human practice. Works of art symbolize by 'referring', and reference has two important species: denotation (in which a label attaches to a particular), and predication (in which a label attaches to indefinitely many particulars). He defines exemplification as the case in which a predicate attaches to something which also refers to the predicate: as in a tailor's swatch, which is both an instance of a pattern, and also refers to that pattern. Expression in art is the special case of exemplification in which the predicate referred to applies only *metaphorically* to the thing that refers to it. For example, a piece of music expresses sadness, by referring to the predicate *sad*, which it also metaphorically possesses.

I say that this is a venture down the old Crocean path, for the reason that it is an elaborate attempt to claim the status of a semantic theory, while removing everything that could make such a theory useful to us. We are told that a work of music stands in a semantic relation to that which it expresses. But there is no implication that the work has semantic structure, as language has; no implication that it is related to its meaning by convention or rules; no implication that we can retrieve the meaning by understanding anything less than the unique work that presents it; no implication that we can put the meaning into words. Nor is it clear that Goodman's approach will pass the tests for a theory of expression that I enumerated in Chapter 6; or that it provides us with anything more than a novel vocabulary for describing the age-old problem, of the inseparability of form and content.

For those and other reasons, I propose to ignore this byway, from which so few return with any clear achievements. There is no reason to forbid a thinker like Goodman from using the term 'reference' as he does. But there is every reason to deny that this word is forced on us, and to deny that a theory of Goodman's 'reference' will be a theory of what we understand, when we understand the expressive content of music.

[30] *Philosophy in a New Key.*

The Analogy Reviewed

What then remains of the analogy with language? The argument of this chapter can be summarized in the following points:

1. Music has structure of a kind. But it is not a syntactic structure.
2. A generative theory of musical structure will not deliver an account of musical understanding.
3. There is no semantic structure in music.
4. Rules in music are not usually conventions, but *post facto* generalizations from a tradition of musical practice.
5. Musical meaning is a matter of expression, and therefore maximally context-dependent.
6. Regularities in expressive meaning arise through a process of making and matching, in which we try to fit artistic gestures to the surrounding context.
7. There are therefore no rules which guarantee expression, even if a background of rule-guidedness may be necessary for the highest expressive effects. Rules have a different role from the grammatical rules of language. If you rewrite the rules (as Stravinsky rewrote the rules of classical music), then you change *the possibilities of expression*.

All those observations tend in a single direction: that the meaning of a piece of music is given not by convention, but by perception. And it is understood only by the person who hears the music correctly—the person whose aesthetic experience comprehends the 'experience of meaning'. This thought brings us to the most difficult of all the topics that we must review: the topic of aesthetic experience.

8 *Understanding*

Understanding music is in part a *cognitive* activity: an activity of mental organization, which collects sounds together and registers them as tones, arranged in a tonal order. That is why the linguistic analogy is so appealing. If we could provide a generative grammar for the musical process, then we should be able to explain the observed human capacity to feel at home with indefinitely many musical experiences, to 'process' even the most unfamiliar sounds and to derive from them the peculiar satisfaction that is so familiar to us, and also so hard to explain. However, the hypothesis remains no more than a formalization of our intuitions, and fails to account for them.

It seems, too, that we cannot attribute representational properties to music. Although musical understanding involves the perception of imaginary movement, it is a movement in which nothing moves. Understanding music requires no recuperation of a fictional world, and no response to imaginary objects. If, nevertheless, we speak of a 'content' in music, this is a matter of 'expression', a concept introduced, but by no means defined, in Chapter 6. We could never explain musical understanding in terms of the expressive content of music, for the very reason that we need a theory of musical understanding before we could begin to see what 'expression', in such a context, means. Moreover, the meaning of music lies *within* it; it can be recovered only through an act of *musical* understanding, and not by an 'assignment of values', of the kind provided by a semantic theory.

Hearing and Playing

We can, however, draw on a number of intuitions, which have been endorsed by our discussion. First, understanding is connected with hearing and with playing. You can hear with understanding; and you can also play with it. These are two ways of manifesting a single capacity. Some people can talk about their musical understanding—presenting complex musicological analyses and critical judgements. (Though what makes a description of a piece of music into an *analysis* is a difficult question, to which I return in Chapter 13.) The ability to think in this way *about* the music is not necessary for understanding it; nor is it sufficient. The expert musicologist may show, through his playing or listening, that he does not understand what he hears, despite his skilled descriptions. The decisive fact is the experience itself. We say that a player can 'play with understanding' because his performance expresses a *way of hearing* what he plays. The performance communicates this way of hearing from performer to listener. (That is why machines, which do not hear music, cannot really play it.)

Ex. 8.1. Ernst Křenek, Eight Piano Pieces, No. 8, Scherzo: (*a*) beginning; (*b*) ending

A composer may put a piece together according to some elaborate intellectual system; but it does not follow that we could *hear* the piece as the system suggests. Consider the little Scherzo by Ernst Křenek (Ex. 8.1). This piece of serial music is organized in a peculiar way: the lower part is the upper part, transposed through three octaves and played in retrograde. But there is no way in which this property of the music can be *heard* in it. You can hear *that* the lower part is the upper part in reverse—in the sense that you can (with considerable effort) recuperate this piece of information from hearing the music—or at least guess that this is what is going on. But you cannot *hear the reversal*, as you hear the theme of the 'Jupiter' Symphony, K. 551, last movement (Ex. 8.2), suddenly reverse itself, or as you hear the imitations, mirrorings, and so on in the 'Goldberg' Variations, BWV988 or the *Art of Fugue*, BWV1080 (Ex. 8.3). It is reasonable to suggest, therefore, that the intellectual understanding of the structure of Křenek's Scherzo is not sufficient to provide an understanding of the piece as music. Perhaps this intellectual understanding is not necessary either: in which case we may begin to wonder whether it is relevant at all.

Ex. 8.2. Mozart, Forty-First 'Jupiter' Symphony, K. 551, finale

Ex. 8.3. Bach, 'Goldberg' Variations, canon at the fifth

Indeed, there is a general question about the relevance of such permutational structures in music. For instance, we know that the music accompanying the film sequence in Berg's *Lulu* runs forwards for two minutes, and then reverses itself, running back to its starting-point. Only at the apex, so to speak, do we hear this happening (Ex. 8.4). After that we soon become indifferent to the intellectual device, precisely because we can no longer hear it. We may wonder why the composer chose to organize the piece in this way: after all, every note in the second half is dictated by the first—*regardless of the way it sounds*. The intellectual rigour seems to imply a musical arbitrariness. If we hear the result as music, this may be despite the structure, and not because of it. (The difficulty here is partly a result of the atonal idiom, which makes it so hard to hear long-range harmonic progressions. Tonal instances of palindromic music—for example Guillaume Machaut's 'Mon fin est mon commencement'—can often be *heard* as palindromic.)

Such examples point to interesting questions about the concept of hearing, and some conclusions immediately suggest themselves. First there is a distinction between the content of a perception, and the conclusions that we draw from it. It is one thing to deduce, from hearing, that a certain event is occurring in the world of sound; it is another to *hear* the event. There is also a distinction between the event that is heard, and the *description under which* we hear it. I may hear the return to the tonic key, but not under that description—even though that is the correct description of what I hear. One of the most vexed questions in music criticism, is the question of 'match' between the content of hearing (the 'description under which') and the musical analysis of the object. Even though I do not hear the return to the tonic *as a return to the tonic* (maybe I lack the concept of a tonic), there is a sense in which the description correctly identifies the content of my perception: it is a description of the intentional object of hearing, and not merely of the material object (the acoustical event) in which it is heard. By contrast, an acoustical description of a musical event—in terms of frequencies and overtones—may completely specify the material object, without describing what we hear, when we hear the event as music. For example, middle C on the clarinet can be analysed in terms of pitch, and the relative prominence of overtones. But that is not a description of what we hear, when we hear the sound of the *clarinet*. The overtone analysis explains what we hear, without describing it.

Furthermore, we must distinguish *intellectual* from *musical* expectations. Theory, analysis, or acoustical information may lead me to expect a certain note or harmony: but such an expectation is not in itself a musical expectation. Consider the Webern Variations, Op. 27. The first three bars use up all of the twelve tones except G sharp (Ex. 8.5). Someone with an acute ear and a knowledge of Webern's serial technique, may hear that this has happened, and, as a result, expect to hear G sharp as the next tone. But this is

Ex. 8.4. (*opposite*) Berg, *Lulu*, film music, point of reversal

Ex. 8.5. Webern, Variations for piano, Op. 27

not yet a *musical* expectation. This G sharp may still sound arbitrary, or even nonsensical; expecting its appearance on *these* grounds has nothing in common with our expectation of the C that follows the B in the last bar of the *St Matthew Passion*, BWV244 (Ex. 8.6). In a well-formed tonal melody

Ex. 8.6. Bach, *St Matthew Passion*, BWV224, concluding phrase

the notes seem to follow of their own accord, so that if you stop at any point before the end, you leave a musical expectation hanging. This experience is of vital importance when it comes to elaborating a theme or creating transitions. Consider the bars which precede the final recapitulation of the theme, in Beethoven's 'Ode to Joy' (Ex. 8.7). Each incomplete phrase has a valency, and summons its completion. We may not know what this completion will be—we may even be surprised by it. But we know that it must sound *right*, and sound right as a response to what preceded it.

This is one reason for thinking that, if there are rules of musical organization, they will be a posteriori, derived from a tradition of musical practice, like the rules of harmony. A priori rules, or conventions, may have a function in the work of this or that composer—as they manifestly do in much modern music. But obedience to them is neither necessary nor sufficient for success. In particular, you cannot give meaning to a musical phrase by convention—as you *can* give meaning to words by convention. This important difference between music and language is one of the reasons for thinking that linguistic theories of musical structure will never really capture what we understand, when we understand sounds as music.

Ex. 8.7. Beethoven, Ninth Symphony in D minor, Op. 125, last movement

Listening

Musical understanding is inseparable from the experience of music—so much, at least, is obvious. But which experience, and how is it obtained? People hear music; they also overhear it in crowded restaurants or super-markets; they sing it, play it, and listen to it. Which of these experiences is our paradigm of musical understanding, and what is its intentional structure?

Cast your mind back to the imaginary origins of music, and you will probably envisage two activities: on the one hand, there is the person who sings aloud, and listens to his singing, or who strikes a hollow object, and listens to its sound; on the other hand, there is the person who stands absorbed in the sounds of nature. Sounds are both made and found; but the latter can enter our music only when we have learned to reproduce them. Music begins when people listen to the sounds that they are making, and so discover *tones*. Of all musical experiences, there is none more direct than free improvisation (whether vocal or instrumental): and this should be understood as a paradigm of *listening*—the form of listening from which music began.

Listening is a relation, between a sensitive organism and a sound. But it can take at least two forms: listening for the sake of information, and listening for its own sake. When you awake in the night, subliminally aware of a creak on the stair, you 'strain your ears' for information. This kind of listening is common to human beings and animals; if it did not occur, hearing would not be a kind of perception. But rational beings have a capacity that no other animals have, which is to listen for the sake of listening: we take 'time off' from our ordinary practical pursuits, and listen to the sounds by which we are surrounded. This kind of listening can be described in two ways: as listening to a sound for the sake of listening, or as listening to a sound 'for its own sake'. These are descriptions of a single phenomenon: for we cannot attend to the act of listening, without attending to the sound itself. And when we attend to the sound with no view to *informing* ourselves, we must inevitably take an interest in *how it sounds*, which is an interest in the act of listening.

Of course, we cannot block our minds to information; but there are two ways in which the information provided by a sound may affect our interest in it. It may displace the sound from our attention; or it may become part of our reason for listening to the sound, and even—in the limiting case— *part of what we hear*. The distinction I have in mind parallels that made above, between the content of hearing, and the inferences that are drawn from it. But it is not a distinction that is exhibited only by the experience of music. Suppose a cry rings out across the water; I ask my companion, 'what noise is that?' and he tells me that it is the song of a curlew. I now listen with new ears, for I should like to know 'what the curlew sounds like': this new piece of information interests me. The cry sounds again and, satisfied, I attend to other things. Now imagine the same circumstances, except that, on hearing the cry for the second time I find myself interested in its sound: I listen again, and it sounds again. I am the more interested, because I know this to be the sound of the curlew; I want to saturate my ears with it; not because I need more information if I am to recognize the sound again, but because its being the sound of the curlew has a special significance for me. I recall a wistful Chinese poem about the curlew; I remember my grandmother recounting how the curlews would come to breed on her farm in early summer, and how their cry would whistle across the moors. I think of the curlew's place in the family of waders, its habits and habitats—and gradually all this information begins to mingle with the sound in my ears, and enhance its significance for me.

I began by listening to the sound for the sake of information; I then listened to the sound for its own sake; finally I began to summon information for the sake of the sound. In the second two cases I treat the sound as intrinsically interesting: it is the focus of my attention. And I enhance its interest for me, by bringing other things to bear on it—so that the *way it sounds* becomes associated in my mind with those other interesting things. Here I am voluntarily changing the 'description under which' the intentional object of hearing is presented.

The transition here is wholly natural, and is of course a paradigm of the attention shift from a practical to a contemplative attitude. Aesthetic interest is a kind of contemplative interest: and we might already wish to describe my interest in the curlew's song as in part 'aesthetic'. What more needs to be said, in order to justify such a description?

Here we should remember an important point, with far-reaching intellectual repercussions. The category of the aesthetic is a philosopher's invention. It came into being, not because of some oft-encountered metaphysical problem, nor through some puzzling usage which philosophy alone could be called on to straighten out. On the contrary, the problems of aesthetics were *discovered* by philosophers, in the course of shaping the ideas of aesthetic interest, aesthetic judgement, and aesthetic experience. Some people might suggest that the problems were not even discovered, but merely invented, and that we should jettison not only the concept of the aesthetic, but also the pseudo-problems that derive from it. Others, less severe, but equally sceptical, will point to the historical circumstances in which this concept came into prominence, and argue that the concept captures no universal or transhistorical component in the human condition—perhaps describing it, as do Eagleton and Bourdieu,[1] as an ideological construct, whose primary function is to fortify a particular political order, and the power-relations that prevail in it.

I shall present an answer to those two kinds of scepticism in Chapter 15. But the premiss upon which they are founded must, I believe, be taken seriously. While Baumgarten did not invent aesthetic interest (what, after all, is Aristotle discussing in the *Poetics*?), he coined the term now used to describe it.[2] It is difficult to find the extra-philosophical constraints on the use of this term—the features of ordinary language, and ordinary reality, that require so elaborate a theory-building gesture. For Kant and his successors, there is a prephilosophical reality to which the study of aesthetics is directed: the 'judgement of taste'. But modern (or at any rate postmodern) people are not so confident that they can identify this judgement, or that it is of any importance in their lives. We must therefore proceed with the greatest caution, if we are to introduce so theory-laden a concept where as yet we have no phenomenon that stands in need of it.

---

[1] Eagleton, *The Ideology of the Aesthetic* (Oxford, 1990); Bourdieu, *Distinction*. The view that the aesthetic is a category of bourgeois ideology has entered music criticism—e.g. in the work of Leppert and McClary, which I discuss in Ch. 13 and elsewhere.

[2] Baumgarten, *Aesthetica*, 2 vols. (Frankfurt an der Order, 1750–8).

When I listen to the curlew's sound, and abrogate the search for information, it is the sound itself that pleases me. Suppose I now detach the sound from its cause, and attend to its tonal properties: I hear it beginning on a certain note and sliding up in a glissando to another. I may notice the interval between these notes—not, perhaps, being able to give it a name, or to identify the two separate pitches, but being able to sing it, play it, recognize it as 'the same again'. Here is a new kind of listening. I am still interested in the sounds, but a double intentionality has developed: my interest is directed simultaneously towards the sounds and towards the tones that I hear in them.

When we attend to sounds for their own sake, it is natural to expect this double intentionality to emerge. If the search for information has been set aside, then our hearing has been freed. We begin to search for pattern, order, and meaning in the sounds that we hear, so as to sustain the contemplative attention that is directed towards them. When we listen to sound for its own sake, therefore, we may begin to hear music. We may pass over from the world of sound into the world of tones; our experience then ceases to be organized in terms of the information contained in it, and acquires a newer and freer organization, whose foundation is metaphor.

Windows and Pictures

Return for a moment to the ordinary case of perception—whether visual, tactile, or auditory. All perception is intentional: it involves the direction upon, and conceptualization of, an object. Even if the concepts involved are themselves purely perceptual (like the concepts of secondary qualities), this process of conceptualization is intrinsic to the perceptual experience, and definitive of the intentional object.

However, the perceptual experience is understood as conveying information about something other than itself. The presentation of the intentional object is ancillary to the process of *finding out*. Concepts applied in perception are also explorations of the material world: they are constantly revised as errors and inadequacies come to light, and the resulting experience is less a picture of reality than a window opened on to it, a transparent medium through which information flows to its cognitive goal. The information is detachable from the experience, and accumulates incrementally as the subject uses his senses to make sense of the world. We can distinguish, here as elsewhere, between understanding and misunderstanding. But the thing understood is not the experience: it is the material world. The experience involves a conceptualization of the world that may be false, misleading, or incomplete. That is what misunderstanding amounts to.

The case of music is very different. The experience is not a window but a picture. The listener is not seeking information about the world: rather, he is allowing the world to play on his perceptions, to feed into them, and to endow them with an intrinsic meaning. The person who listens to sounds, and hears them as music, is not seeking in them for information about their cause, or for clues as to what is happening. On the contrary, he is hearing the sounds *apart* from the material world. They are detached in his perception, and understood in terms of their experienced order: this is what I have referred to as the acousmatic character of the musical experience. All that would intrude from the material world is either blocked out, as when we listen to broadcast or recorded music, or fashioned according to the requirements of the picture in which it is to appear, like the notes made by the orchestra in the concert hall. Think how strange it would be, to listen to those notes as one listens to sounds in daily life. One would hear a squeak from the oboe over there, a drum-beat here, and then a growl from a trombone, a high note on a violin—all so many creaks and murmurs, each with its bit of information to convey, about a person, a place, and a time. But that is not how we hear *music*. On the contrary, the notes in music float free from their causes: one and the same melody begins on that oboe note and flows through to the violin, changing timbre as it moves. The instruments are there precisely to produce this effect, allowed into the picture only because the picture comprehends them and cancels their reality.

What we understand, in understanding music, is not the material world, but the intentional object: the organization that can be heard *in* the experience. In listening to music, we are attending to an appearance, not for the sake of information, but for its own sake. I have no other reason for attending to the music, than the fact that it sounds as it does. *That* is what concerns me; and if I find meaning in the sound, it is a meaning that can be found only by someone who attends to it in the same way, regardless of the desire for information.

Intentional Understanding

The window of perception is an information-gathering device, and information involves conceptualization—the bringing of 'intuitions' under 'concepts', to use the Kantian idiom. But objects can be conceptualized in many ways, depending on our interests. This chair is a collection of mahogany pieces; it is also an ornament and an heirloom. Information useful to one purpose may be useless or inimical to another: as information about the chair's history makes only a negative contribution to my goal of sitting in it. Many of the puzzles of philosophy arise from the failure to see our concepts in terms of the interests that require them, and from our tendency to treat one kind of information as the sole cognitive paradigm.

It is true that we have such a paradigm in natural science, which seeks the best explanation of the world—the description of reality that will explain all that we observe, and in doing so replace our observations. Recent philosophy has made clear the extent to which our common-sense concepts already make room for such a science. Concepts of natural kinds—*dog, tree, gold*—connote real essences; their content is not given by convention, but by the things themselves. The best answer to the question what is meant by 'dog' is given by the true theory of dogs.

The concepts of natural kinds divide nature at the joints. But in classification, as in butchery, we are often more interested in the relation of objects to ourselves than in their causality and constitution. (Compare the way that an animal would be divided, on the one hand by a chef, on the other hand by an anatomist.) Many of our categories record the purpose to which objects may be put, rather than their inner constitution—categories like *table, swing,* or *shelter.* These concepts of 'functional kinds' are of great importance, since they order the world as a sphere of action, and open it to our uses. Other concepts record our contemplative, rather than our practical, interests. (Consider the concept of an ornament, or the concepts of glory, grace, and transfiguration.) Such categories mark out possibilities of action, emotion, and experience that may not be otherwise available—and which may indeed be rendered unavailable by an exclusively scientific view of things.

Classifications which play no part in the scientific world-view may nevertheless be truly or falsely applied. It really is true that the object on which I am sitting is a chair. More interesting is the case of secondary qualities, already touched on in Chapter 1. Things have colours, and judgements of colour may be true or false. Yet there is nothing to colour, besides the disposition that objects have to *appear* coloured to creatures like us. Colour belongs exclusively to the realm of appearances: but there are objective facts about colour, and things really are coloured.

As agents we belong to the surface of the world, and enter into immediate relation with it. The concepts through which we represent it form a vital link with reality, and without this link appropriate action and appropriate response could not emerge with the rapidity and competence that we require. Our everyday concepts have evolved under the pressure of human circumstance, and the attempt to replace them with scientific concepts more open to the underlying truth of things may in fact deprive us of the little competence that we humans have acquired. Consider, for example, the concept of the person: the rational agent with rights, duties, and self-consciousness, who is the focus of our love and hatred, and the pure subject who nevertheless appears mysteriously in the world of objects, watching from a pair of human eyes. What place is there for such a concept in the annals of biology? Where, in the science of the human animal, do we find the freely choosing subject, who exists in his body as the landscape exists in a painted canvas, both there and not there, intimately identified and impassably remote? The problem is a familiar one in metaphysics, and not one that I shall here attempt to answer. Nevertheless, it is important to bear in mind that our concepts function in many different ways, and that the classifications which are effected by them may be entirely cogent from the point of view of practical reason and the moral life, while being wholly useless or misleading for the purposes of physical science. Such is the case with this particular concept of the person. Yet it is true that there are persons, and judgements ascribing personality are every bit as objective, every bit as capable of truth and falsehood, as the axioms of a scientific theory.

Likewise, concepts adapted to the goal of scientific explanation may prove useless or destructive in the moral context. The scientific theory of the human being, when used to view the actions and passions of our friends, estranges us from them, and defeats the goal of human feeling.[3] As many philosophers have argued, in the wake of Kant's theory of freedom, we see human beings in two ways—both as part of nature, and subject to its laws, and as in some sense outside nature, free from 'empirical conditions'. The two ways of seeing humanity are incommensurable and irreducible. The one uses concepts that explain, while the other uses concepts that criticize and justify, like the concept of the person. We should therefore distinguish the world described in the true scientific theory of things (and which contains language-using organisms, disposed to describe themselves and their surroundings in ways that the theory does not endorse) from the world as we perceive, classify, and act on it—the *Lebenswelt*, to use Husserl's idiom.[4] The *Lebenswelt* is not ontologically, but aspectually, distinct from the world of science. It is the world *as represented* by our intentional states of mind— by our perceptions, thoughts, emotions, and motives.

The distinction goes hand in hand with another: that between scientific explanation and 'intentional understanding'. The construction of the *Lebenswelt* is a cognitive process, in which interest-relative concepts and concepts of secondary and tertiary qualities have an important role. These concepts may not, and in all probability do not, apply to the ultimate reality, as science describes it. But they define the intentional objects of our states of mind, in the normal circumstances of living. Intentional understanding is indispensable to us as rational agents; it attempts less to *explain* the world than to make sense of it, as the object of our concerns.

[3] I have tried to show this in detail, for one specific feeling, in *Sexual Desire* (London, 1986).
[4] *The Crisis of the European Sciences and Transcendental Phenomenology*, tr. and introd. D. Carr (Evanston, 1970).

Scientific explanation aims to give a true description of nature, and to identify the laws which govern it. The concepts which guide our scientific understanding may be revised and discarded, as our knowledge improves. From the scientific point of view, it is not the intentional object of perception, but the material object, which we seek to describe; and the true theory of the material object may show the intentional object to be a misrepresentation. This does not mean that science is in conflict with common sense. For common sense contains the seeds of scientific theory. To identify this thing that I see as a tree is already to venture an explanation of my visual images; and the common-sense picture of the world is also an attempt to understand and predict its causal order. Science revises common sense, in the same way, and using the same methods, as common sense revises itself. In the normal way of things, common sense looks out on the world through the very window where science stands. Nevertheless, the world as we perceive it is not constructed only by scientific method. As I have suggested, many of the classifications that we employ, and which identify the intentional objects of perception, have their origin in practical reason, in moral judgement, and in aesthetic interest. These interests play a part in forming the *Lebenswelt* that is at least as important as the part played by explanation. Scientific theories emerge when we put practical and aesthetic considerations to one side, and address the entire manifold of appearances with the single-minded purpose of explaining and predicting it.

Intentional understanding, like scientific understanding, may be improved—through a better grasp of concepts, or through a network of analogies and connections, which enable us to read the world and our interests more clearly. Secondary qualities provide an apt illustration of this. Consider the dispute between Goethe and the physicists concerning colour. The poet was trying to describe appearances, and to elicit their intrinsic order *as* appearances. Helmholtz criticized Goethe, arguing that the poet, by confining his attention to the way things *look*, made it impossible to find the concepts which *explain* his observations.[5] Yet there is something to be learned from Goethe: we understand colours better after reading his account of them, for we are given a way in which to bring together and harmonize the descriptions that experience forces upon us. Wittgenstein[6] suggests that Goethe's theory of colour should be seen as the first step towards a philosophical theory. Goethe is trying to tell us what colours are, by describing what we notice when we see them (relations of complementarity and between-ness, for example; qualities of saturation, pallor, and intensity). The resulting theory

[5] Goethe, *Theory of Colours*, tr. C. L. Eastlake, introd. D. B. Judd (Cambridge, Mass., 1970). Helmholtz, *A Treatise on Physiological Optics*, tr. J. P. C. Southall, 3 vols. (New York, 1924–5) ch. 19.
[6] *Remarks on Colour*, §71.

is not empirical but a priori: it tells us what colours are in themselves, by giving the structure of colour concepts.[7]

Although the emendation of the intentional understanding may lead us in this philosophical direction, philosophy is not always what is needed, by the person who fails to understand the *Lebenswelt*. Consider again the concept of the person. Only with Kant did philosophers begin to become clear about this concept, recognizing persons as the knots, so to speak, in the web of moral relations, whose nature is conferred by their mutual recognition. But the absence of the Kantian philosophy no more prevented people from understanding one another than its presence has overcome their moral ignorance. Interpersonal understanding is a part—the most important part—of our stance towards the *Lebenswelt*, which exists precisely *for* us, as persons. But it is emended less by philosophy than by the enlargement of our sympathies, by moral education, and by the practice of holding one another to account for our acts, omissions, and feelings. A persuasive instance is provided by the common law—the system of reasoned judgement which, proceeding from the particular case, in accordance with the doctrine of precedent, slowly advances towards an implicit system of laws, from the concrete solutions to individual human conflicts.[8] But this process, which discovers legal rights and duties, by asking for the 'why' of human acts, is mirrored also in our moral and customary thinking. And in these areas, philosophy and criticism again have a role to play in the 'emendation of the intentional understanding'.

To give a full theory of intentional understanding would be to cover all of ethics and aesthetics. But it should be evident what I mean, when I say that this kind of understanding exists, that it can be improved by discourse and criticism, and that the knowledge to which it leads is objective, telling us not merely how the world affects us, but how it really appears to creatures who live and die as we do. In understanding the *Lebenswelt*, I come to understand myself, my interests, and the hopes which are rightly mine.

Aesthetic Interest

Aesthetic interests have their own part to play in the formation of our world. For experience is not simply a matter of gaining information about the world, or forming plans to change it. There is a kind of experience which is inherently contemplative, in which sights and sounds are studied for their own sakes, without reference to our immediate cognitive or practical concerns. And since Kant, the term 'aesthetic' has been reserved for experiences of this kind.

[7] See Westphal, *Colour: A Philosophical Introduction*.

[8] See the argument of F. A. Hayek, 'Cosmos and Taxis', and 'Nomos', in *Law, Legislation and Liberty*, i (London, 1973), 35–55 and 94–124 respectively.

All animals have interests. They are interested in satisfying their needs and desires, and in gathering the information required for security and well-being. A rational being employs his reason in the pursuit of these interests, and in resolving, where possible, the conflicts between them. That, according to Hume, is the full extent of reason's writ; for reason is subordinate to our interests, and has no authority to deliver any result apart from the 'relations of ideas'. Kant argued that there are 'interests of reason': that is to say, interests that we have, purely by virtue of our rationality, and which are in no way relative to our desires, needs, and appetites. One of these is morality. Reason motivates us to do our duty, and all other ('empirical') interests are discounted in the process. That is what it *means* for a decision to be a moral one. The interest in doing right is not an interest of my empirical nature, but an interest of reason *in* me. (Hence for Kant, it is an interest of my transcendental self, and in that sense *truly* mine, in the way that no empirical interest can be truly mine.)

Reason also has an interest in the sensuous world. When a cow stands in a field ruminating, and turning her eyes to view the horizon, we can say that she is interested in what is going on (and in particular, in the presence of potential threats to her safety, potential sources of food and drink, and so on), but not that she is interested in the *view*. No animal has ever stood on a promontory and been *moved* by the prospect; no animal has ever longed for the sight of a favourite landscape, or the experience of a favourite sound. A horse may long to get out of the stable and into the field: but this longing is motivated by the sensuous interest in food and freedom.

A rational being, by contrast, takes pleasure in the mere sight of something: a landscape, an animal, a flower—and of course (though for Kant this was a secondary instance) a work of art. This form of pleasure answers to no empirical interest. I satisfy no bodily appetite or need in contemplating the landscape; nor do I merely scan it for useful information. The interest, as Kant puts it, is disinterested—an interest in the landscape *for its own sake*, for the very thing that it is (or that it appears to be). This 'disinterest' is a mark of an 'interest of reason'. We cannot refer it to our empirical nature, but only to the reason that transcends empirical nature, and which searches the world for a meaning that is more authoritative and more complete than the needs of animal life.

We do not have to accept Kant's theory of the 'interest of reason', in order to be attracted by his account of aesthetic experience. The suggestion is this: that rational beings can *discount* their ordinary interests, including the interest in information, and still find an interest in the way the world appears. This disinterested interest feeds on itself, as in the examples I have given. I am trying to match the world to myself and myself to the world, as I search for the order in appearances. Aesthetic interest is not an interest in information. But information always bears on it, since information may enter into the *meaning* of an appearance: it may become part of the 'description under which' the object is presented, the description which defines the intentional object of perception.

As I noted above, however, we should be careful to distinguish the content of an experience, from the conclusions that we draw from it or the states of mind with which it is associated. The archaeologist, sifting through the sand in search of buried artefacts, is seeking information. Each experience is valuable to him, because of what it means: but what it means is something other than itself. Hearing the sound of the curlew, my mind is filled with memories of the Yorkshire moors. These are prompted by the sound, but they exist independently, and survive in my mind long after I cease to hear the sound. We can think of many instances of this kind, in which a thought, a belief, a feeling, or an image is prompted by some experience, while existing independently. Such cases should be contrasted with the kind of double intentionality that is characteristic of the aesthetic experience. When I see the dancers in Poussin's *Adoration of the Golden Calf*, I am not merely prompted by the painting to think of them, or to conjure them in my mind's eye. I see them *there*, in the painting. And when I turn my eyes away I cease to see them. If I retain an image of them it is also an image of the *painting*. The meaning of this painting lies *in* the experience of it, and is not obtainable independently. Nor is the meaning a simple matter of what is represented. I do not see only these dancing figures, and the scene in which they participate. I see their foolishness and frivolity; I sense the danger and the attraction of idolatry, which invites me to cancel all responsibility for my life and soul, and join in the collective dance. A moral idea begins to pervade the aspect of the painting. The figures come before me in a new light, not as happy innocents, but as embodiments of lawlessness, and assassins of the Father. (Hence the feeble appearance of Moses in the distance, as he throws down the tablets of the law.)

The meaning here lies in the perception of the painting. That is why you turn to the *painting* in order to understand the meaning, so as to fall within its gravitational field. Meaning is not an 'association' or a train of images: it is the intentional object of perception, when the painting is the thing perceived. Only by looking at the painting, can this meaning be fully grasped, since it has an irreducibly sensuous component, which is shaped by the image on the canvas. All aesthetic meaning is like that. This fact imposes, as we saw in Chapter 7, a formal constraint on theories of art. When a critic tells us that such and such is part of the meaning of a piece of music, then what he says can be accepted only if we can also experience the music as he describes it. Meaning belongs to a work of art only if it can become the object of the peculiar 'double intentionality' that I described in

Chapter 3. Fanciful allegories may be read into paintings in which they cannot be seen; hidden structures may be perceived in stories in which they cannot be felt; a mathematical order may be discerned in music in which it cannot be heard. Clever critics and analysts who tell us of these things are contributing nothing to our aesthetic interest.

The argument raises the question why this particular kind of meaning, in which thought and experience are inseparable, should be of value to us. Why have we made such a special place in our lives for 'the sensuous shining of the idea'? This is the question which I shall address in later chapters; for the present we must return to the experience of music, which is, I shall assume, an experience motivated by aesthetic interest.

·   Windows, Pictures, and Metaphors

I suggested that aesthetic experience stands to ordinary perception as pictures stand to windows. Ordinary perception looks out on the world, and assesses its utility. Aesthetic perception looks inward to itself, and arranges the world as in a picture, for the effect. This simile will help us to envisage what is distinctive about the act of understanding that occurs in aesthetic perception.

We should first look at the case of pictures themselves. In seeing a picture I may be engaged in an act of straightforward perception—gathering information about the world, and responding to its contents. (This is certainly our normal way of seeing photographs, and perhaps the only way of seeing the images on a television screen.) But there is a particular experience that comes precisely when I stand back from those quotidian interests, and study the aspect of the picture as it is in itself, for its own sake. The world before me at once ceases to be the real world of perception. The real world is replaced by an imaginary world—a world that I perceive without belief. Into this picture the real world may intrude, but only by discarding its reality. Things seen *in* the picture are seen as not really there. The world gathers in this picture as a thing subservient to appearances. In normal perception, by contrast, the appearance is subservient to the world.

As I have already argued, this implies that the concepts which organize my perception of a picture do not literally apply to it—nor do I *think* that they literally apply. They are used in another way, to elicit an order in appearance which is not the order of believing. Nevertheless, without these concepts I could not see what is there to be seen. I must see the man in the picture: and that means applying concepts to what I see, with a view to understanding it. When the world gathers in pictures, it is conceptualized with the very concepts that open the window of sight. But it is not conceptualized as information. This happens too in music, although the case is also distinctive. When, in the normal course of life, I listen to the way things sound, it is the things themselves that interest me, not the sound. And yet the sounds are not conceptualized in terms of the things that emit them. I do not hear the car in its sound, as I see the car in its shape: rather, I hear the sound of a car. Sounds are identified through their normal causes, but are not appearances of their causes. It follows that, when I attend to a sound *for its own sake*, the sound does not take on, for me, the character of its normal cause. When, in the concert hall, I close my ears to the real world, and attend to the sounds that inhabit the air, I do not organize them as 'someone playing the oboe over there', and 'someone playing the violin nearby'. Still less do I hear these events *in* the sounds, as I see the face in the picture. This is the deep reason for thinking that music is not a representational art: not just that we do not understand it in that way, but that we *could* not, since sounds are not organized as *aspects* of the things that emit them.

Nevertheless, when we attend to sounds for the sake of the way they sound, and for no other reason, we are still bound to organize what we hear. This organization has a primitive component: the temporal *Gestalt* has a beginning, a middle, and an end, regardless of the concepts we apply to it. At the same time, the organization of the temporal *Gestalt* tends intrinsically towards a conceptual order—an order of comparison, classification, and 'same again'. When we attend to an appearance for its own sake, the world that we have bracketed comes back in another form, as a conceptual order in the thing perceived. The world is on holiday, and our concepts with it, looking for the place of rest in the imagined picture. We should never enjoy this experience, if it did not in some way communicate to us the life that is ours—either through representation, or through some system of metaphor which implants our life in the thing that we perceive.

The Intentional Understanding of Tones

What is it, then, to undestand or misunderstand a piece of music? And how is this understading amended? By what concepts, arguments, and comparisons do we adjust the object of the musical experience? When is an analysis a description of what we hear or ought to hear, when we hear a piece as music? Such questions will occupy us throughout the following four chapters. But before broaching them, we must draw the argument of the present chapter together.

Musical understanding is manifest first in the apt organization of the musical *Gestalt*—the organization that makes it live for us, and causes us to perceive tones moving in a musical space, rather than mere sequences of pitched sound. The perception of tone and movement can be corrected and criticized. Not only is it within the province of the will, as I argued in

Chapter 2; it also provides the foundation for all higher musical experiences, including those of thematic structure, development, and form. Even in the smallest musical perceptions we can 'hear incorrectly'—by grouping or dividing tones wrongly, by misplacing accent and emphasis, by hearing an up-beat as a down-beat, a background as a foreground, a figure as a theme. And although a good performance aims precisely to guide us to the right perception, no feature of the sounds and their production can guarantee this result, which depends upon the ear of the listener and the musical culture which informs it. The examples given in Chapter 2 should demonstrate exactly how musical understanding, even at this elementary level, may be amended. And if they do not yet tell us what is meant by 'right' and 'wrong', 'correct' or 'incorrect', it is because we stand in need of a theory of aesthetic value, before the practice of criticism and emendation can be fully accounted for.

Indeed, musical understanding would be of little significance—a mere game only—if there were not some larger aesthetic enterprise at stake. Our understanding of music may be rooted in the detailed organization of the musical *Gestalt*, and the careful placing and valuing of boundaries; but it is something more than a mere play of patterns. If we speak of a right and wrong way of hearing musical elements, it is because it *matters* how we hear these things. And it matters because we are interested in musical form and musical content, and attach a deep significance to both.

First, the concept of musical form. Musical events, once ordered rhythmically, melodically, and harmonically as tones, stand in perceivable relations to one another. A phrase may be heard as a variation, version, or elaboration; it may seem to answer or complete another phrase. And our understanding of those relations is comparable to our understanding of gestures, as when a gesture of greeting is embellished or varied in reply. Because the musical surface is organized neither by representational content, nor by syntactical rules, the ability to perceive sameness in difference, and difference in that which is substantially the same, is very hard to describe. Still harder is it to account for the all-important experience of the 'boundary', which I discussed in Chapter 2. Yet these experiences lie at the heart of musical understanding.

Musical boundaries are for the most part semi-permeable, and effect only a partial closure of the phrase. Moreover, they are easily wiped away by succeeding episodes, and no phrase or motif is sealed from the retroactive influence of its successors. One of the most striking features of music in our tradition lies in the ability to prolong the musical movement across a great many inner boundaries, while aiming, nevertheless, at an authoritative final closure. A great symphonic or instrumental movement comes properly home only once, in a gesture that ties up the 'argument'. At the same time, the experience of closure is present in every bar. Theories have been devised, like that of Heinrich Schenker, in order to reduce the musical surface to a single process, hierarchically organized, so that the final closure appears to be intended in all the permeable boundaries that lead to it. Whether this enterprise could ever succeed might be doubted. But the very fact that thinkers have embarked upon it so assiduously—even devoting their lives to it, as Schenker did—is testimony to the extraordinary power exerted by our experience of form. We cannot rest with the idea of musical form as a mere surface pattern, a decorative game, a 'beautiful play of sensations', as Kant ignorantly described it. We experience it as something *deep*, an organizing force which gives sense, direction, and *meaning* to the musical surface. Listening to music would be a fairly pointless exercise, if there were nothing that we took from what we heard, and nothing that we heard in it, besides the garlands of a musical *Gestalt*.

As instrumental music gained ascendancy in the eighteenth and nineteenth centuries, people began to marvel at its power to move us, and to recognize that this power is something quite other than the power of words and pictures. Writers took to describing the organization that we hear in music in the most elevated terms. The Young Hegelian A. B. Marx, for example, praised the *Eroica* Symphony as 'that piece in which musical art first steps independently—without connection to the poet's word or the dramatist's action—out of the play of form and indeterminate impulses and feelings, into the sphere of a brighter and more determinate consciousness'.[9] This brighter consciousness is the Hegelian Idea, of which the symphony is a sensuous manifestation; understanding the symphony, therefore, is a matter of grasping the Idea which unfolds through the musical process. And while, in retrospect, one may dismiss this kind of writing, as a mere mechanical application of Hegelian aesthetics, it is but one manifestation of a widely shared conviction, that the process which we hear in serious music is more like thought than sensation. The example of the Ninth Symphony, in which the musical idea 'breaks the bounds of absolute music', as Wagner put it,[10] seemed to endorse the view that music contains thought in something like the way that words contain thought, and passes over into words when the Idea requires it. And such a claim sounds enormously interesting, until the qualification is added, that the thoughts expressed by music are 'purely musical', and not to be uttered in any form other than that bestowed upon them by the musical work.

The Schenkerian theory of tonality, and the Hegelian aesthetic of the musical Idea, illustrate two sides of the problem of musical understanding. We speak of understanding and misunderstanding music because we recognize

---

[9] *Ludwig van Beethoven* (4th edn., Berlin 1884), i. 271.
[10] *Gesammelte Schriften und Dichtungen*, ed. W. Golther (Berlin, 1926), ii. 61.

that there is something more to musical form than the 'play of sensations'; and we are naïvely disposed to identify this something more both as a 'deep process' revealed in the musical surface, and as a mental 'content', which is recuperated in the act of understanding. Musical form is most easily represented as deep, when it resolves itself into a musical 'content'. (Cf. Diana Rafmann's theory of 'semantic temptation', discussed in Chapter 7.)

Tonality and the 'Description Under Which'

In what sense, however, are these 'deep' facts about music objects of musical understanding? What is the distinction between a musical, and a purely intellectual understanding of a piece of music? And how are form and content recuperated in the act of hearing?

Here we need to revisit the concept of intentional understanding. I remarked that the intentional object of perception is given by the description under which the material object is perceived; from which it might seem to follow that any *other* description of the object is not a description of the intentional object, but at best only of the material object in which it is seen or heard. Suppose, for example, that I see a blue jacket and recognize it as such. Here the intentional object of sight is captured by the description 'blue jacket'; but what I see is, scientifically speaking, a web of fibres of a certain chemical composition, which refracts towards me light of a certain range of wavelengths. The scientific description is not, and could not be, a 'description under which' the jacket is seen; nor does it automatically identify the intentional object (for I might have been seeing the jacket as a black dog); nor does it enhance my *intentional* understanding of the jacket—my understanding of its appearance and uses for me.

Nevertheless, there are ways of amending the 'description under which' an object is presented, which do not look beyond the intentional realm. A description of the precise shade of blue, of the exact style of jacket, of the uses which are implicit in it, of the way in which my interests are addressed by it—such a description does not venture *beyond* my intentional understanding, but amends and amplifies it, as when I describe the jacket as a body-hugging, lady-killing concoction in Prussian blue. Here I am describing the jacket as it is perceived, but not with the description under which it is first perceived by the observer. If the observer accepts the new description, it is not as a hypothesis about the material world, but as a better and fuller characterization of the way the world appears to him. And in the course of accepting this description his perceptions may change.

This bears directly on the understanding of music. One suggestion, frequently made, and of great initial persuasiveness, is that there is an order to be heard in music, that this order is constituted and manifest at the intentional level, and yet that the concepts needed to describe it form no part of the normal 'description under which' the music is heard. We hear anticipation and closure, development and variation, tension and release, and a process which in some way lasts through these things, guiding and guided by them. In the great masterworks this process does not have the character of succession only; it is like an argument, an exploration, which concludes as a narrative concludes, at the point beyond which it cannot go without detracting from its meaning. But the similes used in that sentence, while they arise naturally from the musical experience, are far from indispensable; and the process to which they refer can be described in other and more illuminating ways, which do not merely record our intentional understanding, but also amplify it, by showing exactly *what* we hear when we hear a melody return to its starting-point, or a sequence of dissonant harmonies resolve.

Most music that seems meaningful to us is tonal. While it is a controversial question what tonality consists in, there is no doubt that we recognize tonality, and that our expectations are ordered and guided by it. Under the system of tonality tones, chords, and keys bear constant relations to one another; standard devices can be recognized and used to new effect; harmonic progressions seem to be dictated by the very same principles that control the melodic line; everything has a natural and logical sound—and moreover the 'laws of motion' of this tonal realm seem to be constant from epoque to epoque and style to style. The synthesis according to which harmonies follow from melody, and melody from the harmonic sequence, is as much a feature of Dowland as it is of Wagner and Brahms. The theory of tonality is a persuasive theory of *what* we hear, when we hear the melodic and harmonic process in tonal music; yet the terms of the theory may be entirely beyond the grasp, even of the person who understands everything he hears. The cadence V–I is something that I can hear, even without the language with which I have just described it; nevertheless, the theory of tonality captures and amplifies the intentional understanding of those who hear tonal music correctly. That is its purpose. It is not an *acoustical* theory, since it distinguishes events which are acoustically identical. (For instance, the progression V–I in C major, which is acoustically identical to I–IV in G.) It tells us *what* we are hearing, in hearing cadences, parallels, motions towards and away from a centre, tension and release, and so on. It generalizes from the musical experience, towards descriptions which, however technically phrased, are anchored in the particular experience of 'right' and 'wrong'. And, it gives an inkling of the achievement involved when someone composes tonal music that is not banal or perfunctory, and which wanders in distant and exciting regions before its final coming home.

The theory of tonality is beautiful and satisfying. It also offers to explain many things, in addition to our sense of a 'deep' order in the tonal masterpieces. For example, it seems to explain why it is that a person brought up on one kind of tonal music (that of Mozart, for example) can spontaneously appreciate tonal music in another idiom (be it Palestrina or Chopin, Praetorius or Elgar), without embarking upon some elaborate learning process. Furthermore, it accounts for the history of Western music, while offering to explain why other musics *have* no history, or have been forced into history only by their encounter with the Western tradition. For the tonal system is dynamic: it is a system not of arbitrary rules but of genuine *discoveries* (albeit 'intentional discoveries') which, once made, cannot be undiscovered, but only incorporated or ignored. This is surely what is most impressive about the Western tradition: that composers build upon the achievements of their predecessors, and endeavour to extend the tonal idiom in some new direction, incorporating new harmonies, key-relations, and melodic shapes, while meticulously obeying the rules of classical polyphony.

And perhaps it is this very spirit of experiment and discovery which tempted composers at last to break through the bounds of tonality, into atonal regions which cannot be charted by the old harmonic laws. And perhaps that is why we find atonal music inherently difficult, and strive always to hear in it an order that it seems to defy. At any rate, we should take very seriously the suggestion that tonality contains the key to musical form, and that when we understand a piece of tonal music, it is because we have grasped the tonal order which generates the musical surface.

Imagination and the Human World

In the normal case the intentional order is, like the order of science, an order of the window. The concepts that organize the world's appearance are world-directed; I improve my grasp of them by amending my knowledge of the *world*. That is what happens, for example, in moral education, when I come to know what a person is, and how a person should be treated.

But what happens when concepts are removed from their justifying context, and applied in a systematic metaphor, like the concepts that deliver the intentional realm of music? A metaphor must be understood through the literal usage. I do not understand what life is by hearing life in music; rather, because I know what life is, I can hear life in music. Any improvement in my understanding of this concept is an improvement in my understanding of *life*. If that is so, however, we find ourselves in a quandary. To say that musical understanding is founded in a metaphor, is to cast doubt on the whole idea that we understand *music*, or that the way in which we understand it can be educated or improved. The experience of music comes to seem like the by-product of *other* perceptions—perceptions in which our concepts are formed and put to the test.

This is one reason, I believe, why critics like Hanslick are so resistant to the idea of musical 'content'. For it would seem to imply that the organization of music is of no intrinsic significance. Musical organization is made to depend upon concepts that have no literal application to music, and which derive their sense from contexts in which this peculiar and remarkable experience—the experience of musical form—is wholly out of mind. On the other hand, even Hanslick described music as 'tönend-bewegte Formen' ('forms moved through sound').[11] He too used the metaphor of movement; and he too must say why it is *this* which captures what we hear, when we hear sounds as music.

To answer the objection, we must show that the transfer of concepts of life and movement to music is not merely essential to our hearing of music, but also adds something to our understanding of life. In other words, it is not a gratuitous 'likening' of one thing to another, but an attempt to understand the one through the other—to understand the music through the concept of life, but also life through its embodiment in music.

Return for a moment to the art of painting. It is surely evident that, through the representation of the world in painting, we have achieved an enhanced understanding of the way it appears, and of the concepts *through* which it appears to us: not the least the concept of the face, and of the personality that shines in it. Rembrandt showed us how to discern a whole life in a face, Poussin how to see a world in a gesture. Imaginary worlds are not merely likenesses or imitations: they come before us as equal contenders for our attention. They are on a par with the reality upon which they comment. Indeed, the world in the picture is put to a severer test than the world in the window: it must achieve an order and meaning in *appearance itself*. Its appearance has ceased to be a sign of reality: it has *become* reality, into which the meaning of the world must be distilled. It is true that we can encounter the world in the picture only by deploying obliquely the concepts with which we focus the world through the window. But another order is revealed by this oblique use of concepts, and one that feeds back into the vision from the window. How things seem is subtly transformed by the test of art. Art translates things into pure appearance, so that they lie revealed in their surface. This could not be done, if concepts remained tied to their literal use.

Surely that is the approach that we should take to music too. Just as we learn about the human face from painting, so do we learn about movement and life from music. Not that we learn new *facts*: rather that we come to see movement and life in another way, to sense its inward meaning, and to respond to it as in a dance. Our own life is transfigured as we listen,

[11] *On the Beautiful in Music.*

sensing the movement in ourselves, and the order in appearance that life can achieve. The metaphor that animates our experience is not founded in a bare comparison: it involves an imaginative shift of attention comparable to that which occurs in the appreciation of painting. In listening to music, and experiencing its inner organization, we are also encountering as a pure appearance something which, seen through the window, is not appearance at all.

And here, I suggest, lies the importance of aesthetic experience in general, and of the imaginative act in particular. Our ordinary intentional understanding is subservient to our goals: the order that it discerns is one that opens the world to our projects, dividing it not at the joints, but in the way most useful to moral and practical existence. But there is another way of seeing the world: the way that opens to us when our projects are set aside. Another order then spreads through the realm of appearance, an order that we actively create through our imaginative perception. In perceiving this order, we employ our ordinary concepts, but obliquely, to describe appearances. In a mysterious way, this oblique use of our concepts purifies them, and reconciles us to the world that they describe. It *shows* the meaning of the world, by translating the world into appearance. Imagination cleans the window of perception.

But while this observation should encourage us to look for a theory of musical content in the workings of the imagination, it also reminds us of the dangers involved, in separating the experience of content from the experience of form. Theories of expression, for example, have the lamentable habit of lapsing into silence, when it comes to explaining what is happening *in the music*. Granted the music expresses grief: but why *this* note here? And why *this* harmony, *this* melody, *this* way of developing? Is it not better to hear those things, and to feel—one knows not why—the rightness of their conjunction, than to come up with some description of musical meaning? The ability to produce such a description is neither a necessary nor a sufficient test of understanding; while to hear the rightness or wrongness of the progressions, the formal perfection or imperfection of the melodies, and the inevitability or arbitrariness of the musical line, is usually sufficient. It is surely this capacity to hear music as growing in and through itself, as stating its material, working on it, and coming to a conclusion, that is the central experience. And we have given no more than a hint of what this involves, besides saying that it is based in metaphor, and that it seems to have a paradigm instance in the experience of tonal organization.

At the same time, we speak freely of the 'content' of musical works—even of works that are purely instrumental. Not only do we distinguish meaningful music from that which is comparatively empty—Beethoven from Hummel, Bach from Telemann, Dvořák's *Rusalka* from Lortzing's *Undine*. We also think of the content of a work of music as *specific* to it—so specific, indeed,

Ex. 8.8. Czerny, Sonata in A flat major, Op. 7, second movement

that we are prepared to embrace the Crocean paradox, and deny that content can be separated from form. The distinction here has nothing to do with grammar. From the 'syntactical' viewpoint the keyboard works of Czerny and Hummel are as well formed as anything in Beethoven. But the kind of musical comprehension that is involved in grasping a piece by Czerny (Ex. 8.8) is at best a preliminary to understanding, and by no means sufficient. Suppose that someone really thought this stuff to be comparable to Beethoven (in the parallel passage of the slow movement from Op. 31 No. 2, for example, Ex. 8.9)—thought it, that is to say, to be every bit as meaningful. Should we not say that he had misunderstood, either the Czerny or the Beethoven, or both? At the same time, the content of a work is not something that we *recuperate* from the work, as we recuperate the meaning from a sentence or a story. The one who hears a sentence with understanding is able not merely to paraphrase it, but also to use the information contained in it, in theoretical and practical reasoning. He has acquired a 'mental content', which outlives the experience of the sentence and enters his cognitive repertoire. No such thing happens when we understand music. There is nothing that we can *do* with our musical understanding in the immediate circumstances of life. The content of a piece of music is the intentional object of a purely *musical* perception, and can exist in no other form—even if it has relations and analogies in language.

This too is a source of scepticism—the origin of the view that music means nothing except *itself*. But the scepticism is premature. All we are licensed to conclude is that the meaning of a piece of music does not reside in it in the way that meaning resides in language—not a surprising result, given the argument of Chapter 7. But it remains a task for the theory of

Ex. 8.9. Beethoven, Sonata in D minor, Op. 31 No. 2, second movement

expression, to explain what we could mean by content, when the constraints that we have placed on musical understanding prevent us from thinking that this content can be transferred from a musical to a non-musical expression.

In what follows, therefore, we must develop our initial account of musical understanding, so as to provide not only a theory of tonality and its limits, but also a positive account of musical expression. These are the two primary concerns of the chapters which follow.

9 *Tonality*

Perception is a natural epistemological power of the organism, which depends on no social context for its exercise. The musical experience, however, is not merely perceptual. It is founded in metaphor, arising when unreal movement is heard in imaginary space. Such an experience occurs only within a musical culture, in which traditions of performance and listening shape our expectations. And in *our* tradition—which could fairly claim to be the richest and most fertile that has yet existed—tonality has played the leading role in the building of musical space. No philosophy of music worth the name can ignore tonality, or dismiss the suggestion that it shows us part of what we hear, when we hear sounds as music. Tonality provides a paradigm of musical organization—an organization in which melody is led by harmony, and harmony in turn by melody. And attempts to depart from tonality, or to discard it entirely, seem only to confirm its authority over the musical ear.

For many musicians, however, tonality has become a 'dead language', or a language that can be used only ironically—maybe even sarcastically—so as to neutralize the banality of its overexploited terms. For such musicians, the search for an alternative musical order defines the work of the composer in our time, and sets the agenda for every creative gesture.

The Definition of Tonality

Conceptions of tonality have ranged so widely, that it is now hard to know what is excluded from the category. George Perle, in an influential study, has described the serial music of Schoenberg and his followers as 'twelve-tone tonality',[1] while Roy Travis defines as tonal any music whose 'motion unfolds through time a particular tone, interval or chord'[2]—a definition that leans on metaphor, and which excludes virtually nothing.

[1] *Twelve-Tone Tonality* (Berkeley & Los Angeles, 1977).
[2] 'Towards a New Concept of Tonality', *Journal of Music Theory*, 3 (1959), 26.

There is a reason for these wide definitions. Seeking the essence of Western classical music, writers come up against the fact that it is always departing in some new direction. They therefore try to include within their concept of tonality not only the classical tradition, but all the harmonic experiments which it has engendered. There is a real question, indeed, whether it is possible to describe tonality in a way that allows for non-tonal music.

Putting that question aside, we can attempt to define tonality in two ways—formally, in terms of essential features, or materially, in terms of the tonal tradition. Formally speaking, tonal music is music that is organized around a tonic. Much music—perhaps all traditional music—contains privileged tones, which are emphasized by rhythm, pitch, repetition, or accent, and to which the melody returns. But not all music has a tonic. Music has a tonic only if the following conditions are met:

1. The melodic line feels fully 'closed' only when it comes to rest on a certain privileged tone (the tonic).
2. The final move on to the tonic has (in standard cases) the character of a 'cadence'—a loosening of tension.
3. Octaves are heard as equivalent—so that the effect of closure is duplicated at the octave.
4. Other tones are heard in relation to the tonic—as more or less distant from it, as tending towards or away from it.

Those conditions are not merely stipulative. They attempt to capture a fundamental musical experience—a feature of the intentional world of tones that has been noticed and nurtured by many musical cultures, and which led at last to the discovery of keys, modulations, and triadic harmony. As now understood, of course, tonality means that a piece of music is (at any given moment) in a certain *key*, or else moving between keys, a key being a self-contained melodic and harmonic system. But we should not take so parochial and time-bound an approach to the underlying phenomenon. There is much 'tonicized' music which is either without harmony, or inherently resistant to it—like the folk-music of the Arabian tribes, in which voices can only double the melody at the unison or octave, leading to effects of high comedy when (as was the case in my youth) the Egyptian army would march to the sound of a military band.

Nevertheless, in our tradition, the harmonic potential of the tonic has been paramount. Our scales and keys emerged over many centuries, through the attempt to order tones according to their harmonic affinities. The primary consonances of fourth, fifth, and octave were already recognized in antiquity. The eight modes or 'tones' of Gregorian chant, the tetrachordal scale of the *Musica enchiriadis*, and the hexachord of Guido d'Arezzo (*c.* 990–*c.*1050), show a continuous attempt to build a melodic system based on harmonic affinities.

In all these systems we observe octave equivalence, the privileging of the fourth and fifth, and the division of scale-steps into tones and semitones.

Materially speaking, therefore, tonality is a continuous musical tradition, a kind of collective meditation on the harmonic nature of the *tone itself.* Although this tradition began with the church modes, it took on its dynamic form only later, with the development of Renaissance polyphony, and the acceptance of triadic harmony and species counterpoint, as the leading structural principles in sacred and secular music. Schoenberg argued that the church modes are pre-tonal in conception,[3] since the primary tones (the reciting tone, the leading tone, and the final tone) have no fixed harmonic meaning—unlike the primary tones (tonic, dominant, and subdominant) in more recent music. On the other hand, the modes are orderings of tones according to a principle of octave equivalence, in which neighbouring tones are separated by a whole-tone or a semitone interval. Modal harmonies are built in the same way as tonal harmonies—with the fourth and fifth as primary concords. The tonal scales (major and minor) are themselves modal scales, which, by their peculiar harmonic and melodic potential, have edged the other modes to the musical margin. And when a modal melody appears in tonal music, as in the masses of Taverner and Byrd, or the *Miserere* of Gesualdo, it leaves the surrounding harmonic order unblemished. The modes may not evince tonality; nevertheless, the steady evolution of polyphony from the monophonic chants seemed to press the modes in a tonal direction, steadily removing from them all the angles and inclinations which neutralize the tonic.

Of course much else changed during this process. The fourth, which is considered to be a concord in early modal polyphony (such as that of Léonin at Nôtre-Dame-de-Paris in the twelfth century) ceased, sometime around 1450, to be heard as such. The major and minor third, heard first as dissonant, were already 'imperfect consonances' in Léonin's time, and became paradigms of consonance in the classical period. These facts demand a deep explanation, and it is one of the striking features of the tonal tradition that the explanation is forthcoming. The very same facts which explain the emergence of the 'tonic', as the note towards which all others tend, explain the laws of tonal harmony.

Natural Music

The demand for a deep explanation of harmony is not new. Ancient thinkers found this explanation in the Pythagorean metaphysic of number, and the explanation proved satisfying not only to Plato, Plotinus, St Augustine, and

---

[3] 'Problems of Harmony', in *Style and Idea*, ed. L. Stein, tr. L. Black (London, 1975), 276–7.

Boethius, but to countless theorists of music from Al-Farabi to Zarlino. Three facts stand immovably against it, however: the unacceptable cosmology upon which it is based; the emergence of new experiences of concord (in particular that represented by the minor triad) in which the simple numerical proportions of fourth, fifth, and octave are no longer displayed; and the mathematical impasse contained in the theory itself. For it soon became clear that the perfect intervals (those defined by simple mathematical ratios such as the fifth and the fourth) cannot be used to construct a mode which fits without remainder into the octave. A variety of attempted solutions to this problem can be observed in the Greek, Arabic, and Latin modes, and in the rival systems of tuning which competed with our own until equal temperament prevailed. But the victory of equal temperament was no accident of history: on the contrary, it was the goal towards which musical thinking inevitably tended, as soon as tonality emerged. And it provides a striking illustration of the distinction between acoustical and musical relations.

The history that led to equal temperament is the subject of another book. I shall therefore jump ahead to the acoustical theories of Helmholtz, and in particular to his explanation of the elementary concords in terms of the overtone series.[4] The pitch of a sound is a function of the frequency of the vibrations that produce it. Helmholtz observed, however, that when an object vibrates at a certain frequency, it sets up subsidiary vibrations at higher frequencies, which are natural number multiples of the root frequency— i.e. their frequencies will be multiples of the root frequency by 2, 3, 4, 5, 6, etc. Suppose, for example, that the C two octaves below middle C is sounded. There will sound with it the C an octave above (× 2), the G a fifth above that C (× 3), middle C itself (× 4), the E above middle C (× 5), and then the scale from G, becoming increasingly chromatic as the gaps in the pitch spectrum are filled (Ex. 9.1). This—the overtone series—does not produce a perfect major scale until much higher frequencies are reached: from the point of view of our diatonic system many of the lower 'partials' are out of tune. Nevertheless, Helmholtz thought that he could explain the traditional consonances in terms of the overtone series, and incidentally offer the true ground for the Pythagorean theory of harmony, as depending upon relations between elementary numbers. Consonance arises when two vibrations nest together, so that the peaks of one coincide with peaks of the

Ex. 9.1. The (approximate) overtone series on C

4 *On the Sensation of Tone*, ch. 9.

other. Dissonance is explained by 'beating'—the interference pattern that arises, when the peaks of one wave cross those of the other, alternately augmenting and cancelling its force, so as to set up subsidiary vibrations which trouble the ear. The consonant character of the major triad is explained by the mathematical relation of the frequencies (4, 5, and 6 times the frequency of a hypothetical root). This means that the upper partials of all three tones in the triad will either coincide or nest together without disturbance. The harmonic importance of the triad stems from the fact that it reproduces (through octave displacement) the first (and most prominent) overtones of the root. It is the 'natural' harmony *par excellence*, since its existence is implied in the tone itself.[5]

The well-tempered system should be seen as the unique solution to problems posed by the experience of harmony. We hear certain 'natural' intervals—the consonances delivered by the first five overtones. These are the octave, the fifth, the fourth, and the major third. From these we derive the interval of the whole tone, which divides the fourth from the fifth, and the semitone, which divides the third from the fourth. Hence the melodic distinction between whole-tone and half-tone steps is delivered by the same laws which deliver the primary consonances. A scale built from such steps should therefore return to the octave, via the primary harmonic intervals. If, however, the scale is built upon the perfect consonances, then the scale-steps will be uneven: the semitone between E and F, in the key of C, will be longer than half the whole-tone between F and G. This may not be noticeable for someone who is singing or playing a stringed instrument, and who never changes from the key of C major. But just as soon as you change the tonic, you realize that all other notes must be altered too, so as to come into harmonic relation with it. Movement to another key is therefore impeded by the very tones of the existing key, which cannot survive modulation. Key-relations are endowed, therefore, with a baffling complexity, and separate keys seem both to possess and to reject notes in common.

The solution to this problem is granted by the context-dependence of musical perception. The ear will tolerate departures from the perfect intervals, and will—in context—hear as a fourth or a fifth an interval which is, from the mathematical point of view, only approximate. This capacity is enhanced by the dynamic character that we attribute to tones (as opposed to the pitched sounds in which we hear them). If the octave is divided into twelve equal semitone steps, the resulting imperfect intervals will be heard as versions of the major third, fourth, fifth, and so on, even though only the octave in this system is perfect. Once this equal temperament has been

[5] In addition to the overtones, there are also 'combination tones' which can be heard when two notes sound together. These too confirm the primacy of the triad: see Revesz, *Psychology of Music*, 17–20.

established, the relations between keys become absolutely transparent. Any of the twelve semitones can serve as tonic, with a scale constructed from other tones within the system. All tones belong to all keys—either as members of the designated scale, or as 'accidentals'. Accidentals have the added function of opening avenues into other keys. All major keys are the same in their intervallic structure, as are all minor scales; scales differ only in the choice of tonic. The resulting system produces imperfect intervals—for example, fifths that are slightly higher in frequency than $2 : 3$, and major thirds that are perceptibly sharper than $4 : 5$. But the difference is untroubling, on account of our disposition to hear nearby frequencies as 'versions' of a single pitch. The distortions are invariably overridden by the perceived order, as the ear becomes used to travelling without strain between keys, experiencing the pitch spectrum as a single dimension of discrete and organized places, each with a settled musical character. Hence, when people really *listen* to the sounds that they are making, while attempting to 'add voices' and to move in the musical space defined by the overtone series, they will tend naturally towards tonality, and to the systematic key-relations which equal temperament makes available.

Such, at any rate, was the conclusion drawn by Helmholtz, who believed that the laws of classical harmony derive almost directly from the laws of physics, being attempts to capture in a body of rules, the dynamic properties imparted to pitched sounds by their overtones and combination tones. Music becomes difficult, even incomprehensible, when the upper partials beat against one another, or the notes move, as in atonal writing, in unpredictable steps across the space of music, unguided by consonant relations or the diatonic triads.

Helmholtz's theory of concord and discord is no longer accepted. A major triad in the bass will generate more conflicting overtones than a minor ninth in the upper register; nevertheless, we hear the first as consonant and the second as dissonant. Exactly why remains unclear, although it is plausible to suggest that our experience of consonance and dissonance is dependent upon our sensitivity to the tonal *system*.[6] Indeed, we can see the adoption of equal temperament, and our canon of triadic concords, as evidence of the distinction between sound and tone, and of the consequent impossibility of providing a purely acoustical theory of music. Our modern ways of hearing are conditioned by our sense of the force that lives in tones, which causes us to overlook acoustical impurities in the interests of greater and more varied organization. It is the dynamic properties of the tone itself that determine our experience of consonance and dissonance, and edge us towards the equal temperament which places the whole of tonal space within reach of its every occupant.

[6] Such is the view defended by Revesz, *Psychology of Music*.

In any case, it is difficult to sustain Helmholtz's view of tonality, as the 'natural' language of music. There is plenty of 'natural' music that retains only a distant hint of the diatonic scale: classical Arabian music, of the kind discussed by Al-Farabi, is an evident example. Moreover, the principal instances of 'natural music' in human history have tended to a pentatonic organization of the melodic line. While this preserves the octave, the fourth, and the fifth, it avoids semitones and therefore contains only a part of the diatonic scale, and only two triads (that of the tonic, which may be major or minor, and that of the mediant or submediant). There seem to be other principles at work in the 'natural' organization of music, that lead to this marked preference for the pentatonic scale.

On the other hand, it is interesting that natural harmony *does* move in the direction predicted by Helmholtz, *even when the melody is pentatonic.* This can be heard in Negro spirituals, where the triad is a fundamental harmonic device, obedient to the sense of key, and where added voices follow the overtone series. In such a case the higher notes in the series tend to be emphasized, notably the seventh and ninth—so moving already in the direction of the added note chords which are a standard device of jazz. (The reason for this is presumably that the leading-note has been already flattened by the pentatonic melody.) Such examples (for instance, Ex. 9.2), suggest that, while pentatonic organization is more stable from the melodic point of view, harmonic thinking tends to provide the pentatonic structure with a diatonic frame—the pentatonic melody *becomes tonal*, as in the opening of Vaughan Williams's Fifth Symphony in D minor (Ex. 9.3).

Whatever we think of the various scales used by 'natural music', we should certainly resist any suggestion that this music is *atonal.* Indian, Arab,

Ex. 9.2. Spiritual, 'Oh when I git t'Heaven' (Pentatonic melody, using the flattened seventh of F, but harmonized with a straight F minor triad)

Ex. 9.3. Vaughan Williams, Fifth Symphony in D major, opening

Chinese, and Balinese music are all 'tonicized', singling out a particular pitch and its octave equivalents as the principal tone, and often privileging the fifth above as a kind of dominant. We can most readily make sense of the phenomenon if we follow Reti in recognizing two kinds of tonality: the harmonic and the melodic.[7] Folksong and liturgical chant, in all traditions, tend to focus on a particular tone, to which the melody constantly returns, and which it emphasizes through rhythmic organization, repetition, and caesura. We spontaneously hear this note as the tonic, and construct the 'mode' of the piece on that assumption. The melodic elaboration of this tonic will not, typically, be constrained by polyphony; at most the harmonic dimension will be provided by a drone on the tonic and the fifth above, as in Indian music, or by parallel octaves or fourths, as in early medieval chant. Ornamentation, and free ('melismatic') elaboration, will therefore take the melodic line in directions that would forbid harmonization according to the diatonic tradition of classical music.

When music becomes polyphonic, however, the modes tend to collapse, of their own accord, into the diatonic scales. The stability of the pentatonic scale can be accounted for in this way: that it preserves just those notes of a

---

[7] *Tonality—Atonality—Pantonality* (London, 1958), 15–18.

mode which can be sung together without semitone or tritone dissonances. It is the 'reduced' form to which every folk-mode will tend, just as soon as the voices multiply. It is, in short, a step on the way to the triadic harmony which is the core of Western tonality.

Triadic Tonality

In describing the modes as pre-tonal, Schoenberg meant that they preceded the *triadic* tonality which emerged as voices were multiplied. Harmonic relations then began to arrange themselves not around the fourth, the fifth, and the octave, but around the triad, which quickly established itself as the only fully consonant three-tone chord. By the time of Rameau's *Treatise on Harmony* (1722), the fifth was seen as a sum of two thirds. For Rameau the principle of 'building in thirds' had become the fundamental rule of harmonic structure, so that the dissonant seventh and ninth chords acquired a harmonic identity on a par with that of the triad:

> we could consider thirds . . . as the sole elements of all chords. To form the perfect chord [i.e. the triad], we must add one third to the other; to form all dissonant chords, we must add three or four thirds to one another.[8]

Rameau went on to argue, in a way that subsequent musical practice has fully justified, that the chord on the dominant whose treble lies an octave and a fourth higher, should not be understood as a fourth chord, but as the eleventh chord, whose intermediate thirds have been suppressed.[9] Triadic organization explains the emerging dissonance of the fourth itself; for in the triadic system the fourth is an embryonic 6–4 chord, which demands resolution downwards on to a triad in root position. In the absence of contrary influences, therefore, the upper voice of a fourth leans to the semitone below.

Triadic tonality is often described as a set of conventions, more or less arbitrarily arrived at, and adopted for stylistic reasons. But the history of Western music belies that account. The triad owes its authority to its place in a system, the details of which were not so much made as discovered, through experiments in polyphony. Once discovered, the devices of triadic tonality became part of the repertoire, and instantly recognizable to the musical ear. A logical harmonic progression in Praetorius may remain logical in Bach, in Haydn, in Beethoven, and in Brahms, even if it has, by Brahms's day, become stylistically antiquated. This is why Helmholtz looked for an *acoustical* theory of triadic tonality: a theory that would pass beyond the intentional realm and the accidents of style, to find the roots of tonal organization in the nature of sound itself.

[8] *Treatise on Harmony*, tr. P. Gossett (New York, 1971), bk. 1, ch. 7, p. 39.
[9] Ibid., bk. 2, ch. 11.

Writers differ in their emphasis, but the following features are widely recognized as central to triadic tonality:

1. Key. Being in a key is not simply a matter of having a tonic. A key is a particular kind of organisation *around* the tonic, in which other notes are disposed in relation to it, and the whole system set in the context of other possible keys.[10] The result of this organization is to bring melody and harmony into close and constant relation. Even if Rameau exaggerates, when he writes that 'melody is only a consequence of harmony',[11] there is no doubt that the harmonic structure implied in the major and minor keys dictates the shape and development of tonal melodies. Some writers (Hindemith and Reti among them) believe that this has resulted in a certain melodic impoverishment, and that the endless melisma of the Gregorian chant shows a melodic inspiration that can never be recaptured by those who hear in triads.

2. The diatonic scale. Each key involves certain designated tones: 7, for the major key; 9 for the 'melodic minor', which distinguishes ascending and descending versions of the scale. The whole-tone interval is itself a product of (pre-triadic) tonal thinking, as is the semitone. It is an interesting fact that Schoenberg attempted to break from tonality by the use of all twelve semitones, in a serial organization. Yet the semitone owes its authority to the fact that it is the smallest interval recognized in *tonal* music; since the advent of equal temperament, the semitone has provided the standard unit for measuring intervals—a fact which is fundamental to the theory and practice of atonal music.

The scale depends upon and emphasizes the experience of the octave—a phenomenon that seems to exist in all musical traditions. The octave is heard as 'the same again'—it reproduces, at a higher pitch, the harmonic and melodic potential of the tone an octave below. Helmholtz's theory of harmony offers to explain the consonance of the octave (the frequency ratio $1 : 2$). But it does not explain the identity between its component tones. Triadic tonality involves an attempt to systematize such intuitive experiences of identity, similarity, and remoteness.

3. Non-designated tones. As tonality evolved, it began to extend a reprieve, as it were, to the 'foreign' tones—those excluded from the diatonic scale. By the time of Haydn and Mozart, it was clear that any of the twelve chromatic tones belongs to the key, and can be incorporated as an 'accidental'

---

[10] What is it that we recognize, when we recognize a key? This question is very puzzling, and I hardly know what to say in answer to it. For a psychological theory, which emphasizes the decisive role of octave, fifth, and major third in organizing our harmonic expectations, see Longuet-Higgins, 'Two Letters to a Musical Friend', in *Mental Processes*, 64–81.

[11] *Treatise on Harmony*, bk. 1, ch. 5, p. 22, and bk. 2, ch. 21, which contains Rameau's comprehensive assault on the modes of 'the ancients'.

in the melodic and harmonic structure. However, the role of these non-designated tones is subordinate to that of the designated tones, which define the principal regions of tonal space.

4. The role of the designated tones. Each tone has a character, arising from its relation to the tonic (the first and last note of the scale). Thus the fifth note of the scale, the dominant, points back to the tonic, while also being a place of rest—a place where a melody might linger for a while, without calling for a completing gesture, as in the nursery theme of Ex. 9.4. This special character of the dominant is matched by that of the subdominant (the fourth note of the scale): dominant and subdominant are 'metastable' positions on the scale, juxtaposed to the finality of the tonic. The two tones are heard in relation to the tonic, and we sense the possibilities of movement between them. The nursery theme plays with these auditory relations, with the implied harmony moving first from tonic to subdominant and back again, and then settling on the dominant for its passage home.

5. The circle of fifths and the harmonic scale. It is a striking feature of the diatonic scale that it can be derived in two ways: melodically (by moving stepwise through the octave) and harmonically. In the second case, we begin (in C major) from C, and move to the tone which most perfectly harmonizes with it, the dominant, G. We then move from G to its dominant, D, from D to A, from A to E, from E to B, and from B to F sharp. The result is the diatonic scale on the dominant: G.

If we repeat the process, starting from G, we arrive at the scale of the dominant of G, which is D major. Proceeding in this way, we find that all the major keys are one by one unfolded by the circle of fifths, each new key being related by a fifth to its neighbours. There is, in other words, a remarkable concidence between the harmonic order established by the twelve keys, and the melodic order of the scales which compose them.

If we substitute for the final fifth of the first circle on C (B to F sharp) a diminished fifth (B to F natural) the result is the diatonic scale on the tonic, rather than the scale on the dominant. The sequence of fifths now comes round in a perfect circle, enabling us to move back from F to its dominant C, which was our starting-point (Ex. 9.5). This new (imperfect) circle of fifths can be used to harmonize all diatonic melodies, and to generate the natural-sounding progressions which are the root of classical harmony. It also vividly dramatizes the choice that we must make as we progress round the circle: between staying in the same key, and diminishing

Ex. 9.4. Nursery theme ('Twinkle twinkle little star', 'Ah vous dirai-je maman', etc.)

Modulating

Ex. 9.5. The circle of fifths

the fifth, or substituting either F sharp for F natural, and so moving to the dominant, or B flat for B natural, so moving to the subdominant. It is the subliminal awareness of the diminished fifth which endows the leading tone—B natural—with its unsaturated character, its need for the tonic, in order that its harmonic tension should be resolved. In the diatonic scale, therefore, we find a remarkable synthesis of melodic and harmonic perception, and a key with which to open the whole realm of music.

The presence in the one-key circle of fifths of a flattened fifth may lead us to doubt that the harmonic scale is in any way 'natural'; for it seems as though we are flattening the fifth merely in order to conform to the octave equivalence required by the diatonic scale; in which case the supposed harmonic derivation of the scale from the interval of a fifth is a mere illusion. However, there is another way of looking at the matter. We should see the perfect circle of fifths as *sacrificed* in the diatonic system to the octave. The diatonic scale shows us how to retain both octave and fifth as the primary harmonic affinities, by making one small but necessary adjustment. Moreover, it creates the background against which the perfect circle of fifths is heard as a *modulation* into a neighbouring key which is itself removed by a fifth from the original. (This key being either the dominant or the subdominant.) In a deeper sense, therefore, the diatonic scale can be heard as a system whereby the two primary harmonic affinities—octave and fifth—are worked into the very substance of music, and their intrinsic tension resolved. In medieval music, the diminished fifth was avoided by the device of *musica ficta*—which means, in effect, sharpening or flattening one of the tones, in defiance of the diatonic scale, but without treating the tone in question as genuinely chromatic. The diatonic circle of fifths provides the rationale for this practice, though it is a rationale of which the medievals were ignorant.[12]

6. The relation between major and minor. Major and minor are heard as *versions* of the same key, even though the designated tones are not the same. This effect, which stems from the role of tonic and dominant in establishing a key, has provided composers with one of the most powerful

---

[12] See the explanation of this practice given by R. Donington, *The Interpretation of Early Music* (London, 1963).

means of expression—used with exquisite taste by Schubert in song after song, and with more questionable taste by Strauss in *Also Sprach Zarathustra* (Ex. 9.6). (Though note the proximity of this bathetic gesture to the genuinely tragic opening of Schubert's String Quartet in G major, D887, Ex. 9.7.) One and the same melody can exist in two versions—major and minor—and the change in melodic impulse is felt also as a change in harmonic structure. Familiar examples include the principal theme of Smetana's tone-poem 'Vltava', and the first song in *Winterreise*. This experience of

Ex. 9.6. Richard Strauss, *Also Sprach Zarathustra*, opening

Ex. 9.7. Schubert, String Quartet in G major, D887, opening

identity-in-difference helps to reinforce the status of melody, as a kind of musical individual.

7. The system of triads. This has been an immovable part of the tonal language since the Renaissance, and it is now difficult to hear the relation between the tones of the scale without also sensing the triads that move with them, and which impart to them the harmonic tension that reinforces their melodic tendency. (This is true even of the crudest popular music.)

The system of triads has been the subject of deep and illuminating speculation in our time, and two great (if sometimes dogmatic) works called *Harmonielehre*—one by Schenker and the other by Schoenberg—contain more wisdom than I can hope to summarize. In essence, however, the phenomenon is this: by adding to each tone of the diatonic scale the third and fifth tone above, we form a triad, which, with one exception, creates a consonant harmony, being either the major or minor triad of the key which takes that tone as its tonic. The one exception is the triad on the leading tone (B in the key of C), which, as noted above, has a diminished fifth, and therefore a tritone (the *diabolus in musica*) contained within it. This triad has an unstable quality. It also seems to call for a fundamental tone of the dominant. Add the dominant, and the result is the dominant seventh chord—the mild dissonance which strives to resolve itself by passing to the tonic triad. The subliminal presence of this chord is part of what we notice, when we hear the leading-tone 'tend' towards the tonic.

The triads have a natural order: we are as familiar with the passage from the one to the other, as with the movement from tone to tone. Moreover, they can be inverted, and change their character with each inversion; they can also be spread over many octaves, with similar effect. Hence the chords in Ex. 9.8 are both the same and not the same. Because of this, there can be interesting counterpoint on one chord, as in the prelude to *Rheingold*, or the magnificent conclusion to the first movement of Bruckner's Seventh Symphony. A simple triad may still astonish us, on account of the spaces between its parts, and the places that they occupy in tonal space—as in Ex. 9.9 (the opening of Britten's canticle *Abraham and Isaac*), which is in effect an E flat major triad, with the fifth omitted. Spacing is important in atonal music: indeed, it is one way of creating consonance and dissonance.

Ex. 9.8. Versions and inversions of the C major triad

But it is hard to reproduce this precise effect, of a familiar harmony spread gossamer thin through the whole of musical space. Indeed, atonal dissonances tend to change character quite radically according to their inversions and spacing, so that the four chords of Ex. 9.10, for example, are only with difficulty heard as the same. (The first evokes C major, the fourth E minor, partly because we instinctively search for the diatonic context that would resolve them.)

Ex. 9.9. Britten, *Abraham and Isaac*, opening

Ex. 9.10. Spacing and inversion of dissonant harmony

8. Polyphony and voice-leading. Tonal music came to the triads through polyphony: they are the natural consonances which we discover when three or more distinct voices join together without singing in unison or in parallel motion. This is a very important fact historically, and also aesthetically. The triads are filled with the movement of the voices that produce them. Even in the classical style of J. C. Bach and Haydn, in which the chord has been partly emancipated from counterpoint, it is treated also as a synthesis of voices, each with a natural tendency to move off in some direction. (Consider the sequence of chords which concludes Schubert's famous setting of Heine's 'Doppelgänger', D957, Ex. 9.11. Each note in each successive chord is responding to a note in its predecessor; the chord is an aggregate of voices, horizontally ordered.)

This way of treating harmony emerges from the diatonic scale, whose order is harmonic and melodic at once. Melodies accompanied by block

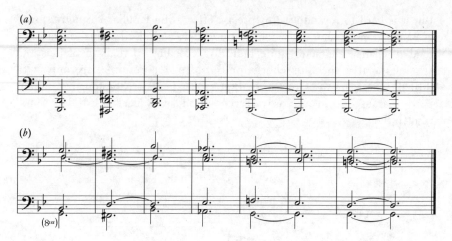

Ex. 9.11. Schubert, 'Der Doppelgänger': (a) concluding chord sequence; (b) the same as heard

chords (strummed, for example, on a guitar) have only one half of tonality, and are far indeed from the sense of a tonal space which is present in almost all works in the classical tradition. This can be seen in one of the most significant aesthetic disasters of modern times—the destruction of folksong by harmony. Even the meandering songs of the Arabs, which are in themselves barely tonal, using modal scales with stretched or contracted intervals, are now heard above diatonic chords. These chords are not voices, and have nothing to add to the vocal line: instead they cancel its native melody, while imprisoning the movement in blocks of synthetic sound.

In Renaissance and classical part-writing, the triad is treated always as part of a *process*, in which tension is created and resolved. The voices come together on a triad or its inversion, and the progression between the triads must make harmonic sense, just as the several voices make melodic sense. Variety and tension are enhanced by the use of suspensions and passing-tones (see below); while the sense of key derives from the fact that each triad is treated as part of the tonal scheme.

9. Chord relations. Although voice-leading has played such an important part in establishing the harmonic value of the individual triads, we must also recognize that the relations between chords have become hypostatized as harmonic progressions, which make sense even when the relations between the voices are imperfect or obscure. The sequence I–V–I, for instance—the move from the tonic triad to the triad on the dominant and back again—is an established harmonic progression, whose instances are not only recognizable in themselves, but also inherently 'closed', even in the absence of effective voice-leading.

Harmonic progressions are not composed only of triads. Seventh chords, altered chords, and chords with augmented and diminished intervals, have slowly acquired stable characters, through their habitual relations with other chords in the diatonic repertoire. Progressions involving these chords belong to the repertoire of all musicians who improvise tonal music, from Bach to Thelonius Monk. Although voice-leading has been marginalized in the study of harmonic progressions, its influence can still be felt. Inversions of a single triad are not always substitutable for one another, and every coherent progression requires genuine voice-leading in the bass.

10. Cadences. These provide a harmonic boundary—whether closure (the perfect cadence), or interruption (imperfect and interrupted cadences). The traditional V–I, IV–I and II–V–I progressions have been so embellished by the tonal tradition, that it would be the work of a chapter to describe the many ways of bringing a harmonic sequence to a cadential conclusion. Consider the particular version of IV–I that resolves almost everything in *Tristan und Isolde*, and brings the work to its close (Ex. 9.12). Or consider the even more spectacular version of IV–I that brings Skriabin's *Poem of Ecstasy* to its triumphant conclusion (Ex. 9.13).

Cadences are an integral part of triadic tonality. Yet it is difficult to describe exactly what they are. Not every V–I is a cadence from dominant to tonic: only when properly prepared, at both harmonic and melodic level, can the *cadence* be heard. The music must have already created in the

Ex. 9.12. Wagner, *Tristan und Isolde*, final cadence

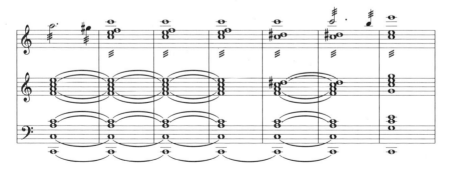

Ex. 9.13. Skriabin, *Poem of Ecstasy*

listener the expectation of home, long before the gesture of arriving there, if he is to hear a *conclusion* in the music. It is arguable, for example, that Chopin, who begins his Prelude, Op. 28 No. 2 in E minor, only to meander into A minor, does not really give an audible cadence at the end of the piece, despite making all the requisite *sounds* (Ex. 9.14). Here we seem to have another of those areas in which what is heard *in* music cannot be fully described in acoustical terms.

Ex. 9.14. Chopin, Prelude, Op. 28 No. 2, conclusion

If you try to imagine what music in our tradition would be without the cadence, and without the 'sense of an ending' that comes with it, you will surely agree that the cadence is not an embellishment, but an integral part of the experience of structure and form. Atonal music can create the sense of an ending—but it is often not by the inner logic of the music, which remains 'unclosed' even beyond the final measure, but by emphasis—a sudden loud chord, for example, a rhythmic climax, or a dwindling into nothingness, as in the final bars of *Wozzeck*. These gestures are far removed from the orderly grammar of a tonal cadence. Again, this is not to deny the reality of musical expectations in atonal music: it is to question whether these expectations can lead towards closure. When the first movement of Schoenberg's Fourth String Quartet, Op. 37, comes to a conclusion, you hear the two hexachords of the basic series played alternately as tone-clusters. But if you know that the movement will end on the hexachord containing C sharp, this is not because the harmony tends in this direction—rather than towards the rival hexachord—but only because the first violin has been insisting on C sharp for three bars, while the other instruments have studiously avoided it. (Ex. 9.15.)

Ex. 9.15. Schoenberg, Fourth String Quartet, Op. 37, first movement, conclusion

11. The independence of the bass. Even when voice-leading ceases to play a major role, the bass voice persists in tonal music as an independent melodic line. The reason for this is not hard to find. Harmonies rest on the bass-line, and are heard in relation to it. Triadic tonality therefore forces the bass into a prominence matched only by the principal melodic voice, and melodic constraints automatically apply to it.

According to Zarlino:

> Just as the earth is the foundation for the other elements, so does the bass have the property of sustaining, establishing, and strengthening the other parts. It is thus taken as the basis and foundation of harmony and is called the bass—the basis and support, so to speak.[13]

The metaphors here convey the fact that Zarlino is describing a musical, rather than an acoustical, function. This is how we *hear* the bass in the tonal system.

12. Modulation. The harmonic presentation of a key opens the way to changes of key, and therefore to one of the most impressive and magical of musical effects. As I argued above, modulation is already implicit in the circle of fifths; its subliminal presence in the diatonic scale is precisely what enables a composer to treat all the chromatic tones as part of the key. The fact that we hear major and minor as versions of the *same* key opens yet another road to modulation, by borrowing triads from the corresponding minor or major scale. Moreover each key has a relative minor or major, whose designated tones are identical with or include those of the key. By reaching into the triadic repertoire of these related keys, a composer finds a rich resource for spontaneous modulation, of a kind that will be heard as both natural and thrilling by a musical person.

Modulation reinforces our sense of the distinction between harmonic and melodic organization. To modulate it is necessary not merely to land on a melodic tone that belongs to another key, but to land on the *chords* of that key. The art of modulation involves the mastery of harmonic progressions.

[13] *Istitutzioni harmoniche* (Venice, 1558; complete edn., 3 vols., Venice, 1589), pt. iii, ch. 58, pp. 281–2.

Hence the use of purely chordal modulation tables in Schoenberg's *Harmonielehre*—Ex. 9.16.

13. The tonal centre and the harmonic field. Tonal music does not derive merely from the notes of the diatonic scale and the harmonies which are implied by them. It uses those phenomena in order to create a tonal centre, which in turn generates the 'field of force' through which the music passes. A triad may dominate a particular passage—not by causing it to modulate, but by making us hear all the harmonies as extensions or elaborations of it. Consider the tonic triad of B flat major, as it appears in the first bar of the aria 'Mache dich, mein Herze, rein', from the *St Matthew Passion*, BWV244 (Ex. 9.17*a*). Here the tonic triad dominates the other harmonies, which renounce their sovereignty in its presence. All the chords in this bar are heard as elaborations of the B flat major triad, even the dominant seventh at the close of it. And the effect continues through the next bar, despite the loss of the B flat pedal, as suspensions carry the music forward to the B flat triad, second inversion, which opens the third bar. It is this very triad which sounds again at the opening of the fourth bar, when, however, the F in the bass is heard as establishing the dominant, so introducing the first genuine shift away from the tonic harmony.

A comparable effect is that of the pedal-point, which causes harmonies to stabilize around a point of rest, from which the music refuses to depart until the bass moves on. Witness the standard device, used to such consummate effect by Bach and Haydn, of the pedal on the dominant, in which a vast array of harmonies can be assembled, as it were, at the door of the tonic, all to come home at once as the dominant gives way. (An example from the opening chorus of the *St Matthew Passion* is given in Ex. 9.17*b*.)

14. Structure and prolongation. 'Mache dich' (Ex. 9.17*a*) would be described by Heinrich Schenker as *prolonging* the initial tonic harmony for two

Ex. 9.16. Schoenberg, *Harmonielehre*, modulation tables

Ex. 9.17. J. S. Bach, *St Matthew Passion*, BWV244 (*a*) 'Mache dich, mein Herze, rein'; (*b*) from the opening chorus

measures, through superficial changes. According to Schenker, there is in all classical tonal music a distinction between structural events, and their prolongations. It is through prolongation that the musical organism grows around its audible frame; but we perceive the frame *as* a frame: individual tones and harmonies stand out in our perception as places *towards which* and *from which* the music moves. This is what gives sense and order to our experience of movement and boundary in music.

Schenker used the distinction between structure and prolongation to build an ambitious and highly controversial theory of music, which derives the foreground of a piece of music hierarchically from the cadence, in accordance with the laws of counterpoint. Such is the importance of this theory, that I postpone discussion of it until Chapter 10, when I shall provide a more philosophical context for its principal claims. It is not necessary to accept the theory, however, in order to recognize the intentional reality from which it derives: the presence in tonal music of an audible structure, composed of tones and harmonies which are heard as 'stations on the way'. Whether these structural events are also hierarchically ordered, in the way suggested by Schenker, is a question which does not yet require an answer.

The Effects of Tonality

To list all the features which endow tonality with its aesthetic character is a task beyond my power and scope. However, I shall quickly review what seem to me to be the most important of these features, and the ones which have contributed most to shaping the metaphors through which we understand the phenomenal space of music.

1. First is key. Normally a piece of tonal music is *in* a certain key, and could be transposed to another key without losing its identity (as with songs). We hear one and the same melody, now in C major, now in E major. This experience of 'same again' should not be confused with the experience (available equally in atonal music) of hearing a phrase or motif at different *pitches*. It is entirely *sui generis*, and gives to our conception of the musical individual a richness and diversity all of its own.

The point is brought home by those rare cases of 'same again' in which one and the same melody appears now in one key, now in another, while remaining at exactly the same pitch. Consider the example from the slow movement of Schubert's last sonata (Exx. 2.60 and 2.61), in which a melody is harmonized first in C sharp minor, and then in E major, with scarcely a single pitch altered. It is the same melody in a new context: and the value, implications, and direction of every single note in it is changed. (You might say that in its second occurrence the melody is composed of completely *different* tones, which happen to be acoustically indistinguishable: for now it begins on $\hat{3}$ of E major, whereas before it began on $\hat{5}$ of C sharp minor.)

Tonality is not present only at one level. A melody may be harmonized in one key, against a rival key in the background. For example, the penultimate movement of Stravinsky's *Rite of Spring* establishes a background tonality of B minor, just before the melody enters in an unambiguous G sharp minor. The background tonality continues undeterred, and leads the music naturally towards the D minor of the sacrificial dance (Ex. 9.18).

As a result of the innovations made by Wagner and his immediate followers, we have become familiar with tonal music that has no settled key,

Ex. 9.18. Stravinsky, *The Rite of Spring*, penultimate movement

but which drifts through keys without emphasizing any of them. Such extended tonality exists in many forms, and in many degrees of emancipation. In the songs of Hugo Wolf, for example, a key may be affirmed at the beginning, and reaffirmed at the end, but with no intervening harmonies that endorse it. We may be reluctant to say that the song is really 'in' the key whose signature it bears: just as we may be reluctant to say that the prelude to *Tristan und Isolde* is really 'in' A minor—not because it is in some other key, but because it is 'in' no key at all. Such new forms of tonality have been explored by Patrick McCreless and others,[14] and form a

[14] McCreless, 'Ernst Kurth and the Analysis of the Music of the Late 19th Century', *Music Theory Spectrum*, 5 (1983); R. Bailey, 'The Structure of the *Ring* and its Evolution', *Nineteenth-Century Music*, i (1977/8), 48–61. Bailey, following McCreless, distinguishes three types of tonality: the associative, the expressive, and the directional.

fascinating subject of musical analysis. They do not constitute a break with tonality, but rather a 'setting in motion' of the tonal centre. They stand to classical tonality as the Baroque architecture of Bernini and Borromini stands to the classical orders: something once fixed and monumental has been uprooted, set in motion, and employed in a wholly new spirit of design.

2. Polyphony and counterpoint. This feature has probably been the most dynamic force in the development of Western music. It was through Renaissance polyphony that harmonic progressions, passing-tones, and suspensions came to the fore. And polyphony led naturally to counterpoint in the tonal tradition. Counterpoint endows simultaneous voices with melodic independence, within a single harmonic structure. In its simplest form—the canon—the independence of the voices is secured by assigning a single subject to each, so that the melody of the first voice is heard again (or in a modified form) in the second. Consider two very different examples: the canon between piano and strings in the Scherzo of Schubert's Piano Trio in E flat major, D929, and the canon on the fourth from Bach's 'Goldberg' Variations, BWV988 (Exx. 9.19 and 9.20). Schubert's canon involves an inspired melody, whose canonical double is instantly recognizable as the same again; and the two parts between them lead the piece through harmonies that seem wholly uncontrived and logical. Bach's canon is more remarkable: for there is scarcely a listener who will fail to notice that the two upper voices are in canon, despite the fact that they are separated by a fourth, and despite the fact that the melody sounding in the one voice is the mirror image of the melody sounding in the other. This kind of lucidity derives to a great measure from the fact that Bach's two melodies are both beautiful and memorable as melodies, and also create between them a kind of question-and-answer sequence which is a fitting embellishment to the underlying harmonic progression.

Ex. 9.19. Schubert, Piano Trio in E flat major, D929, third movement

Ex. 9.20. J. S. Bach, 'Goldberg' Variations, BWV988, canon at the fourth (bass voice omitted)

Polyphony played a major role in generating the harmonic language of modern music. The great composers of the last century continued the practice of their predecessors, by deriving harmonies from the inner voices that move antiphonally between bass and treble. You should not think of the first chord of *Tristan und Isolde* merely as a new acoustical effect—as though nobody had used this *chord* before. Acoustically speaking, they had: witness Mozart, in the Piano Sonata in F major, K. 533 (Ex. 9.21), or Purcell, in *Dido and Aeneas* (Ex. 9.22). Described in one way (which is acoustically, but not *musically* accurate), the 'Tristan' chord is an inverted minor triad with added major sixth. And such a chord forms a natural subdominant harmony in Bach or Purcell, as we see. (Rameau discusses the chord,

Ex. 9.21. Mozart, Piano Sonata in F major, K. 533, first movement

Ex. 9.22. Purcell, *Dido and Aeneas*, 'When I am laid in earth'

therefore, as part of the 'irregular cadence' in the minor.)[15] But the chord was already lifted from that context by Mozart, and used like the A flat seventh two bars later to dislocate the key. (In this use the chord is best described as a half-diminished seventh.) Wagner's originality consists in the way in which the voices that compose this chord promptly move away from it, on to a quasi-resolution that leaves the key only weakly determined, by the dominant seventh of A on which the sequence pauses (Ex. 9.23). The originality of the harmony derives at least in part from its inner counterpoint, and when we speak of the 'Tristan' chord, we really mean the chord in *this* contrapuntal setting. This is perhaps why we can describe its use in

Ex. 9.23. Wagner, *Tristan und Isolde*, prelude

[15] *Treatise on Harmony*, bk. 2, ch. 7.

Götterdämmerung as involving the *same* chord: for although it is 'resolved' differently (that is, on to another dominant seventh), it is still resolved by a chromatic movement of the voices (Ex. 9.24). By the time Berg has come to quote the chord and its 'resolution' in the *Lyric Suite*, however, it has ceased to be the same chord—indeed, it has almost ceased to be a chord entirely, since it is now a vertical statement of set-class 4–27 (the four-tone class of pitch sets, whose members are related to each other as 0258, the numbers denoting semitone steps).[16] This set-class is itself embedded in the twelve-tone series of Berg's work, and generalized in ways which contain no audible reference to *Tristan*: only the strength and familiarity of Wagner's original utterance enables us to perceive bars 26–7 of the last movement as a quotation (see Ex. 9.25). (In none of the instances that I have cited should we describe the 'Tristan' chord as a 'spy', still less as a 'highly amusing fellow', *pace* Schoenberg: see the discussion of the chord above, Chapter 3.) The case illustrates the way in which harmonies appear in Wagner—never merely as chords (as they might in a second-rate recitative), but always as a confluence of voices.

Ex. 9.24. Wagner, *Götterdämmerung*, Act 3

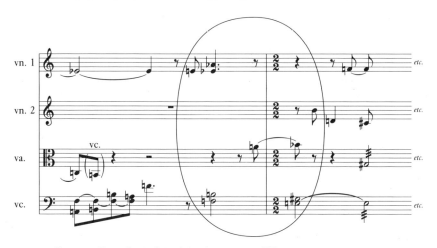

Ex. 9.25. Berg, *Lyric Suite* for string quartet, fifth movement

---

[16] The set-theoretic notation for atonal music is described further in Ch. 13.

The distinction between melody and bass is known in many cultures; so too is the distinction between melody and harmony. But how many cultures pay this kind of detailed attention to the inner voice, and attempt to compose harmonies from independent melodic lines? When composers, during the twentieth century, began to move into new regions of tonality, it was as much as anything the logic of the inner voice that was compelling them, as in the prelude to *Tristan und Isolde*. Witness Walton at the beginning of the Violin Concerto in B minor (Ex. 9.26), in which the two voices of violin and bassoon weave between them the novel harmonic texture over the B minor ostinato. Or Bartók in the Third String Quartet, where harmonies that had never been heard before (or at least, never heard as harmonies), come whispering to us from the three enquiring voices (Ex. 9.27). Such examples suggest that the very force which created tonality—the force of polyphony—was also destined to destroy it.

3. Tension and resolution through harmonic progression. This much-studied phenomenon is of inexhaustible interest, and has inspired some of the most important ventures in music theory, such as Schenker's analytical method. Tension may be built up entirely through suspensions, as in Bach's Prelude in B flat minor from the First Book of the Forty-Eight (Ex. 9.28)—here the sequence climaxes on a diminished seventh chord, before resolving in a cadence to the tonic (in the major). But tension can be heightened and extended, by resolving dissonances into dissonances—i.e. resolving the tension between some of the voices only to create a new tension between others. A sufficiently firm tonal background will enable the composer to augment the tension to agonizing extremes in this way, as in the first movement of Walton's First Symphony.

Some might wonder why we should speak of 'tension and release', when describing tonal progressions. Is this one of those 'indispensable metaphors', that I discussed in Chapter 3? Or is it, as some would argue, a piece of ideology, an attempt to read relations of social power into the surface of music?[17] Clearly, the choice of language here is not neutral: it reflects a particular way of *hearing* music, and one that could be altered or amended. Nevertheless, the relations that we hear in this way, in terms of tension and release, do not depend on that metaphor. Those who hear 'attraction and repulsion', or 'saturation and unsaturation', or 'pain and soothing', still hear a good part of what *we* hear, when hearing harmonic progression. For this thing that we hear lies in the nature of tonality.

Perhaps there can be similar experiences in listening to non-tonal music. Nevertheless, tonality is not an *accidental* feature of music in which

[17] Such is claimed e.g. by S. McClary, *Feminine Endings: Music, Gender and Sexuality* (Minneapolis, 1991).

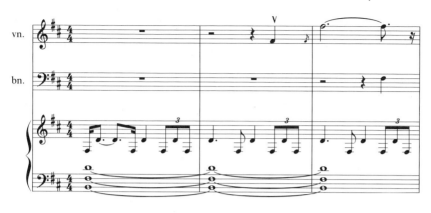

Ex. 9.26. Walton, Violin Concerto in B minor, opening

Ex. 9.27. Bartók, Third String Quartet, opening

Ex. 9.28. J. S. Bach, *The Well-Tempered Clavier*, First Book, Prelude in B flat

harmonic tension is heard. For the principal instrument of tension is the suspended tone. A suspension occurs only when we have a clear sense that one of the voices has delayed moving to its 'rightful' place—i.e. its place in a stable harmony, such as a tonal triad, which requires no further resolution. This is how we hear, for example, the opening of Mozart's Twenty-Second Piano Concerto in E flat major, K. 482 (Ex. 9.29). The delicious clash of tones and semitones might occur in another context, and yet our expectations of resolution be defeated— as in Ex. 9.30, from Britten's *Peter Grimes*. As soon as the prospect of resolution disappears, we cease to hear tension, and hear something else—a sequence of harmonies which are piquant, but also, unlike the suspensions in the Mozart, relaxed and directionless.

Ex. 9.29. Mozart, Twenty-Second Piano Concerto in E flat major, K. 482, opening

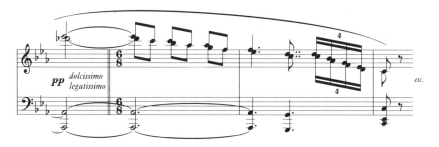

Ex. 9.30. Britten, *Peter Grimes*, Act 3

4. The 'journey through tonal space'. The 'narrative' character of tonal music has been frequently remarked upon.[18] We are dealing here with a fundamental musical experience, and one that is responsible for much of our awareness of structure. Even in the simplest tonal melody, we experience harmonic implications, and arrange the harmonies according to their structural importance. Scarlatti's charming melody in Ex. 9.31 moves through dominant regions twice, before reaching the sub-dominant in bar 4, and coming to a temporary rest on the dominant. Not only do we sense this movement; we also recognize the first two dominant regions as unimportant in comparison with the final one—passing harmonies which merely sustain the melodic line on its way towards the descent on the subdominant. (Hence Scarlatti's impeccable harmonization (Ex. 9.32), using the dominant *minor* triad in bar 3, in order to postpone any sense of resolution, and the ghost of a 'Tristan' chord in bar 4 in order to prolong the subdominant region.) This kind of 'structural hearing' has been singled out by Schenker and his disciples as the key to tonal understanding. And much learned ink has been spilled in the (highly controversial) attempt to describe it.

Music will shift through keys in the course of harmonizing a melody or as a result of voice-leading. But these local shifts tend to take place against a far more slow-moving background, in which a tonal centre is reaffirmed through many superficial changes, to be replaced only gradually by another and rival centre. This slowly shifting centre is the operative device of 'sonata form'—that ideal type of composition to which, as Charles Rosen has shown, very few classical sonata movements actually conform.[19] As

Ex. 9.31. Domenico Scarlatti, Sonata in D minor, L413, melody

Ex. 9.32. Domenico Scarlatti, Sonata in D minor, L413, melody and bass

[18] Schoenberg, *Harmonielehre* (3rd edn., Vienna, 1922), 129; McClary, *Feminine Endings*, 15.
[19] *The Classical Style: Haydn, Mozart and Beethoven* (New York, 1972); and *Sonata Forms* (rev. edn., New York, 1988).

Rosen makes clear, however, the classical style achieves its effects through the creation of successive tonal *regions*, regardless of the overall pattern of the movement. These regions are like fields of force, changing the character of the music as it moves among them. They create the contours of the musical journey, and the sense of being *taken* somewhere, through a soundscape of tones.

Those are not the only effects of tonality in music: but taken together they give rise to a powerful thought: namely, that tonality is not just a *style*, but an *order*, which we hear in music despite the greatest divergences of style. If we compare tonality to a language, it is surely for this reason, that it wholly permeates the life and organization of any piece that displays it, and offers an inexhaustible fund of artistic possibilities. The features that I have listed give us a partial description of what we understand, in understanding tonal music, and seem to justify not only our ways of describing music, but all our ordinary responses to it.

To put the matter simply, the order of triadic tonality is an order of polyphonic elaboration. Tonal harmony enables us to hear simultaneous musical events as similar or varied; as moving together through a common intentional space; as creating tension and resolution, attraction and repulsion; as answering, commenting upon, and questioning each other; as moving with the force and logic of gestures which are mutually aware, and mutually accommodating. Triadic tonality is not a system of conventions, arbitrarily devised, and imposed by fiat; it is the life-giving air which the voices breathe, and through which they move in dance-like discipline. Tonal relations are *audible* relations, constituted intentionally. They operate through the three dimensions of musical organization—rhythmic, melodic, and harmonic—so as to determine the directions and motion of the music in each. In describing the tonal order of a work, therefore, we are describing what is heard, when it is heard as music.

In referring to triadic tonality as an order of elaboration, I have given only a partial account of it. For what exactly *is* an elaboration? And what kind of order is involved? In answer to the second question, theorists have offered hierarchical theories of tonality. That of Lerdahl and Jackendoff has been considered already; that of Schenker will occupy us in the chapter which follows. Suffice it to say that such theories are in general too bold, too comprehensive, and also too restrictive. They are too bold in their postulation of an *underlying* order, which exfoliates in the musical surface. They are too comprehensive in applying equally to music that is heard as supremely ordered, like the sonata movements of Mozart or the mazurkas of Chopin, and that which has no audible logic, like the monologues of Philip Glass. And they are too restrictive in excluding music whose tonal order is constituted entirely on the surface, and in defiance of the traditional laws of harmony—like Benjamin Britten's *Curlew River*, or Dallapiccola's *Il prigioniero*.

As for what is meant by 'elaboration', an illuminating comparison is provided by decorative lines and arabesques, in which the intention is to produce a visual *Gestalt*. We easily recognize one curlicue as a version of, a continuation of, or a response to another; we assign boundaries and movement to each arabesque, and we recognize the visual equivalent of closure—the boundary which is also a completion. We spontaneously perceive the relations between squiggles, and have a clear idea of how a squiggle might be elaborated—through imitation, variation, prolongation, augmentation, and diminution—so as to make a complex and satisfying pattern. Something similar occurs in music; and tonal harmony enables us to extend this order of elaboration through many simultaneous voices, and so to turn ornament into architecture.

Imperfect Tonality

But this very 'order of elaboration' has pushed music through the boundary of triadic harmony, in search of new musical relations. Music has developed beyond traditional tonality in five ways:

1. Extended tonality, of which there are three kinds. The first incorporates into tonal structures passages, melodies, and harmonies that belong to some other musical system: the pentatonic scale in Vaughan Williams, for instance, or the whole-tone scale in Debussy's *Pelléas et Mélisande*. These non-diatonic elements may, as in the Debussy, disrupt the tonal logic, and remove the possibility of a tonal resolution. Nevertheless, they sit within the tonal frame quite happily, because the whole-tone and pentatonic scales overlap in whole or in part with the diatonic scale, and because whole-tone and pentatonic harmonies are acoustically identical with harmonies in the tonal system. (For example, the augmented major triad occurs in both the tonal and the whole-tone system.) Whole-tone sequences are not unknown even in the most traditional tonal melodies—as in the Bach chorale ('Es ist genug') quoted to such effect by Berg in the Violin Concerto (Ex. 9.33). Tovey has

Ex. 9.33. Bach, 'Es ist genug'

even suggested that the whole-tone scale should be seen as an arpeggiated chord, which resolves spontaneously by chromatic steps on to tonal harmonies.[20] Tovey is of course exaggerating; nevertheless, that is how Puccini treats the whole-tone scale in the second act of *Madama Butterfly*, and it is not too far from the treatment accorded to it by Debussy in *Pelléas*.

The second kind of extended tonality is that which has been most fertile in our century: the incorporation of 'wrong notes' into tonal melodies and harmonies—the stretching of musical space, so as to escape the limits of the diatonic scale. From Janáček to Schnittke we find composers refusing to respect the 'designated tones' of the key, and allowing any of the twelve tones to enter into melodic and harmonic relation with the notes of the scale, without treating these 'outside' tones as either accidentals or avenues to modulation. Music that is as tonal in its organization as Schumann may as a result be sprinkled with notes that are ruled out by the old laws of harmony. (Consider, for example, the Gloria of Poulenc, or the symphonies of Martinů.)

Historians of music used once to refer to *Tristan und Isolde* as announcing the break with the tonal tradition, repeating a thought that was placed in their heads by Schoenberg. It is true that the chromatic harmonies of that work often produce uncertainty as to the tonal centre: but such uncertainty is not unknown in the tonal tradition. (Think of the evocation of chaos that opens Haydn's *Creation*, or the way in which Beethoven introduces a key change gradually and by stages, with frequent backward glances to the previous tonal centre (*Grosse Fuge*, Op. 133, e.g.).) The organization of *Tristan* is tonal: even the harmonies are, for the most part, triadic, though usually with an added step of a kind familiar from the classical seventh chord. Consider the chords derived from stacked up thirds in Ex. 9.34. These (which include the 'Tristan' chord) form the basic harmonic repertoire of the *Ring*; but they are used in that work to build a *tonal* organization, and one, moreover, in which background tonality can be clearly distinguished through the superficial veil of chord-colour. *Tristan* should be seen not as the farewell to tonality, but as the harbinger of new kinds of tonal organization. The harmonic movement of the 'Liebestod'—a sequence of third progressions—makes sense only because it is taking the melodic line through tonal areas, none of which has the power to detain the melody, so boundless

Ex. 9.34. Third chords

[20] 'Harmony' in *Musical Articles from the Encyclopedia Britannica* (London, 1944) 67–9.

is its ambition (see Ex. 9.35). Surely we should describe this as tonal music; for what is creating this astonishing sense of freedom, if it is not harmonic progression and keys which are never affirmed, but move spectre-like on the musical horizon, beckoning and vanishing in endless procession?

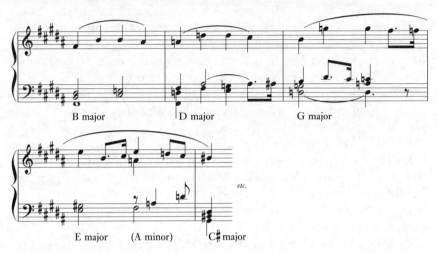

B major   D major   G major

E major   (A minor)   C♯ major

Ex. 9.35. Wagner, 'Liebestod', harmonic scheme

In this respect, however, *Tristan* can be seen as announcing the third and most interesting kind of extended tonality: the 'wandering tonality', in which perfect triads are seldom used, in which rogue chords which demand resolution are left unresolved, and in which, nevertheless, there is a constant reference to a tonal centre—although frequently a shifting centre. A clear illustration is given by Ex. 9.36: the prelude 'Ondine' from Debussy's Second Book. This piece begins and ends in D major, makes much use of the tonic and dominant of D in the bass, and ends on a major triad; but the harmonic textures are constantly pointing away from the key. The sequence of fourth chords in bars 4, 6 and 7, for example, demands resolution into F sharp major or B: a resolution that is not granted. The decorative arpeggios contain playful mixtures of chords, and the muffled third section in F sharp major avoids every triad of that key. Moreover, the jubilant sparkle with which the piece ends is not really a cadence, but a superimposition of the rival triads of F sharp major and D major. If D major unambiguously wins in this decorative contest, it is because Debussy has discreetly affirmed it as the home key, even in those passages which point in an atonal direction. But one looks in vain for a sign that Debussy is guided by the rules of tonal harmony, or is eager to impose upon the music any key structure that does not emerge of its own accord from the competing sonorities of the chords. (Copland's words therefore ring true: 'Debussy . . . was the first composer

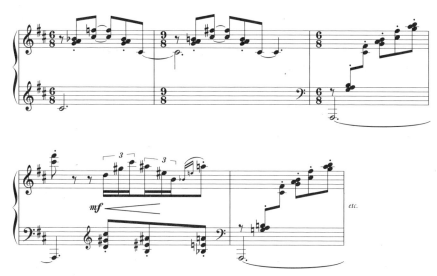

Ex. 9.36. Debussy, Preludes, Second Book, 'Ondine'

of our time who dared to make his ear the sole judge of what was good harmonically.')[21]

Reti has made the interesting suggestion that this kind of wandering tonality derives from a new approach to the melodic line—or rather a very old approach, brought into relation with a newer kind of harmonic thinking. According to Reti, the classical melody, as we find it in Mozart, Haydn, or Beethoven, is shaped by the harmonic syntax of tonality, with antecedent and consequent typically organized around the passage from tonic to dominant and back again. With Debussy, however, we have a return to the melodic tonality of folk music and liturgical chant, in which the melodic line obeys no such harmonic logic.[22] The melodic tonality of the leading voice depends upon chords that depart from the tonal logic without cancelling it entirely. Reti's suggestion is not without merit, in drawing attention to the dual nature of tonal organization—as melodic line and harmonic progression. However, it is worth pointing out that there is no leading 'melodic' voice in the opening bars of 'Ondine', and the logic of the piece is achieved at the *harmonic* level, by the use of chords which we hear more as 'sonorities' than chords of a specific key, since their harmonic meaning is always ambiguous. Debussy's wandering tonality in such passages leads naturally to:

2. Music that uses a rival scale to the diatonic, or a rival system of harmony to the triads and circle of fifths, while retaining a tonal aura. In

[21] *What to Listen for in Music*, 73.
[22] *Tonality—Atonality—Pantonality*, 19–30.

such music the listener may lose the sense of key, and yet still hear the octave as 'the same again', still recognize certain tones as defining points of rest and resolution, still hear dissonances as 'resolved' and harmonic sequences as working towards a conclusion, still hear melodies with oblique but recognizable tonal force. Debussy's short prelude called 'Voiles', written in the whole-tone scale, with a pentatonic middle section, illustrates what I have in mind. But there is little that can be done with these scales, as Debussy realized, without the tonal setting which he elsewhere provides for them. A comparable departure from, and return to, tonality, can be witnessed in Stravinsky's use of the 'octatonic' scale—the scale composed on alternating whole tones and semitones, as in the *Symphony of Psalms*. This contains a variety of triads, both major and minor (Ex. 9.37). In the symphony, Stravinsky emphasizes the triad of E minor (arranged as in Ex. 9.37(*b*): the 'psalms' chord), so that the listener strives constantly to hear either G or E as the tonic, despite the fact that there is no leading note into either key. This enables Stravinsky to achieve a remarkable atmosphere in this work—a kind of hollowed-out tonality, in which movement is contained within static pillars of harmony.[23]

Ex. 9.37. Stravinsky and the octatonic scale: (*a*) octatonic scale on B, with resulting triads; (*b*) *Symphony of Psalms*

More provocative than such recent examples, however, is Skriabin, one of the greatest of modern composers, whose moves away from strict tonality are as interesting as the canonized experiments of Schoenberg. It is worth while to review his case, since it shows a genuine attempt to discompose tonality into its elements, and then to reassemble them.

Although Skriabin began his career as an accomplished composer of tonal music in the tradition of Chopin, he moved further away from traditional

[23] Richard Taruskin has persuasively argued that Stravinsky's use of the octatonic scale dates from his earliest works, and derives from a well-established Russian tradition, exemplified also in Rimsky-Korsakov. See Taruskin, '*Chez Petrouchka*: Harmony and Tonality chez Stravinsky', *Nineteenth-Century Music*, 10 (1987), 265–86.

tonality than any previous composer. Schoenberg broke with tonality: he did not develop it in new directions. It was Skriabin's achievement to retain enough of the tonal language to guarantee that his music would still be intelligible to tonal ears. First, he rejected Rameau's principle, that harmonies should be built in thirds, and used fourths instead. Fourth chords contain suggestions of key. They can also be heard both as resolving into triadic chords, and as the resolutions of starker dissonances. Furthermore, by dint of repetition, they can acquire the character of a 'home chord'— even without a clearly designated tonic. (Consider the Prelude, Op. 67 No. 1, in Ex. 9.38, in which a particular fourth chord gradually takes on the character of home, so that the music seems to venture out from it, return, and, in the last moment, evaporate with a sigh of dispossession.)

Secondly, Skriabin discovered the art of composing lingering melodic phrases which borrow the movement of tonal melodies, while identifying no tone as the tonic, as in the example from the extraordinary Seventh Piano Sonata (Ex. 9.39).[24]

Thirdly, Skriabin's music is full of octaves and powerful pedal-points, which anchor the harmony, and create a kind of substitute for key—a temporary home, which stands to the tonic as a rooming-house stands to a birthplace. Skriabin's music exhibits a kind of 'orphaned tonality'. The

Ex. 9.38. Skriabin, Prelude, Op. 67 No. 1, conclusion (the home chord is marked with an arrow)

[24] A case can be made for saying, however, that this sonata is one of the first compositions to be organized also serially, through permutations of a 'basic set'. See G. Perle, *Serial Composition and Atonality* (2nd edn., London, 1975).

Ex. 9.39. Skriabin, Seventh Piano Sonata in F sharp major

harmonic order that he achieves does not negate tonality, so much as stretch it to its isolated limit. For he retains three of the guiding principles of tonal structure: the principle of harmonic progression, whereby chords arise out of, resolve into, and diverge from one another; the principle of resonance, whereby melodic line and harmonic progression are mutually dependent, with the shape of the melody dictating, and also dictated by, the underlying harmonic movement, as in Ex. 9.39; and the principle of voice-leading in the bass-line, according to which the bass moves melodically to a conclusion, anchoring the harmonies above it. The daring of Skriabin's 'mystical' harmonies lies in the fact that they impose large and barely tolerable harmonic and melodic obligations. With a few exceptions, Skriabin is able to accomodate them within musical structures that proceed with a quasi-tonal logic, often resolving at last (as in the symphonic poem *Prometheus*, which ends in a blaze of F sharp major) in a tonal cadence. There is, indeed, an evolution in Skriabin's piano music towards Schoenberg's conception of a 'unity of musical space'—i.e. a space with no privileged positions, such as are created by tonic and dominant in the diatonic scale. But often, as in the augmented E major chord that concludes *Vers la flamme*, harmonies which are marginal to the tonal directory are used in a manner that creates a strong suggestion of tonal resolution. If the music avoids tonality, this is because it is constantly *veering away* from it—constantly denying a tendency that is implicit in its own musical dynamic.

Skriabin's music illustrates the way in which tonality can be reconstituted from its own ruins. Even when composing without a clear tonal centre, Skriabin gives a kind of ghostly tonal meaning to his music, perpetuating the light of tonality in the world of shadows. And the important point to notice is that the intentional order of Skriabin's music is, like that of tonality, an order of elaboration, projected polyphonically. It is precisely this which causes him, having moved away from triadic harmony, to restore its main effects.

3. Polytonality. Bartók, Stravinsky, and Szymanowski perfected the art of writing in several keys at once: a procedure that loads the harmony with competing tonal centres, while retaining a differentiated musical space, with privileged positions, and points of rest. In general the bass-line of a polytonal work will tend to establish a weak sense of key, as in the passage (Ex. 9.40) from the prelude to Part II of the *Rite of Spring*, which is certainly in D minor. (Note the parallel here with the opening bars of the

prelude to *Pelléas et Mélisande*, in which a similar clash between D minor and colourful keyless (whole-tone) harmonies occurs, but diachronically, and not, as in the Stravinsky, synchronously. See the discussion of the Debussy in Chapter 7, above.)

Sometimes the effect of the bass-line is so strong as to pull everything back into tonal order, as when Szymanowski's first Violin Concerto suddenly finds itself on the dominant of G (Ex. 9.41), and avoids resolving on to the

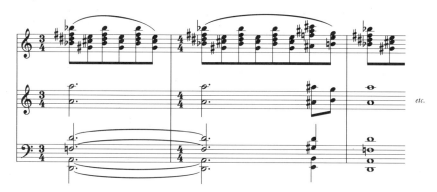

Ex. 9.40. Stravinsky, *The Rite of Spring*, prelude to part II

Ex. 9.41. Szymanowski, First Violin Concerto, Op. 35

tonic only by shifting sideways towards E flat (in which key it lands a few bars later). Polytonal music, when successful, seems to move through harmonic regions exactly as tonal music does. Whenever the opportunity occurs to hear it as passing though a single key, we do so; and the harmonies are like tonal harmonies that have been 'coloured in'. It is received by the ear as a challenge, and the triumph of the listener comes in hearing the latent tonal order.

4. In addition to the polytonality of the early modern masters, Rudolf Reti describes 'pantonality' as a distinct form of tonal organization, and the final and lasting result of the modernist experiments.[25] Reti writes in this context of a 'tonality which does not appear on the surface but is created by the ear singling out hidden relationships between various points of a melodic or contrapuntal web'.[26] Any pitch class can function as a tonic, and a piece may (according to Reti) keep indefinitely many tonics 'in play', without cancelling their primary function, either as the focus of melodic organization, or as the reference point against which the harmonies must be read. It is in terms of such pantonality, Reti claims, that we understand the work of many modern composers—Benjamin Britten, Aaron Copland, Charles Ives, and even Pierre Boulez!

Needless to say, the concept of pantonality is controversial—not least because it suggests that avowedly atonal music may be organized tonally, against the composer's intentions, but in accordance with the instinctive requirements of the human ear. Reti's characterization of pantonality is both dense and vacillating; and, without a clear explanation, which Reti never gives, the idea of a plurality of tonics strikes the reader as incoherent, like the idea of a plurality of monarchs. There is some force, nevertheless, in the suggestion that melody and harmony may point to more than one 'privileged' pitch, and that we might organize the tones in relation to these pitches, much as we do the melodies and harmonies of tonal music. Take away these floating 'tonics', and the musical line becomes 'disaggregated', with neither horizontal nor vertical connections. Melody gives way to sequence, and harmony to simultaneity. Whether Reti's suggestion can be defended, however, must await a more detailed consideration of the atonal idiom.

In all its forms imperfect tonality illustrates the retroactive power of tonal organization. In a chord sequence, Schoenberg wrote, it is often the last which prevails.[27] Play any sequence of chords, however keyless and dissonant, and follow it with a major triad, spaced so as to resolve some of the tensions contained in its predecessor. At once the whole sequence will acquire

[25] *Tonality—Atonality—Pantonality.*
[26] Ibid. 65.
[27] 'Problems of Harmony', in *Style and Idea*, 273–4.

a tonal meaning: the triad is 'read back' into the chords that preceded it. We have acquired the habit of holding dissonances and unrelated chords in a state of 'suspended animation', until the clue to their tonality is offered: only then do we come down firmly on a musical reading. This habit derives in large measure from traditional counterpoint and voice-leading, which cause us to hear dissonance as a stage on the way to a consonant resolution. The more traditionally minded of modern composers—Honegger, Walton, Roussel—can be seen as practitioners of 'dissonant counterpoint', as it has been called, in which the desire for a resolution is kept in indefinite suspense. Dissonant counterpoint provides another route away from tonality, which is at the same time guided by tonal principles and tonal habits of hearing.

Dissonant counterpoint, and the principle that the 'last prevails', have therefore been of some importance in liberating modern music from the stricter forms of tonal composition. It is a judicious use of these devices that causes us to hear Martinů's symphonies, for example, as always centred in a key. To overcome the force of tonality, therefore, we must be more determined than Martinů in chasing the triad from its former haunts, so as to leave them unfrequented even by the ghost of a tonal order.

Atonal Music

While there is music (such as the above kinds) which stretches and conserves tonality, there is also music which decidedly rejects it. Atonality may be unsystematic—a free use of musical elements in defiance of tonal organization. Or it may be founded in some rival musical system, and strive for a rival order to the tonal, a substitute for the organizing principles of the traditional language. Unsystematic atonality has many instances, two of the most important being the early modernist works of Schoenberg, Ives, and Bartók, and the work of postwar radicals in the Darmstadt tradition. The interest of more recent experiments in atonality often resides in novel sonorities, organized in ways which do not permit the experience of musical movement. Music then retreats from the intentional to the material realm; and what we hear, in hearing Stockhausen's *Gruppen*, for instance, is precisely what we do not hear in a Beethoven symphony: a series of sounds, produced by many different sources in physical space, as opposed to a movement of tones which summon and answer one another in a space of their own. (In describing such music, therefore, we cannot refer to 'melodies' or 'motifs', but only to sequences; we cannot identify chords, but only sonorities and 'simultaneities'.)

Systematic atonality is the brainchild of Schoenberg, who advocated the well-known technique of 'serial composition', regarded by many composers, critics, and musicologists as a genuine rival to the tonal system. The desire was to organize the twelve tones of the chromatic scale in such a way as to privilege none of them—to prevent the emergence of a master-tone that would serve as tonic, and thereby to achieve an absolute equality between all regions of musical space. The twelve tones are arranged in a series, which can be inverted, reversed, and transformed in all the ways that are familiar from contrapuntal writing in the tonal tradition. Certain rules of musical syntax are then adopted. Unlike the rules of tonal harmony, these rules have an a priori character: they are laid down in advance, as willed contraints on the composer's practice. In his *Studies in Counterpoint*,[28] Ernst Křenek has provided a statement of some of them. 'A theme', he writes, 'is not necessarily identical with the series; on the contrary, that will only occasionally be the case. Therefore, the caesuras between the themes (or, in general, between the articulated sections of the melodic line) should not coincide with the consecutive entrances of the series.' That 'master-rule' of twelve-tone composition is followed by the equally important rule of repetition, which tells us that 'repetition of a tone is allowed *before* the following tone of the series is introduced, and within the same octave'; otherwise repetition is forbidden, except in trills, tremolos, and similar formations. These rules are necessary adjuncts of the serial technique: without them, the series would cease to be what it is intended to be—the constantly returning *ground* of the musical structure—and become instead a theme, in the classical sense. Once the rules are in place, the rest can be left to the ear of the composer—to ensure that an interesting structure will emerge, which should not be heard as a tonal structure. The serial ordering is the fundamental constraint: the feature which removes what might otherwise be the arbitrary quality of the atonal line, and which orders it as music.

In most cases, systematic atonality replaces both melodic and harmonic organization with an organization by *motif*. The motif is defined without reference to tonal categories, as a set of pitch classes. A pitch class consists of a single pitch, together with all its octave equivalents. A pitch-class set is defined in terms of the distance (measured in semitone steps) between its members, when these have been given a 'normal' order, each interval being transposed by octave equivalence into its smallest version, and the whole sequence arranged so as to proceed from smallest to largest interval.[29] A pitch-class set can be transposed, inverted, arranged in retrograde, and so on, while still remaining the same pitch-class set. It can be spread out 'horizontally', as a 'melodic' device, or 'vertically', as a chord. Much of serial music (especially that of Schoenberg and his disciples) relies on our

---

[28] (New York, 1940).

[29] This method of identifying the building blocks of atonal music was adumbrated by Milton Babbitt, and provided with its full theoretical elaboration by Allen Forte: see the discussion below, Ch. 13.

ability to discern a single motif in all these arrangements: to hear the equivalence between horizontal and vertical forms of a single pitch-class set, and
to recognize the set in its transposed, inverted, and retrograde arrangements.
The assumption is that, when we have learned to hear in this way, a wholly
new kind of musical order will dawn upon us, and tonal expectations will
be finally neutralized.

Considerable skill is required, even so, if the expectations of the tonal
ear are to be thwarted. Chords have to contain minor seconds, tritones, or
sevenths, while avoiding triads; repetition of the motif must not lead to
repetition of a tonally significant note or harmony; the bass-line must be
kept in constant motion. The constraints that emerge from the attempt to
be systematically atonal are almost as great as those contained in the
language of tonality itself. But they arise at least in part by negation, from
the attempt to *avoid* something. Nevertheless the hope was to establish a
new kind of *order* among tones, an order that would present itself to the
musical ear, to be recuperated and enjoyed in the act of listening. If tonal
sounds are heard in this music it will be by accident; the sounds will not
have a tonal *function*, and will therefore not be heard as tonal, when heard
as *tones*. To put the point succinctly, composers wished to find a way of
translating sound into tone, without using the order of tonality. Examples
are familiar, and if I choose one well-known work, it is not because it is in
any way canonical: each composer carried out his own experiments, and
moved in his own way towards an audible organization that would negate
the demands of the ear accustomed to tonality. Webern's *Konzert*, Op. 24,
illustrates the ingenious constraints that a sophisticated composer is able to
extract from the seemingly arbitrary discipline, that requires an equal value
to be placed on all the twelve tones of the chromatic scale. Consider the
first statement of the series in this work (Ex. 9.42). The twelve tones have
been divided into four groups of three, and each group comprises two

Ex. 9.42. Webern, *Konzert*, Op. 24 (*a*) series; (*b*) opening statement

intervals: a major third and a semitone. These intervals can be rearranged, according to the law of octave equivalence, so as to create a constant internal variation in the very motif from which the series is constructed, the four trichords here being related by inversion, retrograde, and retroversion. The series itself is conceived as a motif with three variations; its rhythmical presentation is likewise varied, with a serial ordering of the metrical intervals. What might have been an arbitrary choice in the arrangement of the twelve tones therefore displays itself as minutely ordered, and the listener is invited to hear the series as contained within the smallest musical cell. Webern's technique here was followed by later composers, notably by Milton Babbitt, who divides the series into two hexachords, and plays with the symmetries and correspondence between them, so as to establish the maximum *internal* order in the series itself. This internal order is a kind of substitute for melodic organization: with the proviso that it may be displayed either horizontally, in sequence, or vertically, through the simultaneous sounding of the tones in any group.

It is possible to become sufficiently familiar with these devices, as to recognize the recurrence of a motif, in its transposed, retrograde, inverted and simultaneous versions. And there is often a kind of satisfaction in this. But two questions present themselves. First, is it not true that this new and artificial order is achieved only on the assumption of the old and natural order established by tonality? The twelve tones derive from the tonal scale, which is itself founded upon tonal harmony. And we count them as *twelve*, only because we rely on the phenomenon of octave equivalence, which is itself the fundamental relation in the diatonic scale. Although we can describe what is going on in terms that make no reference to tonality, there is no guarantee that the ear will not surreptitiously hear the musical movement as a movement in tonal space, a movement that lies across that space, clashing with its contours, but nevertheless understood in terms of the very order that it tries in vain to reject. When I hear the first motif of the *Konzert* as a minor ninth followed by a major third, I am hearing *tonally*. (For that is what these descriptions—'major', 'third', and 'ninth'—imply.) Am I therefore *misunderstanding* what I hear? What would it *be* to hear these intervals as the theory requires, namely, as 13 followed by 4? Those numerical concepts have never had a place in the organization of musical space, as my ear achieves it. So how, and for what end, should I introduce them now?

Secondly, there is all the difference in the world, between hearing *that* some process occurs in the world of sound, and *hearing the process*. And there is a further difference between hearing the process as a sequence of sounds, and hearing it as a movement of tones. This last kind of hearing requires metaphorical organization, of the kind that I described in the first three chapters. The order established by Webern, however, makes no reference to such an organization, and deliberately negates the experiences—melodic movement, harmonic tension and release, metrical pulse—which bring it into being. (Notice, for example, that the rhythmic organization is designed so as to impede the experience of a beat, by implanting conflicting metres in the sequence of sounds.) The mere existence of serial order, therefore, does nothing to prove that it is a *musical* order, or that it is the order that we hear, when we hear this piece as music. I have already suggested that the order of triadic tonality is an order *within* the intentional realm: it is an order that we hear, when we hear the music. But there is much information that we gain from hearing tones, which forms no part of their intentional order. For example, the listener in the concert hall hears that the oboe is situated behind the violins; he hears that the timpani are slightly out of tune; and so on. But this information, which can be recuperated acoustically, forms no part of the intentional order that he hears in hearing the sounds as music. Likewise, a person with a good ear may hear that a piece of music is organized serially—he may even take a lively pleasure in this fact—although the serial order is not what he hears, when he hears the intentional relations between the tones.

Indeed, as Edward Cone has shown, the organization of a piece of serial music remains the same, when the piece is reassembled as in a mirror, with each interval replaced by its inversion. Yet the *musical* movement is utterly changed by this transformation. In hearing the movement, therefore, we are responding to something more than the serial ordering: maybe to something completely *other* than the serial ordering.[30] The difficulty suggested by this observation is one to which I return below.

· *The Argument Against Tonality*

Why did composers and critics come to think that systematic atonality should be necessary? Here, briefly, is Schoenberg's argument: tonality is not the 'natural' and inescapable thing which its defenders suppose. It is part of a particular tradition, which was not initially tonal, and which became so only through historical development. In time tonality became a unifying force in music, the principle which enables us to hold a piece of music together as we listen: that is why tonal music is so readily comprehensible. But tonality has now exhausted its potential, and must be replaced if new artistic gestures are to be possible.

Schoenberg writes:

> It is evident that abandoning tonality can be contemplated only if other satisfactory means for coherence and articulation present themselves. If, in

[30] E. T. Cone, 'Beyond Analysis', in B. Boretz and E. T. Cone, *Perspectives on Contemporary Music Theory* (New York, 1972).

other words, one could write a piece which does not use the advantages offered by tonality and yet unifies all elements so that their succession and relation are logically comprehensible, and which is articulated as our mental capacity requires, namely so that the parts unfold clearly and characteristically in related significance and function.[31]

He goes on to argue that there is another principle of unity in music, which he identifies as the motif, whose audible transformations and repetitions can provide just what tonality provided, even when organized according to principles that defy the tonal experience. 'Consciously used, the motif should produce unity, relationship, coherence, logic, comprehensibility and fluency.'[32] The motif is the seed from which everything grows.

Although Schoenberg is surely right to attribute to tonality the power to generate the experience of unity with which we are familiar in classical music, this is not the *only* effect of tonality, nor indeed the most important effect. The effect of unity comes only as a consequence of the journey through tonal space, itself made possible by the harmonic, contrapuntal, and melodic organization of tonal music. Such organization could exist without the experience of unity (as in Liszt's Second Piano Concerto, or the last movement of Bruckner's Eighth Symphony); it is best seen as a *perfection* of tonal writing, rather than an essential part of it. By overlooking everything except unity, abstractly described, Schoenberg makes the task of replacing tonality seem far easier than it is.

Secondly, why should we believe that tonality has exhausted itself? The complaint is made in various ways and tones of voice, being elevated to a comprehensive doctrine by Adorno, who sees the survival of tonality in popular culture as a kind of sickness, connected with the degeneracy of modern capitalist society. Schoenberg writes thus of the diminished seventh chord—the chord which does such stirling work in the recitatives of Weber, and which is still in the back of Wagner's mind as he explores the seventh chords of his later harmony:

This uncommon, restless, undependable guest, here today, gone tomorrow, settled down, became a citizen, was retired a philistine. The chord had lost the appeal of novelty, hence, it had lost its sharpness, but also its lustre. It had nothing more to say in a new era. Thus, it fell from the higher sphere of art music to the lower music for entertainment. There it remains, as a sentimental expression of sentimental concerns. It became banal and effeminate. Became banal! It was not so originally. It was sharp and dazzling. Today, though, it is scarcely used any more except in that mawkish stuff [*Schmachtliteratur*] which sometime later always apes what was, in great art, the important event.[33]

[31] *Style and Idea*, 279.
[32] *The Fundamentals of Musical Composition*, ed. G. Strang (London, 1967), 8.
[33] *Harmonielehre*, 288–9.

That revealing utterance contains the master-thought from which the twelve-tone system grew: the thought that the old devices were exhausted, that they could no longer be used sincerely, but only 'in inverted commas', or else as part of some debased and sentimental musical practice inimical to the aims of art. That is how we must hear them—we whose ears have been educated by the great tradition. Yet is that not a strange thing to say? When we hear the diminished seventh chord in Bach (as in the B flat minor Prelude), or in Mozart (as in the duel scene in Act 1 of *Don Giovanni*) it does not seem banal at all. On the contrary, it is tense, vigorous, dramatic, part of a sublime musical effect. Even in Wagner—in the Ring motif—it is wholly natural, and certainly not *Schmachtliteratur*. So what does it mean to say that this chord has *become* banal, when it is manifestly not banal in the contexts provided by the masters?

Adorno is yet more severe. In *The Philosophy of Modern Music*, a book deeply marked by Adorno's despairing neo-Marxism, he writes:

> Even the most insensitive ear detects the shabbiness and exhaustion of the diminished seventh chord and certain chromatic modulatory tones in the salon music of the nineteenth century. For the technically trained ear, such vague discomfort is transformed into a prohibitive canon.

And he goes on—by way of pressing the advantage in Schoenberg's favour—

> If all is not deception, this canon today excludes even the medium of tonality—that is to say, the means of all traditional music. It is not simply that these sounds are antiquated and untimely, but that they are false. They no longer fulfil their function. The most progressive level of technical procedures designs tasks before which traditional sounds reveal themselves as impotent clichés. There are modern compositions which occasionally scatter tonal sounds in their own context. It is precisely the triads which, in such context, are cacophonous and not the dissonances![34]

The thought reappears in the muddle-headed pages of Ernst Bloch:

> The brilliant and harsh diminished 7th was once new; it gave an impression of novelty and so could represent anything—pain, anger, excitement and all violent emotion—in the music of the classical masters. Now that the radicalism has worn off, it has sunk irretrievably into mere 'light music' as a sentimental expression of sentimental ideas.[35]

Reading such second-hand stuff, you could be forgiven for thinking that there is no greater cliché in the theory of music than the theory that the diminished seventh is a cliché. But clichés have consequences. Adorno, for

---

[34] tr. A. G. Mitchell and W. V. Blomster (New York, 1973), 34.

[35] *Essays on the Philosophy of Music*, tr. P. Palmer, introd. D. Drew (Cambridge, 1985), 98.

example, goes on from this standard example to make some radical and dismissive judgements. He condemns the entire works of Sibelius, whose tonal sounds are, he suggests, mere enclaves in the field of atonality, and therefore entirely false, exhausted, sentimental. For Adorno, tonal implications in a piece of modern music sound as false as would atonal chords in Haydn. But the least we can say in reply to that, is that Adorno has confused two kinds of 'falsehood': the wrong note, and the wrong sentiment.

Adorno admits that the diminished seventh chord, which 'rings false in salon pieces', as he puts it, is correct and full of every possible expression at the beginning of Beethoven's last sonata (Ex. 9.43). What makes it correct, he argues, is the context; not just the context of Beethoven's style, but the historical context, which made this chord into the most extreme dissonance possible for Beethoven. Certainly, Beethoven had none of the modernist's reservations concerning this chord. 'The startling effects,' he wrote, 'which many credit to the natural genius of the composer, are often achieved with the greatest ease by the use and resolution of the diminished seventh chord.'[36] Or does Beethoven reveal, in those words, that he already has an inkling of what Adorno and Schoenberg were later to object to: the danger that this chord, used too often, will become banal?

Ex. 9.43. Beethoven, Piano Sonata in C minor, Op. 111

There is a reason for singling out the diminished seventh, from all the other devices of the tonal tradition. For it is precisely the chord which enabled composers to achieve a temporary suspension of tonality, and therefore to escape into that unified musical space over which Schoenberg wished to claim exclusive sovereignty. A diminished seventh chord is in no specific key: it can move logically into almost any tonal harmony, or into other seventh chords. (Schoenberg argued that it should be treated as a ninth chord, with missing root.[37] Since there is a choice of four possible roots, however, this does nothing to resolve its harmonic ambiguity.) A genius like Mozart can use the diminished seventh to occupy virtually the whole of twelve-tone space, while retaining a remorseless tonal logic, as in Ex. 9.44

[36] Quoted, ibid. 49.   [37] *Harmonielehre*, 234–6.

Ex. 9.44. Mozart, *Don Giovanni*, the Commendatore's summons

from *Don Giovanni*. By singling out the diminished seventh, Schoenberg and Adorno were pre-empting the best reply to their arguments: namely, that tonality contains within itself everything that a composer needs to *escape* from tonal thinking when it 'becomes banal'. While Schoenberg was writing his *Harmonielehre*, composers were still devising fresh uses for his 'undependable guest', who appears as dependable in the lush harmonies of *Rosenkavalier*, as in the tear-stained pages of Janáček (Exx. 9.45 and 9.46). Those two passages are among the most beautiful things composed in our century. And if the one narrowly avoids banality, might we not say that it is all the greater, on account of its daring flirtation with the tasteless?

Ex. 9.45. Richard Strauss, *Der Rosenkavalier*, Act 3, trio

Ex. 9.46. Janáček, *On an Overgrown Path*, 'A Blown-Away leaf'

Schoenberg and Adorno are right to say that there are musical clichés. But can a *chord* be one of them? When the diminished seventh is used in the song 'Walter, Walter', as a substitute for genuine part-writing, a way of maintaining the sense of harmony, as the music slops its way across a dominant pedal, you have an instance of the *Schmachtliteratur* to which Schoenberg was objecting (see Ex. 9.47). But that is not how the chord is used by Strauss or Janáček. Nor is it how Schnittke uses it, in his admittedly vain attempts to recuperate the thrill of Mozart (Ex. 9.48). The chord even crops up, in a surprising context, in Berg's *Lyric Suite* (Ex. 9.49)—where it forms part of a systematic attempt to turn serial organization in a tonal direction. Indeed,

Ex. 9.47. 'Walter, Walter', pop song of the 1930s

Ex. 9.48. Schnittke, *Requiem*

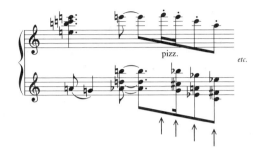

Ex. 9.49. Berg, *Lyric Suite*, first movement

the claim seems to be that the chord has become banal, not because of its use in serious music, but precisely because of its use in popular music; it is the polluting effect of the new kind of popular music which has made the tonal language 'unavailable'. The point is expressed in uncompromising terms by Ernst Křenek:

> The bold harmonic accomplishments of Richard Wagner have long since been incorporated into the normal stock-in-trade of all kinds of *Gebrauchmusik*; and the clever and exquisite tone marvels of Debussy, which engendered bewilderment and uneasiness at the time of their origin, have become primitive tools in the hands of the swing music arrangers of Tin Pan Alley. Naturally the element thus made banal remains relatively untouched in the place where it first appeared. At every performance the Prelude to *Tristan* is as daring and original as it was at its premiere; but . . . no composer can create this same mood any more by identical or similar means.[38]

Suppose that an art critic were to say of a certain shade of red—for instance, that which dominates Matisse's *Red Room*—that it had 'become banal'. Would we understand him? We certainly think that colours have moral characteristics: there are vulgar colours, brash and offensive colours, soothing, modest, and dignified colours. And it is true that the repeated misuse of a colour can give it a hackneyed appearance—like the yellow of the MacDonald's sign, associated with shapes whose vulgarity forms part of their commercial appeal. Nevertheless, any colour, and any shape, can be redeemed from its uses, by the artist who paints them afresh. What would remain of the art of painting if individual shades could be simply deleted from the painter's palette by those who use them tastelessly? In art, context

---

[38] *Music Here and Now*, tr. B. Fles (New York, 1939). Křenek is right to remind us of the influence of Debussy on jazz—esp. modern jazz. But, writing in 1939, he had no idea that popular music would decline to the point where such an influence is no longer conceivable.

is all-important. Matisse's shade of red appears as the colour of walls and furniture in a room, from which contrasts of light and shade have been carefully excised. It does not appear as it would on a tie, or in a Dutch interior. If it is banal in one of these contexts, it does not follow that it will be banal in another. The idea of a colour that is banal *in itself,* and without reference to context, is surely mysterious.

The same goes for a chord. Tonality converts pitched sounds into tones: the diminished seventh chord acquires its musical character from the tonal context in which it occurs. And this reflects a general truth. One and the same chord can appear twice in a single piece of music, while in fact being two different harmonies. In Schenker's analysis of the Prelude in C major from the First Book of the Forty-Eight, the acoustically identical bars 18 and 27 are described quite differently, since they are experienced quite differently, the first as a prolongation of the tonic tonality, the second as a prolongation of the dominant (see Ex. 9.50). Whether or not we agree with Schenker's analysis, he is surely right to imply that the C major triad, understood as the tonic triad, is a quite different musical entity from the dominant triad of F or the subdominant triad of G, even if the sounds of these three chords are—taken out of context—identical. This musical illustration of Frege's 'context principle' is no more than a common-sense recognition of the status of tonality, not as a style, but as a system for the ordering of sounds as music.

And that, surely, is what is questionable in the attack on it. There is no doubt that *styles* can become exhausted—although why this is so, and what our response should be, are complex matters. Tonality is not a language, for the reasons spelled out in Chapter 7; but it is more like a language than it is like a style. It is a system within which styles are engendered. A new style may revitalize some old device, as Janáček revitalizes the diminished seventh chord, precisely by 'making it new'. True, a composer must *earn* the right to use these old devices: and that means forging the style that will freshen them. But what prevents him from doing just that? Why should Messiaen not bring his *Turangalîla symphonie* to a full stop in F sharp major, with a lush tonic triad? Even if this is the same *chord*, acoustically speaking, as that which concludes Skriabin's *Prometheus*, it is not the same musical entity. It has been brought back to life by the music that preceded it, reacquiring its aboriginal joyfulness.

That is only the beginning of an answer to Schoenberg and Adorno. The nagging feeling persists that they are on to something, that a change has occurred, not merely in music, and not merely in the habits of listening and performance, which has put the tonal language in question. This change involves the entire surrounding culture; it can be understood only through a theory of modernity, and only if we look outside the realm of music.

Ex. 9.50. Bach, *The Well-Tempered Clavier*, First Book, Prelude in C major

In Chapter 15, therefore, I shall return to the topic, and try to address the underlying anxiety.

Is There an Alternative?

In the passages quoted from Schoenberg, we find the vehement, though cryptic, belief in an alternative to tonality. This alternative will render music 'logically comprehensible', without depending upon tonal devices. Is there such an alternative? 'Logically comprehensible' might mean simply that there is an intellectual system which explains every note: as we can explain the bass-line of the little piece by Křenek illustrated earlier (Ex. 8.1) by pointing out that it is a transposition of the upper part in retrograde. But since this is not something that you could possibly hear in the music, it does not answer the important question, which is why the composer should have chosen such a technique in the first place. The complaint is reasonably made against the 'serial' techniques introduced by Schoenberg, that they impose an intellectual order on sounds, but not a *musical* order. The order that exists in them is not an order that can be heard, when we hear the sounds as music. As I suggested earlier, this complaint may be right. When hearing the musical organization in serial music, it could be, for all the theoretical baggage that is foisted upon us by Webern and Babbitt, that we are hearing *against* the intellectual structure, and incorporating what we hear into tonal or quasi-tonal categories.

This observation is given in a novel form by Fred Lerdahl. Serial composition, he argues, generates a 'huge gap between compositional system and cognized result'.[39] He illustrates the point through a telling example:

> Boulez's *Le Marteau sans Maître* (1954) was widely hailed as a masterpiece of post-war serialism. Yet nobody could figure out, much less hear, how the piece was serial. From hints in Boulez (1963), Koblyakov (1977) at last determined that it was indeed serial, though in an idiosyncratic way. In the interim, listeners made what sense they could of the piece in ways unrelated to its construction. Nor has Koblyakov's decipherment subsequently changed how the piece is heard . . . The serial organization of *Le Marteau* would appear . . . to be irrelevant.[40]

The reason for this, Lerdahl suggests, is that the *compositional grammar* consciously employed by Boulez in order to generate the piece, is not matched by any corresponding *listening grammar*, unconsciously deployed by the listener in order to comprehend it. He leans, here, on the 'grammar' of tonal music expounded by himself and Jackendoff (see Chapter 7). And

[39] 'Cognitive Constraints on Compositional Systems', in J. A. Sloboda (ed.), *Generative Processes in Music* (Oxford, 1988), 236.
[40] Ibid. 231.

he describes musical comprehension in the terms used by a certain kind of cognitive psychologist, as a matter of forming a 'mental representation' of the musical object. But those ideas are not necessary to his case. It is surely quite reasonable to suggest that the practice of understanding music in our tradition—the practice which effectively *created* music from the array of pitches—corresponds to the tonal language, but not to the atonal substitute. The rules used by the serial composer in constructing a piece, have no counterpart in the process whereby we comprehend it. A 'natural compositional grammar', Lerdahl argues, 'depends on the listening grammar as a source.'[41] In other words, rules of composition, if they are to result in intelligible music, must derive from our way of hearing musical structure, and not from a 'constructivist' theory of composition. Lerdahl goes on to repeat the commonsensical observations upon which his and Jackendoff's earlier attempt at a 'listening grammar' had relied: our demand that the musical surface should be parsed into discrete events, with a metrical organization, symmetries, prolongations, and parallels. (See above, Chapters 2 and 7.) Serial organization does not, in itself, produce these things. It is a permutational system, whereas our 'listening grammar' is elaborational: we organize the musical surface in terms of symmetries and prolongations of a kind that are not typically produced by permutation. There is ample evidence from other fields of cognitive psychology, that permutational arrangements are hard to learn and comprehend, when compared to arrangements based on repetition, elaboration, and symmetry.

Although Lerdahl weakens his case through his assumption that the 'listening grammar' is a form of generative grammar, which imposes a hierarchical organization on the musical surface, his point can be rephrased in less contentious terms. He is not denying that serial organization affects what we hear: but he is denying that this organization is *what* we hear, when we hear serial works as music. In hearing such works we strive to elicit, in their musical surface, an order of elaboration, of a kind typified by triadic tonality. The serial order, however, is an order of permutation, which, even if heard, is not heard as part of the musical surface.

The point should be put in the context of the 'intentional understanding' discussed in Chapter 8. Many acoustical events occur when music occurs, and contribute to the musical effect. But not all of these events form part of *what* we hear, in the intentional sense, when we hear the music. To be part of the intentional object, it is not necessary that a sound be itself discriminated as the particular sound that it is. For example, in an elaborately orchestrated chord we do not hear each instrumental tone: rather we hear a complex tone into which the contributing parts are absorbed. Nevertheless,

[41] Ibid. 235.

the intentional object is, in such a case, *composed* of tones, which are heard as contributions to the whole.

At first sight it might seem as though a serial order could form part of the intentional object, even though it is not heard *as such*, by the listener who hears with understanding. However, the case is very different from that of the orchestrated chord. The purpose of serial organization was precisely to replace the order of tonality with an order which, by treating the twelve tones permutationally, would confer equality on each of them. In other words, it was to endow the musical surface with a new *heard order*. If the serial organization is merely contributing acoustically to a musical surface whose order is not serial at all, then we have not succeeded in producing serial music. Indeed, the possibility remains open that we strive to hear such serially organized music as tonal, and that we understand it by eliciting the ghost of a tonal order.

And as a matter of fact, when Schoenberg describes his alternative to tonal organization, he does not refer to the serial technique. His alternative principle of musical structure is precisely the motif: the smallest element of musical significance, such as the four-note phrase that opens Beethoven's Fifth Symphony. And when he comes to explain, in *The Fundamentals of Musical Composition*, just *how* these motifs are to be used in composing, he takes all his examples from tonal music (mostly Beethoven). Moreover, he shows that motifs can be used to develop a musical surface through 'developing variation', which is his own term for the feature that I have called 'elaboration', the most powerful examples of which are tonal. Not a hint is given as to how a serial organisation might produce the effects to which Schoenberg refers—the 'unity in variety' of the classical style. Only in very rare cases, does the motif in classical music retain its musical identity when displayed as a chord, and motivic organization is almost invariably understood in the context of thematic development, and tonal structure. We should not be surprised, therefore, to find that many musicologists have tried to vindicate 'post-tonal' music, not by endorsing serialism as such, but by showing that serial music may *also* exhibit an elaborational structure, and that *this* is what we hear, when we hear the musical organization.[42]

A useful illustration is provided by one of Schoenberg's own examples, from 'Composition with Twelve Tones'.[43] The two statements of 'Es muss sein!', in the last movement of Beethoven's String Quartet, Op. 135, are

---

[42] See the by now quite heated controversy as to whether serial music exhibits 'prolongations', of the kind theorized by Schenker and his school: J. Baker, 'Schenkerian Analysis and Post-Tonal Music,' in D. Beach (ed.), *Aspects of Schenkerian Theory* (New Haven, 1983); J. Straus, 'The Problem of Prolongation in Post-Tonal Music', *Journal of Music Theory*, 31 (1987) 1–21.

[43] In *Style and Idea*, 221.

followed by a short answering phrase, with which Beethoven completes the melodic line. This phrase, Schoenberg points out, can be derived from the three-note motif by retrograde inversion and transposition. Its flowing character comes from filling in the 'passing tones' (see Ex. 9.51). In this way, Schoenberg hopes to show how the motivic organization which is essential to serial composition develops naturally from the techniques already employed by such masters as Beethoven. But the example shows nothing of the kind. The third phrase of Beethoven's melody owes its character less to its motivic derivation than to its ability to *answer* the motifs which precede; and it answers them first because it completes their incipient progression from F major to B flat major, and secondly because it *elaborates* their truncated movement, by spreading it horizontally through tonal space. The 'passing-tones' are not to be heard as subsidiary parts of the melodic structure, but as fundamental. They endow the motif with its musical character, by propelling it forward towards its goal.

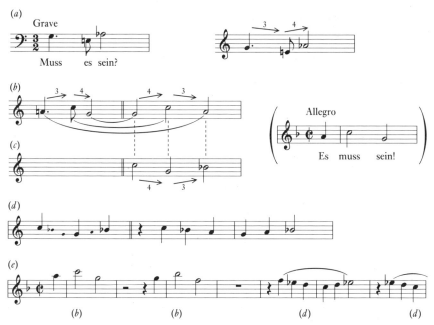

Ex. 9.51. Schoenberg's derivation of theme from Beethoven's String Quartet in F major, Op. 135, fourth movement: (a) motif; (b) transposed inversion; (c) retrograde inversion of (b); (d) the same with passing tones; (e) the theme

It is when we turn to the great works of allegedly atonal music that we see how important this point is. In Berg's Violin Concerto, for instance, the serial organization is subverted by the use of a tone-row (Ex. 9.52) which divides into two distinct and clearly tonal regions: G minor, and B major/

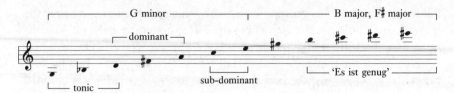

Ex. 9.52. Berg, fundamental series of the Violin Concerto

F sharp major. And from the outset the serial structure is submerged by the surface elaborations. There is a melodic movement, beginning in the first motif on arpeggiated fifths, that sustains itself through repetition and parallelism, and causes us to hear tonal harmonies even in the most discordant of the orchestral chords. When the music comes home at last, to the lovely prayer in which Berg quotes from Bach's setting of 'Es ist genug', it comes home also to the second tonality of the tone-row, and uses all the devices of triadic tonality to which I referred in the earlier sections of this chapter.

This does not mean that the chorale passage from the Violin Concerto does not *also* exhibit a serial order. It does, and—as Joseph Straus has shown—a remarkable one. Straus discovers, in Bach's striking harmonization of the original chorale, three tetrachords (4–19, 4–21, and 4–27 in Forte's index)[44] which are prominent subsets of the twelve-tone series from which the concerto is derived (see Ex. 9.53). 'As we listen to the concerto,' Straus writes, 'the chorale seems to grow out of the series and its transformations . . . the chorale comes to sound like an outgrowth of Berg's serial composition.'[45] Is it not truer to say, however, that the chorale seems to grow out of the melodic and harmonic movement that precedes it? If the *series* is responsible for this, it is partly because of its latent tonal implications. The three prominent tetrachords are by-products of the tonal order, just as they are by-products of the voice-leading in Bach's chorale.

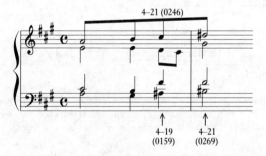

Ex. 9.53. Set-theoretical derivation of J. S. Bach, 'Es ist genug'

[44] A. Forte, *The Structure of Atonal Music* (New Haven, 1973).
[45] *Remaking the Past: Musical Modernism and the Tonal Tradition* (Cambridge, Mass., 1990).

Even when spread out in a single voice, a twelve-tone series invites us to hear an elaborational, rather than permutational order. And this we usually do, unless there is some compelling obstacle. A twelve-tone theme opens Liszt's *Faust* Symphony (Ex. 9.54): but we spontaneously hear this as two phrases, one imitating the other, shifting chromatically through neighbouring augmented triads. True, we do not necessarily hear the passage as an instance of triadic tonality; but by discerning this elaborational structure, we are already moving in that direction, so that Liszt's tonal treatment of the theme comes as no surprise. Another such theme introduces Busoni's *Arlecchino* (Ex. 9.55): we hear this as a sequence of broken triads, departing chromatically from A, and returning to A as tonic: again the elaborational order seems to point in a tonal direction. Or consider the more nearly atonal sequence from Samuel Barber's *Vanessa* in Ex. 9.56, which, in the

Ex. 9.54. Liszt, *Faust Symphony*, motto theme

Ex. 9.55. Busoni, *Arlecchino*, opening

Ex. 9.56. Samuel Barber, *Vanessa*, prologue

first bar of the treble clef, and in the three bars of the bass clef, uses up all the twelve tones except D sharp: here the internal symmetry of the phrases, their repetition, and the convergence of both voices on F sharp, lead us to hear the passage as creating a dominant in the key of B minor. (B minor rather than major, largely because the D sharp has been avoided.) And B minor is the key on which the piece eventually settles, as Barber renounces his atonal rhetoric and begins unaffectedly to sing.

As the Barber passage shows, serialism and atonality are distinct phenomena. It is often a matter of doubt whether Barber's music is tonal; but it is certainly not serial. On the contrary, like many of the great modern composers, Barber was searching for new ways of extending the elabo-rational devices which we hear in tonal music, and new ways of projecting those devices into a polyphonic space. The complaint against serialism is precisely that it gives us no alternative way of organizing such a space.

Thus tonal music could be serially organized: but the serial organization would *not* be the organization that we hear, when we hear the musical order. In a *tour de force* of musical paradoxism, Hans Keller has even argued that the more-or-less twelve-tone passage from Mozart's String Quartet in E flat major, K. 428, in Ex. 9.57, can be derived from a three-tone basic set, by inversion and retroversion.[46] But one thing is surely true: it is not *this* order that we hear, when we hear the passage as music. The chromatic notes here enter as leading-notes on to 'subsidiary dominants'. If Mozart succeeds in using all twelve tones in five bars, this is a by-product of his energetic tonal thinking, rather than evidence of thinking of another kind.

If we ask ourselves whether atonal music can produce the characteristic features of tonal organization, then our answer must surely be sceptical. Consider a few obvious instances:

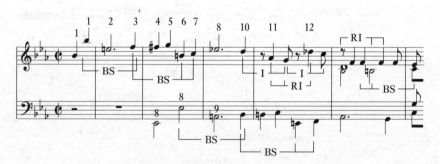

Ex. 9.57. Hans Keller, serial analysis of Mozart, K. 428, first movement (simplified) BS = basic series; I = inversion; RI = retrograde inversion

[46] H. Keller, 'Strict Serial Technique in Classical Music', in *Essays on Music*, ed. C. Wintle (Cambridge, 1994), esp. 172–4.

1. The sense of key. Berg achieves this in the passages mentioned; but only by becoming tonal. All attempts to find an atonal equivalent of key are either contradictory, or involve a move towards the forms of extended or wandering tonality which I described above.

2. Harmonic progressions. Schoenberg wrote of the 'emancipation of the dissonance', meaning that dissonances in atonal music no longer have to be resolved. He was right; but the strange thing is that they cease to sound like dissonances. A dissonance is such only through the implicit contrast with the consonance that resolves it. When there is no resolution, there is no dissonance either. The result is often more like an aimless, mellifluous wandering, which could go anywhere because it is in fact going nowhere, as in the first movement of Schoenberg's Piano Concerto, or Boulez's *Le Marteau sans maître*. It could be argued that Schoenberg has confused the musical idea of dissonance with the purely acoustical idea of discord: but discords are 'emancipated' in all music, and by no one more effectively than the great tonal masters, for whom dissonances are not merely discords, but *harmonies*, which are *arrived at*, by voice-leading away from the concords of the scale.[47]

The notation of pitch-class sets—which I discuss in more detail in Chapter 13—is introduced precisely in order to neutralize the suggestion that atonal music is organized in the way that tonal music is organized. Nevertheless, it needs more than a new notation to abolish the tonal order. Consider the passage from the Berg Violin Concerto quoted in Ex. 9.58. The lyrical character of this passage depends upon the harmonic sequence created by the accompanying figure. The movement between the syncopated right-hand chords sounds right, largely because they are heard as a sequence of suspensions in E flat minor. The first four bars contain all the twelve tones *except* for D, the leading-note of E flat—so emphasizing that we are in some way *at home* in E flat minor. The description of the chords as pitch-class sets does nothing to explain their movement: for example, it does not explain the way in which the A flat in the second bar pulls the other voices down towards it, so that they settle on F, or the similar gravitational influence of the G flat in bar 3. It is these *tonal* properties

---

[47] A similar point is made by Carl Dahlhaus, when he writes: 'emancipation meant that the forward-moving tendency of the dissonance, which made for coherence, was abolished together with the obligation to resolve'. ('Schoenberg's poetics of music', in Dahlhaus, *Schoenberg and the New Music*, tr. D. Puffett and A. Clayton (Cambridge, 1987), 77.) Dahlhaus adds that dissonance is 'isolated' in the atonal idiom, and 'isolation proves to be the reverse of emancipation'. Although atonal music is full of acoustical discords, the circumstances may not be present, in which intentional dissonance can be heard in them. As Zuckerkandl puts it, 'to consider a sound dissonant means to acknowledge its state of inner tension and to be responsive to its *will not to be*' (*The Sense of Music* (Princeton, 1959), 80 ff.). Dissonance is not the kind of thing that can be emancipated.

Ex. 9.58. Berg, Violin Concerto

upon which Berg relies for the movement of the passage, and which enable him to state the inversion of the fundamental series on the violin, as though it were a kind of decorative introduction to a melody.

3. Tension and release. For the same reason, tension and release are marginal in atonal music. Often a kind of uniform nervousness prevails, as in the opera *Le Grand Macabre* by Ligeti, in which an exasperating uniformity of tone defeats every attempt to identify with the action. Since harmonic progression plays no real part in building tension, the composer must rely on other devices. Rhythm, loudness, interval size, and tessitura begin to take over as the vehicles of dramatic movement, leading to a new sense of the psychic meaning of tension. Tension and release are no longer the normal, breath-like phenomenon that we find in Bach or Mozart; they are somehow less in the nature of things, more artificially induced, more rhetorical.

4. Polyphony. Schoenberg and his immediate followers were skilled contrapuntalists. Listen to their music, however, and you will again find that the *audible* counterpoint is precisely that which comes through an incipient surrender to elaborational, rather than permutational, order: it comes when an inner voice *imitates* the upper part; when a motif is passed from one voice to another; when a bass-line stands out as a genuine *bass* to the voices above it. When the inner voices capture our attention, it is for

the same reason that they do so in tonal music—namely, that they create harmony out of coexisting melodies. In the Berg Violin Concerto, it is again the inner voices that call the work to order, and summon Bach's chorale. The intellectual structures of serial atonality, although designed precisely for contrapuntal use, seem unable to generate counterpoint: for the relations are not heard as relations among contrapuntal voices, responding to each other with apt musical gestures. Thus, in almost all serial music, analysis of the permutational structure involves groupings that cut across the polyphonic movement, detaching tones from their melodic and harmonic function, in order to combine them into the sets required by the system.

5. Cadences. It goes without saying that these cannot be duplicated in truly atonal music. Without them, however, the experiences of boundary and closure, on which the organization of the musical surface depends, are more difficult to guarantee. Cadences are the punctuation marks of the musical surface; when they are absent, music does not end, but merely 'breaks off', like a twig snapped from a branch. Unity in music requires both a beginning and an end. Where there is no *perceivable* end, there is no actual end, and therefore no unity.

Attempts to bring atonal music to a perceived conclusion are either quasi-tonal—as in Berg's use of the A minor or major triad over an F, in order to bring each act of *Lulu* to a resolution (Ex. 9.59)—or essentially rhetorical: a noisy climax, or a dwindling into silence. The sense of the tones themselves, as advancing inexorably towards a final resting place, is absent.

Ex. 9.59. Berg, *Lulu*, Act 2, 'Schlußakkord'

6. The journey through tonal space. Evidently this too must be absent from atonal music. Nor is there any clear equivalent to be found. Again, the composer must have recourse to rhetorical devices, in order to create the sense that the music is changing place and character, that it is acted on by dynamic fields of force. Outside the dramatic context—as in *Moses and Aaron*—this sense seems to evaporate. The 'unity of musical space' is in fact an abolition or at any rate a confining of musical space. When the music goes everywhere, it also goes nowhere.

7. But this brings us to the final sceptical question. When we hear *movement* in atonal music, it is precisely *not* the serial ordering that we are hearing. Schoenberg admits as much, when he writes of the 'unity of musical space':

> *The unity of musical space demands an absolute and unitary perception.* In this space . . . there is no absolute down, no right or left, forward or backward. Every musical configuration, every movement of tones has to be comprehended primarily as a mutual relation of sounds, of oscillatory vibrations, appearing at different places and times.[48]

In other words, the 'grouping' required by serial organization forbids the experience of musical movement, as we know it. We are to hear the music as *sounds*, rather than tones, exhibiting an acoustical, rather than a musical, order. Yet this is manifestly *not* what we hear, in hearing atonal music. On the contrary, we strive to organize it in the usual way, to hear themes, motifs, melodies, rather than 'configurations'; harmonies rather than 'simultaneities', tension and release, rather than 'oscillatory vibrations'. Even in a piece as uncompromising as Schoenberg's Violin Concerto (Ex. 9.60), we hear *against* the atonal order. The opening motif on the violin is heard as a phrase, repeated at once in the melodic line and then played twice in inversion; the chords in the lower strings are heard as accompanying harmonies, whose sense may not be apparent, but which are subordinate nevertheless to the melody. The music moves through tonal space with a kind of logic: but it is not the logic of the series. It is the logic of a tune, meditating on neighbouring semitones, in a manner reminiscent of Wotan's farewell. The fact that these semitones can be grouped as a hexachord is of far less significance than the *movement* of the violin from each to each. To hear the serial order we must disregard this movement. We must group first the

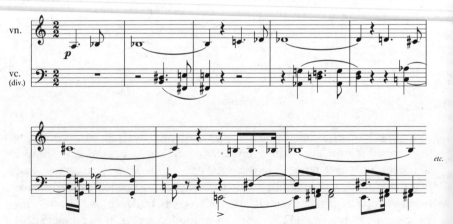

Ex. 9.60. Schoenberg, Violin Concerto, Op. 36, first movement

[48] *Style and Idea*, 113.

opening motif, and then its repeat, with the chords beneath them, so as to form the two hexachords of the series. I venture to suggest that no musical listener will spontaneously do this, and that, if he does do it, the result will sound strange to him. Nor should the performer do it: for the violin melody must be played as though each note grew from its predecessor. As in tonal music, the violinist will lean on the semitone intervals, so that they depart from equal temperament, and lead more effectively onwards. The pseudo-mathematics of the serial system is exploded from the outset, by the fact that this is a concerto for the violin!

In such a case, the constraints implied by the serial order are musically arbitrary. The listener will depend upon the expectations established by tonality, in order to grasp the direction and organization of the music. In particular, he will be relying on the tonal implications of the ascending and descending semitone—the perceived character of *leaning* that these intervals derive from the tradition of tonal harmony. It is surely this character which gives such force and poignancy to Schoenberg's simple tune.

Atonal Expression

Schoenberg presented his move towards atonality as a reaction to the exhaustion, as he saw it, of the tonal language. Artistically speaking, however, it was motivated by an expressive intention: a need to render into audible forms the complex and harrowing emotions that arose with the collapse of spiritual order in Central Europe. It is no accident, I believe, that the most successful pieces of atonal music have been operatic, dramatic, or vocal. There is a formal reason for this success: the prop provided by the song or the drama reduces the need for a *musical* order. Beginning, middle, and end are bestowed by the literary source; and the music can be used to its best effect—as an *expressive* idiom, whose power derives from its repeated defiance of the human ear. It is precisely the juxtaposition of simple human drama, and difficult, massively organized music, that creates the effect of *meaning* something, and something entirely new, in the dramatic works of Berg and Schoenberg. Atonal idioms can be used to invest the most repulsive and trivial situations with an aura of universal significance (as in *Lulu*); they can persuade us that a morbid melodrama (*Erwartung*) offers a glimpse into the deepest regions of Hell; they can endow adolescent narcissism with an air of mystical morality (Harrison Birtwistle's *Mask of Orpheus*); and they can dignify precisely the *Schmachtliteratur* that Schoenberg found so repulsive (*Le Grand Macabre*) by sprinkling it with existential anxiety and the tired old gestures of the avant-garde. But how much of this is achieved by the *music*, and how much depends merely on the contrast between the simple situations and the defiant negation from the pit below?

It is certainly hard to imagine atonal music being used to comic effect: the attempt (as here and there in the Ligeti) invariably falls flat, since comedy requires a background of joy, or at any rate gaiety, emotions which have no home in atonal music. Atonal music in the theatre expresses states of mind that are always partly negative: every lyrical passage is shot through with anxiety; each loving gesture is also a gesture of betrayal; there is no affirmation of life that does not mask a will to deny it. It is as though anxiety were programmed into this music and can never be wholly eliminated. Perhaps we should see atonality exactly in the way that tonality can *not* be seen: namely as a style, rather than a language. It is a style that reflects the epoch which gave birth to it: nihilistic, yet saturated with romantic longing and *nostalgie de la boue*. Like every style, it was destined to exhaust itself, and the attempt to use it today is as likely to lead to cliché as any conscious return to tonality. What is the opening of Ginastera's *Don Rodrigo* (Ex. 9.61) if not an atonal cliché?

This is not to say that the atonal style cannot be rescued from its morbid self-obsession. In late Stravinsky, for example, it is reworked with a pure inspiration, so as to remodel the familiar Stravinskian harmonies and

Ex. 9.61. Ginestera, *Don Rodrigo*, opening

melodic cells. Stravinsky emancipates the atonal idiom, as Berg does: using pitch-class sets which are also chords, and motifs which are also melodies. The result is a reading of serialism *against* itself, so that each harmony and motif contains a kind of pointer towards a distant tonal centre. Stravinsky composed, in his late works, a fitting farewell to serial atonality—a farewell that was matched by Benjamin Britten, in his borrowings from serialism in *The Turn of the Screw*. The subsequent history of music has given no cause to believe in serial atonality, as the new lifeblood of our musical tradition. On the contrary, it has placed a frame around the 'Second Viennese School', and consigned it to musical history.

The State of the Art

Can we really return to tonality—even in its extended versions, even in the form of the 'pantonality' advocated by Reti? Do we not feel a kind of truth in what Schoenberg, Křenek, and Adorno tell us, that the language of tonality is in some way *not available* to people in our condition—meaning, not *spiritually* available? There is nothing that *we* can say by this means, while also *meaning* it. The attempt to do so is either ironical—as in John Corigliano's brilliant 'opera in inverted commas', *The Ghosts of Versailles*—or dull, repetitious, and, yes, banal, like the works of Philip Glass. Occasionally the atonal orthodoxy is defied, with pleasant results, as by Michael Torke in his mesmerizing orchestral pieces. But, when David Del Tredici introduces his acrostic song into *Final Alice* (Ex. 9.62), the critics raise their eyebrows with an anticipatory sneer. 'Pastiche', they tell us; meaning that the melody and harmony are in some sense *borrowed*. It is not Del Tredici who is speaking to us, but an artificial person, put together from the discarded garments of people who—were they alive today—would surely be speaking another language.

That is the thinking which has, since Schoenberg, prevailed, not only among the avant-garde composers, but also among many musicologists and

Ex. 9.62. David Del Tredici, *Final Alice*, 'Acrostic Song'

music critics. To discover what is true in it, and what is false, is one of the hardest tasks in aesthetics. But even if it *is* true, it seems to me, it cannot justify the belief that there is some other language available to the composer than the language of tonality. The argument of this chapter implies that musical understanding elicits an elaborational order in the intentional realm of tones; and that it is no accident if triadic tonality has resulted from our experiments in polyphony. If this polyphonic elaboration can be extended in new directions, it is either because tonality can be extended or because its effects can be preserved through the kind of oblique tonal thinking shown by Skriabin, Stravinsky, Britten, and Berg. The possibility remains that tonal music is the only music that will ever really mean anything to us, and that, if atonal music sometimes gains a hearing, it is because we can elicit within it a latent tonal order.

Such thoughts return us, however, to the question that was left unanswered in Chapter 6: what do we mean by 'meaning', when we refer to the meaning of music? And how can musical organization, as I have described it in this chapter, be a vehicle for meaning things?

10 *Form*

We have seen that music is organized, but not as language is organized; that the musical experience can be amended and deepened without losing its distinctive intentionality; and that there is a central phenonemon—tonality—which provides us with a paradigm of musical order. The question immediately before us is whether this order can be described in less intuitive, and more explanatory, terms, and if so, whether we can arrive at a general theory of musical form.

Levels of Organization

In the opening chapters of this work I argued that music is organized on three primary levels, which are those of rhythm, melody, and harmony. Its organization at any one level is affected by its organization at the others, and by such features as volume, dynamics, and timbre, which add emphasis and colour to the musical surface. On each level the intentional object contains a 'grouping' of elements into motifs, phrases, and patterns, through which the musical movement flows to a full or partial 'closure'. Beats, tones, and chords are heard as directed towards or away from other elements in the sequence to which they intuitively belong, and certain events have the character of boundaries, places of rest, points of arrival or departure. In a great many cases, we seem to distinguish 'structural' elements from the episodes which embellish them—and the distinction between 'structure' and 'prolongation' has, in the wake of Schenkerian theory, become fundamental to musical analysis. Furthermore, harmonic and melodic elements are heard not merely as parts of a sequence, but 'functionally': elements transform the movement to which they are added into movement of another kind, and with another direction. Hence musical movement seems not merely to fill the time in which it occurs, but to span it, to reach across from beginning to end, via recognizable 'stations on the way'. In tonal music, this spanning of time occurs at the melodic, rhythmic, and harmonic levels simultaneously, and in the master-works of our tradition the three simultaneous movements fuse in a single dynamic intention. It is tempting, in view of this, to identify tonality as the key to musical order, and to believe, with Schenker and his followers, that the theory of tonality adumbrates a deep structure that we grasp, when we hear pattern and process in music.

In the last chapter I referred to certain elementary experiences, made available by tonal music: the resolution of dissonance through voice-leading; the preparation and realization of key-changes; the closure of a movement through a cadence; harmonic progressions—and so on. These 'functional' relations between musical events seem to support and perhaps explain the experience of order and implication in what would otherwise be only a sequence of sounds. Although the use of the term 'functional' is, or ought to be, controversial, the difficulties suggested by this usage are generally swept aside, in the interests of a powerful and influential thought, which is that the masterworks in our tradition are especially bold or complex applications of principles which can be heard in the simplest tonal sequence. Musical events act on one another in systematic ways, and what we hear, in hearing structure, is a sequence of transformations, as the musical movement passes through harmonies, keys, melodic devices, and so on, each of which has a standard impact on the material to which it is applied.

Deep Structure

We have encountered a variant of this thought in the 'generative syntax' of Lerdahl and Jackendoff, who argue that the patterns which we recognize in tonal music are the exfoliations of a 'deep structure'. This suggestion does not merely account for the centrality of the tonal idiom, and the difficulties presented to our ears by serial music; it also explains why we can understand an indefinite number of tonal pieces, without learning the trick afresh for each one that we encounter. It offers to explain the unity of musical structures in the classical tradition—the irresistible sense, in a symphonic movement of Haydn or Mozart, that there is a *single* process unfolding through the music, displayed on all three levels of organization. And the presence of deep structure might even suggest a theory of the meaning of music—or at least, an explanation of our *impression* that music has a meaning.

The suggestion is that, in tonal music, we hear the product of a generative process, and unconsciously recuperate the process from the product. We understand tonal music, even though ignorant of the theory which explains it: for this theory is internalized, as a body of tacit, practical knowledge. We no more need to know the theory explicitly, than a computer needs to know the theory behind its software. At the same time, the understanding of tonal music, like the understanding of language, will be a form of intentional understanding—understanding contained in the very perception of its object.

Linear and Hierarchical Order

Some distinctions must here be made, if the suggestion is to be properly examined. The first is that between linear and hierarchical order. Linear order is illustrated by the egg-and-dart moulding in classical architecture, in which egg and dart follow each other in succession, and in which no other order is imputed, besides the alternating sequence. A generative syntax can be given for this pattern, in the following trivial rules:

1. Egg is a well-formed string; dart is a well-formed string.
2. If s is a well-formed string ending with a dart, then the string consisting of s followed by an egg is also well formed.
3. If t is a well-formed string ending with an egg, then the string consisting of t followed by a dart is also well formed.
4. No other string is well formed.

Those four rules generate infinitely many sections of 'grammatical' moulding.

Simple rhythms in music may be understood as linear orderings, in which each element arises in response to its predecessor, according to rules of well-formedness. However, as as we have seen in Chapter 2, many theorists have argued that the linear order of rhythm is either overlaid by, or subservient to, a hierarchical order. Christopher Longuet-Higgins has given a generative theory of metre which accounts for many of the basic orderings that we experience in hearing rhythm, while Leonard B. Meyer, in a distinguished series of books and essays, has argued that both melody and rhythm are hierachically organized: we do not, for example, hear only the basic grouping, or 'primary rhythm', but higher-order groupings, and higher-order fluctuations of emphasis, which subsume the basic elements under a wider time-span. Meyer explicitly connects his theory with that of Heinrich Schenker, who attempts to derive the surface organization of tonal music from a hierarchy of middleground structures, themselves 'composing out' (*auskomponierend*) a single background structure, or *Ursatz*, by a generative process which we internalize when we learn the tonal discourse. Both Meyer and Schenker try to explain the perceived distinction between 'structure' and 'prolongation', by showing that structural events occur simultaneously at the higher as well as the primary level, while prolongations belong only to the primary level—the 'foreground'. However, to return to the distinction made in Chapter 2, Meyer's arguments, if valid, establish only that there is a cumulative hierarchy in rhythmic organization, whereas Schenker's theory imputes a generative hierarchy to music in the tonal tradition. In the case of cumulative hierarchies, the higher levels are perceived only as a *consequence* of the lower levels, and have no generative function. The existence of such hierarchies does not account for musical understanding, which is exhibited at the lowest level of organization—the level which the theory is forced to treat as 'given'.

All planned activity is the result of decisions, arranged hierarchically. Students of business management will be familiar with the 'decision tree', of which Diagram 10.1 is an instance. Suppose a firm has a long-term goal of selling its product in a new market. The directors will be faced with the following choices: either we import the product, or we manufacture it locally. Suppose we manufacture it locally, then we can either build our own factory, or acquire existing facilities; suppose we build our own factory, then we can either import our own staff or hire local labour; suppose we hire local labour, then we can either send the managers to our base for training, or train them at their place of work; if we train them at their place of work, then we must either bring in competent instructors, or obtain them locally. And so on. These decisions form a tree structure, which is such that we could not understand the lower level without relating it back to the higher level, as in the Diagram 10.1:

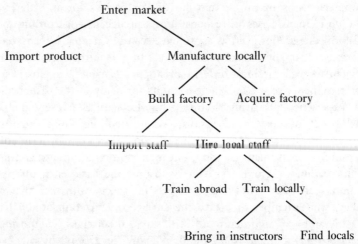

Diagram 10.1

A competitor, wishing to understand his rival's decision, must reconstruct this tree, since no decision can be understood without relating it to the hierarchy from which it flows.

The same kind of hierarchy can be observed in architecture, and is characteristic of all serious reasoned action, whether or not it has an aesthetic goal. And the hierarchy has an important feature in common with generative hierarchies: namely, that lower levels can be understood only through their connection with higher levels. Nevertheless, there is no set of rules—or none that we know of—that would generate from higher levels just those decisions which we observe at the lower levels. In what follows I propose to reserve the term 'generative' for those hierarchies in which recursive application of transformation rules generates lower from higher levels.

Decision trees can be discerned in all forms of rational action, while cumulative hierarchies exist in all forms of *Gestalt* perception, being the natural consequence of our 'rage for order'. Only if musical hierarchies are generative, however, do they impute a deep structure to music. The suggestion that music is organized according to a generative hierarchy would clearly have the most far-reaching implications for the philosophy of music, and cause us to revise many of our prejudices concerning the experience of tones. It is plausible, as we have seen, for certain protomusical experiences, such as the experience of metre. But is it plausible for music as a whole?

Schenker

In offering an affirmative answer to that question (though in rather different terms from those that I have just employed) Heinrich Schenker introduced a new kind of musical analysis, whose professed aim was to derive the musical 'foreground' from a constant 'background', by a series of expansions (the middleground layers). To listen with understanding, Schenker proposed, is to relate foreground to background by the very same route whereby the composer subconsciously derived it. This recuperation of the background is also subconscious; one purpose of musical analysis is to make it explicit— and in doing so, to settle questions of phrasing and emphasis that are left undecided by the score.

From any tone, phrase, or measure, melodic and rhythmic 'diminutions' can be constructed, by inserting passing-tones and ornaments, by altering and dividing the rhythm, or by momentarily exploring the 'neighbour tones' of the given elements. The musical structure of Ex. 10.1*a*, for instance, is preserved in the diminutions of *b*, *c*, and *d*. In hearing these last three, we instinctively recuperate the structure (10.1*a*) from the ornaments, passing-tones, neighbour tones, and subsidiary rhythms which flesh it out. Moreover, we in some sense hear it *as* a structure—as giving the unchanging essence of the phrase, beneath the 'accidents' of its prolongation. In classical variation form we are often given little more than a series of extended diminutions (as, for example, in Handel's 'Harmonious Blacksmith'); and our pleasure in listening depends on our sense of the unchanging essence which is embellished in the variations. But this distinction—between essence and accident—lies on the surface, in the intentional realm of tones. Hearing structure is part of the *phenomenology* of musical perception, rather than a matter of inference or analysis.

Ex. 10.1. Structure and diminution.

Ornaments can succeed or precede the tone which they prolong: an upward apoggiatura precedes the tone, while a trill succeeds it. The phenomenon can be compared to prefix and suffix in natural languages: and it extends to more elaborate diminutions. Schenker's theory begins from the idea that whole sections of music can be heard as subordinate to a particular musical event, either as preparing it, or as elaborating upon it in its aftermath. Consider the opening of Beethoven's 'Waldstein' Sonata, Op. 53 (Ex. 10.2). The first two bars are heard as preparing the G major chord of bar 3, while bar 4 is heard as a prolongation and embellishment of this event. This small-scale use of 'prefix' and 'suffix' is only the beginning of the story; the G major triad of bar 3 is a first inversion; in this context it is heard as distinctly 'unsaturated', anticipating some larger and more inclusive movement. You could, in theory, end a piece on such a chord—Puccini does so, in *Madama Butterfly*, but the effect is as dissonant as a concord can be. Beethoven, however, has prepared, stated, and embellished the dominant of C major, and left it hanging. At once the process begins again, this time preparing the subdominant minor, so that by bar 9 we are expecting the cadence on to an arpeggiated C minor triad that follows.[1]

The bold claim made by Schenkerian theory is that this kind of hierarchical organization is generative. We understand the elements through their derivation from a more fundamental organization, rather than the organization through the cumulative experience of the elements. Schenker went on to propose that the tree which I have just begun ends at a single place—an *Ursatz* or fundamental structure. He even believed that the *Ursatz* is common to all tonal music—or at least, to all master-works in the tonal tradition—and that it consists harmonically of a single I–V–I cadence, and

[1] Those who have studied this movement will know what an obstacle it presents to Schenkerian ways of thinking: a movement in C major which makes virtually no space for the home key except by way of fantastic modulations; whose second subject is announced in E major, making extensive use of C sharp minor harmonies; whose penultimate bars are still toying with C minor, and whose principal theme makes use of the C major triad only by way of 'tonicizing' the key of G major! Still, the first subject is as good an illustration as can be found, of hierarchical organization in music.

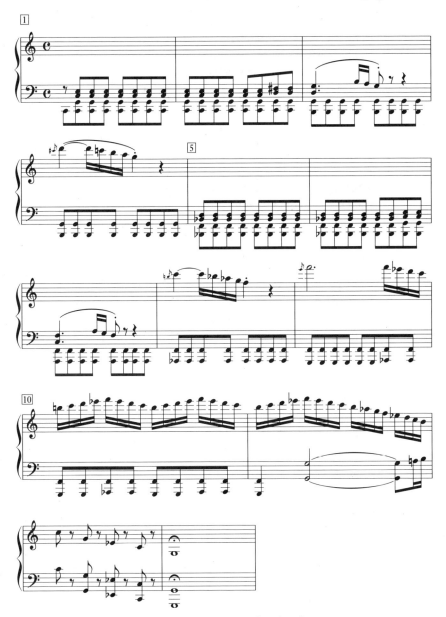

Ex. 10.2. Beethoven, 'Waldstein' Sonata in C major, Op. 53

melodically of a descent on to the tonic beginning either on the third, the
fifth, or the eighth degree of the scale. The whole piece of music is to be
understood as an exfoliation of the triad, in its melodic expansion through
the diatonic scale, and in its harmonic expansion through the dominant–

tonic cadence that is implied in its outer tones (see Ex. 10.3). Each master-work is therefore a kind of extended commentary on the triad, a temporal unfolding, in which the aboriginal harmonic and melodic movement contained in the diatonic scale is spread out through tonal space.

Schenker, who was not inclined to make a modest claim when a bold one would prove more disturbing, therefore asserted that all master-works must be derivable from the triadic *Ursatz*. He offered a few metaphysical and even mystical considerations by way of settling the point, and made passing reference to the series of overtones. However, he was clearly much more concerned, in his actual analyses, with the *middleground* structures—the organization below the surface of the music, which points the way to the deep structure of the composition. The assumption was that the 'fore-ground' (by which he meant not the musical surface, but the organization that we hear in it) can be reduced, via successive middleground structures, to the background progression from which the whole piece derives. We do not *hear* the background: but the foreground is generated from it, by repeated transformations of a rule-governed kind. When we hear the foreground organization, however, we are assigning importance and function to the several musical events, in accordance with a tacit understanding of their derivation. In Schenkerian analysis, the background and middleground structures are represented by graphs, which make non-standard use of standard musical notation. These graphs should be understood, however, as successive levels in a tree-like structure, whose meaning lies in the gener-ative process that is described by it.

In assessing such a theory, we must know how the middleground is derived from empirical observation—in other words, from the musical foreground. Schenker presents a variety of methods, which are of two broad kinds: a method of elimination or erasure, whereby events are removed one by one from the foreground, until another (intermediate) structure remains; and a method of construction, whereby the foreground is built up from a hypothesized deep structure, according to principles which govern the organization of all tonal music. The hypothesis about deep structure is confirmed when the results of the two methods coincide.

Ex. 10.3. The Schenkerian *Ursatz*

The method of erasure seems to proceed in the following way.[2] First we effect a 'rhythmic reduction' of the musical surface, to reveal the underlying melodic and harmonic pattern (the foreground). This first step is in itself highly controversial, since it seems to remove rhythm—the most compelling and immediate of all the ways in which music is organized, and perhaps the only one that really does exhibit a generative structure—from the very object whose organization we are trying to explain.[3] From the rhythmic reduction we then erase those events which are heard as prolongations of other events in the foreground. For example, a melody may pass from one structural tone to another via a series of 'passing-tones' to which can be assigned no special harmonic or long-term function, and which are therefore erased from the structure. In Ex. 10.4, the second subject of Schubert's Eighth Symphony, D759, first movement, the passing-tones (as suggested, at least, by Forte and Gilbert),[4] are those marked with a P. In a similar manner, we eliminate the neighbour-tone elaborations, which occur when a melody lingers above, below, or around a structural tone, without effecting any fundamental change in the direction, harmony, or long-term implications of the music. In Ex. 10.5, following the same authorities, the neighbour-tones are marked with an N.

Other devices which enable us to erase prolongations include the removal of arpeggiations (in which a chord is prolonged through horizontal motion), and 'consonant skips', which prolong melodic tones by leaping from them to a place which is already contained within their harmonic potential. (See the remarks on melodic organization in Chapter 2.) By erasing prolongations we arrive at the 'structure' of the foreground, whose elements are in turn subjected to a similar analysis, so as to arrive at another and deeper middle-ground structure. (Examples of this will be given in Chapter 13: for the moment it is the method, and not the result, which concerns us—though the

---

[2] I am influenced here not only by Schenker's own writings, but by O. Jonas, *Einführung in die Lehre Heinrich Schenkers* (rev. edn., Vienna, 1972); and by the painstaking *Introduction to Schenkerian Analysis*, by A. Forte and S. E. Gilbert (New York, 1982). Less systematic, but of more importance in discussing the *analytical* employment of Schenker's theories, is F. Salzer's *Structural Hearing*, 2 vols. (New York, 1952–62), whose arguments are more relevant to the discussion in Ch. 13, below.

[3] Salzer and others have made a serious attempt to answer the objection that I have just adumbrated: see esp. C. Schachter, 'Rhythm and Linear Analysis', in F. Salzer and C. Schachter (eds.), *Music Forum*, iv (New York, 1976), 281–334. However, Schachter admits that, for Schenker, tonal relations have priority over rhythmic organization, and neither Salzer nor Forte, the two who have done most to place Schenker on the curriculum of musicology in the English speaking world, pays much attention to rhythmic structures in the works cited above, n. 2. Schenker's own approach to rhythm is epitomized by his remark that 'the roots of musical rhythm . . . lie in counterpoint': *Free Composition*, tr. E. Oster (London, 1979), 32.

[4] *Schenkerian Analysis*, 25.

Ex. 10.4. Schubert, Eighth Symphony in B minor, D759, first movement

first moves in Schenkerian analysis can be understood from the lower staffs of Ex. 10.5.) Now, if the theory were merely an elaborate process of elimination, we should suspect it to be little more than a redescription of the phenomenon that it is designed to explain—a way of identifying the perceived junctures and boundaries in a sequence of tones. Hence a method is required in order at the same time to 'construct' the deep structure that we discover through erasure—a method that will show how just *this* structure can be derived from the deep grammar of music.

The deep grammar proposed by Schenker turns out, in fact, to be the surface grammar of classical music: the theory of harmony and counterpoint, in the tradition of Fux.[5] The background is spelt out by two voices, a descending upper part, and an arpeggiated bass-line, moving from tonic to dominant and back again. The middleground is derived by adding voices to this elementary movement, so as to prolong it through intermediate tones and harmonies, which grow from each other in accordance with the

[5] Fux, *Gradus ad Parnassum* (1725); and see Schenker's own profound treatment of species counterpoint in *Counterpoint*, tr. J. Rothgeb and J. Thym, ed. J. Rothbeg, 2 vols. (New York, 1987).

Ex. 10.5. Mozart, 'Linz' Symphony in C major, K. 425, fourth movement

principles of voice-leading—for example, resolving dissonances by stepwise descent. Briefly put, that is what the middleground consists in: a structure in which voices, moving in strict counterpoint, prolong the basic progression.[6] This contrapuntal middleground is not consciously heard. But it *explains* what we hear: we notice it only subconsciously, and only by grasping the surface organization that flows from it.

The test of the Schenkerian theory is that the structure generated by the theory coincides with that which is heard in the music, by the person who

---

[6] According to Salzer, the 'free' counterpoint of the foreground is possible only if it 'appears' (is heard?) as a prolongation of the strict counterpoint which underlies it (*Structural Hearing*, 131).

hears with understanding. In other words, it should identify boundaries and closures in the foreground at just the points where they are heard. But at once a problem arises. There seem to be indefinitely many ways in which, by using the rules of classical harmony and counterpoint, we could derive a perceived distribution of structural and prolonging events from some underlying sequence of middleground patterns. So which do we choose and why? Schenker's postulation of a single *Ursatz* from which all the master-works derive, was designed to constrain our choice of middleground struc-tures: however, except in the case of very short movements, or thematic statements (like the Haydn 'St Anthony' Chorale to which Schenkerians refer *ad nauseam*—see Ex. 10.6), the road back to the supposed *Ursatz* is tortuous, obscure, and soon abandoned. We are left with the vague claim that one among the many competing middleground hypotheses contains the truth about the music's derivation—though we may not know which.

Ex. 10.6. Haydn, 'St Anthony' Chorale

This objection would be of no significance, were it simply repeating the well-known thesis of the 'under-determination of theory by data'.[7] However, there are special features of Schenker's theory which make it vulnerable to the charge of arbitrariness. First, there is no rule-governed deduction of obser-vation from theory; secondly, the theory introduces no genuine theoretical

---

[7] This celebrated thesis, associated with the work of the French physicist Pierre Duhem (*The Aim and Structure of Physical Theory*, tr. P. P. Wiener (Princeton, 1954)), and the philosopher W. V. Quine (see esp. 'Two Dogmas of Empiricism', in *From a Logical Point of View* (2nd edn., Cambridge, Mass., 1961), and *Word and*

concepts. Instead, it uses observation terms (the 'rules' of harmony and counterpoint) as though they were theoretical, merely postulating another and deeper layer of reality to which they supposedly apply. I shall consider these two objections in turn.

Ex. 10.7. Cadence

The theory relies heavily on the idea that musical events are to be understood *functionally*. It is not simply that *a* leads to *b*, which leads to *c*; it is rather that *b* transforms *a*, in such a way that *c* becomes a fitting sequel. For instance, the passage of the alto voice from A to G in Ex. 10.7 transforms what we hear, in such a way that the tenor's move to E (with a neighbour-tone prolongation) sounds both right and conclusive. There is a question, however, as to what the term 'function' means, or ought to mean, in such a context. In mathematics and formal logic, the term 'function' means a rule-governed transformation procedure, which delivers a determinate output (or 'value') for each determinate input (or 'argument'). The function denoted by + in arithmetic, for example, delivers, in respect of every pair of numbers upon which it operates, the sum of those two numbers. The function & in formal logic delivers, for every pair of sentences that it links, another sentence whose truth-value is connected by the truth-table with the truth-values of its parts. (It denotes a function between truth-values, just as + denotes a function between numbers.) We could never capture the perceived 'functionality' of musical elements by such 'rules of transformation', since it is a functionality that depends entirely upon context. Musical elements sometimes *sound* functional in the mathematical sense, and this fact contributes to the perceived distinction between structure and prolongation. But their function is derived not from a priori rules of transformation, but from a posteriori regularities established over time. The impression of rule-governedness is no more than an impression, and, while it feeds upon the extramusical experience of language, it cannot be explained as the experience of language is explained, in terms of genuinely rule-governed transformations operating over determinate syntactical arguments.

Object (Cambridge, Mass., 1964)), is sometimes known as the Quine–Duhem thesis, following the initiative of Imre Lakatos, in 'Falsification and the Methodology of Scientific Research Programmes', in I. Lakatos and A. Musgrave (eds.), *Criticism and the Growth of Knowledge* (Cambridge 1970), 92–195.

When the 'functional' theory of harmony was introduced by Riemann, it was with another idea in mind: the function of a chord, for Riemann, was its role in the harmonic system.[8] This idea is open to serious qualification, as I shall later show. In any case, it is of no use to the Schenkerian, since the function of a chord, in Riemann's sense, is a matter of primary musical observation, and imputes neither deep structure nor rule-governed transformations to the context in which it is heard.

But this leads me to the second objection. For the Schenkerian, the appearance of functionality on the musical surface is the consequence of *real* functional relations in the depths. Yet nothing is said to distinguish this real functionality from the apparent functionality that we hear in the surface. The 'rules' organizing the deep structure turn out to be the very same rules—harmony and counterpoint—that organize the surface. (And, as I have indicated, they are not rules at all, but generalizations from the musical tradition.) The music is doing in the depths exactly what it is doing on the surface; in which case, why say that the foreground is generated by the deep structure, rather than the other way round? The Schenkerian argument seems to be of the following form: *if* this piece of music were organized according to a generative hierarchy, then here is another piece of music which would be higher up (or deeper into) the hierarchical structure. But no reason has been given for thinking, either that music *is* organized generatively, or that any real explanation could be given in this way, for the organization that we hear in the surface.

The point can be brought home by returning to the comparison with language. Linguistics does not merely give sense to the idea of a generative hierarchy; it also explains what is meant by the 'function' of elements in the deep structure. A long tradition of persuasive argument, from Frege, through Tarski, to the model theories and discourse representation theories of recent times, has placed *thought* at the heart of communication, and identified a thought in terms of the conditions for its truth. Language owes its structure to its truth-directed nature. Although there is enduring controversy concerning the deep structure of natural languages, we have a clear means of evaluating any given candidate. We ask whether it can be correlated with a semantic theory which assigns truth-conditions to any well-formed sentence—i.e., a theory which shows how the truth-value of a sentence is determined by the values (referents) of its parts. We understand the functionality of grammatical categories in terms of this criterion. But it is precisely in this respect, as we have seen, that the comparison between music and language fails to hold. And because it fails to hold, the search for a generative theory of musical structure loses its motive. We have no means

---

[8] See Ch. 2 n. 23.

of proving that the 'deep structure' read into music by this or that analytical theory really does have a generative function, no way of showing that the surface is derived from the structure, rather than the structure from the surface.

Indeed, the whole tenor of Schenkerian theory belies the generative hypothesis. For the deep structure is made to 'function' in ways that we understand only because of our prior experience of musical order, in terms of harmony and voice-leading. We read foreground movement into the background, and treat the background as though it were really a vastly stretched-out and ponderous kind of foreground. The 'deep structure' becomes another way of describing long-range relationships in the foreground; but it does not explain them, still less show how they are generated from a root idea.

Nor does the exclusive emphasis on harmony and counterpoint seem justified. Many of our experiences of closure, boundary, and movement depend upon factors like repetition, stress, tempo, volume, and even timbre, which present us at best only with cumulative rather than generative hierarchies. And while the Schenkerian theory involves many subtle—and indeed Ptolemaic—adjustments, in its attempts to show how all these features may be seen to derive, by ever more intricate middleground structures, from the basic *Ursatz*, it is hard to avoid the impression that the theory is being stretched, in the process, to the point of irrefutability, and therefore vacuousness.[9]

Schenker's theory makes certain specific assumptions which, while independent of the hypothesis that music has a generative structure, nevertheless feed into it, and endow it with some of its allure. For example, the theory assumes, not without a superficial air of plausibility, that tonal music is always, in some way, moving towards a final V–I cadence. And this is true of much tonal music—whether taken in larger or in smaller time-spans. It is true, for instance, of Haydn, Mozart, Beethoven, and Schubert; true too of Schumann and Bruckner. But there is tonal music which moves to a subdominant cadence, as in several of Skriabin's sonatas and symphonies; and there is tonal music that is not cadential at all—as in Debussy, Ravel, and their progeny.

Furthermore, the features that Schenker's theory claims to explain—large-scale movement, development, boundaries, and final closure—can be heard in music that is not tonal at all, or at least tonal only to the point which these musical experiences require. (See the argument of Chapter 9.) Even if the claim that there might be an atonal 'language' on a par with the language of tonality is spurious, there is nothing in Schenker's theory to show that it *must* be spurious. Indeed, the obvious lesson to be drawn from

[9] See esp. the argument in E. Narmour, *Beyond Schenkerism: Towards Alternatives in Musical Analysis* (Chicago, 1977).

atonal music is that the order which reveals itself in the musical surface is not understood as the product of a generative hierarchy, but is heard in the surface *regardless* of any 'structural' base.

The second objection that I made to Schenkerian theory suggests a deep difficulty for any comparable theory of musical structure. Schenker, it will be recalled, explains the background and middleground structures in terms of the laws of harmony and counterpoint. The music 'composes out' a single harmonic structure, according to a contrapuntal motion of the voices that are implied in it. But the rules of harmony and counterpoint derive precisely from our understanding of the musical *surface*. They are generalizations from our cumulative experience of what 'sounds right': and the assumption that it is *these* rules which operate at the deeper level constitutes a recognition that we have no other idea of musical structure, than that which we hear in the musical surface. Moreover, when we hear counterpoint, we do not hear a single movement, but several movements, which may be staggered in time, like a canon, or advancing at quite different paces, as in a double fugue, towards boundaries and closures that do not coincide. To hear, in such a music, a single underlying movement, which is unfolding through the complex surface, would be to hear the music wrongly. You could achieve this impression of a single movement, only if you ignored the polyphonic character of the music, and heard it, instead, as a sequence of chords. Only at the harmonic level could it make sense to reduce true counterpoint to a single movement, based on structure and prolongation. At the melodic level, any such reduction would falsify what we hear, and miss precisely what we most appreciate.

In Schenkerian theory melody evaporates from every level except the foreground, whereas harmony endures. Since the harmonic relations in the middle and background levels are just the kinds of thing that can be heard in the foreground too—'sounding through', as it were, the melodic surface— it is inevitable that the 'structure' of the piece will be described in harmonic terms. Melodic features are then either absorbed into the harmony, or hung (often with some strain) on the supposed descent of scale degrees, from $\hat{8}$, $\hat{5}$, or $\hat{3}$ to $\hat{1}$, which forms the melodic *Urlinie*. In true polyphony, however, we hear the opposite of this: namely, a harmonic order which arises from the confluence of several melodies, tracing the outlines of chords as they hurry through them, but owing their impetus and meaning to their own intrinsic force.

Hearing Functionally

Schenkerian theory may be used in order to emphasize and bring into the foreground features of the musical *Gestalt* which might otherwise remain merely latent in our perception. It can be used, in other words, in the 'emendation of the intentional understanding', in ways that I shall later illustrate. If this is possible, it is not because tonal music is organized by a generative hierarchy. Rather, it is because of four important features of the musical surface.

1. When we hear tones, we hear sequences and patterns; but we also hear a process which moves through them, in which individual events, whether melodic, rhythmic, or harmonic, operate upon one another, transforming existing tensions and movements into tensions and movements of another kind and with another direction. A sequence of C major triads sounds; and then, in the bass, a B flat enters—at once the triads change their character, calling now for a resolution, demanding their own extinction, their self-immolation before the chord of F. (Ex. 10.8(*a*).) In hearing such a sequence we assign a harmonic function to the B flat. And although this function is the effect of style, tradition, and habit, it is as much part of the music (conceived intentionally) as are pitch, tempo, and rhythm. It is not governed by rules, being indefinitely sensitive to contextual change; it does not explain the order that we hear in the surface, since it is itself derived from it. Nevertheless, we hear the function just as clearly as we hear the musical event which possesses it.

Ex. 10.8. Functional hearing

Given that we are not to understand the term 'function' here in its mathematical sense, how should we understand it? Riemann identified three harmonic functions, associated with tonic, dominant, and subdominant in the tonal idiom.[10] At the same time there seemed to be no attempt to identify the function of a chord in other terms. The finality imported by

---

[10] The idea that there are three essential harmonic functions—tonic, dominant, and subdominant—has been re-expressed in more phenomenological terms by Y. Sadai, in *Harmony in its Systemic and Phenomenological Aspects* (Jerusalem, 1980), 76–116.

the tonic chord is the finality of the *tonic*; there is no function here comparable to that of a knife or a hammer—i.e. nothing that is done by the tonic chord that could be described without reference to the thing that does it. The functions of tonic, dominant, and subdominant are to be defined precisely in terms of the chords that perform them. Only because Riemann was inclined to regard the three primary chords as performing all the necessary functions of classical harmony, could he refer to other chords as having the *same* function: i.e., as taking on the role of tonic, dominant, or subdominant. But what this role might be cannot be specified, except in terms of our experience of harmony. (Contrast a tool: the function of a knife is cutting—and this can be described without reference to knives, or to any equivalent tool. Indeed, it is because we know independently what this function is, that we can say what kind of tool a knife is. There is no equivalent in the case of harmony: it is only because we know what a tonic chord is, that we can identify the function of the tonic chord.)

In any case, this idea of function, related specifically to the dynamic character of the classical style, has fallen out of favour. Romantic polyphony seems to emancipate chords from the dynamic functions described by Riemann, while at the same time emphasizing the 'virtual causality' which leads us to hear one chord as springing from or summoning another. If we speak of function here, then this usage is imbued with the ruling metaphors of musical perception. For it is only in context that we have any idea of what a given chord is being used to do: no chord is a tool, with a fixed range of uses. Each is heard to *do* something to the musical movement: but *what* it does is not distinct from the movement itself.

We can use the term 'function' to describe the intentional object of the musical experience only by first bending it to the ruling metaphor of musical organization—by placing it within the field of the great 'as if' which translates sound into tone. Harmonies are heard as operations upon a musical movement; but only in context can we say what any given harmony is doing.

2. Our experience of function is influenced, moreover, by our sense of large-scale organization. A passage in C major sounds one way if we are already hearing C major as the home key; but it sounds otherwise if we are expecting a return to E minor—for now C major is not home at all, but an adventure into foreign regions. In such a case the B flat mentioned above would be heard, in all probability, as A sharp, seeking a resolution on to a second inversion triad of E minor, as in Ex. 10.8(*b*).

Music has often been compared to architecture (which Schelling famously described as 'frozen music'). Like the composer, the architect establishes large-scale expectations, within which small-scale events are situated and in terms of which they are understood. A giant pilaster order, such as Michelangelo uses on the Campidoglio, transforms all subsidiary forms of organization. Mouldings, window-frames, subsidiary columns, and even the plain wall itself detach themselves from the giant order, and form 'aedicules', subordinate to the overmastering rhythm of the façade. In just such a way, the large-scale organization of keys and harmonic structures will cause us to hear musical details in relation to them. It does not follow that the details are generated from the large-scale pattern, still less that they are generated in the rule-governed manner suggested by Schenkerian theory—any more than the details of Michelangelo's Palazzo are generated from the pilaster order. We are faced simply with another instance of the context-dependence of the *Gestalt*.

3. At the local level tonal music often exhibits hierarchical order of a kind—an order which lies on the surface, and which we instinctively recuperate when we hear with understanding. Consider again the opening of Beethoven's 'Waldstein' Sonata. This begins with a repeated C major triad leaving us seemingly with no alternative but to hear C as the tonic. But the music at once seems to modulate away towards the key of G, only to begin again on the triad of B flat major, which belongs to neither of those keys. The musical listener is not troubled, however, by this skip from G to B flat major, which appears to him both natural and beautiful, involving no real change of the underlying key. He hears the first bars not as a modulation from C major to G major, but as a preparation for the G major triad, conceived as the dominant of C. In like manner, he hears the B flat triad as a preparation for the triad of F, the subdominant of C (although the triad changes to the minor, so leading us to expect a cadence in C minor, which duly arrives). In short, the listener hears an extended V–IV–V–I progression in C. The first two segments involve the phenomenon that Schenker described as 'tonicization' (*Tonalisierung*) in which the music briefly focuses on a 'secondary' tonic (here successively G and F) while remaining in the original key. The music is organized hierarchically, in the manner suggested by Diagram 10.2:

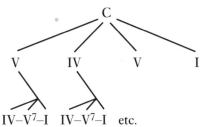

Diagram 10.2

Schenker's theory grew in large measure from the study of this phenomenon, and of the 'harmonic scale step' (*Stufe*), in which the harmonic base shifts from note to note along the scale, tonicizing now this scale degree, now that, but without destroying the underlying sense of key. (A simple example is the prayer which opens the prelude to *Hänsel und Gretel*: Ex. 10.9.)

Ex. 10.9. Humperdinck, *Hänsel und Gretel*, prelude: tonicization of neighbouring scale degrees

When we study the 'Waldstein' Sonata, we see that the metaphor of background and foreground comes to seem more like a literal truth, and the idea that our hearing is informed by a tacit structural hypothesis finds reason on its side. It does not follow, of course, that the foreground is linked to the background by a set of generative rules—although, as I argued in the Chapter 7, a set of such rules could always be produced, regardless of the particular composition of foreground and background structures. (The tree that I have given for the Beethoven is in fact a decision tree, representing a set of decisions on the part of the composer, and a set of unconscious determinations on the part of the listener.) Nevertheless, there is, in such cases, more to 'structural hearing' than a mere *impression* of structure. The music is elaborately dependent upon a sense of key which is established independently of the surface harmonies. (Notice, for example, that the triad of C major—which is the home key of this movement—appears only fleetingly in the first bar of the exposition, and then only in order to announce its resignation.)

4. Finally, we should recognize that, in the small scale, classical music is often organized as Schenker says. Classical melodies frequently rest on a I–V–I progression, which they are heard to prolong through stepwise movement. Examples are familiar—Beethoven's 'Ode to Joy' comes instantly to mind—and I discuss their significance in Chapter 13. They serve to illustrate the movement away from and back to the tonic, which is so important a structural device in classical music, and which has become rooted in the Western consciousness. Nevertheless, the assumption that *large*-scale structure simply prolongs this *small*-scale structure, has never been plausibly defended. The best that we are entitled to assume is that we have, in the I–V–I movement of the classical melody, a paradigm of musical 'syntax' and one which is often imitated at every level of organization in the classical style.

Furthermore, it is only a particular tradition which composes melodies around a I–V–I structure. Folk-melodies may exhibit harmonic shifts along a modal scale, as in the I–ii–I of Greek folk-music, or the I–VII$^\flat$–I of English folksong; they may remain obstinately on one chord until shifting down a third or fourth, to repeat the same melodic pattern; they may be based on a I–IV–I progression, or they may imply no harmonic shift at all. These melodies have been incorporated into our symphonic tradition, or taken as models for symphonic themes (for instance by Tchaikovsky, Enesco, Janáček, and Bartók). There is no evidence that they damage the search for musical unity, or that they lead to works that are in any way less structured than the four-square themes of the classical style.

Implication and Realization

Schenker's theory of structure and prolongation involves, in addition to the hypothesis of generative structure, an emphasis on harmonic progression, on arpeggiation, and on the outer voices (which between them generate the voice-leading movements of the inner parts). It is not surprising, therefore, if the classical repertoire is most often cited in illustration of the theory. The classical style that emerged with the sons of Bach is a style which gives a leading role to harmonic progressions and long-term harmonic relations, while at the same time emphasizing the outer voices, and often preferring implied to actual counterpoint. Even within this range of examples, however, the theory gives only an impoverished account of melody and rhythm, despite the fact that melody and rhythm have a greater claim to the status of musical universals than has harmony.

In a series of impressive works Leonard B. Meyer has tried to give an account of 'structural' ways of hearing which will do justice to melody and rhythm, as forms of musical organization. Meyer recognizes no conflict between his own approach and that of Schenker, although Meyer's disciple, Eugene Narmour, has shown explicitly that Meyer's principles are at variance with many of the more important Schenkerian ideas.[11] Meyer endorses Schenker's distinction between structure amd prolongation. He also uses many of the Schenkerian terms (foreground and middleground; passing-tone and neighbour tone; etc.) as well as the graph notation as a means of identifying latent structures. But this should not lead us to ignore the very real differences between the two approaches. As I have suggested, when Meyer writes of hierarchical order, he is implying the existence neither of a generative syntax, nor even of a 'decision tree'. Rather, he is noting the manner in which small-scale patterns are reproduced or expanded in the larger scale—and the 'height' of any level in the hierarchy is simply a function of the time-span that is covered by it. Meyer's hierarchies are almost invariably cumulative rather than generative.

Meyer describes all three musical dimensions—melody, rhythm, and harmony—in terms of the implications established by musical sequences, and their demand for 'closure'. 'The structure of a composition', he writes, 'is something which we infer from the hierarchy of closures which it presents.'[12] The relation of implication he describes thus: 'An implicative relationship is one in which an event—be it a motive, a phrase and so on—is patterned in such a way that reasonable inferences can be made both about its connections with preceding events and about how the event itself might be continued and perhaps reach closure and stability.'[13] The emphasis on closure is taken further by Eugene Narmour, who wishes to explain musical form entirely in terms of it. 'For the listener,' he writes, 'structure is a result of closure'; and 'closure occurs in various degrees and thus on all levels of music, from low-level motives to the highest levels of musical form. (Indeed, closure is responsible for the emergence of hierarchical levels).'[14] It is clear from that remark, and from the way in which both Narmour and Meyer develop the argument, that the hierarchical levels of musical structure are cumulative rather than generative.

[11] See L. B. Meyer, *Explaining Music* (Berkeley & Los Angeles, 1973); Cooper and Meyer, *Rhythmic Structure of Music;* and E. Narmour, *Beyond Schenkerism: The Need for Alternatives in Musical Analysis* (Chicago, 1977).

[12] *Explaining Music*, 89.

[13] Ibid.

[14] 'On the Relationship of Analytical Theory to Performance and Interpretation', in E. Narmour and R.A. Solie (eds.), *Explorations in Music, the Arts and Ideas: Essays in Honour of Leonard B. Meyer* (Stuyvesant, NY, 1988), 317–40. See also id., *The Analysis and Perception of Basic Melodic Structures: The Implication–Realisation Model* (Chicago, 1990).

In another respect, however, Meyer's emphasis on 'reasonable inferences' should be seen in the same light as Schenker's generative theory. It involves an attempt to lay bare the unconscious mental processes whereby we 'match' the sounds that we hear with a hypothesis concerning their structure. Meyer tries to explain implication in terms of probability, and in earlier work even entertained the thought that information theory and the concept of redundancy could account for tension and release, and hence for emotional 'affect', in music.[15] For Meyer, in his later and more cautious arguments, one musical event implies another by rendering it more or less probable, and closure occurs when that which has been rendered increasingly probable over a time-span of events, duly happens. Meyer tries to show, using largely classical examples, how our expectations are aroused by musical events, so as to enable us to assign probabilities to their successors—as we would assign a high probability to the final C in Ex. 10.10, even if we had never heard Beethoven's Fifth Symphony, Op. 67, or his Third Piano Concerto in C minor, Op. 37. On this view, the structure of a piece of music is not generative but epistemic. It is given by a pattern of diminishing and increasing probabilities, as melody, harmony, and rhythm establish, frustrate, and finally fulfil our musical expectations. The experience of form is, in the end, an extended experience of implication and closure.

There is much that is attractive in Meyer's approach. Nevertheless, the term 'implication', which sustains the burden of his theory of musical understanding, is no more than a metaphor. Meyer assumes that it means here just what it means in scientific inference: event A implies event B to the extent that B is probable, given A. But this invocation of probability theory is without force. Our only grounds for saying that the final C in Ex. 10.10 has been made probable by the preceding events lie in our musical expectations. The probability assigned to the event does not explain our feelings of anticipation and release, but is itself explained by them. It is only because we hear the music in *this* way, that we are inclined to think of the final C as highly probable. We experience 'implication' and closure only because we hear

Ex. 10.10. Beethoven, Fifth Symphony in C minor, Op. 67, last movement

[15] See *Emotion and Meaning in Music* (Chicago, 1956).

musical movement: and the experience of movement, founded in metaphorical transfer, is the real source of the boundaries, closures, and continuities that lie across the musical surface. Moreover, it is only in certain styles—for the most part robustly tonal—that we can anticipate movement with the precision required by an assignment of probability. Yet the sense of 'implication', boundary, and closure persists as an immovable part of musical understanding, even though all judgements of probability are thrown into disarray: think of Szymanowski's First Violin Concerto, for example, or aleatoric music, like Lutosławski's String Quartet, which is every bit as dependent for its effect on our ability to hear movement and boundary as a quartet by Haydn. Furthermore, there is music that is highly predictable in its motion, in which closures are seldom heard—music like Gregorian chant, in which boundaries are dissolved in the sweet self-confidence of a melody that never ends, but only dwindles as it is called away.

Indeed, if the order that we hear in the musical surface were, as Meyer implies, an epistemic order, we should be hard pressed to explain its importance. The pattern of expectations and fulfilments would change from hearing to hearing, to the point where, knowing the piece by heart, we should assign probability 1 to every event in it, and therefore cease to distinguish it from other pieces in the repertoire. More pertinently, Meyer's theory renders the whole experience of music mysterious. Just *why* should we trace these strange patterns through time, if the only motive is to frustrate and fulfil our expectations as to 'what comes next'? Surely there is something more to these patterns than the experience of closure? And surely, this 'something more' is not just a matter of predictability?

In his desire to give a scientific account of musical organization, Meyer has overlooked the thing which makes music interesting: its life. Such predictability as we discern in musical events attaches to them because they form part of a living, breathing, moving organism. The terms that I have used in that last sentence can be replaced by others: but the result will be other metaphors, used to the same effect. Metaphor is here indispensable, since it forms the structure of the musical experience. The sense of closure in music is not the primitive fact, as Meyer would have it: on the contrary, it derives from the experience of movement, which it cannot be used to explain.

And just because this experience of movement is delivered by a metaphorical transfer, we should be suspicious of all attempts to provide rules for the organization of the musical surface. Whatever rules are proposed—whether linear, hierarchical, or epistemic—they will misrepresent the organization of the musical *Gestalt*, which is a spontaneous result of an imaginative act of attention.

The formal relations that we perceive in music neither are, nor result from, a structure below the surface. Form and structure in music are purely phenomenal, and even if our grasp of them can be improved, by an 'emendation of the intentional understanding', the result is an experience of the same kind as the one which stood to be amended: an experience of movement, life, and gesture, reaching through the imagined space of music. Undoubtedly Meyer is right, in arguing that melodic and rhythmic organization are many-layered, and that the phrase-structure of music is far more complex than it might at first appear. But this phrase-structure is given to the musical ear, and our difficulties arise not in hearing it, but in attempting to describe what we hear in terms which capture its complexity.

Form and Gesture

Both Meyer and Schenker attempt to find structural rules and principles which are internal to music—which assume no prior organization of the musical surface. But sounds become music only when organized through concepts taken from another sphere. The organization of music is perceived not merely as movement, but as gesture. The activity which animates the musical surface is that which animates you and me—although transferred to another and inaccessible realm, the realm of pure sound, where only incorporeal creatures live and breathe. Musical activity is not just movement, but the peculiar form of movement that we call action—the confluence of life and rational agency which distinguishes humanity from every other phenomenon in the natural world. This explains the peculiar effect of silence in music: we hear silence as a *Schweigen*, a being-silent. It is not a cessation of action, but action of another kind—refraining, withholding, refusing. Silences in music are always pregnant.

Return for a moment to the Beethoven theme in Ex. 10.10, and study how it continues (Ex. 10.11). Confined within the tonic–dominant harmony that Beethoven prefers for his most energetic statements, it bursts through every rhythmic and melodic pattern that it first establishes, constantly enlarging the upward movement, alighting on new but congenial rhythms with which to descend at last on to the dominant—only to return at once to the tonic with another theme, projected into the foreground by the same indomitable force, the same musical *will*, leading at last to those emphatic strokes which you hear as coming from somewhere behind the melody, and yet integrally a part of it. All this—unpredictable though it was, prior to Beethoven's invention—has an immediacy, a rightness, and a unity that could never be captured in a generative syntax or an epistemic graph. All such theories fall short of Beethoven's thematic invention, for the very reason that they apply equally to the flimsiest musical sequence, and leave out of consideration the factor which creates the power and unity of Beethoven's utterance—the force which drives the music through tonal

Ex. 10.11. Beethoven, Fifth Symphony in C minor, Op. 67, the melodic line continued into the second subject

space, in a gesture of comprehensive affirmation. 'Implications' and 'realizations' here are those which we know from another context and a more familiar world: as when someone slams his fist into the palm of his hand, and at the same time bursts into a smile. The background order of rhythm, melody, and harmony make these implications possible. But they are achieved against that background order, by a process which is not rule-governed but at most rule-guided, and in which rules are not prescriptions but generalizations from the history of style.

The Structure of Atonal Music

The theories considered in this chapter have concentrated on tonal music in the classical tradition. Yet some of the most ambitious experiments in musical form have been atonal; moreover, serialism offers to provide new principles of musical structure, the result of which will be the abolition of tonal expectations, and a reorganization of the musical surface as an array of permutations.

If we look at the techniques followed by the composer, we might come to the conclusion that serial music has a generative syntax, and is derived hierarchically by transformation rules from the *Ursatz*—in this case, the internally ordered twelve-tone series. In fact the syntax does not generate the musical surface but merely forbids certain transformations—in particular, those which lead to the privileging of any given pitch class, and which therefore jeopardize the music's atonality. The real question is whether this syntax corresponds to the structure that is *heard* in the music by the listener who hears with understanding. We could stipulate that this is so— in other words, that nothing else will count as understanding serial music. As the argument of Chapter 9 suggests, however, the principles according to which a piece of music is constructed do not necessarily determine the structure which is heard in it. Serial music is organized in our perception, and it is arguable that it is organized as other music is organized: in terms of phrasing, closure, and boundary; in terms of rhythmic pattern, harmonic tension, and the movement of the melodic line. The serial structure, even if it can be heard, may form no part of this musical organization, which often arises in spite of the serial ordering, and not as a result of it.

In the face of this difficulty, theorists have suggested new forms of organization which can be heard in atonal music. In particular, Allen Forte, following Milton Babbitt, has argued for the importance of pitch–class sets, as objects of our musical perception. I shall outline the theory of the pitch-class set in Chapter 13. For the present we should note merely that these sets can be isolated by the listener only if he first attributes a segmentation to the musical surface. The music must be divided into sections which are musically coherent—that is, audibly 'bounded', whether rhythmically, melodically, or harmonically. This segmentation of the musical surface is presupposed by the description of its atonal structure, and is not determined by it. Pitch-class sets become significant only if they are brought into prominence by the segmentation.[16]

If there is a lesson to be drawn from the argument of Chapter 9, it is that the *Gestalt* organization of music tends in the direction typified by tonality—not because this is how music is constructed but because, *however*

---

[16] See the thorough argument of N. Cook, *A Guide to Musical Analysis* (London 1987), 124–51.

music is constructed, this is how it is heard. Of course, we learn to hear in new ways, and to notice new and challenging musical relations. And this means that the *analysis* of atonal music may require new ways of describing the musical surface. But the claim that atonal music is organized differently, and on different principles, from tonal music has never, to my mind, been substantiated. The only grounds that are offered for this claim are two: first, that the composer uses rival (e.g. serial) principles whereby to compose the musical surface; second that the musicologist uses rival (e.g. set-theoretic) principles whereby to discompose it. Both these grounds are irrelevant. For the argument needs to be made, and never has been made, that these rival principles govern the organization that we hear, when we hear with understanding. As I shall argue in Chapter 13, this argument will always elude us. The organization of the musical *Gestalt*, in terms of movement, closure, tension, and metre, is presupposed, both in the successful use of serial technique, and in the application of any 'atonal' (e.g. set-theoretic) system of analysis. Atonal music as *heard* is organized as tonal music is organized, and differs only in the one respect implied in its name—the absence of a tonic.

Rules, Style and Surface

The argument of this chapter has been somewhat abstruse, and the reader may reasonably wonder what emerges from it, concerning the organization and formal properties of music (whether of music in general, or merely of music in our tradition). The lesson I wish to draw concerns intentional understanding. Although the theory of 'deep structure' remains, and always will remain, an unsubstantiated speculation, it has a permanent appeal to those brought up in our classical tradition. And its effect has been to amend the metaphors through which music is heard: to cause us to listen out for 'structural' events, which stand firm in the phenomenal space, while the movement ebbs and flows around them. It has caused us to assign a special importance to large-scale harmonic shifts, and to listen for harmonic organization, often at the expense of melodic or rhythmic relations. Schools of analysis inspired by the theories of Schenker, Meyer, and others have therefore had an influence which is in no way undermined by the poverty of the theories themselves. The structural analysis of music does not so much describe as create its object—for an intentional object owes its nature to the description under which it is perceived.

The search for deep structure in music is comparable to the search for deep structure in painting, whereby to explain the formal properties of its surface. Suppose you were to describe Manet's *Olympia* in terms of geometrical coordinates in two-dimensional space, assigning a colour to every point. A theory exists which could generate just *this* distribution of colours, from some finite set of equations. But these equations do not describe the deep structure of Manet's picture. For they generate no description of the order that we see, but only a description of the surface *in* which we see it. We see a distribution of colour patches, certainly; but we also see a naked woman on a couch, attended by a black servant with a bunch of flowers. And the formal properies of the picture—its balance, symmetry, unity, and order—all depend upon this second perception, whose content is not mentioned in any description of the painting that can be derived from the 'structural' equations.

In just this way, musical form and organization are subservient to the movement that we hear in the tones, which shapes the musical events into coherent gestures. A theory which assigned deep structure to music would make no mention of this movement, and therefore provide no account of the formal properties of the musical surface. Whenever such a theory seems plausible to us, it is either because, like that of Longuet-Higgins, it falls short of describing the musical *Gestalt*, or because, like Meyer's, it is *constructing* form in the musical surface, following the movement that is already there and perceivable to the musical ear. And the same is true of Schenkerian analysis.

The perception of musical form is indefinitely sensitive to context, like aspect perception in the visual arts. There can be rules for constructing a musical surface; but they will not determine the pattern and order that we hear, since this is something that we contribute, through an act of imaginative attention in which metaphors play an inescapable part. Theories of deep structure are at best extensions of these metaphors; at worst irrelevant gestures towards a theoretical void.

Musical Form

The absence of deep structure makes the organization that we perceive in music all the more extraordinary: this intricate web of connections, which may sustain itself over hours, while creating the irresistible impression of a unified argument and a comprehensive order, is achieved in the very surface that we hear. Music *has no secrets*; and yet its form and meaning elude our most earnest attempts to describe them. Even so basic a phenomenon as rhythm turns out, on examination, to be a multivalent ordering of pulses, in which life and rationality are miraculously fused, as they are fused in the human person. And when we consider the synthesis of rhythm with melody and harmony, in structures which evolve simultaneously in all three dimensions, we are astonished by the complexity of musical organization, and by the effortless clarity with which, in the masterpieces of our tradition, it is displayed to the ear. Is there anything to be said that will explain our interest in this extraordinary phenomenon, and account for the nature of musical form, as an object of intentional understanding? I shall respond to those questions with a tentative theory.

The experience of society shapes everything that we do and feel. We must coordinate our activities with those of other people—so as to fit our gestures, movements, and purposes to theirs, and to make space for them to do likewise. Coordination may have a practical goal, as when we (we British, that is) keep to the left while passing others in a restricted roadway. But it may also be its own goal—as in marching, dancing, and polite conversation, which are always to some extent ends in themselves, and can be means to other ends only when also *treated* as ends. Sometimes, too, coordination is organized around a goal, even though the goal is there for the sake of the coordination, and not vice versa: this, I believe, is the right way to understand organized sports. Dancing and sport illustrate the peculiar pleasure that rational beings take in coordination, a pleasure that rises above every practical purpose. Functionless coordination provides a picture of our social nature: we endeavour to amplify it, to vary it, to embellish it; and as it becomes intricate, so does it change into a spectacle, providing vicarious enjoyment to those who are merely witnesses of its social meaning. Dancing becomes the self-representation of the dance. In watching a finely coordinated troupe of dancers, we are confronted with society in a distilled form, and the result is a kind of vindication of our nature.

The concerted movements of a dance troupe are embodied in separate performers. Each dancer occupies his own space: the harmony between the dancers does not cancel their separation. In music, however, movements coalesce and flow together in a single stream. The phenomenal space of music contains no places that are 'occupied', or from which competing gestures are excluded. Moreover, the aural world is transparent: nothing that occurs in it is blocked from view, and all that flows through it is revealed to the ear as flowing.

Rhythm, even when occurring alone, without pitch, melody, or harmony, provides this experience of coalescence. A rhythm is not one process but many (measure, division, stress, and accent), organized and overlaid by grouping. To hear a rhythm is already to hear a simultaneity of coalescing movements, in a placeless and transparent medium.

Why should this confluence contain so great an appeal for us? Here is a suggestion: the coordination of movement in dancing and marching grants a vision of social order. But the movements here combined are seen as apart from one another, each occupying its exclusive space and expressing its distinct agenda. In music, however, all distance between movements is abolished, and we confront a single process in which multiplicity is simultaneously preserved and overridden. No musical event excludes any other, but all coexist in a placeless self-presentation. And while we can focus now on this, now on that component, we find it impossible to say just what the synthesis involves—just what kind of entity this is, that lives and breathes before us. It is as though these many currents flowed together in a single life, at one with itself. If we search for some natural archetype of this experience, then we find it in ourselves. I know myself too, as a confluence of processes—mental, bodily, emotional—which flow inexplicably yet transparently together. And they form this very thing that I am, which I know immediately and on no basis as 'I', and yet which always eludes my attempts to describe it, disappearing into the wings of every thought or feeling, observing but unobserved. In the experience of music we find our social nature condensed in a single life—a translation of the dance into a unitary process, endowed with the 'transcendental unity' of a perceiving self.

In harmony we hear the conquest of tonal space by simultaneous voices, which are nevertheless also one voice. Harmonies in the tonal tradition are also chords—complex individuals, with their own autonomous relations to one another, which sound right or wrong in sequence. We hear in tonal harmonies the very same drive towards rest and resolution that we hear in melody. But even without the experience of harmony, we are bound to hear music as pressing towards some kind of closure, as divided into phrases, as summoning and answering elements which come after or before. The interweaving of melody and rhythm will force upon us a distinction between 'structure' and 'ornament', and the experience of prolongation is already contained in that of rhythmic measure. Harmony endows the musical surface with a character of tension and release, and with this character comes the experience of passing-tones, as melodies move from one harmonic region to another. Neighbour tones and arpeggiations will likewise be immediately obvious to the musical ear, as it strives to fit melodic line and harmonic meaning into a single movement. And because we hear music as life, we strive also to hear the continuity of life, to hear the small-scale unities of phrase, theme, and progression as parts of the larger patterns which subsume them. Musical form arises through the attempt to provide this instinctive striving of the musical ear with objects that satisfy it; and the traditional 'forms' of music—fugue, sonata, theme and variations, and so on—are the product of a continuous process of making and matching, whereby settled expectations arise in the listener, and are then enhanced, thwarted, or put to new effect as the life of music flows through and over them.

Musical Forms

Words, gestures, and actions are the objects of our deepest feelings: it is through them that we understand the human world, and they have an authority that nothing else can match. In the rush of life, however, they can achieve no completion: they are subsumed by purpose, interrupted and overridden by the torrent of needful things. Only in art do they achieve self-sufficiency, since in art they are removed from the world of practicalities, and isolated from all competitors.

A poet bequeaths his sentiments to words, and the forms of poetry carry the feeling to its completion. The delights of poetry are many; but one of them lies surely in this. Rhyme, metre, and association endow our words with a new order—and one that tends of its own accord to closure. We are offered a picture of what it would be like, for a feeling to have the moral space demanded by it, so as to reach through to its conclusion and realize its nature.

Gestures bequeathed to the dance are likewise rescued from competition and endowed with the space and movement required for their completion. This is one of the delights of dancing, that the gesture moves of its own accord and unimpeded to its goal. We enter the dance so as to free our movements from the fragmentation and disorder of reality.

Movement bequeathed to music has a yet greater freedom. Tones join in sequences, assemble themselves in logical phrases, move through harmonic space without interruption from the outer world. The virtual force that drives the musical movement exists nowhere but in tonal space. The completion of human gesture in this sphere of total freedom excites us beyond anything that we can encounter in our own bodily movement. In music gestures are entirely unimpeded and can project themselves as far as they require for their quiescence.

It is from this experience that the forms of classical music evolved. Phrase-structure grows automatically from the primary organization which transforms sound to tone. Repetition, variation, harmonic progression, and rhythmic organization automatically bring phrases into relation—forming question and answer, statement and development, expectation and resolution.

The forms of music are not a priori structures, imposed by convention, in the manner of a syntax, but traditions, emerging by an invisible hand over centuries of experiment. The same is true of key relations and harmonic progressions. When, in a great sonata movement, relations of key, theme, harmonic progression, and rhythm unfold across a vast time-span, we should see this, not as the unfolding or 'composing-out' of some underlying 'deep structure', but in the way that we see the composition of a painting—as forms and figures in a unified surface, each answering to, completing, or complementing the others. The pleasure that we take in musical forms depends also upon their abstract quality—on their emancipation from the figurative aims which tie painting to the world of objects. Music shows us movement without the thing that moves; it can therefore present us with a reality that we know otherwise only through the workings of consciousness—movements outside physical space, which do not merely coincide but which coalesce as a unity. And these movements find in music a completion which ordinary consciousness denies.

The study of musical form is an attempt to understand the way in which musical gestures can be prolonged and brought to a conclusion. The work of a great critic like Charles Rosen can entirely change our understanding of form—not merely by destroying the neat categories of traditional musicology, but by showing that form is a large-scale working-out of forces that are brought into being by the musical material itself. If it is right to speak, as Rosen does, of a sonata *style*, and of sonata *forms* in the plural, it is because these forms are the long-term consequence of a certain kind of musical gesture. The organization of melody, rhythm, and harmony in the classical style brings into being a phrase-structure which cannot be heard in Bach or Handel, and which demands its own development—a development which is polyphonic but only loosely contrapuntal, and which dramatizes neighbouring keys as areas through which the music passes, rather than places to which it is anchored.

New forms in music cannot be created by fiat or convention. They must grow from a new musical gesture, which means a new style—a new *way of hearing tones, and their organization*. The successful invention of form is a rare achievement. The nocturne would not have existed merely because John Field used that name for his charming and inconsequential piano pieces. The nocturne came into being only with the style that requires just *this* form for its completion—the style of Chopin.

Form and Content

The above account explains musical form as an object of intentional understanding, and makes a tentative suggestion as to the source of our delight in it. But it also returns us to our earlier arguments. Any theory of artistic form raises the question of form and content—of the relation between the structure of the musical *Gestalt* and its meaning. As we saw, there is a philosophical tradition which refuses to countenance the idea of musical meaning, over and above the forms in which it is embodied. For Hanslick, music just *is* 'tönend-bewegte Formen'—a fact which, he implies, both occupies and explains our musical interests. The metaphor of movement, which Hanslick innocently employs, gives the lie to his analysis. For it shows that the formal organization of music can be understood only by the person who relates it, through a metaphorical perception, to the world of life and gesture. The theory of form that I have presented in this chapter therefore also suggests a theory of content, and hints at the truth contained in the equally popular view, that the meaning and value of music lie in its expressive power.

11 *Content*

When Schoenberg turned from tonality, it was because he felt that it was no longer available, as a vehicle for sincere artistic intentions. Recall his animadversions against the diminished seventh: 'it fell from the higher sphere of art music to the lower sphere of music for entertainment. There it remains, as a sentimental expression of sentimental concerns. It became banal and effeminate. *Became* banal!' This thought, which became banal in the writings of Bloch and Adorno, bears directly on our present argument. For notice Schoenberg's way of describing the offending chord: not banal merely, but sentimental and effeminate. The tiredness of a musical gesture becomes a *moral failing*. The composer who works in an exhausted idiom does not merely produce clichés and banalities. His emotional repertoire is confined to the sentimental and the effeminate—to that which is false, undisciplined, self-deceived. Looked at from the philosophical standpoint, such a conclusion is remarkable. For how can this merely *formal* defect in a work of art—that its effects are taken from an 'exhausted' repertoire—lead to so defective a *content*, and to a condemnation, therefore, which is as much moral as aesthetic? Even if Schoenberg is exaggerating, the instinct behind his remark is shared by many, perhaps most, sensitive listeners. Clichés are not merely to be avoided: they are false, unserious, destructive of something that we value—though of what, precisely, it is hard to say.

If we are to make sense of Schoenberg's remark, we must first show how absolute music—music considered in itself and without ancillary text or drama—can express, convey, or contain a state of mind or character. And in returning to the topic of expression we must acknowledge a singular and important truth: that many people who manifestly understand music will deny that it has expressive content, refuse to describe it in emotional or mental terms, and obstinately adhere, like Hanslick, to the view that musical value is to be found in form alone. A theory of expression must show how it is that people can understand the expressive character of a work of music, and yet sincerely deny that *that* is what they understand.

Tentative Conclusions

It is worth summarizing, first the tentative conclusions of earlier chapters, and secondly, the tests which a theory of musical content must pass. For, although our earlier discussions left us with many unanswered questions, they have considerably narrowed the field of enquiry, and marked out the terrain in which a theory of content must be sought.

1. Music does not represent objects or actions, except at the margin.
2. Nevertheless music is often meaningful, in the strong sense that there is something to be understood in it.
3. Listening to music is an expression of aesthetic interest, and music is understood through the aesthetic experience.
4. Music is not a language, even if it is like a language in certain respects.
5. The expressive qualities of a work of music form the most important part of its content.

From those conclusions we can derive certain tests which a theory of content must pass. Four in particular seem important:

(a) Musical meaning is not like the meaning of the Morse code or a semaphore signal. You do not attribute expressive qualities to music merely by devising some code or convention, and thereafter using it as a means of communication. The content of a work of music is given only in the aesthetic experience, which is something over and above the recognition of convention. (The 'semaphore test'.)

(b) The meaning of a piece of music is what we understand when we understand it as music. (The understanding test.) Most existing accounts of expression in music fail this test—or at least, fail to show that they can pass it. We just do not know what is proved by them, or whether anything important is being said—for instance by Peter Kivy, when he points to the way in which the shape of a musical phrase may resemble the 'shape' of an emotion.[1]

(c) The value test. It follows from (3) and (5) above, that expressive qualities are also objects of aesthetic interest to the person who grasps them. This is why we must distinguish the expressive content of a piece of music from the associations, atmosphere, and emotional aura that inhabit its surface. A piece of music might be dreamy and indolent, like the guitar music of Luiz Bonfa, and all the worse for it. But if it *expresses* dreaminess and indolence, as does Debussy's masterly 'La puerta del vino', from the Second Book of Preludes (Ex. 11.1), (although with a bitter tang), then this is a kind of aesthetic success. Bonfa offers us music which has atmosphere, while being *inexpressive* (Ex. 11.2).

---

[1] At least, this is the view which Kivy occasionally seems to defend in *Corded Shell*.

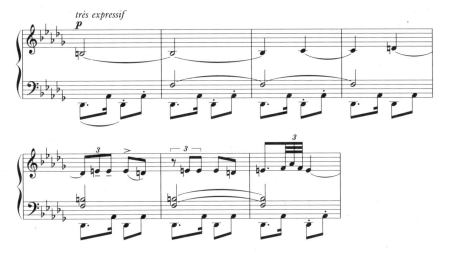

Ex. 11.1. Debussy, Preludes, Second Book, 'La puerta del vino'

Ex. 11.2. Luiz Bonfa (transcribed Carlos Barbosa-Lima), 'In the Shade of the Mango Tree'

Thus there is all the difference in the world between empty music, and music that expresses emptiness, between banal music (like Andrew Lloyd Webber's music for *Cats*) and music that expresses banality (like the brilliant dance sequence from Samuel Barber's *Vanessa*). We speak of expression only where we recognize an *expressive power* in the music. And this recognition of expressive power involves (in the normal case) a judgement of value.

(*d*) The structure test. The expressive quality of a musical work is developed through the music, and the elaboration of the musical line is at the same time an elaboration of the content. Expression does not reside in some passing resemblance or aspect: it is brought into being through the musical argument, and worked into the musical structure.

Those tests are stringent, and I doubt that any theory currently defended could pass them. The difficulties are compounded by two further observations. First, as I noted above, it seems quite possible to understand an expressive piece of music, and at the same time to deny that it is expressive—or at least, to deny that there is anything, besides itself, that the music means. Secondly, and relatedly, we find it almost impossible to detach the meaning from the music and to give it a name. The meaning resides in the music, and—while we have a concept of the 'identity of expression'—it is only in very special circumstances that we are prepared to apply it, and to admit that two separate works of music may express the same thing. *Identifying* the content seems to have little or no role in the appreciation of music. This fact lies behind our preference for an 'intransitive' concept of expression, as I argued in Chapter 6.

Emotion

The use of the term 'expression' to describe the content of music reflects a widespread view that music has meaning because it connects in some way with our states of mind. Yet when Croce first placed the distinction between representation and expression at the heart of philosophical aesthetics, he had no desire to connect art with the emotions. On the contrary, he opposed the *estetica del simpatico*, so eagerly embraced by the empiricists, which places the emotions of the audience at the centre of the aesthetic experience, and reduces art, in Croce's view, to a mere means to stimulation.[2] For Croce a work of art expresses an 'intuition', and he had in mind something like the immediate and preconceptual apprehension of the world which Kant (and Croce likewise) contrasted with the discursive 'concept' required by scientific knowledge.

Other philosophers have departed even further from the common-or-garden use of the term 'expression'. As I remarked in Chapter 6, for Nelson Goodman a work of art can express any 'predicate'—which means (ignoring Goodman's nominalism) any property whatsoever. A work could express blueness, fragility, disease, vastness, indigestion, sadness, or high calorific value. Whatever can be metaphorically exemplified can also be expressed: and there are no a priori limits to metaphor.

It follows that theories of expression in aesthetics are not necessarily theories of the same thing. The relation discussed by Goodman has little to do with that discussed by Croce, or with that which I consider in the present chapter. In what follows I shall consider the expression of emotion in music. For although the meaning of music does not lie purely in its emotional content, the expression of emotion is a paradigm case of musical significance.

---

[2] *Estetica come scienza dell'espressione e linguistica generale* (Palermo, 1902), ch. 12.

It would be foolish to begin such a discussion without saying what emotions are. Limitations of space oblige me to give the briefest summary, drawing on arguments which ought to be sufficiently familiar to readers of contemporary philosophy that I need not repeat them.

First, there is a temptation to think of emotions in terms of their inner or 'subjective' aspect. But, even if this inner aspect exists, it does not constitute the essence of an emotion—or of anything else. Emotions are, like other mental items, publicly recognizable states of an organism. They are identified in terms of their role in a cognitive system, displayed in desires, beliefs, and actions.

Secondly, the human mind is the mind of a person, who is characterized by rationality, responsibility, and self-consciousness. Personality transforms our emotional life, from passive reaction to active dialogue. Rational beings strive to define themselves through their emotions, and enter by means of them into conscious relation with others of their kind.

Thirdly, while emotions include feelings (there is for example, 'something that it is like' to feel fear), it is not 'how they feel' but 'what they do' that is important. In the normal case, an emotion is a motive to action. You act *out of* love, fear, or embarrassment. Our interest in each others' emotions derives in large measure from our interest in 'what makes people tick'. I want to know *why* you did what you did or said what you said: and learning about your emotional state provides an answer.

Fourthly, emotions are intentional states. An emotion is *of* or *about* its object, which has 'intentional inexistence' in Brentano's sense—which is to say that it need correspond to no actual object in the material world. An emotion is a response not to a stimulus, but to a thought. Moreover, each emotion is founded upon certain thoughts which define its 'formal object'— the condition which the intentional object must satisfy, if it is to be the object of *that* emotion. Thus, fear involves the thought that something threatens me, jealousy the thought that someone is a rival, pride the thought that something casts credit on me.

Not all thoughts are beliefs, however, and where belief is absent, so is the motive to act on it. In responding to fiction, I do not believe in the reality of what I read. Yet I respond to it emotionally, and my emotions are founded on thought. In such a case, emotions are shorn of their normal motivating force, and exist in a realm of pure contemplation. There is a real problem concerning the nature of these fictive emotions, and whether we can rightly think of them as we think of their normal and motivating versions.

Fifthly, while animals have emotions, only self-conscious beings have those imaginative thoughts to which I have just referred. In general, the emotions of self-conscious beings have a structure which distinguishes them from the motives of animals. A self-conscious subject is aware not only of the object of a feeling, but also of himself as its subject. He therefore *puts himself into* his emotion, and expresses himself through it. To a varying extent, his emotions are artefacts of his own devising, and grow from thoughts not only about the object, but also about the subject. Hence self-conscious emotions are liable to corruption in ways which are unknown in the animal kingdom. They can become narcissistic, sentimental, bathetic—and it will be a task of later arguments to examine these conditions, and to show their destructive mark in music.

The self-conscious being is therefore involved in his emotional life in a special way. It is probably more nearly true of emotion than it is of any other aspect of human life, that it has the structure laid down as universal law by Hegel. Self-conscious emotion begins in what is subjective, inchoate, 'immediate', and ventures outwards to encounter that which is 'other', objective, resistant to the will. From this encounter the emotion gains in precision or 'determination', and the subject begins to know himself as a motivated being. Emotions *become* what they essentially are, through the process of their public expression. They are formed and amended in dialogue with others; through their 'realization' in an objective order the subject himself is also realized, as an object of his own awareness and decision-making. Hence the expressing of emotion is also a creating of emotion. Through expression the self-conscious subject projects himself into realms of action and perception which give form to his self-awareness. The *Entäußerung* of the emotion is also the coming-into-consciousness of the subject.

Those last thoughts are difficult to state with precision; but they were at the back of Collingwood's mind when he made the concept of expression central to aesthetics, and they suggest an answer to the vexed question why the expression of emotion in art is so important to us. The answer is that art provides us with a means not merely to project our emotions outwards, but also to encounter ourselves *in* them.

Hanslick Revisited

Since emotions have objects, Hanslick argued, the expression of 'definite' emotions in music would require precisely what music cannot offer—the representation of some 'definite' object. The subliminal awareness of this difficulty has reinforced the view that the term 'expression' is properly used of music only intransitively.

How serious is the difficulty? We should distinguish two quite different claims that might be made in these terms. Someone might argue that we cannot identify an emotion as the particular emotion that it is, without identifying its (intentional) object; he might also argue that we cannot express a particular emotion without representing its object. Unless we mean something very special by 'identify' and 'express', neither of those claims is in fact true. I can identify an emotion through its subject: the emotion felt by Jane Smith at 8 p.m. on Christmas Day 1993. And Jane Smith could express that emotion through a cry and a gesture, without thereby identifying its object.

However, identification and expression, so construed, are of no great interest: certainly they do not satisfy our interest in *emotion*. If works of art are to engage our attention through their expressive character, they must acquaint us with a particular emotion, by *articulating* it. And how this is to be done, without the means to portray an object, has yet to be explained.

Imagine a painting, in which a figure is staring out of the canvas towards a point outside it. The figure wears an expression of intense misgiving; his arms are raised as though in preparation to defend himself; his body is poised for flight. Surely it would be perfectly reasonable to construe this figure as in a state of fear. A painter may in this way create a portrait of fear far more expressive than anything that we know from life, without depicting the object feared.

Or consider a painting of a saint, whose beatified countenance looks out from an altarpiece, to nowhere visible. An intense emotion is contained in these features, but towards what is it directed? We imagine those eyes rest-ing on something—something concrete and present to hand, which receives a steady benediction from the face in the painting. We have no knowledge of this object; yet the emotion is there before us, clearly rendered in the subtle flesh-tints of a Duccio or a Simone Martini. In such a case we have no trouble in identifying the emotion that is being portrayed, even without knowledge of its object. The attitude of serene and transfigured acceptance is there before us, vividly portrayed in the paint.

Such examples suggest that there is something narrow-minded in Hanslick's objection. But they also remind us of two significant differences between representational and non-representational art forms. The emotion presented in the painting is *represented* there. But it does not follow that it is also expressed. The first painting portrays a man in a state of fear: but it does not for that reason *express* fear. Perhaps the painting expresses some other and incompatible emotion: anger, or disgust, as in Goya's engravings of the trials of war.

Furthermore, we identify the emotion in the painting through its sub-ject: the fear presented in the painting is the fear of *this* man, who is placed before us by the representation. Another way of interpreting Hanslick's objection is this: music cannot represent the *subject* of an emotion. It therefore deprives us of the *vehicle* of sentiment. We are left with a free-floating emotion for which neither object nor subject can be supplied. In what way can this emotion be real to us?

Works of art very often owe their expressive character to the emotional life of an imaginary subject. In a dramatic monologue we imagine the emotion along with its subject. The same is true in lyric poetry, where the voice of the poet creates a fictitious persona, into whose point of view we momentarily enter through the words. Of course, there are many cases here; a poet like Heine presents us with an imaginary subject who is fully aware of the ironies of his situation, and who therefore gives vent to an emotion from which he also half withdraws; a poet like Browning endows his lyrical persona with a complete dramatic character, in order to place inverted commas around the very feelings that he most intensely conveys— as in 'My Last Duchess', or 'A Toccata of Galuppi'. But even allowing for the complexities of 'romantic irony' (as Hegel called it), we can still acknowledge that the presentation of an imaginary subject is an essential part of lyric poetry, and the foundation of its expressive power.

There is no precise equivalent of the 'represented subject' in music. Nevertheless some writers have found it natural to describe expressive music at least as *the voice* of such a subject: it is as though someone were expressing himself through the music. When writers argue in this way, however, we find that they can say nothing else *about* this subject. He becomes an abstract 'I', the transcendental self that has no empirical identity. The musical self is pure subjectivity, beyond the reach of concepts. Such a suggestion is implied in Schopenhauer's theory, to which I return below.

A Note on Levinson

The difficulty can be grasped through considering a theory put forward by Jerrold Levinson, in an important series of papers.[3] Levinson argues, in a manner not unlike that of the last section, that Hanslick's objection is not fatal to the idea that music expresses emotion. The objection simply reinforces the demand that we say *how* emotion is expressed in music, and what features contribute to its expressive character. Levinson goes on to propose a definition of expression in terms of 'hearing as', in which the 'imaginary subject' plays a prominent role:

> P expresses (or is expressive of) *a* if and only if P is most readily and aptly heard by the appropriate reference class of listeners as (or as if it were) a *sui generis* personal expression of *a* by some (imaginatively indeterminate) individual.[4]

[3] 'Hope in the Hebrides', in *Music, Art and Metaphysics*, 336–75; and 'Musical Expressiveness', in *The Pleasures of Aesthetics: Philosophical Essays* (Ithaca, NY, 1996), 90–125.

[4] 'Hope in the Hebrides', 338.

This definition is subsequently modified, and is never confidently *leaned upon* by Levinson. Nevertheless, it repays study. The core idea is that, in hearing expression, we hear a piece of music as though it were the voice of an imaginary subject, who is expressing (in the non-aesthetic sense of that term) his state of mind. Levinson writes more loosely that music is expressive if it is 'readily perceivable as personal expression'.[5] The person in question is indeterminate, in the sense that nothing else is attributed to him besides the particular emotion, and the act of expressing it. He is like the voice behind the screen in the acousmatic world of Pythagoras. Boiled down to its essentials, the definition tells us that we recognize expression in music, by hearing music as (or as if it were) an expression (in the non-aesthetic sense of the term).

Levinson illustrates his definition with a step by step analysis of the 'Hebrides' Overture, designed to show that a specific emotion—namely hope—is expressed by this music. He writes at first as though the music resembles the posture, attitude, and life of a hopeful person. But he is reluctant to be explicit, presumably because he knows that the music resembles no such thing. (At least, it resembles a duck in a state of gastric distress just as much as it resembles a man in a state of hope.) In fact, Levinson rests his case on the claim that we can (ought to?) hear something *in* the music that resembles the life and gestures of a hopeful man. And that is true: for (if his critical judgement is right) we hear *hope* in the music, and hope resembles hope.

Levinson begins from the idea that we hear the music as (or as if it were) the expression of hope (in the normal sense of expression). But he shifts at once from 'hearing as if it were' to 'hearing in'; it then becomes unclear that the reference to a hopeful *subject* is required. Surely, if a theory of expression is worth anything, it ought to tell us what it *means* to say that we can hear hope in music. Yet Levinson takes that phrase for granted. Moreover, he fails to tell us why it is important to 'hear emotion in' music, or why this fact—if it is a fact—about the 'Hebrides' Overture contributes to its value. In short, he does not show how his definition would pass the four tests mentioned at the beginning of this chapter.

In the normal understanding of the phrase, hearing *x* as if it were *y* should be distinguished from hearing *y* in *x*. For the second, unlike the first, exhibits double intentionality: you must hear *x*, and focus on *x*, at the same time as hearing *y* in it, and focusing too on *y*. I may hear the curlew's song as if it were the cry of a departed spirit, without hearing it as the curlew's song. But if I hear the cry of a departed spirit *in* the curlew's song, I must also focus my attention on the song, and hear it as it is, knowing it *not* to be

---

[5] 'Musical Expressiveness', 90.

the cry of a departed spirit. The two perceptions amalgamate, precisely because there is no competition between them, the one being founded in imagination, the other in belief. There are many subtle gradations here; but the double intentionality signalled by 'hearing in' enables us to dispense with the reference to an imaginary subject. We hear movement in music: but we do not attribute this movement to anything—we do not hear the music as though it were a moving thing. And what goes for motion, goes for emotion too. Levinson's implicit dependence on 'hearing in' enables him to arrive at his analysis of the 'Hebrides' Overture *despite* his definition of expression, and without reference to the feelings of some imaginary being.

There is another, and deeper reason, for rejecting Levinson's 'imaginary subject'. When we hear expression in music, Levinson suggests, this is like hearing another person express his feelings. But in what way like? We have no prior conception of what it would be to express feelings in *music*: if we can think of someone doing this, it is because we have an idea of the expressive character of music, and therefore can imagine someone choosing just *this* piece of music, to convey just *this* state of mind. Our ability to imagine a subject expressing his feelings in just *this* way is predicated upon our ability to recognize the expressive content of the music. Only if we can independently recognize the emotional content of music, therefore, can we embark on the thought-experiment required by Levinson's definition. Once again, the definition *leans upon* a notion of musical expression, and does not provide it.

This difficulty returns us to the Hegelian argument considered in the previous section. The expressive character of art is connected with its role in the *Entäußerung* or 'realization' of our feelings. We encounter works of art as perfected icons of our felt potential, and appropriate them in order to bring form, lucidity, and self-knowledge to our inner life. The human psyche is transformed by art, but only because art provides us with the expressive gestures towards which our emotions lean in their search for sympathy—gestures which we seize, when we encounter them, with a sense of being carried at last to a destination that we could not reach alone, as when a poem offers us the words of love or grief which we cannot find in ourselves. Art realizes what is otherwise inchoate, unformed, and incommunicable. It does this because we recognize its expressive properties, and appropriate them as vehicles of our own emotion. But just what these properties are, and why they contribute to the 'objectifying' of subjective life, are matters which are left unexplained by theories such as Levinson's.

There is another aspect of Levinson's definition that deserves attention: namely, that it is a *definition*, phrased in the peculiar syntax of analytical philosophy, with the 'if and only if' prominently announced. Yet to propose definitions of the terms used in aesthetic description is to make a large assumption. As I argued in Chapter 6, almost every term deployed in describing the aesthetic character of something (its character as an object of aesthetic interest) is transferred from another context. To give a definition of the term in *this* use is to break the connection with its central use, and so to undermine the metaphor. To explain a metaphor is to explain its *point*: and that means not defining it, but explaining the experience that it is designed to convey.

Furthermore, the invocation of a 'reference class' of listeners opens the way to a radical scepticism: how is this class defined and by whom? The natural gloss on Levinson's definition is to identify the reference class as the class of those who are able to discern the expressive content of a work of music. But this would reduce the definition to vacuousness. Behind this difficulty lies another, which is that of finding an objective ground for our judgements of expression. Is there a right answer to the question, what the 'Hebrides' Overture expresses? Since expression, I maintain, is an aesthetic value, we could give a positive answer to that question only if we could also defend the objectivity of aesthetic values.

Hanslick Yet Again

Hanslick is often treated as a 'formalist'—that is, as someone who believes that we understand music in terms of its formal organization—i.e. in terms of the balance, order, and architecture which is achieved through tones. And we have seen that Hanslick ventured a description of the essence of music, as 'tönend-bewegte Formen', an obscure phrase which may be translated 'forms moved through sounding', or 'forms moved through tones'. This might seem to confirm the judgement that Hanslick is a formalist, on account of the prominence given in the definition to form. But form is mentioned only in the context of movement. And this idea of musical movement is an irreducible metaphor, which can be explained only through our response to music. It is associated with other metaphors—and in particular with the metaphor of life. In hearing the movement in music we are hearing life—life conscious of itself; and if, sometimes, we use words like 'expression' to convey the character of this life, is this not merely a natural extension of the metaphor? In short, Hanslick has given us no alternative to the theory that he criticizes: on the contrary, he has tacitly accepted its most important claim—that music is the object of a metaphorical perception, whereby it is lifted from the physical realm of sound and placed in the intentional theatre of our sympathies.

Just as the formalist ends by endorsing the metaphors which lead his opponent to describe music as an expressive medium, so does his opponent tend, under pressure, to retreat from the theory that works of music express precise states of mind. Almost invariably the transitive concept of expression gives way to an intransitive notion of 'expressiveness'. The question *what* is expressed by the music is in the end answered by ostension—by pointing to the particular work, in all its complexity, and saying 'this'. Such a concession to the formalist is not a complete capitulation. But it leaves us without an adequate account of the *point* of expression in music.

The Dance of Sympathy

It is obvious from what I have said that we could understand expression only if we could understand our response to it. The response to expression is a sympathetic response: it is awakened by the presentation of another life, another subjectivity, another viewpoint within the *Lebenswelt*. Much confusion enters into this topic because writers have so unclear a conception of the range of sympathetic emotions.

If you are afraid of a danger, and I too am afraid of it, then our feelings coincide: but neither feeling is the work of sympathy. If, however, you are afraid of a danger, and I, observing your fear, come to share in it while not being afraid for myself, then my fear is a sympathetic feeling. So too is my compassion. (The special case where the response coincides with the emotion responded to is sometimes called empathy—translating the German *Einfühlung*.) Sympathetic emotions have a complex intentional structure. Suppose Mary unjustly accuses William of a misdemeanour, causing William to lose the job which she covets. William will feel anger towards Mary, and a desire for retribution; knowing the facts we will naturally sympathize. But what do we feel, towards what or whom? We sympathize *with* William; but William is not exactly the object of our emotion. For sympathy, in such a case, is also a form of indignation, and the object of this indignation is *Mary*, and her act of injustice. Sympathetic emotions *borrow* their intentionality: it is William's emotion that defines the object of ours.

Furthermore, it is necessary to distinguish our sympathy with William from the impartial indignation with which anyone might respond to Mary's injustice, regardless of sympathy. Indignation is not a form of sympathy, even if it has its origin, as Hume and others suppose, in sympathy. It is abstract, impartial, and targets its object (in this case, Mary) directly, and not through the feelings of another. I sympathize with William in response to his anger; but I am indignant with Mary in response to her act. Of course, the two emotions are hard, in such a case, to distinguish, since sympathy involves not merely a response to William, but an assessment of his situation, and of William as a part of it. If I thought that Mary had acted rightly, then my sympathies would change.

Sympathetic emotions are aroused as easily by imaginary as by real situations. Indeed, they are more fully released in us by fiction than by fact.

In real situations our interests are at stake, and tend to eclipse our sympathies. Fictions occur at an impassable distance, in another and inaccessible world, where the pure archetypes of human feeling expand into a space of their own creation. No fiction can impede or advance my purposes: fictional characters pose no threat; nor can we change their situation. Our feelings towards them are free from the normal cost of sympathy, which is the active need to intervene. In entering a fictional world, we are *exercising* our feelings, but not *acting from* them, for the beliefs necessary for motivation have been ruled out of court. This peculiar exercise of sympathy therefore presents us with the residue of emotion, when the motive has been neutralized—the residue which distinguishes *emotion* from all the other motives in the human psyche. This residue is often referred to as 'feeling'; but it is more than that. It is an active assessment of the world, as a place in which my concerns are engaged. Through the free play of sympathy in fiction our emotions can be educated, and also corrupted. And that is one reason why art matters.

Our response to music is a sympathetic response: a response to human life, imagined in the sounds we hear. However, in the absence of representation there is no precise object of sympathy—neither an imaginary human subject, nor a situation perceived through his eyes. The life in music belongs in the musical process, abstract, indeterminate, unowned except through the act whereby we listeners possess it.

Sympathy is not merely a matter of feeling things. There are sympathetic actions and sympathetic gestures. These gestures may arise in response to a real person, really feeling something—someone who needs help, encouragement, or reprimand. Or they may again arise, as in representational art, to things imagined, which are severed from the world of practical interests. Among actions of this second kind none is more remarkable than dancing. In dancing I respond to another's gestures, move with him, or in harmony with him, without seeking to change his predicament or to share his burden. Dancing is not necessarily an aesthetic response; but it has an intrinsic tendency to become aesthetic: it involves responding to movement for its own sake, dwelling on the appearance of another's gesture, finding meaning in that appearance, and matching it with a gesture of my own.

Plato and Aristotle emphasized the character-forming nature of music partly because they thought of music as something in which we *join*. When we dance to music we move with it, just as we move with other people in a dance. And although there are forms of dancing which break free from the bounds of aesthetic experience—which, by losing all restraint, spill over into erotic or violent action—there is a kind of dancing which parallels acting or singing, in being the producer and the product of an aesthetic response. This kind of dancing resembles our experience in the concert hall, which is itself a kind of truncated dance. When we listen we may tap our feet and sway subliminally; our whole being is absorbed by the movement of the music, and moves with it, compelled by incipient gestures of imitation. The object of this imitation is life—life imagined in the form of music.

When someone dances to music, he responds to the way it sounds. Someone might be 'set in motion' by subdued music, or driven to a frenzy by corybantic noise. But he would be dancing *to* the music only if his movements express his attention to the music. 'Dancing to', in the sense that I am considering, is the name of an aesthetic response.

The dancer who moves with the music moves also with other dancers—and this is part of what he does, even when the other dancers are imaginary. Dancing creates a 'sympathetic space' whose meaning is corporate. (It is part of the pleasure of dancing that you are 'joining in'.)

A ballerina may say, 'when I hear this music, I imagine a bird fluttering about its violated nest; that way I know how to dance to it'. On the other hand, she may simply say, 'This is how I dance to it', and venture no interpretation of her gestures. Similarly, a dancer may describe the music in emotional terms—as an expression of love or grief or anger—and so make sense of it, as the focus of the dance. But someone could dance the very same dance, and feel no inclination to describe the music in emotional terms. Understanding lies in the dance, not in the description.

Dance is a close relative of gesture, and in particular of the formal gestures with which we encounter one another on special occasions, such as weddings and funerals. Manners are a kind of generalized choreography. Consider the gesture of condolence: in performing this I *represent myself* to my grieving neighbour. The distinction can be made (as I shall show in more detail later) between the sincere gesture of condolence and the sentimental fake. We distinguish true compassion, which focuses on another's suffering, from the self-dramatizing pretence of it, whose aim is to display the 'beautiful soul' of the performer. A sincere gesture of condolence is not an expression of grief, but an expression of sympathy for grief: its sincerity consists in its concentration on another's predicament, with a view to *relating* to the other *in* his predicament. Sincerity is therefore a matter of intention: is the gesture aimed at the other in his predicament, or is it aimed reflexively, at the person who makes it? (Contrast the person who is distressed by the victim's distress and tries to comfort him, from the person who makes magnificent display of a vicarious grief, but forgets the victim entirely, and a moment later is found happily engaged in some equally dramatic emotional display towards someone else.) Conventions emerge spontaneously, as David Lewis has shown, from the complex intentions involved in communicating our states of mind.[6] The conventional gestures

---

[6] *Convention* (Cambridge 1969).

at a funeral make possible the sincere expressions of regret and condolence. In learning them you enter into a common culture with your neighbours.

There is no more difficulty in describing the gestures of a dancer as sincere or sentimental than there is in so describing the gestures of condolence at a funeral. In learning the steps of the dance you are learning to represent yourself to others. And in dancing to music you respond sympathetically to an imaginary movement that is itself understood as a movement of sympathy.

Nietzsche wrote of the 'birth of tragedy out of the spirit of music'. More plausibly, we might refer to the birth of drama out of the spirit of dancing. Dancing is the social activity which stands nearest to the aesthetic response— a way of 'being together' which achieves the absorption in the present experience and the saturation of interest, that are the familiar gifts of art. Light is cast on the expressive character of music if we see the response of the listener as a kind of latent dancing—a sublimated desire to 'move with' the music, and so to focus on its moving forms.

In responding to a piece of music we are being led through a series of gestures which gain their significance from the intimation of community. As with a dance, a kind of gravitational field is created, which shapes the emotional life of the one who enters it. We move for a while along the orbit of a formalized emotion and practise its steps. Our truncated movements are also acts of attention: we do what we do in response to the sounds that we hear, when we attend to them aesthetically. If this is what it is to hear the meaning, then hearing the meaning is inseparable from the aesthetic experience. A theory which accounted for the expressive character of music in these terms will therefore pass the first two of the tests outlined earlier. It will also explain the inseparability of form and content in music. As I tried to show in Chapter 10, the experience of musical form is an experience of movements and gestures, detached from the material world, and carried through to their musical completion. In hearing the content of a piece of music, therefore, we are also hearing the form: the life which grows and fulfils itself in tones.

But why is the 'experience of meaning' (as I have described it) so important? Why is it that so many musical people deny the expressive character of music, and why is it that we find it difficult (and usually unnecessary in any case) to put the meaning of music into words—to move from an intransitive to a transitive idea of expression?

Value and Structure

I have given no analysis of the terms 'expression', and 'expressive'. Instead, I have decribed a central instance of the *response* to expression in music. 'Moving with' expressive music is one form of the 'recognition of expression'.

When this recognition occurs the listener may have no words for *what* he recognizes—just as I may respond to your gestures with a spontaneous movement of sympathy, even though I have no words to describe what either of us is feeling. The description of the music as *expressive* is a record of the fact that *this* is how I respond to it—and perhaps a recommendation to others, that they respond in a similar way.

It seems to me evident that you could not respond in the way that I have described, if you were not also attending to the music for its own sake, as the sensory object that it is. The response to expression is an aesthetic response. Furthermore, it is a response that finds intrinsic value in its object: to respond in this way *is* to value the work of music, so that there is no gap between the recognition of expression, and the attribution of aesthetic value. The theory therefore passes the 'value test'.

It also passes the structure test. When you move to music, the music takes charge of your response to it—you are being *led* by it, from gesture to gesture, and each new departure is dictated by the musical development. The response to expression is not the fleeting and casual thing that the analogy theory would seem to imply. You are *in the hands* of the music; your sympathetic response moves in parallel to the musical development, and you may taste the same experience of 'exploration' and 'resolution' that attends the performance of a tragedy. When you hear the transition to the second subject in Schubert's String Quartet in G major D887, and that dance-like but strangely solitary melody breaks through the drama of the major–minor exposition, your sense that this is exactly *right* is generated within the music (Ex. 11.3). This is the musical answer to that fearful

Ex. 11.3. Schubert, String Quartet in G major, D887, first movement, second subject.

opening statement. But it is right too in your response to it: you are being led by the most natural means to enact the lightness and wonder of life just at the point where you should recall it—the point in which fear and foreboding threaten to become morbid. This sympathetic response to the music is also, in a very real sense, an emotional education: you are rehearsing something that it is very hard to feel—the impulse to selfless gratitude for the gift of life, in full awareness that the gift will soon have vanished.

Emotional education does not involve the acquisition of theoretical knowledge nor the gaining of information. That is why we should resist cognitive theories of expression; for, however sophisticated, they miss what is really important—which is the reordering of the sympathies that we acquire through our response to art. The education of the emotions is enhanced by repetition: we seek the experience again and again, because we must exercise our sympathies if they are to be alive at all.

The great triumphs of music, it seems to me, involve this synthesis, whereby a musical structure, moving according to its own logic, compels our feelings to move along with it, and so leads us to rehearse a feeling at which we would not otherwise arrive. Consider Beethoven's Ninth Symphony. The plain, awesome statement of those opening bars leads to an extraordinary musical argument, in which every kind of tragic, defiant, and titanic emotion is shown to have been lying dormant in the initial gesture. There follows a frenzied dance, full of wit and paradox, in which the music recklessly disregards what it has discovered; from thence we proceed to a sublime meditation, full of longing, in double variation form. The three movements leave a memory of contrasted dances, in which the listener's sympathy is led through the possibilities of an heroic solitude. Suddenly we hear a musical negation: the chord of D minor with an added minor sixth and major seventh, commanding a full stop to the dream of isolation. The lines of a recitative then emerge: phrases which take their meaning from the accent of human speech, and which effortlessly lead to the melody of the 'Ode to Joy'. This triumphant affirmation of community is not the cheap trick that it might have been: for it has received the stamp of musical inevitability. We are made to rehearse, in our extended sympathies, a particular movement of the soul. We return from private struggle to public comfort, and we feel this return as natural, inevitable. We sense that it is possible, after all, to explore the depths of human isolation, and still to re-emerge in communion with our fellow men. Beethoven's sincerity lies in the process whereby we are led from isolation to community without a faltering or sarcastic step, without a single cliché or a note that is forced from its natural orbit to do service to a false emotion.

Ineffability and Empathy

But why do so many musical people deny the relevance of descriptions like the one that I have just given? And why are these descriptions so hard to produce, and so inadequate to what we hear, when we encounter a true masterpiece?

The first of those questions is easily answered. The musical response does not consist in the words with which we attempt to capture it. It consists in the many and varied ways in which we move to music, when we 'move with understanding'. You show your understanding not through words, but through listening, and finding yourself compelled by the musical argument. If people refuse to describe their response in emotional terms, it is often because these suggest *wrong ways of listening*—as though we should be interested in something *other* than the music. Properly understood, however, the description of the expressive content in a piece of music *is* simply a description of the music. It is an attempt, through metaphor, to identify what we hear, when we hear with understanding.

Nevertheless, there is something ineffable about the content of music— something that words cannot capture, but which must nevertheless be heard and grasped in our deeper experience of meaning. In Chapter 7 I discussed the suggestion made by Diana Raffmann, that this 'ineffable' quality is the result of semantic disappointment. On the assumption that a generative theory of musical structure, of the kind proposed by Lerdahl and Jackendoff, is in broad measure correct, Raffmann argues that we are inevitably led by our cognitive powers to hear syntactic order in music. But we look in vain for the semantic order that underlies and generates it: hence there arises that peculiar bafflement, that sense of being led to a vast echoing space where meaning should reside, and finding only a scaffolding of tones.

As I suggested, however, we may have the very same experience of ineffability, even when semantic expectations are fulfilled. The lines 'Ô saisons, Ô châteaux | Quel âme est sans défaut?' convey to me an indefinable emotion. Were I to try to identify it, I might point to some *other* work of art: a Corot landscape, for example, or a Fauré chamber movement. This is not because my semantic expectations have been simultaneously aroused and thwarted. It is because expressiveness, in poetry as in music, cannot be detached from its sensuous form. Hence the 'heresy of paraphrase', and the problem of form and content; and hence too the preference for an intransitive over a transitive concept of expression in *all* truly confident descriptions of aesthetic meaning.

What does this ineffability suggest? Let us turn from understanding music to understanding people: for our paradigm of sympathetic interest is surely the interest that we take in our own moral kind. It has often been argued that, in order to understand the gesture, state of mind, or feeling of another, some kind of empathy or *Einfühlung* is required, whereby I imaginatively project myself into his position and see the world through his eyes. Without that act of projection I know only what is 'outer'—body and behaviour—and not the 'inner' reality of another consciousness. This suggestion has been applied to music (for example, by Theodor Lipps), in order to make sense of expressive qualities. And it contains both insight and error.

The original picture offered by the theorists of *Einfühlung* was this: a state of mind has two aspects, that which is revealed in body and behaviour, and that which is 'subjective', captured by the contents of the subject's first-person awareness but by nothing else. The essence of the mental state consists in the second aspect, and genuine knowledge of another's state of mind must involve knowledge of that aspect. But the 'inner' aspect is purely intentional, the object only of 'immediate' awareness, whose nature is falsified by any other mode of cognition. To know it is to know also that its nature cannot be 'discovered', since it is known only as 'given'. How then, can I know in *that* way what is 'given' to *you*? *Einfühlung* is proposed as the faculty whereby I adopt, as it were, the vestiges of your outward expression, and so come to feel in myself the subjective awareness that is yours. I then re-create the intentional object of your first-person awareness, and so know the inner essence of your state of mind. What I then know can be communicated only through the act of *Einfühlung*. I could not describe the intentional structure of this state of mind and thereby make it available in its inner essence to you: nor could I make it available to you *simply* by acquainting you with its 'outer' expression.

The claim is twofold: that there is an objective and a subjective aspect to the mental; and that there is a form of knowledge proper to each. These claims can each be interpreted in two ways: one misleading, the other illuminating. According to the misleading interpretation, there are properties of the mental which are 'purely subjective', and therefore perceivable only from the first-person viewpoint. This way of expressing the theory involves accepting some version—however temperate—of the Cartesian theory of consciousness: the theory which identifies consciousness as essentially 'apart from' the physical world, and irreducible.

But it is not necessary to express the theory in that way: nor should we do so. The Cartesian theory of consciousness is incompatible with one of the most important truths of aesthetics: namely, that our states of mind are brought into being with the means for their expression. It is the *Entäußerung* of feeling in dialogue and social life that endows us with the higher emotions: emotions that exist in and through their social expression, and which are brought to conscious completion in works of art. If we value art it is partly because it introduces new states of mind, by providing the expressive gestures that convey them. We should therefore try to frame the theory of *Einfühlung* without conceding that the mind is 'other' than its outer manifestation. To do this we need only rephrase the theory in terms of the asymmetry that exists, between first- and third-person awareness. My first-person awareness is 'immediate', based on nothing: it therefore involves no recognition of 'subjective' properties that are not available to you. It is immediate knowledge of the very same thing that is known mediately from the third-person viewpoint. The difference between being in pain and merely observing pain in another does not lie in the difference between an awareness of 'subjective' facts and an awareness of their outer expression. It lies in the difference between a first- and a third-person perspective on one and the same state of affairs.

Even on this metaphysically harmless interpretation, however, there is an asymmetry between the two points of view. Someone could have a purely theoretical knowledge of fear, as did Siegfried when he asked Mime to explain the feeling. But he may lack—as did Siegfried—the 'knowledge by acquaintance' which comes only with the *experience* of fear. How could Siegfried acquire this second kind of knowledge—'knowledge what it is like'? One answer is: by *Einfühlung*. There is a kind of response to your face and gestures which makes your first-person perspective available to me. I imagine what it is like to be you, feeling this; I then entertain your emotion within my own point of view. There is nothing to be *said* about what I thereby come to know, for there is no new proposition that I know. But the experience may be of peculiar importance, both as cementing the bond between us, and as helping me to see the force of the reasons that you offer for your actions. Knowing your fear in *that* way I can understand your behaviour. There is a close connection between 'knowing what it's like' and understanding the premises of another's practical reason: understanding not what they are, but *how they weigh with him*.

'Knowledge by acquaintance' lies wholly outside the reach of any third-person perspective; its content cannot be described since it contains no proposition known. If we call it knowledge, nevertheless, it is because it shares with theoretical and practical knowledge the distinguishing mark of knowledge, which is expertise. The one who knows is the one whom we can trust—either because his sincere beliefs are a guide to truth (theoretical knowledge), or because his skills and dispositions are a guide to competent or right conduct (practical knowledge), or because his states of mind are 'the real thing', a guide to how the world appears, when it enters our perception (knowing what it's like). There is no paradox, either in the claim that you have to 'enter into' someone's state of mind in order to know it by acquaintance, or in the claim that what you thereby know is inexpressible. For this kind of knowledge occurs only with the experience itself.

Often *Einfühlung* has for its object not an emotion but simply a facial expression, a gesture, or a frown. Such things may seem peculiarly significant, and, whether by an act of imitation, by the residue of such an act, or by whatever method (who knows, in fact, how it is done?), we 'enter into' them, and transform our observation of another's expression into the imaginative awareness of 'what it is like'. This might lead us to understand someone's outlook and intentions, even though we could not convey our understanding in words. Indeed, *Einfühlung* may give us a complete, but non-discursive, picture of a state of mind which, from the third-person perspective, is barely manifest. This non-discursive awareness is what Croce really meant—or at any rate, what he should have meant—by 'intuition'. And it is plausible to argue, as did Croce, that it is intuitions that are expressed by art.

Suppose that a mimic suddenly arranges his face in a striking expression. I respond with an *Einfühlung* that presents me with the picture of an 'inner world'. Here I might be tempted to say: behind that expression there is feeling. But of course I do not attribute the feeling to anyone, least of all to the actor before me. I have 'entered into' an absent state of mind. In the normal theatrical case, an actor will portray a precise character in precise circumstances, suffering some identifiable emotion. The dramatic context will provide the thoughts through which the object of the feeling can be defined. My act of *Einfühlung* takes place against a background of third-person knowledge, and I feel no hesitation in describing what the actor or his words express. If someone says to me: 'there is a quite definite emotion in these lines', then I might reply to him with a description: 'it is a sentimental remorse over the death of Desdemona'.

But such descriptions, however astute, never seem to capture what is known, by the person who understands the play. We want to add: 'but of course, the important thing is the quite peculiar *shade* of remorse that is conveyed by the lines'. In answer to the question 'what shade?' the critic will eventually have recourse to ostension: '*that* shade!', pointing to the text. It is the desire to emphasize first-person awareness, or 'knowledge what it's like', that causes us to retreat, in this way, from a transitive to an intransitive concept of expression.

Here, then, is the origin of ineffability. Observing a gesture or expression, we may have the experience of *Einfühlung*, of 'knowing what it's like', whereby the gesture becomes, in imagination, our own. We then feel it, not from the observer's, but from the subject's point of view. This experience may provide an intimation of a whole state of mind, regardless of whether the state can be described; regardless of whether 'feeling' is the right name for it; regardless of whether we believe that there *is* another person into whose mental arena we have felt our way. We obtain a first-person awareness of a world that is neither ours nor anyone's. It is a creation of the imagination, prompted by sympathy.

What we know from the first-person perspective ('what it is like') can be known only from that perspective—which is not to say that it is mysterious. Or rather, it is mysterious only in the way that the first-person perspective is mysterious. The ineffability of artistic meaning is, I suggest, simply a special case of the ineffability of first-person awareness—the impossibility of translating 'what it is like' into a description. It is this which explains the effect of 'condensation' in art. In the two famous lines from Rimbaud that I quoted earlier, much is at work besides the literal meaning. The alert reader will ask himself what seasons and castles have to do with each other, and why they prompt the question: 'quel âme est sans défaut?' He will recall that the seasons began, according to traditional Christian belief, only with the Fall and the expulsion from Paradise; that castles represent man's futile attempt to stave off disaster, to render permanent what is fleeting; hence the two ideas suggest the only kind of permanence that we obtain—the permanence of ageing things. The question comes—and the invited answer is not 'none' , but 'none since the Fall'. In two lines the reader has been prepared for Rimbaud's invocation of guilt and sexual transgression ('le coq gallois'). None of this is stated by the poet: but precisely because it is *not* stated, the lines can be understood only by a leap into subjectivity—by attaining the first-person perspective that binds these images together. That is what condensation means, and why it is a value. Without it, poetry would be both prolix and cold, and its readers would stay always on the outside of the poetic vision.

The expressive and the ineffable go together, therefore, not only in music but in poetry too. And if all art aspires to the condition of music (as Schlegel and Pater argued) it is because music achieves the greatest possible distance from the explicit statement, while still inviting us to 'enter into' its expressive content. Understanding music involves the active creation of an intentional world, in which sounds are transfigured into tones—into metaphorical move-ments in a metaphorical space. At a certain point, the listener has the experi-ence of a first-person perspective on a life that is no one's. This 'recognition of expression' is simply a continuation of the imaginative activity that is involved in understanding music: the activity of hearing sounds as figurative life, so that 'you are the music while the music lasts'. That, in short, is why we should see expression as central to the meaning of music.

A Note on Schopenhauer

Discussion of this topic would be incomplete without a reference to Schopenhauer, whose 'metaphysics of music' constitutes one of the boldest attempts to make music central to our self-understanding. Following the Kant of the *Critique of Practical Reason*, Schopenhauer argued that the thing-in-itself, which could not be known as an object since it could not be brought under concepts, could nevertheless be known as a subject, through practical reason. When I make a decision I am immediately aware of my own reality as will, and it is the will that underlies the world of representation. The will is the inner essence of man as it is of everything; it can be known directly, however, only in the first person, and then only because the first-person perspective offers an opportunity for non-conceptual awareness: for an 'immediate' acquaintance with the thing-in-itself.

In poetry and the visual arts we are presented with images of the phenomenal world—the world of 'representations', which are themselves represented in the works of art. But in music, Schopenhauer argues, we are presented with something else. Music is free from concepts; it provides no images of the phenomenal world, but a 'direct' perception of the will itself. In listening to music, therefore, we encounter the very thing that is presented to us through practical reason—the will, of which we have only 'immediate' and non-conceptual knowledge.

This theory is bound up with the transcendental idealism of Kant, and suffers from difficulties of which Kant himself was well aware. Schopenhauer's will, like any 'thing-in-itself', lacks a *principium individuationis*: there is only one undifferentiated and indeterminate will, which lies above and beyond appearances, outside the reach of concepts altogether. Nothing, therefore, can be said about it: not even what Schopenhauer says in his theory of music. To suppose any relation between this will and the concrete phenomena of human emotion is inherently absurd. The will, as Schopenhauer conceives it, is neither cause nor effect, neither process nor substance, neither object nor subject. To refer to it at all is to use the Kantian philosophy as a source of metaphor. Nevertheless, Schopenhauer's metaphor enables him to convey two important facts about music. First, it shows the first-person perspective to be central to the experience of music: our understanding of music is expressly likened to our knowledge of the inner life, when we know it not by description but by acquaintance. Secondly, the theory, divested of its metaphysical assumptions, tells us that, when we hear movement in music, it is a movement that is self-propelled, motivated, purposeful, in the manner of human intention. We hear musical movement as action, and not just as movement.

Properly amended, therefore, Schopenhauer's philosophy of music provides an interesting precursor to the theory presented in this chapter.

Music and Drama

It is often said that music cannot be understood as an expression of emotion, since this is incompatible with its role in opera. Although there are occasions when a character sings out his feelings or when two characters, as in a love duet, join in expressing some common state of mind, the greatest triumphs of music-drama consist precisely in those ensembles in which a single piece of polyphonic writing accompanies many contrasting and incompatible emotions—incompatible in the sense that they could not coexist in a single soul. Think of the sextet from *Don Giovanni*, or the oath of loyalty in Verdi's *Otello*, in which Iago is merely pretending to feel what Otello is feeling truly. Surely the music cannot be expressing all the emotions of the characters involved: the attempt to do that would lead to chaos. Nor can the music be successful if it merely expresses *one* of the relevant emotions, leaving the others unvoiced: for then it would destroy the drama, by displacing most of the characters from the foreground. So why not acknowledge that the music is doing something else—that it is not expressing emotion at all, but simply providing a musical accompaniment to a dramatic action?

Difficult questions are raised by this objection. But the first step in any response to it is to follow Wagner, in comparing the music of an opera with the chorus in a Greek play. The music stands proxy for the listener himself, expressing not the emotions of the characters, so much as a sympathetic response to them. An ensemble is like any other theatrical relationship: it involves many contrasting feelings, to which the listener responds as a whole. When you see two people quarrelling on the stage, you do not necessarily identify with either: nevertheless, you respond to the situation, and your response is a single thing. You become excited as the tension mounts; you form fears and expectations; the two characters seem to dissolve in the quarrel, which becomes the single presence on the stage. If the quarrel were to be accompanied by music, it would be to these feelings—the unified response of the audience—that it should address itself. The music would become excited, full of fear and anticipation, a response to the quarrel and not the voice of either party.

When a composer sets words to music, he is doing something not unlike the person who coins a metaphor. He is bringing one thing *to bear* on another: bringing music to *bear* on a situation identified through words, just as the poet describes one thing in terms of another and so *forges* the relation between them. The ruling principle here is one of appropriateness: does this music *sound appropriate* to the situation? And this is the very same idea of appropriateness that governs figurative language. Does this word *sound right* when applied to this thing? (Is Wednesday fat or lean?) You could say that the music that accompanies a drama is a metaphor for the drama.

Word-setting is like dancing with another person: it involves matching your response to his, answering the social 'valency' which his movements create. This matching process can be observed in all areas of social life: arranging flowers for a wedding, laying a table for guests, dressing for a party, decorating a room. The process has a social reference and a social function. It is our way of acknowledging and deferring to our social nature, in the appearances by which we are surrounded; it is a way of building a public space in our own vicinity, and welcoming others into our world.

The recognition of expression in art is the highest point to which this matching process leads—the point at which we do not simply match things to each other, as in decoration, or ourselves to each other, as in dancing, but things to ourselves. This is in part what the German idealists had in mind, when they saw in art the unifying force between subject and object, the thing which heals the fracture between the self and its world, and restores the alienated subject to the wholeness and innocence from which his journey into knowledge first sundered him. (Such, at least, seems to be implicit in the writings of Fichte and Schelling.) The point can be put less contentiously, in the terms that I have suggested. In artistic expression we find a minute correspondence between an object of contemplation, and the inexpressible 'what it's like' which is the core of our conscious existence. Why we should value this experience is the principal matter that will concern us in the concluding chapters of this work.

Antirealism

The theory of expression defended in this chapter tends in what recent philosophers would call an antirealist direction. Instead of searching, like Levinson, for a definition of expression, in terms of properties and relations of the expressive object, I have given neither necessary, nor sufficient, conditions, nor even criteria in Wittgenstein's sense, for the description of a work as expressive. Rather I have identified a state of mind—the 'recognition of expression'—and its place in the aesthetic experience. The description of the work as expressive is an attempt to articulate this state of mind. It is sincerely asserted only by the person who has the experience of recognition, and it uses metaphors whose point can be seen only by the one who shares, in fact or imagination, the experience that they are designed to convey. To accept the description is to concur in an experience, and not in a belief.

It is no part of my concern to defend such an antirealist theory of aesthetic description. (I have made the attempt in *Art and Imagination*.) In any case, the conflict between realist and antirealist is, in aesthetics, somewhat irrelevant. For the central question, which is decided by neither position, concerns the justification of the aesthetic response. An antirealist does not have to be a subjectivist. He believes that the term 'expressive' describes no property of an object, but serves instead to articulate the feelings of the person who responds to it. Nevertheless he may also believe that there is a right and a wrong response to any particular work, and a form of argument that would justify the one against the other. Conversely the realist, who believes that works of art literally possess expressive properties, may be a subjectivist, believing that no particular response can be rationally preferred, and that there is no argument that will vindicate an aesthetic experience, even when it involves the 'recognition of expression'.

Our discussion has led us therefore into the vexed subjects of criticism and aesthetic value, to which we now must turn.

12 *Value*

Many of our interests, once satisfied, are dropped from life's agenda. When you have conned your law book, you can set it aside. It has performed its function, which was to teach you the law. The same is true of the scientific or historical text: if you refer to it again, it is because your memory is imperfect. The interest in information is satiable; as is the interest in food. But there are interests which are by their nature insatiable, since they have no goal. Aesthetic interest is like this. Someone may say 'I have listened to the "Jupiter" Symphony a hundred times, and each time I find something new in it.' What he means, however, is that each time he finds something old in it: the very same experience calls to him, again and again, and still he repeats it. For there is nothing that he is seeking which could bring his seeking to an end.

An experience to which we are repeatedly recalled, which is imbued with meaning, and which is available to us only when we set our interests aside, sounds very like an experience of value. Indeed, Kant argued, that is what it is. The ideas of right and wrong, which grow from the exercise of freedom, inhabit our aesthetic perceptions. Moreover, if my attitude towards a work of music is truly disinterested, I refer its value to no desire or need, to no empirical predicament of my own: aesthetic value is therefore a form of *intrinsic* value.

But why speak of aesthetic value? Given the scepticism about the 'judgement of taste', as Kant called it, and the growing tendency to regard all aesthetic judgements as groundless or at any rate only arbitrarily grounded, we might find ourselves hesitating to assume that there are aesthetic values. What would justify such a claim? Why is it not enough to describe our various aesthetic *preferences*, and to leave it at that?

Values are preferences; but not all preferences are values. A preference becomes a value when it matters to us in a certain way whether others share and accept it. 'Mattering' is that deep but familiar thing which provides our idea of the 'community of rational beings'—our sense of a shared involvement in the destiny of our kind, and of an investment in the moral order. Our aesthetic preferences become values just as soon as we find *ourselves* in them—just as soon, in other words, as they become part of the attempt to create a place for ourselves in the world, and to situate ourselves among our fellows. For many people, this process of value formation— the transition from subjective preference to the judgement of taste—exists only imperfectly and in truncated form. But in no person could it be entirely dispensed with, without lapsing into a kind of solipsism, an estrangement from the world of objects, in which all relations to things take on a purely instrumental character. Appearances can cease to matter to us only by beginning to dominate our lives, as they dominate the lives of animals. The person who cannot contemplate appearances, surrenders to the trajectory of getting and begetting which makes each merely animal life dispensable.

Consider the genesis of aesthetic value in architecture, the art through which we construct the all-pervasive background to our lives as social beings. We could not possibly know what we are doing, if we began to build without consideration for what looks right and what looks wrong. These experiences of right and wrong define our idea of home. Through them we make sense of our *being with* the strangers upon whom our lives depend. Moreover, it is imperative that we should reach agreement with these strangers. The appearance of your house matters as much to me, your neighbour, as it does to you. When people lose sight of this, they retreat from the public realm: the atomization of the city has begun, and with it the atomization of civil society.

Those considerations apply equally to music. For although music can be understood and heard in private, we should be entirely at a loss if we did not hear it as a social gesture: an appeal to the community of listeners, to seek out and sympathize with the life that resides in tones. It matters to us, what forms of life we listen to; and the preferences of other people also matter. We cannot exist at ease in a world of aliens; we strive instead to extend and enhance the web of sympathy. Taste in music may be as important as taste in friends, in sexual behaviour, and in manners.

The Language of Criticism

We should not be surprised, therefore, that we are as given to making discriminations between musical objects, as between works of architecture, poetry, or fiction. But before examining the grounds for these discriminations, we should explore the language used to make them. Our judgements of works of music are not phrased simply in terms of what is 'good' or 'bad', still less 'beautiful' and 'ugly', but in terms of the aesthetic character of music, as this is revealed to the discriminating ear. The attempt to discriminate leads to new kinds of aesthetic attention, and to new comparisons, new descriptions, and new ways of making sense of what we hear. As a result, the language of criticism and evaluation has become so complex that we cannot hope to embrace it within a single unified theory of aesthetic discourse. Here are some of the elements:

1. Terms which denote aesthetic values, whether positive or negative: 'beautiful', 'sublime', 'elegant', 'ugly', 'unsightly'. Much of traditional aesthetics has been focused on the meaning of these terms. For that is one way of focusing on aesthetic value. The problem, however, is that evaluative terms are rarely used, and make sense only in context, when they tend to give way to idioms whose primary use is not to make aesthetic judgements at all.

2. Terms which describe an object through its effect on us: 'moving', 'exciting', 'uplifting'. We can be moved, excited, and uplifted in many ways, and the use of these terms does not invariably imply an *aesthetic* judgement. Nevertheless, it is significant that aesthetic judgement has such frequent recourse to these 'affective' descriptions.

In describing a piece as moving, I do not mean that *I* am moved by it, nor that the majority are moved by it, nor even that the normal person is moved by it. All such suggestions miss the point of affective language, which is not to describe a response but to recommend it. In describing a work as moving, we are suggesting that the listener *should* be moved by it: not to be moved is to fail to respond as the work demands. And the judgement can be made sincerely only by the person who has himself been moved. Affective language is normative—proposing a 'standard of taste', an ideal of discrimination. Many people are moved by music that is not moving at all, but merely sentimental. The prominence of affective language in the discussion and criticism of art is another sign that aesthetic interest is an interest in value.

3. Terms which describe the aesthetic character of something, without conveying an evaluation. There are at least three levels at which a work of art may be described: as a material object; as an object of perception (the intentional object of our awareness); or as an aesthetic object (the intentional object of the interest which it is designed to satisfy). These various descriptions may seem to conflict. For instance, a painting may be described, from the physical point of view, as a two-dimensional surface, reflecting light of various wavelengths in a specific distribution; and from the aesthetic point of view, as a three-dimensional landscape, containing people, trees, horses, and buildings. It is hard to reconcile these descriptions, and that is one of the reasons why there are philosophical questions about the ontology of art. Some phenomenologists—notably Roman Ingarden[1]—have

---

[1] *Das Literarische Kunstwerk* (2nd edn., Tubingen, 1960); Ingarden recognizes some of the difficulties encountered in the attempt to extend his approach to music. See *The Work of Music and the Problem of its Identity*.

suggested that works of art have a 'layered' nature, each description corresponding to a separate level of meaning. But this contentious idea arises, I believe, from a mistake about aspects. As objects of imaginative thinking, and not of belief, aspects do not conflict with the physical reality in which we perceive them. Oversimplifying, we might say that they are not properties, but projections.

In offering an aesthetic description I characterize a work as an object of aesthetic interest, as when I describe the sharply outlined theme of a fugue by Bach, the balance, intricacy, ardour, or sadness of a melody by Brahms. There is a seemingly infinite variety of terms used in aesthetic description, and philosophers have continually debated what is meant by them. Frank Sibley[2] made the interesting proposal that aesthetic descriptions are not 'conditioned' by the first-order (physical and perceptual) descriptions of the aesthetic object, meaning that there could be no rules of the form: if a work possesses material properties F, G, H, . . . , then it will be sad, intricate, balanced, etc. He went on to argue that there is a distinct kind of property that is ascribed by aesthetic descriptions. Aesthetic properties are not reducible to the material features in which we perceive them; hence they must be discerned by another faculty—aesthetic perception, or 'taste'.

This novel way of reviving a widespread eighteenth-century opinion has the consequence that terms have a different *sense* when used in aesthetic descriptions from their sense elsewhere. If Sibley is right, 'sad', 'intricate', 'balanced', and so on *change their meaning* when used to describe the character of works of art. And that is precisely what we must not say. They have the *same* meaning here, as in their central deployment; but they are being used *metaphorically*. The correct approach to aesthetic description, I believe, is to distinguish clearly between the intentional object of aesthetic interest, and the material object in which it is located. Aesthetic description is an attempt to characterize the intentional object—that which we see, hear, or understand *in* the work of art. The terms deployed in aesthetic description do not describe the material reality at all, but express, and also recommend, a particular response to it. Hence their largely metaphorical character, which arises from the attempt to convey the 'what it is like' of an aesthetic experience.

In criticism, the judgement of value would be presumptuous, even absurd, if it were not accompanied by a sufficient aesthetic description—by which I mean a description that prompts the reader to imagine the experience which compels the evaluation. For this reason, aesthetic description is an immovable part of critical practice, and can be distinguished from aesthetic evaluation only with difficulty, and only at the risk of isolating the

[2] 'Aesthetic Concepts', and 'Aesthetic and Non-Aesthetic'.

evaluative judgement and emptying it of content. The good critic is not the one who ranks works of music in an order of merit, or assigns credit marks to each, but the one who alters our perception of the thing we hear, so as to persuade us of his judgement. Nobody will be impressed by the critic who dismisses the melody in Ex. 12.1 (from *Sheherazade*) as simply bad; but the critic who describes the limpness of the melodic line, the lack of inner voices, and the failure to develop will perhaps gain a hearing. And when he backs up these descriptions with a more detailed account, showing how the limpness of the melodic line infects the whole musical *Gestalt*, he might bring us to agree with him, by persuading us to *hear* the passage as he describes it. Just how the critic should proceed in this enterprise is a controversial question, which I take up in Chapter 13.

Ex. 12.1. Rimsky-Korsakov, *Sheherazade*

4. Aesthetic evaluation does not require the use of specifically aesthetic terms. Far more common than 'beautiful' are the terms that we reserve for everything that elicits our approval: 'good', 'great', 'a triumph', and so on— the assumption being that others will understand the context needed to clarify the judgement, and hence the respect in which a work is being praised or blamed.

5. Our moral judgements tend to focus on the virtues and vices of people. In the same way, aesthetic judgement discovers virtues and vices— often the same virtues and vices—in works of art. Thus we describe works of art as sentimental, cruel, effeminate, vapid; as noble, courageous, self-confident, truthful. Terms denoting virtues and vices are the most important in a critic's vocabulary, the most necessary to critical judgement, and the hardest to understand and justify.

The reader might feel that the variety of critical judgement is so great, that there is no hope of accounting for it in terms of a common theory of its logic, or a common interest that it serves. This sentiment is likely to be compounded by such considerations as these:

a We often praise works of art that we deny to be beautiful. Consider Bartók's *Miraculous Mandarin*: an exciting and brilliant work, full of ugliness and grotesquery, the ugliness of which is an immovable part of the aesthetic effect. For an eighteenth-century thinker it would have been inconceivable that we should attach a positive aesthetic value to *ugliness*. And yet here, it seems, we do just that. (Or should we say that the ugliness is absorbed into, redeemed by, a higher beauty? We have no firm intuitions in the matter, and are to a great extent inventing the language as we proceed.)

b We distinguish the great from the merely good. The great work has an *authority* for us: it stands beyond criticism, a monument to what is possible. There is nothing that could displace Bach's *Well-Tempered Clavier* or the Beethoven Symphonies from their exalted position in the canon of music. They are, to use Matthew Arnold's term, the 'touchstones' against which we try all lesser works, and towards which composers look for their paradigms. Although we have an idea of saintly and heroic actions, our morality does not depend upon imitating them or even recognizing them. Aesthetic values, by contrast, not only reflect our disposition to recognize and cherish what is superlative; they present the superlative as the goal which gives purpose to everything else.

c We recognize many different kinds of aesthetic value. For example, tragedy and comedy appeal to us in quite different ways, and are valued for quite different reasons. One work might be valued for its majesty, another for its sweetness, another for its pathos, and yet another for its scurrilous note of low comedy. Can we really believe that these are all varieties of a single species of value—the 'aesthetic'? On what grounds would we say such a thing?

Aesthetic Value

We speak of aesthetic value because there is aesthetic experience—the experience which arises, when we attend to appearances 'for their own sake'. Whether aesthetic values are objective is a question that I here lay to one side. What matters is that we discriminate among the appearances that prompt our aesthetic interest. In doing so we regard one thing as more rewarding than another, one thing as unworthy of attention, another as beyond the pale. The varied language of criticism, and the motley collection of aesthetic properties and virtues, are precisely what we should expect, given the structure of aesthetic interest. If this interest were goal-directed, then it would distinguish the relevant from the irrelevant features of its object. Aesthetic values would then be instrumental values, as they are, for example, for socialist realists. By so construing them we lose their distinctive character. We arrive at a clear criterion of aesthetic value, only by turning it into value of another kind.

The dangers of 'instrumentalizing' aesthetic objects are well known. If music is good or bad because of its effects, then the act of listening drops out of consideration altogether. The good effects of music might ensue, regardless of whether it is listened to: muzak induces relaxation precisely in those who do not notice it. To the musical, who cannot avoid noticing such things, muzak is exquisite torture.

This does not mean that music *has* no instrumental value; nor does it mean that the instrumental value of music is insignificant. It means only that aesthetic values are not instrumental values. The point can be illustrated through an Aristotelian analogy. Friendship is undeniably useful. A person with friends has support in times of trouble, and joy in times of good fortune. Friendship is one of the greatest benefits that life bestows, and we value it accordingly. But friendship comes only to the person who forgets its instrumental value. If I approach you with an eye to the benefit then I cease to see you as a friend. To gain a friend I must put another's interest before my own; and I must treat him as an end in himself, not as a means to my advantage. On the other hand, by showing my disinterested concern for another's welfare, and so winning his friendship, I avail myself of a powerful means to success and happiness. (La Rochefoucauld's remark, that interest wears many faces, including that of disinterest, need not be interpreted as cynical.)

So it is with aesthetic values. We obtain much that is useful to us through the experience of art. But the experience is available only if we forget the use. We must consider the work of art as an end in itself; only then does it become a means for us.

Similar considerations tell against the idea that aesthetic values are really cognitive values—that the value of a work of art consists in the knowledge, information, or conceptual grasp that is provided by it. For if aesthetic values *were* like that, we should not need to repeat the aesthetic experience. Yet the significance of a truly meaningful work seems to grow with every encounter, so that these very words, tones, or lines become indelibly engraved in our perception, as the essence of the thing we love. Cognitive interests are satisfied by the acquisition of knowledge and information: once acquired, cognitive states dispense with the means whereby we obtain them. The instrument of learning—the textbook, diagram, or exercise—becomes a husk, in Hegel's image, which we throw away when we have grasped what it contains.

Our experience of art is not like that. Philosophers who wish to rank the aesthetic with the scientific, as a branch of our cognitive activity, therefore stand under a heavy onus to tell us exactly why it is, that a thing valued solely as a source of knowledge, should retain its interest beyond the point when the knowledge has been acquired. So far as I know, this onus has never been discharged—certainly not by Nelson Goodman, whose cognitive theory of aesthetic interest looks plausible because his nominalist metaphysics makes it impossible to describe exactly *what* we are supposed to learn from a work of art, when we grasp its semantic import.

At the same time, there is something that we learn from art—and the argument of Chapters 10–11 enables us to account for this. Art provides us with 'knowledge by acquaintance' of states of mind which we can otherwise glimpse only in their mutilated forms. The work of art lifts human feeling free of everyday life, and endows it with artistic form. The human gesture, translated into tonal space, moves of its own accord towards completion: and in moving with it, we imagine what it would be like, to live our lives completely. This imaginative response is also a form of knowledge. But it is knowledge by acquaintance and as such inseparable from the experience of the work of art. Although it offers knowledge, therefore, the work is not a means to information.

Aesthetic Judgement

Only a comprehensive aesthetics could answer the question, whether judgements of aesthetic value are capable of objectivity. But we should at least be clear what the question means. In one sense aesthetic judgement is subjective—for it consists in the attempt to articulate an individual experience. But in another sense it is objective, for it aims to *justify* that experience, through presenting reasons that are addressed impartially to all beings with aesthetic understanding.

However, a judgement can aim at justification without achieving it, and the crucial question is whether the achievement is possible. The question is often obscured because writers tend to confuse the concepts of objectivity and truth. Aesthetic judgement is understood and accepted not through a change in belief, but through the acquisition of an experience—in the case of music, an experience of hearing. It would be misleading to suggest that the critic aims to prove the *truth* of his judgement: he is telling us what to hear and what to feel, not what to think. Yet this does not remove the hope of objective validity.

The Kantian theory of moral judgement may help to clarify the matter. Kant held that moral judgements are imperatives—and therefore incapable of being true or false. They describe only an ideal world, not the actual world. Yet they are objective, since moral judgements may be valid for all rational beings, irrespective of their particular desires. The validity of a moral judgement consists in the fact that a rational being can dissent from it only by misunderstanding what it says.

Kant's theory is of course highly controversial. But it offers us a useful idea of objectivity; it suggests how objectivity may be present even where truth is not the goal. Could we introduce a parallel notion of objectivity into the field of aesthetic judgement? Many philosophers—including Kant—have thought that we cannot, precisely because the endpoint of discussion is here an experience. A critical argument is accepted only persuasively, as it were, when the opponent has been brought to share the critic's experience, and to concur in saying, yes, *that* is how it is. This close connection with experience already suggests that no critical conclusion can be reached by the application of a rule; each case is unique and must be judged in its own terms. Any other kind of judgement ignores the defining character of the aesthetic experience—as the experience of *this* individual work, judged for its own sake and as it is in itself. (This observation led Kant to his cele- brated 'antinomy of taste': for it seems as though taste is pulled in two contradictory directions, towards the apprehension of the individual as unique and incomparable, and towards a grounding in reasons, which must be 'valid for all rational beings' and therefore universal.)

This essential reference to experience may be compatible with the claim to objectivity. Judgements of secondary qualities, for example, make essential reference to experience—to how things look or feel or sound. Nevertheless they are objective: there is a right answer to the question whether this book is brown or red. It is red if it appears red in standard conditions to the standard observer: our judgements of secondary qualities are founded in the spontaneous 'agreement in judgements' among normal observers. The theory of aesthetic perception argues that the objectivity of aesthetic judge- ment is founded in exactly the same way—in the 'agreement in judgements' of mature observers.[3] But such an approach is at best indecisive. Even if there were *de facto* agreement in aesthetic judgements, this would not establish their objectivity. For a person can be reasoned out of a critical interpretation: he can be brought to see or hear the work in a different way, and so to revise his judgement. No *reasoning* can change a person's perception of colour, and it is precisely the involuntary and passive nature of the expe- rience of colour that prompts us to speak of colour as a quality in the object.

We say that one must 'see for oneself' in aesthetic judgement: but this use of the word 'see' is very different from that which describes the expe- rience of colour. For one thing, it is not true that you *must* see for yourself in order to make judgements of colour: I can take another's word as proof of the colour of something. Indeed a blind man can make colour judgements, since he too knows that the colour of something is given by the way it looks in normal conditions to normal observers. If the aesthetic judgement *must* be made at first-hand, it is because it is not a description of a quality. It is, rather, the expression of the aesthetic experience—and the judgement is sincerely made only by the person who has the experience expressed by it.

Furthermore, the aesthetic experience is founded on a complex act of understanding. You do not 'see' that a work of art is sad, sentimental, or

---

[3] See F. N. Sibley, 'Objectivity and Aesthetics', *Proceedings of the Aristotelian Society*, suppl. vol. (1968).

sincere unless you understand it. No understanding is required in order to see that a picture is red. Aesthetic understanding is multiform; it can be educated, criticized, and changed through rational argument. Hence any 'agreement in judgements' among critics may lie only on the surface: it may mask wholly incompatible experiences, founded in wholly contradictory accounts of the work's aesthetic qualities. Such 'agreement' cannot be the foundation of objectivity.

There is, it seems to me, no future for the theory of aesthetic perception, and no hope of establishing the objectivity of aesthetic judgement by reference to some 'common sense' of mankind. Nor do I find much solace in another eighteenth-century notion, put to ingenious use by Anthony Savile[4]—the 'test of time'. For though it is true that great works of art satisfy the test of time, and are loved and appreciated for as long as people have the education necessary to understand them, this is not a criterion of aesthetic value, but a consequence of it. The very fact that different critics, at different periods, may give quite incompatible accounts of the masterpieces, will cause us to doubt that this diachronous 'agreement in judgements' is any more a proof of objectivity than the synchronous agreement of our own contemporaries.

Rather than explore this vexed question completely, I shall make a very general suggestion as to where we might look for the foundations of aesthetic judgement. Subsequent chapters will, I hope, lend some plausibility to it; but they certainly will not constitute a proof of the view, that aesthetic judgements may sometimes be valid for all humanity—or even for all members of a particular tradition or culture.

Granted that there are no universal rules of taste, there is nevertheless a difference between the person with taste, and the person without it. Consider again the case of moral judgement. On some views morality consists of a set of rules of conduct; and the philosophical problem is how to justify these rules. This legalistic approach does not, however, capture the real intuitions of moral beings, most of whom would be reluctant to 'lay down the law', in the form of absolute rules of conduct, even if they find no difficulty in recognizing acts which merit praise or blame. And the ability to recognize such actions stems from an ability to distinguish good people from bad—to recognize moral virtue *in* action, to recognize that a particular action expresses dispositions that one should emulate and praise, dispositions towards which we 'warm', in the manner uniquely characteristic of moral beings, as we warm to another's courage, decency, generosity, or selflessness. If this thought is true—and there is a long tradition of moral philosophers from Aristotle on who have defended it—then we can understand what is right

---

[4] *The Test of Time: An Essay in Philosophical Aesthetics* (Oxford, 1982).

and wrong, not because we possess some catalogue of rules, but because we understand the motives and feelings that constitute vice and virtue. Understanding virtuous people we can, when the occasion arises, imagine what *they* would feel and do. The ensuing precept is reached indirectly, and without reference to any universal rule. But it may, for all that, be objective, like the notion of virtue from which it stems. For if it can be shown (as Aristotle tried to show) that our ideal of virtue is not arbitrary but on the contrary imposed on us by the very nature of rational choice, then our moral judgements will be well grounded, based in reasons which no person can reasonably reject. Aristotle argued that we all have reason to aim at happiness (fulfilment), which he defined as 'an activity of the soul in accordance with virtue'; since virtue is the prerequisite of fulfilment, the actions and feelings of the virtuous person are those which we should emulate and share.

If the argument of Chapter 11 is right, then taste is not simply a set of arbitrary preferences. It is a complex exercise of sympathy, in which we respond to human life, enhanced and idealized in artistic form. Good taste is not reducible to rules; but we can define it instead through a concept of virtue: it is the sum of those preferences that would emerge in a well-ordered soul, in which human passions are accorded their true significance, and sympathy is the act of a healthy conscience.

On this basis, we can distinguish between those objects of aesthetic interest which are fitting and those which are not. In making such a distinction we are conducting an imaginative experiment: what kind of a person must I be, I ask myself, in order to sympathize, or identify, with *this*? In condemning pornography or gratuitous violence as objects of aesthetic attention, it is such an 'experiment of the imagination' that directs us. And the resulting condemnation, I maintain, is well founded, and a part of good taste. The person with good taste turns instinctively away from certain things, since they 'contaminate' his conscience, and tempt him towards sympathies that he should not have. As Pope expressed it:

> Vice is a monster of so frightful mien,
> As to be hated needs but to be seen;
> Yet seen too oft, familiar with her face,
> We first endure, then pity, then embrace.
> (*An Essay on Man*, ii. 217–20.)

Works of art may fail, then, in two ways: either through failing to interest us, or through inviting an interest of which we disapprove. It is the second kind of failure that is the most difficult to discuss, and also the most urgently in need of discussion. Before considering it, however, it is important to say something about the first kind of failure, which will bring our discussion back to the topic of musical aesthetics.

Musical Competence

Whatever the field of endeavour, people display their incompetence in one of two ways: either by failing to achieve what they intend, or by adjusting their intentions. In music these two kinds of incompetence are abundantly familiar, and form the prime target of musical criticism. Thus Nietzsche, in his grandiose *Hymn to Friendship*, offers us an example of the first kind of incompetence (Ex. 12.2). The composer has mastered certain stock rhetorical gestures, but lacks the sense of musical structure that will enable him to develop and elaborate his sparse ideas. Not every 'falling short' in music is quite so pronounced. For example, the last movement of Bruckner's Eighth Symphony fails to 'come off': its enormous themes and structures do not, in the end, cohere, and a certain disorder makes itself heard beneath the majestic musical surface. But if this is failure, it is failure of quite another order from Nietzsche's. Bruckner should be compared to the mountain-climber who has halted just short of the summit; Nietzsche with the amateur who stands triumphant on some lower prominence, failing to notice the mountain that still towers above.

Success and failure are sometimes hard to analyse. A cadence may 'sound weak'; a melody may seem trite or boring; a harmonic sequence may sound illogical or forced. But we may not know how to justify those judgements, or how to bring another person to agree with them. This difficulty lies in the nature of things: aesthetic values are discerned only through aesthetic experience. To persuade another to notice them, you must persuade him to hear things as *you* hear them. Reasoning in favour of an aesthetic judgement involves mounting an argument whose conclusion is not a thought,

Ex. 12.2. Nietzsche, *Hymn to Friendship*

nor an action, but an *experience*. Critical reasoning is a matter of bringing things to the reader's attention, making comparisons and contrasts, with the hope that the aesthetic aspect will 'dawn'. Ostension forms a large part of such reasoning, which may be described as a prolongation of the command: 'listen!' or 'look!'. Listen, for example, to the weakness of the cadence in Ex. 12.3, from the last song in *Nuits d'été*, and notice how it causes the delicate irony of Berlioz's musical line suddenly to discharge itself. Or

Jeu - ne bel - le, Dit - es, où vou - lez vous al - ler?

Ex. 12.3. Berlioz, *Nuits d'été*, No. 6, 'L'Ile inconnue'

listen to the way in which Beethoven prolongs the transition between first and second subject in the first movement of the *Eroica*. (Ex. 12.4: Leonard Bernstein gave a public lecture with orchestra, in which he played the transition without the passage that prolongs it, saying 'this is what a lesser composer might have done'. He then played the piece as Beethoven had written it; and the audience recognized, without further discussion, what mastery really means. This was a paradigm of criticism, and awakened many people to the truth about Beethoven's genius.)

The more common form of incompetence is that in which the artistic intention is scaled down to match the artistic means. Rather than do large things badly, composers prefer to do small things well. Fibich, for example, whose harmonies seem to admit of too little variety, and to move with too little inner compulsion, to sustain any large-scale symphonic development, purposefully turned from the larger forms, to the little pansies for piano—the *Nálady, dojmy a upomínki*—which stand with the opera *Šárka* as his artistic monument. These pieces offer single ideas—a melody, a harmonic sequence, a motif, or accompanying voice—into which the composer concentrates his musical personality (see Ex. 12.5). By pruning away whole dimensions of musical thought and experience, he naturally forbids himself the greatest of effects. If the result is interesting, it is so in a way that cannot match the interest of a Brahms intermezzo or a Chopin nocturne.

Judgements of competence are of great importance in musical criticism. An incompetent performer is judged by the standard of aesthetic interest;

and it is a standard against which even the emptiest pop music can be measured. A pop song in which the bass-line fails to move; in which an inner voice is mutilated; in which rhythm is generated mechanically, and

Ex. 12.4. Beethoven, *Eroica Symphony*, Op. 55, first movement, transition from first to second subjects: (*a*) the transition begins; (*b*) prolongation of concluding phrase from (*a*)

Ex. 12.4. (c) third transitional episode; (d) second subject

Ex. 12.4. (e) transition without prolongation

with neither syncopations nor accents in the vocal line—such a song may well be judged inferior on those grounds alone. If we are to sustain our interest, even in music as empty as that of U2, we may reasonably demand a greater mastery of the medium, and a greater awareness of how sound transforms itself to tone.

Clearly, however, judgements of competence form only one small corner of musical criticism. Far more important are the judgements of *significance*, and of the value of the aesthetic effect. Nobody could fault the last movement of Tchaikovsky's Sixth Symphony in B minor, Op. 74, on grounds of competence—this is one of the supreme achievements of the master's style, in which not a note remains unjustified by its place in the structure. And

Ex. 12.5. Fibich, from *Nálady, dojmý a upomínki*

many listeners would agree with James Huneker, in praising the movement's emotional content:

> Since the music of the march in the *Eroica*, since the mighty funeral music
> in *Siegfried*, there has been no such death music as this 'adagio lamentoso',
> this astounding torso, which Michelangelo would have understood and
> Dante wept over. It is the very apotheosis of mortality, and its gloomy
> accents, poignant melody and harmonic colouring make it one of the most
> impressive of contributions to mortuary music. It sings of the entombment
> of a nation, and is incomparably noble, dignified and unspeakably tender.[5]

For some listeners this movement is 'mortuary music' in quite another
sense: a kind of ghoulish brooding which lacks both the dignity of grief and
the tenderness of true affection. For such listeners the movement seems to
be demanding an emotion that is best avoided—namely, a collusive and self-
centred depression, decked out in the noble garments of mourning. To
judge the movement in this way is not to doubt Tchaikovsky's competence—

[5] *Mezzotints in Modern Music*, quoted in S. Lipman, *Music and More* (Boston,
1992), 221.

on the contrary, it is to acknowledge it, and to recognize the questionable power of his art.

The Judgement of Taste

That last suggestion throws us into the central problem of aesthetic value, which is, why do aesthetic values matter? What is the connection between our aesthetic discriminations and the rest of our lives? Are we free to pursue our musical tastes, regardless of where they might lead? Or is there something more at stake, besides the love of music?

Eighteenth-century writers, who certainly thought there was more at stake, referred, as I have done, to the concept of 'taste'. Taste was not construed as a kind of refined choosiness, like the taste of the wine connoisseur, but as a systematic posture in the life of the rational being. I exercise my taste through literature, music, and the arts; and also through my manners, remarks, and social demeanour. There is taste in friends as well as in hobbies. And by displaying my tastes I display my soul. The tasteless remark, for example, is a revelation of character, a window on to the attitude of the one who utters it, which may change for ever the way in which he is perceived. That is why taste and virtue are connected.

If we could establish that 'taste' referred to the *same* faculty in each of those cases, then we should have established something important about the aesthetic judgement: it would become as fully and immediately an expression of character as our taste in friends or jokes. The one with bad taste in music would be, to that extent, open to condemnation, just like the one who associates with low company or delights in coarse humour. In the remainder of this book, I shall build on the suggestion made above, and sketch an argument for the view that taste in music matters as much as taste in other things, that the education of taste is of primary moral significance, and that the decline in musical taste is just the catastrophe that it seems to be.

We should begin by studying our reaction to bad taste—for example, to such kitsch as the guitar music of Luiz Bonfa (Ex. 11.2), or the film scores of Vangelis. Such music prompts that peculiar 'yuk' feeling, the sense of being contaminated, which sends spasms of recoil through the body. The 'yuk' feeling is a common social response: to obscenity, to disgusting habits, to unwanted attentions. Perhaps the most important instance of it is the response to an unwanted sexual advance. When a woman feels disgust that *this* man should put his hand on her knee, something of great moral significance occurs. It is not that she dislikes having a hand on her knee: she does not want the hand of *this* man on her knee. Her revulsion is not like the physical revulsion that we feel when we step barefoot on to a slug. It is the refusal to be drawn into and compromised by another's desire.

When people experience the 'yuk' feeling from music, they often have a comparable sense of being drawn into a relationship that is repugnant to them. They are being compromised, presumed upon, placed in an alien ambience. This experience of contamination is at the same time a *social* response. To avoid it, people may place around the offending work of art an ironical fence of inverted commas, dismissing it with a smile as 'kitsch'.

In literary criticism the point is thoroughly familiar. Literary critics do not confine their observations to the purely sensory dimension—the formal arrangement, rhyme-scheme, use of metre, accent, and imagery. They study the way in which a poem directs itself towards the life portrayed in it. A poem is describing or invoking something; it is also taking up an attitude. A wrong word is not just one that sounds wrong, but one that reveals some failure to observe, some insensitivity to the experience conveyed, some emotional ignorance or coldness. We should not be surprised by this: after all, it happens in life too—one word may show that someone is professing a love or sympathy that he does not feel, or which he appropriates for some self-dramatizing purpose. Reading poetry is a way in which we become sensitive to this, and so understand how and when to extend our sympathies.[6] The judgement of taste, which guides us in our reading of poetry, is the very same judgement that governs our choice of friends.

We think of music in a similar way. And in opera and song it is easy to understand why. Consider the passage from 'Un bel dì vedremo', in which Butterfly, expressing her faith in Pinkerton's return, conveys not only her love for him but also the self-deception upon which it has been built (Ex. 12.6). You cannot fail to be touched by this situation. But Puccini wishes you to be *overwhelmed* by it—to put aside all critical distance, and to give way to an unlimited sympathy for the heroine, as she displays her innocent heart. Moving in one stride out of G flat major into B flat minor, he mobilizes the orchestra around a subdominant cadence, using the major triad for rhetorical effect, so as to break decisively through the barrier of G flat on to G natural, before stepping as suddenly back again. The orchestra works on the G flat melody in double octaves and, having squeezed out the last drop of emotion, collapses on a limp V–I cadence. Of course, it works. But some listeners, not without reason, find the passage highly questionable. Are not these rhetorical devices too pat, too obvious? Is not that final cadence a sign that the composer has not really been thinking, as he allows the rhetoric to carry him away—that he has allowed the music to exhaust its movement before achieving a conclusion, as though Butterfly's emotion were too short-winded to deserve our sympathetic grief? Are we not being artificially stirred

---

[6] Cf. T. S. Eliot's description of the critical intelligence, 'of which an important function is the discernment of exactly what, and how much, we feel in any given situation' ('Wordsworth and English Poetry', *Egoist*, 4 (1917), 118–19).

Ex. 12.6. Puccini, *Madama Butterfly*, 'Un bel dì vedremo'

into an attitude that the situation does not justify, so as to wallow in a sympathy that is as self-deceived as Butterfly's pathetic hope?

Those are rhetorical questions, and I shall not answer them. But they illustrate the point that I have in mind: namely, that the judgment of taste in music is in the end no different from the judgement of taste in poetry. We can recognize the precise way in which our sympathies are being enlisted by a piece of music, and condone or recoil from it accordingly. The critic can ask us to hear the passage from *Madame Butterfly* differently: to hear a false-hood, an inflation of effect, where previously we heard the natural outpouring of innocent love. He may do this in a variety of ways: by musical analysis, by description, or by comparison with some other and more genuine instance. He might invite us to compare 'Un bel dì vedremo' with the 'Willow Song' from Verdi's *Otello*, in which the continuous musical thinking forbids any false emotion. The restraint of Verdi's melodic line, the finesse with which it is controlled and enhanced by the inner voices, and the absence of any stock effects or rhetorical devices, all work together, opening our hearts to Desdemona's situation, until, utterly aghast, our ears are assailed by that final and devastating cry (Ex. 12.7).

Ex. 12.7. Verdi, *Otello*, 'Salce, salce'

In the two examples, the invitation is to identify with a character. But like other forms of dramatic art, music can also set you at a distance from the subject portrayed. In *Die Schöne Müllerin*, Schubert's music stays just slightly apart from the central character and his misfortunes. The Miller's awakening joy, his love and jealousy, his despair and self-destruction, are perceived out of the corner of the music's eye, so to speak. Nature occupies the foreground, and the Miller's story occurs in it as do figures in a Poussin landscape, their drama softened by the vastness of the light. Consider the last song, in which the waters of the brook close over the Miller, and sing his final lullaby (Ex. 12.8). The music, with utter simplicity, weaves together the movement

Ex. 12.8. Schubert, *Die Schöne Müllerin*, D795, 'Des Baches Wiegenlied'

of the brook, the love of the Miller, and the distant call of hunting-horns, drawing the dead man and his rival together, so that the brook flows over both and the listener is set at a distance from this little tragedy. There is a rightness in this which opens the possibilities of feeling.

Absolute Music

In opera and song we have representation, achieved through the words, and therefore a subject-matter *towards which* the music is inviting our response. But these cases of applied music say nothing about pure or 'absolute' music, in which neither words nor drama provide an object to our emotions. We recognize that there is good and bad taste in absolute music. But does taste have the same moral resonance as it has in my examples? And if not, why should taste matter?

The theory of expression that I developed in Chapter 11 offers an answer to that sceptical question. Music is a companion, and an object of sympathy. It *invites* us into its orbit, so as to share in its manners and outlook, and to 'join in' a particular form of life. That description is of course metaphorical. But it is a natural record of something that we all know, and of which Plato had an inkling, in his impetuous desire to ban from the ideal republic all but the sober and virtuous modes of music. To understand the point it is useful to return to Plato, and also to our previous discussion of the dance.

According to Plato, music is mimetic of human character. His term *mimēsis* is crucially ambiguous between the three forms of meaning that I distinguished in Chapter 4: imitation, representation, and expression. Nevertheless, he believed that the presentation of character in music leads to another act of *mimesis* in those who sing or dance to it: they 'enter into' the spirit of the music, learning to imitate the character that it imitates. *Mimēsis* is the process whereby habits are acquired—both good and bad; music therefore plays a role in the education of character. People who dance or march to the Dorian mode are learning to hold themselves as honourable citizens should hold themselves; those who dance to the Phrygian mode are releasing what is lowest and wildest in their nature, and learning to imitate the intemperate soul.

Plato's theory depends upon two crucial assumptions: first that the 'imitation' of character by music is the same phenomenon as the 'imitation' of character by a person; secondly, that our interest in music involves the kind of engagement that is characteristic of dancing, singing along, or joining in. Although the first of those assumptions is clearly false, the second, I have argued, contains a grain of truth. And Plato is surely right to think that dancing is a reflection of social character. Listen to a gavotte from the late Renaissance, and imagine the mores of the people who danced to it (Ex. 12.9).

Ex. 12.9. Praetorius, *Terpsichore* (1612), Gavotte, No. 2

Then listen to a track by Nirvana, and imagine the mores of the people who can dance to *that*. Surely, you will not be tempted to think that these two sets of people could live in the same way, with the same habits of mind and character, and the same ways of responding to each other in the circumstances of social life.

The transition from the Viennese waltz, to ballroom dancing, to ragtime, to the Charleston and Tango, to swing, to rock, and on to all the successors of rock, tells us much about the moral transformation of modernity. Love, sex, and the body are perceived differently now; courtesy and courtship have disappeared from dancing just as they have disappeared from life. The Platonic campaign against the reign of Dionysus could no longer be seriously fought, since the idea of dancing as a form of *order* and self-control—the idea embodied in the Greek chorus and preserved in the formation dances of our ancestors—is dead. Dancing has become a form of social and sexual release— or else a spectator art, something that *others* do, to be contemplated in passive silence. Moreover, in a very important sense, the dances observed on the stage, as in a ballet, are not real dances, but representations of the dance. And while there are places where you can go for waltzes, polkas, or highland reels, you do not so much dance there as 'dance' in inverted commas, conscious of your separation from the real life of the body in modern conditions.

There is nothing strained or unnatural in that fragment of the social history of dancing; yet it is far from being morally neutral—any more than the condemnation of modern corybantic dancing given by Ernst Bloch in *The Principle of Hope*, or by Allan Bloom in *The Closing of the American Mind*. And it shows clearly why taste in dancing is continuous with the moral life, of a piece with our taste in company and lifestyle. If, therefore, our response to absolute music is a kind of latent dancing, it is surely unproblematically true that taste in music matters, and that the search for objective musical values is one part of our search for the right way to live.

13 *Analysis*

The science of sound says nothing about tonal space, musical movement, or the language of tonality: music is absent from the scientific theory of the world. Yet music exists. Like the figures in a painting, the characters in fiction, and the smile on a face, music occupies a part of the phenomenal foreground, and is as real for us as any other feature of the *Lebenswelt*. How, then, should music be described, in order to capture its character as *music*? And what is the connection between description and criticism?

Readers of such journals as *Music Theory* will know how widely the net of scholarship is cast, and how various are the questions posed and the methods used to answer them. It is scarcely conceivable that any one person should be competent in all the areas of thought and knowledge that might legitimately be described as 'musical analysis'; nor is there likely to be agreement as to which of those areas are central, or which have most to tell us concerning the meaning of music. In such a situation, however, a philosophical overview is our only way to know what we *should* know, in advance of knowing it.

Musical analysis occurs in the following contexts:

1. The psychology of musical perception. This branch of cognitive psychology seeks to explain our perception of phrase-structure, metre, and key-relations; our preference for certain harmonies and progressions; our ability to hear parallels and variations; our acceptance of the diatonic scale and the system of triads as natural; and so on. As we have seen, some writers have sought for generative structures in tonal music—structures that would explain how the listener is able to process such music, so as to form an intelligible 'mental representation' of its form. Others have studied the processing of information in musical performance, and the 'feedback' mechanisms that enable a performer to adjust what he is doing in the act of doing it.

There are those who argue that the cognitive psychology of music is destined to replace the philosophy of music, or at least to dictate the philosophical agenda.[1] However, not only is cognitive psychology in great need of a philosophical underpinning; it is also unlikely that a theory of musical understanding could be derived from it. To describe the mechanism whereby we 'process' music into cognitively stable and durable structures is not to explain what we are *looking for* in those structures, what it means to prefer one to another, or why this preference matters. In other words, it leaves the aesthetics of music unaffected. By contrast, a generative theory of language structure would tell us exactly how information is encoded in, and retrieved from, syntactical forms: such a theory would tell us not only what we are looking for in language, but also how we find it. (Note, however, that a generative theory of language structure would still not explain our understanding of *poetry*.)

2. Musical analysis. I shall reserve this term for the attempt to describe music as an object of aesthetic interest, and to show how the tonal surface is constructed.

Musical analysis is a highly controversial practice, divided into conflicting schools. To some extent the conflicts are a matter of emphasis; but they also reflect deep aesthetic preferences, and even philosophical, moral, and religious disagreements. A writer like Rudolph Reti seeks to show the way in which a musical surface is derived from thematic motives. To analyse one theme as an elaboration, continuation, augmentation, or diminution of another is, on Reti's view, to show something of intrinsic interest, since it bears on our aesthetic attention. By contrast, a theorist like Heinrich Schenker tries to penetrate below the perceived surface of the work, to its underlying structure. Schenker believed that his kind of analysis was able to explain not only the experience of musical unity, but also the eternal significance of music, its metaphysical status as an art of organized sound, and the value of the great master-works in our tradition. There is, however, no need to accept all of Schenker's claims on behalf of his procedures, in order to agree with some of them.

Others, either more sceptical or more empirical, have argued for a view of musical analysis as a kind of ostension: we *point* to the features that we wish the listener to attend to, so that the structure *emerges* in his perception, without being described. Indeed there are those (Hans Keller, for instance) who believe that the attempt to describe the musical structure will always falsify it, since the structure is real only as *lived* by the listener.

3. Music criticism. In addition to describing the musical surface, we might also try to judge it—to show just what is good or bad in it, and just what it means. Analysts like Donald Tovey were not content merely to describe 'what is going on' in a classical symphony. They wanted their readers

[1] e.g. Raffman in *Language, Music and Mind*.

to enjoy what they heard, to see how important it is, and to discriminate between the trivial and the profound, the sentimental and the genuine, the bad and the good. Is this possible? That is one of the deepest questions in aesthetics, and it has two parts: first, are there aesthetic values, in addition to aesthetic preferences? Secondly, is there any way of justifying our judgements of aesthetic value? I believe that we must give a positive answer to both of those questions, although it is hard to prove the point. This positive answer is quite clearly assumed in any musical criticism worth the name. Consider the following passage, from Tovey's description of the Beethoven Violin Concerto:

> With all its light-heartedness and comparative simplicity of form, the finale is the truthful outcome of its sublime antecedents. To complain that it is not the finest movement in the concerto is to make the mistake exposed a considerable time ago by Plato, when he derided the argument that 'since purple is the most beautiful colour, and the eyes the most beautiful feature, therefore in every statue the eyes ought to be painted purple'. In no art-form is it so constantly a mistake to expect the last part to be the 'finest' as in the concerto form. To find the *right* finale to a scheme so subtle and delicate as that of a classical concerto is of itself a crowning stroke of genius. And there is no finale which more boldly and accurately gives the range, so to speak, of the whole, than this most naïvely humorous of rondos. Besides its first theme, we must quote the transition with the pendulous introductory notes from which witticisms are to arise on its later occurrences (e.g. the only two pizzicato notes for the solo violin in the whole concerto) [Ex. 13.1], the main theme of the first episode or second subject in dialogue between the violin and the orchestra [Ex. 13.2], and the pathetic childlike second episode with its fully formed melody in two parts, each of which is repeated by the bassoon [Ex. 13.3].[2]

Note the easy way in which Tovey works his critical judgement into his description of the music, and uses the description in order to justify what he

Ex. 13.1. Beethoven, Violin Concerto in D major, Op. 61, third movement, bars 44–9

[2] *Essays in Musical Analysis*, iii. 94–5.

Ex. 13.2. Beethoven, Violin Concerto in D major, Op. 61, third movement, bars 58–62

Ex. 13.3. Beethoven, Violin Concerto in D major, Op. 61, third movement, bars 126–30

says. Here the passage from judgement to analysis and back again is not merely natural; it provides the analysis with its purpose, and removes all arbitrariness from the description. Yet, without the background assumption, that there really *is* such a thing as aesthetic value, and that a work of music can be described in such a way as to *show* its value, the passage would be arbitrary at best.

This background assumption causes some musicologists to veer away from criticism, proposing 'value-free' analysis, as a haven from 'subjective' judgement. It is as though theory were able to dissect the work of music, like the surgeon who explores the bodies of both saint and sinner while passing judgement on neither. But a willed neutrality is itself a kind of judgement, and critics with a political agenda are rightly suspicious of scholarship which forbids us to ask the pressing questions—questions concerning meaning and value—which trouble our listening habits.

Recent controversy in the theory of literary criticism has likewise made it difficult to look neutrally on the pursuit of neutrality. Marxists, structuralists, Foucauldians, and feminists are eager to expose the ideological mask of the surrounding culture, and what is neutrality, if not a mask? Radical critics propose a new agenda for criticism, and we must ask ourselves whether this agenda is coherent, and if so, whether it can be brought to the study of music.

4. Musical aesthetics, as exemplified by this work. This is a metastudy. It does not analyse music, but asks what analysis could achieve; it does not evaluate music, but asks whether evaluation is possible; it does not explain the cognition of musical structures, but asks what we understand when we understand them as *music*. In Kantian parlance, musical aesthetics is a *critical* discipline; it describes the nature and limits of our thought about music.

It is difficult to hold those four practices apart. Nor should we strive officiously to do so; for the divorce between analysis and criticism proves fatal to both. The prospect of criticism is precisely what enables us to distinguish a relevant from an irrelevant analysis, while criticism which is not rooted in analysis quickly degenerates into bombast. The mutual dependence of analysis and criticism can be witnessed in what is perhaps the first analytical study devoted to a single masterpiece—E. T. A. Hoffmann's review of Beethoven's Fifth Symphony,[3] in which the author tries to prove that the work contains the essence of romanticism.

Likewise, there would be little point in a psychology of music that was not founded in a conception of aesthetic experience, and which did not, therefore, raise in its own way the questions of musical aesthetics.

Kinds of Analysis

Analysis attempts to build a bridge from the sound structure to the aesthetic experience. It follows that there will be as many things to analyse in music as there are aesthetically interesting features to be heard in a sound, when it is heard as music. Analysis could therefore easily get out of hand. For who could describe everything contained in a bar of Mozart? The assumption is that the analyst will discriminate between salient and peripheral features; between things which go without saying, and things that might well be missed; and between important and unimportant episodes.

Analysis ought to tell us what we should be listening for in a work of music, in order to receive its full effect. It describes the musical surface—but in such a way that certain features stand out as prominent, while others sink into the background. Analytical description can be undertaken in many ways, because aesthetic interest *leaves nothing out*. Every perceivable feature of a work of art is embraced by the aesthetic response to it: and it is a matter of critical argument, whether this or that feature should be given the prominence which a particular analysis confers on it. When the intoxicating force of theory is felt, this point tends to be forgotten. All kinds of structural relations occur in music, and can be 'brought to the surface' by a patient analysis. But there is a real question as to whether it is *these* that we should be attending to, or whether, on the contrary, we should ignore them in favour of something else.

Consider the passage in Ex. 13.4 from Schoenberg's Third String Quartet, Op. 30. The ostinato accompaniment contains all the pitch classes that fail to occur in the melodic line (divided here between first violin and cello). It would be natural to stress this fact when considering the piece as an exercise in twelve-tone composition. But is it *this* that we should bring into prominence when we listen? If we do so, we shall find it harder to hear the

---

[3] Contained in *E. T. A. Hoffman's Musical Writings*, ed. D. Charlton, tr. M. Clark (Cambridge, 1989), 234–51.

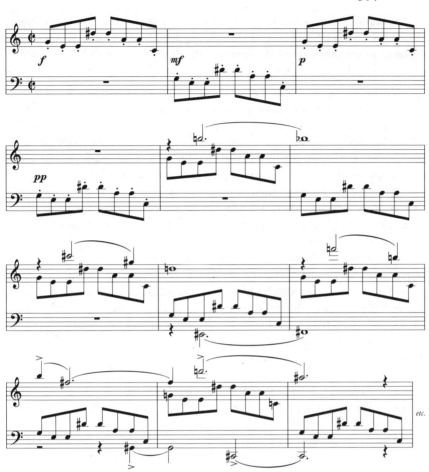

Ex. 13.4. Schoenberg, Third String Quartet, Op. 30

underlying *tonality* of the passage, as it hovers between E and B minor. Another analyst, therefore, will be intent on showing the tonality of E minor which is implicit in the ostinato (based on abridged, non-triadic versions of the tonic, subdominant, and dominant seventh of that key), and the beautiful B minor movement of the melodic line. Some may say that we should not rule between these rival analyses, and that it is part of the richness of the piece that it admits of both of them. Nevertheless, they derive from conflicting ways of hearing. The choice between them is a *critical* choice, since the two ways of hearing prompt quite different responses.

It is evident in any case, that the analysis of tonal music will not follow the same principles as the analysis of genuinely atonal music: whatever we think about the ultimate value of the flight from tonality, it invites us to hear in new ways, by attending to new features of the auditory surface. The motif, construed in atonal terms, as an ordered pitch-class set, will be the prime variable in any theoretical description. Bearing that in mind, I propose to divide musical analysis into the following broad kinds:

1. Chord grammar: the identification and labelling of harmonies, actual and implied, according to the standard roman numeral notation. This descriptive exercise is not always as easy as it seems, but since it aims merely to describe what we hear, its relevance is unquestionable. However, it is doubtful that it could ever be a sufficient instrument for the analysis of musical form, since it is indifferent to the distinction between structural and non-structural harmonies, says nothing about melodic and rhythmic organization, and delivers only a very simplified account of harmonic progressions.

2. Analysis of tonal centres, modulations, and the 'journey through tonal space' in classical music. Such analysis occurs in much traditional criticism— notably in the works of Tovey, and, more recently, in Charles Rosen's impressive studies *The Classical Style* and *Sonata Forms*.

3. Motivic analysis, which shows how the audible structure of a piece is derived from basic elements or motifs. This has been practised most thoroughly for tonal music by Rudolf Reti: but it can be applied equally to atonal music, in which context it seems to have displaced all other analytical procedures, for reasons that I touch on below.

4. Schenkerian analysis: the analysis of tonal music in the manner of Heinrich Schenker, who believed that the unity and cogency of a tonal work could be displayed by his generative theory of foreground structures (see Chapter 10). Schenkerian analysis exists in three forms: as a generative theory of tonal music; as an instrument for the analysis of musical unity in the tonal tradition; and as an *ad hoc* addition to thematic and harmonic analysis, which emphasizes *latent* structure. Considerable confusion has entered musical theory from the failure to distinguish these separate enterprises. The first, which belongs to the cognitive psychology of music, has little relevance to analysis and is in any case unfounded, as I have argued in Chapter 10. The second is or would be relevant, if it had the remotest chance of success; while the third, in my view the only successful application of Schenker's techniques, can be understood and practised without recourse to the quasi-generative theory.

5. Critical narrative, of the kind practised by Tovey and others, which sacrifices theory to description. The aim is to get the reader to *hear* what is there, to notice details and connections, and to respond to their musical significance. Although this is frequently called analysis, it could also be described as criticism. In the end, some may argue, the theories provided by (1), (2), (3), and (4) can be justified only by showing their relevance to an analysis of kind (5): a description of what can be heard in the musical surface.

6. Ideological analysis, in which works of music are subjected to the 'hermeneutics of suspicion'.[4] Under the influence of Marx, Adorno, Foucault, feminism, and the 'new historicism', American musicology has begun to treat musical works as ideological productions, whose meaning lies in their social function. It is a philosophical question whether ideological analysis tells us anything about the meaning of a work of music, or whether it is something more than amateur sociology.

7. Others. There are as many schools of analysis as there are candidates for a job in musicology, and it is no part of my intention to consider all the methods that have been proposed in recent years. At a certain period the disease of semiosis attacked the musical world, producing the works of Ruwet and Nattiez that I discussed in Chapter 7. Deryck Cooke's attempt to decipher the 'language' of music belongs with these, as do the related theories against which I have already argued. In what follows, therefore, I shall consider only the six kinds of analysis mentioned above. I believe, in any case, that they raise all the *basic* questions; by understanding how they proceed, and how they ought to proceed, we shall have an outline grasp of musical analysis in all its forms, and also of the arguments available to a critic who wishes to found the judgement of a piece of music in a description of its audible surface.

Chord Grammar

Chord grammar is of two kinds—roman numeral notation and figured bass. The first identifies a chord in terms of its root, its modality, and the surrounding key. Thus V in C major is the triad of G major, iii in the same key the triad of E minor. The name of the chord is then supplemented, where necessary, with arabic numerals and accidentals. These signs will, in the normal case, identify the bass note, together with the salient notes above it. Thus IV$^6_4$ in C minor is the triad of F major, in its second inversion. The numerals and accidentals follow the conventions established by figured bass—i.e., the numerals measure the intervals in terms of scale-degrees from the bass, while the accidentals indicate raised or lowered intervals.

In a figured bass, however, the bass-line is identified in musical notation, and the figures are purely descriptive, conveying no information as to key, and no hypothesis as to the functional nature of the harmony. To describe a chord as VI$^6_!$ in C is to make a far-reaching judgement as to its function in the harmonic structure; to notate it as 6 under a bass note of C sharp is to make no such judgement: the resulting chord could as well be I of A major, or an altered I of C sharp minor, etc.

[4] P. Ricœur, *Freud and Philosophy: An Essay on Interpretation*, tr. D. Savage (New Haven, 1970).

Figuration is, in fact, simply another form of musical notation: no more an *analysis* of the music than the notes which spell it out. It tells us nothing about the function of the harmonies which it prescribes, and can be seriously misleading when applied to chords that arise from pedal-points or passing-tones, in which the bass may be quite unrelated to the harmonies that are superimposed above it. Consider for example, the passage from Haydn's String Quartet, Op. 74 No. 2, last movement, in Ex. 13.5. The figures here accurately identify the notes in the chords. But they fail to specify their harmonic function, and convey the entirely misleading impression that Haydn is engaged in producing daring modernistic harmonies—such at least is the natural inference to be drawn from the figure $^{\sharp8}_{5}$. In fact this figure refers to a passing-chord in a sequence of diminished sevenths over a tonic pedal—nothing very unusual, and in the context hardly even dissonant.

Passages like Ex. 13.5 also illustrate the inadequacy of roman numeral notation. It is possible, with a little strain, to assign a roman numeral to each chord in the sequence of diminished sevenths. But the result will tell us very little about what is going on in this passage, in which the ruling harmony of I endures while other 'unasserted' harmonies play across it, marking out possibilities to which the music refuses to move. We have no difficulty in *hearing* this. But to describe it, and to describe it in a way that captures the subtle movement and the careful sculpting of tonal space—'hic labor, hoc opus est'! Not surprisingly, therefore, much musical analysis in our century has been devoted to giving a functional account of harmony—an account which will show whence harmonies arise and whither they lead, and which will enable us to understand the force that binds them together. And many theorists now follow Schenker in distinguishing a structural harmony from a harmony that merely embellishes, prolongs, or varies the harmonic movement.

Ex. 13.5. Haydn, String Quartet, Op. 74 No. 2, last movement

The Journey through Tonal Space

All tonal music moves to its conclusion through regions of tonal space. To listen to it as it demands, we should be in some measure aware of *what is happening* at any moment. This does not mean that we should be able to name the keys and their relations, or identify the harmonies in accordance with the traditional nomenclature. Our awareness of the music is *recognitional*, like our awareness of a face: we know where it is going and from whence it comes, and, if the music is successful, the transition seems natural to us and satisfying.

Man-che Thrän' aus mei- nen Au-gen ist ge-fal-len in der Schnee; Sei - ne Kal-len

Ex. 13.6. Schubert, *Winterreise*, D911, 'Wasserfluth'

An analysis may add to this awareness by describing its object more completely: by showing *what it is* that engages our interest, when we hear the musical journey. Consider Schubert's song 'Wasserfluth', from *Winterreise* (Ex. 13.6). At the seventh bar of the melody, the listener will hear the musical line ascending to its natural ceiling (the E in the next bar): he will expect it to reach that ceiling and fall away from it—for he will have felt the musical value of that high E in its previous two occurrences, as marking a limit to the musical ascent, and also to the grief of the poet. But when the melody reaches that E for the third time, the listener hears a sudden shift in harmony: the E is no longer the conclusion of something, but a transitional point: the voice breaks through it to the F natural beyond. The listener will be intensely aware of this harmonic shift, even if he is unable to describe it, except perhaps as a sudden tension which disrupts the melody. Tonal analysis tells us that the chord which harmonizes that high E on its third occurrence is a dominant seventh of the neighbouring key of A minor. It compels the listener to hear the E as fifth scale degree of A minor, rather than the eighth of E minor; moreover, the harmony shifts again, from the dominant seventh to a diminished seventh (here an implied minor ninth) which cancels the F sharp of the original key, and forces the voice upwards on to F.

The analysis is a very simple one. But it illustrates the way in which a description of the music is also a description of the *intentional object of hearing*. The analyst is not *explaining* our experience, as a psychologist might; he is describing it—describing what we hear, when we hear the song correctly. Someone might wonder how it is, that the description of the intentional object of hearing should use concepts that are not available to the listener himself. But, as I argued in Chapter 8, there is nothing strange in this. Just as someone may recognize a certain colour, without having a name for it, so might he recognize harmonies, and harmonic relations, while lacking the vocabulary which describes them. In analysis of this kind, the concepts that are used to identify what is heard are themselves intentional concepts: they describe the *appearance* of sound, when it is heard as music. (In this they differ, for example, from an account of chords in terms of their interlocking overtones: an account that might *explain* what we hear, but which does not describe it.)

Moreover, we should again distinguish the two ways in which the appearance of a sound may be characterized: the acoustical and the musical. An acoustical description refers to pitched sounds and their secondary qualities. A musical description refers to the tones that we hear in those sounds, and to their audible relations in musical space. An acoustical description of the passage from 'Wasserfluth' would recognize no distinction between the first and the third occurrences of the top E: they are the same sound, with the same acoustic qualities. A musical description, however, would distinguish them, as I have done: the first being $\overset{8}{8}$ of E minor, the second $\overset{\wedge}{5}$ of A minor. The parallel here is with the distinction between a chromatological and an iconographical description of a picture.

Why should we engage in analysis, if it does not take us any further than the intentional object of hearing? Would not ostension be just as useful? (This was, presumably, Hans Keller's view.) Here we should return to the concept of intentional understanding, introduced in Chapter 8. We may study appearances, not as sources of information about other things, but as they are in themselves. This requires concepts and figures of speech, with which to discuss the way things look, and the way things sound, without advancing to a judgement about the way things are. In such a study we describe appearances and also reorder them, through discrimination and comparison. There is a sense in which colours look the same to the ordinary eye and to the eye of the painter, and a sense in which they do not look the same. The painter's long habit of discriminating colours, naming them, and situating them in contexts where their expressive potential is brought to the fore, generates an increased intentional understanding: he *sees colours differently*, through concepts and comparisons which shape and record their aesthetic character.

A similar process occurs in the analysis of tonal music. The ordinary listener certainly will hear the shift of the high E in Schubert's 'Wasserfluth' from the tonic of E minor to the dominant of A minor; but he may not hear the full potential of that shift. Analysis shows *what* is heard, when the tone is heard with fuller understanding. It may change the experience of the listener, in something like the way that the experience of colour is changed when we learn to paint with it.

This is made clear by the 'problem cases'. The last of Janáček's first series of piano pieces entitled *On an Overgrown Path* ends on an inversion of the 'Tristan' chord (Ex. 13.7). In what key is this? E major, like the increasingly anguished prayer-theme (Ex. 13.8)? Or C sharp minor, like the owl's call that negates it (Ex. 13.9)? You can hear the passage in either way, so that it sounds inconclusive and ambiguous. Here, where you have a choice of musical experience, an analysis may actually change what you hear. The cycle of pieces as a whole shows a definite preference for C sharp (minor or major): although C major and E minor are powerfully represented in the most

Ex. 13.7. Janáček, *On an Overgrown Path*, 'The owl has not flown away', bars 114–15

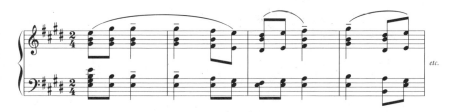

Ex. 13.8. Janáček, *On an Overgrown Path*, 'The owl has not flown away', bars 13–16

Ex. 13.9. Janáček, *On an Overgrown Path*, 'The owl has not flown away', bars 34–6

dramatic episodes. On the other hand, the tonality of E major is pushed to the fore by arpeggiation and massive triads. To decide the question, we must therefore study the whole tonal journey, through which the final piece takes us, and the way in which each successive harmony is resolved, denied, or discarded.

The masters of classical composition constantly present us with such analytical problems. It is tempting to dismiss them, with the thought that they are not real problems, but merely academic exercises. If analysis belongs to intentional understanding, however, it must address itself to problems that are already there, in the musical *Gestalt*. Consider bar 5 of the Prelude in C major from the First Book of Bach's Forty-Eight (Ex. 13.10 (*a*)). Is this the submediant of C, or the supertonic of G? Acoustically they are identical—the A minor triad. But musically they are distinct. This measure would involve the supertonic of G only if the piece has already modulated to G (the dominant). It has certainly done so by the time of bar 6. So where does the modulation occur? The answer matters, since there is again a choice involved: I can hear bar 5 as the end of one sequence, or as the beginning of another. Since there is no melody in the strict sense, but only gently arpeggiated

Ex. 13.10. J. S. Bach, *Well-Tempered Clavier*, First Book, Prelude in C major

triads, the parsing of the surface is a matter of extreme delicacy, and very much depends upon our conception of the tonal journey.

We should remember that the experience of music is available, only because music is also *performed*. And how it is performed will depend upon the way in which it is assembled in the mind and fingers of the performer. Analysis deeply influences performance; and many performances of Bach today testify to this influence. Yet the right analysis is presumably the one which contains within it, not only a prescription for hearing correctly, but a prescription for playing correctly too. (This point has been forcefully argued by Edward Cone.)[5]

Bach's Prelude, which announces one of the greatest works of art in existence, is arresting, even shocking, in its economy of musical resources: a succession of arpeggiated chords, nothing more. Yet it rises to one of the most exquisite climaxes in all music, and moves with a compelling logic from bar to bar. Deciding on the tonal centre at bar 5 is important for understanding the drama and logic of this piece. We need to know where the transitions naturally occur, which bars to hear as preparations, and which to emphasize in our attention as adding a new force and direction to the movement. What, for example, happens at bars 22 and 23, where the bass-line moves between two tones that do not belong to the key of C major (Ex. 13.10(*b*))? Should we emphasize these rogue notes, should we try to retire them into the background, or should we, like Czerny, in his edition of the Forty-Eight, interpellate another measure between them, with G in the bass and an arpeggiated C minor triad, in order to make them part of a chromatic movement?

Motivic Analysis

Tonal Music The Bach Prelude lends itself to the techniques of tonal analysis, precisely because it is nothing more than harmony in motion: if there is an implied descant here, it is of far less importance than the movement which projects itself upwards from the bass line into the rippling arpeggios. Gounod's Ave Maria certainly does not bring out the implied descant (see Ex. 13.11). It *imposes* a redundant melody on this delicate structure, and thereby submerges it. 'A piece of sacred pop music,' Adorno called it, 'featuring one of those Magdalenes notable equally for their penitence and their seductiveness.'[6] One can see what Adorno means, even if the Ave Maria does not deserve his scorn. Gounod's melody can be heard as a kind of analysis of the Bach Prelude—though an analysis that no one today would

---

[5] Cone, *Musical Form and Musical Performance*.

[6] 'Commodity Music Analysed', in *Quasi una Fantasia*, tr. R. Livingstone (London, 1992), 37.

Ex. 13.11. Gounod, Ave Maria, melody (transposed into C, to begin at bar 5 of Bach's Prelude, Ex. 13.10)

find acceptable. This melody is not an implied voice but an *antiphonal* voice, one which is in tension with the musical movement.

But of course there is more to tonal music than harmonic sequences; nor are these the only important *structural* features of the classical style. Music contains themes, composed of phrases and motifs, which can be shifted, transposed, enlarged, and diminished, in ways that are not only recognizable, but inherently interesting. A motif may be spread-out horizontally, as a melody, or vertically as a chord. (See Ex. 13.12, the curse motif from the *Ring*.) It may be altered in rhythm or accent, without ceasing to be itself; it may be scattered through musical space, before eliding with a melody, as in the prelude to *The Cunning Little Vixen* (see Exx. 2.29–2.31). All these familiar effects have given impetus to analysis. Some, such as Rudolf Reti, have made as great a claim for thematic analysis as others have made on behalf of tonal structure, hoping to find the clue to the ineffable unity of the masterworks in the transformations of musical molecules.

Ex. 13.12. Wagner, *Ring* cycle (*a*) the 'curse' motif; (*b*) vertical statement of the same, absorbed into the 'fate' motif at the end of *Götterdämmerung*

Consider the first movement of Beethoven's String Quartet in F major, Op. 135 (Ex. 13.13(*a*)). This seems to have no definite theme, but begins, rather, from a set of fragmentary phrases, which together produce one of the most striking statements of F major in the whole of music. Reti analyses

Ex. 13.13. Beethoven, String Quartet in F major, Op. 135: (a) opening bars

Ex. 13.13.   (b) Reti's analysis (i) motif II (ii) secondary motif (iii) motif I
(iv) phrase constructed from motif I with passing-tones (v) analysis of melodic line

these phrases in the manner shown in Ex. 13.13(b), discerning two leading
motifs, from which, he argues, the whole sequence is derived, whether
directly, as in bars 1–10, or by inversion, as in bar 16.[7] The analysis is ingenious, and to a certain extent persuasive. But why do we agree with it? And
what does it show?

[7] *The Thematic Process in Music* (London, 1961), 206–14.

There are three possible replies to the first of those questions. First that Reti has described Beethoven's compositional process, the analysis being an hypothesis as to how the movement was put together; second that the analysis is an account of the hidden structure of the piece, regardless of whether Beethoven so intended it, and regardless of whether this structure can be heard in the musical surface. Finally, the analysis could be read as a description of what we hear, could hear, or ought to hear when we hear with understanding. Only the third of those readings will explain why the analysis is relevant to the music as *music*. Doubtless, if the analysis is persuasive, it would be natural to assume that it is also a true account of Beethoven's intentions: an artistic intention is revealed in the work that expresses it.[8] But the structure cannot be more 'hidden' than this implies. Otherwise it will cease to be part of the musical surface, and therefore cease to be part of what we understand in hearing the music.

What does the analysis show? Reti advanced the bold hypothesis that the unity of musical works could be accounted for entirely in terms of an underlying *thematic* economy. We hear the musical surface as generated from a handful of motifs, and this enables us to hold it together in our experience, and also to appreciate its organic form as it grows from these musical seeds.

There are certainly occasions when thematic analysis suggests an account of musical unity. Consider Bach's Two–Part Invention in D minor, BWV775, entirely constructed from three phrases by repetition, canon, inversion, and elaboration (Ex. 13.14). Once you understand what is going on, you feel the rightness of what Bach is doing: the musical surface appears inevitable, logical, and unified like a mathematical proof. On the other hand, the example is exceptional: only Bach could have achieved with such simplicity of means an effect which is so compelling. And the reason is evident: Bach seldom wrote a phrase that is not marked by a supreme melodic and harmonic inspiration. The first theme of this invention is nothing more than an ascending and descending D minor scale: but with a magical octave transposition at its harmonic crux. The listener is gripped at once by this melody, and led through the 'proof' by it. A composer who did what Bach did in this invention, but using phrases that had neither the simplicity nor the subtlety that came so naturally to Bach, would certainly achieve no comparable experience of unity.

When we turn to the Beethoven we see yet more clearly how much has been left out by the thematic analysis. Not only the tonal structure of the piece, but also the peculiar Beethovenian force that welds the phrases together, shaping the melodic line through rhythm and counterpoint. A lesser

---

[8] Not for the first time in this book, I avoid discussion of the so–called 'intentional fallacy'.

Ex. 13.14. Bach, Two-Part Invention in D minor, BWV775: (*a*) motifs; (*b*) opening bars

composer, using Beethoven's sparse materials, and weaving them into the fabric of his work as thoroughly as Beethoven did, would not achieve an effect of unity. On the contrary, the result would probably be the kind of chaos so often heard in the thematically highly organized chamber works of Hindemith.

If thematic analysis provides no general account of musical unity, what *does* it provide? The only cogent answer is this: an improved way of hearing the musical surface; a knowledge of the musical relations that inform the auditory *Gestalt*; in short, the kind of intentional understanding which is the aim of tonal analysis as I have described it. Although books of music theory often refer to separate and even conflicting analytical 'methods', it seems to me that the techniques deployed by Tovey, Rosen, and Reti are complementary parts of a single enterprise, the goal of which is to bring the listener to hear *what is going on* in the musical surface. They do not provide a theory of musical unity: at best they prompt us to hear music in such a way that its aesthetic character emerges. And if the music has a character of unity (which is sometimes, but not invariably, the case) an analysis should help us to hear that too. Motivic analysis tries to identify the primary gestures, from which the musical action is formed. It provides us, therefore, with an account of the musical *material*. Whether the work is unified depends not only upon the material, but also upon how that material is treated.

Atonal Music

Motivic analysis is not confined to tonal music. Whether or not Schoenberg was right, in his declared belief that the motif could become the single factor in generating musical unity, displacing harmonic progression and tonal architecture, he was certainly right that the jettisoning of tonality leaves us with little besides the motif and its transformations, through which to comprehend the musical surface.

But what exactly *is* a motif in atonal music? Our normal ways of describing motifs are replete with tonal implications. We describe the intervals between the tones as 'minor third', 'fourth', and so on; we identify individual tones as the 'seventh of the dominant', or the 'subdominant mediant', and so on. And that is how we *should* describe motifs, if we are to make sense of them in tonal music. Beethoven's Op. 135 opens with a motif that leads by two passing-tones to the seventh of the dominant; this is followed by another motif, beginning on the tonic and falling a minor third on to the third of the dominant. That is how we hear the passage; and that is how it should be described.

So how should we analyse motifs in atonal music? We must find a way of describing the relations between tones that is entirely divested of tonal implications—otherwise our analysis will carry precisely the implication that we wish to avoid: namely, that the music is really, in some latent way, tonal. One suggestion—originally made by Milton Babbitt, and worked out in considerable detail by Allen Forte[9]—is that we should identify motifs through an ordering of the intervals involved in them. The procedure is as follows. First we reduce all the audible pitches to twelve 'pitch classes'—the chromatic notes in an octave. 'Octave equivalence' means, according to Babbitt and Forte, that we can fully identify all motifs by representing their pitch intervals within a single octave range. (The interval between middle C and the top E of 'Wasserfluth' is reducible to the smallest interval between C and E, since all Es are 'equivalent': it is therefore an interval of four semi-

[9] *Structure of Atonal Music.*

tone steps.) In tonal music the twelve chromatic pitches have many different names, and function very differently depending upon the surrounding key. B is emphatically *not* the same tone as C flat. This kind of context-dependence is not exhibited in atonal music; hence we can treat each of the twelve pitch classes as a single musical entity, whose sole relation to other such entities lies in the interval between them (and all that flows from this). We then count this interval in semitone steps, using an arithmetic like that of the clock-face, based on the modulus of 12. Intervals can be ordered—showing the direction between pitches—or unordered, describing merely the distance. Finally, we can arrange intervals into classes, again relying on octave equivalence. The interval between middle C and the G that tops the treble staff is + 19 (when ordered) or 19 (when unordered). But the ordered pitch-class interval is + 7 (C to G), which, because of octave equivalence, becomes 5 (i.e. G to the C above) when the pitch-class interval loses its ordering.

We can now describe motifs in terms of the pitch-class intervals between their components. To describe chords we adopt the same technique, first reducing them to their 'normal form', by writing them within a single octave, in such a way that they are most tightly packed 'to the left'. For example, the chord C, E, F, F sharp, can be arranged in four different ways within a single octave; the preferred way is that which places E at the bottom, as in Ex. 13.15. This way of writing sonorities is no more than a convention, though there are those who object to it, because it is insensitive to factors that strongly influence our experience of harmony: the spread of a chord, and the various inversions. Nevertheless, by this device, Forte is able to provide a language for describing motivic organization, and the sonorities that derive from it, without implying the existence of any other organization than that which is contained in the intervals. From the perspective of atonal music, the essential characteristic of both a motif and a chord is that each comprises a set of pitch classes—a set being a collection with no specific order or contour. Pitch-class sets themselves belong to higher order sets containing all their transpositions, inversions, retrograde transformations, and retrograde inversions: all the sets which are transformationally equivalent to the given set, under the procedures recognized in serial organization. There are only finitely many such 'set-classes' for any given number of tones, and Forte's theory provides a numerical procedure for labelling them. Thus the class of four-member sets related by the intervals 0258 is assigned the number 4–27: the twenty-seventh of the four-tone set-classes in Forte's table. The

Ex. 13.15. 'Normal' ordering of a chord

number 4–27 might also be described as the 'Tristan' chord, which it contains as a member.

In Ex. 13.16 from Webern's *Konzert* for nine instruments, Op. 24, the
same pitch-class set occurs four times—the four occurrences being 'transpo-
sitionally equivalent'. The use of the set in this repetitive way provides, we
are encouraged to believe, one of the basic principles of atonal structure.

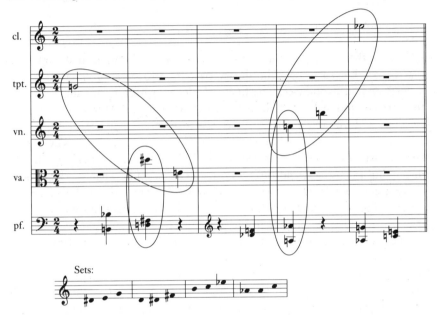

Ex. 13.16. Webern, *Konzert*, Op. 24

When we hear atonal organization, we hear the arrangement and rearrange-
ment of a pitch-class set, and in certain cases the relations between sets
established in the fundamental series—for instance the internal relations
between the two hexachords of a twelve-tone sequence. Perhaps this is what
Schoenberg really had in mind, when referring to the 'motif' as the new
source of musical unity. Set-theoretic analysis can show exactly how a piece
of atonal music is derived from the motifs which are its primary material.
And it does seem that much atonal music deploys members of a single set-
class, in ways that resemble the use of the motifs in Beethoven's Op. 135.
Ex. 13.17 gives the opening of the first of Schoenberg's *Three Piano Pieces*
Op. 11, with a number of pitch-class sets circled. Each of these sets belongs
to a single set-class. It is important to recognize that this piece of music is
atonal, but not organized serially. The set-theoretic analysis shows the role of
the set in ordering the musical surface, without implying that the music
exhibits a serial ordering.

Ex. 13.17. Schoenberg, *Three Piano Pieces*, Op. 11 No. 1

Forte's theory of post-tonal music has been widely applauded. But what exactly is achieved by it? The theory contains two parts: a descriptive procedure, and an hypothesis. The first provides us with a means for describing the surface of atonal music. It avoids all unwanted suggestions of an implied tonality, and yet recognizes the effect of octave equivalence, transposition and inversion in shaping our experience of musical 'sameness'. The second asserts that this description is also a description of what we hear or can hear in the musical surface, and furthermore a description of what we *should* hear, if we are to obtain the experience of musical order. About the second of those claims we should, I think, be sceptical. There may indeed be people who can hear *that* a piece of music is composed from a single set-class, and can hear the extent to which the piece is *saturated* with the set-class. But, as I have tried to show in Chapters 8 and 9, there is a subtle distinction between hearing *that* something is the case, and actually hearing it—the distinction exemplified by the Brahms variation in Ex. 13.18, in which the listener is likely to hear *that* the bass-line is sounding the melody in canon, without actually hearing the melody. Sets are not obviously the kinds of things that

Ex. 13.18. Brahms, Variations on a Theme by Schumann, Op. 9

we hear, when we hear music, even though we may hear that they are present, and train ourselves to recognize their occurrence in a variety of 'horizontal' and 'vertical' arrangements. (Consider again Exx. 9.52 and 9.58 from the Berg Violin Concerto, discussed in Chapter 9.)

More importantly, a piece of music can be related to any number of pitch-class sets, depending upon how we choose to divide the surface. To single out a particular set is already to suppose the existence of boundaries and segmentation. As Nicholas Cook has shown, Forte's set-theoretic analysis of Stravinsky's *Excentrique* requires an entirely counter-intuitive segmentation of the musical surface, in which the longest silence in the piece, lasting for two bars, is ignored, and tones to either side of it are grouped in a single pitch formation.[10] Since all listeners will hear a boundary at this place, and group the tones to either side of it with their predecessors or successors, the set-theoretic analysis seems to misrepresent the musical movement. Indeed, we can accept it only if we read the music *against* the movement—in other words, we must discount a feature that is essential to the character of the piece as *music*. (The same is true, it seems to me, of the embryonic analysis that I have given of Schoenberg's Op. 11 No. 1.)

The focus on pitch-class sets may therefore promote deviant ways of hearing atonal music. A set can appear as a chord, as a sequence, in retrograde or inverted, as part of a melodic line or as an overarching structural device. If *this* is what we must notice, in order to hear the musical organization and unity, then we must perforce renounce the habit of polyphonic hearing; we must isolate the set wherever it appears, breaking it free from the horizontal line, and treating it indifferently as chord or sequence. Even if this can be done, it is entirely unclear that the result will be an experience of *musical* unity, or indeed an experience of unity at all. The least that can be said is that motifs, understood in this way, are not the same phenomena as the motifs that abound in tonal music, where motifs form part of the musical movement.

The set-theoretic analysis of atonal music must therefore be regarded with a certain measure of suspicion: for if it is an analysis of the intentional object of the listener's experience, it may set that experience outside the musical sphere, or at any rate, on the margins of it. If, on the other hand, it is an analysis of the material organization of the *sounds*, regardless of our musical experience, it is not an analysis of the music. In fact, set-theoretical analysis offers a striking proof of the eccentricity of much atonal music. For it aims to describe the *actual* order of the music: and the result is a description of nothing that it would be interesting to hear. The dry pseudo-science of the language draws our attention only to what is most lifeless in the music, and

[10] Cook, *Guide to Musical Analysis*, 138–51.

seems precisely to forbid us to hear its expressive power. Here, for example, is Milton Babbitt, describing pieces by Stravinsky:

> The pitch collection from which the serial unit of the Gigue from the *Septet* is formed is so constructed that maximum identification of pitch content is achieved by transposition by an interval of 5 or 7; this reflects the compositional design of the movement, with the serial unity employed as a thematic entity in what may be described as a succession of fugal entries. In *In Memoriam* the transpositions effecting maximum intersection are 1 and 11, reflecting the fact that the succession of serial units is in the vocal part, as a linear succession . . . The Ricercar of the *Cantata* employs a six note collection which permits maximum intersection of pitch content by inversion at the interval 6, which is employed by Stravinsky in the initial statement of forms of the collection, while the collection of the *In Memoriam* is inversionally symmetrical, thus permitting total pitch intersection at the interval of 4.[11]

Those mathematical observations are like the observations of a chemist, analysing the pigments in a painting. The facts are interesting: but do they constitute an analysis of the work of art? If the correct way to describe atonal order issues in no description of the *music*, then atonality is a departure from music, rather a novel form of it.

There is much more to be said about the analysis of atonal music, and about set-theoretical structure in tonal or quasi-tonal music—such as the music of Skriabin and Bartók. Before returning to the subject, however, it is necessary to consider again the theories of Heinrich Schenker.

Schenkerian Analysis

Schenker's analyses of the 'master-works' of classical music were largely unnoticed in his lifetime, or, if noticed, dismissed as the weird hieroglyphs of an isolated mystic. Schenker thought of himself as showing the hidden order and unity in the tonal classics, and displaying just why and how they are among the greatest achievements of the human spirit. Today, however, there is a dispute among both Schenkerians and their opponents, as to just what Schenker's theory is a theory *of*. And the dispute carries over into the practice of Schenkerian analysis. At certain points Schenker tells us that the analysis is actually *part of the work of music*. In other words, he is describing something that belongs to the work, and which is being discerned for the first time. Most people would recoil from that suggestion, which seems to imply that nobody heard the classics rightly, until Schenker came to describe them. In any case, there now seem to be three quite different, and probably incompatible, uses of Schenkerian analysis:

[11] 'The Structure and Function of Music Theory', in Boretz and Cone (eds.), *Perspectives*, 10–21.

1. As the foundation for a 'generative grammar' of tonal structure. So used, the theory is implausible, for reasons given in Chapter 10. Moreover, it implies that the cognitive process whereby we organize music in our perception takes only the *complete work* as the meaningful unit. This is not only counter to musical experience—in which the single melody and the single harmonic sequence seem to be far more important as primary units of cognition—but also suggests superhuman cognitive capacities. Moreover, conceived as a 'generative grammar', the theory loses all force as a critical instrument. *All* tonal music would have to conform to the Schenkerian paradigm, whether good or bad, expressive or empty, unified or disorderly. The peculiar effect that *Schenker* wished to account for—the experience of total integration in which every part exists by necessity and under the irresistible impulse of an artistic idea—would then have to be explained by another theory, and another type of analysis.

2. As an account of the hidden structure of the great masterpieces. This is certainly how Schenker interpreted his theory. But at once a problem is encountered: to what extent is the structure hidden, and in what way? In general Schenkerians divide into two classes in answering this question. There are those who believe that the middleground and the background are not heard, or heard only subliminally; and there are those who believe that the middleground at least, and perhaps the background too, can be 'brought forward' into perception, so as to augment or change the intentional understanding that is constitutive of the musical experience. The first class of Schenkerian has a hard job explaining why it is important to describe these structures that we do not hear: why they are any more relevant to the analysis of music than descriptions of the back of the canvas are relevant to the analysis of a painting. The second class has a hard job convincing us that we really can hear the middleground, let alone the background, of a particular master-work.

Consider Schenker's analysis of the Bach Prelude in C major, from the First Book of the Forty-Eight (Ex. 13.19). The foreground has been reduced to a sequence of chords—harmonies that we certainly *do* hear in the music. But the only middleground structure that we are given is something far removed from this: a plain and uninteresting cadence, which can tell us, at best, to attend to the harmonic sequence at bars 21-4. *Why* we should single out those bars is far from clear. And even if we do single them out successfully, we surely do not hear what is represented in the middleground graph. In response to this observation, the Schenkerian may retreat from saying that we actually *hear* the middleground, and refer instead to the middleground as a hidden structure that explains our musical understanding, as a generative grammar might. It is by this constant retreat from intentional description, to structural explanation, that Schenkerian analysis in its original form maintains itself in being.

Ex. 13.19. Schenker's graph-analysis of Bach's *The Well-Tempered Clavier*, First Book, Prelude in C major, showing foreground (above), middleground and background (below).

This is brought out by asking ourselves precisely what we learn from Schenker's analysis of the prelude. Certainly, it teaches us to emphasize in our hearing the long pedal on the dominant, and it shows us why bars 18, 27, and 31, for example, sound so different, even though they are, acoustically speaking, exactly the same. Having worked through Schenker's analysis we cannot fail to be familiar with the journey through tonal space, and with the way in which harmonies are prolonged through passages which do not explicitly state them. The analysis of the triad sequence in the foreground is also interesting, in revealing just which notes of each chord are being held over. But it seems to be independent of the theory through which it is presented. Furthermore, Schenker does not know quite what to say about those problematic bars, in which F sharp is followed by A flat in the bass-line. He simply puts them in brackets, and concocts a weird explanation, based on Bach's way of notating them in the autograph, as to why we should exclude them from the *true* foreground structure.

3. As an instrument of small-scale analysis. Many of the difficulties encountered by Schenkerian analysis derive from its astonishing ambition—which is to derive the entire surface of a piece from a single cadence. But we can reject that ambition, and still find something suggestive in the idea of a hidden or latent structure, operating over smaller or larger passages, to hold the musical movement together. We then effectively dispense with Schenker's theory of the *Ursatz*, and operate entirely at the level of the middleground, picking out the significant tones and harmonies, and linking them so as to suggest the real logic of the musical movement.

Indeed, we can trace the hidden layers back to the *Ursatz* only in the smallest pieces, such as the Bach Prelude that I have been considering. Occasionally, with a I–V–I melody, we can give a kind of middleground and background unhesitatingly, as in the analysis of the theme of Beethoven's 'Ode to Joy'—taken from Zuckerkandl (Ex. 13.20).[12] But this is because the Schenkerian analysis is describing a cadence that we all hear in the music. The theory does not (in its original form) attribute this kind of background structure to a single theme. The theory has become plausible, only because of a massive reduction in its ambitions.

In this reduced version, Schenkerian analysis concentrates on the distinction between structurally important episodes and their prolongations. According to Felix Salzer, the distinction between structural and prolonging harmonies represents 'the instinctive perception of the truly musical ear'.[13] Moreover, 'the concept of structure and prolongation is the outstanding factor in which tonal coherence is based'.[14] Certainly, if you make your musical examples small enough, it is not difficult to endow them with a Schenkerian shape. However, the theory of the *Ursatz* is no part of this modified theory; it has become a mere speculation, which does no analytical work, since the analysis would be unaffected by its truth or falsehood. If the idea of such a background persists, it is as a kind of dogma—the I–V–I cadence acquires the status of

[12] *Man the Musician*, 174.   [13] *Structural Hearing*, 13.   [14] Ibid. 28.

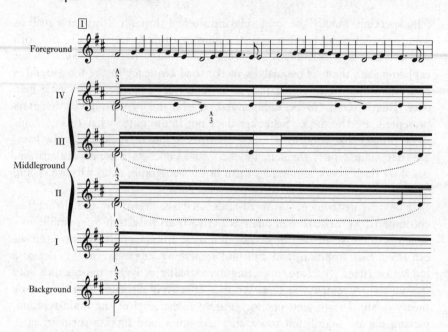

Ex. 13.20. Schenkerian analysis of Beethoven's 'Ode to Joy', from Zuckerkandl, *Man the Musician*

prime mover, becoming as abstract and unknowable as God himself. The procedure of analysis then reverses the original theory. Instead of generating foreground from background, it moves from foreground to middleground and *stops there*.

By way of illustration I shall consider an unusual and interesting example, taken from Christopher Wintle.[15] Sieglinde, exhausted by her flight from Hunding, falls into a fitful sleep, during which she is troubled by a nightmare, re-enacting the trauma of her mother's death and father's disappearance. Wagner's musical presentation of Sieglinde's state of mind is one of his many psychological triumphs (Ex. 13.21). The passage begins from a powerful discord, the dominant minor ninth (B flat major in the key signature, but B flat minor to the ear). A series of arpeggiated triads, the rocking theme of Sieglinde's sleep, continues the subdued dissonance over the dominant pedal, until the harmony ascends through three consecutive diminished sevenths, in which all twelve tones are thrown down before the listener. The sense of key is disrupted and the vocal line filled with anguish, as Sieglinde starts up from her nightmare and the music returns to the original chord.

Wintle describes the first chord of the passage quoted (which is, in fact, a vertical statement of the 'lightning' leitmotif that precedes it) as 'the source-chord'. He analyses the passage as follows, referring to his own graphs of foreground and middleground (Ex. 13.22):

> When the thunder and lightning music is first heard, the source-chord's diminished seventh (d.i) is prolonged by neighbour-note movement (d.ii). The counter-structure to which these two diminished sevenths belong is completed at bars 13–19; as the middleground shows, the third diminished seventh (d.iii) immediately precedes the return to the source-chord. In the foreground of bar 19, furthermore, all three diminished sevenths can be heard in rapid succession. Metaphorically speaking, Sieglinde's anxiety has welled to the surface, and 'worked itself out'. By contrast, the middleground shows that, in the first eight bars of the dream, the triads of Sieglinde's sleeping motif decorate the source-chord (and project a Lydian G-flat mode as they do so); indeed, the bass F of the chord retains the ominous timpani roll from the thunder and lightning music. In bars 8–13, the bass composes out the interval F to A of the source-chord (each step supports a transposition of this chord). The goal of the motion is no more than a second inversion of a D minor triad, which in turn is transformed into the middleground diminished seventh (d.iii). Although the triads search for a wished-for resolution, they never escape the gravitational pull of the anxiety-promoting diminished aspect of the source-chord.[16]

[15] 'Analysis and Psychoanalysis: Wagner's Musical Metaphors', in J. Paynter *et al.*, *Companion to Contemporary Musical Thought* (London, 1992), 650–91.

[16] 'Analysis and Psychoanalysis', 665.

Ex. 13.21. Wagner, *Die Walküre*, Act 12, Sieglinde's dream

(a)

(b)

'Source chord' bars 1– 8   9   11

(c)

Ex. 13.22. Christopher Wintle, Schenkerian analysis of Ex. 13.21: (a) foreground; (b) middleground; (c) diminished chords

That passage forms part of an illuminating attempt to uncover the Freudian dream-work in Wagner's music. In such circumstances, when the unconscious takes centre stage, we should naturally expect the music to have both an overt and a covert structure. But what precisely *is* the middleground that Wintle discerns behind the foreground of the music? Any attempt to show the foreground as *generated* from the middleground has been abandoned. The middleground is simply a representation of salient musical materials, in an ordered relation that suggests how the movement established by one of them is prolonged by another. It represents nothing that we do not hear in the music—or do not begin to hear, as soon as we have understood the analysis. The crucial facts to which Wintle draws our attention—the latent diminished harmony, the function of the 'source-chord' in producing and controlling it, the inability of Sieglinde's sleep-sodden triads to dampen the anxious forward movement—these can be described and understood without the theory.

The redundant parts of Schenkerian analysis result from its vast ambition. Any attempt to apply it will always involve a reversal of its theoretical claims, a move back from the musical surface to what lies behind it. In making that move we search, not for a 'deep structure' in the linguist's sense, from which the surface might be generated, but for a *latent* structure—a structure that can be heard in the music, as we hear Wagner's diminished seventh harmony leading away from the dominant minor ninth and back to it.

The distinction between deep and latent structure is of the first importance in understanding just what a musical analysis could achieve. Deep structures *explain* surface structures, by showing how they are derived in a rule-guided way from something simpler than themselves. But latent structures do not *explain* surface structures: they are part of them. Nor are they necessarily simpler than the surface structures, or related to them by any rule-governed process. They are the structures that we can be brought to *hear* in the surface, as we broaden our musical understanding, and begin to notice relations that are more subtle than those which immediately strike the ear. An analysis of latent structure is also a piece of music criticism. For it aims to bring into salience what is important in the music, and to lead us to hear with greater understanding. It effects an adjustment in the intentional object—and could indeed be compared with the work of psychoanalysis, in bringing into consciousness the full matter of the musical response.

Of course, the true Schenkerian will dismiss that argument, as he would dismiss Wintle's imaginative use of the theory. He will argue that middle-ground cannot be detached from background, but must always be seen as part of a generative sequence. But this retreat to the high ground of speculation exposes the theory to some awkward questions. By what criterion is a Schenkerian analysis to be verified? Since there are conflicting Schenkerian accounts of any single work of music, which is to be preferred and why? If background exists, why must it always consist in a melodic line that begins from tonic, mediant, or dominant, with a dominant cadence below? Could there not be a subdominant movement in music? And how is the analysis to be applied to those works of stretched tonality which have shaped the styles of modern music?

Schenker asserted quite dogmatically that all master-works *must* conform to his system. He did not seek for counter-examples: a work that did not conform to the system would be simply dismissed as unworthy of attention. It does not follow that conformity to the system is a *sufficient* condition of artistic value. (To give a Schenkerian syntax for 'Baa baa black sheep' is child's play.) But it is a necessary condition. Our experience of the master-works is an experience of organic unity—of a structure that exfoliates from a tiny seed of musical meaning, and always the same seed.

But is the experience of musical unity really like that? Consider, for example, the unity achieved through the use of a ground bass, as in Bach's D minor Chaconne for solo violin; or the unity that informs Skriabin's *Poem of Ecstasy*: a unity of force and movement, pressing towards a distant subdominant cadence. Or the musical unity of *Götterdämmerung*, Act 3, which begins in F major and ends in D flat major; or that of Chopin's Second Ballade, Op. 38, which begins in F and ends in A minor. Musical unity is not the simple and uniform thing that Schenker describes: and it is part of artistic genius to achieve this unity, even when the tonic changes from scene to scene and from movement to movement, as in a classical symphony.

The Critical Narrative

If it is necessary in a work of musical aesthetics to consider such technical matters as Schenkerian analysis, it is because they bear on the concept of musical understanding. All the theories that I have considered return us to the same point. Either they describe what is hidden, in which case they are at best psychological hypotheses; or they describe what is present or latent in the musical surface, in which case the technicalities can usually be discarded, or else persist as extended metaphors to which no theory corresponds. But what exactly is meant by the 'musical surface', and what does 'latent' mean?

Listening is a cognitive activity; but it is not one single activity. We should distinguish the following mental acts:

1. Hearing a sound.
2. Hearing a sound and inferring its cause: 'I heard a crash, and deduced that she had fallen'.
3. Hearing the cause: 'I heard her fall'.
4. Hearing sound A, and deducing a relation to sound B.
5. Hearing tone A, and deducing a relation to tone B.
6. Hearing the relation between A and B, as when I hear a variation in music.
7. Hearing A *in* B, as when I hear an inner voice in a sequence of chords.
8. Hearing A and being reminded of B.

The first four cases concern our ordinary cognitive relation to sounds. Cases (5)–(8), however, belong more specifically to the experience of music. As an example of (5) consider the film music of *Lulu*. At the apex I hear the music reversing; I go on to trace similarities with what has gone before, only in reverse order; finally I deduce that the second half of the piece is the mirror image of the first. As an example of (6) consider the perceived relation between the four-note motif of Beethoven's Fifth Symphony, first movement, and the theme of the Scherzo. As an example of (7) consider the way in which the opening theme of Beethoven's *Eroica Symphony*, last movement, is heard in the 'second subject' (Ex. 13.23). As an example of (8) consider the concluding phrase of Schubert's first 'Suleika' song, D720, which recalls the unanswered question of the opening bars (Ex 13.24). All these experiences, with the possible exception of the first, are musically significant. The Scherzo of Beethoven's Fifth Symphony elicits from us a powerful sense of recognition. The second subject of the Variations from the *Eroica* springs more fully

Ex. 13.23. Beethoven, *Eroica Symphony*, Op. 55, last movement

Ex. 13.24. Schubert, 'Suleika I', D720: (*a*) the question; (*b*) the answer (slower)

to life, when we hear the first subject striving to burst out of it into the open. And the recollection of the earlier phrase in the Schubert song enables us to perceive that Suleika's question does, at last, have an answer.

Now all of those experiences can be obtained without analysis. Nevertheless analysis can help us to enjoy them. Someone can be brought to hear things differently, by an analysis which forges at the theoretical level, the relation which he must perceive with his ears. The theory serves as a scaffold with which to rise to this higher and more complete perception. But once the relation has been established in experience, the theoretical scaffolding can be thrown away. Nor does it matter that one theory rather than another should have been used for the job. What matters is the experience with which the analysis concludes. The experience is the criterion which distinguishes mere paper theory from an understanding of the musical surface. True analysis is also a synthesis, a building of the intentional object through comparisons and contrasts that can be *heard*. By describing the musical surface, we also rearrange it; that which previously appeared as an accompanying figure becomes part of the melody; that which lingered in the background comes into the foreground as a key element of the musical argument; that which was first heard as a modulation to the dominant, becomes a prolongation of the tonic harmony; that which sounded like a passing discord (the 'source-chord' in Wintle's example) suddenly stands out as the ruling harmony.

The musical surface is the intentional object of hearing, as this is constructed in the act of aesthetic attention. And to say that a given structure is 'latent' within it, is to say that it can become part of that intentional object, and *should* become part if we are to hear the music correctly. If there is a difficulty in saying any more than this it stems from the general difficulty of discovering a language of pure appearances: a language that will identify the full complexity of an intentional object, when it is the object of aesthetic, rather than practical or theoretical attention. In attempting to characterize this thing we are driven to use irreducible metaphors: metaphors of unity, organism, growth, and life, which seem totally compelling when properly formulated, but which forbid translation into other and more theory-laden terms. When theory takes over, as in Forte's set-theoretic analysis of atonal music, the result is often difficult to understand as an analysis of the *music*, rather than a description of the *sounds*.

Criticism, Value, and Ideology

Analysis makes sense, therefore, only as a prelude to criticism. Criticism begins and ends in an elaborate act of ostension. The critic asks us to *notice* certain things, and to hear them differently. He also describes these things, using metaphors that come naturally to us, when studying the life and movement that we hear in music. The background assumption is that the critic's readers share in the musical culture, which forms the bedrock of communication; in this culture are planted all the varieties of our musical experience; and the words we use in communicating and recommending the forms of musical understanding are addressed to others whose ears have been educated as ours have been.

But that account of the critic's task is open to a familiar objection. For it seems to place our musical culture beyond criticism—unquestionable, because assumed in every question. This 'sanctifying' of existing things, it will be said, is ideological. To attribute absolute value to a musical culture is to conceal its historical nature. It is also to leave unquestioned the relations of power which graced themselves with this cultural halo. Surely, the true task of the critic is to see beyond such ideological constructs, and to place works of art in relation to the historical conditions that produced them, so as to expose their real social and political significance. If art and culture are the great deceivers of mankind, then the critic must assume the role of unde-ceiver, enabling us to perceive truly what has been enchanted, mystified, and hallowed in the interests of power.

It is not the truth of the theory implied in that paragraph which prompts me to respond to it, but its enormous and continuing influence. It can be found in many versions: the critical theory of the Frankfurt school; Adorno's defence of modernism against the 'musical fetish'; Foucault's 'histories' of bourgeois institutions; contemporary American feminism; the 'new histori-cism' in literary theory; and the moves towards a politicized musicology— whether Marxist, in the manner of Christopher Ballantine or feminist in the style of Susan McClary.[17] Its original—the Marxian theory of 'ideology'—has been frequently exposed to devastating criticism. Nevertheless, this seems to have no impact on Marx's successors, who owe their following less to the truth of what they say, than to the political agenda implied in it.

So compelling is this agenda, that those who have adopted it seldom pause to examine either the concept of ideology, or the belief that ideology is the creature of power. Consider the following passage from Stephen Greenblatt, a leading exponent of the 'new historicism':

> In all my texts and documents, there were, so far as I could tell, no moments of pure unfettered subjectivity; indeed, the human subject itself began to seem remarkably unfree, the ideological product of the relations of power in a particular society. Whenever I focussed upon a moment of apparently autonomous self-fashioning, I found not an epiphany of identity freely chosen but a cultural artifact. If there remained traces of free choice, the choice was among possibilities whose range was strictly delineated by the social and ideological system then in force.[18]

Everything that is most questionable has here been *built into the language*: not as the conclusion of an argument, but as part of the syntax. Would it be possible for such a writer really to recognize 'autonomous self-fashioning', if he cannot find it in Shakespeare? And what does he mean by a 'social and ideological system'? There is a kind of somnambulism in the phrase 'ideological product of the relations of power in a particular society'—a phrase which points unobstructed to the preconceived conclusion. All the products of a society are effects of the power that orders it: how could they not be? And all 'culture' is ideological. So exactly what is being ruled out by the author's 'findings'?

It is not surprising to discover that, in debates arising within the 'new historicism', the beliefs which stand most to be criticized are left unscathed. Here, for example, is a protest against Greenblatt from a fellow 'historicist':

> Again and again, the new historicists pose an important (if by now somewhat rhetorical) question: are early modern cultural differences (of blood, gender, class, ethnicity, virtue, religion) natural and essential, or cultural and constructed? 'Cultural and constructed', they respond consistently and rightly, and then go about discovering the social system producing and

---

[17] Ballantine, *Music and its Social Meanings* (New York, 1984); McClary, *Feminine Endings*. Of similar tendency, though ranging more widely over the vast literature of postmodern 'theory', are C. Abbate, *Unsung Voices: Opera and Musical Narrative in the Nineteenth Century* (Princeton, 1991), and L. Kramer, *Music as Cultural Practice 1800–1900* (Berkeley & Los Angeles, 1990), and *Classical Music and Postmodern Knowledge* (Berkeley & Los Angeles, 1995).

[18] *Renaissance Self-Fashioning: From More to Shakespeare* (Chicago, 1980), 256.

integrating these differences. But by posing this question so insistently, they drown out another important question that might also be addressed: how did early modern women and men, circulating in this field of socially constructed differences, manage to create new sorts of differences and even (at rare moments) to affiliate themselves with oppositional collectives that challenged the system of privileges prescribed by the dominant social order?[19]

The writing is animated by the same political agenda, and the 'theory' of ideology is left unquestioned. The appearance of scientific rigour is induced by a concealed tautology—'are cultural differences cultural?'—which enables the writer, by a sleight of hand, to smuggle in 'cultural and constructed', as though these were coextensive terms. (And note the unexplained contrast to 'natural and essential': as though culture were not natural to us.) The writer assumes that differences involve a 'system of privileges', that this system is 'prescribed' by a 'dominant social order', and that when people escape the grip of that dominant order it is by 'affiliating' themselves to 'oppositional collectives': all these assumptions are again built into the syntax, and could be removed or questioned only by destroying the very impulse of the writer's thought. Not only do they depend upon an untenable theory of history; they betray a sentimentality about the nature of political action which lies at the opposite pole from true cultural criticism.

A treatise on musical aesthetics is not the place to mount a reply to the Marxist theory of history. But a few remarks are necessary, if my argument is not to be dismissed as another piece of ideology. Consider the view that everything cultural is also a 'construct': what does this mean? Presumably that culture arises as a consequence of social life, and would not exist in a state of nature. But, for reasons made evident by Hegel and Wittgenstein, the rational being is also a construct in this sense. Only in the condition of society does language emerge, and only through language can the self define itself, as an object of its own awareness. Furthermore, we should distinguish 'constructs' which are chosen, from those which arise by an invisible hand. Some of 'culture' is the unintended by-product of social order; but much of it, including art, is freely intended. And that which is freely intended is always more than ideology, even if it is also ideology. A work of art may express and endorse the social conditions which gave rise to it; but it may also question them. And if it is a great work of art, it will transcend them entirely, to see into the human heart. Its meaning as *ideology* may be what interests us the least, when we see it as a work of art. The masses of Palestrina are important, not because they mystify those princely powers on which the Counter-Reformation depended, but because they present, in musical form,

[19] J. Holstun, 'Ranting at the New Historicism', *English Literary Rensaissance*, 19 (1989), 198.

an astonishing human experience—an experience of serene belief in the midst of tumultuous change, of timeless stasis in the stream of time—so helping us to understand this feeling and know it as a well-grounded psychic possibility. We are led not to share the feeling, but to sympathize. As to whether it is right or wrong to feel such things, how can we know, except through the critical meditation on the possibilities of emotion which is the true business of art?

And if the music of Palestrina is *ideology*, then what is wrong with ideology? Is this music not the stuff of human life, and as good a justification as any that might be offered, for those 'power-relations' which engendered the genius of Palestrina?

In fact, if we look at the results of ideological criticism, we find nothing very new. Susan McClary, for example, who explores the 'process of gender construction' in the music of Monteverdi, is just as concerned as a traditional critic would be, to show us how we should *hear* the music.[20] She justifies her judgement by arguing that Monteverdi's melodic line embodies conceptions of the masculine and feminine. And this is true. Has it not always been a part of hearing the human voice correctly, that we should understand the vision of sexuality that is projected by the musical line? It is a further question, whether the music is also endorsing the vision; and a further question still whether the endorsement is contentious. Those questions were addressed long before critics had been seduced by the Marxian theory of ideology. Consider Kierkegaard's study of *Don Giovanni*. Mozart's music cleverly shows us, Kierkegaard suggests, the demonic springs of Don Giovanni's seductiveness. But it also stands at a distance from the character, isolating him in a field where he may be judged. The music does not protect or sanctify a *culture*, still less a way of life; rather it turns the moral force of music upon a human experience, and shows this experience as it is *lived*. Only those steeped in our musical culture can understand Mozart's message: but the message is universal. Nor does it follow that the culture cannot be questioned from its own vantage point. What is *Die Meistersinger*, if not an attempt to dramatize through music, the very crisis that has put music in question?

Or take another of Susan McClary's examples—the presentation of the heroine's sexuality in Bizet's *Carmen*. It is undeniable that the music projects a particular conception of Carmen, using compelling folk-rhythms and chromatic melodies (as in the famous 'Habanera'), in order to emphasize her threatening quality. And the threat is real, working its way into the soul of José and slowly undermining it. (It is not as though nobody had noticed this before.) But what follows? When it comes to describing the *meaning* of Bizet's work, McClary does exactly what any other critic would do: she shows how

[20] *Feminine Endings*.

the drama is conveyed through the music, and how the simple tonality of José's love is undermined by the vacillating cadences which are Carmen's musical gift to him (Ex. 13.25). The sociological theory is dropped from the agenda. For the music presents Carmen and José as real individuals, bound in a real but disastrous love. It is at *this* level that we judge it, and the music neither excuses the weakness of the hero, nor condemns the strength of the heroine. We are presented with the object and the instrument of judgement; but it is we who judge. It is when a work falsifies feeling, that we cast judgement on *it*.

Ex. 13.25. Bizet, *Carmen*, 'Flower Song'

The inherent weakness in ideological analysis is often concealed by a crucial ambiguity in terms like 'expression' and 'meaning'. As I argued in Chapter 6, these terms may be used in a purely diagnostic way—as when the sociologist describes Heavy Metal as expressing the frustration of modern youth.[21] In this use the term 'expression' applies to music, regardless of its aesthetic impact. Heavy Metal expresses frustration in just the way that the hooting of car-horns expresses the impatience of stranded drivers. This judgement has no bearing on the nature, meaning, or value of any particular piece of Heavy Metal, which would express frustration in this sense, even if entirely empty, boring, and uninspired. But, as that last sentence shows, terms like 'expression' and their cognates are used also to describe the content of works of art. In this use they are immovably connected with aesthetic judgement. Ideological criticism often seems to be describing the content of a work of art: when it does so, however, it is no longer engaged in the search for ideology—which makes no distinction between expressive and inexpressive instances. Christopher Ballantine's attempt to show that Beethoven's music expresses the will and aspiration of the rising bourgeoisie proceeds by

[21] See e.g. Walser, *Running with the Devil*, and Simon Frith, *Sound Effects: Youth, Leisure and the Politics of Rock 'n Roll* (New York, 1981).

distinguishing Beethoven from his limp contemporaries, by showing the peculiar strength and confidence of his style, and arguing that Beethoven's music expresses in the aesthetic sense the spirit of the French Revolution.[22] This judgement is *not* a piece of Marxist sociology, even if it is derived from the Marxian caricature of history. It is a piece of criticism, inviting us to hear the revolutionary spirit in Beethoven's music, and to judge accordingly. It is proved or disproved not by adducing sociological facts and theories, but by critical argument, describing the shape and structure of melodies, harmonies, and rhythms, and the musical movement that is projected through them.

Analysis and Meaning

It is important to confront a charge that is often made (by Susan McClary among others) against the traditional forms of analysis. It is said that, in analysing a piece, we avoid the question of its *meaning*: we treat it precisely as though it had no meaning, or as though meaning were the least important of its features. This avoidance of meaning appears as an ideologically motivated *turning-away* from the questions which really matter, or which ought to matter, when approaching the products of a culture. And if so many music-lovers are attracted instead by politicized forms of criticism, this is partly because no alternative is commonly defended.

It seems to me that the complaint stems from a narrow view of analysis. What I mean may be clarified by an example of motivic analysis. Schoenberg[23] observed that, by octave transposition, the opening theme of the first movement of Brahms's Fourth Symphony in E minor, Op. 98, could be written as two series of thirds, the first descending, the second ascending (Ex. 13.26). This observation, simple though it is, proves to be truly illuminating, not just of the form and structure of Brahms's movement, but also, and concurrently, of its meaning. Although it is extremely difficult to hear the

Ex. 13.26. Schoenberg, analysis of the first theme from Brahms, Fourth Symphony in E minor, Op. 98

[22] *Music and its Social Meanings.*
[23] 'Brahms the Progressive', in *Style and Idea*, 398–441, esp. 406. See also Erwin Stein, 'Some Observation on Brahms's Shaping of Forms', in *Orpheus in New Guises* (London, 1953), 96–8.

melody *as* a progression of thirds, the analysis points to a living principle of development within the music—a force that can be heard as driving both melody and harmony relentlessly onwards.

Consider the second motif of the transition section, the strong, bleak fanfare in B minor, that disrupts the rhythm and effects a momentary pause in the surging development of the initial material (Ex. 13.27). This theme interpolates a semitone into the structure of thirds (see Ex. 13.28). And it is this semitone that Brahms uses to initiate the antiphonal passage between strings and woodwind, creating the sequence of broken third chords which contain so much of the emotion of this work (Ex. 13.29). Even when the melodic line breaks free from the discipline of thirds, as in the transitional theme which immediately follows the fanfare, the bass continues to obey it, in massive broken third chords that recall the Wagner of *Siegfried* and *Götterdämmerung* (Ex. 13.30). And the sequence of descending thirds again comes to the fore in the more langorous second subject (Ex. 13.31).

Ex. 13.27. Brahms, Fourth Symphony in E minor, Op. 98, bars 53–7

Ex. 13.28. Brahms, Fourth Symphony in E minor, Op. 98, bars 73–5

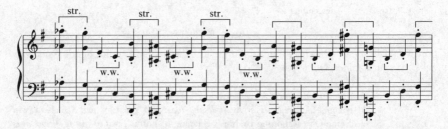

Ex. 13.29. Brahms, Fourth Symphony in E minor, Op. 98, bars 79–84

Ex. 13.30. Brahms, Fourth Symphony in E minor, Op. 98, bars 57–64

Ex. 13.31. Brahms, Fourth Symphony in E minor, Op. 98, bars 95–102

In the course of the development the opening motif of the descending third is expanded from a group of two tones to a group of three, as in Ex. 13.32, harmonized in thirds. This little cell gives Brahms the climax of the development, which he prepares from the fanfare in the masterly way illustrated in Ex. 13.33. From this climax emerges a triplet figure (Ex. 13.34), which Brahms promptly uses to create a lyrical variation of the opening theme, with the original concealed in the off-beats which sound in the bass (Ex. 13.35).

This is but a glimpse into the astonishing order of this movement. But it is also a glimpse into its meaning: it shows Brahms leading the listener to 'hear in thirds', and to respond to the logic of the musical line, as it

Ex. 13.32. Brahms, Fourth Symphony in E minor, Op. 98, bars 157–60

Ex. 13.33. Brahms, Fourth Symphony in E minor, Op. 98, bars 192–206

Ex. 13.34. Brahms, Fourth Symphony in E minor, Op. 98, bars 217–18

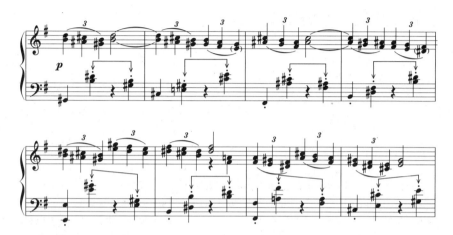

Ex. 13.35. Brahms, Fourth Symphony in E minor, Op. 98, bars 219–26

exfoliates from that tiny cell of two notes. The effect is one of the most powerful in all romantic music, of tragic feeling that is nevertheless utterly controlled, and utterly in control. And that *is* the meaning of the music: the aural presentation of a sincere and solemn gesture—a gesture which never betrays itself as a pretence, which never stumbles, as it unfolds with unanswerable authority the complete motive to action, and the justifying narrative which brought it into being. The listener is presented with an instance of human integrity, in which a life is concentrated in a timeless instant. And recalling the gesture from which this narrative began, he will notice that it was not a *minor* third at all, but a *major* third, whose minor harmony entered only when the gesture was complete. Here is the truth of our condition, and it is hardly surprising that the same musical devices recur in the song 'O Tod, wie bitter', in which Brahms acknowledges the inescapable grief of being human: or rather, the grief that we escape only by unscrupulous shallowness towards self and other.

There is much more to be said about criticism. But first we must explore the nature of the musical culture in which we participate, and try to ascertain whether, and to what extent, it offers a paradigm of the musical experience.

14 *Performance*

Making and listening to music were once social activities, with religious or ceremonial connotations, and the music of our classical tradition bears the imprint of the Christian culture from which it grew. Liturgical chant and a capella responses; courtly madrigals and dances; sung masses and chorales; hymns and brass bands—all testify to the social and religious uses of music, and we might be reasonably suspicious of a philosophy which identifies silent *listening* as the primary musical experience. It is only at a certain period of history that the public concert began to emerge as the principal musical forum; and even if an audience was present when Renaissance musicians performed, there is a real historical question, as to when this audience *fell silent*.[1] Moreover, the new kind of listening—listening in private to a performer recorded miles away and years ago—so completely severs music from its social context, that one may reasonably doubt that the experience of music has remained the same since the invention of the gramophone.

Nevertheless, music remains a performance art, and the polyphonic character of music in our tradition means that most performances are also social events—occasions of 'making music together'. As Alfred Schutz has argued, musical performance provides a paradigm of 'non-semantic communication'— of a 'mutual tuning-in relationship' which transcends the barrier of 'I' and 'thou' into the realm of 'we'.[2] This relationship binds those who play together, and also the musicians and their audience.

When considering this social relation, we must be careful to distinguish free improvisation from a performance with a score. When musicians improvise together, obeying no instructions other than those which they agree either explicitly beforehand, or tacitly in the course of playing, an extraordinary feat of coordination occurs. It is as though human movements were lifted free

---

[1] See J. Johnson, *Listening in Paris, a Cultural History* (Berkeley and Los Angeles, 1995).

[2] 'Making Music Together', in *Collected Papers*, (The Hague, 1964), ii. 159–78.

from the bodies in which they originate and released into tonal space, there to achieve a togetherness beyond anything that could qualify our bodily life. The audience moves in response to this, whether by dancing or by following the musical pulse, and much of the significance of an art form like jazz resides in the spontaneous eruption of social feeling which this sympathetic movement engenders.

The jazz performer is, in a sense, also the composer, or one part of a corporate composer. But to describe free improvisation in that way is to assume that composition is the paradigm case, and improvisation secondary. It would be truer to the history of music, and truer to our deeper musical instincts, to see things the other way round: to see composition as born from the writing-down of music, and from the subsequent transformation of the scribe from recorder to creator of the thing he writes. Jacques Derrida has famously criticized Western civilization as 'logocentric'—privileging speech over writing, as the purveyor of human intention.[3] The criticism is the opposite of the truth: writing has been so privileged by our civilization, in religion, law, and politics, as well as in art and literature, that we tend to lose sight of the fact that written signs owe their life to the thing which is *written down*.

Is there anything important in common between the band of musicians, improvising around a formula to an audience of dancers, and the modern concert orchestra playing from sheet music to a silent crowd? We can cast light on the relation between these phenomena through a religious parallel. We should see the 'elementary forms of the religious life' in Durkheim's terms, as providing the collective 'we' which ensures the protection and survival of the tribe. In this elementary form religion is like a collective dance, in which the tribe moves together, invoking the god who incarnates himself in the ritual—perhaps in the body of the priest or shaman. But religion changes character with the discovery of writing and the sacred text. Now the voice of God speaks from another and more distant region—a region beyond this world, which we address through formalized rituals and readings from the 'word of God'. The priest ceases to impersonate the deity, and becomes instead a mediator. The worshippers stand in hushed silence, hanging on the sacred words, which are the words of no mortal present, but of an observer in transcendental regions, speaking a higher language and calling his flock to glory.

The parallel is tendentious. But it helps us to understand two extraordinary modern phenomena. First is the rock concert, in which an audience moves excitedly in time to the rhythm, its eyes fixed upon the performers, who are the full and final object of attention, the living embodiment of the music's spirit. Second is the classical orchestral concert, in which the performers vanish behind their ritual dress, and only the conductor—

---

[3] *Marges de la philosophie.*

himself in formal costume, and with his back to the audience—retains the charisma of his priestly office, while the audience sits motionless and expectant, wrapped in an awed silence, and focusing not on the performers, but on the music which makes use of them. The silence of the concert hall is a *substantial* silence, which lives and breathes with the music. The rise of the public concert has made this substance into one of the composer's primary materials—and in the symphonies of Mahler we find silence shaped by the surrounding tones and placed before us like a mirror, in which we see our own astonished faces.

In the next chapter I shall say more about concerts, their quasi-religious function, and the listening culture that depends on them. Before doing so, however, we must address the more technical issue of the nature of performance in a tradition of written music, and the relation between performance and work.

Work and Performance

The performer inevitably leaves a mark on what is heard. If we are to retain the concept of a *work* of music, therefore, we must distinguish those features which belong to the work, from those which are added in performance. If we could not make this distinction, we should have no conception of the work as something distinct from its performances, with an aesthetic character that remains unaltered at different places and different times. In jazz and rock this distinction is not easily made: performances are 'versions', and the work may have little meaning or character of its own, being identified entirely with the musicians who play it. In the tradition of Western art music, on the other hand, the distinction between work and performance has become fundamental to the musical experience.[4] Each performance is judged against the aesthetic potential of the work, which it must 'realize' if it is to deserve our applause. Even if we were to devise a mechanical means of translating a score directly into sound, this too would be a performance, to be judged by comparison with the human version, as adding to and altering the work's aesthetic properties.

Since the score underdetermines the performance, however, the question of authenticity arises in any tradition where music is written down. There are indefinitely many things that we hear when we hear a performance that have

---

[4] There are those who argue that this distinction is itself a mark of the listening culture, and neither fundamental to the art of music, nor separable from the 'bourgeois' economy which has promoted it. See C. Dahlhaus, *Foundations of Music History*, tr. J. B. Robinson (Cambridge, 1983), and *Idea of Absolute Music*; Goehr, *Imaginary Museum of Musical Works*. For reasons given in Ch. 15, I reject this historicist approach.

either no notation, or a notation that is indeterminate or incomplete. Consider tempo markings (other than those specified by metronome figures), dynamic markings, markings like *espressivo*, 'mit gutem humor' (Schumann) or 'comme un léger et triste regret' (Debussy). These remind us that the performer is not merely producing the sounds specified in the score: he is interpreting the score, and is animated by a musical intention that may either harmonize or compete with the intention of the composer. Moreover, like every set of instructions, a score must be followed, and—outside the context provided by a tradition of performance—it is entirely unclear what this 'following' amounts to. (Cf. Wittgenstein's sceptical argument about rule-following, which prompts the conclusion that it is the practice that makes the rule, and not vice versa.)

Those observations raise again the question of the ontology of the musical work. I argued in Chapter 4 that the identity of musical works is determined not by nature but by convention. The most convenient way of identifying them is as temporally ordered patterns of pitched sound. Whether we call such patterns 'types' or 'kinds', or whether we identify them as abstract individuals like numbers or letters of the alphabet, is a matter of indifference, just as it is a matter of indifference in the case of single sound events. What matters is that such patterns can be 'realized' in performance, just as the design of a car is realized in the individual machines that emerge from the production line, and the text of a literary work is realized in a reading of it. Whether we choose to say, with Goodman,[5] that all and only those features that are notated in the score identify a performance as a performance of *that* particular work is again a matter of convention. But we should be loath to follow Goodman's strict criterion of identity, for several reasons—first because it is indifferent to the distinction between mistakes and departures; secondly because it privileges the written score over the sounds described by it, and so, as I have suggested, reverses the true order of things.

We can, if we wish, describe the individual performances as 'tokens' of the 'type': this way of speaking is neither more nor less clear than the distinction between type and token. Rather than settle on any particular idiom, however, it is enough to recognize that a performance aims to present the particular pattern, as an object of intrinsic interest. And to do this, it must contain more features than are specified in the pattern, and may, within the established conventions, deviate from the pattern without ceasing to be a performance of *it*. However, the aim of the performance is not *merely* to produce a particular pattern of pitches, but to present those pitches as music, and therefore to make whatever additions and adjustments are required by a musical understanding. Performance is the art of translating instructions to produce certain *sounds* into an organization of *tones*.

[5] *Languages of Art*, ch. 5.

On this view considerable latitude in performance is permitted, without change to the identity of the work. For example, since our perception of pitch is, in the normal case, a perception of *relations* of pitch, any performance which preserves the relations specified by the composer will be a performance of his work. A transposed performance of a song is not the performance of *another* song, but a performance of the *same* song in another key. This is not to say that transposition does not alter the aesthetic character: indeed it does, and in many cases destroys the song entirely—as Schumann's cycle *Frauen-liebe und Leben* is destroyed when transposed for a bass voice. Nevertheless a transposed rendering of this song cycle is still a rendering of Schumann's work, and not a new composition.

Within limits, tempos can be varied without destroying the pitch pattern of a work, so that one performance may last half as long as another, and still be a performance of the same work. Pitch relations are also indifferent to instrumentation, so that—again within limits—the instrumentation of a work may vary from performance to performance without changing its identity. Since there are no *metaphysical* constraints on the concept of identity in this application, there is no way of ruling out such variations a priori: only taste and tradition can decide. There are philosophers (Jerrold Levinson, for example) who have tried to build into their criteria for the identity of musical works some specification of the 'performance means'.[6] But as has been conclusively shown by Peter Kivy,[7] the attempt does not and cannot succeed. The resulting criterion of identity will always fall apart—there is nothing in the concept of a pitch pattern that determines the timbre that will most perspicuously realize it. Hence performances of the *Well-Tempered Clavier* on a piano, on a harpsichord, by a quartet of brass or woodwind, or by the Swingle Singers are all performances of the *Well-Tempered Clavier*. (The case of performance should, however, be contrasted with those of transcription and arrangement, which are discussed below.)

This does not mean that instrumentation is unimportant, or that change of instrumentation will not change the aesthetic character of a work. For many people, Bach's *Well-Tempered Clavier* would be destroyed by the Swingle Singers—and even by a string quartet, which, in Hindemith's view, would turn this great and weighty utterance into a series of pleasant minia-tures.[8] But that only implies what we already knew—that numerical identity does not determine sameness of aesthetic character.

---

[6] Levinson, 'What a Musical Work Is', 'What a Musical Work Is, Again', and 'Authentic Performance and Performance Means', in *Music, Art and Metaphysics*, 63–88, 393–408, and 215–66 respectively.

[7] 'Orchestrating Platonism', in *Fine Art of Repetition*, 75–94.

[8] *Composer's World*, 105.

Authentic Performance

How might we distinguish authentic from inauthentic performances? And what special value, if any, attaches to the authentic performance? There would be little point in the distinction, if we could not think of authenticity as a value—as something at which we might aim, not just for curiosity's sake, as we might aim to reconstruct the taste of a Roman supper, but as part of our appreciation of the music. If authentic performance means simply 'the kind of performance that the composer himself might have heard', then it is difficult to see the point of reconstructing it, since most of the performances will have been quite inadequate. It is for this reason that attempts to define authenticity (e.g. those of Stephen Davies and Peter Kivy) tend to rely, first on an idea of the composer's intentions, secondly on a notion of the 'ideal' or 'optimal' realization of them. Here is the definition offered by Davies:

> A performance will be more rather than less authentic if it successfully (re)creates the sound of a performance of the work in question as could be given by good musicians playing good instruments under good conditions (of rehearsal time etc.), where 'good' is relativized to the best that was known by the composer to be available at the time, whether or not those resources were available for the composer's use.[9]

On this definition authenticity is a matter of degree, as it is for Kivy.[10] Some might reject it outright, on the grounds that a composer's intentions are either unknowable, or irrelevant: the composer vanishes behind his work, which is the sole and sufficient witness to its meaning. But such arguments, whether presented through the old-fashioned allegation of an 'intentional fallacy', or through the newfangled mystique of deconstruction (the 'death of the author'), should not detain us, for reasons which I have already given. Like any human product, a work of music is imbued with the signs of intention, and our recognition of intention affects and is affected by our perception of the musical surface. Others might worry over the words 'good' and 'best', in Davies's definition: do these refer to talent, skill, musicality, taste, or what? But that objection too need not detain us, since the composer's intention can be appealed to in this matter too.

The real problems, with this as with any similar account, are two: first, that while the composer intended certain *sounds* to be produced, by way of a performance of his work, he also intended those sounds to be heard as music—in other words, as organized in the way that music is organized. His

---

[9] 'Authenticity and Musical Performance', *British Journal of Aesthetics*, 27 (1987), 45.

[10] 'On the Concept of the "Historically Authentic" Performance', in *Fine Art of Repetition*, 117–36. Kivy has recently expanded his thoughts in *Authenticities: Philosophical Reflections on Musical Performance* (Ithaca, NY, 1995).

instructions specify a pattern of pitched sounds, since that is all that can be physically identified, and therefore all that can be physically reproduced. But both he and the performer know that the music is to be identified *intentionally*: it is the order that we hear *in* those sounds. And musicianship consists in bringing that order to the fore, even at the cost of acoustic accuracy. The composer could not have intended merely that the performer should produce the pattern of pitches that he specified, whether or not the life of the music is heard in them. And it is begging the question to assume that any particular combination of instruments, any particular manner of performance, any particular collection of physical sounds (specified in terms other than their pitch relations and temporal organization) would be the one in which the life of the music would be most clearly perceived and most immediately responded to. Glenn Gould's performances of Bach are far removed from any that would be countenanced by the 'early music' specialists: but they are animated by the intention to be *true* to Bach's musical inspiration.

Secondly, the definition neglects what one might call the 'historicity of the human ear'. How things sound depends upon who is listening, and upon the tacit comparisons that animate his perception. A single pattern of vibrations in the air will not sound the same to one who has lived quietly in the country, hearing only horse-drawn carriages and the cries of animals, and to one who has lived always in a modern city among busy streets crammed with motor cars. More to the point, the same musical sounds will be received differently by someone who knows only the works of Bach and his predecessors and by someone who has been brought up on Brahms, Wagner, and Liszt. Even if we could reproduce exactly the vibrations in the air that Bach's choir and orchestra at Leipzig might have generated, there is no way of determining that we should hear those vibrations as he heard them, or that we should hear *in* them the musical life that *he* heard. Music is a living tradition, and we compare musical works in our hearing not only with works that are contemporary with them, but with works that came before and after. To us the 'Goldberg' Variations anticipate the Diabelli Variations—that is how they sound, and one reason why we wish to play them on the piano. For Bach they could not have sounded like that.

Performance and Culture

The search for authenticity must take account, too, of the cultural background from which music emerges. Music is not insulated from the rest of life. A musical culture thrives when music enters our lives as a day-to-day companion—when we dance to it and sing along with it; when we apply it in worship and recreation, in work and in play. As those social relations change, so will our perception of music. A galliard or a gavotte to which people once danced will not sound to our ears as it did to theirs: for we have only an imperfect conception, not merely of how we should dance to this music, but of the social background which gave sense to this kind of dancing. Of course, we can learn about those things: but to possess scholarly knowledge of a culture is not in itself to belong to it. Besides, the argument might force us to the conclusion that authentic performance requires the creation of authentic social conditions—in which case authenticity is a historical impossibility. (Thus Dolmetsch, who performed on his home-made lutes and viols while dressed in Elizabethan costume, described the music which he resuscitated as 'quite beyond the reach of modern people'.)[11]

Furthermore, the composer is as aware as we are of the fact that music is part of, and develops with, the rest of social life. Bach wrote 'French' and 'English' suites, an 'Italian' concerto, as well as liturgical music for a faith that he did not share. Those musical appropriations of neighbouring cultures were not designed as 'authentic' renderings, but as tributes to a social context that was not his own. Likewise Mozart's 'alla Turca' idiom, his country dances and conscious pastiches of Handel in *Don Giovanni* were appropriations which freely played with the music of other places and other times, and played too with the social context implied in them. To perform these works now, we too must play: but from a different vantage point, and understanding the social context through new contrasts and across an ever-increasing distance.

Musical performance, in short, involves an ongoing dialogue between composer and performer, a dialogue across generations, in which the dead play as great a part as the living. Such is the nature of every healthy culture, and just as the composer lays down instructions for the performer, so does the performer, in his turn, instruct the composer, setting the piece in a new social and musical context, and dressing it accordingly. So vivid is our sense of this dialogue between generations, that we do not, in practice, confine ourselves to a study of the composer's actual intentions. We are just as interested in his hypothetical intentions: what *would* he have wanted, we ask ourselves, if he were living now, in this society, and with an audience like this? Would he have wanted his music to be played on 'authentic instruments' by musicians who must struggle to master them, or would he prefer it to be played on the instruments that have come (often for the best of aesthetic reasons) to replace them? Would Bach have wished us to finger out his fugues on a reproduction harpsichord, or on the Steinway grand to which we are accustomed, and which is, for us, the medium through which Beethoven, Chopin, and Bartók also make their way to our ears? We may not

---

[11] See the description of a Dolmetsch house-party in A. C. Benson's *Diary*, ed. P. Lubbock (London, 1926), for 7 Mar. 1913. Although Dolmetsch became a symbol of the early music revival, his instruments and performance practice are now often criticized as inauthentic.

have clear answers to those questions: but they are real questions neverthe-less. In a living culture, the dead are still present among the living. And sometimes they provide evidence of their hypothetical desires. (We know, for example, that in later life Bach was much taken by the newly invented forte-piano, for the very reasons that might have led him, had he lived another century and a half, to be taken by the Steinway grand.)[12]

None of that suggests that we cannot produce a workable definition of the authentic performance. But it does suggest that the authentic performance will not, in itself, provide a standard, or give access to the true musical iden-tity of the work performed. This fact is of considerable importance, in the light of the 'early music' movement, and the fashion for playing 'early' music on instruments of the period. For even if we are convinced that the com-posers were themselves satisfied with those instruments (in which case, why was so much effort devoted to improving them?), we cannot assume that a modern player will be able to express his musical instincts by means of them as well as would a player who knew no alternative.

The same goes for ornaments and embellishments. At a certain stage, having convinced themselves that the habit of playing stringed instruments with continuous vibrato was a nineteenth-century innovation, advocates of authenticity decided that 'early' music should be played strictly without vibrato—which was to be used at most only when a contemporary player might have used it, to emphasize a cadence, or as a kind of incipient trill. Since modern players rely on vibrato to correct their ears, so as to 'feel' their way to the designated pitch, the result may be a wooden and cacophonous sound which, even if nearer acoustically to the sound originally intended, is much further musically from anything that the 'early' composer would have countenanced. For the composer did not intend his performers to produce sounds only: he intended them to produce tones, and to convey those rela-tions between tones which are the life and soul of music.[13]

---

[12] See C. Wolff, 'New Research on Bach's *Musical Offering*', *Musical Quarterly*, 57 (July 1971), 379–408.

[13] Authenticity means many things. But if we define it in *acoustical* terms (i.e. in terms of the material object of musical interest, rather than the intentional object), we are likely to foster musically *inauthentic* performances. Thus J. O. Young defines an authentic performance as 'one which causes the air to vibrate as it would have vibrated at the time of composition' ('The Concept of Authentic Performance', *British Journal of Aesthetics*, 28 (1988)). Such a definition is a recipe for the grossest violation of the composer's real intentions, for reasons well set out by Kivy in *Authenticities*.

The Museum Culture

When a culture dies it is ceremonially buried in a museum. I placed the word 'early' in inverted commas, precisely because there is nothing genuinely early about Buxtehude, Gibbons, Purcell, or Bach. On the contrary, to the extent that the musical culture which they enjoyed is still alive, and to the extent that we too can share in it, they remain our contemporaries. To isolate them as instances of 'early music' is already to officiate at their burial—as Rameau dismissed all music prior to his own as music of 'les anciens'. It is to deny the transparent truth that they were doing the same thing as Mozart, Beethoven, Brahms, Wagner, and Stravinsky—namely, creating sound patterns which can be heard as music. Bach's counterpoint can be heard in Mozart's and in Beethoven's; the Brahms symphonies show the very same submission to the principle of voice-leading that we know from the *Well-Tempered Clavier* and the *Art of Fugue*. We could not understand Stravinsky or Berg if we did not also hear Bach's unmistakable accents sounding through them. And to suppose that, in order to acquaint ourselves with the music of Bach, we must lay down the instruments with which we perform the music of his great successors, is to do a terrible injustice to the greatest musician who has ever lived.

The dispute over authentic performance began in the last century, and was already in full swing by 1848, when F. C. Griepenkerl and A. B. Marx fought each other through the pages of the *Allgemeine Musikalische Zeitung* over editions and performance styles for the music of Bach.[14] By then, the 'Academy of Ancient Music' had been founded in England, borrowing the word *ancien* to describe the music of Handel. By degrees, 'early' music entered the curriculum of the Humboldtian university, to fall under the spell of Hegelian scholarship. Musicologists began to take a 'historicist' view of their subject. To study the music of the past, it was assumed, we must return it to its historical context, and fix it within a period.[15]

The inspiration for this historical musicology came in part from the new academic discipline of art history, with its tacit assumption that periodization and historical analysis are the primary way to understand 'the art of the past'. The art historians divided up their territory according to the Hegelian precepts of Burkhardt, Wölfflin, and their successors. The history of art was sliced into 'periods'—Renaissance, Mannerist, Baroque, Rococo, Romantic, Neo-Classical—which were embellished with a weight of Hegelian theory, until they came to be accepted as the stages of an ineluctable spiritual journey. Each period was construed in terms of a single *Zeitgeist*, and if you happened

[14] 50 (1848), nos. 5 and 10.
[15] See T. Adorno, 'Bach defended against his devotees', in *Prisms*, tr. S. Weber and S. Weber (Cambridge, Mass., 1967; repr. Boston, 1990).

to be born in 1640, nothing could conceivably transport you from the 'Baroque' frame of mind which it was your historical destiny to express.

When, in their search for academic *Lebensraum*, the scholars lighted on music, they decided that music must be squeezed into the same card-index as had been devised for the history of art. Henceforth Bach was to be known as a Baroque composer, just as Wren was a Baroque architect, Rubens a Baroque painter and Milton a Baroque poet. A concept invented by Burkhardt and Wölfflin in order to make a fine but important distinction between styles of architecture was elevated into a spiritual category, and tied immovably to the chronology of Western culture.

Nothing is conveyed by the description of Bach as a 'Baroque' composer: such analogies as there might be between his music and the buildings of Bernini or Fischer von Erlach are either too stretched or too superficial to cast any light on his musical genius. The sole effect of this label has been to imprison Bach's soul in the period that gave birth to his body, and so to consign his music to a glass case in the museum of culture.

In more recent years, and since the flamboyant gestures of Dolmetsch and friends, a multitude of groups has sprung up, devoted to the task of historically 'authentic' performance. The scholarly intention is revealed in their names: London Baroque Ensemble, Concentus Musicus, Musica Antiqua Cologne, The Parley of Instruments, Collegium Aurium, the Consort of Musicke, the Orchestra of the Age of the Enlightenment, or such twee extravagances as Les Arts Florissants and La Grande Écurie et la Chambre du Roi—a title worthy of Molière's *Précieuses ridicules*. Such groups may have begun with the benign intention of extending the repertoire. But the effect has frequently been to cocoon the past in a wad of phoney scholarship, to elevate musicology over music, and to confine Bach and his contemporaries to an acoustic time-warp. The tired feeling which so many 'authentic' performances induce can be compared to the atmosphere of a modern museum. A painting receives its final tribute from the scholar only in the form of a catalogue entry. Hence it is assumed that the proper place for a painting—even for a minor painting—is not on the wall of a private house, where it can bestow joy and dignity on the life surrounding it, but in the gallery of some great museum, to be gaped at by weary multitudes, as they wander from picture to picture in a state of well-informed fatigue. Likewise, the works of the 'early' or 'ancient' composers have been confiscated by scholarship. They no longer have a place in our homes, played on our own familiar instruments, but are arranged behind the glass of authenticity, staring bleakly from the other side of an impassable screen. Yet how absurd it is, even to *think* of Bach as 'early' music—Bach, whose voice sounds as fresh and clear in the music of Stravinsky and Schoenberg as in that of Mozart, Beethoven, Mendelssohn, and Brahms.

None of this is to deny that the original performances of Bach's works were very different *acoustically* from those inauthentic but exuberant renderings that we associate with Otto Klemperer, Karl Munchinger, and Wilhelm Furtwaengler. Nor is it to deny the interest of any attempt to 'reconstruct' the sound that Bach's own musicians would have made under his direction in Leipzig. But there is a deep reason for thinking that this 'reconstruction' can never capture Bach's intentions. As Peter Kivy eloquently puts it:

> Bach was not reproducing an eighteenth-century performance of his work, he was giving one. Bach was not reviving a tradition, he was living one. He was not 'following the rules': he was in the dynamic process of making and breaking them. And those that he was 'following' he was not following in the sense in which I follow Mattheson's instructions for ornamentation, or Heinichen's for realizing a figured bass, but in the sense in which one follows rules when they have been internalized and are part of one's blood and bones. Bach was not an outsider to a tradition he was trying to reconstruct, but part of the living tradition that *we* are trying to reconstruct. Thus, what our time traveller would hear in Leipzig [at Bach's own performance of the *St Matthew Passion*] would be a performance full of the spontaneity, vigour, liveliness, musicality, aesthetic imagination that critics of the 'early music' movement find lacking in its 'authentic' performances.[16]

I would only add that we do not need to reconstruct the 'living tradition' to which Kivy refers, for we are still part of it—though for how much longer I do not know. It is precisely because the tradition of Western music still lives that we can gain access, through the music of previous generations, to states of mind that we no longer encounter in our daily experience. The unbroken tradition of polyphonic writing enables us to hear, in Victoria's great *Responsories for Tenebrae*, exactly *what it was like* to believe as Victoria believed, seeing the world in terms of the Christian drama. This experience is overwhelming: it redeems for us a moment of past time, which could never be redeemed by factual knowledge. It makes a vanished experience present in our own emotions, and instructs us, through the imagination, in spiritual possibilities that our lives deny. Such experiences could not be obtained, if musical performance were merely a kind of scholarly reconstruction. Every performance would then be an affirmation of the distance between the audience and the music. Performance should be part of a tradition: a practice which is constantly amended in the light of new examples, which in turn owe their life to what has gone before.[17]

The above reflections suggest that the access to the past that we obtain through musical performance is not enhanced, but on the contrary often

---

[16] *Fine Art of Repetition*, 128–9.

[17] See T. S. Eliot, 'Tradition and the Individual Talent', in *The Sacred Wood* (London, 1920), for the classic account of tradition in artistic matters.

diminished, by surrendering to the call of scholarship. The 'authetic' performer, using 'authentic' instruments, is imitating someone long-since dead, and acting from aesthetic motives that were unavailable to his vanished predecessor. We might enjoy the result, but not in the way that the original audience enjoyed the original performance. For the music is now presented to us under an aspect of 'pastness', and enjoyed partly on that account. Richard Taruskin has put the point in another way:

> even at their best and most successful, or especially at their best and most successful, historical reconstructionist performances are in no sense recreations of the past. They are quintessentially modern performances, modernist performances in fact, the product of an aesthetic wholly of our own era, no less time-bound than the performance styles they would supplant.[18]

The reference to modernism is exact. For the authentic performance arises from a consciousness of the past which is available only to those who feel themselves irremediably sundered from it. And it expresses the same kind of censoriousness that motivated the early modernists. The authentic performance is a kind of tacit reprimand of the audience. Listeners to Beethoven's Ninth, thinned with white spirit by Roger Norrington and painted in fast brush-strokes on the air, are *meant* to be shocked. They are *meant* to understand the vulgarity of their taste, in wanting the full-throated brass of a modern orchestra, and the silken saturation of ten- or twenty-fold strings.

Composer and Audience

It was the growing conflict between composer and audience that hardened the hearts of the modernists. The history of Schoenberg's concerts in the Vienna of the 1900s is too well known for readers to feel much sympathy for those who disrupted them. And it is hardly surprising if Schoenberg acted and wrote thereafter as though audiences should hear his music only as a stern rebuke. Even in 1946 he was writing as though the audience had no legitimate part to play in the creation and understanding of music, and as though it entered the equation only by overhearing a dialogue between the composer and his inner voice:

> Those who compose because they want to please others, and have audiences in mind, are not real artists. They are not the kind of men who are driven to say something whether or not there exists one person who likes it, even if they themselves dislike it. They are not creators who must open the valves in order to relieve the interior pressure of a creation ready to be born. They

[18] 'The Musicologist and the Performer', in D. K. Holoman and C. V. Palisca (eds.), *Musicology in the 1980s: Methods, Goals, Opportunities* (New York, 1982), 113.

are merely more or less skilful entertainers who would renounce composing if they did not find listeners.[19]

It is as though the priest, disgusted with his sinful congregation, has turned away from them entirely, so as to communicate with God alone.

Schoenberg's attitude suffers from the same defects as the cult of authentic performance. The composer's intention is not to produce a pattern of sounds, but to create a living musical movement. Even when writing for himself, the composer is writing for an audience: for music is the intentional object of a human experience, and exists only as heard. To think the audience away is to think away the composer's intention. For how can you intend to produce music, if you have no conception of the listener in whom this music lives?

The problem for the modernist composer is not solved, therefore, by rejecting the audience. Nor is it solved by appealing to existing audiences— whose expectations are for those 'banal' and 'sentimental' gestures which the true artist can no longer provide. To create modernist music, the composer must also create the modernist audience. And the real question is whether such a thing is possible—indeed, whether audiences are ever truly *created*, and whether they could be created in *our* cultural conditions.

Versions and Transcriptions

The process of musical dissemination creates versions, variants, and transcriptions as a by-product. We make an intuitive distinction between the transcription which is the *same* work of music as the original, and the transcription which is *another* work, derived from, but not identical with, its parent. The vocal score of an opera, in which the orchestral parts are transcribed for piano, is surely not another work. The ruling intention of the transcriber is to preserve the pattern of pitched sounds as the composer intended it, but without the instrumental colour. The intentions of the *orchestrator*, however, may derive from a critical interpretation of the work, a desire to emphasize features that the composer's original leaves in the background. When Schoenberg orchestrated Bach's Chorale Prelude, BWV 654, he retained all the pitched sounds, and the temporal pattern of their arrangement, but used the orchestral timbre in such a way that the musical order that is heard in those sounds is radically different from the musical order that would be heard in them in any other version. He read a *motivic* structure into a piece that is normally heard according to the traditions of tonal counterpoint.[20] Is this a *new* work of music? By the criterion of identity

---

[19] 'Heart and Brain in Music', in *Style and Idea*, 54.

[20] Joseph Straus comments that 'in cases like these Schoenberg is not so much revealing a motivic structure as imposing one'; *Remaking the Past*, 47.

that I have been assuming in this chapter, we should have to say that it is not; yet a serious effort of recomposition went into making it, and the result is a genuine aesthetic achievement. It is only because questions of identity do not ultimately matter that we can live with this result.

A contrasting case is that mentioned in Chapter 4: the orchestration of Chopin's C sharp minor Waltz, Op. 64 No. 2, which occurs as part of the collective effort known as *Les Sylphides*. The orchestrator discovers an implied inner voice in Chopin's original, and discreetly introduces it: the result is a new sound pattern. Yet it is one that moves as music just as the original moves. In a sense the result is the opposite of that achieved by Schoenberg: *another* work of music, but one in which we hear the same musical movement. Finally there is the case exemplified by Ravel's brilliant orchestration of Mussorgsky's *Pictures at an Exhibition*, in which new pitches and inner voices are supplied abundantly, while retaining the overall harmonic, melodic, and rhythmic structure. Here is a new work of music, which is new both acoustically and musically. Yet it is still heard as a *version* of Mussorgsky's original.

The most interesting cases are those in which, in order to preserve the *aesthetic* identity of an original, the transcriber is compelled to recompose it, introducing new pitches and patterns in order to re-create the old effect. An instructive instance is provided by the D minor Chaconne for solo violin by Bach. This is undeniably one of the most noble and profound utterances for solo violin in the history of music, and a remarkable study in implied harmony. Its effect of titanic strain, as of a giant Atlas, bearing the burden of the world's great sadness, is inseparable from the way in which the performer must stretch across the four strings of the instrument, to provide as many voices as can be produced by it, and to imply as many more. The performer's effort must be heard in the music, but heard too as *part* of the music. The brilliance of Bach's writing was precisely to achieve that effect: to make the difficulty of the piece into a quality of the music, rather than a matter of virtuosity. The music is intrinsically difficult, but not because it is showing off: rather, because difficulty is inseparable from its message.

This piece has been transcribed at least four times: for violin and piano by Schumann; for piano, left hand, by Brahms; for piano, two hands, by Busoni; and for full orchestra by Stokowski. Schumann's version is seldom performed, because it removes the tension from the piece. The implied harmonies are provided by the piano, so too are decorative passages of accompaniment; but the distribution of the difficult chords between the two instruments negates the sense of struggle. Brahms, by contrast, retains the aesthetic character, and his transcription is a model of its kind. By making the one hand stretch across the keyboard, and by filling in the harmonies to form chords that would naturally demand two hands for a comfortable performance, and which must therefore be arpeggiated, he re-creates the strain of Bach's original, and the expressive burden that goes with it. Moreover, he achieves this effect without separating the performer from the musical structure: the difficulty is experienced, as in Bach's original, as a property of the music. Busoni attempts something similar: although, in order to make the music sound as though it is reaching beyond the instrument, to a vaster space which cannot be captured by it, he must add embellishments of his own, massive octave doublings, chords of a vastness that all but drown the melodic line. The result is brilliant: but it is a new work of music, scarcely a transcription. The Brahms can still be heard as a transcription of Bach; the Busoni is definitely Bach–Busoni, as it is referred to in the repertoire. As for Stokowski's version: some would dismiss it as a vulgar travesty. But, in its own way, it remains faithful to the titanic original: the problem being that the individual players have an easy time of it, and only the conductor is strained.

All those transcriptions will count as new works of music, by the criterion that I have offered. But their relation to the original is not merely accidental: they are *versions* of it, attempts to realize, in another medium, its musical essence. Here we see a striving to reproduce a similar musical experience, through dissimilar sounds. Simply to play the notes of Bach's original on the piano would be to lose its effect: the result would be nothing, or next to nothing, as music. To arrange the original as Brahms does is to be *truer* to Bach's artistic intention than one could be simply by performing his violin score on the piano.

Transcriptions play an important part in a living musical culture, by placing instruments in dialogue, and making the repertoire into common property. They overcome the 'pathos of distance' of the concert hall, and democratize the musical experience. They also promote our sense that harmony, melody, and movement belong to the essence of music—while instrumentation is accidental.

This distinction between essence and accident involves a metaphor. Although Husserl imagined that we could find the 'essences' of things in the intentional realm, it is now apparent that, if there is any useful distinction to be made between essence and accident, it is in the material realm alone.[21] At the intentional level essence is no more than an *impression* of essence. Yet this factitious distinction between 'essence' and 'accident' informs our entire experience of music. If recordings present a challenge to our musical culture it is not so much that of 'mechanical reproduction'; it is rather that they make transcription superfluous, an optional addition to musicianship, instead

---

[21] See Husserl, *Ideas: General Introduction to Pure Phenomenology*, tr. W. R. Boyce Gibson (London, 1931), ch. 1. Modern ideas of essence involve a resuscitiation of the 'real essence' of Locke—as in S. Kripke, *Naming and Necessity*, and D. Wiggins, *Sameness and Substance* (Oxford, 1980).

of a necessary part of the distribution of the musical experience. By playing the Beethoven Symphonies in an arrangement for piano duet you come to understand them as tonal structures, in a way that is increasingly difficult for people whose only experience of these works is through polished performances on polished discs. For such people the distinction between essence and accident is beginning to fade from the musical experience. Beethoven's Sixth Symphony becomes inseparable in their memory from a particular performance, and no other performance sounds right to them. All features of that one performance are now essential; and therefore none are essential, since the distinction between essence and accident no longer applies. A fertile metaphor has gone from the world.

Paul Ziff has pointed out that, while we apply the concept of identity to both persons and works of music, we also distinguish *versions* of a single piece of music, but not versions of a person.[22] Indeed, the concept of the identity of the musical work—of numerical sameness of individual compositions—is of less importance to us than the concept of a version. We distinguish versions from departures, and our sense of one musical object as a version of another has an important part to play in the aesthetic experience. Performances are not versions; but versions are made for performance, and they reflect the need to descend from the abstract particular which is the work of music to the concrete event which is its realization, through intermediate steps which may themselves involve a creative act, an imaginative meditation on the original as the composer defined it.

The importance of versions is brought out by another musical practice—improvisation, which frequently takes a melody, a harmonic sequence, or some combination of those as its point of departure. An improvisation is a performance: it may be recorded, or even written down. But the listener should hear that this music is being created *now*, in the act of performance. The performance is not a realization of some independently existing prescription. It is the aesthetic object itself. But it is also an elaboration of musical ideas which have or could have an independent life. In the jazz repertoire, for example, we find many versions of a single idea (a melody, a sequence of harmonies), elaborated in such a way that it is precisely the elaboration that captures our attention.

This points to another difficulty in the way of the 'historically authentic performance'. Many pieces in the classical repertoire started life as improvisations, and were originally performed by musicians steeped in the art of improvisation, and ready at every moment to depart from a written score on some frolic of their own. If we are to perform Bach's pieces as they were performed in his day, we should entrust them only to players who had

---

[22] 'The Cow on the Roof', *Journal of Philosophy*, 70 (1973), 713–23.

mastered seventeenth-century harmony and counterpoint, whose fingers, feelings, and style have been shaped in the practice of improvisation as were those of Bach's contemporaries. But even if someone did learn, now, to improvise in such a way, he would be consciously improvising in a dead idiom, and the result would be imbued with an irony and inauthenticity that are wholly modern. In fact, our modern 'authentic' performers pay little or no attention to improvisation, and have no competence to sit before an audience, as Bach did or as a jazz musician might, and produce version upon version of some skeletal theme.

Improvisation, transcription, and arrangement acquaint us with another important distinction within the intentional realm—the distinction between musical material, and what is done with it. The world of tones is occupied by a variety of quasi-individuals—melodies, phrases, motifs, and harmonies—which are the primary objects of the experience of 'the same again'. Our understanding of music is shaped by our acquaintance with these quasi-individuals, which serve as the materials from which works are composed. They can be repeated, embellished, varied, transposed, orchestrated, while remaining in essence the same. Through such practices as transcription and improvisation we 'internalize' the experience of musical material: our feeling for the musical individual, the 'unit of significance', becomes robust and durable. In all of us melodies and harmonies reside as the enduring stuff of music, because we ourselves have transcribed them into our inner voice, and because we have acquired the habit of detaching them from the larger musical structures, and perceiving them as individuals.

A living musical culture is not merely a culture of performance. It involves arrangement, improvisation, embellishment—a constant creative playing with its own material. When this stance towards the material of music fades away, the experience of form also begins to suffer. We are amazed and exhilarated by Beethoven's formal achievements—like the first movement of the *Eroica*—because the material which they organize lives separately in us. *Le Marteau sans maître* gives no comparable experience, since it contains no recognizable material—no units of significance that can live outside the work that produces them. (Could there be an arrangement of *Le Marteau* for solo piano? A free improvisation for jazz combo? A set of variations for string quartet? A fragment whistled in the street?)

Notes towards a definition of Musical Culture

'A musical culture', in the apt words of Nicholas Cook, 'is a tradition of imagining sound as music.'[23] Such a tradition is founded in the following practices:

---

[23] *Music, Imagination and Culture* (Oxford 1990), 223. See also the illuminating reflections of R. Sessions, in *The Musical Experience of Composer, Performer, Listener* (Princeton, 1950), esp. 97–104.

1. Composition, which is the bringing into being not of musical works only, but also of the musical materials from which works are constructed. (Some composers are known, like Cole Porter, only for their tunes.)

2. Performance, which is of two kinds: the realization of a musical work in obedience to the composer's instructions, and free improvisation, which may have another work as its point of departure.

3. Making music together: the special kind of performance in which performers make music for their own pleasure, and move together in a manner that is mediated by the music.

4. Making music for others: the kind of performance in which an audience is involved, whether dancing or singing along, or silently listening.

5. Transcription, arrangement, and embellishment—practices which distribute material through all the forms and media of music.

6. The application of music to every-day life: in dance, song, work, and worship. This application would be impossible without the habit of arranging, embellishing, and improvising. That habit existed in Bach's day, and was one of the factors which created the unity between high and popular culture. Nowadays, the habit is confined to popular culture, while the performance of 'serious' music is steadily becoming ossified by scholarship. The cult of authentic performance is one sign of the divide between serious and popular music, and one sign of the impending death of a musical culture.

7. Listening, as the core experience of all participants—composer, performer, audience, and dancer—and the forum in which the musical object lives.

Those practices all contribute to the emergence of the phenomenon that I have been discussing in this book: the phenomenon of tone, as an intentional entity distinct from the material sound in which we hear it. As the shadow of scholarship falls across them, however, such practices lose their spontaneity. They are fully themselves only when lived, rather than merely studied. Were they to disappear, there would be nothing of music to study. There would be sounds, meticulously arranged according to pitch, temporal order, and timbre. There would be an elaborate art, or at least a science, of sound effects. But the habit of perceiving sounds as musical individuals, of hearing the movement that brings them to life, and understanding the form that fulfils their inner impulse—this habit would vanish.

15 *Culture*

The ways of poetry and music are not changed anywhere without change in the most important laws of the city.

(Plato, *Republic*, 4.424c)

When I work for a living, my activity is a means to an end: making money, or 'producing value', as the Marxists prefer. When I play, however, my activity is an end in itself. Play is not a means to enjoyment; it is the very thing enjoyed. And it provides the archetype of those activities in which man is 'at home with himself', sheltered from the anxieties of survival, as a child is sheltered by his protectors—activities like sport, conversation, ceremonies, festivals, and art. Schiller, noticing this fact, exalted play into his paradigm of intrinsic value. With the agreeable and the good, he remarked, man is merely in earnest; but with the beautiful he *plays*.[1]

There is an element of paradoxism in Schiller's remark. But you can extract from it a thought that is far from paradoxical. If every activity is a means to an end, then nothing has intrinsic value. The world is then deprived of its *sense*—it becomes a system of means without a meaning, in which we are caught up and enslaved by the accident of birth. If, however, there are activities that are engaged in for their own sakes, the world is restored to us, and we to it. Of these activities, we do not ask what they are *for*; they are sufficient in themselves. The sum of such activities composes a culture: by engaging in them we constitute the human world, transforming it from a system of means to one of ends, from an unchosen destiny to an elected home. Play, as Schiller suggests, is a paradigm case; and its association with childhood reminds us of the essential exhilaration and innocence that attend all 'disinterested' interest. If work becomes play—so that the worker is fulfilled in his work, as I am fulfilled in writing this book—then

[1] *Letters on the Aesthetic Education of Man*, tr. E. Wilkinson and L. A. Willoughby (Oxford, 1967), 105–6.

work ceases to be drudgery and becomes instead the 'restoration of man to himself'. Those last words are Marx's, and contain the core of his theory of 'unalienated labour'—a theory which came to him from Schiller, via Hegel and Feuerbach.

In order to understand such activities as play, conversation, or dancing, we must distinguish purpose from function. A sociobiologist will insist that play has a function: it is the safest way to explore the world, and to prepare the mind and body for the serious trials of later life. But its function is not its purpose. The child plays because he wants to play: play is its *own* purpose. Indeed, if you make the function into a purpose—playing for the sake of learning, say—then you cease to play. You are now, in Schiller's words, 'merely in earnest'. Likewise, the urgent man who converses in order to gain or impart some piece of information, to elicit sympathy, or to tell his story, has ceased to converse.

This distinction between function and purpose is most clearly shown by the core fact of every human culture, which is friendship. As I argued in Chapter 12, friendship has a function: it binds people together, making communities strong and durable; it brings advantages to those who are joined by it, and fortifies them in all their enterprises. But make those advantages into your purpose and friendship is gone. Friendship is a means to advantage, but only when not treated as a means. The same is true of everything worth while: love, learning, sport, and art itself. Meaning lies in intrinsic value; we possess it by finding the thing that interests us for its own sake; and such an interest must be disinterested, in the manner of every activity where we are not 'merely in earnest'. At the same time, intrinsic value, and the pursuit of it, are means to the highest human end: namely happiness—that elusive but abundant thing which we obtain only so long as we do not pursue it.

Culture and Religion

Art is the product of leisure; leisure the product of safety; and safety the product of friends—not those intimate friends whose faces fill one's day-to-day perception, but the others, most of them unknown, who will risk their lives when danger threatens, and who will uphold the law in times of peace. Only the assurance that such friends exist brings security to ordinary mortals; participation in a culture is one way of obtaining this assurance, since it is one way of seeing the world through the eyes of a 'first-person plural'.

In traditional societies, religious observance played a vital role in securing this first-person plural: indeed, if Durkheim is to be followed, this is the function of religious observance (although once again the function and the purpose do not, and cannot, coincide). Observance concerns our comportment in this world, our posture towards others and towards objects. It is manifest in the sanctity that attaches to custom and ceremony and to the objects, times, and places that are marked by them. It shows itself in the experience of awe, and in the fact that certain things are not to be done, not to be touched, not to be spoken of, regardless of the calculations that prompt us to disobey. Religious observance fills the mind with ideas of purity and defilement, and gives to the moral decree its force of absolute command, turning temperance to chastity, courage to martyrdom, and justice to the extremes of self-denial. For the secular spirit good is opposed to bad; for the religious spirit, good is opposed to evil. While each may pursue the good and avoid its opposite, only the religious spirit feels the repugnance and the pollution that we know as the sense of sin. Only the religious person experiences his condition as 'fallen' and, in that very experience, feels a longing and a hope that transcend the boundaries of everyday morality.

Anthropologists have described many kinds of religious observance. Despite the diversity, we can discern an interesting pattern, which is roughly this:

First, the experience of pollution, separation, or 'fall': the sense that I am cast out and excluded, through some fault for which I must atone. Sometimes this is a moral fault—a crime that would be recognized as such even without the vantage point of religion. Often, however, the religion that cures the fault also creates it—as with the Greek *miasma*, or with the pollution that comes from eating some forbidden animal, or with the idea of 'original sin' (i.e. of a fault that is mine by nature, and inescapable).

Second, the *sacrifice*, which is the primary ingredient in the process of atonement. Something is 'offered' at the altar, though not necessarily to anyone in particular; and this offering is a custom, regularly repeated and framed by ceremonial gestures.

Third, the *ritual*, which transforms the offering from a 'natural' object into something 'supernatural' and holy. Ritual is shrouded in the sanctity that it creates. Its words and gestures are archaic, mysterious, and all the more imperative because they have come down to us unexplained. The voice of our ancestors speaks through the ritual, and the one who seeks to change or distort what is done at the altar commits the primary act of sacrilege. Ritual is therefore understood as the visible presence of a supernatural power.

Fourth, by a wondrous inversion, which is perhaps the archetype of all miracles, the sacrifice becomes a *sacrament*, something offered *from* the altar to the mortal who offers it, and which translates him from pollution to purity, from separation to communion, from fall to redemption. I give the god to himself, in order to receive him.

I do not say that such a pattern is displayed by all religions: but it provides the central experience in our own tradition, and is the theme, whether revealed or hidden, of much Western art. It enables us to understand, not only the proximity of religious and aesthetic experience, but the role of each in defining and sustaining a common culture.

The religious experience is not disinterested—at least, not in the manner of the aesthetic experience. We do not participate in religious rites merely so as to contemplate their meaning in the detached way that we would contemplate a play or a painting. We are genuine *participants*, who are engaged for the sake of our salvation and with a view to the truth. Nevertheless, there are interesting similarities with the aesthetic experience. Although the purpose of an act of worship lies beyond the moment—in the form of a promised salvation, a revelation, or a restoration of the soul's natural harmony—it is not entirely separable from the experience. God is *defined* in the act of worship far more precisely than he is defined by any theology, and this is why the forms of the ceremony are so important. Changes in the liturgy take on a momentous significance for the believer, for they are changes in his experience of God.

The religious rite resembles the aesthetic experience in other ways too. It is inexhaustible and endlessly renewable. The person who goes once to Mass, and comes away with the thought 'now I know what it means, and I need not go again', either has not seen the point of it, or else does not believe. Even if he is able thereafter to remember every gesture and every word; even if he gives the most subtle and persuasive commentary on the associated theology and doctrine, he still has not understood the ritual. The meaning of the Mass is inseparable from the experience and must, for the believer, be constantly renewed. You enter the frame of mind in which you 'cannot have enough of it'; not because you look forward to it—on the contrary, you might, like Amfortas, dread it to the point of preferring death—but because you belong to it, and it to you.

There is another, and more elusive, comparison between the aesthetic and the religious. The subjective nature of aesthetic experience goes hand in hand with an implied idea of community: in thinking everything away except this unique and present object, and in addressing myself to it with all my interests discounted, I am also opening my mind to its meaning—not for me only, but for the kind of which I am a member. The aesthetic experience is a lived encounter between object and subject, in which the subject takes on a universal significance. The meaning that I find in the object is the meaning that it has for all who live like me, for all members of my 'imagined community', who share our 'first-person plural' and whose joys and sufferings are mirrored in me. As Kant puts it,[2] aesthetic judgement makes appeal to a 'common sense': it frees me from the slavish attachment to my own desires. I come to see myself as one member of an implied community, whose life is present and vindicated in the experience of contemplation.

---

[2] *Critique of Judgement*, tr. J. C. Meredith (Oxford, 1952), pt 1, sect. 20.

In the religious experience too there is an implied but partly absent community: for the religious rite implicates not the living only, but the dead and the unborn. The religious stories concern people long since departed; the ceremony of participation unites me with my own dead, and also with those who have not yet been born. Changes in the ritual are disturbing, partly because they suggest that the community may be cut short by time, that the words and gestures that I employ are no better than provisional, and that we shall all be forgotten. They threaten the authoritative nature of the first-person plural by which I am subsumed. Ritual has a timeless quality, for it affirms the community as something permanent, absolved from death and decay. It is essentially life-affirming, even when, and especially when, as in a funeral, it comes face to face with death.

I remarked that the religious rites and ceremonies are means to salvation, and not ends in themselves. But my brief survey of the phenomena suggests that this is too simple an account. For it is only through their *intrinsic* value that the rituals obtain this redemptive quality. The recital of the sacred text, the performance of the sacred rites, and the offering of the sacred gifts are *mysteries*, things which are intrinsically meaningful, but whose meaning cannot be openly expressed. Religion consists in the performance of these things, punctiliously and for their own sakes, without thought for what is gained. (That is what is meant by 'piety'.) The doctrine of salvation is a kind of metaphor: a way of presenting the believer with a full sense of what is at stake in the performance of holy actions.

The term 'culture' has been appropriated for two distinct but related ends. The anthropologist uses it to mean the customs and rituals that seal the bond of membership—the 'common culture' that distinguishes 'us' from 'them'. The critic uses the term to mean the expression of the human spirit in art, architecture and aesthetic convention—the 'high culture' that may not be common to every member of the community, and which may reflect the peculiar conventions of a courtly or *haut bourgeois* lifestyle. This might lead us to think that the term is simply ambiguous, and that when critics write of cultural decline they are referring to a process that could occur while leaving the rest of social order quite unaffected. In fact, however, almost all those who write about the fate of high culture see it as integrally connected to the fate of society. Like Adorno or Leavis, they regard high culture as symptomatic of social life, and offer diagnoses which purport to show why it matters, not just to the connoisseur but also to the philistine, that poetry or music should have suffered some calamitous decline. The above sketch of the religious experience helps to explain this attitude. The religious experience is the archetype of all experiences of membership—of all those experiences which are essentially 'shared', and which affirm the first-person plural that protects and endorses our endeavours. Yet its seat in the human psyche is adjacent to that of the aesthetic experience: it involves a comparable search for meaning, and a comparable straining to hear, in the most intimate experience, the distant voices of the tribe. Here are two versions of the 'dance of sympathy'. And the difference between them is explained largely by the fact that, in the religious experience, the 'real presence' comes through faith, while in aesthetic experience it depends upon imagination. Hence the value of aesthetic experience in modern life: that which we could otherwise obtain only through grace (as a gift of faith), we can summon here by an act of will.

Art and Allusion

In *The Birth of Tragedy*, Nietzsche speculates on the religious origin of tragedy, and comes up with the following suggestion. The worshippers of Dionysus cast off their worldly concerns and join in a dance. This dance is an invocation of the god and he is present in it. All music derives from this desire to dance together, in a community that embraces each of us, and cancels our separation. The chorus that we form tells us the story of the god; and also the story of those who separate themselves from the pure communion, so as to embark on some fatal project of their own. Out of the dance there steps the tragic hero, whose fate appals and fascinates his fellow dancers in the chorus. He acts apart, affirms himself, and is destroyed, sinking back into the unity from which he briefly emerged, purged by death of his 'original sin', which was the sin of originality. There lies the consolation of the tragic dance, that the individual transgression is enacted at a distance, accepted, and at last overcome.

The same experience can be repeated in the theatre. The audience dances by proxy, through the chorus of the play. The tragic hero is the centre of the represented action. The god himself has been quietly hidden away. But it is essentially the same experience. And maybe it is the same experience when a priest recounts the tale of Christ's passion, reminds his congregation of their sins and the separation from God that sin engenders, and then invites them to a common 'sacrifice'. In each case the same story is told: the ideal community, the act that separates us (whether error or sin), and the ultimate restoration as the community is reconstituted—not now a community of the living, but one that includes the dead and the unborn. The tragic hero who passes over to the dead is like the worshipper who joins them in his worship.

I have extemporized on Nietzsche's pregnant suggestion, since it takes us again over the ground that we have just crossed, and helps us to see it from another perspective—that of a society in which high culture and common culture were not, as they are for us, distinct realms of experience, but part of a continuous social engagement, whose essence was the life-affirming religion of polytheism. The use that Nietzsche himself makes of those ideas is not one that I endorse. Nevertheless, he saw that the aesthetic experience belongs with the religious experience—and hoped, in his later philosophy, to vest in the aesthetic all that the religious could no longer contain. At the same time, he went on to misread the aesthetic experience as a *defiance* of the 'herd', a means to rediscover in solitude and isolation the strength of spirit that comes to ordinary mortals only when united in a crowd, and only when fortified by a doctrine that undermines the threatening presence of the hero. The insightfulness of *The Birth of Tragedy* resides precisely in what the later writings deny: the perception that the aesthetic experience contains the very same intimation of community that is contained in the experience of religion. A light shines from it into the inner realm, dispelling our isolation, and outlining the otherwise hidden forms of common sentiments. That which is revealed to me in aesthetic experience is revealed as inalienably mine, and also as yours and his and hers: as the common property of all who enter the dance of sympathy. This, I believe, is the *cultural* significance of the silent audience in the concert hall, as it is of the silent listener at home. And it also explains the compelling need for applause in the concert hall: the need for the audience to release into the public air the enormous weight of social emotion that has grown in silence.

If we see aesthetic experience in this way, we begin to understand why allusion and elusiveness are such important components of its object. To explain is to alienate: it is to show something as 'outside', observed but not internalized, as in an historical narrative or a scientific textbook. It is to prefer conception to experience. Allusions, unlike explanations, automatically import a social context—common knowledge, common references, common symbols—which are embodied together in a common experience. In understanding an allusion we become maximally aware of the community which the experience of meaning implies.

An allusion is designed to be noticed: it expressly summons one work into the orbit of another. The author need assume no prior knowledge of his source; for he may himself take charge of his reader's education, as did Eliot with the footnotes to the *Waste Land*, and with the wonderful essays through which he rewrote the canon of English Literature. Allusions exploit familiarity, and also create it, binding the literary culture into a many-stranded web. Literary forms are themselves allusive: heroic couplets point the English reader to Dryden and Pope, as does the sonnet to Shakespeare, Donne, and Wordsworth; while the unrhymed pentameters of Tennyson stand in the shadow of Milton, looking constantly upwards to that towering presence. The intentions of the author play with the expectations of the reader; and it is thus that a literary culture arises, as a complex meditation on the givenness of human life.

Allusion may be used to make a contrast—as in Pope's allusion to *Paradise Lost*, in Book II of the *Dunciad*:

> High on a gorgeous seat that far outshone
> Henley's gilt tub, or Fleckno's Irish throne,
> Or that where on her Curlls the Public pours
> All bounteous, fragrant grains, and golden showers,
> Great Tibbald sat.

Here the allusion to Satan in his majesty conveys a complex judgement on Tibbald, and also reinforces the view that these minor talents are minor precisely through their self-esteem—through the sin of pride. But allusion may be used to opposite effect, as in Eliot's reference, through style and imagery, to the Brunetto Latini passage in *Inferno*, in the last of *Four Quartets*. The 'familiar compound ghost' is the creature of sustained allusion, the spirit of European civilization itself, flitting through the ruined wartime dawn, to urge on us the strange thought that this hell is proof of our salvation.

Rather than study our own tradition, however, it is more pertinent to take an unfamiliar literary culture—a culture whose inward vision must be understood from outside. Consider, then, the Japanese haiku—that mysterious seventeen-syllable utterance, in which a whole world is suggested by words that refrain from describing it. Here is an example by Shigeyori:[3]

> yaa shibaraku
> hana ni taishite
> kane tsuku koto
>
> Hey there, wait a moment
> before you strike the temple bell
> at the cherry blossoms.

To understand this poem you must capture the allusion to the Noh play *Miidera*, and also to a certain poem in the classical anthology entitled *Shin Kokinshu*. In the first of these a madwoman, about to strike the temple bell, is stopped by a priest with the words 'Hey there, wait a minute! What are you, a mad woman, doing striking the bell?' (a speech which, in the original, contains all the words of the first line and the third). The poem from the *Shin Kokinshu* supplies the remaining words: it describes the fall of cherry blossoms at evening while the temple bell is struck. The reader must experience the fusion of these two allusions in a single revelation: the striking of the temple bell, which is the symbol of eternal things, becomes the very act of madness that precipitates the fall of mortal beauty. Without the allusions, it is impossible for these words to convey such a meaning: with them, they

---

[3] Taken from D. Keene: *World within Walls: Japanese Literature of the Pre-Modern Era 1600–1867* (London 1977). Shigeyori's haiku is deviant, in containing six syllables in the final line, instead of five.

suggest not only a poignant thought about the human condition, but also a community of people who share this thought, and who are comforted by sharing it.

A high culture flourishes by drawing on such connections: by creating artistic paradigms and a fund of expressive artefacts which identify and enlarge the responses of educated people. It exists through the constant exercise of taste—the matching of one word or gesture to another, of one experience to another, according to a sense of what is appropriate, decorous, or revealing. Through taste we strive to realize the implied community which gives sense to the aesthetic experience: our matching of thought to thought and image to image is also a matching of person to person, the active creation of the first-person plural to which we aspire.

This process of matching informs all the higher forms of social life—not only art, but also games, jokes, ceremonies, and customs. Another Japanese example is instructive—the ancient game called 'listening to incense' (*ko wo kiku*), in which one person mixes incense, while others try to match its scent with a line from the classics. This is an instance of something that we have already encountered in the realm of music: a metaphor which is not even a word—in this case a perfume predicated of a state of mind, itself identified by allusion. And the point of the game lies in the confederacy of sentiment that it expresses and inspires.

Jokes too, which provide the most vivid examples in daily life of the exercise of taste, depend upon allusion, and when we laugh at them, it is because we discover through them that we *belong*: we find ourselves *with* the joke, seeing the world from the same communal eyes, and suddenly at home even in what is most absurd and incongruous. Wit is not what Pope says it is—'what oft was thought, but ne'er so well express't'—since true wit creates the thought with its expression. The matching of words in the witty remark is an inseparable part of the thought—it creates a verbal cadence, which is also a posture towards reality.

Wit propagates the sense of membership. Like a flash of lightning, an allusion shows avenues beyond the present moment, crowded already with our listening fellows. It brings us back from our solitude, into a world of public discourse and shared experience. All art is thus; and all styles develop allusively. Genres and forms are established by the echoes which are heard in them, and which give normality and naturalness to the metres, rhymes, and verse schemes of a literary tradition.

The process is not confined to words. In every sphere where the aesthetic understanding is employed, allusion claims its sovereign overview. Nothing illustrates this fact so well as the classical tradition in European architecture—a system of visual reference and cross-reference of unparalleled power and simplicity, which has endured through renewals and variations, for 3,000 years. The classical idiom exerts its power even over those who have not studied it, offering satisfaction to the ignorant eye as much as to the eye of the expert. The Orders, with their proportions and details, implant themselves in the perceiving psyche. Plinth, cornice, entablature, column, capital, and mouldings serve not merely to mark out the proportions of the walls and the juncture of the storeys. They divide the building into intelligible sections, invest it with light and contrast, create a play of shadows and a minute life of familiar detail, so that the wall is simultaneously in motion before us, and serenely at rest. Anyone who has witnessed the effect, however unconsciously, has absorbed a visual repertoire, the first move in a constantly evolving game of echo and allusion. The Orders have been described as a language—but the term is as misleading here as it is when used of tonality. In the classical styles of architecture we witness something more flexible and more complex than a body of grammatical rules: we witness a *tradition*, developing under the ceaseless impulse of the allusive sensibility, and endowing the city street with the life and outlook of an imagined community of people. The classical styles provide a background to the city's unceasing industry, standing amid the bustle of present life with the posture of permanent things—the real presence amid the living of the unborn and the dead.

What I have said about allusion, community, and taste applies equally to music. But because music reaches across the boundaries created by language, it seems to effect an enlargement of our world-view, a reaching out to others whom we could understand in no other way than this one, through their spontaneous absorption into the dance of sympathy. Stravinsky was inclined to the view that a musical culture requires the kind of aristocratic audience which, he imagined, had created through its patronage the *bon goût* of the classical style.[4] In so arguing he failed to take into account the many *uses* of music outside the court—the universalizing tendency of music, as it flows into every activity and into every corner of the human world, with the same resistless impulse as the market economy. Although it is true that the European aristocracy did much to support and encourage the development of our music, it depended, in this as in everything, on the bourgeois, who provided the goods. A musical culture arises because people associate in order to make and listen to music. It exists, as all art exists, by virtue of the surplus which creates the conditions of leisure. It therefore depends on the market, on the division of labour, on the manifold achievement of economic cooperation, whereby man has freed himself for some hours in every day from the arduous task of self-reproduction. (When Pascal tells us that all man's troubles come from his inability to sit quietly at a desk, he forgets the communal effort that was required to produce that desk, and the leisure of the one who sits at it.)

[4] *Poetics of Music*, 73–5, 117–19.

The process of cooperation whereby people generate a durable surplus is the very same process as that which creates the town—the commercial centre in which people of different classes, different interests, even different languages, come together in order to exchange their goods. The town is the solvent of human differences, the only conceivable forum in which sympathies can be constantly enlarged. The idea of universal humanity emerged in the European Enlightenment, not through the aristocracy, but through the encounter of the aristocrats with their bourgeois mentors. It is in honour of this idea that townsmen devote so much energy to constructing churches, assembly halls, ballrooms, and theatres. Into these institutions the spirit of music is injected: it is sung in church, whistled at work, danced to in the ballroom, and played in private and public gatherings. It is the universal idiom which, being 'free from concepts', can be understood by anyone who is open to the influence of the surrounding world. And it is through the diverse uses of music in the universalizing culture of the European city that the manifold allusiveness of music arose. We recognize the various dance forms; we distinguish a march from a gallop; we know the ancestral meaning of trumpet and horn, the harmonies of hymns and the chorale melodies which come to us through the works of Bach. This constantly developing repertoire of musical uses ensures that our music is multiply allusive, that scarcely a chord or a phrase can be composed without at once summoning a web of cross-reference, and without gesturing to the new form of community—the community beyond language—which is the great achievement of bourgeois civilization.

Here we can at last lay to rest the idea of tonality as a language—a system of quasi-syntactical rules, organizing the notes of music in ways that happen to please us, but which are in themselves as baseless and a priori as any syntax, and which therefore may be discarded in favour of some newer and fresher idiom. Tonality is no more a language than is the classical idiom in architecture. It is a tradition, developing by echo and allusion, so as to comprehend ever-wider and more varied applications of its living movement. If we can capture in a system of rules the immense body of knowledge contained in the tonal tradition, then this a fortunate accident. The rules will be a summary of past practice, rather than prescriptions for the future; tonality itself will be neither constrained nor explained by them.

And if a Schoenberg should declare that this old language is now unmeaning, he will no more be able to replace it with a new set of rules than tonality itself could survive by such a prescriptive method. The new rules will be merely arbitrary until they have grown beyond rules, to become a tradition of self-perpetuating allusions, in which the listener recognizes not only the call of tone to tone across the space of music, but also the call to himself, as the spiritual medium in which all this commotion occurs.

Thoughts on Adorno

Among the many writers who have meditated on what they have taken to be the decline of musical culture in the modern world, few have been more influential than Theodor Adorno, whose extraordinary attempt to explain the banality, as he saw it, of the tonal idiom through a Marxian critique of capitalist society, has inspired not only musical modernists, but also all the many writers and composers who have associated the avant-garde in art with the revolutionary vanguard in politics. It may no longer be necessary to argue against the Marxian theory of history. But it is still pertinent to defend the bourgeois order, and to oppose the naïve idea—fostered by countless modern writers from Matthew Arnold to Jean-Paul Sartre—that bourgeois culture is essentially philistine, and that the ways of 'getting and spending' are inimical to the higher life.

Adorno's claim is that late capitalism has generated, as part of its ideology, a 'mass culture', the function of which is to distract people from the truth of their condition, and to provide them with a blanket of sentimental clichés. This mass culture contains an important musical component, derived from the last degenerate platitudes of the tonal language. This provides, in the place of the true musical object, a kind of 'fetish', an illusory substitute for musical thought, which demands nothing of the listener beyond a cheerful acquiescence in its sugary harmonies and undemanding rhythms, so that the listener adopts the line of least resistance, to become a 'willing purchaser' of the consumer product.[5] In such a situation, the artist must 'reflect without concessions everything that society prefers to forget'.[6] He must be a modernist, working in conscious defiance of the 'culture-industry', in order to break the spell of domination that is contained in the musical fetish. For Adorno, this meant that the modern composer must adopt the twelve-tone system of Schoenberg, achieving a complete emancipation from tonality and its pernicious charms, so reversing the 'confiscation of art' which had proceeded apace through the nineteenth century, as bourgeois culture gradually colonized the aesthetic impulse in order to satisfy the needs of a new dominant class.

The musical fetish, in Adorno's conception, has ceased to be art and become *ideology*. Ideology is a mask, a system of illusions, which serves to veil the historical nature of the social reality. Fetishized music promotes the false consciousness that rests content with a less-than-human existence, and which endows exploitation with the changeless authority of nature. True art

---

[5] *Über der Fetischcharakter in der Musik*, in *Dissonanzen: Musik in der verwalteten Welt* (Gottingen, 1956), tr. in A. Arato and E. Gebhardt (eds.), *The Essential Frankfurt School Reader* (New York, 1978), 78.

[6] *Philosophy of Modern Music*, 14.

sees through this veil, and is therefore a critical force; to understand it is also to understand the imperfection of our present arrangements, and to see beyond them to the possibilities of change.

I offer that as the briefest summary of a position that is embellished by Adorno, Horkheimer, and Bloch with many baroque variations, and many suggestive asides. But it captures the aspect of the Frankfurt school that has become a musicological commonplace. It also contains the two ideas that I wish to refute, and whose persistence has been especially damaging: the idea of mass culture as a 'bourgeois' product, and of modernism as the only available answer to it. The first of those ideas is based in a sociological theory, the second in a philosophy of art.

The sociological theory tells us that capitalism, and the rise of the bourgeois class, has produced an ever-enlarging gulf between serious art and mass entertainment, the first designed for the connoisseur, the second produced as an ideological sop for the exploited masses. Adhering to the Marxian typology of events, Adorno locates the transition to capitalism at the end of the eighteenth century, arguing that *The Magic Flute* is the last work of music in which high and popular culture coincide.[7]

If that theory were true, we should expect to find an extensive 'pop' culture emerging in the nineteenth century, whose adherents shun the concert hall and the opera-house, and whose favourite music employs only facile harmonies, automatic rhythms, and catchy melodies, avoiding all pretence at musical form. But we do not find this at all. What Adorno says of *The Magic Flute* could with more reason be said of *Hänsel und Gretel* or *Porgy and Bess*; while the popular music of the nineteenth century was to a great extent the product of the harmonic, melodic, and formal discoveries of the classical tradition—consider, for example, the Strauss family, Gilbert and Sullivan, Balfe, or Offenbach, whose *Tales of Hoffmann* is not only a paradigm of popular entertainment, but also an unforgettable work of art. This popular culture has been eclectic, adopting with the same cheerful catholicity the latest parlour song and the piano transcriptions of Liszt. But such is the nature of popular culture, founded as it is on intuitive rather than reflective judgement. Like every living culture, it soon tires of what is merely fashionable, and finds itself, in time, with a repertoire of genuine masterpieces, such as the waltzes of Johann Strauss the younger, and the operettas of Offenbach.

If you ask yourself seriously, when the transformation of popular music began, the answer would surely be in the twentieth century, with the reduction of the jazz and blues tradition to a set of repeatable melodic and

---

[7] A strange judgement, incidentally, of an opera which hides its meaning from popular perception. See J. Chailley, *The Magic Flute, Masonic Opera*, tr. H. Weinstock (London, 1972).

harmonic formulae, held together by a continuous 'beat'. This was not a bourgeois phenomenon at all, and had less to do with the triumph of capitalism than with the triumph of democracy. Nor does it illustrate the need for an 'ideological' music with which to mollify the exploited masses. The masses themselves produced this music—and a version of it arose in every quarter of the civilized world, including those 'socialist countries' whose official policy was to unite popular and serious music in a common, forward-looking idiom (a policy which made popular music tedious and serious music banal). There is no simple explanation as to why this new form of music arose, although clearly the invention of gramophone and radio had something to do with it, as did the rise of the new democratic man, whose belief that he is entitled to his tastes, however uninstructed, has undermined the confidence of high culture, and questioned its claim to be 'higher'. It is precisely because people have been freed from 'domination'—that is, from a society constrained from above—that the mass culture of which Adorno complains is here to stay. High culture is now the province of a minority; those with ears must guard them from the white noise of modern life, and exercise them only in private, or among those like-minded listeners whom they encounter in the concert hall. It is the *collapse* of bourgeois culture that has brought about the situation that Adorno deplores—the loss of that spontaneous habit of domestic music-making and collective singing which made our ancestors so acutely aware of the voice in music, and so eager to harmonize melodies with counter-melodies, and to provide a bass-line which was something more than a summary of a sequence of chords.

As for Adorno's second claim, it seems to me to reflect a romantic misconception. Art cannot be the critical instrument that he requires it to be, simply by defying the aesthetic expectations of those whom it seeks to criticize. If Schoenberg was a critic of bourgeois musical culture, then he was a singularly ineffective one. For his music has been received only to the extent that it has found its place in the great 'bourgeois' tradition—the tradition of concert-hall and opera-house; while his experiments in atonality are the study of a small band of bourgeois intellectuals, many of them academic representatives, like Milton Babbitt, of the new 'leisure class'. Avant-gardism invariably leads, in time, to the loss of an audience. And since music exists only as heard, it is ontologically dependent upon the audience that will enjoy it, and therefore on a living musical culture. Avant-gardism can therefore never be the key to aesthetic renewal.

I do not intend this as a criticism of Schoenberg's music—who can doubt the genius of the composer who gave us *A Survivor from Warsaw* or *Moses and Aaron*? But we must take seriously, I believe, the very situation that Schoenberg dramatized in that last work—the situation in which the audience is lost to deeper meanings, and the meanings themselves decay, becoming a residue and a burden in the consciousness of the one who seeks to express them, lacking as he does the voice that would make them live for others.

Avant-gardism should be understood, I believe, as the last gasp of a romantic illusion: the illusion of the artist as separated from society, possessed of new and astonishing truths which raise him above the lives of ordinary mortals and endow him with the attributes of judgement: a scourge and a redeemer to whom all is secretly permitted. As the Romantic movement lost its initial confidence, it strove to perpetuate itself in both art and politics, by contrasting its ambitions with the dullness and subjection of the ordinary 'bourgeois' world. *Épater le bourgeois* became the signature of the disaffected artist, the guarantee of his social credentials, whereby he demonstrated his aristocratic entitlement and his contempt for the rising middle class. Under the dual influence of Marx and Flaubert, the bourgeois emerged from the nineteenth century transformed out of all recognition from his humble origins. He was the 'class enemy' of Leninist dogma, the creature whom we are commanded by history to destroy; he was also the philistine, the enemy of the artistic spirit, the one who negated through his all-pervasive mediocrity, the sole remaining path to human salvation—the path of art. It is *against* this caricature of the bourgeois that the avant-garde has always defined itself, often accompanying its aggressive posturing with the fiction that the avant-garde is inwardly at one with the proletariat, the uncomprehended champion of the uncomprehending oppressed. These romantic illusions can be seen at work in Apollinaire and Breton, in Brecht and Sartre, and in Adorno too.

The avant-garde defines itself against the bourgeois, and therefore creates the bourgeois as the fictional object of a renewable contempt. This negative self-identity explains what is perhaps the most curious feature of the musical avant-garde in our century: its use of technicalities, both theoretical and practical, in the justification of its novel sounds. Serialism should not be understood as the 'emancipation of the dissonance', for, as I have argued, that emancipation never occurred. It should be seen as a kind of elaborate *pretence* at musical discipline: a congeries of rules, canons, and theories, and a mock exactitude (manifest at its most comic in the scores of Stockhausen and the set-theoretic musicology of Babbitt and Forte) which strives in vain to overcome the listener's sense of the arbitrariness and senselessness of what he hears. The affectation of artistic order is a mask for an inner disorder. True musical constraint depends not on intellectual systems, but on custom, habit, and tradition—on the forms of a common musical culture which create the currency of allusion. It depends, in short, precisely on the 'bourgeois' audience which the avant-garde set out to destroy.

We should see Adorno's hostility to that bourgeois audience in the quasi-theological terms that I earlier used to describe the aesthetic experience. Observing the world of commodity capitalism, and finding in it only a 'fetishized' art, and an illusory community, Adorno summoned the new music as a spiritual purge. The serial language had been purified of 'ideological' devices, while the language of tonality had become a mystifying fetish. Inevitably, therefore, Adorno romanticized the avant-garde, believing that its idiom was essentially free from ideology, as the idiom of science is free. It gives us the *truth* of our condition, without the mystifying images. Moreover, it contains the promise of a new community, a community of the liberated. Its secret aim is social revolution. Atonality becomes, in Adorno's fraught and *klagende* prose, the harbinger of a new religion, in which people will see one another as they really are. The very gestures wherewith the avant-garde offends the people, show it to be the peoples' friend. One may sympathize with this: but is it not also a tissue of illusions, as blind to social realities as the anti-bourgeois posturings of a Foucault or a Sartre?

Adorno pinned his hopes (which were not hopes at all, but only the wistful frame around his imprecations) on the proletarian revolution. This Messianic transformation was to loosen the chains of false consciousness, and its musical avatar had been sent to us in the twelve-tone idiom of Schoenberg. Belief in the revolution was the last great religious idea of our civilization— and the most dangerous, in conscripting religious feeling to an earthly cause. Yet, precisely because it was to be tested in the human world, the idea quickly lost its congregation. The emancipation of mankind has occurred— not by revolution, which has only retarded the process, but by the relentless working of those forces against which Adorno's heart rebelled: 'bourgeois' democracy, the free market, and the mass media which confer an equal value on every person, since each of us is no less than a customer and also no more. Only in the places where revolution triumphed, was the vision preserved of that higher and more spiritual life which is the object and the source of artistic feeling. But it was preserved in the catacombs, a secret shrine at which to pour out all the grief and anguish which were the poisoned gift of revolution. We encounter this vision in Arvo Pärt and Henryk Górecki; elsewhere, however, it has vanished—vaporized in the noonday sun of capitalist democracy.[8]

At the same time, Adorno sets before us a great and pressing problem: the problem of cultural renewal. How, if at all, can a musical culture be renewed in the face of decay: or is every cultural decline a terminal decline, as the Spenglerians would argue? Although there is a limit to what a philosopher can say in answer to that question, it is so pressing that the argument of this book would be seriously incomplete if I were to ignore it.

[8] Those last sentences summarize an experience that is hard to convey in a work of philosophy—even though philosophers need to be familiar with it. I therefore refer the reader to a work in which I have tried to convey the experience more directly, 'The Seminar', in *A Dove Descending and Other Stories* (London, 1991).

In *Die Meistersinger* Wagner portrays, in schematic form, the components of a musical culture—although it is a culture that stands in need of a restoring hand. In the idealized bourgeois community of Nuremberg music serves as a lingua franca, uniting and harmonizing the many occupations upon which the life of the town depends. There is a division of labour, and a division of musical labour too, in this perfected market economy. But the labour has become mechanical, and the wholeness of rational conduct is jeopardized. The apprentice David provides to the aristocratic interloper Walther a touching decription of the current musical conventions: the frozen ornaments of a local style, in which variety is also a monstrous uniformity. Each idiom, each detail, each constraint, participates in a common musical substance—the substance of tonality, whereby these diverse musical entities are brought together into a harmonious whole. Tonality is the symbol of the broader harmony of the town, the invisible hand of cooperation which is the true gift of a bourgeois culture. But tonality has exhausted itself—or at any rate, the tonality of Nuremberg.

Walther therefore looks on the musical life of Nuremberg with contempt, seeing in it no more than its shabby provinciality, its arbitrariness, and its monotonous sameness of flavour. The rules which David teaches to him are no more than the ossified remainders of practices which impede the artistic impulse, and place a barrier between him and the prize: the muse Eva (who is, however, the daughter of Nuremberg's leading citizen). His own musical idiom separates him from the hidebound burghers. His is a free-flowing, constantly modulating, unstructured melody, in which the principal ingredient is feeling—or so it seems to him. When at last he contemptuously rejects the title of 'Master', and with it the civic pride of the Nurembergers, it is in order to show his freedom from the pettifogging constraints of a dead musical tradition—a tradition that had 'become banal'. For a moment he stands isolated, sole member of an aristocratic avant-garde.

But what had brought him to this point? Only the persuasive power of his song, which had carried the people with it, establishing its reality as music by creating the audience that would hear it as such. Walther's success lay in the creation of an intelligible musical idiom. In being understood, however, his song became part of the culture that he had spurned. When Hans Sachs rebukes the Junker for his haughtiness, he gestures to the meaninglessness of an art that has no audience, an art that defies the community of listeners, and the local attachments that unite them. Such an art, he implies, is nothing in itself, and also, in its nothingness, a kind of cancer in society. By scorning the common culture of the town, it scorns also the social existence which makes culture of any kind possible. The aristocratic contempt for the market-place is a two-edged weapon which, wounding the community, wounds also itself. For it damages the common life upon which all individual gestures, however original, however sublime, depend for their significance.

Ex. 15.1 (a) Wagner, *Die Meistersinger*, theme of the Mastersingers; (b) Beethoven, Diabelli Variations, Op. 120, first variation

Walther acquiesces, and receives his reward. And in truth he has deserved it. For throughout the opera, fragments of his *endlose Melodei*—turns of phrase, chromatic questions and answers, a free restlessness of ornament and rhythm—have been slowly seeping into the surrounding music, and rescuing it from the exhaustion of which it stood accused. The chorus begins again, and reaffirms the mutual dependence of the old and the new, the original and the conventional, reminding us that the pompous C major theme of the Mastersingers, with its melodic and harmonic allusion to Beethoven's first Diabelli variation, is, in fact, the natural bass-line to Walther's song (Exx. 15.1, 15.2 and 15.3). Tonality triumphs, and, in its triumph, is also transformed. Such, Wagner masterfully suggests, is the process of cultural renewal—not a defiance of the moribund tradition, but a breathing into it of life—not alien life either, but life that is natural to it. The implication is that, if our musical culture is to continue, it is not by discarding tonality, but by renewing it.

Historicity and Aesthetic Judgement

It is surely evident that culture—whether high or low, aristocratic or popular—is a historical phenomenon, not merely in the sense that it comes into being and passes away, but in the more interesting sense that it develops in response to itself, and by reflection on its own past and achievements. But this historicity also contains a paradox. What people value in one period they may find ridiculous in the next; and what today seems dignified and honourable may tomorrow seem senseless and corrupt. But to the one who has them, values are universal, indefeasible, absolute, and transhistorical. The Marxian resolves this paradox through the theory of ideology: the values of

Ex. 15.2. Wagner, *Die Meistersinger*, prize song, first version, as 'love' motif

Ex. 15.3. Exx. 15.1 (*a*) and 15.2 together

an epoque exist through their function, which is to consolidate the economic infrastructure. They can perform this function only if they are accorded the absolute status that transforms them from wishes to commands. Nevertheless their claim to absolute validity is an illusion, which vanishes with the economic order that produced them. In retrospect they have no more authority than the gods of antiquity or the fairies who inhabited the glades.

Such a theory undermines what it seeks to explain. The claim to validity that is contained in all our values begins to seem spurious, when portrayed as an ideological device. In like manner, the sociologist Pierre Bourdieu and the critic Terry Eagleton have tried to represent the entire concept of aesthetic value as a particular 'moment' in the unfolding of bourgeois culture, to be accounted for, along with the rest of that culture, in terms of the economic transformation that placed the bourgeoisie on top of the pile.[9]

[9] Eagleton, *The Ideology of the Aesthetic*; Bourdieu, *Distinction*. The foundations for this approach to aesthetic interest are again to be found in the Frankfurt School. Horkheimer, e.g., writes that 'the pure aesthetic feeling is a reaction of the atomised private subject . . . [aesthetic judgement] is the judgement of the individual abstracted from overriding social standards' (*Neue Kunst und Massenkultur* (1941), in A. Schmidt (ed.), *Kritische Theorie* (Frankfurt am Main, 1968), ii. 513).

It is undeniable that the *term* 'aesthetic', in its modern meaning, is an invention of the Enlightenment; the suggestion is that the same is true of the *concept*, and also of the phenomenon described by it. When Kant presented his great theory of the disinterested interest, he was, it is argued, not describing a human universal at all; instead, he was presenting, in philosophical idiom, a piece of bourgeois ideology. This 'disinterested' interest becomes available only in certain historical conditions; and it is available because it is functional.

Why is aesthetic interest functional in 'bourgeois' conditions? There seem to be two answers to this question in the writings of Eagleton and Bourdieu. The first goes as follows: by the fiction of intrinsic value, the human world is deprived of its historicity. The 'disinterested' perception of nature, of objects, of human relations, renders them permament, ineluctable, immune to change. The bourgeois order is thereby inscribed into nature and rendered sacrosanct. This 'making holy' of things can be understood as an attempt to represent a transient social order as natural and therefore permanent. The idea of an aesthetic interest therefore encourages us to retain unaltered the economic relations which made the human world. This ideological device is all the more pernicious, it might be said, in concealing the truth of man's relation to man and to objects in the bourgeois order: for, while rejoicing in the fiction that both men and things are valued as 'ends in themselves', the bourgeois treats everything and everyone as a means. That which is seen as most holy, is at the same time treated as most expendable; and the ideological lie facilitates the material exploitation.

The second explanation turns on the concept of 'taste', which features in the writings of Bourdieu as part of the comprehensive social practice which he calls 'distinction'—the practice of presenting and representing oneself to others as other than them. Taste and high culture are part of the 'struggle' of the 'dominant class' to remain dominant, by producing instruments of exclusion which will protect its monopoly of social power. The aesthetic impulse—the impulse to value objects not as means or instruments, but as ends in themselves—is fundamental to the manufacture of social distinctions. For it is only when valued as ends that objects can be understood as expressing the power and status of those who possess them. For Bourdieu, as for Eagleton, the idea of intrinsic value is an elaborate fiction, designed to inscribe the class interest of the bourgeoisie on the face of nature; and for Bourdieu too this fiction finds its most revealing expression in Kant's theory of aeshetic interest, as a form of disinterested contemplation:

> Totally ahistorical . . . , perfectly ethnocentric . . . , Kant's analysis of the judgement of taste finds its real basis in a set of aesthetic principles which are the universalisation of the dispositions associated with a particular social and economic condition.[10]

[10] *Distinction*, 493.

Parallel 'insights' inform the writings of *marxisant* critics like Barthes and nominalist historians like Foucault. They fall ready-made from the Marxian literary machine, and owe their appeal to the political agenda which instantly engages with them. The details of my pastiche may not be exactly right: but it accurately reflects the method. The question is whether this method really poses a challenge to philosophical aesthetics, and if so, whether the challenge is one that should be met in the context of my present argument.

Notice, first, that the claim against the judgement of taste is far stronger than the one typically made against moral values. It is common for Marxists to argue that moral values are historically determined, by the economic conditions that render them functional, while also accepting that people must *have* moral values: perhaps even adding that there is some core of morality which is a genuine universal, since it is functional in all possible economies. The argument that I have just given purports to show not merely that aesthetic values are historically determined, but that the very *idea* of aesthetic value is a transient attribute of bourgeois ideology: that other cultures, equally rational, have no such conception, and recognize no such interest as the one that I have been at pains to describe. This strong claim is, I believe, highly implausible. Or at least, it is certainly ill-conceived to think that the interest Kant was describing in the *Critique of Judgement* is peculiar to bourgeois society as *we* know it. Plato is describing the same kind of interest in the *Republic* and the *Ion*; Aristotle is describing it in the *Poetics*, and Nogami is describing it in his *Art of Noh*. (I take only three of uncountably many instances.)

Be that as it may, however, philosophers and critics certainly present different and often conflicting theories of the aesthetic experience. And there does seem to be an interesting new departure in Kant, Schiller, and their followers: an elevation of the aesthetic to a position that had hitherto been reserved for religion. Indeed Kant explicitly assimilates the two domains, although not in the way that I assimilated them earlier in this chapter. How should we respond to this fact?

A useful comparison can be made with mathematics. Pure mathematics is not a human universal: only in certain historical and economic conditions do people break free from the prison of counting, and begin to treat numbers as abstract objects, bound by intrinsic laws. But once the discovery has been made, pure mathematics develops according to its own inner logic, and regardless of the interests that it may thwart or serve. The truths of mathematics are universal, but it is only in certain conditions that people will discover them.

Equally pertinent is the case of law, towards which rational beings have an intrinsic propensity, just as they have a propensity towards mathematics. This does not mean that all rational beings recognize the existence of laws, or that laws are everywhere the same. Nevertheless, once awakened, the search for law proceeds with a logic of its own, making and unmaking the surrounding social context. The Marxist attempt to reduce law to a functional superstructure, as though its sole claim to our attention lies in the economic relations which it holds in place, falls before the fact of common law. Common law arises spontaneously from the attempt to do justice, and proceeds according to its own intrinsic logic—the doctrines of precedent and *stare decisis*, and the rules of natural justice. Economic relations have been shaped by this law, as much as law by economic relations. Only when we grasp the autonomous principles of judicial reasoning, will we understand why property-relations in the modern world are as they are. The common law may be a product of history; but it is also a producer of history, and owes its authority to principles which influence human thinking always and everywhere.

Similar remarks should be made concerning the judgement of taste. The aesthetic impulse is latent in rational nature, arising from the need to complete our instrumental reasoning with a conception of the end. It may lie dormant for centuries, or express itself only in an impure and 'applied' way—as in the customs and costumes of the tribe. Once noticed, however, the aesthetic experience expands to fill the moral space available. It is only in certain cultural conditions—those which the bourgeois order most readily promotes, by promoting the prosperity which is the root of leisure—that this flowering of the aesthetic impulse can occur. The impulse flowers in many ways, and its products are marked by the surrounding culture, since they are merely the highest and most self-conscious manifestations of it. But taste is as natural to humanity as law or mathematics, and just as free from the 'ideology of domination'. There are good philosophical reasons for agreeing with the Kantians, that the aesthetic and the religious are proximate phenomena, complementary attempts to make sense of the world as home. Conceptions of home may differ from tribe to tribe: but the root distinction between safety and danger, between love and hostility, is a human universal, and requires of every society that emancipates itself from need that it spread its image before itself in poetry, architecture, image-making, and music.

The art of music, I have argued, could not exist without the aesthetic experience through which we perceive it. Music is *intrinsically* aesthetic; and any society that makes music is already taking an interest, however primitive, in something that has no purpose but itself. A tribe may use music in order to dance: but dancing is (in the normal case) an aesthetic response, a response to the music as music, a way of according intrinsic value to a string of sounds, experienced as tones. A musical culture arises whenever music enters into the life of the tribe, to become a system of allusion, and a way of 'joining in'. Dancing is not the purpose of music, but a way of adopting its lack of purpose.

The Flight from Banality

But this returns us to the topic of value, which we left with that discon-certing thought of Schoenberg's, that the tonal language has 'become banal', and that it is, as such, confined to 'sentimental gestures'. What do these judgements mean, how true are they, and what should be our response to the cultural condition which is implied by them?

In the study of language the concept of banality is familiar under the labels 'cliché', and 'hackneyed' usage. The *Oxford English Dictionary* describes a cliché as 'a stereotyped expression, a commonplace phrase'. Eric Partridge, in his *Dictionary of Clichés*, adds that a cliché is an *outworn* commonplace, and contrasts clichés with proverbs which, although often repeated, retain their value on account of the wisdom which resides in them. Clichés, he implies, are not merely outworn: they are empty, pointless, a sign of thoughtlessness. Unlike a proverb, which distils a truth of which we stand always to be reminded, a cliché blunts or obscures the message that it is used to convey. Of course, clichés can be used to great effect, as by Geoffrey Hill and Samuel Beckett. Consider Hill's description of a search for the bodies of drowned men along the seashore: 'Quietly they wade the disturbed shore; | Gather their dead as the first dead scrape home.'[11] What is disturbing in this is precisely the cliché—'scrape home'—but used now, not as a worn-out figure of speech, but as a literal description of a horrible fact. The reader is jolted into awareness of the thing described, just as the cliché is jolted out of its customary inattentiveness. But the example shows just what is wrong with a cliché in its normal occurrence—namely, that (to use a cliché) it skates over the thing described, negating not only thought, but the emotion that is founded on thought, and which is our real and obligatory tribute to life. A literature of clichés is therefore a literature without worth: for it instils in the place of a real response to the world a habit of emotional complacency.

It is an interesting fact about human beings that they try to avoid banal-ity: or at least, to avoid being accused of it. The banal remark is not just an impediment to conversation. It is a sign that the speaker is not truly inter-ested: or at least, that his interest is running in channels that have been laid down in advance. At the same time, the effort not to be banal is costly. A life of undemanding platitudes is, on the whole, easier to get through, less trau-matic, less troubled, even if less interesting than the life lived with one's faculties always freshly attuned. That is one reason why we react so adversely (when we discern it) to banality in art. For art is the realm in which the effort is made *for* us, and in which we are interested precisely because it shows us human feeling in its higher form. We follow the words of the poet, knowing when they are merely compelled by the metre, and when, on the

---

[11] 'The Guardians', in *Collected Poems* (London, 1986), 39.

contrary, they are compelled by the thought. For we want to know, not merely that he *means* it, but that *this* (whatever it may be) can actually be *meant*. That is the wonderful experience that awaits the reader of *Little Gidding*, *Le Bateau ivre*, or the *Duino Elegies*.

Cliché has a comparable effect in the work of music—an effect of deadening, of making easy what should be difficult, and of cancelling the possibilities of real emotion. Adorno is surely right in his view that much of the music of modern mass culture is saturated with banality: harmonies, melodies, and rhythms frequently have that easy, unthinking, platitudinous quality, which leaves the listener either thoughtlessly placated, or profoundly displeased. And yet there is also something hasty and *un*discriminating in this dismissal of an entire subculture, as though we could not distinguish the cheerful and life-enhancing sound of Louis Armstrong from the monsters of Heavy Metal.

It is not constant use that makes a cliché. The word 'apple' has been used by me, you, and our companions countless times: but, in its ordinary literal meaning, it could never be a cliché, because it *does not pretend to any effect*. It is doing its ordinary job of work, and makes no claim to expressive power. The phrase 'apple of my eye' is, however, although used far more rarely, a cliché. For it is pretending to be expressive when it has lost the power of being so. It makes a promise of effect which it can no longer fulfil.

In a similar way, standard devices in the classical style are not in themselves clichés: rather, they form part of the grammar of musical utterance. Cliché comes only with the pretence at an effect. Even the arpeggiated tonic chord, followed by the arpeggiated dominant, is not a cliché, however many times we hear it. Think of the opening of *Eine Kleine Nachtmusik*, K. 525, (Ex. 15.4) and compare it with the theme from Mozart's Twenty-First Piano Concerto, K. 467 (Ex. 15.5). In both examples you encounter this simplest of harmonic and melodic devices. Yet these are among the most expressive statements in all music: not banal, even now when we have heard them uncounted times, even now that the second has appeared as background music to a sentimental film (*Elvira Madigan*). (Consider, in this connection, the ideas of the hackneyed, and of kitsch: only in a very specific social context can these have a meaning for us: the context in which art has become an instrument of self-knowledge and self-criticism.)

Cliché involves a stereotype, an unthinking bid for effect which falls short of meaning anything. Although Berlioz's introduction of the 'Dies Irae' into the *Symphonie fantastique* is not a cliché, it is a cliché to use the theme, as Liszt does in his *Totentanz*, in order to provide a hasty shorthand for the macabre. Yet the theme is saved from cliché by Rachmaninov in his Paganini Rhapsody, by a set of musical inverted commas: it regains some of its aura of surprise, when it breaks into the demonic flow of Paganini's obsessive melody,

Ex. 15.4. Mozart, *Eine Kleine Nachtmusik*, K. 525

Ex. 15.5. Mozart, Twenty-First Piano Concerto in C major, K. 467, slow movement

and clothes the master-violinist in the devil's costume. But could it be done again? Could a modern composer now write a set of variations on the 'Dies Irae', or introduce the theme into one of his compositions, while avoiding banality? Such questions puzzle us. For we are inclined to agree with Schoenberg, that certain devices have 'become banal' and are therefore no longer available to the true artistic spirit. (Perhaps the expressive density of Dallapiccola's idiom in *Canti di prigionia* enables him to make appropriate use of the chant; but it is interesting that Penderecki, in his own work entitled 'Dies Irae', avoids quoting from the chant entirely.)

How does a musical device 'become banal'? The mere fact of repetition does not bring this about. The D minor chord with added minor sixth and major seventh that opens the last movement of Beethoven's Ninth Symphony will never 'become banal'—at least not in *that* particular appearance. But maybe it *is* banal when Tippett quotes it in the finale of his Third Symphony. On the other hand, the *misuse* of a piece of music does not make the music banal; the four-note theme that opens Beethoven's Fifth has not 'become banal' merely because of the hackneyed way in which people other than Beethoven have chosen to apply it, any more than 'the winter of our discontent', which is a cliché in the mouths of politicians, is a cliché in the mouth of Shakespeare's Richard III.

A musical device becomes banal when it is *borrowed*, but not earned. Mozart's melodies, which seem to spring forth effortlessly from the tonal language, possess a freshness and simplicity that is entirely free from rhetoric. But take these melodies, break them down into their expressive phrases, and reassemble them as Spontini does in *La vestale*, and the result is empty cliché (Ex. 15.6). The melodic line is no longer the free outpouring of musical feeling, but a concatenation of effects, each made real by Mozart, and each made unreal when used again, outside the context that led to its discovery. By Spontini's day the classical style was a thing of the past, which could be borrowed as a set of rhetorical devices, but which had lost its spontaneity.

Thus we find that musical devices are constantly regenerated, as each new idiom appropriates them. Consider the turn, singled out as a permanent but constantly changing expressive gesture by Edward Said.[12] The turn was a pure ornament in seventeenth-century music: an embellishment which the performer could choose to perform as he thought fit. By the time of Bach it had been incorporated into the melodic line, as in the arioso variation from the 'Goldberg' Variations, Ex. 15.7. The inimitable effect of grace created by the initial turn coincides here with an exquisite meditative sadness, as though the turn were not merely emphasizing that first note, but causing the music to linger around it, reluctant to move away.

By Mozart's day the turn has been emancipated entirely from its role as ornament, and become an essentially melodic device, as in the opening theme of the Clarinet Trio, K. 498, Ex. 15.8. It has acquired, thanks to the forward-going movement of classical harmony, a free and open character. It does not linger, but on the contrary moves things on, sometimes with an unprecedented dynamism, as in the opening theme of Beethoven's 'Emperor' Piano Concerto, Op. 73, Ex. 15.9, which introduces the turn as a major structural motif, on which the entire movement depends.

But this new self-confidence was inseparable from the classical style. By the time of Wagner the turn has been recreated yet again, not as a forward-going melodic device, but as a lingering, caressing expression of a transcendental desire—as in Isolde's 'Liebestod', Ex. 15.10. This very same effect can be found in Bruckner (the slow movement of the Seventh Symphony), but transformed by the warm tone of the strings into a full-hearted prayer to the Godhead (Ex. 15.11). Such a history has all but exhausted the potential of so small a device; so should we be surprised if Mahler, using it again and again, in a manner typified by the last movement of the Third Symphony (Ex. 15.12), should, by the time of the Ninth symphony (Ex. 15.13), come so close to kitsch—lingering in these soft farewells too long and too deliciously?

[12] Said, *Musical Elaborations*. For an illuminating discussion of the Wagner turn in romantic music, see D. Newlin, *Bruckner, Mahler, Schoenberg* (New York, 1947), 136–207.

Ex. 15.6. Spontini, *La vestale*, 'Les dieux prendront pitié'

Ex. 15.7. Bach, 'Goldberg' Variations, BWV988, variation no. 13

Ex. 15.8. Mozart, Clarinet Trio in E flat major, K. 498

Ex. 15.9. Beethoven, Fifth 'Emperor' Piano Concerto in E flat major, Op. 73, first movement

Ex. 15.10. Wagner, *Tristan und Isolde*, Act 3, 'Liebestod'

Ex. 15.11. Bruckner, Seventh Symphony in E major, slow movement

Ex. 15.12. Mahler, Third Symphony in D minor, fifth movement

Ex. 15.13. Mahler, Ninth Symphony in D major, last movement

That is presumably what Schoenberg and Adorno mean, when saying that certain devices have 'become banal'. A modernist, whose music requires 'the striking out of cliché and rhetoric', as Adorno puts it,[13] would surely avoid this gesture—and even the whole tonal language from which it is shaped. Yet Tippett, in his Triple Concerto, revives the Wagner turn in one of the most poignant melodies written in recent times—and the effect is neither sentimental nor banal, but fresh and startling (Ex. 15.14). Such an example must surely make us suspicious of the accusation against tonality—the accusation that the tonal system itself is no longer available. At least, it is a hard accusation to uphold, and we still need an argument for it.

Ex. 15.14. Tippett, Triple Concerto

Sentimentality

We are now in a position to see why banality and sentimentality are so closely connected, why both are aesthetic defects, and how both can be displayed not merely by representational art, but by abstract art as well. (Think of the reams of abstract kitsch produced by American painters, much of it now stored in the cellars of the Metropolitan Museum of Modern Art.)

Just as it would be a mistake to define 'sad' as applied to music simply in terms of musical qualities, so would it be a mistake to define sentimentality in purely musical terms. In describing a piece of music as sad or sentimental I am using a predicate which, in its primary occurrence, applies to people. It is this primary use that must be defined.

In one of the few serious attempts by a philosopher to analyse sentimentality, Michael Tanner outlines four characteristics, as he sees them, of sentimental people: (1) they respond with extreme readiness to stimuli; (2) they appear to be pained, but actually enjoy their pangs; (3) they respond with equal violence to disparate stimuli at an amazing pace; (4) they avoid following up their responses with *appropriate* actions. It is characteristic of a

[13] *Die Tildung von Cliché und Floskel*, T. W. Adorno and H. Eisler, *Komposition für den Film*, in Adorno, *Gesammelte Schriften* (Frankfurt am Main, 1976), 40.

sentimental person to respond with gushing emotion to a stranger's misfortune, but to do nothing to remedy the stranger's lot, moving on at once to the next object of emotion with an inner serenity that is only lightly perturbed by the superficial storms.[14]

There is a recognisable syndrome captured by those four characteristics, to which we can add: (5) sentimental people respond more warmly to strangers than to those who are close to them, and are more heatedly concerned by abstract issues which demand no personal sacrifice, than by concrete obligations that cost time and energy to fulfil. (Dickens is a master at portraying this characteristic, perhaps because it was one that he shared.) Tanner offers, as a diagnosis, the suggestion (taken from Wilde) that sentimental people are attempting to have their emotions 'on the cheap': by which he means, having the pleasure of an active emotional life, without the cost of it. But what *is* the cost? Tanner does not explicitly say; and perhaps there is no general answer—the cost varying from emotion to emotion, and circumstance to circumstance. The cost of love, for example, includes all of the following: the trouble of caring for another, of anticipating and satisfying his desires; the pain of jealousy, when his love declines or wavers; the agony of grief should he leave or die. Far easier to fill one's world with those casual affections which can be turned on and off at will, and to live *du côté de Guermantes*, where real sacrifices are displaced by *petits soins*.

But that suggests another, and deeper, description of what the sentimentalist is up to. He is not so much feeling something as *avoiding* it. He is not feeling what he pretends to feel, and he prefers to pretend, for the pretence is deeply motivated. Sentimental emotions are *artefacts*: they are designed to cast credit on the one who claims them. The sentimentalist is courting admiration and sympathy. He wishes others to credit him with a warm heart and generous feelings; but he does not wish to pay the price that those things demand. That is why there is sentimental love, sentimental indignation, sentimental grief and sympathy; but not sentimental malice, spite, envy or depression, since these are feelings which no-one admires.

Sentimentality, so described, is a vice. Not only does it place someone at a distance from reality; it also involves an overevaluation of the self at the cost of others. The other person enters the orbit of the sentimentalist as an *excuse* for emotion, rather than an *object* of it. The other is deprived of his objectivity as a person, and absorbed into the subjectivity of the sentimentalist. The other becomes, in a very real sense, a means to emotion, rather than an end in himself. Although Kant tried to banish the emotions from their central place in the moral life, it is far easier to understand his great injunction, to

[14] M. Tanner, 'Sentimentality', *Proceedings of the Aristotelian Society* (1976–7), 127–47.

treat others as ends and never as means only, if we restore emotions to their rightful place in our existence. For then we may recognize the distinction between the one who uses others to feed his own emotional fires, and the one who is open to the reality of other people, and as a result loves and hates, grieves and pities not for the sake of feeling some pleasurable simulacrum of those things, but purely for the other's sake, and because these emotions are called forth irresistibly by the reality to which he responds. *That* is what it is, to treat another as an end in himself: and the cost of true morality is the cost of responding in such a way.

The sentimentalist is therefore a paradigm immoralist. His carefree existence is not a happy one: for it lacks the essential ingredients—love and friendship—on which happiness depends. The sentimental friend is not a friend: indeed, he is a danger to others. His instinct is to facilitate tragedy, in order to bathe in easy sympathy; to stimulate love, in order to pretend to love in return, while always reserving his heart and mind, and calculating to his own advantage. He enters human relations by seduction, and leaves them by betrayal.

Sentimentality exists in art as well as in life; and it is as much an aesthetic as a moral defect. Expression in art involves an invitation to sympathy. The characteristic of sentimental art is that it invites us to pretend to an emotion, without really feeling it. It gives the trappings of emotion without the real and costly fact of it. One sign of this, as Leavis has powerfully argued,[15] is a vague and unobservant portrayal of the object of feeling. The world of the sentimental work of art is an excuse for emotion, but not a full-bodied object of it. It is schematic, stereotyped, smoothed over by the wash of sentiment, deprived of the concrete reality that would show the cost of really feeling things. In a sentimental romance, like Alain Fournier's *Le Grand Meaulnes*, the beloved is deprived of all but the vaguest human attributes, and becomes an *excuse* for love—but a narcissistic love, in which the subject meditates on his own emotion. In the sentimental expression of grief, death serves as the *excuse* for mellifluous feelings, in which the concrete reality of loss is obliterated. (See Leavis's discussion of 'Hereto I come to view a voiceless ghost' (Hardy), in which the object of grief is conjured in all her painful, imperfect and reproachful reality.)[16] To respond to the invitation in such works is to join in their self-indulgence; it is to prefer, in imagination, the self-dramatising pretence of emotion, over the self-critical reality.

Sentimentality in art therefore goes hand in hand with cliché and banality. Sentimental art is always reaching for effects, but since—in a deep sense—it is *feeling nothing*, it cannot derive these effects from its subject-matter, or from

[15] 'Thought and Emotional Quality', *Scrutiny*, 13 (1945), repr. in Leavis (ed.), *Selections from Scrutiny* (Cambridge, 1968), ii. 211–30.

[16] 'Reality and Sincerity', in *Scrutiny*, 19, (1952–3), repr. in *Selections from Scrutiny*, ii. 248–57.

its own expressive life. They must be borrowed, therefore, like costumes. And that is precisely the origin of the cliché—the borrowed gesture, which has become the formula for an emotion which it cannot recreate.

Furthermore, banality and sentimentality feed upon each other. We are all to some extent sentimentalists: for human kind cannot bear very much reality. And banalities help not merely to give expression to our sentimental pretences, but also to gain other people's complicity in them—to sustain a kind of collective illusion, with which we cloak our common heartlessness. The sentimentalist makes direct appeal to his kind: you are like me, he reminds us; these clichés that I utter are your clichés too. However, by accepting them we can appear noble in each other's eyes, without the cost of being so. Let us, then, pretend.

That, in brief, is the reason for Schoenberg's admittedly exaggerated aspersions on the diminished seventh chord. In using this chord, and the language of which it is a part, the composer is summoning up a world of easy pretence, in which both composer and audience shirk the question of whether they are really feeling anything, or whether there is really anything to feel. Such a language could never be used to capture and reflect upon the realities of modern life, or on the unprecedented calamities which inspired *A Survivor from Warsaw* or the *Quatuor pour le fin du temps*.

Instrumental Music, and the Culture of Listening

Schoenberg was referring to a chord, implying that its banality would be apparent even in instrumental music: and that here too banality and senti-mentality conspire. And there is no doubt that we do judge instrumental music in this way, despite the lack of a represented object, and despite our reluctance to identify an emotion that is being sentimentalized. From the extremes of sugary romance (Mantovani and his Strings), to the just too self-indulgent rendering of a profound emotion (Tchaikovsky's Sixth); from flagrant eroticism (Strauss's *Don Juan*) to the mere hint of come-hitherish-ness (Mendelssohn's 'Spring Song'), we hear sentimentality in instrumental music just as clearly as we hear it in the human voice. The argument of the previous chapters establishes, I hope, that there is nothing truly strange in this. But it does not tell us why we are so alert to the phenomenon, or indeed how we recognize it. Why is it that a wholly abstract art can arouse such violent responses—including the 'yuk' feeling with which we react to what is morally contaminating?

The question returns us to the nature of musical culture, and of our culture in particular. Music has many social uses: in worship, dancing, marching, and as an accompaniment to labour. It is plausible to suppose that dancing and singing came before silent listening in the scheme of things, and that singing for a purpose (e.g. in an act of worship, or in battle) came before the pure strophic song. Yet, by a seemingly inexorable process, instrumental music gradually took over from the voice, just as silent listening took over from song and dance. Music seemed to fulfil its destiny by freeing itself from its worldly uses, while continuing to allude to them in ever more refined and ever more suggestive gestures. After Beethoven it became impossible to think of the human voice as the source of music, or of song as the goal of melody. From Weber onwards the opera is in the process of becoming symphonic music: the voice is no longer accompanied by the orchestra, but redeemed by it, lifted free from its natural condition and remade as a member of the symphony of instruments. The voice is removed from the physical space of human action, to reappear in the acousmatic space of music.

As I suggested in Chapter 14, this displacing of song and dance from the central place in music-making has a profound spiritual significance. Music is heard as though breathed into the ear of the listener from another and higher sphere: it is not the here and now, the world of mere contingency that speaks to us through music, but another world, whose order is only dimly reflected in the empirical realm. Music fulfils itself as an art by reaching into this realm of pure abstraction and reconstituting there the movements of the human soul. Only through a culture of listening can this strange transformation occur: but once it begins, it feeds on itself, each new work being conceived as a further extension of that other-worldly voice which speaks to us in tones. And the experience of this voice becomes the more important to us as the sense of a spiritual and religious community dwindles. Music is free from the obligation to represent the empirical world; hence it can gesture to the true community, precisely when that community is vanishing. The implied community which can be glimpsed in music is finer, nobler, and more generous in its feelings than anything that we could know. The encounter with it leads to the peculiar, quasi-religious reverence of the recital room and the concert hall.

It is understandable that we should be so alert to the things which pollute this higher community with the debris of our baser attitudes. The invitation to sympathy that is uttered in the voice of pure music is one that we are eager to accept; but the slightest cliché or banality, the slightest borrowing of some stock effect, makes us doubt the voice's sincerity. We encounter the temptation to pretence, and to the community established by pretence—that complicitous humbug which is the goal of sentimentality. Even if that is how our *lives* must be, we can surely be spared such an experience in art. For we enter the realm of art of our own accord and precisely so as to understand what *might* have been, had we been free from the tyranny of habit.

Instrumental music also provides us with a paradigm of order: in the great works of pure music gestures follow logically, completing one another. The musical logic shows us what it is like to live something completely and to its conclusion, without the flitting between states of mind which is the norm of sentimental compromise. It is from instrumental music that we derive our most overwhelming experience of form. And when, as in the later operas of Wagner, this experience of purely musical form gathers into itself the workings of a drama, the effect is so overwhelming that only religious language can describe it.

Tonality and Postmodernism

When a device becomes banal it is, to the true artist, *no longer available*. It must be written out of his style—or, if retained, used against itself, as in the clichés exploited by Samuel Beckett and Geoffrey Hill.[17] In this way, Adorno and Schoenberg argued that tonality is no longer available, and that all of music must be derived anew, from some other grammar. However, the failure of serial atonality to attract an audience has caused both composers and critics to be suspicious of the modernist project—not just of the avantgardism of its main proponents, but of the very idea of an art that self-consciously situates itself in the present and the future, and seeks to rid itself of the past.

At the same time, the return to tonality has had a peculiar character. What we find in Del Tredici, John Adams, Robin Holloway, and Alfred Schnittke is not tonality, but 'tonality' in inverted commas: somehow the composer does not treat the tonal idiom as his predecessors had treated it. It is treated not as the true language of music, compelled by the very art of sound, but only as one 'style' among many. (Thus in John Corigliano's *The Ghosts of Versailles*, passages of pure Mozart—or, if you prefer, pure 'Mozart'—alternate with dodecaphonic sonorities and piercing tone-clusters.) To treat tonality as a style is precisely to belie its reality, as the 'force of nature' in music: tonality is not an effect of style since it is the ground of any style that uses it.

We encounter here a peculiar quagmire that at least deserves a map, if not a passage through: the quagmire of the postmodern condition, concerning which volumes have already been written (obsession with itself being one of the characteristics of the postmodern condition). What exactly do the 'postmodernist' inverted commas mean? When a composer uses them, is he exemplifying a renewed attachment to tonality, or, on the contrary, distancing himself from tonality, like one who picks it up with rubber gloves?

---

[17] I have analysed Beckett's use of cliché in 'Beckett and the Cartesian Soul', in *The Aesthetic Understanding* (London, 1983), 222–41. See also C. Ricks's profound study of Beckett's language, *Beckett's Dying Words*.

Umberto Eco offers a clever definition of postmodernism which is pertinent here. The postmodernist's attitude, he writes, is

> that of a man who loves a very cultivated woman and knows he cannot say to her, 'I love you madly', because he knows that she knows (and that she knows that he knows) that these words have already been written by Barbara Cartland. Still, there is a solution. He can say, 'As Barbara Cartland would put it, I love you madly.' At this point, having avoided false innocence, he will nevertheless have said what he wanted to say to the woman: that he loves her, but that he loves her in an age of lost innocence. If the woman goes along with this, she will have received a declaration of love all the same.[18]

But will she? Surely, in circumstances like these, both man and woman are playing at love: for the 'innocence' to which Eco refers is part of love, and the loss of it makes love impossible. You do not recover innocence by placing it in inverted commas: at best the result is the kind of *faux naif* whose finest musical expression is in the songs and symphonies of Mahler— works which are often treated with suspicion for this very reason.[19]

If it is true, therefore, that all attempts to recuperate tonality end in inverted commas, tonality, as the forthright and self-believing thing that it has to be if it is to exist at all, is irrecoverable. It is at this point that the argument must run into the sand, however. For who can say whether the postmodernist is right? Who can know that some new composer might not emerge tomorrow, who causes tonality to live again? Or should we endorse the vision of Thomas Mann in *Doktor Faustus*, arguing that we exist at the end of something, and that the only artistic gestures that remain to us are either ironical or directed towards the 'taking-back' of our culture? If it is true that we can no longer compose tonally, except in inverted commas, then, since tonality is the irreplaceable core of music, we can no longer compose, but only 'compose'. This would be startling proof that after all music is an expressive art. For it would demonstrate that composition is possible only in a condition of emotional innocence. The fact that an innocent stance towards the world is unavailable, makes music uncomposable. That which music must express has gone from the world; and so music too must go.

It is undeniable that our musical culture has undergone many radical changes since the great period of the nineteenth century. Even if we can avoid the inverted commas, we cannot recover the innocent ear of a Ravel or a Humperdinck: sophisticated composers, who nevertheless did not 'choose' their styles with a knowing irony from the set of past alternatives, but composed as they had to, in order to express what they felt. If we criticize

---

[18] *Reflections on 'The Name of the Rose'*, 112.

[19] Wittgenstein gives voice to this suspicion, in characterisically dismissive tones, in the notes on *Culture and Value*.

the nostalgia of a Vaughan Williams or the populism of a Shostakovich or a Khachaturian, it is because we recognize in these things another aspect of sentimentality. The lingering backward glance towards that which can never be recovered (and which is falsified in the very yearning for it) has been the greatest vice of English music in our century. Like every form of sentimentality, it involves a 'turning-away' from the present reality, a desire to lock emotions into a narrow and predetermined world of fantasy, a world which *you yourself* control. That which is invoked in a nostalgic work like *On Wenlock Edge* is presented as *no longer available*. It is the object of feelings which belong nowhere except in fairyland, and which, because there is no possibility of living them, cost nothing. How different this kind of writing is from those real invocations of peasant life in Janáček, in which a vanishing form of life is presented in all its raw vitality, and where the impulse to sympathy involves a real moral commitment. Compare Ex. 15.15 and Ex. 15.16: both pieces deploy allusions to folk culture—parallel fifths in the Vaughan Williams, and a pentatonic melody in the Janáček. Yet the first has a sepia-toned quality, exhumed from a drawer of sad mementoes, while the second is fresh, simple, and sincere, as though discovered for the first time.

Great art, we are inclined to believe, involves some affirmation, however qualified, of the actual. The faint sarcastic smile of the postmodernist is as

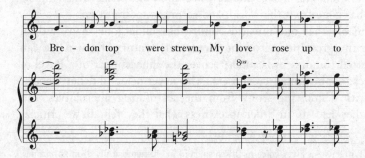

Ex. 15.15. Vaughan Williams, *On Wenlock Edge*

Ex. 15.16. Janáček, *Diary of One who Disappeared*, 'Farewell my birthplace'

incompatible with greatness as is the helpless nostalgia of a Havergal Brian or the sentimental sweetness of a Rodrigo. Postmodernist irony is simply a more sophisticated way of avoiding the question of modern life—the question of what we are to affirm in it, and what deny. If art ceases to affirm life, then it loses its point: after all, life is all that we have. Even when it turns its thoughts to death, true art seeks a path to affirmation. Schubert's meditations on death, in the last piano sonata, D960, the slow movement of the String Quintet in C, D956, and the incomparable String Quartet in G major, D887, are among the profoundest testimonies in art to the beauty of life and the pain of losing it: they are also true gestures of acceptance—since that which is accepted is neither sentimentalized nor set aside, but confronted in all its unspeakable darkness. Mahler achieves another kind of acceptance in *Das Lied von der Erde*: a poignant and resigned farewell, which is also a 'yes' to existence (although not the urgent 'yes', full of wanting, that we find in Schubert). (Note the added sixth which wars, however feebly, against the triad in Mahler's final chord: the slight raising of the body for that last glimpse of life: Ex. 15.17.) Every true requiem has this life-affirming quality, and it is no small achievement on the part of Benjamin Britten to have dragged his music through the charnel-house of the Somme, to emerge at the end of the *War Requiem* with the sublime setting of 'Let us sleep now'. You may, perhaps, object to those banal tritones in the boys' choir

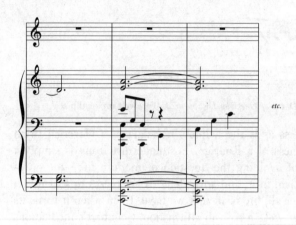

Ex. 15.17. Mahler, *Das Lied von der Erde*, conclusion

(Ex. 15.18); but these too have their purpose, and lead at last to a surprising and beautiful cadence (Ex. 15.19). Here is a genuine addition to the repertoire of musical consonance, comparable to that offered by Stravinsky at the end of his *Symphony of Psalms* (Ex. 15.20.) Such life-affirming works have been by no means as rare in late twentieth-century music as the pessimists would have us believe: think of Tippett's Triple Concerto, Messiaen's *Turangalîla symphonie*, Elliot Carter's Concerto for Orchestra (a work which succeeds in turning an uncompromising modernism to the service of joy), and Nicholas Maw's *Vita Nuova*. More recently, composers like Judith Weir, Robin Holloway, and David Matthews have written works which, in the interests of a serious and unsentimental affirmation, have returned to tonal regions, and sought (or at any rate 'sought') for plots in the vast tonal landscape which have not been ploughed into sterility.

Ex. 15.18. Britten, *War Requiem*

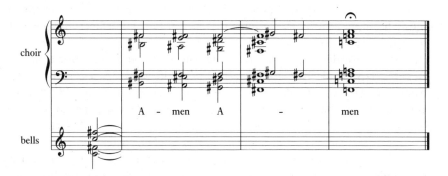

Ex. 15.19. Britten, *War Requiem*

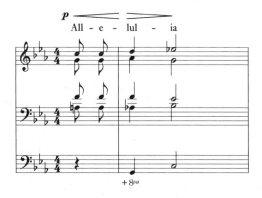

Ex. 15.20. Stravinsky, *Symphony of Psalms*

This affirmation of life is not easy to make, however: for life can be affirmed only in the plural—art endorses life only through the 'we' of the implied community, which redeems the death and grief of the mere individual. Sentimentality becomes the norm when a culture declines, since it veils the underlying absence, the lack of that first-person plural which gives sense to art. To 'purify the dialect of the tribe' is then the most urgent and the hardest of artistic undertakings. It can be done only through the equivalent of fasting and prayer, for it involves an imaginative forgiveness, a reacceptance of the commonplace, in full consciousness of its insufficiency.

The Consumer Culture

Those thoughts may perhaps strike a chord in the lover of 'classical' music—the music which asks to be heard, but never overheard. Unfortunately, however, they make no contact with the music which is the daily diet of postmodern society: music which hums in every public place, and which is poured into every silence, lest silence be heard. Before concluding, it is fitting to consider popular music, and the quite peculiar condition into which music has been put, by the seeming disappearance from ordinary listening of the judgement of taste.

Plato, the reader will recall, wished to ban certain kinds of music from his Republic—particularly those associated with the wild dances of the cory-bants. In Plato's view, abandoned movement bespeaks an abandoned soul, and the 'care of the soul' is the first task of politics. Aristotle was not so keen on banning things. Nevertheless, he too believed that music has character, and that when singing or dancing we imitate this character and make it our own. Few matters are more important to the educator than the music which his pupils sing or dance to. In this, the Greeks thought, as in every habit, we must separate virtue from vice, which means distinguishing music that fulfils our nature, from music which destroys it.

Not many people would now endorse those ancient attitudes. Perhaps only Allan Bloom, in *The Closing of the American Mind*, has been willing to stand beside Plato, in dismissing the Dionysian pop music of our times as the enemy of moral order. But Bloom's despondency about popular culture rang hollow: the music that he deplored animates the world of enterprise; it is the voice of modern America, humming in homes, offices, and factories throughout the nation, encouraging those who provide the surplus upon which Bloom and his kind depend. Only in a democratic culture can a poor child rise to the rank of tenured professor, to collect a salary consonant with his self-opinion in return for reading the Great Books, and thinking the Great Thoughts, which he would have read and thought in any case.

This democratic culture is the real meaning of the 'postmodern' age. Modernism, with its priesthood of the avant-garde, was the last gasp of the aristocratic world-view. Such a view is no longer tenable, not because it is false, but because the conditions are no longer in place, which would enable us to live it. The democratic culture of America is also a geopolitical force. Turn on the radio anywhere in the world, and you will hear the sounds of rock, grunge, and Heavy Metal. American popular music flows through the ether like the voice of mankind itself; and while local attempts to block the public ear may enjoy a brief success, they depend on unsustainable efforts of coercion. If you were to ask what really brought down the Berlin Wall, the answer would surely include some reference to American popular culture, which had so captivated the hearts of the young that their impatience to join that enchanted world would brook no further delay.

Democratic culture presses us to accept every taste that does no obvious damage. A teacher who criticizes the music of his pupils, or who tries to cultivate, in the place of it, a love for the classics, will be attacked as 'judgemental'. In matters of aesthetic taste, no adverse judgement is permitted, save judgement of the adverse judge. This attitude has helped America to survive and flourish in a world of change. An aristocratic culture has an instinctive aversion to what is vulgar, sentimental, or commonplace; not so a democratic culture, which sacrifices good taste to popularity, and places no obstacles whatsoever before the ordinary citizen in his quest for a taste of his own. This is the culture whose 'political theology' has been so carefully constructed by Rawls in his *Theory of Justice*—the culture in which 'conceptions of the good' belong to the private sphere, and the public sphere has no other business than to guarantee fair treatment for everyone, without regard for private tastes.

Bloom would have agreed with Adorno in nothing besides a certain lyrical despondency. But it was Adorno who first rejected the popular scene, describing it as part of the 'false consciousness' with which capitalism distracts us from the truth of our condition. He was not referring to REM, U2, or AC/DC. He was dismissing the melodious and sophisticated music of our parents and grandparents: Gershwin, Cole Porter, Rodgers and Hammerstein; Louis Armstrong, Glenn Miller, and Ella Fitzgerald. This blanket condemnation aroused no more sympathy at the time than does Bloom's today. But it also shows how important judgement is. For those things dismissed by Adorno are better in every way than the things dismissed by Bloom; and whatever argument can be levelled against grunge and Heavy Metal will surely leave the innocent melodies of our parents and grandparents quite unaffected. Castigating all popular music is not merely counter-productive; it shows the very same atrophy of judgement as the surrounding popular culture.

But how should we judge that which repudiates judgement? There *is* a literature devoted to pop music, and it frequently offers a verdict on its subject. But it is a verdict founded in acceptance, both of the music and of the lifestyle of its adherents. Writers who look for the 'meaning' of Heavy Metal tend to argue in the manner of Robert Walser,[20] referring to the alienation and frustration expressed by this music—while making no real distinction between the expressive and the inexpressive instances, so removing the term 'expression' from the context of aesthetic judgement. (See the argument in Chapter 6, the section entitled 'Expression and Ideology'.) Criticism gives way to the anthropology of subcultures, each of which is entitled to its

[20] See *Running with the Devil*.

'conception of the good', and none of which can be judged from a point of view outside itself.

It seems to me, however, that there is nothing very compelling in that aesthetic relativism. In a democratic culture, people believe themselves to be entitled to their tastes. But it does not follow that good and bad taste are indistinguishable, or that the education of taste ceases to be a duty. It is only the abstract nature of music that seems to rescue it from criticism: we have no difficulty in seeing why a taste for pornographic videos may be adversely judged, or why we might wish to protect our children from acquiring it. In so far as pop music is attached to words and images it may attract similar criticism—as indeed, 'rap' music, with its message of sustained aggression, and the violent images of the music video have attracted criticism. But the sympathetic reader of my argument will recognize that words and images do not exhaust the meaning of music. On the contrary, they reinforce a message which is shaped and projected through tones.

We can best understand the point by once again returning music to its hypothetical origins in dance. It is obvious that dancing has social conse-quences—particularly on the attitudes through which men and women come together in quest of a partner. Traditional dances had to be *learned*—often by a long process which began in childhood. (Think of the gavotte, the gig, or the stately saraband.) They were not forms of abandon, but exercises in self-control. They required the dancer to understand steps, patterns, formations, and sequences; they required him to fit his gestures to the movement of his partner and to the pattern of the whole. In formation dancing, you also relinquish your partner to dance with others whom you may not know. In this way the sexual motive is moderated in its very invocation. The dancer may be prompted by desire, but he is dancing with people for whom he has no such emotion, acknowledging their existence as sexual beings with gestures of innocent courtesy. A girl might dance with her lover's friend or father, with her own brothers, uncles, and neighbours, clarifying—not in her mind only, but also in her body—her posture towards the other sex. The formation dance is dignified; but it is also lively—in the true sense of that word—far more lively than anything to be seen on MTV. (If you doubt this, then it is time to learn some Highland reels.) This liveliness is in fact the other side of dignity: it comes about when the body dances, and the soul along with it. The formation dance is also the enactment of a moral idea, a vision of peaceful community which serves to tame the sexual instinct and to overcome its impetuosity.

Formation dances gave way, in time, to the paired forms of waltz, polka, and schottische, in which only the steps need to be learned. These forms were at first regarded as immoral. Even so, they permitted the dancer to take a partner of any age or status, to dance without hint of a sexual motive, and to represent himself as an embodied person, rather than an abandoned body. The conception of the dance as a social rather than a sexual occasion lasted well into our century. It survives in the ballroom waltz, the foxtrot, and even the tango and the Charleston, which require such knowledge and control as to become a display more of skill than of sexuality—and also occasions of innocent fun. If such dances are familiar today, it is rather as flamenco is familiar. They have become forms of ballet. But ballet is not so much dancing as the *representation* of dancing. It is an activity for experts, and takes place on an elevated stage, removed from the world of the audience, who sit immobilized below.

There are now few occasions when a young man can dance with his aunt, or a young girl with her boyfriend's father. Dancing has become a sexual exhibition, since the music available for dancing has no other meaning besides release. It requires neither knowledge nor self-control, for these would impede the democratic right of everyone to enter the fray. Hence no one really dances with anyone else; instead, each dancer exudes a kind of narcissistic excitement which requires no acknowledgement from a partner besides similar gestures of display. The ethos of such a dance is well captured by the immortal words of the group Nirvana:

> I lease it, lease, yeah.
> Ev'ryone is how old?
> Pick me, pick me, yeah.
> Ev'ryone is waiting.

The dance becomes a lapse into disorder, a kind of surrender of the body which anticipates the sexual act itself. This decay of dancing is a necessary consequence of democratic culture, and an irreversible feature of the postmodern world. And it goes hand in hand with a decay in musical resources. The gestures that attend the new forms of dancing require an abdication of music to sound: to the dominating beat of the percussion, and to such antiharmonic devices as the 'power chord', produced by electronic distortion. Melodies become brief exhalations, which cannot develop since they are swamped by rhythm, and have no voice-leading role. Consider the actual tune sung by the late Kurt Cobain to the words I have quoted: fragments in a kind of B minor (though harmonized for the most part with an E major chord played anyhow), with only a ghostly resemblance to melody. No movement passes between the notes, since all movement is generated elsewhere, by the rhythm guitar. And this melodic deficiency goes hand in hand with a loss of harmonic texture. In the soup of amplified overtones, inner voices are drowned out: all the guitarist can do is create an illusion of harmony by playing parallel fifths. (The number, called 'Dive', the chorus of which invites the fan to 'dive in me', it to be found in the album *Incesticide*).

At the same time, this music has enormous power over its typical audience, precisely because it has brushed aside the demands of *music*, and replaced them with demands of another kind. The audience does not listen *to* the music, but *through* it, to the performers. The group members become leaders of an 'imagined community'—the community of their fans. Television, which brings distant things into close-up, while holding them behind an impassable screen, emphasizes this experience, endowing the singer with the epiphanous aura of the shaman, dancing before his tribe. The relation between the musicians and their fans is tribal; and any criticism of the music is received by the fan as an assault upon himself and his identity.[21] It is not a metaphor to describe Kurt Cobain as an idol: on the contrary, he is simply one among many recent manifestations of the Golden Calf. His music exists in order to blow away the external world, to create an imaginary living-space, where the fan can move freely, endowed with miraculous powers. If the music sounds ugly, this is of no significance: it is not there to be listened to, but to take revenge on the world.

The Decline of the Musical Culture

Our civilization is bound up with music as no other that the world has known. In social gatherings, whether sacred or secular, formal or informal, ceremonial or friendly, music has played a dominant role. It is an invitation to join, an expression of the feelings and hopes of the participants. It lends dignity and harmony to our gestures, and raises them to a higher level, where they can be understood and emulated. Whether singing hymns in church, whistling a tune in the street, or sitting rapt in a concert hall, we are enjoying the expression of human life—but in an enhanced and perfected form, which offers a mirror to our understanding.

Of course, music is of many kinds, and not all has the expressive power or moral refinement of Bach, Mozart, and Schubert. Moreover, the gradual sundering of 'highbrow' and 'lowbrow', 'classical' and 'popular' has left a gap between the language of serious music and the ears of the young—a gap that was once filled with hymns, carols, and musicals, but which is now empty except for the works of Sir Andrew Lloyd Webber, whose popularity, however, is a vivid reminder of the continuing need for melody and harmony, in a world suborned by rhythm. This no man's land between high and popular culture was vacated only recently. Debussy bequeathed his harmonies to jazz, and jazz its rhythms to Stravinsky. Gershwin, Milhaud, Constant Lambert, and Bernstein wrote music that is neither highbrow nor lowbrow,

[21] See S. Frith, 'Towards an Aesthetic of Popular Music', in Leppert and McClary (eds.), *Music and Society*.

while even the Broadway musical is grounded in harmony and counterpoint. The long tradition of musical utterance, which enabled our parents to hum with equal facility an aria by Mozart or a melody of Nat King Cole, was a precious icon of humanity. You can hear it still in the Beatles or Buddy Holly, and to sing or move to this music is to take one step across the divide between popular and classical culture. You are beginning to think and feel *musically*— with an awareness of the voice not as a sound only, but as an expression of the soul. Compare the breathless gestures of Nirvana with the melody in Ex. 15.21—'She loves you', by the Beatles—in which the music moves effortlessly through the harmonic field of G major, with phrases that answer and develop their predecessors, and which open the implied harmony at every juncture on to vistas of neighbouring keys—B minor, E minor, C minor, and D.

Ex. 15.21. The Beatles, 'She loves you'

A musical culture introduces its participants to three important experiences, and three forms of knowledge. The first is the experience of melody— of musical thinking, as it begins in tonal space and leads onwards to an apt conclusion. In singing a melody we understand the relation between phrases, the way in which tone calls to tone across the imagined space of music. Melodies have character, and in singing them we imitate the forms of human life. Musical education teaches us to be alert to this character, and to understand that the rightness or wrongness of a tone is the rightness or wrongness of a gesture. In singing we rehearse our social nature, just as we do in dancing. And it matters that we should sing in courteous and cheerful ways.

The second experience is that of harmony—of voices sounding together, moving in concord, creating tensions and resolutions, filling the tonal space with an image of community. Classical harmony provides us with an archetype of human sympathy. The ability to notice a bass-line, to feel the rightness of the notes and of the harmonies that erupt from them, is the ability to respond to a wider world, to value the other voice, and to situate both self and other in a moralized universe. There is all the difference between harmony formed through voice-leading, and harmony formed by hitting strings without regard to the relations among the inner parts—as in the characteristic figure for acoustic guitar in Ex. 15.22, from 'Losing my Religion' by REM, in which no triad is ever inverted, and nothing moves between the chords, so that all is absorbed in rhythm. Ex. 15.23 gives a typical cadence from Cole Porter ('I've got you under my skin'). Notice how the composer postpones the dominant seventh chord that might have come in at the final syllable of 'reality', and prolongs the cadence over seven bars, slipping sideways through B flat minor to F minor, and thence to the minor ninth on B flat, in order to bring the music home. This is not contrived at all, since the musical movement is shaped entirely by the melody, and by the voice-leading of the inner parts, which summon these harmonies from the tonal space in a relaxed response to the humour of the words.

Ex. 15.22. REM, 'Losing my Religion', chord sequence for acoustic guitar

The third experience is that of rhythm—by which I mean something other than the all-pervasive beat, on which the shapeless cries of the singer are hung as on wires of steel. (See Ex. 15.24, from 'Losing my Religion': a shapeless tune which has lost all movement of its own.) I mean the pulse of human life, displayed in measure, syncopation, and accent. Rhythm is a play of heartbeats, which reaches to all mankind. You hear it in jazz, and in the great works of classical music—a delicate display of accents which invites us to dance. Beat is not rhythm, but the last sad skeleton of rhythm, stripped bare of human life.

Nobody who understands the experiences of melody, harmony, and rhythm will doubt their value. Not only are they the distillation of centuries of social life: they are also forms of knowledge, providing the competence to reach *out* of ourselves through music. Through melody, harmony, and rhythm, we enter a world where others exist besides the self, a world that is full of feeling but also ordered, disciplined but free. That is why music is a character-forming force, and the decline of musical taste a decline in morals. The *anomie* of Nirvana and REM is the *anomie* of its listeners. To withhold all judgement, as though a taste in music were on a par with a taste in ice-cream, is precisely not to understand the power of music.

Ex. 15.23. Cole Porter, 'I've got you under my skin'

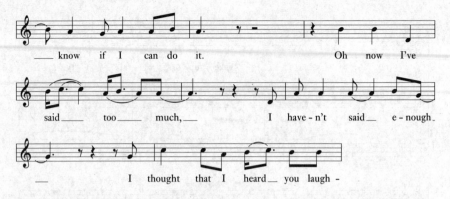

Ex. 15.24. REM, 'Losing my Religion'

In the first Pythian Ode Pindar evokes the lyre of Apollo, reminding us that music is god-given, and hated by the beings to whom the love of Zeus does not extend. Music soothes, cheers and pacifies; it threatens the power of the monsters, who live by violence and lawlessness. Those lonely, antinomian beings are astounded by music, which speaks of another order of being—the order which 'the footstep hears, as the dance begins'. It is this very order that is threatened by the monsters of popular culture. Much modern pop is cheerless, and meant to be cheerless. But much of it is also a kind of *negation* of music, a dehumanizing of the spirit of song.

Theories of cultural decline are two a penny, and it is no part of philosophy to provide them. Nevertheless, we should be doing scant justice to the subject of this chapter, if we did not, in conclusion, try to understand the process that has brought us to our present pass. Marxists typically divide culture into two components: one belonging to ideology, and serving to induce our acquiescence in existing things; one transcending ideology, to become a critical instrument, an unsettling and destabilizing force, which furthers the cause of social revolution, and prepares us for a better world. Contemporary popular culture belongs to the first of those categories: it is, in the Marxist view, the opiate of the consumer society, decadent precisely because that society is decadent. The true art of our time, according to writers like Bloch and Adorno, is the questioning, critical, forward-looking art of the avant-garde, in which the existing social realities are put in question, and the ground is prepared for something new.

Such a view is no longer believable: the consumer society is characterized by its extraordinary stability. It is able to receive the deft thrusts of history with a buoyant equilibrium, to survive all Jeremiads, to re-emerge from every downpour with the same untroubled countenance, acknowledging that the critic too deserves his place in the democratic order. Modernism did not overthrow the consumer culture: it merely inoculated it against modernism, which now floats around the system accompanied by its own friendly anti-bodies. What I have described is not the *decadence* of popular music, but its final *freedom*—its breaking-loose from the channel of taste, into the great ocean of equality, where the writ of taste no longer runs. The postmodern world denatures music only because it denatures everything, in order that each individual might have his chance to buy and sell. Popular music ceases to be music, just as sexual love ceases to be love: nothing less than this is required by the new form of life—life 'in the present moment'. And the alienation that comes from this life—the fear, inadequacy, and anger that attend the attempt to live without the blessing of the dead—is itself expressed by the popular culture and reabsorbed by it. The cheerlessness of so much pop music is therapeutic: an acknowledgement that we live *outside* society, that we too, in granting equality to every human type, have become monsters, and that a monster is an OK thing to be.

There is therefore more than a grain of truth in Nietzsche's view, according to which high culture belongs to the 'pathos of distance' established by an aristocratic class. Culture embodies the will of that class to perpetuate its own distinction, and to glorify its power. It declines when the aristocratic class renounces the will to power, becomes rotten with guilt and self-doubt, and finally succumbs to the equalizing tendency of the herd.[22] Nietzsche implies that no *new* culture will come in place of the old, except through conquest. Democratic man is essentially 'culture-less', without the aspirations that require him to exalt his image in literature and art. The postmodern world is the world that follows the death of the 'last man'—the last human being who has attempted to *better* himself, and to strive towards the inequality which is the mark of the truly human.

There is an element in the picture which Nietzsche refuses to acknowledge. Like the Marxist, he attaches culture to the wrong roots—namely, to the power-relations that prevail in a society. In fact, culture is the natural elaboration of a first-person plural, which expresses itself in the first instance through religious forms and a conception of the sanctity of places and times, persons and offices, customs and rites. A culture is grounded in a religion, develops with the religion, and grows away from it only to mourn its loss. When people lose their faith, and cease to experience their social membership in sacral terms, the culture begins to wither, like the leaves on a tree that has been felled—which may, however, sprout for a year or more beyond its cutting down. Although Nietzsche is right in identifying taste with the demands of privilege, and in seeing art as perpetuating the idea of a 'higher' state, he fails to see that this idea is the gift of religion, which heals the

[22] *Beyond Good and Evil*, tr. R. J. Hollingdale (Harmondsworth, 1973), ch. 9, 'What is Noble?', sect. 257.

divisions of rank and class, and releases the highest aesthetic inspiration into the veins of society. The postmodern world is not merely democratic; it is essentially irreligious, since that is what 'life in the present moment' requires. It has become deaf to the voice of absent generations, and lives in the thin time-slice of the now, calling over and over the same tuneless utterance—'the loud lament of the disconsolate chimera'.

It is not only art and music that have undergone a fatal metamorphosis in these new conditions. The human psyche itself has been thrown out of orbit, as the world is swallowed by its own representations. The television screen has ceased to be a summary of distant episodes, and become the criterion of reality itself. Events are real to the extent that they can be captured on a videotape, and made available in playback. But when the really real is endlessly repeatable, nothing truly happens. The river of time ceases to murmur in the psychic background, and a zombie-like disengagement spreads like a fungus over the human will. Life becomes episodic, like a soap opera, and its parts can be reorganized according to a rule of substitution. Any part of life has its equivalent, which will 'do just as well', and the attachment to particulars—to spouses and lovers, to projects and ambitions, to sacred places and true communities—begins to seem faintly comic, especially in playback. That is what Adorno really meant, I believe, by the 'fetishization' of culture.

In such a condition it is inevitable that people should lose all sense of a sacral community, so as to become locked in the isolation of their own desires. The social world, which remains a necessary *image*—for how else can we live with our isolation?—becomes sentimentalized. It is also inevitable that the products of popular culture should be uniform and mutually substitutable—using always the same devices, the same phrases, the same references to a world that is not to be questioned, save in a sentimental and self-regarding way. It is further inevitable that the religious impulse, which finds no outlet to the transcendental, should find solace in idolatry, and that popular culture should involve the worship of idols. There, in brief, is the explanation of popular music as we currently know it. In the condition in which we find ourselves, it is inevitable that popular music should be both sentimental and idolatrous.

The Music of the Future

The avant-garde persists only as a state-funded priesthood, ministering to a dying congregation. We have seen the demotion of serialism from the obligatory language of modern music to a stylistic eccentricity in free competition with the tonal styles; we have witnessed too the renunciation of experiment for experiment's sake and the attempt to integrate the modernist discoveries into a lingua franca that will be not so much post-tonal as pantonal. Atonal music proved unable either to find an audience or to create one. Its harsh interdictions and censorious theories threatened the musical culture, by disparaging the natural bourgeois life on which it depends.

At the same time, a new bourgeois audience is emerging—one which does not feel the force of modernism's bleak imperatives. It is as yet a fragile audience: its ears muddied by pop music, its body starved of rhythm, and its soul untutored in religious hope. Yet it has encountered the old musical culture, and been inspired by it. We should not be surprised if this new audience prefers easy homophony to complex polyphony, endless repetition to continuous development, block chords to voiced harmonies, regular beat to shifting accent, and boundless chant to bounded melody. For such are the expectations fostered by popular culture. Nor should we be surprised if the new audience is animated by a religious longing, while being unable to distinguish the religious from the religiose, content with a sentimental image of a faith that, in its real version, stands too severely in judgement over the postmodern world-view.

Such an audience finds in the morose spirituality of Górecki the perfect correlative of its musical taste. For his is serious music, with a promise of release from the alienated world of popular culture, yet composed as pop is composed, with monodic chanting over unvoiced chords (see Ex. 15.25). It is as though serious music must begin again, from the first hesitant steps of tonality, in order to capture the postmodern ear. There is no doubt that, thanks to composers like Górecki and Tavener, the bourgeois ear is again being opened to music. Nevertheless, the thinness of this new music reminds us of the great task which lies before the art of sound: the task of recovering tonality, as the imagined space of music, and of restoring the spiritual community with which that space was filled. I doubt that this act of restoration

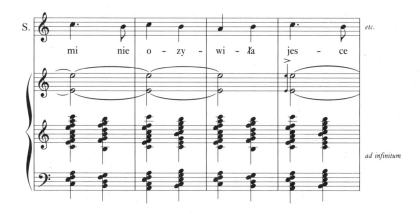

Ex. 15.25. Górecki, Third Symphony, Op. 36

can be accomplished in Taverner's or Górecki's way: a musical equivalent of *Four Quartets* is needed—a rediscovery of the tonal language, which will also redeem the time. Many of our contemporaries have aimed at this—Nicholas Maw, John Adams, Robin Holloway, and Alfred Schnittke. But none, I think, has yet succeeded.

Bibliography

ABBATE, CAROLYN, *Unsung Voices: Opera and Musical Narrative in the Nineteenth Century* (Princeton, 1991).

ADORNO, THEODOR W., *Prisms*, tr. S. Weber and S. Weber (Cambridge, Mass., 1967; repr. Boston, 1990).

—— *Philosophy of Modern Music*, tr. A. G. Mitchell and W. V. Blomster (New York, 1973).

—— *Über der Fetischcharakter in der Musik*, in *Dissonanzen: Musik in der verwalteten Welt* (Gottingen, 1956), tr. in A. Arato and E. Gebhardt (eds.), *The Essential Frankfurt School Reader* (New York, 1978).

—— *Quasi una Fantasia*, tr. Rodney Livingstone (London 1992).

—— and EISLER, HANS, *Komposition für den Film*, in Adorno, *Gesammelte Schriften* (Frankfurt-am-Main, 1976).

AL-FARABI, *Kitab al-mousiqi al-kabir* (Cairo, 1923).

ALPERSON, PHILIP (ed.), *What is Music? An Introduction to the Philosophy of Music* (University Park, Pa., 1994).

ALSTON, WILLIAM P., *The Philosophy of Language* (Englewood Cliffs, NJ, 1964).

ANSCOMBE, G. E. M., *An Introduction to Wittgenstein's Tractatus* (London, 1959; 3rd edn., London, 1967).

ARISTOTLE, *Categories*; *De Anima*; *De Generatione et Corruptione*; *Poetics*: all in J. A. Smith and W. D. Ross (eds.) *The Works of Aristotle Translated into English* (Oxford, 1910–52).

AUGUSTINE, St., *De Musica*, ed. and tr. R. C. Taliafero (New York, 1947).

BABBITT, MILTON, *Words about Music* (Madison, Wisc., 1987).

—— 'The Structure and Function of Music Theory', in Boretz and Cone (eds.), *Perspectives*, 10–21.

BAILEY, ROBERT, 'The Structure of the *Ring* and its Evolution', *Nineteenth-Century Music*, 1 (1977/8), 48–61.

BAKER, JAMES, 'Schenkerian Analysis and Post-Tonal Music', in Beach (ed.), *Aspects of Schenkerian Theory*, 153–88.

BALLANTINE, CHRISTOPHER, *Music and its Social Meanings* (New York, 1984).

BAR-ELLI, G., 'A Note on the Substitutivity of Notes', *Analysis*, 41/1 (Jan. 1981), 27–32.

BARTHES, ROLAND, *Éléments de sémiologie* (Paris, 1959), tr. as *Elements of Semiology*, by A. Lavers and C. Smith (London, 1967).

BARTÓK, BELA, *Hungarian Folk Music*, tr. M. D. Calvocoressi (London, 1931).

BATTEUX, CHARLES, *Les Beaux-Arts réduits à un même principe* (Paris, 1746).

BAUMGARTEN, A. G., *Aesthetica*, 2 vols. (Frankfurt an der Oder, 1750–8).

BEACH, DAVID (ed.), *Aspects of Schenkerian Theory* (New Haven, 1983).

BEARDSLEY, MONROE C. and WIMSATT, W. K., 'The Intentional Fallacy' in Wimsatt, *The Verbal Icon*.

BELL, J. S., 'Bertleman's Socks and the Nature of Reality', *J. Phys.* (Paris), 42 (1981), 41–61.

BENDER, JOHN, 'Music and Metaphysics: Types and Patterns, Performances and Works', *Proceedings of the Ohio Philosophical Association* (Apr. 1991).

BENNETT, JONATHAN, *Kant's Analytic* (Cambridge, 1966).

—— *Events and their Names* (Oxford, 1988).

BENSON, A. C., *Diary*, ed. Percy Lubbock (London, 1926).

BERGSON, HENRI, *The Creative Mind*, tr. Mabelle Andison (Westport, Conn., 1946).

BESANÇON, ALAIN, *L'Image interdite* (Paris, 1993).

BLACK, MAX, *Models and Metaphors: Studies in Language and Philosophy* (Ithaca, 1962).

—— 'More about Metaphor', in A. Ortony (ed.), *Metaphor and Thought* (2nd edn., Cambridge, 1993).

BLOCH, ERNST, *Essays on the Philosophy of Music*, tr. Peter Palmer, introd. David Drew (Cambridge, 1985).

—— *The Principle of Hope*, tr. Neville Plaice, Stephen Plaice, and Paul Knight, 3 vols. (Oxford, 1986).

BLOOM, ALLEN, *The Closing of the American Mind* (Chicago, 1989).

BOETHIUS, *De institutione musica*, tr. C. M. Bower and Claude V. Palisca, as *Boethius' 'Fundamentals of Music': An Introduction and Translation* (New Haven, 1989).

BORETZ, BENJAMIN, and CONE, E. T., *Perspectives on Contemporary Music Theory* (New York, 1972).

BOURDIEU, PIERRE, *Distinction: A Social Critique of the Judgement of Taste*, tr. Richard Nice (London, 1984).

BRAND, MYLES, 'Identity Conditions for Events', *American Philosophical Quarterly*, 1 (1977), 329–77.

BROOKS, CLEANTH, *The Well Wrought Urn* (London, 1949).

BUDD, MALCOLM, 'Understanding Music', *Proceedings of the Aristotelian Society*, suppl. vol. (1985).

—— *Music and the Emotions: The Philosophical Theories* (London, 1985).

—— *Values of Art* (London, 1995).

CAVELL, STANLEY, *Must We Mean What We Say?* (New York, 1969).

CHAILLEY, JACQUES, *The Magic Flute, Masonic Opera*, tr. Herbert Weinstock (London, 1972).

CHOMSKY, NOAM, *Aspects of the Theory of Syntax* (Cambridge, Mass., 1964).

—— *Syntactic Structures* (The Hague, 1969).

CLARKE, ERIC F., 'Structure and Expression in Rhythmic Performance', in Howell, Cross, and West (eds.), *Musical Structure*, 209–36.

COKER, J. WILSON, *Music and Meaning* (New York, 1972).

COLLINGWOOD, R. G., *The Principles of Art* (Oxford, 1938).

CONE, EDWARD T., *Musical Form and Musical Performance* (New York, 1968).

—— 'Beyond Analysis', in Boretz and Cone (eds.), *Perspectives*, 72–90.

COOK, NICHOLAS, *A Guide to Musical Analysis* (London, 1987).
—— *Music, Imagination and Culture* (Oxford, 1990).
COOKE, DERYCK, *The Language of Music* (Oxford, 1959).
COOPER, DAVID, *Metaphor* (London, 1986).
COOPER, W. GROSVENOR, and MEYER, LEONARD B., *The Rhythmic Structure of Music* (Chicago, 1960).
COPLAND, AARON, *What to Listen for in Music* (New York, 1939).
CROCE, BENEDETTO, 'Beaumarchais's Cherubino and the Countess', in *Philosophy, Poetry, History: An Anthology of Essays*, tr. and introd. Cecil Sprigge (London, 1966), 900–7.
—— *Estetica come scienza dell'espressione e linguistica generale* (Palermo, 1902), tr. Douglas Ainslie as *Aesthetic as Science of Expression and General Linguistic* (New York, 1922).
DAHLHAUS, CARL, *Esthetics of Music*, tr. W. Austin (Cambridge, 1982).
—— *Foundations of Music History*, tr. J. B. Robinson (Cambridge, 1983).
—— *Schoenberg and the New Music*, tr. D. Puffett and A. Clayton (Cambridge, 1987).
—— *The Idea of Absolute Music*, tr. R. Lustig (Chicago, 1989).
DAVIDSON, DONALD, *Essays on Actions and Events* (Oxford, 1980).
DAVIES, STEPHEN, 'Authenticity and Musical Performance', *British Journal of Aesthetics*, 27 (1987).
Musical Meaning and Expression (Ithaca, NY, 1994).
DERRIDA, JACQUES, *Marges de la philosophie* (Paris, 1972).
DESCARTES, RENE, *Compendium musicae* (Utrecht, 1650).
DONINGTON, ROBERT, *The Interpretation of Early Music* (London, 1963).
DUHEM, PIERRE, *The Aim and Structure of Physical Theory*, tr. Philip P. Wiener (Princeton, 1954).
DUMMETT, MICHAEL, *Frege: Philosophy of Language* (London, 1973).
EAGLETON, TERRY, *The Ideology of the Aesthetic* (Oxford, 1990).
ECO, UMBERTO, *Reflections on 'The Name of the Rose'*, tr. William Weaver (London, 1994).
EISLER, HANS. See ADORNO, THEODOR W. and EISLER, HANS.
ELIOT, T. S. 'Wordsworth and English poetry' in *Egoist*, 4 (1917), 118–19.
—— *The Sacred Wood* (London, 1920).
EVANS, GARETH, *Collected Papers* (Oxford, 1993).
FODOR, JERRY A., *The Language of Thought* (New York, 1975).
FORTE, ALLEN, *The Structure of Atonal Music* (New Haven, 1973).
—— and GILBERT, STEVEN E., *Introduction to Schenkerian Analysis* (New York, 1982).
FREGE, GOTTLOB, 'The Thought: A Logical Enquiry', in Strawson (ed.), *Philosophical Logic*, 17–38.
—— 'On Sense and Reference', tr. Max Black, in M. Black and P. T. Geach (eds.), *Translations from the Philosophical Writings of Gottlob Frege* (2nd. edn., Oxford, 1960), 56–78.
FRITH, SIMON, *Sound Effects: Youth, Leisure and the Politics of Rock 'n Roll* (New York, 1981).
—— 'Towards an Aesthetic of Popular Music', in Leppert and McClary (eds.), *Music and Society*, 133–150.

FUX, JOHANN JOSEPH, *Gradus ad Parnassum* (1725), tr. and ed. Alfred Mann with the collaboration of John St Edmunds, as *Steps to Parnassus: The Study of Counterpoint* (London, 1944).

GARDNER, HELEN, *The Art of T. S. Eliot* (London, 1949).

GEACH, P. T., *Logic Matters* (Oxford, 1972).

GOEHR, LYDIA, *The Imaginary Museum of Musical Works* (Oxford, 1992).

GOETHE, J. W. VON, *Theory of Colours*, tr. C. L. Eastlake, introd. Deane B. Judd (Cambridge, Mass., 1970).

GOODMAN, NELSON, *Languages of Art: An Approach to a Theory of Symbols* (Oxford, 1969).

GREENBLATT, STEPHEN, *Renaissance Self-Fashioning: From More to Shakespeare* (Chicago, 1980).

GREENE, DAVID B., *Temporal Processes in Beethoven's Music* (New York, 1982).

GRICE, H. P., 'Meaning', *Philosophical Review*, 66 (1957), 377–88.

GRIEPENKERL, FRIEDRICH CONRAD, 'J. S. Bach's chromatische Phantasie', *Allgemeine Musikalische Zeitung*, 50/5 (16 Feb. 1848), 97–100.

GURNEY, EDMUND, *The Power of Sound* (London, 1880).

HANSLICK, E., *On the Beautiful in Music*, tr. and ed. G. Payzant (Indianapolis, 1986).

HATTON, ROBERT S., *Musical Meaning in Beethoven: Markedness, Correlation and Interpretation* (Indianapolis, 1994).

HAYEK, F. A., 'Cosmos and Taxis', and 'Nomos', in *Law, Legislation and Liberty*, i. (London, 1973), 35–55 and 94–124 respectively.

HEGEL, G. W. F., *Aesthetics: Lectures on Fine Art*, tr. T. M. Knox, 2 vols. (Oxford, 1975).

—— *The Phenomenology of Spirit*, tr. A. Miller and J. N. Findlay (Oxford, 1977).

HELMHOLTZ, HERMANN VON, *On the Sensation of Tone*, tr. Alexander J. Ellis (London, 1885; repr. New York, 1954).

—— *A Treatise on Physiological Optics*, tr. J. P. C. Southall (3 vols., New York, 1924–5).

HESTER, MARCUS B., *The Meaning of Poetic Metaphor* (The Hague, 1967).

HILL, GEOFFREY, *Collected Poems* (London, 1986).

HINDEMITH, PAUL, *A Composer's World* (Cambridge, Mass., 1952).

HIRBOUR-PAQUETTE, L. See NATTIEZ, J.-J, and HIRBOUR-PAQUETTE.

HOBBES, THOMAS, *De corpore*, in *Thomas Hobbes opera philosophica*, ed. Sir Thomas Molesworth, ii.

HOFFMAN, E. T. A., *E. T. A. Hoffman's Musical Writings*, ed. D. Charlton, tr. M. Clark (Cambridge, 1989).

HOLOMAN, D. KERN, and PALISCA, CLAUDE V., *Musicology in the 1980s: Methods, Goals, Opportunities* (New York, 1982).

HOLSTUN, JAMES, 'Ranting at the New Historicism', *English Literary Renaissance*, 19 (1984).

HORKHEIMER, MAX, 'Neue Kunst und Massenkultur' (1941), in Alfred Schmidt (ed.), *Kritische Theorie* (Frankfurt-am-Main, 1968), ii. 313–32.

HOWELL, P., CROSS I., and WEST R. (eds.), *Musical Structure and Cognition* (London, 1985).

HUSSERL, EDMUND, *Ideas: General Introduction to Pure Phenomenology*, tr. W. R. Boyce Gibson (London, 1931).

—— *The Phenomenology of Internal Time Consciousness*, ed. M. Heidegger, tr. James S. Churchill (The Hague, 1964).

—— *The Crisis of the European Sciences and Transcendental Phenomenology*, tr. and introd. David Carr (Evanston, Ill., 1970).

INGARDEN, ROMAN, *Das Literarische Kunstwerk* (2nd edn., Tubingen, 1960).

—— *The Work of Music and the Problem of its Identity* (1928), tr. A. Czerniawski, ed. J. G. Harrell (Berkeley & Los Angeles, 1986).

JACKENDOFF, RAY. See LERDAHL, FRED and JACKENDOFF, RAY.

JAMES, WILLIAM, *The Principles of Psychology*, 2 vols. (New York, 1890).

JOHNSON, JAMES, *Listening in Paris, a Cultural History* (Berkeley & Los Angeles, 1995).

JOHNSON, MARK, and LAKOFF, GEORGE, *Metaphors We Live By* (Chicago, 1980).

JOHNSON, SAMUEL, *Lives of the English Poets* (Everyman Edition; London, 1925).

JONAS, OSWALD, *Einführung in die Lehre Heinrich Schenkers* (revised edn., Vienna, 1972).

KANT, IMMANUEL, *Critique of Pure Reason*, tr. N. Kemp Smith (London, 1929).

—— *Critique of Practical Reason*, tr. T. K. Abbott (London, 1879).

—— *Critique of Judgement*, tr. J. C. Meredith (Oxford, 1952).

KEENE, DONALD, *World within Walls: Japanese Literature of the Pre-Modern Era, 1600–1867* (London, 1977).

KELLER, HANS, *Essays on Music*, ed. Christopher Wintle (Cambridge, 1994).

KIERKEGAARD, SØREN, 'The Immediate Stages of the Erotic or the Musical Erotic', *Either/Or*, tr. David F. Swenson and Lillian Marvin Swenson, rev. Howard A. Johnson (New York, 1959), i. 43–134.

KIM, JAEGWON, 'Causality, Identity and Supervenience in the Mind–Body Problem', *Midwest Studies in Philosophy*, 4 (1979), 31–49.

—— 'Events as Property Exemplifications', in M. Brand and D. Walton (eds.), *Action Theory* (Dordrecht, 1980), 159–77.

—— 'Psychophysical Supervenience', *Philosophical Studies*, 41 (1982), 51–70.

KIVY, PETER, *The Corded Shell: Reflections on Musical Expression* (Princeton, 1980).

—— *Sound Sentiment: An Essay on the Musical Emotions* (Philadelphia, 1989).

—— *Music Alone: Philosophical Reflections on the Purely Musical Experience* (Ithaca, NY, 1990).

—— *Sound and Semblance: Reflections on Musical Representation* (Ithaca, NY, 1991).

—— *The Fine Art of Repetition: Essays in the Philosophy of Music* (Cambridge, 1993).

—— *Authenticities: Philosophical Reflections on Musical Performance* (Ithaca, NY, 1995).

KOFFKA, KURT, *Principles of Gestalt Psychology* (New York, 1935).

KÖHLER, WOLFGANG, *Gestalt Psychology: An Introduction to New Concepts in Modern Psychology* (New York, 1947).

KRAMER, LAWRENCE, *Music as Cultural Practice 1800–1900* (Berkeley & Los Angeles, 1990).

—— *Classical Music and Postmodern Knowledge* (Berkeley & Los Angeles, 1995).

KŘENEK, ERNST, *Music Here and Now*, tr. B. Fles (New York, 1939).

—— *Studies in Counterpoint* (New York, 1940).

KRIPKE, SAUL, 'Semantic Considerations on Modal Logic', *Acta Philosophica Fennica*, 16 (1963), 83–94.

—— *Naming and Necessity* (Oxford, 1980).

KURTH, ERNST, *Musikpsychologie* (Bern, 1947).

LAKOFF, GEORGE. See JOHNSON, MARK AND LAKOFF, GEORGE.

LAKATOS, IMRE, 'Falsification and the Methodology of Scientific Research Programmes', in I. Lakatos and A. Musgrave (eds.), *Criticism and the Growth of Knowledge* (Cambridge, 1970), 92–195.

LANGER, SUZANNE, *Philosophy in a New Key* (Cambridge, Mass., 1942).

—— *Feeling and Form* (New York, 1953).

LEAVIS, F. R. (ed.), *Selections from Scrutiny*, 2 vols. (Cambridge, 1968).

LEE, C. S. See LONGUET-HIGGINS, H. C., and LEE.

LEIBNIZ, G.W., *Philosophical Essays*, tr. and ed. Roger Ariew and Daniel Garber (Indianapolis, 1989).

—— *Gottfried Wilhelm Leibniz: Philosophical Papers and Letters*, tr. and ed. L. E. Loemker (2nd edn., Dordrecht, 1969).

LEIBOWITZ, RENÉ, 'Pélleas et Mélisande ou les fantômes de la réalité', *Temps modernes*, 305 (1971), 891–922.

LEPPERT, RICHARD, and MCCLARY, SUSAN (eds.), *Music and Society: The Politics of Composition, Performance and Reception* (Cambridge, 1987).

LERDAHL, FRED, 'Cognitive Constraints on Compositional Systems', in John A. Sloboda (ed.), *Generative Processes in Music* (Oxford, 1988).

—— and JACKENDOFF, RAY, *A Generative Theory of Tonal Music* (Cambridge, Mass., 1983).

LEVINSON, JERROLD, 'Properties and Related Entities', *Philosophy and Phenomenological Research*, 39 (1978), 1–22.

—— *Music, Art and Metaphysics* (Ithaca, NY, 1990).

—— *Work and Œuvre and Other Essays* (Ithaca, NY, 1996).

LEWIS, DAVID, *Convention* (Cambridge, 1969).

LICKLIDER, J. C. R., 'Basic Correlatives of the Auditory Stimulus', in S. S. Stevens (ed.), *Handbook of Experimental Psychology* (New York, 1951), 1002 f.

LINDHOLM, B. See SUNDBERG, J. and LINDHOLM, B.

LIPMAN, SAMUEL, *Music and More* (Boston, 1992).

LISZT, FRANZ, *Gesammelte Schriften*, ed. L. Ramann (Leipzig, 1880–3).

LONGUET-HIGGINS, H. C., *Mental Processes: Studies in Cognitive Science* (Cambridge, Mass., 1987).

—— and LEE, C. S., 'The Perception of Musical Rhythm', *Perception*, 11 (1982), 115–28.

MCCLARY, SUSAN, 'On Blasphemously Talking Politics during Bach Year', in Leppert and McClary (eds.), *Music and Society*, 13–62.

—— *Feminine Endings: Music, Gender and Sexuality* (Minneapolis, 1991).

MCCRELESS, PATRICK, 'Ernst Kurth and the Analysis of the Music of the Late 19th Century,' *Music Theory Spectrum*, 5 (1983).

MCDOWELL, JOHN, 'On the Sense and Reference of a Proper Name', in Mark Platts (ed.), *Reference, Truth and Reality* (London, 1980), 141–66.

—— *Mind and World* (Cambridge, Mass., 1994).

MCFETRIDGE, IAN, *Logical Necessity and Other Essays*, ed. John Haldane and Roger Scruton (London, 1990).

MAHLER, ALMA, *Memories and Letters* (2nd edn., London, 1968).

MARX, A. B., *Die Lehre von der musikalischen Komposition*, 2 vols. (Leipzig, 1837–42).

—— 'Sebastian Bach's chromatische Phantasie', *Allgemeine Musikalische Zeitung*, 50/3 (1848), 33–40.

—— 'Tradition und Prufung', *Allgemeine Musikalische Zeitung*, 50/10 (1848), 153–160.

—— *Ludwig van Beethoven* (4th edn., Berlin, 1884).

MATTHESON, JOHANN, *Der Vollkommene Capellmeister* (1734), ed. Margarete Riemann (Kassel, 1954).

MEYER, LEONARD B., *Emotion and Meaning in Music* (Chicago, 1956).

—— *Explaining Music* (Berkeley & Los Angeles, 1973).

—— See also COOPER, W. GROSVENOR, and MEYER.

MILL, J. S., *System of Logic* (London, 1943).

MONTAGUE, RICHARD, *Formal Philosophy*, ed. and introd. Richmond H. Thomason (New Haven, 1979).

MORRIS, CHARLES W., *Foundations of the Theory of Signs* (New York, 1938).

NARMOUR, EUGENE, *Beyond Schenkerism: The Need for Alternatives in Musical Analysis* (Chicago, 1977).

—— *The Analysis and Perception of Basic Melodic Structures: the Implication-Realization Model* (Chicago, 1990).

—— 'On the Relationship of Analytical Theory to Performance and Interpretation', in Eugene Narmour and R. A. Solie (eds.), *Explorations in Music, the Arts and Ideas: Essays in honor of Leonard B. Meyer* (Stuyvesant, NY, 1988), 317–40.

NATTIEZ, J.-J., *Fondements d'une sémiologie de la musique* (Paris, 1975).

—— and L. HIRBOUR-PAQUETTE, 'Analyse musicale et sémiologie: A propos du Prélude de Pelléas', *Musique en jeu*, 10 (1973), 42–69.

NEWLIN, DAVID, *Bruckner, Mahler, Schoenberg* (New York, 1947).

NIETZSCHE, F. W., *The Birth of Tragedy* and *The Case of Wagner*, tr. Walter Kaufmann (New York, 1966).

—— *Beyond Good and Evil*, tr. R. J. Hollingdale (Harmondsworth, 1973).

NOGAMI, TOYOICHIRŌ, *Nō no hanashi* (The Art of Noh) (Tokyo, 1938).

NORTON, RICHARD, *Tonality and Western Culture: A Critical and Historical Perspective* (University Park, Pa., 1984).

PALISCA, CLAUDE V. See HOLOMAN, D. KERN, and PALISCA.

PARFIT, DEREK, *Reason and Persons* (Oxford, 1984).

PARTRIDGE, ERIC, *A Dictionary of Clichés* (London, 1940).

PEACOCKE, CHRISTOPHER, *Sense and Content* (Oxford, 1983).

PEIRCE, C. S., *Selected Writings*, ed. Philip P. Wiener (New York, 1958).

PERLE, GEORGE, *Twelve-Tone Tonality* (Berkeley & Los Angeles, 1977).

—— *Serial Composition and Atonality* (2nd edn., London, 1975).

PLATO, *The Republic*, ed. and tr. G. M. A. Grube (London, 1981).

—— *The Laws*, ed and tr. T. J. Saunders (Harmondsworth, 1975).

PLOTINUS, *ENNEADS*, in *The Enneads of Plotinus*, tr. Stephen McKenna, foreword by E. R. Dodds (London, 1969).

PRATT, CARROLL C., *The Meaning of Music: A Study in Psychological Aesthetics* (New York, 1931).

PUTNAM, HILARY, *Mind, Language and Reality: Philosophical Papers*, ii (Cambridge, 1975).

QUINE, W. V., *From a Logical Point of View* (2nd edn., Cambridge, Mass., 1961).

—— *Word and Object* (Cambridge, Mass., 1964).

RAFFMAN, DIANA, *Language, Music and Mind* (Cambridge, Mass., 1993).

RAMEAU, JEAN-PHILIPPE, *Treatise on Harmony*, tr. Philip Gossett (New York, 1971).

RAWLS, JOHN, *A Theory of Justice* (Oxford, 1971).

RETI, RUDOLF, *Tonality—Atonality—Pantonality* (London, 1958).

—— *The Thematic Process in Music* (London, 1961).

REVESZ, G., *Introduction to the Psychology of Music*, tr. G. I. C. De Courcy (Norman, Okla., 1945).

RICHARDS, I. A., *The Philosophy of Rhetoric* (London, 1936).

RICKS, CHRISTOPHER, *Beckett's Dying Words* (Oxford, 1995).

RICŒUR, PAUL, *La Métaphore vive* (Paris, 1976), tr. as *The Rule of Metaphor: Multi-Disciplinary Studies of the Creation of Meaning in Language*, by R. Czerny, K. McLaughlin, and J. Costello (Toronto, 1978).

—— *Freud and Philosophy: An Essay on Interpretation*, tr. D. Savage (New Haven, 1970).

RIEMANN, H., *System der musikalischen Rythmik und Metrik* (Leipzig, 1903).

—— *Elementar-Schulbuch der Harmonielehre* (Leipzig, 1906).

—— *Musiklexikon* (Leipzig, 1909).

ROSEN, CHARLES, *The Classical Style: Haydn, Mozart and Beethoven* (New York, 1972).

—— *Sonata Forms* (revised edn., New York, 1988).

ROUSSEAU, J.-J., *Essai sur l'origine des langues* (Geneva, *c*.1760), tr. as *On the Origin of Language*, by John H. Moran and Alexander Gode (Chicago, 1986).

—— *Dictionnaire de musique*, ed. V. D. Musset-Pathay, 2 vols. (Paris, 1824).

RUWET, NICOLAS, *Langage, musique, poésie* (Paris, 1972).

SADAI, YIZHAK, *Harmony in its Systemic and Phenomenological Aspects* (Jerusalem, 1980).

SAID, EDWARD, *Musical Elaborations* (London, 1991).

SALZER, FELIX, *Structural Hearing*, 2 vols. (New York, 1952–62).

SAUSSURE, FERDINAND DE, *Cours de linguistique générale* (Paris, 1966).

SAVILE, ANTHONY, *The Test of Time: An Essay in Philosophical Aesthetics* (Oxford, 1982).

SCHACHTER, CARL, 'Rhythm and Linear Analysis', in Felix Salzer and Carl Schachter (eds.), *Music Forum*, iv (New York, 1976), 281–334.

SCHAEFFER, PIERRE, *Traité des objets musicaux* (Paris, 1966).

SCHENKER, HEINRICH, *Harmonielehre* (Berlin, 1906), tr. E. M. Borgese, as *Harmony* (Chicago, 1954).

—— *Das Meisterwerk in der Musik*, 3 vols. (Munich, 1925, 1926, 1930).

—— *Five Graphic Musical Analyses* (New York, 1969).

—— *Free Composition*, tr. Ernst Oster (London, 1979).

—— *Counterpoint*, tr. John Rothgeb and Jurgen Thym, ed. John Rothbeg, 2 vols. (New York, 1987).

SCHILLER, FRIEDRICH, *Letters on the Aesthetic Education of Man*, tr. E. Wilkinson and L. A. Willoughby (Oxford, 1967).

SCHMIDT, ALFRED (ed.), *Kritische Theorie*, 2 vols. (Frankfurt-am-Main, 1968).

SCHOENBERG, ARNOLD, *Harmonielehre* (3rd edn., Vienna, 1922).

—— *The Fundamentals of Musical Composition*, ed. Gerald Strang (London, 1967).

—— *Style and Idea*, ed. Leonard Stein, tr. Leo Black (London, 1975).

SCHOPENHAUER, ARTHUR, *The World as Will and Representation*, tr. E. F. J. Payne, 2 vols. (New York, 1969).

SCHUTZ, ALFRED, *Collected Papers*, 2 vols. (The Hague, 1964).
SCRUTON, ROGER, *Art and Imagination* (London, 1974).
—— *The Aesthetic Understanding* (London, 1983).
—— *Sexual Desire* (London, 1986).
—— *A Dove Descending and Other Stories* (London, 1991).
SEARLE, J. R., *Speech Acts* (Cambridge, 1969).
SESSIONS, ROGER, *The Musical Experience of Composer, Performer, Listener* (Princeton, 1950).
SIBLEY, F. N., 'Aesthetic Concepts', *Philosophical Review*, 68 (1959), 421–50.
—— 'Aesthetic and Non-Aesthetic', *Philosophical Review*, 74 (1965), 135–59.
—— 'Objectivity and Aesthetics', *Proceedings of the Aristotelian Society*, suppl. vol. (1968).
SLOBODA, JOHN A., *The Musical Mind: The Cognitive Psychology of Music* (Oxford, 1985).
STEIN, ERWIN, *Orpheus in New Guises* (London, 1953).
STRAUS, JOSEPH, 'The Problem of Prolongation in Post-Tonal Music', *Journal of Music Theory*, 31 (1987), 1–21.
—— *Remaking the Past: Musical Modernism and the Tonal Tradition* (Cambridge, Mass., 1990).
STRAVINSKY, IGOR, *Poetics of Music, in The form of Six Lessons*, tr. A. Knodel and I. Dahl, pref. by G. Seferis (Cambridge, Mass., 1970).
STRAWSON, P. F., *Individuals* (London, 1959).
—— *Freedom and Resentment and Other Essays* (London, 1974).
—— (ed.) *Philosophical Logic* (Oxford, 1967).
STUMPF, CARL, *Tonpsychologie*, 2 vols. (Leipzig, 1883).
SUNDBERG, J., and Lindholm, B., 'Towards a Generative Theory of Melody', *Svensk Tidskrift for Musikforskning*, 52 (1970), 71–88.
TANNER, MICHAEL, 'Sentimentality', *Proceedings of the Aristotelian Society* (1976–7), 127–47.
TARSKI, ALFRED, *Logic, Semantics and Metamathematics*, tr. J. H. Woodger (new edn., Oxford, 1956).
TARUSKIN, RICHARD, 'The Musicologist and the Performer', in Holoman and Palisca (eds.), *Musicology in the 1980s*, 101–17.
—— '*Chez Petrouchka*: Harmony and Tonality chez Stravinsky', *Nineteenth-Century Music*, 10 (1987), 265–86.
TOVEY, SIR DONALD, *Essays in Musical Analysis*, 7 vols. (London, 1935).
—— *Musical Articles from the Encyclopedia Britannica* (London, 1944).
TRAVIS, ROY, 'Towards a New Concept of Tonality', *Journal of Music Theory*, 3 (1959), 257–84.
VAN APPLEDORN, M.-J., 'Stylistic Study of Debussy's Opera *Pelléas et Mélisande*', Ph.D. diss., University of Rochester, NY.
WAGNER, COSIMA, *Diaries*, ed. Martin Gregor-Dellin and Dietrich Mack, tr. Geoffrey Skelton, 2 vols. (London 1978–80).
WAGNER, RICHARD, *Gesammelte Schriften und Dichtungen*, ed. W. Gottler, 16 vols. (Berlin, 1926).
WALSER, ROBERT, *Running with the Devil: Power, Gender and Madness in Heavy Metal Music* (Hanover, 1993).

WALTON, KENDALL L., 'What is Abstract about the Art of Music?', *Journal of Aesthetics and Art Criticism*, 46 (1988), 351–64.

WEST, M. L., *Ancient Greek Music* (Oxford, 1992).

WESTPHAL, JONATHAN, *Colour: A Philosophical Introduction* (2nd edn., London, 1991).

WIGGINS, DAVID, *Sameness and Substance* (Oxford, 1980).

WIMSATT, W. K., *The Verbal Icon: Studies in the Meaning of Poetry* (Lexington, Ky., 1954).

WINTLE, CHRISTOPHER, 'Analysis and Psychoanalysis: Wagner's Musical Metaphors', in John Paynter, Tim Howell, Richard Orton, and Peter Seymour (eds.), *Companion to Contemporary Musical Thought* (London, 1992), 650–91.

WITTGENSTEIN, LUDWIG, *Tractatus Logico-Philosophicus*, tr. D. F. Pears and B. F. McGuiness (London, 1961).

—— *Philosophical Investigations*, tr. G. E. M. Anscombe (Oxford, 1953).

—— *The Blue and Brown Books* (Oxford, 1958).

—— *Remarks on Colour*, ed. G. E. M. Anscombe, tr. Linda L. McAlister and Margarete Schattle (Oxford, 1977).

—— *Culture and Value*, ed. G. H. Von Wright, tr. Peter Winch (Oxford, 1980).

WOLFF, CHRISTOFF, 'New Research on Bach's *Musical Offering*', *Musical Quarterly*, 57 (July, 1971) 379–408.

WOLLHEIM, RICHARD, *Art and its Objects* (2nd edn., Cambridge, 1980).

—— *Painting as an Art* (London, 1987).

WOLTERSTORFF, NICHOLAS, 'The Work of Making a Work of Music', in Alperson (ed.), *What is Music?*, 101–30.

WRIGHT, CRISPIN, *Frege's Conception of Numbers as Objects* (Aberdeen, 1983).

YOUNG, JAMES O., 'The Concept of Authentic Performance', *British Journal of Aesthetics*, 28 (1988).

ZARLINO, G., *Istituzioni armoniche* (Venice 1558; complete edn., 3 vols., Venice, 1589).

ZIFF, PAUL, 'The Cow on the Roof', *Journal of Philosophy*, 70 (1973), 713–23.

ZUCKERKANDL, VICTOR, *Sound and Symbol*, tr. Willard R. Trask (London, 1956).

—— *The Sense of Music* (Princeton, 1959).

—— *Man the Musician* (vol. ii of *Sound and Symbol*), tr. Norbert Guterman (Princeton, 1976).

Acknowledgements

The author and publisher are grateful for the following kind permissions.

G. Schirmer Inc., for permission to quote from

Arnold Schoenberg, Fourth Quartet, Op. 37, Copyright © 1939 (Renewed) by G. Schirmer Inc. (ASCAP). Reproduced by permission (Ref. PLo81096)

Arnold Schoenberg, Violin Concerto, Op. 36, Copyright © 1939 (Renewed) G. Schirmer Inc. (ASCAP). Reproduced by permission (Ref. PLo81096)

Samuel Barber, *Vanessa*, Op. 32, Copyright © 1957 (Renewed) by G. Schirmer Inc. (ASCAP). Reproduced by permission (Ref PLo81096)

Warner/Chappell Music Ltd., for permission to quote from

Stripe/Mills/Berry/Buck, 'Losing my Religion', © 1991 Night Garden Music, Unichappell Music Inc., USA. Reproduced by permission of International Music Publications Ltd.

Cole Porter, 'I've got you under my skin', © 1936 Chappell-Co Inc., Buxton Hill Music Corp., USA, reproduced by permission of International Music Publications Ltd.

Boosey & Hawkes Music Publishers Ltd., for permission to quote from

Benjamin Britten, *Abraham and Isaac*
Benjamin Britten, *Peter Grimes*
Benjamin Britten, *War Requiem*
Alberto Ginastera, *Don Rodrigo*
Henryk Górecki, Third Symphony, Op. 36
Richard Strauss, *Der Rosenkavalier*
Igor Stravinsky, *The Rite of Spring*
Igor Stravinsky, *Symphony of Psalms*
David Del Tredici, *Final Alice*
Ralph Vaughan Williams, *On Wenlock Edge*

Richard Birnbach Verlag, for permission to quote from

Arnold Schoenberg, *Erwartung*, Op. 17, © Verlag Dreililien (Richard Birnbach), D-82166 Lochham

Universal Edition Ltd., for permission to quote from

Anton Webern, Variations for piano, Op. 27
Anton Webern, Concerto for 9 Instruments (*Konzert*), Op. 24
Bach (arr. Webern), 'Ricercar' from the *Musical Offering*
Arnold Schoenberg, Third String Quartet, Op. 30
Arnold Schoenberg, Three Piano Pieces, Op. 11
Alban Berg, *Lulu*
Alban Berg, Violin Concerto
Alban Berg, *Lyric Suite*
Béla Bartók, Third String Quartet
Karol Szymanowski, First Violin Concerto, Op. 35
All © Universal Edition Ltd.

Schott and Co., for permission to quote from

Sir Michael Tippett, Triple Concerto
Igor Stravinsky, Symphony in Three Movements
Igor Stravinsky, *Symphony of Psalms*
György Ligeti, Trio for violin, horn, and piano
Paul Hindemith, Concerto for trumpet, bassoon and strings
All © Schott and Co. Ltd.

Derry Music Co. USA, for permission to quote from

Paul Desmond and Dave Brubeck, 'Take Five'

Editions Durand S.A. and United Music Publishers Ltd., for permission to
quote from

Olivier Messiaen, *Turangalîla symphonie*

Music Sales Ltd., for permission to quote from

John Lennon and Paul McCartney, 'She loves you'
© 1963 Northern Songs. All rights reserved. International Copyright Secured.

Peters Edition Ltd. London, for permission to quote from

Richard Strauss, *Also Sprach Zarathustra*, Op. 30
© Copyright assigned 1932 to CF Peters
Alfred Schnittke, *Requiem*
© 1977 Edition Peters Leipzig

Oxford University Press for permission to quote from

Sir William Walton, Violin Concerto
© 1945 Oxford University Press

Faber Music Ltd. for permission to quote from

Ralph Vaughan Williams, *Pastoral Symphony* (No. 3)

Index of names

Subject Index

abstract art 121–2, 131
abstract objects 11, 104, 113–5
accent 29–30
acoustics 64
acousmatic experience 2–3, 11–15, 19–79, 115, 221
action 9, 79, 103 n., 107–8, 113–14
aesthetic description 370–6
aesthetic interest 5, 97, 138, 148–9, 153–4, 168–9, 219, 225–8, 357, 369–70, 396, 460–1, 475–8
aesthetic judgement 369–70, 376–9
aesthetic value 374–6,
  see also value
affective terms 153, 154–5
African music 38
aleatoric music 111, 332
allusion 463–4
analysis 211–12, 392–437
animals 102
Arabian music 16, 242, 245–6, 254
architecture 33, 120–1, 127, 262, 311, 312–13, 326–7, 370, 447–8, 465–6
aspect perception 44, 84, 86–9, 93–4, 108–15, 122, 123, 160–5, 229, 372
association 145–8, 227 n.
atonal music 256–7, 265, 281–5, 294–307, 323 n., 335–6, 396–8, 411, 416, 471–2, 506–7
avant-gardism 468–72, 504, 506

Balinese music 245–6
banality 285–94, 479–85, 487–8, 489
beat 24, 470, 502
Bell's theorem 5

causality 9–10, 19–20, 39, 68, 73–7, 79
Chinese music 245–6

chord, nature of 65–70, 399–400
chord grammar 308, 399–400
circle of fifths 249–50
cliché 285–94, 479–81, 487–8, 489
closure 45–6, 230–1, 309, 330–3
cognitive science 189–99, 295, 392–3
cognitivism 153–4, 375
colour 1–2, 15, 20–1, 402–3
combination tones 243 n.
consonance and dissonance 242–5, 301
content 236–8, 343–68
cosmology vii, ix, 63–4
counterpoint 318, 324
critical theory 150, 428
criticism 370–6, 393–9, 426–8, 433, 497–500
culture 292–3, 438–40, 444–50, 455–6, 457–508

dance 130, 338–9, 355–7, 367, 391, 444–5, 456, 462, 467, 478, 488–9, 498–9
Darmstadt 281
decision trees 312–14
diatonic scales 240–47, 248
dispositions 5
dissonance *see* consonance
'dissonant counterpoint' 281
'dot works' 193–4
down-beat and up-beat 26–8, 42

early music movement 444–50
Einfühlung, see empathy
elaboration 271–2
emotion 346–8, 354–7, 359, 485–8
empathy 360–4
equal temperament 21–2, 243–5
essence 5–6, 453–4
events 9–13, 105–7
evocation 145–6